PICTURE SOURCES UK

To the memory of
Ann Novotny (1936-1982)
Picture Researcher, Editor and Photo Historian

PICTURE SOURCES UK

Editor
Dr Rosemary Eakins

Associate Editor
Elizabeth Loving

Macdonald

A Macdonald BOOK

© Macdonald 1985
The essays, 'Pictures and the Law', and 'An Introduction
to Picture Research' © Rosemary Eakins 1985

First published in Great Britain in 1985
by Macdonald & Co (Publishers) Ltd
London & Sydney

A member of BPCC plc

British Library Cataloguing in Publication Data

Picture sources U.K.
    1. Pictures – Catalogs   2. Libraries – Great
    Britain – Directories
    I. Eakins, Rosemary II. Loving, Elizabeth
    025.17'71   Z5939

    ISBN 0-356-10078-2

Filmset

Printed and bound in England by
Netherwood Dalton & Co. Ltd., Huddersfield

Editor: Sara Wheeler
Designer: Kate Poole
Indexers: David Lee and Alice Mackrell

Macdonald & Co (Publishers) Ltd
Maxwell House
74 Worship Street
London EC2A 2EN

Acknowledgements

The Editors wish to thank the following people for
their assistance during the preparation of this
book: Caroline Mitchell, Suzanne Williams, Diana
Morris, Kathy Lockley and Kate Poole, who are the
Picture Department at Macdonald; The Society of
Picture Researchers and Editors, and in particular
Milly Trowbridge, Jane Puttick and Jenny Speller,
and also Jenny de Gex, Marianne Taylor, Vanessa
Whinney, Jessica Johnson, Stella Martin, Rose
Hill, Brigitte Arora, Jane Freebairn-Smith, Diana
Korchien, Caroline Masom, Liz Strauli, Mary
Fane, Frances Vargo, Linda Proud and Mia
Stewart Wilson. Special thanks go to Susan Griggs.

Contents

How to use the Directory

There are three methods of access to the information contained in the Directory:

- The entries
- The subject index
- The collection index

The entries are arranged alphabetically within chapters by name of collection and give concise details based on information provided by the sources themselves. Each entry is arranged under the following headings:

Items tells you the number, range of sizes and types of pictures in the collection.

Dates of subject matter gives the historical scope of the collection.

Dates of photographs tells you when the photographs were taken: an agency that specifies 1970 to the present will not have photographs of the Festival of Britain in 1952.

Subjects have been grouped into logical categories or listed alphabetically.

Access and conditions tells you how and when you may use the collection. In every case a preliminary phone call is advisable. Collections open to qualified researchers may require a formal letter of introduction.

Advertising Availability of material for advertising falls into two categories: some museums and libraries stipulate no advertising use; some sources state that some material is available for advertising use, recognizing that without model releases, advertising use in many cases is impossible.

Black-and-white and colour material Commercial picture agencies will usually lend their transparencies and prints. Small organizations or non-commercial sources, however, often do not maintain files of prints or transparencies and have to make them for you on demand. In these cases it is advisable to ask if there is likely to be a delay in providing material. In the meantime, photocopies may be available for which a small charge is usually made – well worth it in order to have material on hand for reference.

Reproduction rights fees are charged for permission to publish visual material on a sliding scale depending on how the pictures are used.

Service fees (sometimes called handling fees) are charged by most commercial sources and cover the cost of paperwork, filing and re-filing, postage and handling of the batches of material sent out to clients.

Holding fees are charged by commercial and non-commercial sources and usually come into effect after a free holding period of from one to three months. Such fees are designed to prevent picture users from holding material unnecessarily and do not apply when material is being held for publication.

Research fees are usually negotiable and are normally charged only for large projects.

Copyright Collections that do not own the copyright on the pictures they hold often expect the researcher to contact the copyright owner and obtain permission to use the material before they will deliver prints.

Picture credits A credit line is expected by most picture sources; many even specify the exact wording.

Number of staff includes the supervisor, but not all staff are necessarily engaged in services to clients.

The subject index refers you by entry numbers to a choice of sources for any given subject. You should also refer to the general category for that subject. For example, if you look up the subject 'rain forests', you will be directed to a list of specific sources and you may also look at the general category 'geography (tropical)'.

The collection index is the alphabetical key to collections and sub-collections whose name you know and about which you need further information.

Editors' Note
The intention of the editors was to include every major source of illustrations in the UK that makes its material available for reproduction. Our criteria were, firstly, that the

material be available for commercial use and not for research purposes alone; secondly, that in the case of individual photographers, they should have either unusual or comprehensive specialities or large collections open during normal business hours. Some non-commercial sources, however, did not wish to be included because they are short-staffed and felt that any increased demand on their resources would only lead to unsatisfactory service.

Although a number of museums and art galleries are included as picture sources, the emphasis is on material available from their library or photographic archives rather than on works of art in their collections.

All information was checked before going to press, but personnel, telephone numbers and even addresses are, of course, liable to change.

Pictures & the Law

COPYRIGHT

Origins of copyright

Copyright is the exclusive right granted by law to publish, sell or distribute a literary or artistic work; it is conferred automatically when a writer puts words on paper or a photographer releases the shutter of a camera. This right remains the property of the authors or originators of a work for a limited period of time so that they can control the use of it and receive payment for it. The purpose of the law is to prevent the unauthorized publication or reproduction of a photograph, painting, novel or piece of music; in this sense, it is a negative law. A manufacturer of goods or provider of services finds it relatively easy to insist on payment before completing an order, but a photographer or an artist must show work to the public and as a result expose it to the danger of plagiarism or piracy. Now more than ever it is very easy to make copies of pictures and of the written word, and it is very difficult to control distribution of those copies. Plagiarism, it is safe to say, has always been condemned by public opinion, but as long as plagiarism meant copying a work in longhand with a quill pen it did not present too serious a problem.

The invention of the printing press changed matters. The first printed book in Europe was probably the Vulgate Bible printed at Mainz in Germany sometime before August, 1456. The art of printing spread from Germany to Italy and then to France and Switzerland before William Caxton learned it from a printer in Cologne and returned to England to set up his press at Westminster in 1476 or 1477. By 1480 he had produced at least thirty books, a folio edition of Chaucer's *The Canterbury Tales* among them.

The speed with which the new presses could make multiple copies alarmed Parliament and they soon imposed control and cen-sorship on the printers. They feared that the printed page might be employed to spread heresy and sedition. By 1538 a printer needed a licence to print a book, and in 1557 The Company of Stationers was formed by a charter of Queen Mary. The purpose of the Company had nothing to do with the protection of authors; it was designed to prevent the dissemination of sedition and heresy against the Roman Catholic Church by means of printed pamphlets. Thereafter only members of the Stationers' Company could print books. The Company was also empowered to seize and destroy prohibited books and to make by-laws governing the printing trade. In 1559 Queen Elizabeth, equally concerned to prevent sedition, confirmed the charter of The Stationers' Company. But there was still nothing to protect the writer, nor was there for another century. In 1641 an ordinance was passed prohibiting the printing of any book without the consent of the owner of the copy. For the first time authors had some protection, but only until their work was published, after which it passed completely out of their control. Protection for the authors, however, was not a major interest of the lawmakers, for they were still primarily concerned with censorship and control of printing. In 1643 the Long Parliament passed another ordinance providing the further restriction that no book could be published without a licence from a Licenser appointed by Parliament. Milton's *Areopagitica* (1644) was a passionate plea for the freedom of the press in direct response to this ordinance.

For another fifty years little changed except that the authority of The Stationers' Company dwindled and it was less able to control the widespread activities of piratical printers who ignored the law. In 1694 the last of the licensing laws lapsed and all restraint was removed. The printers were acutely distressed now by their inability to protect their property and were obliged to petition Parliament for legislation. In 1709 an Act for the Encouragement of Learning was passed (taking effect in 1710), said to have been drafted in its original form by Jonathan Swift. For the first time the law gave authors the right to property in their own work. In the case of old books, the authors alone could publish them for a period of fourteen years, renewable for a second period of fourteen years if the author were still living. In other words, an author had a monopoly on the right to make copies for a period of up to twenty-eight years; for the first time, a legal copyright was vested in the creator of a work.

Despite this recognition of the author, the new law was in fact a law for booksellers. During the sixteenth century, the printers had been in a position of power, but had gradually been eclipsed by the booksellers whose employees they had become. The printer still printed the books, but the bookseller published them and it was in fact the booksellers who owned copyright in their wares, for authors customarily sold their work outright to the bookseller/publisher. The means were there to protect the authors, but they had yet to realize it and take advantage of the new law. Despite the fact that the law spoke of two terms of copyright of fourteen years each, the bookseller/publishers of the eighteenth century believed firmly that in common law perpetual copyright belonged to the author or to the bookseller to whom it had been assigned. A series of legal battles were fought over the next seventy years on this very matter, booksellers taking action against those who they thought infringed their privileges, and not until 1774 by a decision in the House of Lords were the provisions of the 1710 law finally upheld.

The 1710 act also marked the beginning of the copyright libraries, for it provided that nine copies of every book printed should be delivered to The Stationers' Company for the use of universities and libraries, a requirement maintained to the present day. The publisher of every book published in the United Kingdom is required to send one copy to the trustees of the British Museum within a month of publication. In addition, on written demand a copy must be supplied to each of the following libraries: the Bodleian Library, Oxford; University Library, Cambridge; the National Library of Scotland; the Library of Trinity College, Dublin; and, in the case of some books, the National Library of Wales. Between 1710 and 1911 when the next major copyright law was passed, some forty acts enlarging the scope of copyright were enacted, and during the nineteenth century authors came into their own, their rights in their work firmly established unless they chose to transfer them to someone else. The act currently in force is the Copyright Act of 1956 and it in turn is awaiting revision. The Government has published a Green Paper (1981) and various interested committees on copyright have been formed in order to offer advice and recommendations during the revision process.

Copyright and photographs

Copyright in a photograph exists from the moment a photograph is taken and it belongs to one of two persons. If a photographer is self-employed or an amateur, he or she owns the copyright. If a photographer is being paid to take photographs (i.e. working for hire), then the copyright belongs to the person paying, who is the commissioner of the work. The law provides that the author of a photograph (owner of copyright) is the person who owns the material on which the photograph is taken (negative or transparency) at the moment when it is taken. Subsequent physical possession of a photographic print, negative or colour transparency has nothing whatsoever to do with ownership of copyright. A photographer working for hire frequently retains the negatives when the job is finished, but the copyright still belongs to the commissioning person or company. A photographer might decide to retire and present all of his or her photographs and negatives to a museum, but unless copyright is assigned to the museum along with the photographs, then it remains with the photographer.

No one may publish any copyright photographs in any form – book, magazine, newspaper, television or film – without permission, nor may anyone make and distribute multiple copies. The only exceptions to this rule are that a photograph may be (1) shown in an exhibition, (2) projected on the screen as part of a free lecture, (3) published in a book or periodical accompanying criticism or review of the photograph or of an exhibition in which it is shown — as long as the review is of the photograph itself and not of the subject of the photograph and (4) reproduced as a single copy for purposes of private study. These four cases are considered fair dealing and do not infringe copyright.

Sometimes copyright in commissioned work is shared by the photographer and the commissioner. A magazine, for instance, may wish to keep copyright in the photographs published, but will return all of the unpublished material to the photographer. The two should draw up a written agreement to the effect that the magazine holds copyright in the published work, but although it commissioned all of the photographs, it assigns copyright in the unpublished material to the photographer. This, by the way, is *not* joint copyright. Joint copyright refers only to a work that has been created by two or more authors.

Copyright has nothing to do with payment and everything to do with control. Confusion may arise because a professional photographer earns income by giving permission for work to be copied or published in consideration of a fee. Charging a fee is entirely discretionary; a photographer may permit publication of a photograph free of charge.

Copy negatives and copy prints

What happens when a photograph is in turn photographed, producing what the trade calls a copy negative from which copy prints can be made? Some people mistakenly believe that a new copyright is thereby established, forgetting that the copyright is in the original image on the original negative, the work itself, and not in any copies that may be made. If a photograph is still in copyright, the making of a copy negative is legal if carried out by the owner of the copyright, and illegal if carried out by anyone else without permission. It is also illegal to copy a photograph from the pages of a book or

magazine in which it has been published. Copy negatives and copy prints are often made of historical photographs for which the original negative may no longer exist, but if copyright on the original photograph has expired, then the copy negative and copy photograph are also out of copyright. A picture agency holding such historical photographs and lending them for purposes of publication charges a fee for their use but the fee has nothing to do with copyright. It is merely a rental fee charged by one who has possession of a commodity to another who wishes to make use of it.

Portrait photographs

If you commission a photographer to take your portrait photograph, then you own the copyright in that photograph, even though the photographer keeps the negative. The photographer may not make any use of the portrait except in the four ways listed previously. As the copyright owner, you may give permission for the portrait to be published and may charge a fee; but you will probably have to pay a fee to the photographer for a print if you do not want to part with your own print. Since the photographer has the negative and took the photograph in the first place, he or she may feel justified in charging you a considerable fee. If you commission a photographer to take your portrait but neglect to pay the bill, you still own the copyright. The photographer may sue to recover the fee, but cannot claim or win the copyright.

If a photographer approaches you and offers to take your portrait free of charge and you agree, then the copyright in your portrait belongs to the photographer. If you are a famous person, a photographer might photograph you without your knowledge or permission and then allow your portrait to be published widely and collect fees for its use. If you find that your portrait is appearing in an advertisement or in some editorial context that is libellous, you may have recourse to legal redress, but this has nothing to do with copyright law, which will not have been infringed.

Photographs of works of art

Photographs of works of art or other objects that may be in copyright pose another problem. If the work of art and the photograph are both out of copyright, then obviously there are no difficulties. If the work of art is out of copyright, but the photograph was taken within the last fifty years, then the photograph is in copyright and may not be reproduced without the permission of the copyright holder. The work of art might belong to an individual or an organization, such as a museum which may charge a fee as well, but that fee has nothing to do with copyright unless the person or museum owns the copyright in the photograph. If the work of art is still in copyright, in most cases a photograph of it is probably in copyright too. (Copyright in a work of art, however, lasts for the life of the artist plus fifty years; copyright in a photograph lasts for fifty years from the end of the year in which it is taken. It can happen, therefore, that the photograph is out of copyright but the work of art is not.) When both photograph and work of art are in copyright, both the photographer and the artist are entitled to a fee and permission to publish must be sought from each of them. In this case publishers might feel that they are paying twice for the same thing, but reflection should remind us that two separate creative acts by two people are involved, each deserving and entitled to protection.

Some kinds of art objects may be photographed and published without infringement of copyright: architecture and structures; exhibitions; sculpture, woodwork and mosaics if they are permanently installed in a public place or place open to the public (i.e. a place which may be entered without payment). You may not, however, publish photographs of the following items without first gaining the permission of the copyright holder: paintings; sculpture (except as described above); drawings; sketches; engravings, etchings, aquatints, mezzotints, silkscreen and other types of print; book illustrations; arts and crafts such as textile fabrics, goldsmiths' and silversmiths' work; jewellery; pottery; porcelain and glass; furniture and woodwork; ironwork and other metalwork; architectural designs and plans; costume designs, textile designs, and other design plans. The only exceptions to this rule are those four mentioned on page 10.

Works of art by nationals of other countries are governed by the copyright laws of those countries and may be covered by one or both of the international copyright conventions – the higher standard Berne Convention of 1886 (revised, Paris, 1971) and the UNESCO-sponsored Universal Copyright Convention of 1952 (revised, Paris, 1971) – if the countries are signatories. To clear copyright for works of art by foreign artists, contact Design and Architects Copyright Society (DACS), St Mary's Clergy House, 2 Whitechurch Lane, London E1 7QR. (Tel: (01) 247 1650). DACS represents the following copyright societies: SPADEM and ADAGP (France), Beeldrecht (Holland), Bildkunst (West Germany), SABAM and SOFAM (Belgium), SGAE (Spain), SPA (Portugal), SIAE (Italy), Hung Art (Hungary), VAAP (USSR), VAGA (USA).

Duration of copyright

Copyright law protects the holder of copyright and ensures control over the work so that its creator may profit from it. The duration of copyright also takes into consideration that the family of the holder has some claim to profit as well. But this term is finite, for the law intends that the public as a whole should benefit from the work of creative artists.

The present British copyright law became effective in 1957 (it was enacted in 1956), and it had to make provision for photographs taken before its passage as well as for those taken afterwards. Photographs taken before 1 June 1957 remain in copyright for fifty years from the end of the calendar year in which they were taken. For example, a photograph taken on 13 May 1940 remains in copyright until 31 December 1990 and comes out of copyright on 1 January 1991. Photographs taken after 1 June 1957 remain in copyright perpetually until they are first published; once they have been published they remain in copyright for fifty years from the end of the calendar year in which they were first published. Therefore a photograph taken on 16 September 1965 and published in November 1965 remains in copyright until 31 December 2015 and comes out of copyright on 1 January 2016; a photograph taken in 1958 and not published until 1985 remains in copyright until 31 December 2035 and comes out of copyright on 1 January 2036.

To say the least, this system could lead to paralysing uncertainty as it is often impossible to tell whether or not a photograph has ever been published. But since any photograph taken as recently as 1957 is still in copyright whether published or not, the problem will not arise until 2008. Perhaps the law will have been revised by then and this clumsy provision changed. Other countries within the European Economic Community make term of copyright in a photograph the lifetime of the author plus a set number of years: in West Germany, for example, copyright expires seventy years from the end of the year in which the author dies.

The important fact to retain from the provisions for duration of copyright is that all photographs enter the public domain after fifty years and may be published freely by anyone; for example, on 1 January 1989, all British photographs taken at any time before 31 December 1938 come out of copyright.

Crown Copyright

Photographs and works of art published by or under the control of the sovereign or any government department are under Crown Copyright. The duration of Crown Copyright is for fifty years from the end of the calendar year in which the photograph is published. If the photograph is unpublished, copyright is perpetual until it is published and then lasts for fifty years. Therefore published government photographs taken on or before 31 December 1938 come out of Crown Copyright and into the public domain on 1 January 1989.

Some points to remember

When the law says a photograph, it means a transparency or a negative (black-and-white or colour) and not a print, which is a licensed copy made from a negative.

An idea cannot be copyrighted; copyright law deals with things, not with ideas. Copyright is legally a negative right; it allows you to stop people from making copies. It is also an economic right, allowing you to exact a fee in exchange for permission to make copies.

Unless the contract of employment states otherwise, if a photographer is on the staff of a company, the copyright in the photographs taken during working hours belongs to the company and the copyright in photographs taken in private time belongs to the photographer.

Distinguish carefully between reproduction rights and copyright. Payment of a reproduction rights fee to the owner of a photograph does not guarantee that you are not in violation of copyright if you publish it (the owner of the photograph may not own the copyright). Payment of a fee to the owner of copyright does not guarantee you access to a photograph (the owner of copyright may not own the negative or any prints). If the same person owns the copyright and the photograph and sells you reproduction rights, this in no way affects his or her ownership of copyright. If you want to use the same photograph again in a different publication, you must seek permission and pay a new fee.

Copyright and stock photography

Picture agencies (also called photo agencies, photo libraries and stock houses) provide clients with photographs for reproduction whose copyright is unencumbered and act as agents for professional photographers. For a fee they license the client to reproduce the photograph within precisely defined limitations, usually for one edition only of a book (or one issue of a magazine or advertisement insertions in a specified number of newspapers) to be distributed within a prescribed area and in a prescribed number of languages. A photograph might be licensed, for example, for one-time use hardback UK and Commonwealth English language, or one-time use paperback world all languages.

Some commercial fine-art picture libraries provide photographs of modern works which are still in copyright and direct the user to the copyright owner. The user must then negotiate permission with the owner and perhaps pay fees both to the library and the copyright owner. The same procedure must be followed in dealing with many small libraries and museums.

Finding the copyright holder

The occasion inevitably arises when you have the perfect photograph for your purposes, it is clearly still in copyright, and the photographer has vanished leaving no forwarding address. As long as you can prove that you tried to find him or her and are willing to pay for permission to reproduce the photograph, it is safe to publish it. The wisest procedure is to send a letter by registered post to the copyright owner's last known address so that it will eventually come back to you as proof of your good intentions.

OTHER LEGAL PROBLEMS

Model releases: Advertising

A model release is a document signed by a person appearing in a photograph and giving permission for that photograph to be used for the purpose described in the model release. The principal use of the model release is in advertising photography, for you may not exploit someone's appearance for commercial purposes without permission. It is very important that the model should be fully informed about the use that will be made of the photograph. An action was successfully brought by a model who had signed a routine model release. She had posed for an advertisement for a vitamin supplement for pregnant women, but the photograph was later retouched to make the model appear pregnant. She sued the client, claiming that she was

unmarried, had never been pregnant and had been caused great distress by such misrepresentation; and she won.

The use of photographs on the cover of books and magazines is usually considered advertising since the purpose is to sell the product. Therefore a model release should be signed for use on a cover of any photographs of a living person.

Old photographs may present problems too unless you can be sure that every person in the photograph is dead. Suppose you are doing a series of advertisements for a brewery, the theme of which is nostalgia for the good old days of the 1950s. A photograph of people dancing might seem an appropriate choice, but if their faces are all clearly visible, you are taking a real risk. The advertisement implies that all of the people think that the brewery's beer is a fine product, but suppose one of them is a teetotaller, has never tasted alcohol, and campaigns against alcoholic beverages. You may very well have a lively legal action on your hands and the chances are you will lose it.

Model releases: Editorial

Model releases are not usually necessary when photographs of living people are published for editorial purposes, defined as publication for the imparting of news or information. There are, however, some cases in which a model release is essential. If there is any chance that the person whose photograph is published will feel that his or her privacy has been invaded, then you must consult that person and obtain a model release before publishing the photograph.

Invasion of privacy occurs when publication of a photograph or a caption, although perfectly true, causes embarrassment, grief or distress to the subject. Let us suppose that you require a photograph showing someone expressing extreme grief. Even if you hired a professional actor to pose for your photographer, the results might be quite unconvincing. So you look for a photograph of the real thing, and in the files of a news photo agency you find an old photograph of a woman standing outside the ruins of a burned house in which her child has died. It all happened thirty years ago and the photograph shows precisely the expression you need. If you publish that photograph you may not be misrepresenting the truth, but if the woman sees it she may have grounds for a case for invasion of privacy. You might argue that the photograph appeared in a newspaper when the fire happened and therefore to reuse it is not an invasion of privacy. But an event that was news thirty years ago is not news any longer. A court might very well feel that it was wrong to bring the matter up again and cause the woman undue suffering by reminding her of the unhappy event.

Tremendous problems can arise in the attempt to illustrate subjects that are criminal, distressing or controversial. Again, it is possible to use posed models, but nine times out of ten, that is what they look like. Consider the implications in illustrating child or wife battering, glue sniffing, drug taking, prostitution, or indeed deformity, mental illness, disease, sexual deviation or abnormal psychology. Medical textbooks used to solve this problem by printing little black rectangles over the faces of patients in the photographs. There are, of course, other ways around the problem and the commonest is to photograph the subjects in such a way that their faces remain in shadow and unrecognizable. Another way is through very tactful negotiation, carefully-worded model releases and responsible and considerate use of the photographs.

In practice, publishers take calculated risks with some photographs. If they are wise, they weigh up the possible consequences and sometimes even seek legal advice before proceeding to publish.

Libel

Libel is defined as any written, printed or pictorial statement that damages a person by defaming his or her character or exposing him or her to ridicule. Extreme cases in which an innocent citizen is labelled a homicidal madman are perfectly clear, but care must be taken when the distinctions are more subtle.

An educational publisher planned a book on teaching methods to be illustrated with photographs showing good and bad teaching. Photographs were taken in a classroom with teachers who agreed to appear as bad teachers and signed model releases. The publisher's lawyers advised against publishing the photographs because they thought that the teachers might change their minds even years later and complain that their professional reputations had suffered. Professional models were hired and the photographs were re-taken.

Publishers are apt to overlook the fact that holding someone up to ridicule is another form of libel. During the vogue for publishing still photographs from silent films with mocking captions, a former silent film star, long since retired and in her extreme old age, found herself mocked and ridiculed in this fashion. In her youth in the 1920s she had had a distinguished career and was regarded as a serious actress. She sued the publisher on the grounds that her serious work had been ridiculed, and she won a large settlement.

Last words on the law

The best legal advice is that you should so conduct your affairs as not to need it. In dealing with the publication of visual material, there are many pitfalls; copyright violation, libel, invasion of privacy, loss and damage of original material, unlicensed exploitation of subjects. In addition, there are grey areas in the copyright law with resultant unresolved arguments about their interpretation. Finally, the law of precedent does not yet offer much guidance in photographic matters. There have been a few cases, but not enough to offer any clear guidelines.

• Never copy copyright photographs from a printed page. Always obtain the permission of a photographer or picture agency before reproducing a photograph either in print or on the screen. Always publish the photographer's, agency's or museum's credit line.

• In your transactions with other countries, remember that each has its own copyright law. Some countries, among them China, Taiwan and Peru, are not signatories to the Berne Convention, which means that they consider themselves free to copy anythings they choose. Others are gradually revising their own copyright laws with the intention of eventually achieving a genuinely international law. In the meantime, however, national laws remain dissimilar and you should proceed carefully.

• Always obtain a model release for any advertising use of a photograph of living people, including appearance on a book or magazine cover, and also for editorial use of a photograph, the subject matter of which may cause distress to the subject. Even if you *have* obtained a model release, remember that it only licenses you to use the photographs as specified in the model release. Unauthorized or libellous use of the photographs invalidates the model release.

Suggestions for further reading

Copyright Act, 1956. 4 & 5 Elizabeth II, Ch. 74. HMSO

A Brief Guide to Photographic Copyright. Committee on Photographic Copyright, 2 Amwell End, Ware, Herts, SG12 9HN

Gibbs-Smith, Charles H., *Copyright Law Concerning Works of Art, Photographs and the Written and Spoken Word* (Museums Association Information Sheet No. 7). Museums Association, 87 Charlotte St, London W1P 2BX, 1978

Whale, R. F., *Copyright: Evolution, Theory and Practice*. Longman: London, 1972

Copinger and Skone James on Copyright. Sweet and Maxwell: London, 1971

An Introduction to Picture Research

Picture research as a profession has gradually been gaining the recognition it deserves, due in part to the good work of professional associations such as The Society of Picture Researchers and Editors (SPREd) in the UK and The American Society of Picture Professionals (ASPP) in the US. Publishers who once expected authors to provide illustrations at their own expense now employ staff or freelance picture researchers, thereby acknowledging that picture research is too important to be left to the inexperienced.

Following World War II, colour photography gained enormously in popularity, helped by technical advances in film speed, for example, and by improved colour-printing techniques. As a result, the illustrated book began to come into its own. Books with pictures in them were, of course, nothing new, but by and large the pictures had played a primarily decorative role. The true illustrated book, however, offered an integration of words and pictures, telling different but complementary stories, giving different kinds of information which still provided a coherent whole. Television contributed to this increase in visual awareness, as viewers gained in sophistication. The profession of picture research was born in response to a demand for greater richness and accuracy of images in all of the communications media. In the very first illustrated books, a woodcut of a town or a king stood for any town and all kings; later on, illustrations became more varied but were usually anachronistic. Today readers and viewers alike expect high standards of quality and accuracy and indeed sometimes seem under the illusion that high quality professional photographs exist of every event in the world's history.

Picture researchers today are widely employed throughout the publishing industry.

Some publishers, especially those publishing illustrated partworks, maintain picture research departments; others employ freelances. Picture researchers also work for magazine and newspaper publishers and those who work freelance develop clients in a variety of other fields as well, including exhibition design, public relations, advertising and even jigsaw puzzle manufacturing. Picture researchers also work for the non-print media; they are employed by television producers, documentary and feature film makers and for makers of all kinds of audio-visual productions.

What do picture researchers do?

Picture research proceeds most successfully when the picture researcher takes part in the planning stages of the project, whether it is a book, magazine article or film. There are two reasons for this early involvement: to save money and to make the best use of time. In fact, a time/money ratio operates in many picture research projects; overnight miracles are possible but they are expensive. Given plenty of time, however, a good picture researcher can sometimes find fresh material from little used and relatively inexpensive sources that may be slow to deliver prints or transparencies. The picture researcher should therefore attend early meetings about the project and contribute to the preparation of a budget and a schedule. This will prevent such disasters as scheduling the research on a book about cultural anthropology for the summer months when all of the university anthropologists have gone to New Guinea to take more photographs, or financial fiascos such as befell a provincial publisher who sought a freelance picture researcher to provide him with twenty-five colour photographs of a famous political dynasty;

he had worked out a budget to pay for the pictures and for the researcher and was dismayed when no one would take on the job. His budget was not enough to pay for photographs from even the cheapest source, let alone for a researcher's time.

Once the budget and schedule have been worked out, the picture researcher should be provided with the manuscript, or with as detailed an outline of the project as is available, from which to draw up a picture list. The list, of course, should be a cooperative venture to which editor, author, and picture researcher all contribute. Time will be saved, however, if the picture researcher makes the first list and then all three work together to refine it. A picture researcher routinely sees thousands and thousands of pictures on every subject imaginable, remembers a surprising number of them and where they are and is skilled at translating abstract concepts into visual terms. While reading the manuscript, the picture researcher draws on a remarkable visual memory, lists possible illustrations and alternatives, and notes what points in the text can and cannot be illustrated. A good picture list should have two or three times as many items on it as will actually be published in order to allow flexibility as research proceeds. The nature of the list depends also upon how the illustrations are to be distributed in the book. Will they be integrated with the text or used as inserts? What is the proportion of black-and-white and colour, and where will each occur? The list will also indicate possible sources for each picture, and the next task is to break it down by source. The researcher can then start the process of visiting picture sources within reach and writing to those too far away for a personal visit. Picture research should be done in person whenever possible and not on the telephone, especially when any volume of material is to be collected. There is no substitute for personal visits to picture sources. Agency staff, however helpful, will not understand what is needed as clearly and comprehensively as the picture researcher, and they will not think of the variety of alternatives possible. Furthermore, in the very process of looking through the files, alternative, better and unexpected solutions to picture problems will present themselves.

Dealing with all of these matters can take a great deal of time, but the experienced picture researcher can usually predict approximately how much time is needed for a project. The prediction is based on a series of variables involving the subject matter of the pictures and hence the sources that must be approached. Picture research proceeds most quickly when all of the material can be found in commercial picture agencies and when the budget is big enough to pay for professional photography throughout. Some subjects, however, cannot be illustrated entirely from photo agencies, and others not at all. In these cases the time required to carry out research, order prints and transparencies and clear rights and permissions is much longer. Obtaining material from public libraries, museums, art galleries, corporate archives, government sources and private collections can be very time consuming indeed. Arranging for material from private collections is probably the most difficult and time consuming task of all. Private collectors of paintings seem invariably to have departed on a world cruise at the very moment you write to them seeking permission to publish a photograph of one of their paintings. Further problems arise when it turns out that the painting has been sold to yet another private collector who must be found and approached. After selecting batches of pictures from each source, the researcher edits this material a second time back in the office and returns the unwanted pictures to their owners. The remaining pictures are then organized into a logical sequence and an editorial meeting takes place involving some combination of picture researcher, editor and author. This process is repeated with manageable groups of pictures until all the necessary illustrations have been chosen.

At this point the picture researcher's task is far from finished. The selected pictures must be given a final careful inspection for print quality. Are they good enough for reproduction? Are they marked or scarred in any way that will show up when reproduced? Can better prints be ordered? In the case of colour transparencies, each one must be inspected with a hand lens for scratches or any undesirable pictorial detail easily overlooked on a 35mm transparency that would spoil the effect when enlarged. Is caption information needed and is it available, accurate and reliable? Picture agencies cannot guarantee accurate captions, and indeed most have a disclaimer to this effect in their delivery notes. Next, the researcher makes a list of final selections and notifies each of the suppliers in writing of the number of their pictures being used, the relative proportion of the page they will occupy (quarter page, half page, full page, double-page spread), the rights required (UK only, UK and Commonwealth, world English language, world all languages), the date of publication and when to submit the invoice.

As soon as page proofs are available the researcher should check the captions for accuracy. Other problems and details may have to be dealt with at this point. Some organizations and photographers stipulate that reproductions of paintings in their collections may not be cropped in any way, that details from the paintings may not be reproduced without permission, and that no type may overlay any part of the picture. The picture researcher must make sure that these points have been observed, thereby preventing complaints or fines or even legal action. Some professional photographers also forbid cropping of their work – the French photographer Henri Cartier-Bresson insists upon this point.

Museums and living artists sometimes also insist that they must approve the colour proofs of a reproduction before they permit publication, which can present a real problem when material must be sent back and forth from one country to another with deadlines approaching. One editor remembers sending four different colour proofs, one after the other, to the wife of a famous painter, only to have each one rejected. In despair the editor sent proof number one for a second time; a letter came back saying, 'At last! you've got it right!'

The next task is to compile an accurate list of picture credits to be published in the book or at the end of the magazine article. Some museums and picture agencies stipulate that their picture credits appear beside the picture, a sore point for many publishers who prefer to place all the picture credits together at the beginning or end of the book.

The penultimate task for the picture researcher is to return pictures to the suppliers after use. In the case of a book this procedure must wait until material comes back from the printer, probably near the actual publication date and many months after selection. It is essential that photographs be examined and counted immediately so that any problems of damage or loss can be taken up with the printer without delay. Valuable colour transparencies are most at risk during the reproduction process. Sometimes they are sprayed with a fixative to hold them on the drum during colour separation and must be carefully cleaned before they are returned to their owners. Sometimes they are scratched; sometimes they are removed from their mounts and replaced incorrectly or not at all. When all the pictures are clean and accounted for, they are returned with covering letters to the suppliers and the job is nearly complete. The very last task is to make sure that copies of the book are despatched as promised; some libraries and museums waive their fees in exchange for a copy of the publication and others make receipt of a free copy part of the agreement.

What should a picture researcher know?

The best picture researchers have both a very wide range of general knowledge and a good visual sense. People often ask what is the best educational background for a picture researcher and the answer is that while any subject speciality is bound to be useful, perhaps the most useful is modern history. A knowledge of the liberal arts is clearly important and so is familiarity with political, cultural and social history. Some projects, it is true, involve only contemporary material, but many involve historical pictures to a greater or lesser degree. A detailed visual knowledge of the past is essential. Some picture researchers specialize in fine art or science; others are expert generalists who can tackle all subjects. A good visual sense enables a picture researcher to spot errors in captions, for example, and to say with confidence that a photograph was not taken in 1925 but nearer to 1933, or to sort out confused identifications in group photographs, or even to look at a photograph with no caption at all and judge that it was taken in the Kent countryside around 1890. A visual sense cannot be learned, but it can be sharpened by experience and application. Training in the fine arts helps educate the eye and alert it to matters of form, composition, balance and proportion, but more often than not picture researchers must choose illustrations for the information they contain and only secondly for aesthetic qualities. An accurate visual memory is a vital necessity, and this faculty too grows with experience. A skilled researcher can pair a photograph in the hand with one seen in a file a few years before in order to produce a striking comparison on the page. Imagination plays a vital part in this process, as the researcher thinks of fresh uses for pictures remembered from the past. Asked to find a photograph to illustrate religious awe, one picture researcher remembered a photograph she had seen years before in a United Nations collection. It showed a man praying, his forehead against the floor, at the foot of a towering wall covered with beautiful and intricate Islamic designs in the Shah Mosque. The photograph was filed away under 'Architecture: Iran' (and not, of course, under religious awe), but the visual memory and imagination of the researcher produced it as a fresh and very successful means of illustrating the subject and avoiding visual clichés which everyone had seen many times before.

Functions of pictures

A good and imaginative choice of precisely the right picture cannot be made unless the picture researcher understands the function the picture must fill when it is published. The question, 'Why are you searching for these pictures?' must constantly be borne in mind (and there are at least five answers) or the wrong selection may be made. Pictures appear on books and magazine covers, on record sleeves and in advertisements in order *to sell* the product – to attract the readers' or browsers' attention quickly and to hold it. Various techniques are used to this end, one of the most common being the use of a portrait photograph that makes eye contact with the potential buyer. Direct advertising is one way in which pictures help to sell products; they can help in more subtle ways as well. Some books contain handsome colour photographs whose main function is to sell the book; photographs in cookery books, for instance, even the step-by-step pictures, really provide very little information about cooking but they do sell cookery books. New or revised editions of books frequently have fresh pictorial material precisely for the purpose of helping sales.

In textbooks, do-it-yourself books, instruction manuals and other factual material, pictures are used *to inform:* they supplement the written word by providing information that cannot be supplied with lucidity and precision by words alone. The criteria for choosing pictures to inform are above all accuracy and clarity; for manuals and do-it-yourself publications, extraneous and possibly confusing visual information must be kept to a minimum. For textbooks, audio-visual teaching materials or documentaries of any kind, the major criterion is, of course, accuracy, and the picture researcher must be careful to avoid historical anachronisms. Sometimes, however, they are unavoidable. Design considerations, for instance, may dictate that a page must contain a picture when the only subject capable of illustration on that page has no contemporary image. An anachronistic rendition of the subject has to be used, but the caption should explain this clearly.

Pictures are also used *to decorate*, and for this purpose aesthetic considerations predominate in the design to please and delight the viewer. In this category are posters, greetings cards, calendars and reproductions intended for framing. Similar to this function is the use of pictures *to entertain* the reader or viewer. The pictures in many humorous or heavily illustrated coffee-table books fall into this category.

Perhaps the most vital use of pictures is *to persuade*, to serve, as print historian William Ivins wrote, 'as tools in the struggle for opinion'. Photographs help win votes for a political party, help raise money to relieve famines and floods and to find cures for disease, to save wildlife and to protect the environment. When persuasion is the purpose of an illustration, the picture researcher must find material that has the necessary emotional impact.

In most cases, some combination of these five functions of illustrations is at work (to entertain *and* to sell, to inform *and* to persuade), but for the purposes of determining the overall impression a selection of pictures is required to make, it is helpful to consider them separately. Once this initial analysis is made, an assessment of the relative importance of each follows, and the desired visual effect and emotional tone is more clearly perceived. Harold Evans' book, *Pictures on a Page* (Heinemann: London, 1982) is the best account available on how to understand and edit photographs.

What kinds of pictures are there?

When the subject to be illustrated is anything other than purely contemporary, the variety of kinds of pictures available to the researcher is overwhelming. The enormous expansion of literacy in the nineteenth century and the consequent appetite for information among the new readers gave rise to daily and weekly newspapers and magazines in unprecedented numbers. A partiality for illustrations as well as text was gratified with the appearance of the first issue of the *Illustrated London News* (14 May 1842); French and German illustrated monthly magazines followed a year later. The illustrations were provided by engravings on wood or metal, sometimes based on eyewitness sketches or earlier artwork of one kind or another. By the 1860s, photographers were beginning to produce news photographs and these were copied by the engravers, for it was not yet possible to reproduce photographs on the printed page. The magazines dealt with and illustrated every subject imaginable. All of this material is now free of copyright restrictions and is available to picture researchers. But this wealth of material is only the beginning. All conventional fine art is available: oil paintings, fine-art prints, watercolours, lithographs, mezzotints, engravings on copper, zinc or steel plates, and drawings. Through the medium of photography, other art forms are available as well: sculpture, ceramics, pottery, mosaics, murals, stained glass, architectural details, cave paintings, tapestries, needlework, embroidery, samplers, and even graffiti. In collections of ephemera, the researcher can explore the vast visual resources of trade cards, advertisements, postcards, cartoons, greetings cards, package labels, calendars,

playing cards, and wallpaper. In libraries, there are illuminated manuscripts, illustrated maps, architectural and engineering drawings, architectural perspectives. Even postage stamps, currency and stock certificates yield useful and interesting visual material.

To this almost limitless wealth of visual images, we can add the contributions of photography from the 1840s to the present: early daguerreotypes (often exquisite in quality and detail), tintypes, ambrotypes and calotypes, photographs printed from paper and then from glass and finally from film negatives, colour photographs, stills from motion pictures, stereographs, X-rays, multi-exposure stroboscopic photographs, aerial photographs, satellite photographs, infra-red photographs, and holographs.

The problem is no longer how to find a picture of a given subject but to decide what kind of picture of it best suits the purpose. The modern researcher needs, therefore, to be familiar with different print-making techniques, for example, and to be able to judge how well each will reproduce. Prints are made from wood, metal, silk screens and stone, and in each case the material is worked in a different way. Woodcuts are made by carving away the wood into relief with a sharp chisel, metal is engraved by a sharply-pointed tool called a burin or etched with acid, stone is coated with grease (colour crayons) and ink, and silk is used as a stencil. Each of these techniques produces a different kind of line and each has advantages and disadvantages when it comes to reproduction. Early woodcuts stand up well to reduction in size without much loss of detail, but if enlarged too much they look crude and unattractive. The fine lines of an engraving on metal can stand a great deal of enlarging, but if reduced too much lose character. Crayon lithographs, designed to be printed in colour, do not reproduce well in black-and-white; the lines tend to become fuzzy. Hilary and Mary Evans' *Sources of Illustration 1500-1900* (Adams: London, 1971) gives a good account of the different kinds of prints and so does *Prints and Printmaking: An Introduction to the History and Techniques* by Anthony Griffiths (British Museum Publications: London, 1980). Photographs could not be reproduced on the printed page until the development of the half-tone process toward the end of the nineteenth century. Dozens of individual efforts were made to refine and perfect a screening process and a primitive half-tone reproduction of a photograph of Central Park appeared in an American newspaper in 1880, but it was not until about 1900 that the process had been refined to the extent that more photographs than engravings were being published.

It is worth mentioning here, perhaps, that while it is quite possible to photograph engravings successfully from the pages of old books and magazines and perfectly legal if they are out of copyright, trying to copy photographs from a printed page is usually unsuccessful as well as illegal. The half-tone process by means of which they are reproduced breaks the image down through a fine screen into tiny dots in order to obtain gradations of tone. If this image is rephotographed and then rescreened for reproduction, one pattern of dots is superimposed on another. If the screening is coarse, the result can be a moiré pattern, and if fine, the quality may be blurred and muddy.

Some knowledge of the history of photography is essential to a picture researcher, who must be able to judge which events and people may and may not have been documented photographically. It comes as a surprise to most people, for instance, to learn that a photograph (a daguerreotype, in fact) exists of the first Duke of Wellington! The first photograph, the result of work by two Frenchmen, Louis Daguerre and Nicéphore Niepce, was taken in 1839, but the technical limitations of the new medium restricted early photographers to portraits, architectural views, still lifes and landscapes. The required exposure time of the first photographic plates was too long to arrest any movement and those who sat for their photographs had to submit to a headbrace to prevent movement and consequent blurring of the image. Photographers documented the Crimean War and the American Civil War, but the slow and cumbersome wet-plate technique of the time prohibited any kind of action shots. Picture researchers must be ready for the unrealistic requests of editors who want 'real action

shots' of these conflicts. With the refinement of the half-tone process for reproducing photographs, newspapers and magazines began to demand more and more photographs and the first news photo services appeared, supplying pictures of news and sports events, politicians and entertainers, and people in far distant countries. The wire services appeared on the scene in the early 1920s, producing at first rather crude photographic prints suitable only for newspaper reproduction with its very coarse screens. As cameras themselves became lighter, smaller and more versatile, the profession of photojournalism developed from the pioneer struggles of the early photographers. The best book on the subject is *The History of Photography 1685-1914* by Helmut and Alison Gernsheim (Thames and Hudson: London, 1969); also a very fine piece of work is Beaumont Newhall's *The History of Photography* (Secker and Warburg: London, 1973).

Finding the right source

The usefulness of *Picture Sources UK* and its comprehensive subject index is obvious, and it will solve many picture problems. For sources of pictures outside the United Kingdom, other directories exist. For France, consult *Répertoire des collections photographiques en France* (La Documentation Française: Paris, 1980). American picture sources are described in *Picture Sources 3* (1975) and its successor *Picture Sources 4* (1983) (Special Libraries Association, 235 Park Avenue South, New York, NY 10016). *The Picture Researcher's Handbook* by Hilary and Mary Evans (Saturday Ventures: London, 1979) includes British and world commercial picture sources, and *World Photography Sources* edited by David Bradshaw and Catherine Hahn (Directories: New York, 1982) also attempts worldwide coverage.

The present volume makes no pretensions to be exhaustive on the subject of fine art. For detailed reference, consult the *Museum Yearbook* (The Museum Association, London) for UK museums, and for worldwide coverage *The Directory of Museums* (Macmillan: London, 1975) and other similar works. On the subject of fine art, the great auction houses Sotheby's and Christies are extremely helpful in providing information concerning the whereabouts of works of art that have passed through their hands; so in fact are most galleries. British trade associations are listed in *Trade Associations and Professional Bodies of the United Kingdom* by Patricia Millard (Pergamon Press: Oxford, 1979). If you cannot find a copy of it, make enterprising use of the telephone directories. If you have to find photographs of steeplejacks you might vainly try 'steeplejacks' in the directory and then 'Association of Steeplejacks'. Turning to 'National', however, your persistence is rewarded and there is the National Federation of Master Steeplejacks; surely they will be able to direct you to photographs of steeplejacks. *Willing's Press Guide* (IPC Business Press Ltd, London) is published annually and is an invaluable resource, listing the name, address and telephone number of every newspaper (national and regional) and magazine in the UK and of principal publications throughout the world. If you must have a photograph of a specific pub in Inverness and none of the London picture agencies have it, try ringing up one of the Inverness newspapers. They probably employ a photographer who would be more than willing to take the photograph for you in his or her spare time, and it will cost far less than dispatching someone from London on a full day rate. *Willing's* will also put you in touch with an amazing number of special interest periodicals. When all of the agencies specializing in natural history fail to produce a picture of a glass catfish, *Willing's* will lead you to the *Aquarist and Pond Keeper* and eventual success. Large corporations are likely to have photographs of their products and activities round the world and also archives concerning the history of their industry. *Hollis Press and Publications Annual* (Hollis Directories Ltd) lists news contacts, information sources, public relations consultancies, reference and research sources, and services for the communications industry and the media. It is a very useful book.

In-depth photographic coverage of special subjects can be elusive, but a little conventional research in a library with a good collection of illustrated periodicals should help. Periodical and biographic indexes, especially *A Reader's Guide to Periodical Literature* (1900-) *Popular Periodical Index* (1973-) and *Biography Index* (1946-), with a little patience will lead you eventually to an illustrated article on your subject. The periodical should give you picture credits or at least the name of an expert somewhere who should be able to help.

Using the source

Once you have determined the most likely source of the material you need, research on the premises may be more difficult than anticipated. No two picture libraries file their material in quite the same way. Some libraries have had their systems imposed on them by the very complexity of their material. The BBC Hulton Picture Library, for example, has dozens of collections acquired at different times; some are news photo files, others the work of single photographers, and still others have a subject orientation. The pictures are still held in these separate collections, and the BBC Hulton Library does not allow researchers into the files because their system takes too long to learn. Some picture libraries do not hold many black-and-white prints and the researcher must choose black-and-white negatives to be printed up. It takes a considerable amount of skill and experience to read black-and-white negatives successfully, and such research can be a slow and rather daunting business. Museum collections of photography are apt to be filed by the name of the photographer, and it is as well to be forewarned about this and not arrive expecting a subject approach to the material. Some museum collections, however, are lovingly catalogued down to the last detail of the last print and some even have duplicated copies of their catalogues available for a small fee. Some of the large news-gathering agencies, swamped by the sheer volume of material they hold, toss photos into boxes or file-folders labelled with only the very broadest subject classifications.

Computer cataloguing and video discs are beginning to appear in more and more picture libraries and they perform some tasks to perfection; both of these systems, however, have shortcomings and if not carefully used can hinder rather than help image finding. On a video disc a large number of pictures can certainly be scanned very quickly, but an experienced picture researcher can go through four or five hundred black-and-white prints just as quickly, putting some aside for a second look during the process, and returning them to the pile as better images replace them. The problem with computer cataloguing is simply that any moderately complex photograph can be catalogued in so many different ways and under so many headings that the game simply isn't worth the candle when it comes to logging it all into a computer. The photograph, let us say, is a turn-of-the-century streetscene, showing people, shops, children, dogs, traffic. It can be indexed under the name of the town, the name of the street, the name of the photographer, under social history, trade, transport, horse-drawn vehicles, shops and shopping, policemen, greengrocers, butchers, shoe shops, costume and fashion, architecture and so forth. Then someone will come along and want the photograph for none of the above elements but for quite another one, very likely overlooked by the cataloguer. Picture researchers often feel that the best way of cataloguing pictures is to group them under large, fairly simple subject headings. This permits the researcher to look through large numbers of pictures quickly and easily.

Picture researchers and editors must understand the difference between the commercial agencies organized to provide material as quickly and efficiently as possible and the museums, libraries and government or corporate archives that may provide pictures as a courtesy but whose primary function is definitely not the provision of a service to publishers. The commercial agencies are in business to provide images at a profit and to do it more quickly and efficiently than their competitors; their speed and efficiency is provided in return for a fee. The function of museums and libraries is largely archival and custodial; they are concerned to preserve their collections and to make them available to scholars. Many museums and libraries have no in-house photographic service, nor do they keep duplicate prints or transparencies on file even when they do possess either a photographic record of their collection or a collection of photographs. Consequently, researchers may have to wait for weeks or even months for material to be photographed or for prints to be made from existing negatives, captioned and mailed. These organizations are more often than not desperately short of staff; many of them have extensive and interesting picture collections but cannot afford to employ a picture librarian and may even be unfamiliar with the problems of archival care of photographic material or even with photographic terminology. Such problems prevent these bodies from offering the range of services of a commercial agency; a researcher should approach them with a courteous understanding of their problems and by not making unrealistic demands may well be rewarded with enthusiastic cooperation and interesting and fresh visual material.

Whether you are visiting a picture agency or contacting one too far away for a personal call, be as specific as you possibly can with your requests. It is not good practice to send out enormous and undigested lists of requests, and it provokes a very negative response from understaffed and overworked non-commercial collections. You should know approximately which agency or source will have what kind of pictures and tailor your list accordingly.

Delivery notes – legal contracts?

When a commercial picture agency sends a consignment of photographs to a client, it encloses a delivery note that details the number and nature of the pictures consigned. This note normally has printed on it the terms and conditions that the agency stipulates must govern the transaction between agency and client. It is generally accepted that by accepting delivery of the pictures, the client agrees to the terms and that the delivery note has the status of a legal contract. The client should read the delivery note carefully if he or she lacks experience in dealing with picture agencies, and even experienced picture users should closely examine delivery notes from new agencies.

A delivery note may have as many as twenty clauses on the back; the ones that are most important are those to do with copyright, holding fees, damage and loss fees and caption information. The client is warned that the agency owns the copyright and/or represents the copyright holders and that publication of the pictures without permission is illegal. The agency usually grants permission to publish on payment of its invoice and therefore publication of a picture before payment of the photographer's or agency's invoice may technically be an infringement of copyright. There is, however, a great deal of discussion on this point and it remains to be cleared up by revision in the law. In practice, however, payment of the invoices usually takes place near the time of publication, perhaps shortly afterwards.

Agencies and photographers usually lend pictures to publishers free of charge for a month, sometimes longer. The free holding period is stipulated on the delivery note and so is the weekly charge which will be made for holding the material after the free period has expired. Most agencies are quite willing to extend the free holding period if the client rings them up and explains that more time is needed. The holding fee is seldom charged to a regular client who deals responsibly with an agency, keeping them informed of needs and returning material as quickly as possible. The holding fee exists to protect the agency and the photographer from the client who puts the photographs in a drawer and forgets about them for six months, during which time the agency is denied the opportunity of selling them elsewhere. Holding fees, however, can mount up extremely quickly when large numbers of photographs, especially colour transparencies, are held. A careless client may easily receive an invoice for a thousand pounds for holding fees, so it is wise to examine the delivery note, discover what the holding fees are and make a few calculations. The fees are usually charged weekly for each colour transparency or black-and-white photograph. Some agencies charge holding fees for photographs which have been published but not returned to the agency within one month of publication of the book or magazine. Under normal circumstances, photographs should be back in the publisher's hands before the actual publication date, but if material is printed abroad there can be a delay. If this is the case, having the courtesy to telephone and explain the delay to suppliers

may prevent this additional charge.

Fees for the loss or irreparable damage of photographs vary from agency to agency and for an original colour transparency may run to several hundred pounds. In considering these fees, remember that in the case of colour material the transparency is the original (no negative is involved). Duplicate colour transparencies can be made from the original, but most publishers prefer to work with originals for the sake of good quality. Furthermore, good duplicate colour transparencies are quite expensive and duplicating large numbers of transparencies in a collection would be prohibitive. In the case of black-and-white photographs, as long as the negative has not been lost or badly damaged, additional prints can be made relatively cheaply.

The fee for the loss of a colour transparency represents compensation in two ways: first, for the loss of any future income from the transparency and, second, for the expense of replacing it. A good photograph taken by a professional photographer will sell more than once. Ten sales are a modest expectation, and some photographs sell many more times than that. A loss fee of a few hundred pounds might be the equivalent of from one to five sales, and seen in this light, the loss fee is not unreasonable, although anyone who has been careless or unfortunate enough to lose 25 or 30 original transparencies will doubtless have other opinions. The expense of replacing a photograph or transparency varies widely. A spectacular colour photograph of Mount Everest is clearly not in the same price range as a spectacular colour photograph of Piccadilly Circus on a sunny day. But wait a moment – if clients want a colour photograph of Piccadilly Circus, the chances are that they want it looking the way most people expect – with the Eros statue in the middle. For some time Piccadilly Circus was without Eros, which was being restored, and the middle of the famous Circus was occupied by wooden fences and barriers. Replacing the photograph would have had to wait until Piccadilly Circus was back to normal and any sales of a photograph of it would have been lost. Replacing even those photographs that can be replaced locally is not as simple as it seems as first, not to mention the expense of mounting an expedition to the Himalayas or the impossibility of rephotographing people who have grown old or died or events that cannot be restaged. The loss fee has to compensate for all of these eventualities, and it is designed to strike some sort of mean between the possible and the impossible.

Inexperienced buyers of photography are occasionally heard to complain about the fact that agencies and photographers put a disclaimer in the terms and conditions of their delivery memos concerning captions. They usually say that while they make every effort to provide correct caption information, they cannot guarantee it. Picture professionals, however, who are aware of the circumstances under which professional photographers work and of the volume of photographs that may flow, for instance, through a professional newsgathering picture agency, realize the sheer impossibility of guaranteeing accuracy of captions. There are too many photographs, too many people involved and too little time. Photographers usually have a few specialities up their sleeves, but they cannot be expected to have accurate and encyclopedic knowledge about everything they photograph. There are, of course, exceptions to the rule, as some natural history photographers, for example, are experts in ornithology and are willing to provide and guarantee the Latin names of their birds.

The question of the photographer's and agency's credit line is beginning to receive more attention and more agencies and photographers stipulate in their delivery note that a fine is payable if the credit line is omitted. Deliberate omission of credit lines shows disregard for the work of talented professionals. A photographer showing published work to a potential client is at some disadvantage if the publisher has thought so little of the photographs that no name is attached to the work. A credit line has the further function of helping other potential users find the photographer or agency should they want to publish the work themselves. The amount of the fine for omission of credit line varies, but it can be double the normal reproduction rights fee.

Photocopies

Because of recent enforcement and discussion of the copyright rules governing photocopying, many of the smaller libraries and museums are nervous about using the process. It is not, however, an infringement of copyright if you make one photocopy of an image for purposes of reference and it is always useful to build up a collection of photocopies whenever you have the opportunity. When ordering a print from a museum or a library it is sound practice to enclose a photocopy if possible to avoid mistakes.

Pictures on the screen

Feature films, television and audio-visual productions all use still as well as motion pictures. The terminology can be a little confusing. If you are working in the print media, then a still is a frame from a motion picture printed as a black-and-white or colour photographic print. These stills are widely distributed for publicity purposes. If, however, you are working in films or television, then a still is *any* photograph that is not part of a motion picture film or video tape. Television documentaries even of contemporary subject matter must rely on still photographs, and historical subjects, of course, do so to a much greater extent. Some documentary films have been made up entirely of still photographs. Photographs can also help establish a mood, period, or setting either at the beginning of a film or within it, often more effectively than a motion picture sequence. A comedy series set during World War II, for example, might well have a title sequence made up of still photographs. A sequence of filmed photographs can also be used to show the passing of time and to act as a bridge or bridges linking episodic material. If the problem were to suggest the passing of five years, a date flashed on the screen might give the information, but would suggest little of the effect that the passage of time has had on the characters. A sequence of photographs chronicling those five years in terms of fads and fashions, events both serious and silly, sports figures and entertainers, not only indicates time passing but indicates it in human terms.

Picture research for the screen involves one consideration irrelevant to the print media: for how long will the picture appear? This affects the choice of photographs, and the picture researcher needs to know how the photographs will be used before making a selection. It is possible, for instance, to choose a photograph of great visual complexity, a wide-angled streetscene, for example, in which dozens of different people and events and encounters are recorded. Such a photograph can be explored by a skilled cameraman zooming in on a detail, panning along a series of shop-fronts, travelling back and forth, cutting from one group to another to remarkable effect. In this case, the photograph is chosen for complexity and richness of detail and it will be held on the screen, in one form or another, for a relatively long period of time.

Photographs can be used in quite a different way to show the passing of time or the development of an idea. For a New Year's Eve television programme, for instance, the producer might want to review the events of the year just past. A mixture of film footage and stills is required, and the stills can be flashed on the screen at a rate of one per second, or even faster, with various cuts and dissolves for variety. If the photographs are going to be used at such a pace, however, they must be chosen expressly for such use. The subject of the photograph must be instantly recognizable; it must be more or less front and centre in the photo, and there can be no distracting or confusing elements in the picture. The only way to edit photographs for such use is to deal them into a pile like playing cards at about the same pace as they would appear on the screen, and if you cannot tell at a glance what the picture is, discard it. Between these two extremes of exploring a photo leisurely and flashing it quickly, lies a middle ground and in one and the same film you might use photographs in three different ways and at three different speeds.

The shape of a television screen or a cinema screen also has some effect on picture research for these media. Of course photographs can be cropped within reason, but there is less flexibility than on the printed page which not only permits but needs some white space. The picture researcher has to bear in mind the shape of the screen and generally avoid extremely vertical or horizontal pictures, unless they are to be combined in a multiple image.

Negotiating fees for film and television use of photographs is always a problem because prices are usually based on how many times the photographs will be shown. A commercial, for instance, may be shown in the London area for a specific number of weeks, but may later appear regionally as well. The difficulty is in keeping track, yet buying rights to show the photograph for an unlimited period would certainly be prohibitively expensive.

Original research

Good picture research cannot be carried out by scanning other published works on the same subject and producing the same material slightly reshuffled. Checking the picture credits in published material, however, is always worthwhile, for it may lead to a source that is new to you. Of course, it is not always possible to find new material; there is only one photograph of Pavlov's dog and everyone has to use it. Whenever time and the budget permit, however, the good researcher counsels original research, even if it means some travelling. In some cases, such travel is economical, for one or two days spent at the right source are worth a week of letter writing and telephone calls trying to patch together a selection of pictures from inappropriate sources. Original research brings fresh and interesting material to readers and viewers and increases the prestige and profitability of the material illustrated.

General Picture Collections

1 • ABERDEEN UNIVERSITY LIBRARY

MacBean Collection

Special Collections Department
King's College, Aberdeen AB9 2UB
Tel (0224) 40241 Telex 73458

Enquiries to Myrtle Anderson-Smith, Keeper of
Special Collections

Items 3530: sepia photographic prints, fine art
prints

Dates of subject matter *c.* 1688 to 1750

Dates of photographs 1860–1900; prints 1700–
1900

Subjects Photographs: Scottish scenery and
historical sites in most counties; prints: Scottish
history including Jacobite connection, portraits,
battlefields, maps, caricatures, towns, buildings

Access and conditions Open to the public by
appt (tel); closed for the last week in June. All
material available for editorial reproduction and
for advertising. No loans; b/w prints available for a
fee. Reproduction rights fees charged. Staff will undertake some research.
Printed catalogue available: Mabel D. Allardyce,
Aberdeen University Library MacBean Collection,
Aberdeen University Studies No. 126, Aberdeen
University Press, 1949.

George Washington Wilson Collection

Queen Mother Library, Meston Walk, Aberdeen
AB9 2UE
Tel (0224) 40241 Telex 73458

Enquiries to Myrtle Anderson-Smith, Keeper of
Special Collections

Items 40,000: glass negatives, b/w original
photographs

Dates of photographs 1860–1908

Subjects Scotland with emphasis on Aberdeen
and the north-east, landscapes, crofting, fishing,
portraits, tourism; England, South Africa,
Australia, Gibraltar and the Mediterranean area
surrounding it

Access and conditions Open to the public by
appt (tel); closed for the last week in June. All
material available for editorial reproduction and
for advertising. No loans; b/w prints available for a
fee. Reproduction rights fees charged. Staff of three
will undertake some research. Partial subject card
catalogue available.

2 • ACE PHOTO AGENCY

22 Maddox Street, London W1R 9PG
Tel (01) 629 0303 Telex 266801 MEXCO G

Enquiries to Head Librarian

Items Over 100,000: colour transparencies
(35mm, 2¼″, 5″ × 4″, 10″ × 8″), b/w original
photographs, b/w negatives, 3-D colour
transparencies

Dates of subject matter Modern, with some
historical material

Dates of photographs 1940 to present

Subjects World geography (122 countries);
natural history including plants, animals, climatic
conditions, natural phenomena, sunsets, skies,
seascapes; aerial photographs, architecture,
agriculture, industry and technology including
space travel, oil rigs, alternative energy sources;
transportation, sport, performing arts including
classical and rock music, theatre; personalities,
fashion, human behaviour, family life, leisure and
holidays, abstracts, photojournalism

Access and conditions Open to qualified
researchers by appt, Mon-Fri 9.30–6. All material
available for editorial reproduction and for
advertising. B/w and colour material loaned free of
charge for one month. Photocopies and Polaroids
available. Reproduction rights, service and holding
fees charged; service fees deductible from use fees.
Staff of five will undertake research; fee negotiable
for large projects. All material copyright. Printed
subject catalogue.

3 • ADAMS PICTURE LIBRARY

17/18 Rathbone Place, London W1P 1DF
Tel (01) 636 1468

Enquiries to Carol White

Items About 500,000: colour transparencies
(35mm, 2¼")

Subjects People including men, women, babies,
children, families, groups, human interest, posed
models; sports and games, camping; entertainment
including carnivals, theatre, music and dance;
agriculture, industry, people at work, commerce,
shopping and markets, transport; natural history
including flora and fauna and especially domestic
animals, birds, butterflies, micro-biology,
landscapes, seascapes, sunsets, weather and sky,
aerial views; architecture including historical and
modern buildings, churches, houses, interiors,
furnishings; *objets d'art*, fine art; world geography
including London, England, Scotland, Wales,
France, Greece, Venice; special effects including
reflections, textures, silhouettes, lighting effects;
humour and ephemera

Access and conditions Open to qualified
researchers Mon-Fri 9–6. All material available for
editorial reproduction and almost all for
advertising. Colour material loaned free of charge
for four weeks. Reproduction rights, service and
holding fees charged. Staff of two will undertake
research. All material copyright.

ADESPOTON *see* JO BOND WORDS AND
PICTURES

4 • ALDUS ARCHIVE

Maxwell House, 74 Worship Street, London
EC2A 2EN
Tel (01) 377 4669

Enquiries to Kate Poole, Librarian

Items 75,000: colour transparencies (35mm,
5" × 4", larger), b/w original and copy photographs,
illustrated books

Dates of subject matter Prehistory to present

Dates of photographs 19th century to present

Subjects Agriculture, aircraft (historical and
modern), American history (War of Independence,
Civil War, presidents, immigration, black history,
politics, women's movement, personalities,
everyday life, fads and crazes), antiques (glass,
ceramics, furniture, silver, textiles, carpets,
jewellery, clocks, kitchenware, collectibles), art
(reproductions of famous paintings, sculpture),
astronomy, beauty and health (keep fit, diets and
slimming, cosmetics), BPCC company
photographs, chess (history of the game, chess
pieces), cinema (film stills and posters),
communications and language (development of
language and writing, printing, codes, symbols,
long-distance communications), cookery (stock
pictures, step-by-step techniques), crafts and
hobbies (gardening, painting, pottery, needlework,
papercrafts, collage, beadwork, candle-making,
fabric-printing and dyeing, brewing and wine-
making), crime (Jack the Ripper, executioner's
block, drug-smuggling, judge on the bench, etc.),
ecology (pollution, soil erosion, conservation),
education (primary school children, practical
classroom projects), energy, exploration (early
explorers, North and South America, Africa, Far
East, Australia, the Poles, mountaineering, space
travel, gambling (historical and modern),
geography (topography and people of most
countries), geology (earth's crust, minerals,
phenomena, earthquakes, volcanoes, etc.), home
repairs and decoration, human behaviour (love and
romance, sex, marriage, family life, man in society,
psychology, dreams, etc.), industry, manufacture
and occupations (especially newspapers and
printing, hotel management), Jewish history,
medicine and surgery (historical and modern,
hospitals), motor cycles (historical and modern),
mountains (Switzerland, Austria, Spain, India,
Scotland), music (musical instruments, pop stars of
the 1960s and 1970s), mysteries (Loch Ness
monster, flying saucers, Bermuda Triangle,
Atlantis, leylines, etc.), natural history (prehistoric
life, animals, birds, insects, marine creatures),
police work, science and invention (history of
inventions, modern technology), secret societies
and cults, sport (athletics, gymnastics,
showjumping, horse-racing, cricket, soccer, Rugby
football, golf, tennis, judo, squash, fishing, motor
racing, skateboarding), supernatural (ghosts,
poltergeists, alchemy, witchcraft, black magic,
vampires, monsters, werewolves, zombies,
spiritualism, faith-healing, Uri Geller, astrology,
reincarnation, ESP), weapons and warfare
(battleships, submarines, planes, helicopters,
gliders, tanks, field transport, bombs, guns,
missiles, medals, uniforms); bound copies of *Punch,
John Bull, Sphere, Illustrierter Beobachter,
Berliner Illustrierte, Simplicissimus, Deutsche
Illustrierte, Münchner Illustrierte Presse, Kölnische*

Illustrierte, L'Illustration, Le Cri de Paris and others

Access and conditions Open to qualified researchers by appt (tel), Mon-Fri 10–6. All material available for editorial reproduction and for advertising. B/w and colour material loaned free of charge for one month (longer periods negotiable). Photocopies available. Reproduction rights, holding and service fees charged; service fees deductible from use fees. Staff will undertake some research. Printed catalogue.

5 • BRYAN AND CHERRY ALEXANDER PHOTOGRAPHY

Poorhouse Cottage, 33 Mount Pleasant, Arundel, West Sussex BN18 9BD
Tel (0903) 882897

Enquiries to Cherry Alexander

Items About 20,000: colour transparencies (35mm), b/w original photographs

Dates of subject matter Contemporary

Dates of photographs 1971 to present

Subjects World geography, the Arctic (Greenland, Canada, Lapland, USSR) including people and lifestyles, fur clothing, traditional hunting from dogsleds and kayaks, reindeer herding, flora and fauna, glaciers and ice, eskimo art, social change (snowmobiles and video games), polar bears; the Antarctic including penguins, seals and underwater photos of aquatic life; whaling off Newfoundland and the Faeroes; Sweden including glass-blowing, elk-hunting, iron-ore mining; United Kingdom including Royal Warrant holders, underground London, London taxis, fishing industry (Grimsby trawlers), New Forest, Scottish islands including Shetland, North Uist, Islay and its whisky industry, Shillay and breeding of grey seals, Rhum and highland ponies, tweed-weaving and hand-spinning, deer-stalking, the salmon industry including wild and farmed fish; Mali including the Dogon (masked dancing and religious ritual, cicatration and tribal medicine, agriculture and crafts); southern India including the Todas (costumes and architecture, water buffalo as basis of religion, agriculture), Badagars, Irulas, Kotas and Paniyas; USA including Zabriskie Point, White Sands Park and Missile Range, cotton harvest, cattle auction, cowboys; Norway, Denmark, Nepal, Jamaica, France, Canada

Access and conditions Open to qualified researchers by appt (tel). Most material available for editorial reproduction and for advertising; photographs used in Time-Life Books require permission of Time Inc. as well since copyright is held jointly. B/w and colour material loaned free of charge for one month. Reproduction rights and service fees charged; service fees deductible from use fees. Staff will undertake some research. All material copyright.

6 • BERNARD ALFIERI PICTURE LIBRARY

Dunglass, Water Lane, Bookham, Leatherhead, Surrey KT23 3QQ
Tel (0372) 53160

Enquiries to Bernard Alfieri

Items About 60,000: colour transparencies (35mm, 7 × 6 cm), b/w negatives, b/w original photographs

Dates of subject matter BC to present

Dates of photographs 1921 to present

Subjects Horticulture including flowers, trees, shrubs, fruit, vegetables, house plants, cacti and succulents, plant propagation, garden maintenance, garden appliances, greenhouses, garden work step-by-step, flower sections and diagrams; Wisley, Kew, Valley and Dunglass Gardens; photographic copies of old flower prints and early colour illustrations; agriculture including old farming methods, ploughing, reaping, thatching, stringing and hopfields, hop-kilns, hop fruit and blossoms; craftsmen including Chiltern wood-bodgers, crabpot-makers, Sussex trug-makers, bowl-turners, wood-carvers, lace-makers; rural scenes including old cottages, watermills, windmills, quintains, stocks, old buildings; landscapes including Pembroke National Park, Exmoor, Dartmoor, Lake District, Yugoslavia; some natural history including dogs, cats, lion cubs, elephants, butterflies and moths; history of photography including Lacock Abbey and the work of Fox Talbot, early cameras, work and apparatus of Eadweard Muybridge (San Francisco before the earthquake, animal locomotion), work of Lumière brothers, infra-red and polarized light, specialized cameras; pottery including early pots, Roman pots, modern potters at work; measuring devices including sun dials, sand glasses, early mechanical clocks; museum subjects including old typewriters, the first gramophone from Edison, old musical instruments, early cooking tools; prints of old London

Access and conditions Open to qualified researchers by appt (tel). All material available for editorial reproduction; some for advertising. B/w and colour material loaned free of charge for one month. Reproduction rights and holding fees charged; no service fees. Staff will undertake some research; negotiable fee for large projects. All material copyright.

7 • J. CATLING ALLEN PHOTOGRAPHIC LIBRARY

Hope House, 29 Lovaine Place, North Shields, Tyne and Wear NE29 0BU
Tel (0632) 583701

Enquiries to Rev. John Catling Allen

Items 50,000: colour transparencies (35mm), b/w original photographs

Dates of subject matter BC to present

Dates of photographs 1961 to present

Subjects Israel, Jordan, Syria, Lebanon, Egypt, Iran, Iraq, Turkey, Cyprus, Greece, Malta, and Italy with emphasis on archaeological and Biblical sites, excavations, ruins, artefacts, architecture including churches, mosques, synagogues, temples, tombs, pyramids, ziggurats, religions (Christianity, Islam, Judaism), town and country life, markets, bazaars, harbours, human interaction, occupations, agriculture, irrigation; Britain with emphasis on medieval abbeys and priories, cathedrals and churches, historic sites and remains, general landscape coverage; travel coverage of Austria, Canada, France, Gibraltar, Portugal, South Africa, Spain with emphasis on places of pilgrimage and historic sites

Access and conditions Open to qualified researchers by appt (write). All material available for editorial reproduction and for advertising. B/w and colour material loaned free of charge for one month. Reproduction rights, holding and service fees charged. Research undertaken. All material copyright. Duplicated catalogue available.

8 • ANDES PRESS AGENCY

31 Silverbirch Court, 33 Middleton Road, London E8 4BW
Tel (01) 249 8072 Telex 893347 CAFOD G

Enquiries to Carlos Reyes or Val Baker

Items 200,000: b/w original and copy photographs, colour transparencies (35mm, 5″ × 4″), colour photographic prints

Dates of subject matter Stone age to present

Dates of photographs 1975 to present

Subjects UK including geography, industry, education, ethnic minorities (black and Asian communities), health care (National Health Service, handicapped people), social and political issues (demonstrations, Greenham Common, Campaign for Nuclear Disarmament), politicians and personalities, police and prisons (Wormwood Scrubs, Wandsworth and Ford prisons); children, teenagers, men and women, old people; performing arts (ballet, Nureyev, National Ballet of Cuba, Moscow Classical Ballet, Ekaterina Maximova, musicians, orchestras, instrumentalists, composers); religion including Church of England and Roman Catholic churches, church leaders from many countries, Pope John Paul II, bishops, clerics, priests, nuns, seminaries, pilgrimages, conferences, ecumenical services, ordinations, Polish, Ukranian and Italian congregations in London, painting, sculpture and stained glass; international organizations including Amnesty International, British Amnesty, Catholic Fund for Overseas Development, Catholic Institute for International Relations, Paxon Christi, Society of St Vincent de Paul, Society for the Protection of Unborn Children, Trocaire; world geography including Argentina, Bolivia, Brazil, Chile, Colombia, Costa Rica, Ecuador, Nicaragua, El Salvador, Guatemala, Honduras, Panama, Peru, Venezuela, the Philippines, Thailand, India, East Timor, Kenya, China, Mexico, France, Afghanistan, Ethiopia including refugees, African political and religious leaders

Access and conditions Open to the public by appt (tel), Mon-Fri 9.30–5.30. All material available for editorial reproduction and for advertising. B/w and colour material loaned free of charge for two months. Reproduction rights and holding fees charged. Staff will undertake some research. All material copyright.

9 • KEN ANDREW

17 Bellrock Avenue, Prestwick, Strathclyde KA9 1SQ
Tel (0292) 79077

Enquiries to Ken Andrew

Items 30,000: colour transparencies (35mm), b/w original photographs

Dates of subject matter Prehistory to present

Dates of photographs 1955 to present

Subjects Scotland, including architecture, ancient monuments, geology, geography, social history, transport, natural history, weather, forestry, town planning, industry, landscape; special collection on Scottish mountains

Access and conditions Open to qualified researchers by appt (tel). All material available for editorial reproduction and for advertising. B/w and colour material loaned free of charge for two months. Reproduction rights fees charged. Staff will undertake research. All material copyright.

10 • ART DIRECTORS PHOTO LIBRARY

Image House, 86 Haverstock Hill, London
NW3 2ND
Tel (01) 485 9325, 267 6930

Enquiries to Jack Stanley, Managing Director

Items About 500,000: colour transparencies (35mm, 5″ × 4″, larger), b/w prints, lantern slides, postcards

Dates of subject matter BC to present

Dates of photographs 1979 to present

Subjects Comprehensive collection covering all aspects of contemporary life including landscapes, urban views, seascapes, climatic conditions, geography worldwide, agriculture, horticulture, flowers, fruit, vegetables, ecology, wildlife, aircraft, transport, medicine, architecture, industry, trade, finance, including the oil industry and computers and their application in business and industry, entertainment, restaurants, food, public houses, hotels, social groups, interiors, sports including American football, basketball and baseball, and the Los Angeles Olympics

Access and conditions Open to the public by appt (tel), Mon–Fri 9.30–5.30. All material available for editorial reproduction and for advertising. B/w and colour material loaned free of charge for three weeks. Reproduction rights, holding and service fees charged; service fees deductible from use fees. Staff of five will undertake some research. All material copyright. Printed catalogue available free of charge.

11 • ASPECT PICTURE LIBRARY

40 Rostrevor Road, London SW6 5AD
Tel (01) 736 1998, 736 0981 Telex 297606 POLYIS G

Enquiries to Derek Bayes and Angela Bush, Directors

Items Over 150,000: colour transparencies (35mm, 5″ × 4″), b/w original photographs

Dates of subject matter Prehistory to present

Dates of photographs Contemporary

Subjects Geography (worldwide coverage), social change, family life, tribes, human interaction, poverty, famine, agriculture, industry, ecology, energy, personalities, cities, skylines, architecture, religion, science, technology, medicine, microchips, electronics, weather, space exploration, solar system, sun, natural history, animals, farm horses, wild life, parks, scenics, sports, ballooning, fine art, photography, special effects, macro-photography, underwater photography

Access and conditions Open to qualified researchers by appt (tel), Mon–Fri 9.30–5.30. All material available for editorial reproduction and for advertising. B/w and colour material loaned free of charge for one month. Reproduction rights, service and holding fees charged. Staff of four will undertake research; fee negotiable for large projects. All material copyright.

12 • ASSOCIATED PRESS LIMITED

12 Norwich Street, London EC4A 1BP
Tel (01) 353 1515 Telex 262887

Enquiries to Photo Librarian

Items About two million: b/w original photographs, colour transparencies (35mm, 5″ × 4″), b/w copy photographs, colour photographic prints, glass negatives, unprinted film negatives

Dates of subject matter BC to present

Dates of photographs 1920s to present

Subjects News coverage with emphasis on personalities, sport, royalty, conflicts and military activity, crime, politics, demonstrations, strikes, industry, aircraft, shipping

Access and conditions Open to qualified researchers by appt. All material available for editorial reproduction but not for advertising. No loans; b/w prints and duplicate colour transparencies available for a fee. Photocopies available. Reproduction rights fees charged; service fees charged for large projects. All material copyright. Card catalogue for b/w material available.

13 • AVIEMORE PHOTOGRAPHIC

Main Road, Aviemore, Highland PH22 1RH
Tel (0479) 810371

Enquiries to Stewart Grant

Items 10,000: b/w original photographs, colour transparencies (35mm, 120mm)

Dates of photographs 1974 to present

Subjects Highlands of Scotland including agriculture, natural history (domestic animals and wildlife), architecture, towns, the River Spey and the Spey Valley; tourism including golf, fishing, sightseeing, tourists, landscapes, lochs, watersports, pipe bands, mood shots, snow scenes, winter sports including skiing, indoor and outdoor curling; Cairngorm ski area; Highland Games

Access and conditions Open to qualified researchers by appt (tel). All material available for editorial reproduction and for advertising. B/w and colour material loaned free of charge for two months. Reproduction rights, service and holding fees charged. Staff will undertake research; fee charged for large projects. All material copyright.

14 • BANDPHOTOS

25 Longdown Road, Farnham, Surrey GU10 3JL
Tel (0252) 713022 Telex 858623 TELBUR G

Enquiries to Picture Librarian

Items 200,000: b/w original and copy photographs, colour transparencies (35mm, 2¼")

Dates of photographs 1960 to present

Subjects Show business personalities, animals, world geography (112 countries) and also agriculture, antiques, archaeology, art, astronomy, auctions, automobiles, aviation, books, botany, ceremonies, children, circuses, climatology, collections, communications, competitions, conferences, costumes, cowboys and Indians, courts and judges, crimes and trials, dams and bridges, dance, disasters, education, elections, entertainers, exhibitions, expeditions, fashions, finance, hobbies, hovercraft, immigrants, inventions, jewellery, medicine, military, museums, music, patterns and

abstracts, people, police, pollution, power, personalities, prize-winners, religion, safety, scouting, sea shells, seasons, shipping, shops and stalls, space, sports, strikes and demonstrations, traffic, theatre, transport, toys, underwater photography, world wars, writers and authors

Access and conditions Open to qualified researchers by appt, Mon-Fri 9–5. Most material available for editorial reproduction but not for advertising. B/w and colour material loaned free of charge for one month. Reproduction rights, service and holding fees charged; service fees deductible from use fees. Staff will undertake research.

15 • BARNABY'S PICTURE LIBRARY

Barnaby House, 19 Rathbone Street, London W1P 1AF
Tel (01) 636 6128/9

Enquiries to Mary Buckland, Managing Director

Items About two million: b/w original photographs, colour transparencies (35mm, 5" × 4", larger)

Dates of subject matter Prehistory to present

Dates of photographs c. 1840 to present

Subjects World geography including every country in the world and small states and islands, special collection on the USA; MUSTOGRAPH COLLECTION (1900–1945) on the British Isles including comprehensive coverage from abbeys to Christmas scenes; HITLER COLLECTION; general picture collection including abbeys, abstracts, agriculture, aerial views, air forces, animals (zoo, wild), armies, art, antiquities, architecture, archaeology, babies, birds, bridges, butterflies and moths, cacti, cathedrals, castles, camping, caravanning, cats, ceremonies, churches, commerce, communications, customs, Christmas, children, cattle, chalk carvings, cottages, contrasts, diving, domestic life, dams, drinking vessels, doors, donkeys, education, entertainment, exhibitions, farming, fashions (old and new), ferns, fireworks, flowers and plants, fishing, frontier posts, flags, fences and walls, fruit and blossoms, gardens, gambling, graphics, girls, goats, handicrafts, health and welfare, hedges, holiday villas, houses, history, historic prints, horses and ponies, harvesting, inns and signs, insects and bees, inland navigation, indoor games and hobbies, industries (oil, timber, steel, etc.), London, libraries, lighthouses and ships, marine life, magic, men,

mills, miniature and model villages, maritime
industries and occupations, monuments and
statues, natural disasters, navies, nature, night
scenes, parks, people, personalities, public services,
primitive agriculture, pollution, pigs, poultry,
reflections, reptiles, religions, roof tops, roads,
rivers, rural crafts, Roman remains, science,
sculpture, sport, still-life, stately homes, safaris
and big-game hunting, space flights, skies and
clouds, sunsets, snow scenes, spiders, swans, shops
and stores, teenagers, timepieces and clocks, toys,
transport (rail, road, water), tropical beaches,
trains and trams, towns and villages, viniculture,
landscapes (rivers, lakes), wars and battles,
waterfalls, women, weather, waves and seascapes,
windmills, woodland scenes, trees, youth
organizations, yoga, zoos

Access and conditions Open to qualified
researchers, Mon-Fri 9.30–5.30. All material
available for editorial reproduction and for
advertising. B/w and colour material loaned free of
charge for one month. Photocopies available.
Reproduction rights, service and holding fees
charged. Staff of eight will undertake research for
a fee.

16 • BBC HULTON PICTURE LIBRARY

35 Marylebone High Street, London W1M 4AA
Tel (01) 927 4735, 927 4737 Telex 265781 DATAPIC

Enquiries to David Lee, Librarian

Items About nine million: b/w original and copy
photographs, fine art prints, glass negatives, colour
transparencies (35mm, 5″ × 4″, larger), illustrated
maps, daguerreotypes, lantern slides, postcards,
stereographs, cuttings and tearsheets, illustrated
books

Dates of subject matter Prehistory to present

Dates of photographs 1830s to present

Dates of prints etc. 16th century to present

Subjects World history and geography, with
emphasis on the history, social history and
geography of the United Kingdom and former
territories of the British Empire, including the
following more detailed subjects: accidents, actors
and actresses, aerial views, agriculture, animals,
anthropology, archaeology, architecture, armed
forces, art and art history, automobiles, aviation,
ballet, business, cities, commerce, communications,
costume, crime, demonstrations, education,
entertainment, ethnology, exploration, fashion,
films and filming, food and cooking, furniture,
gardens, geography and geology, history (all
periods), industry, interior design, the law, maps,
medicine, music and musicians, natural history,
news events, performing arts, personalities,
photography, police, politics and politicians,
portraits, prisons and prisoners, psychology, radio
shows, railways, religions (including Christianity),
royalty, rural life, schools, science and technology,
ships and shipping, sports, television, theatre,
topography, towns and villages, transport (all
kinds), travel, universities, wars (very wide range),
weather; London agents for The Bettmann Archive
(New York); work by the following photographers
(those marked PP were *Picture Post*
photographers): Gordon Anthony, Baron, Hans
Baumann (Felix Man) PP, Felice Beato, G. C.
Beresford, Bill Brandt PP, Cabot, Julia Margaret
Cameron, Lady Iris Capell, John Chillingworth PP,
Crosslé, E. E. Dennis, Denis De Marney, G.
Deutsch PP, Val Doone, W. and D. Downey,
William England, Jack Esten PP, Daniel Farson
PP, Herbert Felton, Tim Gidal PP, Zoltan Glass PP,
William Grundy, Bert Hardy PP, Charles Hewitt
PP, Garry Hogg, Hopkins PP, Kurt Hutton PP,
Kleboe PP, Le Grice, Serge Lemoine, McCombe PP,
Heywood Magee PP, Felix Man PP, Ernest Mills, F.
J. Mortimer, Leo Pirk, Kenneth Rittener, George
Rodger PP, Sasha (Alexander Stewart), Humphrey
Spender PP, Alexander Stewart (Sasha), D. R.
Stuart, Studio Lisa, Reinhold Thiele, Alex
Watkinson, Woollcombe; the following collections:
GORDON ANTHONY (c. 1935–1955), theatre; BARON
(1935–1956), ballet, society portraits; BEATO,
China, Crimea, India, 1850s–1860s; BERESFORD
(1900–1930s), society portraits; CABOT (c. 1945–
1950), aerial views, cloud studies; CAPELL (1961–
1971), European travel; CHITTY (c. 1900–1910),
foreign travel; COOPER-HUMPHREYS (c. 1900),
furniture, art objects; CROSSLÉ (1930s–1970s),
travel; *DAILY EXPRESS* (1965–1975), news pictures;
E. E. DENNIS (1920s–1930s), natural history; DE
MARNEY (c. 1940–1958), theatre; DIXON SCOTT
(1945–1950), British landscape; VAL DOONE
(1930s–1940s), British landscape; W. & D. DOWNEY
(c. 1860–1938), society portraits; WILLIAM ENGLAND
(c. 1859), North America, Ireland, France; *EVENING
STANDARD* (c. 1940–1980), news pictures, fashion,
personalities; *EXPRESS* and *LONDON EXPRESS*
(c. 1927–1938), news pictures; HERBERT FELTON
(1920s–1940s), British and foreign topography and
buildings; G.P.A. (General Photographic Agency,
1920s–1946), news photographs; DUDLEY GORDON
(c.1943), British and foreign topography; LE GRICE
(1930s), world topography; WILLIAM GRUNDY'S
ENGLISH VIEWS (c. 1855); HENRY GUTTMAN (c. 1930),

miscellaneous; DR OTTO HERSCHAN (19th century), early photographs; GARRY HOGG (1930s–1970s), travel; ICE HOCKEY COLLECTION (1947–1958); SERGE LEMOINE (1970–1981), British royalty; SEYMOUR LINCOLN (1920s–1930s), British and foreign topography; LONDON STEREOSCOPIC CO. (c. 1860–c. 1910), places, portraits, humour; ERNEST MILLS (1900s–1920s), portraits; F. J. MORTIMER, seascapes and British Edwardian seaside; PHILLIPS (early 1900s), society portraits; PICTURE POST (1938–1957), news and features by famous photographers; PIRK (20th century), world travel; RISCHGITZ, miscellaneous, engravings and photographs; KENNETH RITTENER (20th century), British topography; ROBINSON (AUTOTYPE) SERIES (c. 1910–1935), topography, seaside; JOHN SANI (1980s), British topography; SASHA (1924–1940), theatre, social life; D. R. STUART (1931–1970), sport, particularly rugby and golf; STUDIO LISA (1936–1954), British royalty; THIELE (1900–1910), Boer War, world travel, sporting personalities; TODD (1890–1900), East Africa, British Columbia, big-game hunting; TOPICAL PRESS (1900s–1957) wide-ranging general news photographs; TUNBRIDGE-SEDGWICK PICTORIAL PRESS (1939–1945), theatre and society; ALEX WATKINSON (1946–1966), British and European topography; WOOD (c. 1900–1914), Far East topography, war; WOOLLCOMBE (20th century), interiors, etc.

Access and conditions Open to qualified researchers by appt (tel), 9.30–5.30. All material available for editorial reproduction; most available for advertising. B/w and colour material loaned free of charge. Photocopies available. Reproduction rights fees charged; service fees charged only when no material is used. Staff of 24 will undertake research for an hourly fee (minimum charge 15 minutes); first half hour free of charge.

17 • IVAN J. BELCHER COLOUR LIBRARY

34 Berry Croft, Abingdon, Oxfordshire OX14 1JL
Tel (0235) 21524

Enquiries to Ivan J. Belcher

Items About 6000: colour transparencies (2¼″, 5″ × 4″)

Dates of subject matter 1875 to present

Dates of photographs 1956 to present

Subjects Geography and landscape of England and Wales with special emphasis on London, Oxford, Windsor, Henley, Thames Valley, the Cotswolds and the Chilterns; special collections on Inland Waterways, rivers, canals, locks and river craft, veteran and vintage transport, steam traction engines, railways, cars, buses, vans, cycles, fairground equipment, shire horses and horse ploughing, power-stations, paddle-steamers; and also canoeing, castles, children, churches, cottages, country houses, country pubs, dancers, dogs, fairgrounds, flowers, fishing, gardens, glamour, harbours, holiday scenes, horses, inns, cats and kittens, morris dancers, posed models, pub signs, roses, rowing, sailing, seascapes, scrambling, speedboats, special effects, swans, windmills, woodlands

Access and conditions Open to qualified researchers by appt (tel). All material available for editorial reproduction and for advertising. Colour material loaned free of charge for one month. Reproduction rights fees charged. Staff will undertake research. All material copyright. Card catalogue available.

18 • BERNSEN'S INTERNATIONAL PRESS SERVICE LTD (BIPS)

9 Paradise Close, Eastbourne, East Sussex BN20 8BT
Tel (0323) 28760

Enquiries to Patricia Ann Habets, Photo Librarian

Items About one million: b/w original photographs, colour transparencies (35mm), unprinted film negatives

Dates of subject matter Prehistory to present

Dates of photographs 1945 to present

Subjects News features with emphasis on human interest, new inventions and discoveries, technical subjects for the general press, oddities and animal stories; following is a selection from the index: accidents, acting, actors and actresses, agriculture, aviation, airports, America (North and South), animals (in the wild, in zoos), art and artists, ballooning, Belgium, birds, unusual buildings (worldwide), camping, children (schools, diseases of, playgrounds, precocious), caravans, Christmas (extensive coverage), clothing and fashion, cooking and recipes, deafness, dentistry, Egypt, Eire, evangelists, exhibitions (trade and world), fish and fishing, furniture, garages, Greece, health, helicopters, hobbies, hospitals, houses, inventions, Italy, jewellery, judo, laboratories, libraries, magic and magicians, manufacturing, medicine and medical sciences (especially new discoveries and new treatments), motoring, murders, music, night clubs, nutrition, operations, optical, paints and painters, posed models, railways, religion, robots, safety, schools, science, slimming, sports, toys, traffic, transport (all forms), travel, USA, variety artists, vaudeville, watches and clocks, water, whisky, witchcraft, X-rays, yachting, zoos

Access and conditions Open to qualified researchers by appt Mon-Fri, 8.50–12, 1–5. All material available for editorial reproduction and for advertising. B/w and colour material loaned free of charge for two months. Reproduction rights fees charged; service fees charged only when no material is used. Staff of four will undertake some research.

19 • JOHN BETHELL PHOTOGRAPHIC LIBRARY

89 Fishpool Street, St Albans, Hertfordshire
AL3 4RU
Tel (0727) 50112

Enquiries to John Bethell

Items 25,000: colour transparencies (9 × 6 cm), b/w original photographs

Dates of subject matter 300 BC to present

Dates of photographs 1969 to present

Subjects English landscape and architecture especially in London, Buckinghamshire, Essex, Middlesex, Hertfordshire, Berkshire, cities and universities of Oxford and Cambridge; castles of England and Wales; country houses of England

Access and conditions Open to qualified researchers by appt. All material available for editorial reproduction and for advertising. B/w and colour material loaned free of charge for three months. Reproduction rights and holding fees charged. Staff will undertake research; fee charged only if nothing is used. All material copyright.

20 • BETTER WORLD PICTURE LIBRARY

10 Upstall Street, London SE5 9JE
Tel (01) 733 1806

Enquiries to Jane Postma

Items 10,000: b/w original photographs, colour transparencies (35mm)

Dates of photographs 1950s to present

Subjects City life including parks, building sites, architecture, shops and shopkeepers, markets, housing estates, buses, Stoke Newington; Edinburgh; London (inner city) communities, youth and community centres, adventure playgrounds, schools (Africa and London), language centres; leisure activities, sports, entertainment, recreation, tourism; festivals (Cameroon, China, London); demonstrations and marches; street buskers; current affairs, social change (especially Africa and China), police; music and musicians (jazz, popular, traditional Irish and African); conservation and ecology, management, animals (Africa, zoos), tropical rain forest; family life, children at play, at school; appropriate technology; British birds; Kenya; special collections on post-war Europe (1950s), Glasgow doss-houses, Quarriers Homes (orphanage at Bridge of Weir in Scotland), black community in Bath, social change in a Cameroon rural village, China (since 1960s), north-west Scotland, Iceland

Access and conditions Open to qualified researchers by appt, Mon-Fri 9.30–6. All material available for editorial reproduction and for advertising with the library's approval. B/w and colour material loaned free of charge by arrangement. Reproduction rights, service and holding fees charged. Staff will undertake research.

21 • NICK BIRCH PHOTO LIBRARY

34 Chantrey Road, London SW9 9TE
Tel (01) 737 1985

Enquiries to Beverley Birch

Items 200,000: colour transparencies (35mm, 2¼″), b/w original photographs

Dates of photographs 1975 to present

Dates of subject matter Prehistory to present

Subjects Acrobats, Africa, agriculture including sowing, harvesting, livestock, agricultural shows, vegetables, poultry, fruit, vineyards, coffee, figs, sheep (a year in the life of a sheep-farming community), Albania, animals including circuses, farm animals, wildlife, zoos, archaeological sites (prehistoric, Greek, Roman, industrial), architecture and buildings, birds, boats, boat-building, dry docks, bridges, Britain, brass bands and orchestras, cafés and restaurants, canals and locks, castles, China, cemeteries, circus performers, cities and urban life, urban people, clowns (including circuses, parks, fairs, streets, theatres and schools), costumes, crafts and trades (baking, basket-weaving, carving, cobbling, embroidering, pottery, tailoring, taxidermy, textile weaving, thatching, sheep shearing), social conditions (urban decay, factories, communities), demonstrations and parades, drama (children and youth, rehearsals, workshops, puppets), drought, land erosion, land abuse, education (schools, playschemes, playgrounds, colleges and universities), elections (posters, propaganda, meetings and rallies, polling), entertainment (street fairs, circuses, amusement arcades, competitions), fairs, fairgrounds, fêtes, festivals, farming, fishing, (boats, ports, harbours, primitive and commercial fishing, trawling, loading and unloading, markets), forts and fortresses, France, frescoes and murals, gameparks (Kenya), gardens, graffiti, slogans, hedgerows and wildflowers, housing (conditions, vandalism, building and demolition, troglodyte houses, trulli, etc.), illuminations and decorations, industries, occupations (building, ceramics, coffee, engineering, foundries, journalism, meat production and abattoirs, mining and quarrying, printing, steel, science and technology, laboratories, medicine, textiles, tanning, decaying industries), Italy, Kenya, landscapes and geological features (mountains, volcanoes, cliffs, coasts, lakes and rivers, seas and oceans, forests, land and water controls, soil erosion, volcanic areas and lava flows), leisure and recreation, London, markets, shops and foodstalls (including French and Italian), megaliths and dolmens, Muslims and mosques, people (adults at work and recreation, children at work and recreation including drama and musical instruments), political slogans, banners, marches, pollution, docks, Portugal, poverty and slums, railways, trains and stations, religion and religious festivals, rural and village life and people, salt pans (sea) and labourers, social conditions, sports (athletics, basketball, boules (petanque), climbing, cricket, cycling, football, gymnastics and spartakiade, karate, motorbikes, showjumping, skateboarding, trampolining, wrestling), street-scenes, steam engines, parades, rallies

Access and conditions Open to qualified researchers by appt (tel), Mon-Fri 9.30–5.30. All material available for editorial reproduction and for advertising. B/w and colour material loaned free of charge for one month. Reproduction rights, holding and service fees charged; service fees deductible from use fees. Staff will undertake research.

22 • BIRMINGHAM PUBLIC LIBRARIES

Central Library, Chamberlain Square, Birmingham B3 3HQ
Tel (021) 235 4511 Telex 337655 BIRLIB G

History and Geography Department

Tel (021) 235 4549

Enquiries to Philip N. Allen, Head of Department

Items About 250,000: postcards, lantern slides, b/w original photographs, illustrated maps, glass negatives, posters, illustrated books, stereographs

Dates of photographs 1890 to 1910

Subjects SIR BENJAMIN STONE COLLECTION of photographs (1890 to 1910) of everyday life, buildings, manners and customs, mostly in the British Isles but also in Africa, Asia, Australasia, Europe, North and South America; MARSTON RUDLAND COLLECTION of engraved portraits of monarchs and religious personalities up to 1900; collection of topographical postcards

Access and conditions Open to the public Mon-Fri 9–8, Sat 9–5. All material available for editorial reproduction and for advertising; copyrighted material must be cleared with copyright owner. No loans; b/w prints available for a fee. Photocopies available. Reproduction rights fees charged. Staff will undertake limited research. Card catalogue.

Early and Fine Printing Collection
Language and Literature Department

Tel (021) 235 4227

Enquiries to Nesta Jenkins, Head of Department

Items Unknown number: illustrated maps, illustrated books

Dates of subject matter 13th to 20th centuries

Subject matter Medieval manuscripts (13th to 15th century); books of 19th-century photographs including books by Francis Frith and Roger Fenton; maps and atlases printed before 1701; illustrated books including hand-coloured examples and works on topography and natural history; important collection of children's books

Access and conditons Open to the public, Mon-Fri 9–8, Sat 9–5. All material available for editorial reproduction and for advertising: copyrighted material must be cleared with owner of copyright.

No loans; b/w prints and colour transparencies available for a fee. Photocopies available at the discretion of the Department Head. Reproduction rights fees charged. Staff will undertake limited research. Card catalogue.

23 • THE ANTHONY BLAKE PHOTO LIBRARY

54 Hill Rise, Richmond, Surrey TW10 6UB
Tel (01) 940 7771

Enquiries to Trisha Mitchell Vargas

Items About 15,000: colour transparencies (35mm, 10″ × 8″, 5″ × 4″)

Dates of photographs 1960 to present

Subjects Food and wine: raw foodstuffs, step-by-step cooking processes, finished dishes from simple meals to flamboyant Haute Cuisine, Nouvelle Cuisine, Cuisine Minceur, wholefoods; Italian, Indian, Chinese, Greek and French food in detail, Mexican, Middle-Eastern, Hungarian, Scandinavian, Pacific, Corsican food in a range of subjects, British and American food in great detail, including many regional dishes; agriculture; food processes including smoking, home-preserving, curing, cooking, baking, butchery; fishing industry, fish farming, shellfish; restaurants, pubs, wine bars, cafés, diners; shops general and specialist; markets in several countries; Bordeaux, Burgundy and Champagne wine areas in particular, and many other French subjects; comprehensive coverage of Italian wine areas; trimming, spraying, netting of vines, vendange (wine harvest), bottling, pressing, châteaux, grape pickers working and at lunch; wide range of wines and other drinks, alcoholic and non-alcoholic; geography including towns and cities in many countries, land and seascapes, flora and fauna, sunsets, people (portraits and activities), shells, boats and sailing, naval subjects; industry, weather, science, sports, hobbies, hunting

Access and conditions Open to qualified researchers by appt (tel). All material available for editorial reproduction and for advertising (permission of subject required for advertising use). Colour material loaned free of charge for one month. Reproduction rights, service and holding fees charged; service fees charged only when no material is used. Staff will undertake research. All material copyright.

24 • BODLEIAN LIBRARY

Oxford OX1 3BG
Tel (0865) 244675 ext 406

Enquiries to Joanna Dodsworth, Publications Officer

Items B/w original and copy photographs, colour transparencies (35mm, 5″ × 4″, larger), glass negatives, original cartoons, illustrated maps, posters, greetings cards, illustrated books, illuminated manuscripts

Dates of subject matter Prehistory to present

Subjects Material drawn from the collection of the Department of Western Manuscripts, some of the Oxford colleges and other owners. Series A consists of unmounted strips of 35mm colour transparencies (also available mounted) drawn from single manuscripts or from manuscripts on one subject. A strip consists of as few as four or as many as 259 frames, although most are about 25–30 frames. Series B consists of individual colour transparencies of single pages from some of the most famous items in the Library. Most of the manuscripts in the collection date from the 14th and 15th centuries, but there are Greek manuscripts and papyri from the 1st century AD and examples of modern calligraphy from 1961. The manuscripts have many provenances and include examples of the following: Greek, Byzantine, Anglo-Saxon, Irish, Medieval, Romanesque, Renaissance, Flemish, Italian, French, English, German, Polish, Dutch, Slavonic, Hungarian, Portuguese, Mexican. Subjects illustrated or illuminated in these manuscripts provide a detailed portrait of life in medieval Europe and include: religion, lives of the saints and the Virgin Mary, Books of Hours, clerical and monastic life; romances and tales of chivalry including the Romance of the Rose, tales of the Trojan War, the Romance of Alexander, Arthurian legends, Middle English romances, providing illustrations of sports, hunting, warfare, costume, crafts, trades, courtship, musical instruments, domestic pursuits, portraits, plants and animals; treatises on alchemy and medicine, including herbals and providing images of early science and medical practice, plants; bestiaries showing both real and fabulous animals. JOHN JOHNSON COLLECTION OF PRINTED EPHEMERA (16th to 20th centuries) (advertisements and other printed matter): especially rich for the social history of the 19th and 20th centuries; includes Theodore de Bry's engravings (1590–1592) of the Americas (hand-coloured), a history of printing, and also posters, entertainment, children and education, costume, valentine cards, politics and social welfare, farming and food, industries and products, transport, shipping, trade, communications, World War I, religion, etc.; THE HARDING COLLECTION: 19th-century music covers and 18th- and 19th-century broadsheets illustrated with woodcuts; illustrative material on a wealth of subjects including military history, costume, emigration, politics, etc.; THE HENRY MINN COLLECTION (*c.* 1890 to *c.* 1950): photographs of Oxford and some of Oxfordshire, especially of buildings subsequently destroyed. Apply to Dept. of Western Manuscripts, Room 132. Index in preparation.

Access and conditions Open to qualified researchers, Mon-Fri 9–5 (closed week beginning August Bank Holiday and from Christmas Eve to Jan 2). Reader's ticket not needed for slide collection (film strips) and index, but required for research in the Library. Appointment advisable for consulting iconographical index to illuminated manuscripts. All material available for editorial reproduction and for advertising with the permission of the relevant Keeper. No loans; b/w prints and duplicate colour transparencies available for a fee. Photocopies available. Reproduction rights fees charged. Staff will undertake research; small fee charged for long projects. The Publications Officer encourages picture researchers not to send xeroxes of images published frequently (unless absolutely essential), but to describe the kind of material needed and enlist the help of the Publications Officer's staff to find fresh and appropriate images. Printed and card catalogues available.

25 • ANNE BOLT PICTURE LIBRARY

24 Sale Place, London W2 1PU
Tel (01) 262 7484

Enquiries to Anne Bolt

Items 50,000: b/w original photographs, colour transparencies (2¼")

Dates of subject matter Roman times to present

Dates of photographs 1955 to present

Subjects The Caribbean; North Africa including Tunisia, Morocco, coastal Algeria; Gibraltar, Malta, South of France, Spain, Portugal, Italy, Yugoslavia, Budapest, Scandinavia; Bali, Gambia; castles, churches, sports, leisure, people at work, industry including oil, bauxite, asphalt

Access and conditions Open to qualified

researchers by appt (tel), Mon-Fri 9–6. All material available for editorial reproduction and for advertising. B/w and colour material loaned free of charge for one month. Reproduction rights, service and holding fees charged. Staff will undertake research.

26 • JO BOND WORDS AND PICTURES

ADESPOTON FILM SERVICE

Clump Bottom House, Little Wittenham, Abingdon, Oxfordshire OX14 4RA
Tel (086730) 7371

Enquiries to Jo Bond

Items 20,000: colour transparencies (35mm, 2¼"), b/w original photographs, colour photographic prints, colour negatives

Dates of subject matter 300 BC to present

Dates of photographs 1960 to present

Subjects Geography (worldwide coverage), social change, politics, demonstrations, poverty, psychology, ecology, medicine, accidents, human interaction, family life, anthropology, industries, agriculture, schools, sport, religion, architecture, seasons, natural history, science, local radio broadcasting, film-making, portraits of adults and children

Access and conditions Open to qualified researchers by appt only (tel). All material available for editorial reproduction and for advertising. B/w and colour material loaned free of charge for 28 days. Reproduction rights, service and holding fees charged; service fees deductible from use fees. Negotiable research fee charged for large projects. All material copyright.

27 • MICHAEL BOYS SYNDICATION

Red House, Newbourn, Woodbridge, Suffolk IP12 4PX
Tel (047336) 333

Enquiries to Pamela Boys

Items 300,000: colour transparencies (35mm)

Dates of photographs 1963 to present

Subjects Interiors and design, work of interior designers worldwide; food and wine including still life of ingredients and finished dishes, wine-growing areas of France and Italy, vineyards, bottles of wine, etc.; gardens, posed models

Access and conditions Open to qualified researchers by appt, Mon-Fri 9.30–5.30. All material available for editorial reproduction and for advertising. Colour material loaned free of charge for one month. Reproduction rights, service and holding fees charged. Staff of three will undertake research; fee charged for large projects.

28 • BRITAIN ON VIEW PHOTOGRAPHIC LIBRARY

BRITISH TOURIST AUTHORITY

Thames Tower, Blacks Road, London W6 9EL
Tel (01) 846 9000 Telex 264305 BTAMAR G

Enquiries to Jill M. Moore, Photographic Librarian

Items About 280,000: b/w original photographs, colour transparencies (35mm, 2¼", 5" × 4")

Dates of photographs 1970 to present

Subjects Geography of the United Kingdom including all counties of England, Wales, Scotland and Northern Ireland and the following islands: Jersey, Guernsey, Herm, Sark, Isle of Man, Lundy Island, Isles of Scilly, Isle of Wight, Caldy Island, Eigg and Rhum, Isle of Skye, Shetland Isles, Isle of Arran, Isle of Bute, Great Cumbrae Island, Island of Iona and Isles of Islay, Mull, Staffa, Oronsay, Tiree, Ulva, Barra, Harris, Lewis and Uist; the following miscellaneous and specialized subjects: agriculture, animals, beach scenes, bed and breakfast, birds, brass bands and silver bands, butterflies, cabaret, Christmas, clubs, concerts, conferences, crafts and industries, discotheques, educational establishments, Eisteddfods, exhibitions, fairs, festivals, filming, flags, flowers and foliage, food and drink, forest parks, galleries (England, Scotland, Wales, London), Highland games and gatherings, inns and hotels, Jubilee souvenirs, letter boxes, lochs, literary associations, markets, models of the Queen's Beasts, museums, old customs and traditions, organised tours, parking meters, pubs, pub signs, restaurants, Royal Shakespeare Theatre, shops and shopping, shows, signs, snow scenes, sports and pastimes, theatres, travel (by air, rail, road, water), types and characters, personalities, Welsh choirs, wildlife parks, witch scarecrows, zoos; London including general scenes, the military (Blues and Royals, Coldstream Guards, Guards Division, Grenadier Guards, Irish Guards, Junior Guardsmen, King's

Troop, Life Guards, State Trumpeter, Scots Guards, Welsh Guards, Chelsea Pensioners, Queen's Bodyguard, Royal Military School of Music, Yeoman Gaoler, Yeoman Warder), and ceremonies (Beating the Retreat, Changing the Guard, Children of the Chapel Royal, Company of Pikemen, festivals, Garter Ceremony, Lord Mayor's Show, Opening the Legal Year, Royal Residences, State landaus, State Opening of Parliament, Tower of London ceremonies, Trooping the Colour, Van Horse Parade); BRITISH AIRWAYS COLLECTION (1973 to present): whole fleet including Concorde, take-off and landings, interiors and exteriors of planes, planes on tarmac, crews (no foreign scenes). Note: the BTA now houses the ENGLISH TOURIST BOARD COLLECTION of transparencies.

Access and conditions Open to qualified researchers, Mon-Fri 11–4. All material available for editorial reproduction and for advertising; some photographs for editorial use only. B/w material not loaned; b/w prints available for a fee. Colour material loaned free of charge for one month. Reproduction rights, service and holding fees charged. Staff of four will undertake research for clients not resident in London. All material copyright.

29 • THE BRITISH LIBRARY

Great Russell Street, London WC1B 3DG
Tel (01) 636 1544

Department of Manuscripts

Enquiries to the Keeper of Manuscripts, ext 644

Items Over 75,000: manuscripts, illuminated manuscripts, map and music manuscripts, autographs, charters, rolls, b/w original photographs, colour transparencies

Dates of subject matter Late classical period to the present

Dates of photographs Modern

Subjects The history, art, music, science and literature of Western civilization in manuscripts and early books, including Magna Carta, the Lindisfarne Gospels, a 1623 First Folio of Shakespeare's plays, the 4th-Century Codex Sinaiticus, a preliminary version of *Alice in Wonderland* with Lewis Carroll's own illustrations, autograph material by Lord Nelson including two logbooks from *HMS Victory*, an eye-witness account of the execution of Mary, Queen of Scots, manuscripts collected by Robert and Edward Harley and Sir Robert Cotton

Access and conditions Open to qualified researchers holding a British Library Reader's Pass or Temporary Pass and a supplementary pass for the Dept of Manuscripts, Mon-Sat 9.30–5. Some material available for editorial reproduction and for advertising, subject to copyright restrictions. No loans; b/w prints and duplicate colour transparencies available for a fee. Photocopies available. Reproduction rights fees charged. Staff will undertake limited research. Printed and card catalogues available; see *British Library Reference Division Publications Catalogue*.

Department of Printed Books

Enquiries to Douglas Webb, ext 509

Items About seven million: b/w original and copy photographs, colour transparencies (35mm, 5″ × 4″, larger), colour photographic prints, glass negatives, daguerreotypes, postcards, illustrated maps, unprinted film negatives, posters, greetings cards, architectural drawings, cuttings and tearsheets, illustrated books

Subject matter Prehistory to present

Photographs Mid-19th century to present

Subjects The Department of Printed Books is the comprehensive copyright deposit library of the UK and also holds large collections of printed foreign books and periodicals. Subdivisions of the Department include music, maps, postage stamps and official publications. As well as incunabula and later printed books, the collections contain photographic and pictorial material of all kinds and ephemera. The subject matter is encyclopedic; its use is restricted by relative fragility of the material and by copyright law, but otherwise is available.

Access and conditions Open to qualified researchers holding a British Library Reader's Pass or Temporary Pass, Mon-Sat 9.30–5. Some material available for editorial reproduction and for advertising, subject to copyright restrictions. No loans: b/w prints and duplicate colour transparencies available for a fee. Photocopies available. Reproduction rights fees charged. Staff will undertake very limited research. Copyright clearance is responsibility of user. Printed and card catalogues available.

Department of Oriental Manuscripts and Printed Books

14 Store Street, London WC1E 7DG
Tel (01) 636 1544 Telex 21462

Enquiries to B. Bloomfield, Keeper

Items About 40,000 manuscripts and 400,000 printed books including illuminated and decorated manuscripts and calligraphic texts, b/w prints, colour transparencies

Subject matter c. 1500 BC to present

Photographs Modern

Subjects Manuscripts and printed books in oriental languages ranging in area from Morocco to Japan; illustrated Hebrew Mss from medieval Europe and the Middle East; Persian, Turkish and Arab miniature paintings; illuminated Korans and Persian and Turkish Mss; Indian paintings in Mss in various styles including Mughal, Sultanate, Deccani, Rajput, Pala and Jain; illustrated Buddhist and Hindu Mss from India, Nepal, Tibet and South-east Asia; illustrated Chinese and Japanese Mss; engravings, etc., in early Hebrew printed books; blockprints from early Chinese printed scrolls; Japanese prints in books; illustrations in 17th- to 19th-century books printed in the East; early Chinese writing materials of bone, bamboo, silk and paper; Chinese and Japanese scrolls, palm leaf and bark Mss from India and South-east Asia, Indian copper-plate charters, Tibetan xylographs, Islamic Mss with original binding

Access and conditions Open to qualified researchers holding a British Library Reader's Pass or Temporary Pass, Mon-Sat 9.30–5. Material available for reproduction subject only to conservation requirements. No loans: b/w prints and duplicate colour transparencies available for a fee. Special service and rates available to publishers. Reproduction rights fees charged. Staff of 20 will undertake limited research. Card and printed catalogues available, including N. M. Titley, *Miniatures from Persian Manuscripts*, BL Publications, 1977; N. M. Titley, *Miniatures from Turkish Manuscripts*, BL Publications, 1981; J. P. Losty, *The Art of the Book in India*, BL Publications, 1982.

BRITISH TOURIST AUTHORITY and **ENGLISH TOURIST BOARD** *see* BRITAIN ON VIEW PHOTOGRAPHIC LIBRARY

30 • MICHAEL BUSSELLE'S PHOTO LIBRARY

Shropshire House, 179 Tottenham Court Road, London W1P 9LF
Tel (01) 734 3460

Enquiries to Michael Busselle

Items 25,000: colour transparencies (35mm), b/w original photographs

Dates of photographs 1950 to present

Subjects World travel, especially Sri Lanka, USA (west coast, California, Los Angeles), Morocco, Spain, Italy, France (wine regions, Paris), landscapes, industry, recreation, posed models, abstracts

Access and conditions Open to the public by appt (tel). All material available for editorial reproduction and for advertising. B/w and colour material loaned free of charge for 15 days. Reproduction rights, service and holding fees charged. Staff will undertake research.

31 • CHARLES R. BUTT

79 Hazelwood Close, Cambridge CB4 3SW
Tel (0223) 321614

Enquiries to Charles R. Butt

Items 18,000: colour transparencies (35mm), b/w original photographs

Dates of subject matter Prehistory to present

Dates of photographs 1953 to present

Subjects Middle East including Oman, Sudan, Iraq, Dubai, Bahrain, Jordan, Lebanon, Turkey; Nepal and India; Greece and some of the Greek Islands, Italy and Sicily, Paris, Canada (Quebec and Ontario), USA (Rhode Island, Bicentennial celebrations, Massachusetts, Wyoming, Connecticut, New York City), Mexico; ships and aircraft; UK including London, Hertfordshire, Essex, Cambridgeshire, Kent; b/w coverage Holland, Belgium, Cyprus, Aden and West Aden Protectorates

Access and conditions Open to qualified researchers by appt (tel). All material available for editorial reproduction and for advertising. B/w and colour material loaned free of charge for four weeks. Reproduction rights fees charged; other fees negotiable. Staff will undertake research. Card catalogue.

32 • CAMBRIDGE UNIVERSITY LIBRARY

West Road, Cambridge CB3 9DR
Tel (0223) 61441

Enquiries to Photography Department

Items About two million printed books; unknown numbers of manuscripts, b/w original photographs, colour transparencies, lantern slides, postcards, illustrated maps, fine art prints, art reproductions, posters, press cuttings and tearsheets

Dates of subject matter Prehistory to present

Subjects The Library is both a university and a copyright library. The subject matter is encyclopaedic. The Library possesses a Gutenberg Bible (c. 1450), the only perfect copy of Caxton's *Golden Legend*, and the *Codex Bezae* Ms. of the Gospels. Among the collections are BISHOP MOORE'S LIBRARY of 30,000 volumes presented to George I in 1715, the BRADSHAW COLLECTION of Irish Books (1870–1886), the WADE COLLECTION of Chinese books, the ACTON HISTORICAL LIBRARY (60,000 volumes) presented by Viscount Morley (1902) and a collection of incunabula.

Access and conditions Open to qualified researchers only *via* the Admissions Office. Some material available for editorial reproduction and for advertising subject to copyright restrictions. No loans; b/w prints and duplicate colour transparencies available for a fee. Photocopies available for a fee. Reproduction rights fees charged.

33 • CAMERA PRESS LTD

Russell Court, Coram Street, London WC1 0NB
Tel (01) 837 4488, 837 9393 Telex 21654

Enquiries to B/w or Colour Library

Items About three million: b/w original and copy photographs, colour transparencies (35mm, 5″ × 4″)

Dates of subject matter Prehistory to present

Dates of photographs 19th century to present

Subjects Worldwide photojournalism and documentary photography, events and personalities, current news, politics and politicians, government and elections, demonstrations, wars (Boer War to Vietnam, Falklands), travel, transport (road, rail, air, sea), industry, education, sports, theatre, film and television personalities, film stills, space (NASA photographs), religion, cities and urban problems, natural history, posed models, portraits (86,000), feature sets (35,000); special collection on British Royal Family; representatives for Xinhua Chinese News Agency, Tass, Novosti, MTI (Hungary) and others

Access and conditions Open to qualified researchers by appt (tel), Mon-Fri 9.30–5.30. All material available for editorial reproduction; for advertising only photographs with model releases. B/w and colour material loaned free of charge for two months. Reproduction rights, service and holding fees charged. Staff of five will undertake research.

Women's Interest Section

Enquiries to Lesley Winston and Denise Weaver, Sales Representatives

Items 4000: colour transparencies (35mm, 7 × 6 cm, 2¼"), b/w original and copy photographs

Dates of subject matter 1950s to present

Dates of photographs 1950s to present

Subjects DIY, fashion, beauty, health and exercise, gardening, food, interiors, babies and children, families, pregnancy and childbirth, couples, handicrafts; syndication for German, French and Swedish magazines including *Votre Beauté*, *Schöner Wohnen*, *Hauser*, *Zuhauser*, *Petra*, *Für Sie*

Access and conditions Open to qualified researchers by appt (tel), Mon-Fri 10–6. All material available for editorial reproduction; for advertising only photographs with model releases. B/w and colour material loaned free of charge for two months. Reproduction rights, service and holding fees charged. Staff will undertake research.

34 • CAMERAPIX HUTCHISON LIBRARY

8 Ruston Mews, London W11 1RB
Tel (01) 229 2743

Enquiries to Michael Lee, Manager

Items About 500,000: colour transparencies (35mm, 2¼"), b/w original photographs

Dates of photographs 1965 to present

Subjects Worldwide coverage of geography, urban and rural life, industry, religion,

architecture, current events, transport, flora and fauna, alternative technology and medicine, education, civilizations, medicine, aid and disasters, tribal peoples, festivals, arts and crafts, political movements, ecology, family life, anthropology, poverty, natural history, childbirth and babies, family relationships, death, agriculture, sport, tourism, personalities, drugs, mining, weather, weddings and marriage; comprehensive collections on Mecca, the Hadj, the Holy Cities of Islam, East African wildlife, South American Indians, African tribal people, African droughts of 1975 and 1984/5, cultural life of Asia (dance, festivals, architecture, everyday life), cocaine from the highlands and forests of South America through all processes to arrival in Florida, North Vietnam during the war, endangered tribal people (list available), changes and destruction of the Amazon Forest from 1960 to the present, juxtaposition of traditional and contemporary heads of state, contemporary life in and around the Pacific (New Pacific), religions of the world; comprehensive coverage of Pakistan, Sudan, Ethiopia, Nigeria, Brazil, Colombia, Tanzania and Kenya; work by Mohammed Amin, Michael MacIntyre, J. Von Puttkamer, Sarah Errington, Felix Greene, Nancy Durrell McKenna and others; MOSER/TAYLOR COLLECTION: historical and anthropological material on Colombian Indians

Access and conditions Open to qualified researchers by appt (tel), Mon-Fri 10–6. All material available for editorial reproduction and for advertising. B/w and colour material loaned free of charge for one month. Reproduction rights, service and holding fees charged; service fee deductible from use fees. Staff of three will undertake research. All material copyright.

35 • J. ALLAN CASH PHOTOLIBRARY

74 South Ealing Road, London W5 4QB
Tel (01) 840 4141

Enquiries to Alan Denny, Library Manager

Items 300,000: b/w original photographs, colour transparencies (35mm, 5" × 4", 6" × 6"), unprinted film negatives

Dates of subject matter Prehistory to present

Dates of photographs *c.* 1955 to present

Subjects Worldwide coverage (162 countries) of all subjects including: abbeys, abstracts and patterns, agriculture, aircraft, airports, amusement parks, anchors, animals (domestic, farm, wild), antiques, art and artists, architecture, aquariums, astronauts, babies, balloons, bands, bazaars, beaches, beer and brewing, bells, bicycles, biology, birds, blooms and blossoms, boats, body painting, bonfires, botany, bridges, buildings, bulldozing, bullfights, buses, business, cabaret, cable cars, cafés, camping, canals, cannons, caravanning, carnivals, cars and car museums, castles, cathedrals, cattle, caves, cemeteries, ceremonies, chairs, chair lifts, chandeliers, children, chimneys, china and pottery, churches, cliffs, climbing, clocks, clouds, clowns, coal and coalmining, coastlines, coffee, construction industry, contemporary life, costumes (national), cooking, coral, cotton growing, countryside, crafts and craftsmen, cranes, crops, crowds, cruising, customs, dairying, dams, dancing (tribal, folk, national, ballroom, etc.), decorations, demonstrations, deserts, diving, docks, dolls, drugs, eating, embroidery, electronics, entertainment, erosion, events, expeditions, eyes, fabrics, faces, farming, factories, fairs, ferries, festivals, fires, fireworks, fish, fishing, fjords, flags, floods, flowers (wild, cultivated, artificial), food, fortresses, fountains, fruit, funerals, gates, gardens, geology, geysers, gypsies and nomads, girls, glaciers, glass, gliding and hang-gliding, golf and golf courses, gravestones, guards, guides, guns, gymkhanas, handicrafts, harbours, harvesting, hats, hedgerows, helicopters, herbs, highland games, hiking, hippies, historical buildings and sites, hobbies, homes, holidaying, hospital scenes, hotels, housing, hunting, huts, ice, icebergs, ice-skating, idols, illuminations, industry, inns, insects, irrigation, jazz, jewellery, jousting, Jubilee, jungle, kites, knitting, laboratories, lace, lakes, lamps, lighting, lanterns, landscapes, leather, leaves, leisure, lighthouses, lightning, locks, markets, marinas, masks, medical scenes, military, mines and mining, monasteries, monks, moon, mosques, motoring, motor cycling, motorways, mountains, mountaineering, music and musicians, natives, nature conservation, natural history, neon signs, new towns, night scenes, night-clubs, oases, oil industry (drilling, rigs, refining, shipping), orchestras, painting, palaces, parades, parks, pearl diving, peasants, peat, pedestrians, picnics, piers, pilgrims, plantations, police, pollution, postmen, postboxes, pottery and ceramics, power stations, processions, protests, pubs, pygmies, pyramids, quarries, queues, quays, race courses, railways, rainbows, rapids, reflections, religion, reptiles, restaurants, rites, rivers, roads, rock formations, rock groups, roofs, rope, royalty, rubber industry, USSR (pre-War), ruins, safari, sailors, sand, schools, science fiction, sculpture, seas, sea life, shadows, ships, ship-building, shops and shopping, shrines, shrubs, signs, skiing (resorts, children, clothing, lifts, action), skies, skyscrapers, slums, snow, snow scenes, soldiers, space travel, sport, springs, squares, stadiums, stations, statues, streets, students, sun, sunsets, sunrises, sunbathing, supermarkets, surgery, swamps, swimming (pools, on cruise ships, in sea), tailoring, theatres, timber, tombs, towers, toys, tourists and tourism, trade, traffic, traffic wardens, trains, transport, travel, trees, tribes, tunnels, umbrellas, uniforms, universities, utensils, valleys, vegetables, villages, villas, vines and vineyards, volcanoes, warriors, water, waterfalls, weather, weaving, weddings, weirs, wells, wildlife, wine, windmills, winter sports, wood carving, woods, work, World War II (especially the UK), worship, yachts, zebra crossing, zoos, zoology

Access and conditions Open to qualified researchers by appt (tel), Mon-Fri 9–5.30. All material available for editorial reproduction and for advertising (model releases not always available). B/w and colour material loaned free of charge for two months. Reproduction rights fees charged; service fees charged only when no material is used. Staff of five will undertake research.

36 • CELTIC PICTURE LIBRARY

4 Rhodfa Gwilym, St Asaph, Clwyd LL17 0UU
Tel (074574) 395

Enquiries to Ann Thomas

Items Over 10,000: colour transparencies (35mm, 2¼″)

Dates of photographs 1979 to present

Subjects Wales and its people including wildlife, rural life, farming, forestry, castles, landscapes, geography, geology, ancient monuments, culture, crafts, national customs, townscapes, sport, railways, industry, tourism

Access and conditions Open to qualified researchers by appt. All material available for editorial reproduction and for advertising. Colour material loaned free of charge for two months. Reproduction rights fees charged. Staff will undertake research in collection. All material copyright.

37 • CENTAUR FEATURES

7 Ryelands Close, Caterham, Surrey CR3 5HY
Tel (0883) 46545

Enquiries to Richard Parker

Items About 4000: colour transparencies
(2¼″ × 3¼″)

Dates of photographs 1960 to present

Subjects Children in school, at fairs and fêtes, at
Christmas and other holidays, at home, at jobs and
crafts, with animals, with toys, at sports, playing,
discotheques, water scenes, mother and child shots,
camping, portraits, some black and Asian children.

Access and conditions Open to qualified
researchers by appt (tel), Mon-Fri 10–7. All
material available for editorial reproduction and
for advertising. Colour transparencies loaned free
of charge for one month. Reproduction rights and
holding fees charged. Staff will undertake
research. All material copyright.

38 • CENTRAL OFFICE OF INFORMATION

Photographs Library, Hercules Road, London
SE1 7DU
Tel (01) 928 2345

Enquiries to Photo Librarian

Items 250,000: b/w original photographs, colour
transparencies (35mm, 5″ × 4″, larger), colour
photographic prints

Dates of subject matter Prehistory to present

Dates of photographs *c.* 1920 to present

Subjects United Kingdom geography,
government, industry, business and commerce,
armed forces, social history, foreign aid
programmes, prisons, health care, medical
research and hospitals, London theatre exteriors
(recent), personalities (politicians, civil servants),
science, topographical material including sites,
major towns (architecture and streetscenes),
archaeology, agriculture, aerial views,
entertainment, Royal Opera House, Covent
Garden, including performances, back stage
workers, wig-makers, etc. (1984), Falklands War,
British dependencies, etc.

Access and conditions Open to the public by
appt (tel), Mon-Fri 10–4. Most material available
for editorial reproduction and some for advertising
(no model releases); some material must be cleared

with relevant government department. No loans;
b/w prints and duplicate colour transparencies
available for a fee. Photocopies available.
Reproduction rights and service fees charged. Staff
will undertake limited research. Non Crown
copyright material must be cleared by user.

CENTRAL PRESS LTD *see* THE PHOTO
SOURCE

39 • CENTRE FOR WORLD DEVELOPMENT EDUCATION

128 Buckingham Palace Road, London SW1W 9SH
Tel (01) 730 8332

Enquiries to Penny Hooker, Press and
Information Officer

Items 22,000: b/w original photographs, colour
transparencies (35mm) microfiche

Dates of subject matter Prehistory to 1980

Dates of photographs 1960 to present

Subjects Developing countries of the third world
e.g. Africa, India, Bangladesh, Sri Lanka, Brazil,
Thailand, etc., including agriculture, development,
education, food, fishing, children, health, housing,
industry, irrigation, technology, people, roads,
towns, trade, water supplies; WORLD BANK
COLLECTION of photographs on microfiche (prints
can be ordered from Washington)

Access and conditions Open to the public by
appt (tel), Mon-Fri 9.30–5. All material available
for editorial reproduction and for advertising.
B/w material loaned free of charge for one month;
colour material rented for a fee. Reproduction
rights fees charged; no service or holding fees.
Refundable deposit required from commercial
users. Staff will undertake limited research for
out-of-town requests only; search fee charged.

40 • CITY SYNDICATION LTD

47 Fleet Street, London EC4Y 1BJ
Tel (01) 583 0080

Enquiries to David Fowler, Managing Director

Items About 10,000: b/w original photographs,
colour transparencies (35mm), glass negatives

Dates of photographs 1977 to present

Subjects Portraits and action photographs of leading personalities in all fields, especially politics, trade unions, sports, show business, pop music, industry, Royal Family; some general subjects, architecture, events; Crawley area (Sussex) street scenes (1905)

Access and conditions Open to qualified researchers by appt (tel), Mon-Fri 9.30–5.30. All material available for editorial reproduction and for advertising. B/w and colour material loaned free of charge for one month. Photocopies available. Reproduction rights and holding fees charged. Staff will undertake research.

41 • CIVIC TRUST

17 Carlton House Terrace, London SW1Y 5AW
Tel (01) 930 0914

Enquiries to Saskia Hallam, Librarian

Items 10,000: colour transparencies (35mm), b/w original photographs

Dates of photographs 1957 to present

Subjects Urban environments, town schemes and environmental improvements; Civic Trust award-winning schemes, some before and after photographs; housing and commercial buildings; land use, restoration and conservation; good architectural design; material filed by geographical location

Access and conditions Open to the public by appt (tel), Mon-Fri 9.30–5.30. All material available for editorial reproduction and for advertising. B/w and colour material loaned free of charge for three weeks. Reproduction rights and service fees charged. Staff will undertake research.

42 • PETER CLAYTON ASSOCIATES

41 Cardy Road, Boxmoor, Hemel Hempstead, Hertfordshire HP1 1RL
Tel (0442) 67400

Enquiries to Peter Clayton

Items 70,000: colour transparencies (35mm), b/w original photographs

Dates of subject matter 200,000 BC to present

Dates of photographs 1950 to present

Subjects Archaeology (sites and objects) especially Egyptology and the Mediterranean areas, north-west Europe and North Africa; numismatics of all periods, but especially ancient coins; world travel with emphasis on history including Britain, France, Germany, Austria, Tunisia, Algeria, Libya, Morocco, Spain, Italy (Rome, Pompeii, Herculaneum, Sicily, Corsica), Greece (Tiryns, Mycenae, Crete, Athens), Turkey, Malta, Yugoslavia, Syria, Bulgaria, Poland, Rumania, Czechoslovakia, USSR, South Africa, East Africa, Zimbabwe, Ethiopia, Persia (Iran), Iraq, Mexico, Guatemala, Honduras, Peru, Ecuador, Norway, Sweden, Denmark, Iceland, Siberia, Mongolia

Access and conditions Not open; written requests only. All material available for editorial reproduction and for advertising. B/w and colour material loaned free of charge. Reproduction rights fees charged. Staff will undertake research.

43 • STEPHANIE COLASANTI

38 Hillside Court, 409 Finchley Road, London NW3 6HQ
Tel (01) 435 3695

Enquiries to Stephanie Colasanti

Items 50,000: colour transparencies (2¼″), b/w original photographs, colour photographic prints, unprinted film negatives

Dates of subject matter Prehistory to present

Dates of photographs 1970 to present

Subjects World geography including Austria, France, Germany, Yugoslavia, Greece and the Greek Islands, Cyprus, Italy, Madeira, Morocco, Tunisia, Turkey, Israel, Egypt, Kenya, Seychelles, Canada, USA and Hawaii, Mexico, the Caribbean, Jamaica, Barbados, Bahamas, India, Thailand, China and Hong Kong, Switzerland; sports, winter sports, children, people, animals, towns, carnivals, flowers, agriculture, landscapes, seascapes, sunsets, travel, deserts, markets, archaeology, religion, ancient civilizations

Access and conditions Open to qualified researchers by appt (tel), Mon-Fri 9–6. All material available for editorial reproduction and for advertising. B/w and colour material loaned free of charge for one month (two weeks to advertising agencies). Reproduction rights, service and holding fees charged. Staff of two will undertake research; fee negotiable for large projects. Card catalogue available.

44 • COLORIFIC!

Garden Office, Gilray House, Gloucester Terrace, London W2 3DF
Tel (01) 723 5031 Telex 943763 CROCOM G CLR

Enquiries to Shirley Le Goubin

Items About 200,000: colour transparencies (35mm, 5″ × 4″, larger), b/w original photographs

Dates of photographs 1936 to present

Subjects World geography, natural history, travel and exploration, agriculture, architecture, education, religion, medicine, social problems, pollution, engineering, technology, industry, business, aviation, space exploration, food and cooking, games, entertainment, performing arts, art and artists, sports, military, police and criminals, ships and shipping, archaeology, ethnology, astrology, mythology, seasons, personalities, people, human interaction, psychology, children, youth, old age; London agents for Black Star, Contact Press Images, *Discover Magazine*, *Life Magazine*, NASA, Phototake, Rainbow, *Sports Illustrated*, Wheeler Pictures, Zapruder Collection, Visages (Los Angeles), Vision (NYC), JB Pictures (NYC), Cosmos (Paris), Focus (Germany), Grazia Neri (Italy), Lehtikuva Oy (Finland)

Access and conditions Open to qualified researchers by appt (tel), Mon-Fri 9.30–5.30. All material available for editorial reproduction; some restriction on advertising use. B/w and colour material loaned free of charge for one month. Reproduction rights, service and holding fees charged. Staff of four will undertake some research. Printed catalogue available.

45 • COLORPIX PHOTOGRAPHIC LIBRARY

35 Elgin Crescent, London W11 2JD
Tel (01) 229 6694

Enquiries to Ron Carter

Items About 25,000: colour transparencies (35mm, 60mm, 2¼″, larger)

Dates of subject matter Prehistory to present

Dates of photographs 1975 to present

Subjects Geography worldwide including people, places, lifestyles, religion, architecture, arts, industry, agriculture, history; special collection on Australian history; fashion, posed models

Access and conditions Open to qualified researchers by appt (tel), Mon-Fri 9.30–5.30. All material available for editorial reproduction and for advertising. Colour material loaned free of charge for three months. Reproduction rights and holding fees charged. Staff will undertake research. Printed catalogue.

COLOUR LIBRARY INTERNATIONAL
see THE PHOTO SOURCE

46 • COLOURMASTER

10-12 Kelvin Way, Crawley, West Sussex RH10 2SD
Tel (0293) 515381

Enquiries to Pauline Mullanny, Librarian

Items About 60,000: colour transparencies (35mm, 5″ × 4″, larger), postcards

Dates of photographs 1965 to present

Subjects Geography and tourism of England, Scotland and Wales including cities, towns, villages, countryside, castles and cathedrals, churches, rivers, lakes, mountains, coastline, harbours, National Parks, wildlife, folk customs

Access and conditions Open to the public by appt, Mon-Fri 8.30–5. Some material available for editorial reproduction and for advertising. No loans; duplicate colour transparencies available for a fee. Reproduction rights fees charged. Staff will undertake some research.

47 • ELIZABETH-ANN COLVILLE PHOTOGRAPHS

10 Steele's Road, London NW3 4SE
Tel (01) 722 5834

Enquiries to Elizabeth-Ann Colville

Items 10,000: colour transparencies (35mm), b/w original photographs, colour photographic prints, glass negatives, daguerreotypes, postcards

Dates of subject matter Prehistory to present

Dates of photographs 1960 to present

Subjects World geography including Australia, Bahamas, Bermuda, Canada, Denmark, Fiji, Finland, France, Germany, Guam, Hawaii, Holland, Japan, Mexico, Morocco, New Zealand,

Norway, Panama, Poland, Spain, Sweden, Switzerland, Tunisia, USA, USSR, Yugoslavia, UK including stately homes, towns, landscapes, museums, historic sites; aircraft, animals, art, ballooning, birds, conservation, botany, gardens, bonsai, fungi, cars, cats, children, dogs, fireworks, folk festivals, fish and fishing, golf, horses, mills (wind/sail), railways, sailing, ships, shipping, snow, still-life

Access and conditions Open to qualified researchers by appt (tel), Mon-Fri 9–5. All material available for editorial reproduction and for advertising. B/w and colour material loaned free of charge for one month. Reproduction rights and holding fees charged. Staff will undertake research. Photographer available for assignment; museum work a specialty.

48 • COMMONWEALTH INSTITUTE (COMPIX)

Kensington High Street, London W8 6NQ
Tel (01) 603 4535 ext 293

Enquiries to Compix Librarian

Items 10,000: colour transparencies (35mm, 2¼″)

Dates of subject matter Prehistory to present

Dates of photographs c. 1970 to present

Subjects Commonwealth countries: agriculture, architecture, arts and crafts, beaches, festivals, flora, industry, landscapes, people, towns, villages, cities and wildlife in Antigua, Australia, Bahamas, Bangladesh, Barbados, Belize, Botswana, Brunei, Canada, Cayman Islands, Cyprus, Dominica, Fiji, Gambia, Ghana, Gibraltar, Grenada, Guyana, Hong Kong, India, Jamaica, Kenya, Lesotho, Malawi, Malaysia, Malta, Mauritius, Nauru, Nigeria, Papua New Guinea, St Lucia, St Vincent, Sabah, Seychelles, Sierra Leone, Singapore, Solomon Islands, Sri Lanka, Swaziland, Tanzania, Uganda, Vanuatu, Zambia, Zimbabwe

Access and conditions Open to the public by appt (tel), Mon-Fri 10–5.30. All material available for editorial reproduction and for advertising. B/w and colour material loaned free of charge for one month. Reproduction rights, service and holding fees charged. Staff will undertake some research.

49 • COMMONWEALTH SECRETARIAT PHOTOGRAPHIC LIBRARY

Marlborough House, Pall Mall, London SW1Y 5HX
Tel (01) 839 3411 Telex 27678

Enquiries to Dinah Akello, Assistant Publications Editor

Items About 2000: b/w original photographs, unprinted film negatives, colour photographic prints, posters, cuttings and tearsheets

Dates of photographs 1948 to present

Subjects Commonwealth including food production, rural development and industry in member countries, export market development (trade fairs), meetings of ministers of health, education and justice, meetings of Commonwealth Heads of Government, meetings of study groups

Access and conditions Open to qualified researchers by appt (write), Mon-Fri 9.15–5.30. Some material available for editorial reproduction, but not for advertising. B/w and colour material loaned free of charge for one month. No reproduction rights fees charged. Staff of five will undertake limited research.

50 • WADE COOPER ASSOCIATES

32A Alva Street, Edinburgh EH2 4PY
Tel (031) 226 3222

Enquiries to John Orton, Director

Items 20,000: colour transparencies (35mm, 2¼″, 5″ × 4″), b/w original photographs, glass negatives

Dates of subject matter 1860 to present

Dates of photographs 1860 to present

Subjects Aspects of contemporary Scottish life including sports, fishing, industry (e.g. oil), with emphasis on landscapes; many English counties; special collections on Africa, Austria, Afghanistan, Canada, Egypt, France, Fiji, Finland, Greece, Holland, India, Italy, Majorca, Malta, Monaco, Morocco, Nigeria, Norway, Peru, Pakistan, Sweden, Spain, Sri Lanka, Singapore, Thailand, USA, Virgin Islands, Yugoslavia; wild, domestic and farm animals, insects, aerial shots, boats and ships, ballet, crafts, food, gardens, plants, flowers, geology, interiors, industry, professions, social groups, sports including fishing, skiing, water-skiing, sailing, windsurfing, mountaineering (some early material), athletics, motor racing, transport including early aircraft and horse-drawn and motorized vehicles and locomotives, contemporary aircraft, cars, lorries, motor cycles

Access and conditions Open to qualified researchers, Mon-Fri 9–5. All material available for editorial reproduction and for advertising. B/w and colour material loaned free of charge for one month; some b/w prints and duplicate colour transparencies available for a fee. Reproduction rights, service and holding fees charged; service fees deductible from use fees. Staff of four will undertake some research; negotiable research fee charged. All material copyright.

51 • *DAILY TELEGRAPH* COLOUR LIBRARY

135 Fleet Street, London EC4P 4BL
Tel (01) 353 4242 ext 3686 Telex 22874
TELESYNDIC LONDON

Enquiries to John Davies, Colour Library Manager

Items About 500,000: colour transparencies (35mm, 5″ × 4″)

Dates of subject matter Prehistory to present

Dates of photographs 1965 to present

Subjects Worldwide geography (especially London, New York and Canada), architecture (industrial, domestic, modern), agriculture, science and technology, industry (general, oil, fishing, timber, gas, power, ship building, mining), pollution, transport (rail, air, road, sea), religion (including Mecca, the Hadj), demonstrations, health and medicine, service (police, fire, air/sea rescue), entertainment, fashion, sport, military, landscapes (winter, autumn, spring, summer, trees, skies, sunsets, rivers, seascapes, volcanoes, deserts, tropics, mountains), people (children, the elderly, posed models, crowds, holidays, nationalities), animals, personalities; SPACE FRONTIERS LTD COLLECTION: spaceflight and astronomy including rocket launches, deep space and orbital views of earth and its regions (including the UK), men and machines in free space and on the moon, fly-by views of planets, Viking on Mars, orbital images of the Sun, shuttle, images of Earth from UK, European and Japanese resource centres and space agencies, telescope views of planets, galaxies and nebulae by SFL and AD Astrofotografie of West Germany, space art by Don Dixon of California, colour enhancements (computer and photographic), earth surface pictures of natural phenomena (aurora, clouds, sunsets)

Access and conditions Open to qualified researchers by appt (tel), Mon-Fri 10–5.30. All material available for editorial reproduction and for advertising. Colour material loaned free of charge for one month. Reproduction rights, service and holding fees charged. Staff of five will undertake research.

52 • DAS PHOTO

Cherry Trees, Queen's Road, Bisley, Woking, Surrey GU24 9AW
Tel (04867) 3395

Enquiries to David Alexander Simson

Items 110,000: b/w original photographs, colour transparencies (35mm), colour photographic prints

Dates of subject matter 2000 BC to present

Dates of photographs 1970 to present

Subjects World geography, transport, industry (petroleum, motor cars, steel, hemp, sisal), energy and fuel crisis, education (schools, languages), demonstrations, police, animals, social problems, poverty, three-day week, people, artisans, craftwork; Peru, Ecuador, Colombia, Bolivia, Venezuela, USA, Central America, Mexico, Caribbean, UK, France, Spain, Sweden, Norway, Denmark, Holland, Italy, Germany, Belgium, Azores (Flores and Horta), Turkey, Israel, Egypt, Iraq, Syria, Jordan, Saudi Arabia; special subjects: archaeology, transatlantic, sailing trip, Spanish language and culture, folklore and world festivals, European fleamarkets, big motorbikes, biblical mythology, Amazon jungle, Islamic world

Access and conditions Open to qualified researchers by appt (tel), Mon-Fri 9–5. All material available for editorial reproduction and for advertising. B/w and colour material loaned free of charge for one month. Photocopies available. Reproduction rights fees charged. Staff of three will undertake research. All material copyright.

53 • JAMES DAVIS PHOTOGRAPHY

30 Hengistbury Road, New Milton, Hampshire BH25 7LU
Tel (0425) 610328

Enquiries to Jackie Roberts, Library Manager

Items 35,000: colour transparencies (35mm, 2¼″, 5″ × 4″), b/w original photographs

Dates of subject matter Prehistory to present

Dates of photographs 1960 to present

Subjects World geography (183 countries), abstracts, agriculture, archaeology, architecture, art and artists, aviation, biology, botany, business and commerce, ceremonies, cities, cooking, crowds, customs, dancing, demonstrations, education, energy, entertainment, expeditions, food and drink, gardens, geology, harbours, human interaction, industry, interiors, medicine, meteorology, military, motor cars, music and musicians, natural history (animals and plants), people, poverty, recreation, religion, royalty, seasons, science and technology, ships and shipping, social problems, space, sport, transport, travel, waterways

Access and conditions Open to qualified researchers by appt (tel), Mon–Fri 9–5.30. All material available for editorial reproduction and for advertising. B/w and colour material loaned free of charge for one month. Reproduction rights and service fees charged; service fee deductible from use fee. Staff of three will undertake research. Photographers available for assignment.

54 • DOUGLAS DICKINS PHOTO LIBRARY

2 Wessex Gardens, London NW11 9RT
Tel (01) 455 6221

Enquiries to Douglas Dickins

Items About 130,000: colour transparencies (35mm, 2¼″), b/w original photographs, postcards, press cuttings and tearsheets, illustrated books

Dates of subject matter 5000 BC to present

Dates of photographs 1942 to present

Subjects World geography, especially India, Indonesia, Canada, USA; travel and tourism including scenic views, resorts, hotels, leisure activities; anthropology including physical types from five continents; architecture including cities and housing, primitive housing in Borneo, Sulawesi, Africa, India; agriculture especially in the tropics and including rice, sugar, cattle, fishing; natural history (animals, plants) emphasis on Kenya, Uganda and Madagascar; religions including Hinduism, Islam, Buddhism, Jainism,

Shintoism, Taoism, Christianity, Judaism; social life, markets, schools, sports, music; special collections of temples, forts and palaces of India, folk dances of India and the Far East; historical sites (ancient Egypt, Iran including Isfahan, Persepolis, Shiraz, Borobudur in Java, the Angkor Wat in Cambodia, Cuzco and Macchu Picchu in Peru, China including Peking, buried cities of Anuradhapura and Polonnaruwa in Sri Lanka, Taxila and the Karakoram Highway in Pakistan, Kyoto in Japan, and Seoul and Kyongju in Korea)

Access and conditions Open to qualified researchers by appt, Mon–Fri 9–6. All material available for editorial reproduction and for advertising. B/w and colour material loaned free of charge for one month. Reproduction rights and holding fees charged, service fee charged only when no material is used. Staff will undertake research.

55 • C.M. DIXON

The Orchard, Marley Lane, Kingston, Canterbury, Kent CT4 6JH
Tel (0227) 830075

Enquiries to M. Dixon

Items 60,000: colour transparencies (35mm, 6 × 6 cm, 9 × 6 cm, 5″ × 4″), b/w original photographs, colour photographic prints

Dates of subject matter Prehistory to present

Dates of photographs 1950 to present

Subjects Agriculture, architecture, archaeology, art, cattle, children, churches, climbing, clouds, coalmining, coastline, crops, crosses, dolmens, engineering, everyday life, farming, fisheries, food, fossils, glaciers, horses, industry, landforms, landscape, mosaics, mountaineering, mythology, occupations, ports, pottery, rock-climbing, rocks, science and technology, ships, tourism, transport, volcanoes, vulcanism, zoos; world geography including Austria, Bulgaria, Crete, Cyprus, Czechoslovakia, Denmark, Dubai, Eire, Ethiopia, Finland, France, Great Britain, Greece, Holland, Hungary, Iceland, Israel, Italy, Madeira, Majorca, Minorca, Malta, Morocco, Nepal, Norway, Romania, Rhodes, Russia, Sicily, Spain, Sri Lanka, Sweden, Switzerland, Tunisia, Turkey, USSR, Uzbekistan, Yugoslavia; special subjects: ancient civilizations, archaeology, ancient art, folk art, architecture (Greek, Roman, Etruscan, Scythian, Celtic, Viking, Byzantine, Romanesque, neolithic, paleolithic), agriculture, geography, geology, meteorology, mountains, occupations, scenic views, travel, world religions

Access and conditions Open to qualified researchers by appt. All material available for editorial reproduction and for advertising. B/w prints available for a fee; colour material loaned free of charge for one month. Photocopies available. Reproduction rights, holding and service fees charged. Staff of two will undertake research. All material copyright.

56 • DUNDEE COLLEGE OF EDUCATION

Gardyne Road, Dundee, Tayside DD5 1NY
Tel (0382) 453433

Enquiries to Wyllie Fyfe, Co-ordinator of Learning Resources

Items 5000: colour transparencies (35mm), b/w original photographs, colour photographic prints

Dates of photographs 1970 to present

Subjects Art and crafts, biology, economics, education, psychology, educational technology, geography, health education, history, home economics, library, mathematics, modern languages, physical education, religious education, technical education – all material prepared for tape/slide presentations

Access and conditions Open to the public by appt (write) Mon-Fri 9–5. All material available for editorial reproduction and for advertising. No loans; b/w prints and duplicate colour transparencies available for a fee. Reproduction rights fees charged. Staff of two will undertake some research. Printed catalogue available of transparencies only.

57 • DUNDEE UNIVERSITY LIBRARY

University Library, Dundee, Tayside DD1 4HN
Tel (0382) 23181 ext 4094 Telex 76293

Archives and Manuscripts Department

Enquiries to Joan Auld, Archivist, ext 4094

Items About 7000: b/w original and copy photographs, colour transparencies (35mm), colour photographic prints, architectural drawings, postcards, glass negatives, lantern slides, technical drawings, fine art prints, drawings and watercolours, ephemera

Dates of subject matter 4th century to present

Dates of photographs c. 1850 to present

Dates of non-photographic material c. 1830 to 1970

Subjects Industries, especially textiles (linen and jute) and engineering, particularly all aspects of cultivation, processing and manufacture of jute in India, Pakistan and Dundee, textile machinery, steam engines, rice milling machinery, factories, mills housing, company staff and workforce including a few of company fire brigade; geology, natural history (particularly insects and birds), horticulture especially raspberry growing; biblical animals and birds; scenes illustrating the Bible especially by Matson Photo Service; American Civil War, World War I especially British and French Red Cross and prisoner-of-war camps; transport, horse-drawn vehicles and automobiles; medical conditions (particularly skin diseases and physical deformities, also tattoos), scientists, medical practitioners, academics; geography including views, people, buildings in Dundee, Tayside, India, Pakistan, the Middle East, Far East, South and East Africa, USA, Canada, Polynesia, Hebrides, Shetland

Access and conditions Open to the public by appt (tel), Mon-Fri 9–5. All material available for editorial reproduction and for advertising subject to copyright clearance. No loans; b/w prints and duplicate colour transparencies available for a fee. Photocopies available. Reproduction rights fees charged. Staff will undertake some research.

Michael Peto Collection
Photographic Department

Enquiries to Stanley Turner, Library Photographer, ext 4096/7

Items About 132,000: unprinted film negatives, b/w original photographs, colour transparencies (35mm, 2¼")

Dates of photographs 1946 to 1970; some earlier

Subjects Complete photographic work of Michael Peto (1908–1970, born in Hungary, lived and worked in London 1946–1970) and comprising photojournalism, people at work (Britain, India, Israel, Korea), politicians, businessmen, artists, workmen, refugees, gypsies, children, East End of London mid 1940s, politics in Hungary c. 1946; extensive coverage of ballet, especially rehearsals, Prospect Theatre productions; historic and newsworthy events 1950s and 1960s, extensive coverage for Save the Children

Access and conditions Open to qualified researchers by appt (write), Mon-Fri 9–5. All material available for editorial reproduction and for advertising. Contact prints loaned free of charge for three months; b/w prints and duplicate colour transparencies available for a fee. Photocopies available. Reproduction rights fees charged. Staff will undertake some research. Card catalogue available.

58 • EARTHSCAN PHOTO LIBRARY

3 Endsleigh Street, London WC1H 0DD
Tel (01) 388 0736

Enquiries to Shana Magraw

Items 10,000: b/w original and copy photographs, colour transparencies (35mm), postcards

Dates of photographs 1960 to present

Subjects Development and environment in the Third World, including desertification, deforestation, fuel wood crisis, alternative energy, water, sanitation and health problems, agriculture, irrigation, cities, migration, urban problems, mud buildings (worldwide), general village life

Access and conditions Open to qualified researchers by appt (write), Mon-Fri 9.30–5.30. All material available for editorial reproduction and for advertising. B/w and colour material loaned free of charge for two months. Photocopies available. B/w prints and duplicate colour transparencies available for a fee. Reproduction rights, service and holding fees charged; service fees deductible from use fees. Staff will undertake research.

59 • EAST MIDLANDS TOURIST BOARD

Exchequergate, Lincoln LN2 1PZ
Tel (0522) 31521

Enquiries to Margaret Fotheringham, Information Officer

Items Colour transparencies (35mm), b/w original photographs

Dates of subject matter Prehistory to present

Dates of photographs Contemporary

Subjects Tourism in Derbyshire, Leicestershire, Lincolnshire, Northamptonshire and Nottinghamshire including historic houses

Access and conditions Open to qualified researchers by appt (write), Mon-Thurs 9.30–5.30, Fri 9–5 (answerphone 1–2). All material available for editorial reproduction and for advertising. B/w and colour material loaned free of charge. Reproduction rights fees charged at the Board's discretion. Staff will undertake limited research.

60 • ROBERT ESTALL PHOTOGRAPHS

14 Oak Village, London NW5 4QP
Tel (01) 267 1605

Enquiries to Robert Estall

Items 35,000: colour transparencies (35mm, 7 × 6 cm, larger)

Dates of subject matter 3500 BC to present

Dates of photographs 1960 to present

Subjects Archaeology including standing stones, stone circles and megalithic sites; transport including roads, trucks, trains, hovercraft, historic commercial vehicles; cheese and cheese production; animals (domestic and farmyard); trees and forestry; travel and general documentary coverage of Antigua, Austria, Bahamas, Canada (extensive coverage), Corfu, Crete, England, France, Germany, Holland, Ibiza, Italy, Yugoslavia, Madeira, Majorca, Malta, Minorca, Portugal, St Lucia, Scotland, Spain, Switzerland, USA

Access and conditions Open to qualified researchers by appt (tel), Mon-Fri 9.30–5. All material available for editorial reproduction and for advertising. Colour material loaned free of charge for two months. Reproduction rights, service and holding fees charged. Staff will undertake some research. All material copyright.

61 • EUROPEAN GEOGRAPHIC SURVEY

Crowhurst Farm House, Battle, East Sussex TN33 9PU
Tel (04246) 3922, (01) 736 7980

Enquiries to Tim Sharman

Items 5000: colour transparencies (35mm), b/w original photographs

Dates of subject matter Prehistory to present

Dates of photographs 1979 to present

Subjects Eastern Europe including geography, landscape, agriculture, industry, economy, fishing, forestry, shops and offices, apartments, houses, cottages, villages, farms, town planning, national parks, palaces, castles, churches, markets, rivers, mountains, people (officials, professionals, children, families, etc.) in Hungary, Romania, Czechoslovakia, Bulgaria, Poland, Yugoslavia, East Germany; Western Europe (mainly France, Germany, Austria and the Benelux countries) including agriculture, landscape, townscape, villages

Access and conditions Open to qualified researchers by appt (tel), Mon-Fri 9–5. All material available for editorial reproduction and for advertising. B/w and colour material loaned free of charge for one month. Reproduction rights and holding fees charged. Staff will undertake some research. Photographer available for assignments. All material copyright.

62 • GREG EVANS PHOTO LIBRARY

25 Rose Street, London WC2E 9AE
Tel (01) 836 4854

Enquiries to Greg Evans

Items 80,000: colour transparencies (35mm, 7 × 6 cm)

Dates of subject matter Prehistory to present

Dates of photographs 1979 to present

Subjects World geography, agriculture, aircraft, animals, architecture, beaches, birds, fancy dress, flowers and plants, food and restaurants, entertainment and recreation, posed models, hotels, music, night-clubs and discotheques, people (babies, children, families, older couples), ships, skiing, sports, soft focus, sunsets; Afghanistan, Andorra, Australia, Austria, Belgium, Bulgaria, Canary Islands, Canada, Caribbean, China, Corsica, Cyprus, Denmark, Egypt, Fiji, Finland, France, West Germany, East Germany, Gibraltar, Greece, Holland, Hong Kong, Hungary, India, Iran, Ireland, Israel, Italy, Japan, Kashmir, Liechtenstein, Luxembourg, Macao, Maldives, Malaya, Malta, Mexico, Madeira, Monaco, Morocco, Nepal, New Zealand, Norway, Pakistan, Philippines, Poland, Portugal, Romania, Sardinia, San Marino, South Africa, Singapore, Sri Lanka, Spain, Sweden, Switzerland, Tahiti, Thailand, Turkey, UK (England, Scotland, Wales), USA, USSR, Yugoslavia

Access and conditions Open to qualified researchers by appt (tel), Mon-Fri 9–5. All material available for editorial reproduction and for advertising. Colour material loaned free of charge for three months. Reproduction rights fees charged. Staff of three will undertake research.

63 • MARY EVANS PICTURE LIBRARY

1 Tranquil Vale, London SE3 0BU
Tel (01) 318 0034

Enquiries to Picture Librarian

Items Two million: b/w and colour prints and engravings, colour transparencies (9 × 4 cm), glass negatives, lantern slides, postcards, original cartoons, greetings cards, illustrated books, ephemera, illustrated journals (British and foreign)

Dates of subject matter Prehistory to *c.* 1939

Subjects World history, especially people, places, events, science, industry, trade, transport, entertainment, sport, behaviour, daily life, natural history; special collections: advertising, animals and birds, anomalous phenomena, costume, paranormal, portraits, sex, spiritualism, UFOs, witchcraft, women's rights; and also accidents, archaeology, architecture, art, astronomy, bathing, canals, cartoons, characters, children, Christmas, community services, cooking, country life, crime, customs, dancing, death, dentistry, drinking, drugs, education, electioneering, emigration, engineering, entertainments, environment, exhibitions, exploration, fairs, fairy tales, farming, fantasy, fiction, fires, fishing, food and drink, freaks, furniture, games, gardening, girls, heating, household, hunting, inventions, law, life-saving, lighting, love, machines, magic, manufacture, medicine, military, money, monsters, morals, museums, music, mythology, natural phenomena, nudes, ornament, parties, photography, plants, politics, post office and postage, prehistory, press, printing, propaganda, prostitution, punishment, racing, religion, riding, scenery, seaside, secret societies, servants, ships, slavery, slum life, society, streets, technology, theatre, toilet, tourists, travel, warfare, working conditions, zoology; SIGMUND FREUD FAMILY COLLECTION; HARRY PRICE COLLECTION: cases investigated by Price (a psychical investigator); SOCIETY FOR PSYCHICAL RESEARCH COLLECTION

Access and conditions Open to qualified researchers by appt (tel), Mon-Fri 9.30–5.30. All material available for editorial reproduction and for advertising. B/w and colour material loaned free of charge for one month. Photocopies available. Reproduction rights fees, service and holding fees charged. Staff of nine will undertake research; fee for large projects.

64 • *THE EVENING ECHO*

Newspaper House, Chester Hall Lane, Basildon, Essex SS14 3BL
Tel (0268) 22792

Enquiries to Sue Webb, Chief Librarian

Items 500,000: b/w original photographs, unprinted film negatives, press cuttings and tearsheets

Dates of subject matter 12th century to present

Dates of photographs 1972 to present

Subjects Basildon and environs including South Woodham, Ferrars (new town), Southend-on-Sea, Canvey Island; local history, streetscenes, agriculture, ploughing, tractors, farming, local personalities and elections, politicians and celebrities (Gemma Craven, Helen Mirren), sports, industrial estates (Marconi Avionics, Carreras Rothman, Standard Telephones and Cables, Yardley's, Gordon's Gin, etc.); special collection of 1953 east coast floods and Canvey Island oil and gas terminals

Access and conditions Open to the public by appt (tel), Mon-Fri 2–4.30. Some material available for editorial reproduction and for advertising. B/w prints available for a fee. Photocopies available. Reproduction rights fees charged. Staff of three will undertake limited research.

65 • CHRIS FAIRCLOUGH COLOUR LIBRARY

16 Worcester Road, Guildford, Surrey GU2 6SZ
Tel (0483) 69289

Enquiries to Chris Fairclough

Items 200,000: b/w original photographs, colour transparencies (35mm, 2¼")

Dates of subject matter Prehistory to present

Dates of photographs 1975 to present

Subjects Geography worldwide (25 countries), industry, agriculture, cities and streetscenes, countryside, landscapes, seascapes, natural

history, people; special subjects include Australia, New Zealand, Indonesia, Hong Kong, Fiji, Western Europe, UK and USA

Access and conditions Open to qualified researchers by appt (tel), Mon-Fri 9–6. All material available for editorial reproduction and for advertising. B/w material loaned free of charge for 30 days, colour for 60 days. Reproduction rights, service and holding fees charged; service fees deductible from use fees. Staff will undertake research. All material copyright.

66 • FEATURE-PIX COLOUR LIBRARY
TRAVEL PHOTOGRAPHIC SERVICES LTD

21 Great Chapel Street, London W1V 3AQ
Tel (01) 437 2121

Enquiries to Gerry Brenes

Items 400,000: colour transparencies (7 × 6 cm, 5" × 4")

Dates of subject matter Prehistory to present

Dates of photographs Recent

Subjects World geography for the travel market, worldwide countries, cities and resorts, food and drink, hotels, historic sites, beaches, skiing, walking, sailing

Access and conditions Open to qualified researchers by appt (tel), Mon-Fri 9–5.30. All material available for editorial reproduction and for advertising. Colour material loaned free of charge for 28 days. Reproduction rights and holding fees charged; service fees charged only when no material is used. Staff of two will undertake some research.

67 • *FINANCIAL TIMES* PICTURE COLLECTION

Bracken House, 10 Cannon Street, London EC4P 4BY
Tel (01) 248 8000 ext 3484 Telex 895 4871

Enquiries to Non Morgan

Items About 500,000: b/w original and copy photographs, unprinted film negatives

Dates of subject matter Prehistory to present

Dates of photographs *c.* 1970 to present

Subjects Photojournalism with financial

emphasis, portraits of heads of state, political and economic figures, managing directors; countries (worldwide) including banking, stock exchanges, industries, agriculture, education, transport; general subjects including advertising, agriculture, aviation, animals, antiques, archaeology, army, art and artists, astronomy, auctions, awards, ballet, banks, bicycles, birth control, boats and boating, bombing, books, bread, brewing, bridges, broadcasting, building societies, business schools, calculators, campanology, canals, caravans, carpets, castles, catering, cathedrals, cemeteries, cement, ceramics, ceremonies, charities, chemicals and chemical industry, chess, cinemas, clocks, clothing industry, clubs, coaches, coal industry, coffee, coins, commodities, computers, confectionery, conferences, Conservative Party, construction industry, cosmetics, cranes, credit cards, cricket, crime, crowds, currency, custom and excise, dairy produce, dams, defence, demonstrations, devolution, diamonds, disabled persons, distilleries, diving, docks, domestic appliances, drink, drought, drugs, economy, education, elections, electricity, electronics industry, engineering, European Economic Community, exhibitions, expeditions, explosives, factories, fairgrounds, fashion, fertilizers, film industry, fires and fire fighting, fish and fishing, flags, floods, food, football, footwear, forestry, furniture, gambling, games, garages, gardening, gardens, gas, glass, gold, golf, helicopters, hijacking, holograms, holidays, horse-racing, horticulture, hospitals, houses and housing, hovercraft, hydrofoils, immigration, industrial relations, insurance, investment, jewellery, Labour Party, lasers, law, Liberal Party, libraries, management, man-made fibres, meat, medicine, mentally-handicapped, metal industry, microelectronics, military, mines and miners, missiles, mosques, motor cars, motorcycles, motor industry, motorways, mountaineering, museums, music, National Front, NATO, Navy, Nobel prizes, nuclear energy, offices and office equipment, oil industry, opera, optical fibres, paper, pensioners, photography, Plaid Cymru, plastics industry, platinum, police, pollution, Pope John Paul II, post office, poultry, power boats, power stations, press, printing, prisons, publishing, pumps, rabies, race relations, radio, railways, records and recordings, refugees, religion, reservoirs, riots, road haulage, robots, rowing, rubber, Rugby, sailing, sand yachting, satellites, scientific instruments, scrap metal, sculpture, security, sewage, shipping and shipyards, shooting, shops, showjumping, shows, silk, silver, Silver Jubilee, signwriting, skateboarding, skating, ski sports, snooker, Social Democratic Party, social services, solar energy, space, spinning and weaving, spying, squash, stamps, stately homes, steam engines, steel industry, stockbrokers, General Strike 1926, submarines, sugar, summit meetings, supermarkets, swimming, tailoring, tanks, taxidermy, taxis, tea, telecommunications, telephones, television, tennis, terrorism, textile industry, theatre, timber, tobacco industry, tourism, toys, trade unions, traffic, trains, tribunals, tunnel (Channel), underground transport, unemployment, United Nations, vandalism, video systems, viewdata, warehouses, waste disposal, watches, water supply, weapons, windmills, windsurfing, wine, wool, word-processing systems, World War II aircraft, yachting, zoo animals

Access and conditions Open to the public by appt (tel), Mon-Fri 10–1, 2–5. All material available for editorial reproduction and for advertising subject to copyright clearance. B/w prints available for a fee. Photocopies available. Reproduction rights and service fees charged. Staff will undertake some research. Colour material handled by Robert Harding (qv).

68 • FOREIGN AND COMMONWEALTH OFFICE LIBRARY

Photograph Collection

Sanctuary Buildings, 20 Great Smith Street, London SW1P 3BZ
Tel (01) 212 0663, 212 0732

Enquiries to John Fagan

Items About 10,000: b/w original and copy photographs

Dates of photographs *c.* 1850 to present

Subjects Life in former British colonies, official and domestic, from 1850s to the present, but emphasis before 1960; material filed by country and by names of persons, with a large miscellaneous section; major collection of British Commonwealth material with bias towards officialdom; Royal Tours especially pre-1939, ceremonies, indigenous customs (tribal dancing, receptions); topography of former colonies, buildings and especially public buildings, e.g., Barbados 1872–1884, Bahamas 1890, government house in Bermuda 1932, buildings in Toronto 1856; general coverage of Canada, Australia, New Zealand, Nigeria, Palestine, St Helena, Seychelles,

Hong Kong, Zanzibar; China including siege of Peking during the Boxer Rebellion (1900) and social life of the Commissioner of Customs in Peking (1890)

Access and conditions Open to the public by appt, Mon-Fri 9.30–5.30. All material available for editorial reproduction but not for advertising. No loans; material may be copied by outside photographers. Photocopies available. No reproduction rights fees charged.

69 • FORMAT PHOTOGRAPHERS

25 Horsell Road, London N5 1XL
Tel (01) 609 3439

Enquiries to Jane Harper

Items 40,000: b/w original photographs, colour transparencies (35mm)

Dates of photographs 1960 to present

Subjects Documentary photography and photojournalism in Britain with emphasis on political and economic affairs, including health, education, housing, social welfare, demonstrations, trade unions, peace, anti-racist and women's movements, black and Asian culture, society and political movements; youth cultures; childcare and child development, issues affecting women, women's work and changing roles, gay and lesbian issues, personalities and politics, human relationships; political and trade union personalities, British coalmining industry, music and musicians including rock, especially 1960s British rock, reggae, blues, jazz; Ireland (north and south); general social, economic and cultural coverage of Africa, India, Central America, Far East, Middle East, Israel, Caribbean, Europe, USA, USSR; photographs by Brenda Prince, Sheila Gray, Pam Isherwood, Raissa Page, Joanne O'Brien, Jenny Matthews, Maggie Murray, Val Wilmer

Access and conditions Open to qualified researchers by appt (tel), Mon-Fri 10–6. All material available for editorial reproduction and for advertising (with some restrictions). B/w and colour material loaned free of charge for one month. Photocopies available. Reproduction rights, service and holding fees charged. Staff will undertake some research; service fee charged for more than ten prints.

70 • FOTOBANK INTERNATIONAL COLOUR LIBRARY LTD

INCORPORATING ENGLAND SCENE

32 Kingly Court, London W1R 5LE
Tel (01) 734 2915, 734 4764 Telex 25367

Enquiries to Trevor Parr

Items About 200,000: colour transparencies (35mm, 7×6 cm, $5'' \times 4''$)

Dates of subject matter Prehistory to present

Dates of photographs 1980 to present

Subjects United Kingdom life and activities, landscapes and cityscapes, towns, villages, cities, customs, countryside, traditions, people; world travel, safaris (especially Kenya), landscapes, families, children, sports, animals, couples, posed models, industry, business

Access and conditions Open to qualified researchers by appt (tel), Mon-Fri 9–6. All material available for editorial reproduction and for advertising. Colour material loaned free of charge for 28 days. Reproduction rights, service and holding fees charged. Staff of five will undertake some research. Printed catalogue available.

71 • THE FOTOMAS INDEX PICTURE LIBRARY

74 Newman Street, London W1P 3LA
Tel (01) 636 4148

Enquiries to J. de la Mare

Items Over 150,000: b/w original photographs, colour transparencies, glass negatives

Subjects World history up to about 1910 including art, architecture and landscaping, ceramics, calligraphy and manuscript illumination, tapestries and textiles including the Bayeux Tapestry, interior decoration and furniture, sculpture and carving, metalwork, goldsmiths and silversmiths, satire and caricature including works by Hogarth, Rowlandson, Gillray and Cruikshank, portraits (filed by name and profession), prints and drawings, paintings, sports, games and pastimes, hunting and racing, music, titlepages, scores, instruments and players, theatre, music hall and circuses, politics, Parliament, finance, labour, trade unions, migration and slavery, naval and military, police, crime and punishment, social problems, law courts, treaties, education and schools, religion, Christianity, Biblical events and people, ceremonies, books, portraits, persecutions, Jews, Quakers, Islam, astrology, ethics, witchcraft, libraries, museums, newspapers, events in Britain, Europe, Africa, the Americas, the Middle and Far East, Royal occasions, topography, exploration, maps and plans, views of London, the British Isles, Europe, etc., titlepages and extracts from printed books, heraldry, seals, autographs, technology, agriculture, household management, food and drink, cooking, advertising, accounting, commerce, manufacturing industries, metals, textiles, chemicals, paper and printing, building, chimney sweeping, transport and communications, costume, daily life, marriages and funerals, customs, medicine, surgery, anatomy, mining, civil, steam and hydraulic engineering, alphabets and dictionaries, mythology and legend, astronomy, physics, alchemy, chemistry, botany, zoology; material photographed in the British Museum, the Wallace Collection and museums and private collections throughout Britain

Access and conditions Open by appt. Material available for editorial reproduction and for advertising. B/w and colour material loaned for a fee. Reproduction rights fees charged. Compulsory credit line.

FOX PHOTOS LTD *see* THE PHOTO SOURCE

72 • PETER FRAENKEL'S PHOTOGRAPHS

2 Amherst Avenue, London W13 8NQ
Tel (01) 997 2572

Enquiries to Peter Fraenkel

Items About 20,000: colour transparencies (35mm), b/w original photographs

Dates of subject matter 3000 BC to present

Dates of photographs 1970 to present

Subjects Geography of the developing countries of Africa and Asia, including people, scenery, cities, towns, villages, industry, transport, history, agriculture, plants and animals in Algeria, Angola, Benin, Botswana, Dahomey, Djibouti, Egypt, Ethiopia, Gambia, Ghana, Ivory Coast, Kenya, Lesotho, Malawi, Mali, Morocco, Namibia, Niger, Nigeria, Senegal (Dakar), South Africa, Spanish Sahara, Swaziland, Tanzania, Togo, Tunisia, Western Sahara, Zambia, Zimbabwe, Afghanistan,

Bahrain, China, Hong Kong, India, Indonesia, Iran, Laos, Macao, Nepal, Oman, Pakistan, Seychelles, Sri Lanka, Thailand, Turkey, United Arab Emirates (Dubai)

Access and conditions Not open; mail requests only. All material available for editorial reproduction and for advertising. B/w and colour material loaned free of charge for one month. Reproduction rights, holding and service fees charged; service fee deductible from use fee. Staff will undertake research. All material copyright.

73 • GLASGOW UNIVERSITY LIBRARY

Special Collections Department

Hillhead Street, Glasgow G12 8QE
Tel (041) 334 2122   Telex 778421

Enquiries to Phillip Escreet, Keeper of Special Collections

Items About 100,000: b/w original photographs, illustrated books, architectural drawings, colour transparencies (35mm), stereographs, calotypes (prints and negatives), carbon prints, lantern slides, glass negatives, daguerreotypes

Dates of subject matter Prehistory to present

Dates of photographs *c.* 1840 to present

Subjects Medieval illuminated manuscripts; illustrated printed books from late 15th-century to the present day with emphasis on emblem and fête books depicting stately processions, festivals, marriages, coronations, and funerals, mainly of the 16th to 18th centuries; portraits, landscapes and views, especially of Edinburgh, Glasgow, St Andrews, Durham and Newhaven; travel pictures of Italy, France, Belgium, Spain, Switzerland, Scandinavia, USSR, China, Japan, the Holy Land, North Africa, India, Australia and Tasmania; calotype prints, calotype negatives, glass negatives and carbon prints by Davis Octavius Hill; James McNeill Whistler, his work and his family; lantern slides of Ur, Petra, the Holy Land, Mecca and Medina; memorabilia and Mss of Sir Thomas Browne; Scottish Universities Antarctic and other expeditons, *c.* 1903 to 1911; Scottish theatre production photographs (20th-century) including portraits, the Citizen's Theatre, Glasgow

Access and conditions Open to the public by appt (tel), Mon-Fri 9.15–4.45, Sat 9.15–12.15. All material available for editorial reproduction and for advertising. B/w prints available for a fee; colour transparencies loaned free of charge or duplicated for a fee. Photocopies available. Reproduction rights fees charged. Staff will undertake limited research. Printed catalogue of manuscripts and books available.

74 • JOHN GLOVER PHOTOGRAPHY

2 Struan Cottages, Church Fields, Witley, Godalming, Surrey GU8 5PP
Tel (042879) 3322

Enquiries to John Glover

Items 25,000: colour transparencies (35mm)

Dates of subject matter BC to present

Dates of photographs 1975 to present

Subjects Gardens; wild and cultivated flowers; landscapes throughout the British Isles; villages, castles, ancient monuments; babies and young children

Access and conditions Open to qualified researchers by appt (tel), Mon-Fri 9–5. All material available for editorial reproduction and for advertising. Colour material loaned free of charge for one month. Reproduction rights fees charged. Research undertaken. All material copyright.

75 • HENRY GRANT

34 Powis Gardens, London NW11 8HH
Tel (01) 455 1710

Enquiries to Henry Grant

Items About 108,000: b/w original and copy photographs, colour transparencies (35mm)

Dates of subject matter 1948 to present

Dates of photographs 1948 to present

Subjects Education from pre-schools to universities, including playgroups, nursery schools, infant schools, junior schools, secondary schools, public schools, special schools, technical schools, adult education, further education, teacher training, polytechnics, industrial training, art schools and colleges, drama schools, music schools, museums, English as a second language (all aspects including multi-racial); trades and professions, political activities including demonstrations, CND, voluntary services, transport, industrial archaeology; European geography including France, Italy, Yugoslavia, USSR

Access and conditions Open to qualified researchers by appt, Mon-Fri 9.30–5.30. All material available for editorial reproduction; some for advertising use. B/w and colour material loaned free of charge for one month. Reproduction rights, service and holding fees charged. Staff will undertake research; negotiable fee for long projects. All material copyright.

76 • RAY GREEN PHOTO LIBRARY

18 Cringle Drive, Cheadle, Cheshire SK8 1JJ
Tel (061) 428 4053

Enquiries to Ray Green

Items About 10,000: colour transparencies (35mm), b/w original photographs

Dates of subject matter AD 200 to present

Dates of photographs 1950 to present

Subjects North of England life and events: sports including soccer, Cup Finals, cricket, fishing, horse-racing, golf, motor-car racing, cycling, boxing, yachting, athletics; industry, mines and miners, mills, factories, workers, nuclear plants; sociology, working-class life, blacks, immigrants; transport, docks, ports, boats, airports, planes; soldiers and uniforms; medical subjects; people, children, babies, crowds; education, schools and universities; architecture, towns, cities, houses, churches, cathedrals; agriculture and meteorology; geography, seaside, Lancashire and Yorkshire countryside, Lake District, Isle of Man, Ireland; actors and the theatre, television, *Coronation Street*, the Beatles, John Lennon and Yoko Ono; art and artists, L. S. Lowry; Buddhists

Access and conditions Open to qualified researchers by appt (tel), Mon-Fri 9–6. All material available for editorial reproduction and for advertising. B/w and colour material loaned free of charge for one month. Reproduction rights, service and holding fees charged; service fee deductible from use fee. Staff will undertake research.

77 • SALLY AND RICHARD GREENHILL

357 Liverpool Road, London N1 1NL
Tel (01) 607 8549

Enquiries to Sally Neal

Items About 200,000: colour transparencies (35mm), b/w original photographs

Dates of photographs 1970 to present

Subjects Documentation of contemporary life, social change and problems in the UK and abroad, urban scenes, industry, agriculture, education, medicine, leisure, religion, transport, poverty, environment, family life, teenagers, old people, everyday scenes; Germany (especially handicrafts), Greece, India, Afghanistan, USSR, Albania, Sri Lanka, Singapore; special collections on Modern China (from 1971), Hong Kong, the USA, and child development including pregnancy, birth, and family life

Access and conditions Open to qualified researchers by appt (tel), Mon-Fri 9.30–5. All material available for editorial reproduction; some restrictions on advertising use since most material has no model releases. B/w and colour material loaned free of charge for one month. Reproduction rights, service and holding fees charged. Staff of three will undertake research.

78 • SUSAN GRIGGS AGENCY LTD

17 Victoria Grove, London W8 5RW
Tel (01) 584 6738/9/0 Telex 934386

Enquiries to Sandra Schadeberg

Items About 200,000: colour transparencies (35mm)

Dates of subject matter Prehistory to present

Dates of photographs 1967 to present

Subjects World geography (140 countries), industry and commerce, science and technology, transport (air, rail, road, sea), architecture, agriculture, sport, religion, people and personalities, medicine, natural history and the following categories: abstracts, accidents, animals, animal care, antiquities, antiques, aphrodisiacs, archaeology, armoury, art, auctions, banks, behaviour, birds, boats and ships, boatbuilding, books, bridges, cafés and restaurants, camping, candles and lighting, cars, cemeteries, clocks and timepieces, clothing, computers, conservation, crafts, dance, death, demonstrations and protests, dereliction and decay, deserts, disasters (drought, earthquake, floods), drugs, eating and drinking, education, energy crisis, entertaining, entertainment, fairs, fêtes, carnivals, farming, fire, fireworks, fishing industry, flowers, food and drink, funerals, furniture and furnishing, gambling,

gardens and patios, geology, glass and glass-blowing, graffiti, posters and signs, grooming, health and exercise, hotels, industrial archaeology, insects, interior decorating and design, irrigation, jewellery, law, maps, memorabilia, military, mining, mountains, museums, music, occult, oceanography, parades and pageants, people (babies, birth, breastfeeding, with mother, with father, children, couples, crowds, elderly, families, posed models, hippies, housewives, men, occupations, students, teenagers, tourists, women), plants (grasses, shrubs, cacti, indoor plants), pollution, pornography, poverty, prostitutes, race relations, reading, reflections, refugees, religious architecture and art, religious festivals and orders, sea and seascapes, seaside resorts and holidays, seasons, shops and shopping, sky, clouds, moon, sun and sunsets, sleeping, smoking, sports and recreations (archery, athletics, ballooning, bellringing, boating, bowling, brass rubbing, bullfighting, canoeing, climbing, cockfighting, cricket, cycling, dog-racing, drag-racing, falconry, fishing, football (soccer, Rugby, American), gliding, go-karting, golf, hang-gliding, highland games, hiking, horse-driving, horse-jumping, horse-racing, horse-riding, horse-trotting, hunting and shooting, jai alai, judo, kite flying, motor cycling, motor racing, painting, parachuting, polo, pony trekking, rowing, sailing, sandracing, stock-car racing, surfing, swimming, table games, tennis, underwater sports, watersports, pedaloes, snorkling, water parachuting, water-skiing, wrestling, sumo, still life, superstitions, swimming pools, taxidermy, toys and games, trees, volcanoes, war, water, weather, weddings; London representatives for *Photofile International* (qv)

Access and conditions Open to qualified researchers by appt (tel), Mon-Fri 10–6. All material available for editorial reproduction and for advertising (with a few restrictions). Colour material loaned free of charge for one month. Reproduction rights, service and holding fees charged. Staff will undertake research. Photographers available for assignment.

79 • GUILDFORD MUNIMENT ROOM

Surrey Record Office, Castle Arch, Guildford, Surrey GU1 3SX
Tel (0483) 573942

Enquiries to Shirley Corke, Archivist in Charge

Items 14,000: b/w original and copy photographs,

unprinted film negatives, posters, architectural drawings

Dates of subject matter *c*. 1750 to present

Dates of photographs 1856 to present

Subjects DODGSON FAMILY COLLECTION: Lewis Carroll and his family, a few photographs by Lewis Carroll, sketchbook of drawings of children; VULCANISED FIBRE COLLECTION: manufacturing processes (1950s–1960s); ONSLOW COLLECTION:, watercolours and drawings of churches and houses (18th–20th century); parish deposits including photographs of local churches, choirs and vicars; HESTAIR DENNIS COLLECTION (b/w prints and glass negatives) of vehicles including lorries, fire engines, etc., and motor mowers (*c*. 1911–1970s); village of Merrow local history and architecture

Access and conditions Open to the public by appt (tel), Tues-Thurs 9.30–12.30, 1.45–4.45, Sat (1st & 3rd in month) 9.30–12.30. Most material available for editorial reproduction and for advertising subject to copyright clearance. No loans; b/w prints and duplicate colour transparencies available for a fee. Photocopies available. Reproduction rights fees payable to owners of copyright. Staff will undertake limited research.

80 • ROBERT HAAS PHOTO LIBRARY

11 Cormont Road, London SE5 9RA
Tel (01) 735 4577

Enquiries to Robert M. Haas

Items About 20,000: colour transparencies (35mm), illustrated maps, fine art prints

Dates of photographs 1974 to present

Subjects World geography and photojournalism, including extensive coverage of the Netherlands, the Greek Islands, Morocco, New York City, the Scottish Oil Industry; and also Notting Hill Carnival, Thames Flood Barrier, teddy boys and girls, kite flying, cemeteries including old Highgate, bricklaying, traction engines, Regent's Park mosque, discos, demonstrations, Manchester, castles, pigeons, Gatwick airport, Harrods, pubs, steel bands, squatters, Gloucester, Oxford, Jubilee celebrations, housing, children, supermarkets, Fleet Street, English landscape, transport, custom cars, Spain, crowds, rivers, Stock Exchange, Wye Valley, medicine, graffiti, Scottish pipers, Edinburgh, Eton College, container ships, rough seas, ramblers, pollution, Cutty Sark, Flying

Fortress aircraft (B-17), canoeing, family groups, gardens, motorbike football, swimming pools, couples, agriculture, winter landscapes, parachuting, London Parks, Coventry, London police, Karl Marx's grave, Tilbury docks, trees, immigrants, construction sites, St Katherine's Docks, Greenwich Observatory, Big Ben, weirs, Royal Marines, Anti-Nazi League demonstrations, *Burghers of Calais* (Rodin), wakes of ships, children with real guns, taxis, joggers, fire eaters, the British Public (daily life), people

Access and conditions Open to qualified researchers by appt (tel), Mon-Fri 9–5. All material available for editorial reproduction and for advertising. B/w and colour material loaned free of charge for one month. Reproduction rights and service fees charged. Staff will undertake some research. Photographer available for assignment.

81 • SONIA HALLIDAY PHOTOGRAPHS

Primrose Cottage, Bates Lane, Weston Turville, Buckinghamshire HP22 5SL
Tel (029) 661 2266

Enquiries to Sonia Halliday

Items 95,000: colour transparencies (35mm, 7×6 cm, $5'' \times 4''$), b/w original photographs, fine art prints

Dates of subject matter 2000 BC to present

Dates of photographs 1964 to present

Subjects Stained glass of England and Europe (complete glass and sculpture of Chartres Cathedral); material illustrating the Old and New Testaments in all media (glass, mosaics, paintings, etc.); extensive coverage of Israel including aerial photography and all major Biblical sites including St Paul's journeys; Cyprus, Egypt, Greece, Israel, Jordan and Turkey including archaeology, agriculture, ethnology, geography and industry (e.g. cotton, tobacco, wine from the field to the end product); Turkish illuminated manuscripts from the Topkapi Palace Museum, Istanbul; Islamic and Christian manuscripts from the Bibliothèque Nationale, Paris; steel engravings of the Middle East (1840) hand-painted by Laura Lushington; miniature paintings of daily life in China, Turkey and Hindustan (1811); Tassili cave paintings; Angers tapestries; Byzantine and Roman mosaics and murals; natural history including mammals and butterflies (captioned with Latin names), flowers, trees, landscapes, African wildlife; special collection on African Bushmen; cloudscapes, seascapes, etc.; general coverage of Afghanistan, China, Crete, Ethiopia, France, Great Britain, India, Iraq, Italy, Nepal, Persia, Portugal, Sicily, Spain, Syria, Tunisia, Yugoslavia

Access and conditions Open to qualified researchers by appt (tel), Mon-Fri 8–6. All material available for editorial reproduction and for advertising. B/w and colour material loaned free of charge for one month. Reproduction rights fees charged. Staff of three will undertake research.

82 • TOM HANLEY

61 Stephendale Road, London SW6 2LT
Tel (01) 731 3525

Enquiries to Tom Hanley

Items About 20,000: b/w original and copy photographs, colour transparencies

Dates of photographs 1947 to present

Subjects Geography, tourism, economics, trade, industry, agriculture, lifestyles; Saudi Arabia, Jeddah, Riyadh, Dammam; Philippines, Manila, Cebu, Davao, Zamboanga, Bagio, the rice terraces, primitive tribes, Hundred Islands, villages; Brazil, Rio de Janeiro, San Paolo, Bel Horizonte, Ouro Preto, Itaipu, Iguacu and Falls; USA, Los Angeles, San Francisco, Seattle, Chicago, Pittsburgh, Miami; Canada, Prince Edward Island, Quebec, Montreal, Toronto, Ottawa, Calgary, Edmonton, Vancouver; South Korea, Seoul, Ulson, Pusan, Kyongju, Bomun, Yeosu, Popjusa, Songnisan, Korea Folk Village; China, Peking, Shanghai, Hangzhou; Taiwan, Taipei, Kaohsiung, Hualien, Taroko Gorge; Japan, Tokyo, Hakone, Kyoto; Hong Kong; Malaysia, Kuala Lumpur, Banting, Kluang; Singapore; Abu Dhabi, Dubai; Iceland, Reykjavik, Westman Isles (Heimaey), Gulfoss; Sweden, Stockholm, Gothenborg; Holland, Amsterdam, Rotterdam, the Hague; Belgium, Brussels, Antwerp; India, Bombay, Calcutta, Madras, Delhi, Benares, Lucknow, Jaipur, Udaipur, Cochin, Konarak, Khajurao, Kerala, etc.; West Germany, Frankfurt, the Rhine, the Mosel, Heidelberg, the Neckar, Augsburg, Bavaria, Royal castles; Seychelles, Mahe, Praslin, Bird Island, La Digue; Cayman Islands, Grand Cayman; Greece, Athens, Salonika; Bahrain; pop musicians of the 60s and early 70s, jazz musicians, blues singers and other vocalists; general coverage including beaches, airlines, traditions, hotels, restaurants, pregnancy,

children, medicine and doctors, politicians, events (e.g. the removal of London Bridge to Arizona, rowers across the Atlantic, sailors around the world, foot and mouth disease in Britain, World War I trenches at Vimy Ridge)

Access and conditions Open to qualified researchers by appt (tel), Mon-Fri 9–6. All material available for editorial reproduction and for advertising. B/w and colour material loaned free of charge for one month. Reproduction rights, service and holding fees charged. Staff will undertake research; fee for long projects.

83 • JOHN HANNAVY PICTURE COLLECTION

2 Sandycroft Avenue, Wigan, Lancashire WN1 2BG
Tel (0942) 45838

Enquiries to John Hannavy

Items 10,000: b/w original and copy photographs, colour transparencies (35mm, 2¼″, 5″ × 4″), stereographs, colour photographic prints, postcards, glass negatives, daguerrotypes, lantern slides, illustrated books

Dates of subject matter Prehistory to present

Dates of photographs 1840 to present

Subjects British architecture including castles, churches, stately homes, etc; industrial archaeology of north-western England, steam railways; landscape and gardens; Victorian photographic collection (1860–1900) including work by Francis Frith and Francis Bedford and others, portraits, coloured seaside views, mid-19th-century stereo views by G. W. Wilson and others, views of the Middle East including Egypt and the Holy Land by Felice Beato and Langhai (Egyptian photographer, active 1860–1880s in Egypt, the Holy Land, the Middle East); history of photography including examples of almost every photographic process and stage in the development of photography (1840–1920)

Access and conditions Not open; postal and telephone inquiries only. All material available for editorial reproduction and for advertising. B/w and colour material loaned free of charge for one month. B/w prints available for a fee. Reproduction rights, service and holding fees charged; service fees deductible from use fees. Staff will undertake research. Computer catalogue.

84 • HANNIBAL HOUSE PHOTOGRAPHIC LIBRARY

Department of the Environment, Property Services Agency, Room 401, Hannibal House, Elephant & Castle, London SE1 6TD
Tel (01) 703 6380 ext 3469

Enquiries to Raymond Simmons, Librarian

Items About 60,000: b/w original photographs, colour transparencies (5″ × 4″, larger), colour photographic prints, art reproductions, unprinted film negatives

Dates of photographs 1947 to present

Subjects Structures in the United Kingdom under the supervision of the Dept of the Environment, including ancient monuments, palaces, abbeys, government buildings, historical buildings, pictures and paintings, murals and frescoes, parks, ceremonies including State Opening of Parliament, Investitures, etc.

Access and conditions Open to the public by appt (write), Mon-Fri 9–4. Most material available for editorial reproduction and for advertising. B/w prints and duplicate colour transparencies available for a fee. Reproduction rights fees charged. Staff will undertake some research.

85 • ROBERT HARDING PICTURE LIBRARY LTD

17A Newman Street, London W1P 3HD
Tel (01) 637 8969

Enquiries to Jenny Pate

Items 280,000: colour transparencies (35mm, 5″ × 4″), b/w original photographs

Dates of subject matter Prehistory to present

Dates of photographs 1960 to present

Subjects Geography worldwide including cities and towns, deserts, forests, mountains, polar regions, rivers, volcanoes, geology; racial and tribal groups, customs, festivals, education, religion, crafts, tourism; agriculture, trade, industry, archaeology, art, architecture, construction, energy, food, sport, transport; climatic conditions, natural history including mammals, birds, insects, marine life; special collections include the RAINBIRD ART LIBRARY, Tutankhamun and Chinese exhibitions in London, EQUINOX BOTANICAL LIBRARY, *FINANCIAL TIMES* colour library (trade, industry, commerce, commodities, cities worldwide), VICTOR KENNETT'S LIBRARY (Leningrad)

Access and conditions Open to qualified researchers by appt (tel), Mon-Fri 9.30–5.30. All material available for editorial reproduction and for advertising. B/w and colour material loaned free of charge for one month; b/w prints and duplicate colour transparencies available for a fee. Photocopies available. Reproduction rights and holding fees charged; service fees charged for postal orders. Staff of three will undertake research. Most material copyright.

86 • RONALD J. HARRISON-CHURCH

40 Handside Lane, Welwyn Garden City, Hertfordshire AL8 6SJ
Tel (0707) 323293

Enquiries to Ronald J. Harrison-Church

Items 10,000: colour transparencies (35mm), b/w original photographs, glass negatives, lantern slides, press cuttings and tearsheets, postcards

Dates of photographs b/w 1940 to present, colour 1956 to present

Subjects World geography, especially landscapes, towns, economic activities and infrastructures; Africa including Morocco, Tunisia, Egypt, Sudan, Ethiopia, Djibouti, Mauritania, Senegal, Gambia, Mali, Niger Republic, Guinea, Sierra Leone, Liberia, Ivory Coast, Ghana, Togo, Benin (Dahomey), Nigeria, Chad, Cameroon, Equatorial Guinea, St Helena, Kenya, Tanzania, Seychelles, Zambia, Zimbabwe, Mozambique, Mauritius, Madagascar, South Africa; Canada, USA, Mexico, Venezuela, Brazil, Uruguay, Madeira, Grand Canary, Jordan, Turkey, Israel, Maldives, India, Sri Lanka, Singapore, Malaysia, Thailand, Indonesia, Philippines, Hong Kong, Macao, Japan, USSR, UK, Eire, France, Monaco, Andorra, Belgium, Netherlands, Luxembourg, West Germany, Switzerland, Austria, Portugal, Malta, Spain, Gibraltar, Italy, Yugoslavia, Greece, Norway, Sweden, East Berlin, Poland, Czechoslovakia, Turkmenistan, Uzbekistan

Access and conditions Open to qualified researchers by appt (write). All material available for editorial reproduction and for advertising. B/w and colour material loaned free of charge for one month. Reproduction rights, service and holding fees charged. Staff will undertake some research. Catalogue available.

87 • HAWKLEY STUDIO ASSOCIATES LTD

3 Weston Close, Ballfield Road, Godalming, Surrey GU7 2EY
Tel (04868) 22366

Enquiries to Nick Nicholson

Items 2000: colour transparencies (2¼", 5" × 4"), b/w original photographs, glass negatives

Dates of subject matter 1500 to present

Dates of photographs 1963 to present

Subjects English, Dutch and German dolls and dolls houses (18th- to 20th-century) and work by contemporary British doll makers; country properties of all periods (medieval, Regency, Victorian, etc.) including cottages, small estates, castles; town houses; European crafts including shell work, beadwork, feathers, découpage (paper cut-outs) from *c.* 1750 to present; 20th-century embroidery

Access and conditions Open to qualified researchers by appt, Mon-Fri 9–5.30. All material available for editorial reproduction and for advertising. Colour material loaned free of charge for one month; b/w prints available for a fee. Reproduction rights fees and holding fees charged. Staff will undertake research.

88 • HEART OF ENGLAND TOURIST BOARD

2-4 Trinity Street, Worcester WR1 2PW
Tel (0905) 29511

Enquiries to Jenny Reddaway (colour), Christine Tustin (b/w)

Items About 6500: colour transparencies (35mm), b/w original and copy photographs

Dates of subject matter Prehistory to present

Dates of photographs 1974 to present

Subjects Gloucestershire, Hereford, Worcester, Shropshire, Staffordshire, Warwickshire and West Midlands scenic views, tourist attractions, modern theme parks, industrial archaeology, crafts including candle making, stone carving, brass rubbing, glass blowing, pottery, corn dollies, jewellery; historic houses including Packwood, Baddesley Clinton, Shugborough, Hagley Hall, Attingham Park, Weston Park, Stanway Hall, Upton House; events including Three Counties Agricultural Show at Malvern, medieval fairs, morris dancing; cathedrals including Coventry, Hereford, Gloucester, Lichfield, Worcester; churches and villages, canals, markets, customs, Warwick Castle

Access and conditions Open to qualified researchers by appt (tel), Mon-Fri 9–5. All material available for editorial reproduction and for advertising. B/w and colour material loaned free of charge for one month. Reproduction rights and holding fees charged. Staff will undertake some research, time permitting. Card catalogue.

89 • BARBARA HELLER PHOTO LIBRARY

INCORPORATING FAY GODWIN'S PHOTO FILES

36 Camden Square, London NW1 9XA
Tel (01) 267 1034

Enquiries to Barbara Heller

Items About 20,000: colour transparencies (35mm, 2¼"), b/w original photographs

Dates of subject matter Prehistory to present

Dates of photographs 1960 to present

Subjects Archaeology, art and culture of ancient civilizations of the Near and Far East and of primitive societies; families, housing, agriculture, markets, education, transport, dances, ceremonies in Hong Kong, Thailand, Indonesia, Tanzania, and Kenya (including Masai life and the age-grade Eunoto and Olngesher ceremonies); archaeological sites of Mexico; landscapes, daily life, archaeological sites and architecture in Afghanistan, Iran, Morocco, Pakistan, Turkey, Soviet Central Asia and the Caucasus; Egypt and the Sudan in the 1930s including archaeological sites and aircraft of the period; geology and archaeology of the United Kingdom including curious natural formations, stone circles, and occult and esoteric subjects; comprehensive coverage of Greek archaeological sites; Tibetans in exile, including daily life, religious ceremonies, and rituals of the monks and the community, their monastery in southern India, Dharamsala (present home of the Dalai Lama), spread of Tibetan Buddhism in the west; Ottoman calligraphy (15th to 20th century); Ottoman, Turkish, Persian, Syrian, Egyptian, Mesopotamian and Byzantine ceramics (9th to 18th centuries); Russian and Greek icons (12th to 17th centuries); Islamic painting including Ottoman miniatures, illuminations and portraits; Thracian, Anatolian, Caucasian and Persian kilims; Ottoman, Egyptian, Syrian, Persian and Byzantine metalwork (12th to 18th centuries); Mount Athos, including the monastic community, buildings, isolated hermitages, monks and ceremonies, Byzantine art treasures; Ottoman, Coptic, Egyptian, Persian, Indian and Seljuk textiles (3rd to 19th centuries); Great Zimbabwe, including the Royal Palace or Great Enclosure, the Valley Enclosures and the ridge ruins; FAY GODWIN'S PHOTO FILES: landscapes of Great Britain, industry including workshops, mills and factories of Yorkshire and North Sea oil, contemporary society including dole queues, the aged, social services, adult education, schools, pubs and clubs, animals including farm and domestic and guide dogs for the blind, portraits of British and American writers, miscellaneous subjects including Iceland, Paris, skiing, West Indies, trees, moods, nature patterns, humour

Access and conditions Open to qualified researchers by appt (tel), Mon-Fri 9.30–5.30. All material available for editorial reproduction and for advertising. B/w and colour material loaned free of charge for 60 days. Photocopies available. Reproduction rights and holding fees charged; service fee charged only when no material is used. Staff will undertake some research. Catalogue in preparation.

90 • JOHN HESELTINE PHOTOGRAPHY

7 Cedar Way, Camley Street, London NW1 0PD
Tel (01) 387 5114, 609 2012

Enquiries to John Heseltine

Items About 20,000: colour transparencies (35mm, 7 × 6 cm, 5″ × 4″)

Dates of photographs 1979 to present

Subjects British landscape and coast, including gardens, people, food, cities, towns, countryside, abstracts, agriculture and farming, cars and motoring, computers, food and drink, industry, people at work and leisure, modern architecture, illustrations of photographic techniques; travel in USA, Western Europe, especially France, Italy and Spain

Access and conditions Open to qualified researchers by appt (tel), Mon-Fri 10–6. All material available for editorial reproduction and for advertising. Colour material loaned free of charge for one month. Reproduction rights and holding fees charged; service fees charged only when no material is used. Staff will undertake research. All material copyright.

91 • CLIVE HICKS PICTURE COLLECTION

72 Brentham Way, London W5 1BE
Tel (01) 997 7974, 994 6477

Enquiries to Clive Hicks

Items 50,000: b/w original photographs, colour transparencies (35mm), illustrated books

Dates of subject matter Prehistory to present

Dates of photographs 1960 to present

Subjects Architecture and landscape of the United Kingdom and Eire, European architecture and landscape; prehistoric monuments (excluding excavations and material in museums), Celtic and Dark Age sites, early Christian sites; medieval cathedrals, abbeys, castles and churches including sculpture and stained glass; bridges of all periods, development of social housing

Access and conditions Open to qualified researchers by appt, Mon-Fri 9–5. B/w and colour material loaned free of charge for one month. Photocopies available. Reproduction rights fees charged; service and research fees negotiable. Staff will undertake research. All material copyright.

92 • THE JOHN HILLELSON AGENCY LTD

Wheatsheaf House, 4 Carmelite Street, London EC4Y 0BN
Tel (01) 353 4551

Enquiries to John Hillelson

Items 700,000: b/w original and copy photographs, colour transparencies (35mm), glass negatives, art reproductions

Dates of subject matter Prehistory to present

Dates of photographs 1855 to present

Subjects Geography (worldwide coverage), social change, politics, demonstrations, poverty, ecology, medicine, accidents, human interaction, family life, archaeology, anthropology, industries, agriculture, schools, sport, music, religion, personalities (including writers, artists), television personalities, seasons, natural history and science, animals, films and filming, fine art, aerial photography; special collections on China, USSR, India, Asia, Islam; the JOHN HILLELSON COLLECTION of 19th-century topography and wars and especially photographs by John Thomson, James Robertson, Samuel Bourne and Felice Beato; photographs by Brian Brake, Dan Budnik, Gisele Freund, Georg Gerster, Jacques-Henri Lartigue, Erich Lessing, Fred Mayer, Roland and Sabrina Michaud, Marc Riboud, Raghubir Singh, Howard Sochurek; London agent for Magnum, Sygma and *L'Illustration*

Access and conditions Open to qualified researchers by appt (tel), Mon-Fri 10–5. All material available for editorial reproduction and some for advertising. B/w and colour material loaned free of charge for one month. Reproduction rights, service and holding fees charged. Staff of five will undertake research.

93 • PAT HODGSON LIBRARY

Jasmine Cottage, Spring Grove Road, Richmond, Surrey TW10 6EH
Tel (01) 940 5986

Enquiries to Pat Hodgson

Items About 10,000: b/w original and copy photographs, fine art prints, illustrated books, book illustrations (colour)

Dates of subject matter Prehistory to present

Dates of photographs 1960 to present

Subjects History, archaeology, ancient civilizations, 19th-century social history, topography of Greece, Turkey, Egypt, Holland, Luxembourg; witchcraft, magic, the occult

Access and conditions Open to qualified researchers by appt, Mon-Fri 9–6. All material available for editorial reproduction and for advertising. B/w material loaned free of charge for one month. Photocopies available. Reproduction rights, service and holding fees charged. Staff will undertake research.

94 • GEOFF HOWARD

23 Risborough Close, London N10 3PL
Tel (01) 883 5018

Enquiries to Geoff Howard

Items About 30,000: b/w original photographs, colour transparencies (35mm)

Dates of subject matter About 500 AD to present

Dates of photographs 1970 to present

Subjects Religion including faith healing, Irish pilgrimages, christenings, weddings, Divine Light Mission, Church customs and traditions, temples and worship in Hong Kong, Bangkok, Japan, including religious dances; dance including ballet schools, Roy London Ballet, Ballet Rambert, London Contemporary Dance, Extemporary Dance, Royal Ballet, Maina Gielgud, Moving Being, social dancing, go-go dancers, pop festivals, jiving, Irish traditional dances, Highland Scottish dances; architecture of English towns including Chichester, Richmond (Yorks), Tewkesbury, Ludlow, Stamford (Lincs), Totnes, Warwick, Saffron Walden, Beverley (Yorks), Bradford-on-Avon, Berwick-on-Tweed, Lewes, Whitby, Durham, Bury St Edmunds, Sandwich, Devizes, Cirencester; performing arts including festivals (1973, 1974, 1975) in Southampton and at the Serpentine Gallery involving ritual theatre, improvised theatre and improvised painting; philosophers including A. J. Ayer, Stephen Dworkin, Sir Isaiah Berlin, Ernest Gellner, Charles Taylor, Antony Quinton, Bernard Williams, Willard V. Quine, Brian Magee; general subjects including human interaction, personalities, society, London markets, London SE16, Hong Kong, Bangkok, Japan, Johannesburg, Washington, Nairobi, Ulster, factories, health, etc.

Access and conditions Open to qualified researchers by appt (tel), Mon-Fri 9–6. All material available for editorial reproduction and for advertising. B/w and colour material loaned free of charge for one month. Photocopies available. Reproduction rights, holding and service fees charged; service fees deductible from use fees. Staff will undertake research in answer to specific requests.

95 • JOHN HOWARD

Thorpe Lane, Tealby, Lincolnshire LN8 3XJ
Tel (067383) 292

Enquiries to John Howard

Items About 4000: b/w original photographs,

colour transparencies (35mm, 6 × 6 cm), colour photographic prints, postcards, unprinted film negatives

Dates of subject matter Roman times to present

Dates of photographs 1950 to present

Subjects Education including primary and secondary British schooling and curriculum, teacher training, science teaching; veterinary work, general practice; boats and sailing (UK and Eire); landscape, especially Lincolnshire and Tennyson's Lincolnshire, Roman Lincoln, village life; general subjects including people at work, crafts, agriculture

Access and conditions Open to the public by appt (tel), Mon-Fri 9–7. All material available for editorial reproduction and some for advertising. B/w and colour material loaned free of charge for one month. Reproduction rights and holding fees charged. Staff will undertake research.

96 • CHRIS HOWES PHOTOGRAPHS

51 Timbers Square, Roath, Cardiff, South Glamorgan CF2 3SH
Tel (0222) 486557

Enquiries to Chris Howes

Items 30,000: colour transparencies (35mm, 6″ × 6″, 9″ × 6″), b/w original photographs, colour photographic prints, postcards, fine art prints

Dates of subject matter 17th century to present

Dates of photographs 1960 to present

Subjects Caving worldwide including modern caving in the United Kingdom and Eire at Swildon's Hole, Ogof Ffynon Ddu (South Wales), Wookey Hole, Peak Cavern; cave diving gear, people in caving activities; cave fauna (bats, insects), cave landscapes (karst, limestone); history of caving (17th-century engravings, photographs) in France, Czechoslovakia, Switzerland, USA; natural history including microscopy, insects, amphibians, birds; conservation including coal tips before and after, canal cleaning, wastelands cleaning, new path cutting through forests; education including schools, classrooms, playgrounds, school activities in South Wales

Access and conditions Open to qualified researchers by appt (tel). All material available for editorial reproduction and for advertising. B/w and colour material loaned free of charge for one month. Reproduction rights fees charged. Staff will undertake research. All material copyright.

97 • JOHN AND PENNY HUBLEY PHOTOGRAPHIC AND EDUCATIONAL SERVICES

12 Shaw Lane, Leeds, West Yorkshire LS6 4DU
Tel (0532) 755486

Enquiries to John and Penny Hubley

Items 40,000: b/w original photographs, colour transparencies (35mm)

Dates of photographs 1975 to present

Subjects Third-world countries in Africa (Zambia, Zimbabwe, Lesotho, Kenya, Nigeria), the Caribbean (Jamaica, Barbados, Trinidad, St Kitts, Montserrat) and north and south India including development, urban life, rural life, social problems, health, education, nutrition, agriculture, foods, food processing, home economics, women, children, child development, industry, mining, economic crops, water, sanitation, transport, culture, religion; United Kingdom, child development, ethnic minorities

Access and conditions Open to qualified researchers by appt, Mon-Fri 9–5. All material available for editorial reproduction and for advertising. B/w and colour material loaned free of charge for one month. Reproduction rights, service and holding fees charged. Staff will undertake some research.

98 • ILLUSTRATED LONDON NEWS PICTURE LIBRARY

20 Upper Ground, Stamford Street, London SE1 9PD
Tel (01) 928 6969 Telex 8955803

Enquiries to Debbie Moore

Items About three million: illustrated magazines, original cartoons, unprinted film negatives, b/w original and copy photographs, colour transparencies (35mm), art reproductions, press cuttings and tearsheets

Dates of subject matter Prehistory to present

Dates of photographs 1842 to present

Subjects Social and political history especially from 1842 to the present but including earlier material (b/w engravings and photographs); British and foreign geography, portraits, animals, etc. (colour); illustrations indexed as follows: accidents, advertisements, aerial photography, Africa, agriculture, Air Forces, Americas, animals,

Antarctica, anthropology, antiques, archaeology, archery, architecture, armies, art, artists, Asia, astronomy, athletics, auctions, Australasia, aviation, ballet, ballooning, banks, bankers, banquets, balls, behaviour, bicycles, biographies, biology, birds, botany, bowling, boxing, British Isles, broadcasting, buildings, bullfighting, canals, cars, cartoons, castles, cats, cathedrals, caving, ceramics, ceremonies, chemistry, children, China, Christmas, churches, cinema, circuses, cities, civic dignitaries, clocks, clubs, coaches, commerce, communications, computers (history of), conservation, construction, cookery, costumes, country houses, cricket, crime, croquet, customs, cycling, dancing, decorations, demonstrations, disasters, docks, drink, drugs, education, EEC, electricity, emigration, engineering, Europe, executions, exhibitions, expeditions, explorers, family life, famous houses, fashion, fencing, festivals, fêtes, films, financiers, fires, fish, fishing, flowers, folklore, food, football, forestry, fortifications, fountains, funerals, furnishings, gambling, games, game shooting, gardening, geology, girls, glamour, glass, gliding, gold, golf, government, greetings-card subjects, greyhound-racing, gymkhanas, harbours, high society, highwaymen, history, historians, holiday scenes, homes, honours, horse-racing, horse-riding, horse shows, horticulture, hotels, housing, humour, hunting, immigration, India, industries, inns and pubs, interiors, inventions, inventors, Ireland, jewellery, kites, lamps, law, libraries, lighthouses, literature, London, maps, markets, medicine, meetings, military, minerals, mines, monsters, monuments, motor cycles, motor racing, mountains, mountaineering, museums, music, music hall, mythology, nature, navigation, navies, nudes, *objets d'art*, oceanography, occupations and employment, oil, opera, opium, parachuting, paranormal phenomena, parks, people, pets, philately, photo features, photography, pirates, politicians, politics, pollution, polo, porcelain, pot-holing, poverty, prams, primitive cultures, printing, prisons, processions, psychology, Punch and Judy, puppets, radio, railways, receptions, refugees, restaurants and cafes, revolutions, river, roads, rocks, romance, rowing, royalty, Rugby, rural life, sailing, sailors, schools, science, scientists, sculpture, sea, sex, seaside, ships, skating, skiing, show business, smoking, social relief, social welfare, sociology, space exploration, soccer, soldiers, sport, statesmen, stock exchange, strikes, suffragettes, surfing, swimming, target shooting, television, tennis, theatre, towns, toys, transport, travel, treasure, trees, trophies, unemployment, United Nations, villages, volcanoes, valentines, wars, watches, weapons, weather, weddings, windmills, winter sports, women, wrestling, zoos; material in the collection is drawn from *The Illustrated London News*, *The Graphic*, *The Illustrated Sporting and Dramatic News*, *The Sphere*, *The Bystander*, *The Sketch*, *The Tatler*, *Britannia and Eve*, *Sport and Country*, *The Illustrated War News*; THOMAS COOK TRAVEL ARCHIVE: history of travel and tourism in photographs, posters, original cartoons, (b/w and colour), engravings and ephemera; hotels, resorts, beaches, sports, ships, aircraft, motor cars, coaches, railways, passengers and travellers in UK and abroad, especially on the Nile

Access and conditions Open to the public by appt (tel), Mon-Fri 9.30–5.30. All material available for editorial reproduction and for advertising. B/w and colour material loaned free of charge for two months. Photocopies available for a fee. Reproduction rights and holding fees charged; service fees charged when no material is used. Staff of three will undertake research. Card catalogue; printed catalogue.

99 • IMAG

Longwood House, Cadewell Lane, Torquay, South Devon TQ2 7AG
Tel (0803) 615422

Enquiries to Pamela Whitehead

Items About 10,000: colour transparencies (35mm, 6 × 4½ cm), unprinted film negatives, b/w original photographs

Dates of subject matter Prehistory to present

Dates of photographs 1954 to present

Subjects World geography, United Kingdom, Antarctica, Bali, Burundi, Canada, Canary Islands, Egypt, Gabon, Greece, Germany, Hong Kong, India, Italy, Java, Kenya, Nepal, New Zealand, North Sea, Norway, Seychelles, Spain, Sri Lanka, Sudan, Somalia, Suez, Tanzania, Thailand, Uganda, Zanzibar, Zaire; agriculture and farming including walking haystacks and yak-milking in Nepal, rice paddies in Bali, dairy herds and stubble-burning in UK; domestic animals; anthropology including Balinese Gamelan dance, Hindu tooth-filing ceremony, Full Moon processions in Sri Lanka; antiquities and archaeology including Taj Mahal in India, Kistvaen Burial Chamber UK, the Gold Buddha of Wat Trimitr in Thailand; architecture; ceremonies and customs; costume; crafts including silk-spinning (Thailand), thatching (UK) and sculpture (Bali); deserts including an oasis in the Thar Desert of Rajasthan (India), the Bahi Depression and badland topography in Tanzania; energy; engineering; environment and pollution including hedgerow destruction, rubbish tip infilling, poisoned ponds, oiled birds; holidays and tourism; industry including open-cast china clay mining (UK), oil exploration, exploration drilling (Canada); mountains including Everest and Ama Dablang (Nepal), Kala Pattar, glaciers in the Himalayas and New Zealand; natural history; people including Maori warriors in New Zealand and Wagogo Maidens in Tanzania; photography; polar regions including Antarctic icebergs, leopard seals, pack ice; religion; science; oceans and seas; sociology; sports and games including salmon fishing in Scotland, marlin fishing in New Zealand, native fishing in Java; transport; volcanoes and thermal areas in Uganda, Tanzania, Zaire, New Zealand; weather including floods, monsoons and monsoon erosion

Access and conditions Open to qualified researchers by appt (tel), Mon-Fri 9.30–5.30. All material available for editorial reproduction and for advertising. B/w and colour material loaned free of charge for one month. Reproduction rights and holding fees charged. Staff of three will undertake research.

100 • THE IMAGE BANK

8 Charing Cross Road, London WC2H 0HG
Tel (01) 240 5603/4 Telex 894839 TIBG

Enquiries to Pat Eaton, Head Librarian

Items 450,000: colour transparencies (35mm, $2'' \times 2''$, $5'' \times 4''$, larger)

Dates of photographs 1960 to present

Subjects World geography and travel including all continents, scenics, people, lifestyles, tourist attractions, special effects and abstracts, markets (special collection), landscapes, agriculture, sunsets and sunrises, summer and winter, lakes, forests; industry including oil, chemical, mining, iron and steel, computers, food; medicine including

hospitals, patients, research and laboratories; transport including rail, road, airplanes, shipping, docks; sport including skiing, windsurfing, hot-air balloons, fishing, etc.; leisure activities including hiking, horse-riding, eating and drinking, holidays, beaches; health and fitness, beauty care; professional and working people, couples (close-up, indoors, outdoors, young, middle-aged, old), men, women and children

Access and conditions Open to the public by appt (tel), Mon-Fri 9.30–5.30. All material available for editorial reproduction and for advertising with a few restrictions. Colour material loaned free of charge for 30 days. Reproduction rights, service and holding fees charged. Staff of eight will undertake research; fee for lengthy projects.

101 • IMAGES COLOUR LIBRARY LTD

Kingswood House, 180 Hunslet Road, Leeds, West Yorkshire LS10 1AF
Tel (0532) 449807

Enquiries to Richard Robinson

Items About 20,000: colour transparencies (35mm, 7×6 cm, $2\frac{1}{4}''$, $5'' \times 4''$)

Dates of subject matter Prehistory to present

Dates of photographs 1976 to present

Subjects British landscapes and views, industry, commerce, agriculture, transport, sport, natural history, sunsets, seascapes, cloudscapes, seasons, travel, food, families, couples, children, posed models, world geography; special collections: archaeology including major Egyptian, Greek and Roman sites throughout Europe and the Near East; geological sites in the British Isles; occult subjects including spirit photography, witchcraft; drawings and paintings by Arthur Rackham

Access and conditions Open to qualified researchers by appt (tel), Mon-Fri 9–5.30. All material available for editorial reproduction and for advertising. Colour material loaned free of charge for one month. Reproduction rights, service and holding fees charged; service fees deductible from use fees. Staff of four will undertake research. Printed catalogue.

102 • IMAGES PHOTOGRAPHIC AGENCY

86A Westgate, Grantham, Lincolnshire NG31 6LE
Tel (0476) 60645

Enquiries to Matt Limb

Items About 3000: b/w original photographs, colour transparencies (35mm, 5″ × 4″), colour photographic prints

Dates of subject matter Contemporary

Dates of photographs 1984 to present

Subjects Agriculture, farming, rural life; field sports, mountaineering and rock climbing; English villages

Access and conditions Open to the public by appt (tel), Mon-Fri 9–6 (tel). All material available for editorial reproduction and for advertising. B/w and colour material loaned free of charge for three months. Reproduction rights and holding fees charged. Staff will undertake research. Photographer available for assignments.

103 • IMPACT PHOTOS

74 Clerkenwell Road, London EC1M 5QA
Tel (01) 251 5091/2

Enquiries to Patricia Lee, Librarian

Items Over 35,000 colour transparencies (35mm)

Dates of photographs Contemporary

Subjects Worldwide geography, agriculture, industry, science and technology, hospitals, health, social welfare, natural history, plants and animals, religion, demonstrations and protests, political conferences, terrorism, transport (air, rail, road, water), weather and natural phenomena, sport and recreation, crafts, museums and galleries, clubs, concerts, films and television, theatre, shops, restaurants, hotels, food and drink, guest houses, customs, parades, royal events, military events, shows and fairs, fashion, people and personalities, royalty, Papal visits; horticultural collection of photographs by Pamela Toler

Access and conditions Open to qualified researchers by appt (tel), Mon-Fri 10–6. All material available for editorial reproduction and for advertising. Colour material loaned free of charge for one month. Reproduction rights, service and holding fees charged. Staff will undertake research.

104 • INTERFOTO PICTURE LIBRARY LTD

Southbank House, Black Prince Road, London SE1 7SJ
Tel (01) 582 3060 Telex 8951462

Enquiries to Ken Shirley, Director

Items 75,000: colour transparencies (7 × 6 cm, 5″ × 4″), b/w original photographs, glass negatives, lantern slides, postcards, unprinted film negatives

Dates of subject matter 1940 to present

Dates of photographs 1940 to present

Subjects Worldwide feature material including working life, industry, personalities, sport, transport, holidays, still life, scenics, wild life, travel; small archive of b/w photos (1950–1969), life style, family life, clothes, hairstyles, streetscenes, working life

Access and conditions Open to qualified researchers by appt (tel), Mon-Fri 9.30–5. All material available for editorial reproduction and for advertising. B/w and colour material loaned free of charge for negotiable period. Reproduction rights, holding and service fees charged. Staff will undertake some research; negotiable fee for large projects.

INTERNATIONAL FREELANCE LIBRARY *see* REPORT AND INTERNATIONAL FREELANCE LIBRARY

105 • INTERNATIONAL PHOTOBANK

23 Barrs Avenue, New Milton, Hampshire BH25 5HL
Tel (0425) 620359

Enquiries to Peter Baker

Items 85,000: colour transparencies (35mm, 6 × 6 cm), b/w original photographs

Dates of photographs 1964 to present

Subjects World geography including Australia, Austria, Balearic Islands, Belgium, Bermuda, British Isles, Canada, Canary Islands, Channel Islands, Corfu, Crete, Cyprus, Denmark, Egypt, Eire, France, Gambia, Germany, Gibraltar, Greece and Greek Islands, Hawaiian Islands, Hong Kong, India, Italy, Kenya, Madeira, Malta, Monaco, Morocco, New Zealand, Norway, Pacific Islands,

Portugal, Singapore, Spain, Sri Lanka, Sweden, Switzerland, Thailand, Tunisia, Turkey, USA, West Indies, Yugoslavia

Access and conditions Open to qualified researchers by appt (tel), Mon-Fri 9–5.30. All material available for editorial reproduction and for advertising. B/w and colour material loaned free of charge for 28 days. Reproduction rights, service and holding fees charged. Staff of four will undertake research.

106 • RAYMOND IRONS PICTURE LIBRARY

35 Langbourne Mansions, London N6 6PR
Tel (01) 348 1805

Enquiries to Raymond Irons

Items 500,000: b/w original and copy photographs, colour transparencies (35mm, 2¼″), glass negatives, fine art prints, art reproductions, posters

Dates of subject matter Contemporary

Dates of photographs 1945 to present

Subjects Animals in zoos, children, landscapes, posed models; faces of nature (unusual faces in rocks, trees, hedges); first 365 days, the life of a child every day from birth to first birthday; deep sea fishing, trawling for cod and life on board trawlers; British Isles, Spain

Access and conditions Open to qualified researchers by appt (tel), Mon-Fri 9–5. All material available for editorial reproduction and for advertising. B/w and colour material loaned free of charge for four weeks. Reproduction rights, service and holding fees charged. Staff will undertake research.

107 • ISLE OF MAN TOURIST BOARD

13 Victoria Street, Douglas, Isle of Man
Tel (0624) 74323 Telex 627793 MANINF G

Enquiries to Peter Kneale

Items 5000: b/w original photographs, colour transparencies (35mm, 5″ × 4″, larger), colour photographic prints, unprinted film negatives, posters

Dates of subject matter 1800 to present

Dates of photographs 1947 to present

Subjects Isle of Man scenery, towns, villages, recreation, sports including bowls, golf, etc., for tourists, Isle of Man TT motor cycle race, transport including trains, trams, horse-drawn vehicles, the Laxey Wheel (huge water wheel built about 1800)

Access and conditions Open to qualified researchers by appt, Mon-Fri 9–5. All material available for editorial reproduction but not for advertising. B/w and colour material loaned free of charge for six months. Photocopies available. No reproduction rights fees charged. Staff will undertake some research.

108 • JARROLD COLOUR PUBLICATIONS

Barrack Street, Norwich, Norfolk NR3 1TR
Tel (0603) 660211 Telex 97497

Enquiries to Maureen Jones, Photo Librarian

Items 100,000: colour transparencies (35mm, 5″ × 4″), b/w original photographs, postcards

Dates of subject matter 11th century to present

Dates of photographs 1950 to present

Subjects Architecture including cathedrals, churches, houses; landscapes of the British Isles; natural history including domestic pets (cats, dogs, others) and horses

Access and conditions Open to qualified researchers by appt (write), Mon-Fri 8.30–5. All material available for editorial reproduction and for advertising except in competing publications. Colour material loaned free of charge for one month. Reproduction rights and holding fees charged. Staff of four will undertake research.

109 • CAMILLA JESSEL

Riverside House, Riverside, Twickenham, Middlesex TW1 3DJ
Tel (01) 892 1470

Enquiries to Camilla Jessel

Items 4000: b/w original photographs, colour transparencies (35mm)

Dates of photographs 1963 to present

Subjects Children, child development (physical, emotional and cognitive) including birth and pregnancy, newborn babies, babies in intensive care, psychology of play, children in hospital and at clinics, child-minding, children in need, race relations and children together, disabled children and adults, autism, mentally handicapped children, gypsy and traveller children, Vietnamese refugee children, African children, South American shanty-town children; arts, especially music and dance including Royal Ballet School, Royal Ballet adults and children on stage, child musicians, orchestral musicians, rehearsal and recording sessions; some older people; acupuncture

Access and conditions Open to qualified researchers by appt. All material available for editorial reproduction and for advertising with some restrictions. B/w and colour material loaned free of charge for six weeks. Reproduction rights and holding fees charged; service fees charged only when no material is used. Staff will undertake research. All material copyright

110 • KAPPA

14 Market Square, Winslow, Buckingham
MK18 3AF
Tel (029671) 4648 Telex 826715 AERO G

Enquiries to Francesmary Kirby and Mark Kay

Items About 15,000 colour transparencies (35mm, 6 × 6 cm, larger)

Dates of subject matter 16th century to present

Dates of photographs 1980 to present

Subjects Abstracts, animals, architecture, activities, babies, beaches, boats, Britain, business, buildings, birds, children, churches, clouds, cottages, crafts, Cyprus, dancing, discotheques, doors, engines, engineering, England, exhibitions, fairs, fields, fireworks, food, follies, frost, flowers, Finland, France, games, Germany, Greece, harbours, harvesting, hobbies, holidays, horses, horticulture, houses, ice, industry, infants, inns, islands, landscapes, light, locomotives, London, machinery, Malta, moon, motoring, mountains, night-clubs, Norway, offices, parents, parks, pets, photography, plants, railways, riding, rivers, roads, rocks, sailing, sand, seascapes, ships, shrubs, snow, Spain, Sweden, swimming, sports, textures, tourists, towns, trees, tractors, traffic, transport, trains, vegetables, vehicles, villages, walls, wood, water, water sports, weather, winter

Access and conditions Open to qualified researchers by appt (tel), Mon-Fri 9.30–4. All

material available for editorial reproduction and for advertising. Colour material loaned free of charge for one month. Reproduction rights, service and holding fees charged; service fees deductible from use fees. Staff of three will undertake research. Photographers available for assignment. All material copyright. Compulsory credit line.

111 • KENNETH KEANE

9 Dalriach Court, Oban, Strathclyde PA34 5EH
Tel (0631) 62708

Enquiries to Kenneth Keane

Items 6000: b/w original photographs, colour transparencies (35mm, 5″ × 4″) colour photographic prints

Dates of photographs 1960 to present

Subjects Photojournalism, especially in Scotland, but also England, Germany, Norway, etc., including landscapes, industry, farming, fishing boats, castles, bridges, road accidents, mountain rescues, fires, Scottish scenic views, rivers, distilleries, Scottish personalities and politicians, docks, harbours, hydroelectric power stations, military including the Royal Marines in Norway, RAF rescue helicopters, railways, steam engines in Britain and Turkey, overhead electric pylons, cattle and sheep sales, towns, villages, vintage cars, last Clyde ferry at Yoker, yachting marinas, steam rollers, tractors, aircraft, Greenham air show, ferries, canals, lochs, ancient monuments; Germany, Hamburg, Wilhelmshaven; some work distributed by Camera Press, Syndication International, and Images Colour Library (Leeds) qv

Access and conditions Not open; telephone and mail requests only, Mon-Fri 8–6. All material available for editorial reproduction and for advertising. B/w and colour material loaned free of charge for one month. Reproduction rights, service and holding fees charged. Staff will undertake research.

KEYSTONE PRESS AGENCY *see* THE PHOTO SOURCE

112 • KINORY PHOTOGRAPHY

34 Clairville Gardens, London W7 3HZ
Tel (01) 840 1884

Enquiries to Yochanan Kinory or Susan Heeks

Items About 15,000: colour transparencies (35mm, 7 × 6 cm, 2¼″), b/w original photographs, colour photographic prints

Dates of subject matter 100 BC to present

Dates of photographs 1970 to present

Subjects Geography (United Kingdom and Israel), archaeology including megaliths, castles and ruins (UK) and Hellenistic, Roman and Byzantine sites in Israel; industrial archaeology including canals, locks, viaducts, abandoned mines, quarries, railway lines, stations and bridges (UK); contemporary and historical architecture including castles, cottages; people, markets, street vendors, religions, tourists in Israel; UK customs and crafts including well dressing, thatching, coracle racing, wool production in a restored rural mill; natural history including wild plants, habitat and geographical location, cultivated plants, gardens, agriculture, invertebrates, moths, butterflies, other insects, molluscs, birds, mammals

Access and conditions Open to qualified researchers by appt (tel), Mon-Fri 9–5. All material available for editorial reproduction and for advertising. B/w and colour material loaned free of charge for four weeks. Photocopies available. Reproduction rights, service and holding fees charged; service fees deductible from use fee. Staff will undertake some research.

113 • KYLIN PRESS LTD

Darbonne House, High Street, Waddesdon, Nr Aylesbury, Buckinghamshire HP18 0JA
Tel (0296) 651411

Enquiries to Gerry Tomlinson

Items 70,000: b/w original photographs, glass negatives, postcards, stereographs, press cuttings, illustrated books, prints, engravings, printed ephemera

Dates of subject matter 300 BC to present

Dates of photographs 1850 to present

Subjects Rare and unusual prints of all subjects, history, events, trades and crafts, personalities, transport, sports, inventions, men and women, architecture, animals (real and fabulous), including ice-skating on the frozen Thames, General Tom Thumb, Vincent Lunardi (first man to fly in England), a Parisian omnibus of 1853, working Victorian lace-maker, emigrants bound for the New World

Access and conditions Open to qualified researchers by appt (tel), Mon-Fri 9.30–5.30. All material available for editorial reproduction and for advertising. B/w prints, PMTs and bromides available. Photocopies available. Reproduction rights and service fees charged. Staff will undertake research. Computer index available.

114 • ANTHONY J. LAMBERT

38 Chiltern Street, London W1M 1PH
Tel (01) 487 5451

Enquiries to Anthony J. Lambert

Items About 20,000: b/w original and copy photographs, colour transparencies (35mm), glass negatives, lantern slides, postcards

Dates of subject matter 1870 to present

Dates of photographs 1870 to present

Subjects Railways worldwide, historical and contemporary; worldwide geography (40 countries), landscape, architecture including historic and domestic buildings, transport; China including people, buildings, landscapes, transport, work, shops in Shanghai, Soochow (near Nanking), Beijing, Tientsin, Kweilin, Changsha, Guangzhou

Access and conditions Open to qualified researchers by appt (tel), Mon-Fri 9–5. All material available for editorial reproduction and for advertising. B/w material loaned free of charge for three months; colour material, for one month. Photocopies available. Reproduction rights and holding fees charged. Staff will undertake research.

115 • LAMBETH PALACE LIBRARY

London SE1 7JU
Tel (01) 928 6222

Enquiries to Librarian

Items Over 200: b/w original and copy photographs, colour transparencies (35mm), postcards, architectural drawings, illustrated books

Dates of subject matter *c.* 900 to 1950

Dates of photographs *c.* 1960 to 1980

Subjects Medieval manuscripts including Biblical scenes, armour, Arthurian legends, battles including Agincourt, Burghers of Calais, costume, animals, musical instruments; settlement of Ulster in the early 17th century; printed books with illustrations of witchcraft, clerical scenes and services, costume; churches; Elizabethan history including letters by Elizabeth I and leading figures of the period

Access and conditions Open to the public by appt (write). All material available for editorial reproduction but not for advertising. B/w prints available for a fee. Colour transparencies loaned for a rental fee. Photocopies available. Reproduction rights fees charged. Staff will undertake limited research. Card and printed catalogues.

LANCASHIRE PICTURE AGENCY *see* SCOPE PICTURE AGENCY

116 • THE LAST RESORT PICTURE LIBRARY

57 Fawnbrake Avenue, London SE24 0BE
Tel (01) 274 4428

Enquiries to Dick Makin

Items 12,000: colour transparencies (35mm, 6 × 6 cm, larger), colour negatives, unprinted b/w film negatives

Dates of subject matter 2600 BC to present

Dates of photographs 1975 to present

Subjects Architecture, UK and world, interiors and exteriors, including restaurants and hotels, resorts, bridges, ecclesiastical and industrial buildings; natural history including plants (garden flowers, trees, lichens, mosses, ferns, indoor and tropical plants, wild flowers, fungi, shrubs, grass, crops, vegetables and fruit), insects including butterflies and moths, spiders, fish, amphibians, animals including farm animals, horses, cats, birds; occupations and people at work including artists, sculptors, potters, musicians; sports and recreation

including winter sports; people including children and babies, the elderly; transport including roads and motor cars, motorbikes, bicycles, railways, ships, aircraft, space; agriculture including farm machinery; technology including industrial machinery, electronic, domestic appliances, computers, media hardware; food and wine; world geography including cities, towns and villages, tourism, landscapes, beachscenes, mountains, parks, seascapes, rivers, marshes, fens, quays, lakes and lochs, skies; general subjects including Devon pottery, porcelain and pottery, jewellery, prints, guns, model soldiers, toys, machines, copper and brass, heraldry, costumes, furniture, sculpture, musical instruments, swords, glass, gold and silver, signs, boxes, tins, clocks, militaria

Access and conditions Open to qualified researchers by appt (tel), daily 9–6. All material available for editorial reproduction; most available for advertising. B/w and colour material loaned free of charge for one month. Photocopies available. Reproduction rights and holding fees charged. Staff of three will undertake research. Computer catalogue.

117 • ANDRÉ LAUBIER PICTURE LIBRARY

4 St James Park, Bath, Avon BA1 2SS
Tel (0225) 20688

Enquiries to André Laubier

Items About 32,000: colour transparencies (35mm, 6 × 6 cm, 2¼″), b/w original and copy photographs, colour photographic prints, illustrated maps, stereographs, posters, greetings cards

Dates of subject matter Prehistory to present

Dates of photographs 1935 to present

Subjects Geography and travel in the UK (especially the West Country and Wales), France, Austria, Italy and Spain; natural history including seasons, animals, horses, zoos, birds, cranes, swans, plants, botany, gardens, arboretum, flowers; agriculture, farming; cities, towns and villages, architecture, art and artists, sculpture, stained glass; industries; religion, abbeys, cathedrals, churches; transport, canals; sports, showjumping, fishing, gymkhanas, boating, boat clubs; tourism, beaches, castles, fairs, markets;

people, crowds, on streets, spectators, babies, children, families, youth, human interest; customs, ceremonials, Christmas, costumes, crafts; abstracts, special effects, diffraction, experimental photography

Access and conditions Open to qualified researchers by appt (write). All material available for editorial reproduction and for advertising. B/w and colour material loaned free of charge for one month. Reproduction rights, service and holding fees charged. Staff will undertake some research.

118 • ANDREW LAWSON PHOTOGRAPHY

Gothic House, Church Street, Charlbury, Oxfordshire OX7 3PP
Tel (0608) 810654

Enquiries to Andrew Lawson

Items 10,000: colour transparencies (35mm), b/w original photographs

Dates of photographs 1970 to present

Subjects London's traditional ceremonies, pageantry and uniforms including Lord Mayors, Life Guards, Pearly Kings and Queens, Oak Apple Day, Doggett's coat and badge race, quit rents, Druids, street signs and trade signs, street furniture, statues, charity children, salerooms and markets, buskers, entertainers, parks and gardens, the Thames, graves and memorials; British shops and shopfronts nationwide including façades and displays, eccentric shopkeepers, butchers, bakers, candlestick makers; craftsmen including bell founders, farriers, woodturners, gunsmiths, silversmiths, top-hat makers, tailors, bookbinders, etc.; English countryside including houses great and small, countrymen and landscapes, churches, castles, coastlines, towns and villages

Access and conditions Open to qualified researchers by appt (tel), Mon-Sat 9–6. All material available for editorial reproduction and for advertising. B/w and colour material loaned free of charge for one month. Photocopies available. Reproduction rights, holding and service fees charged; service fees deductible from use fees. Staff will undertake research.

119 • LINK PHOTOREPORTAGE LIBRARY

4 Comeragh Road, London W14 9HP
Tel (01) 381 2433, 381 2261

Enquiries to Orde Eliason

Items About 20,000: b/w original photographs, colour transparencies (35mm), postcards

Dates of photographs 1978 to present

Subjects Contemporary life, social change, politics, demonstrations, sport, personalities, geography, human interaction, music; special collection on Midlands youth groups, counter culture, American boys summer camp, Namibia Bushmen; agents for SAMFOTO (Oslo), ALFAFOTO (Copenhagen), ARGUS (Hamburg), and AFRAPIX (Johannesburg)

Access and conditions Open to qualified researchers by appt (tel), Mon-Fri 9.30–5.30. All material available for editorial reproduction and for advertising. B/w and colour material loaned free of charge for 30 days. Reproduction rights and holding fees charged. Staff will undertake research.

120 • THE BILLIE LOVE COLLECTION

112 Weir Road, London SW12 0ND
Tel (01) 673 3711

Enquiries to Billie Love

Items 10,000: b/w original and copy photographs, colour photographic prints, colour transparencies (35mm, 2¼"), stereographs, lantern slides, glass negatives, postcards, autochromes, ambrotypes, daguerreotypes

Dates of subject matter Prehistory to 1966

Dates of photographs 1840 to 1966

Subjects The English at home and abroad (1869 to 1910) in India, Egypt, Siam, China, Norway, Middle East, France, etc.; everyday life in Britain and pictures of Eastern Europe, USSR, Poland, Estonia and Albania in the 1920s and 1960s; the HOBHOUSE COLLECTION of life in a country house, Hadspen Hall in Somerset; the HELEN BIGGAR COLLECTION of pictures of the sculptor and film-maker (1930s); the WYLIE COLLECTION of photographs taken by an English civil engineer working in Egypt (1900–1914); early colour photographs from Photochrom of Zurich; photographs by Francis Frith, George Washington Wilson, James Valentine and Francis Bedford

Access and conditions Open to qualified researchers by appt (tel), Mon-Fri 9–6. All material available for editorial reproduction and for advertising. B/w and colour material loaned free of charge for one month. Reproduction rights, service and holding fees charged. Staff will undertake some research.

121 • THE MACQUITTY INTERNATIONAL PHOTOGRAPHIC COLLECTION

7 Elm Lodge, Stevenage Road, London SW6 6NZ
Tel (01) 385 6031

Enquiries to William MacQuitty

Items 270,000: colour transparencies (35mm), b/w original photographs, unprinted film negatives

Dates of subject matter BC to present

Dates of photographs 1920 to present

Subjects Worldwide geography, landscapes, climatic conditions, archaeology, architecture, historic monuments, animals, birds, fish, insects, reptiles, flowers, fruit, orchids, cacti, vegetables, gardens, agriculture, religion, transport, human interaction, arts, crafts, sports, customs

Access and conditions Open to qualified researchers by appt (tel), Mon-Fri 9–5. All material available for editorial reproduction and for advertising. B/w and colour material loaned free of charge for one month. Reproduction rights and holding fees charged; service fees charged only when no material is used. Staff will undertake some research. Photographers available for assignment. All material copyright. Printed catalogue available.

122 • MAGNUM OPUS

Chesterton Mill, French's Road, Cambridge
CB4 3NP
Tel (0223) 60956

Enquiries to Martin or Cherie Rayner

Items 6000: colour transparencies (35mm, 5″ × 4″)

Dates of photographs 1980 to present

Subjects Underwater coverage of coral and tropical marine life in the Red Sea, Indian Ocean, off the Maldives and Brazilian coast; general coverage including children, British garden flowers, traction engines, travel coverage of Sri Lanka and India with special section on Indian transport; abstracts of laser light refraction, computer software, micrographs of silicon wafers and plant sections

Access and conditions Open to qualified researchers by appt (write), Mon-Fri 9-5.30. All material available for editorial reproduction and for advertising. Duplicate colour transparencies loaned for a fee. Reproduction rights and service fees charged. Staff will undertake research for a fee. All material copyright. Printed catalogue in preparation.

123 • MANSELL COLLECTION

42 Linden Gardens, London W2 4ER
Tel (01) 229 5475

Enquiries to George Anderson

Items About two million: b/w original and copy photographs, engravings, b/w and colour prints and lithographs, hand-tinted b/w photographs and engravings, colour transparencies (2¼″)

Dates of subject matter Prehistory to 1945

Subjects History and topography, past events and people including fine and performing arts, portraits and personalities, sport and recreation, science and technology including medicine, zoology, meteorology, botany and astronomy, transport including ships, motor cars, railways, air-balloons, gliders and airplanes, agriculture, education, schools, universities, literature, music, dancing, social issues including child labour, strikes, riots, trade unions, slavery, exploration, customs, religion, Biblical illustrations, mythology, the occult, architecture, communications, costume, food and drink, cooking, furniture and interiors, houses, cartoons and humour, men and women, families, children, lawyers and the law, policemen and criminals, naval and military; photographs by Samuel Bourne, Roger Fenton, E. O. Hoppé, Dorien Leigh, W. F. Mansell, Richard N. Speaight and others; full sets of *ILN*, *Punch*, *L'Illustration*; London representatives of Alinari

Access and conditions Open to qualified researchers by appt (tel), Mon-Fri 9.30–5.30, closed 12.30–1.30. All material available for editorial reproduction and for advertising. B/w and colour material loaned free of charge for one month. Reproduction rights, service and holding fees charged. Staff will undertake some research.

124 • JOHN MASSEY STEWART

20 Hillway, London N6 6QA
Tel (01) 341 3544

Enquiries to John Massey Stewart

Items About 21,000: b/w original and copy photographs, colour transparencies (35mm), lantern slides, postcards, illustrated maps, fine art prints, posters, greetings cards, press cuttings and tearsheets, illustrated books

Dates of subject matter 40,000 BC to present

Dates of photographs 1961 to present; Russian material 1880 to present

Dates of maps and fine art *c.* 1650 to present

Subjects Reportage and topography including art and architecture, agriculture, artefacts, everyday life, geography, history, transport, town and country, people and places, natural history, folk dance, museum items; special collection on the Soviet Union including art, architecture, agriculture, economy, ethnic peoples, folk dance, history, landscape, museum items, natural history; Baltic States (Riga, Talinn, Vilnius), Central Asia and Kazakhstan (Alma Ata, Ashkhabad, Bukhara, Chardzou, Kara Kum desert, Repetek, Samarkand, Tashkent), European Russia (Leningrad, Moscow, Pavlovsk, Pereslavl, Peterhof (Petrodvorets), Rostov Velikii, Suzdal, Vladimir, Yaroslavl, Zagorsk), Siberia and Soviet Far East (Akademgorodok, Lake Baikal, Bratsk, Irkutsk, Khabarovsk, Nakhodka, Novosibirsk, Sayan mountains, Yakutia), Transcaucasia (Armenia, Azerbaidjan, Georgia: Caucasus, Sukhumi, Tbilisi, Yerevan), Ukraine (Bakhchisarai, Crimea, Gurzuf, Karkhov, Kiev, Odessa, Yalta), history of Tsarist Russia and the Tsars, personalities, ethnography, costumes, views, maps, artefacts, Revolution, Civil War, Soviet period; Mongolia including Chujirt, Gobi Desert, Karakorum, Ulan Bator nomadic and city life, herds, herdsmen, wrestling, etc.; China including Canton, Nanking, Hangchow, Peking, Shanghai, Wuhan, communes, countryside, cities, Workers' and Children's Palaces, education, opera, October 1st display, arts, antiquities; Andorra, Austria, UK including Jersey, Cambodia including Angkor, Canary Islands, Czechoslovakia, Denmark, East Germany, Finland, France, Germany, Gibraltar, Holland, Hong Kong and Kowloon, India, Iran, Ireland, Italy, Japan, Korea, Lapland, Madeira, Norway, Portugal, Spain, South Korea, South Vietnam, Sweden, Switzerland, Thailand

Access and conditions Open to qualified researchers by appt (tel), Mon-Fri 10–5.30. All material available for editorial reproduction and for advertising. B/w and colour material loaned free of charge for one month. Reproduction rights, service and holding fees charged. Staff will undertake research.

125 • S. & O. MATHEWS PHOTOGRAPHY

Stitches Farm House, Eridge, East Sussex TN3 9JB
Tel (089285) 2848

Enquiries to Oliver or Sheila Mathews

Items 12,000: colour transparencies (35mm, 7 × 6 cm), b/w original photographs

Dates of subject matter Prehistory to present

Dates of photographs 1974 to present

Subjects British life and landscape, architecture, agriculture, environment, natural history and habitats, coast and sea, rivers, villages and towns, gardens, garden and wild flowers, fungus, people, churches and castles, cottages and houses; Norway landscapes and scenic shots

Access and conditions Open to qualified researchers by appt (tel), Mon-Fri 9–5. All material available for editorial reproduction and for advertising, with some restrictions. B/w and colour material loaned free of charge for one month. Reproduction rights fees and holding fees charged. Staff will undertake research.

126 • RICHARD MCBRIDE PHOTOGRAPHY

32 Sandholes Road, Brookfield, Strathclyde PA5 8UR
Tel (0505) 26559

Enquiries to Pamela McBride

Items 2000: b/w original photographs, colour transparencies (35mm)

Dates of photographs 1970 to present

Subjects Alternative sources of energy including solar energy, wind energy, biomass energy, energy technologies; natural environments including mountains; land use and natural resources, air pollution, water pollution, acid rain; UK and Scottish landscapes, US landscapes including California and Washington state; protest and demonstrations over environmental problems

Access and conditions Open to qualified researchers by appt (tel). All material available for editorial reproduction and for advertising. B/w and colour material loaned free of charge for three months. Reproduction rights, service and holding fees charged. Staff will undertake research; fee for large projects. Catalogue in preparation.

127 • DEREK McDOUGALL PHOTOGRAPHY

7 Killermont View, Killermont, Glasgow G20 0TZ
Tel (041) 945 2706

Enquiries to Derek McDougall

Items 10,000: colour transparencies (35mm, 7 × 6 cm)

Dates of photographs 1980 to present

Subjects Scotland including landscapes, architecture, historical buildings, sites and monuments, cities, towns and villages; north of England including Newcastle upon Tyne, Carlisle and the Lake District; tourist coverage of the Isle of Man

Access and conditions Open to qualified researchers by appt (write). All material available for editorial reproduction and for advertising. Colour material loaned free of charge for six months (prints fees charged). Reproduction rights fees charged. Research undertaken. All material copyright.

128 • BILL MEADOWS PICTURE LIBRARY

14 Winchester Avenue, St Johns, Worcester WR2 4JE
Tel (0905) 22956

Enquiries to Bill Meadows

Items Over 12,000: b/w original photographs, colour transparencies (35mm, 6 × 6 cm, 7 × 7 cm), colour photographic prints

Dates of subject matter Prehistory to present

Dates of photographs 1960 to present

Subjects Geography, landscapes and tourism of England, Scotland and Wales, archaeology and stone circles, historic sites including Hadrian's Wall, industrial archaeology, buildings and construction, roads, bridges, factory interiors, agriculture

Access and conditions Open to qualified researchers by appt (tel), Tues-Fri 9–5, mail and telephone requests preferred. All material available for editorial reproduction and for advertising. B/w and colour material loaned free of charge for one month. Reproduction rights, service and holding fees charged. Staff will undertake some research.

129 • ERIC G. MEADOWS

8 Orchard Avenue, Harpenden, Hertfordshire AL5 2DP
Tel (05827) 61508

Enquiries to Eric Meadows

Items 31,000: b/w original photographs, colour transparencies (35mm, 5″ × 4″, 2¼″)

Dates of subject matter 1600 BC to present

Dates of photographs B/w 1943 to present; colour 1970 to present

Subjects Bedfordshire and Hertfordshire local history and landscape including buildings, churches, mansions, cottages, places of interest; northern and western Scotland, landscapes and rural scenes

Access and conditions Open to qualified researchers by appt (tel). All material available for editorial reproduction and for advertising. B/w and colour material loaned free of charge for three months. Reproduction rights and holding fees charged. Staff will undertake research.

130 • MERCURY PRESS AGENCY LTD

1st Floor, Abbey Buildings, 77/79 Victoria Street, Liverpool L1 6DE
Tel (051) 236 6707 Telex 628606

Enquiries to Rosemary Blyth or Ann Fillis

Items About 50,000: b/w original and copy

photographs, colour transparencies (35mm), unprinted film negatives

Dates of photographs 1974 to present

Subjects Contemporary photojournalism including social change, politics, demonstrations, poverty, psychology, ecology, medicine, accidents, human interactions, family life, industry, agriculture, schools, sport, theatre, music, religion, architecture, personalities; Toxteth riots, Liverpool, July 1981; Pope John Paul II visit to Liverpool, May 1982; International Garden Festival, Liverpool, 1984; Walton sextuplets; Everton and Liverpool football clubs

Access and conditions Open to the public by appt (tel), Mon-Fri 8–6.30. All material available for editorial reproduction and for advertising. B/w prints available for a fee; colour transparencies loaned free of charge for one month, after which a rental fee is charged. Reproduction rights and service fees charged; new clients charged in advance. Staff will undertake research. Photographers available for assignment.

131 • MEXICOLORE

28 Warriner Gardens, London SW11 4EB
Tel (01) 622 9577

Enquiries to Ian Mursell, Director

Items About 2500: colour transparencies (35mm), posters, illustrated books

Dates of subject matter BC to present

Dates of photographs 1979 to present

Subjects Mexico including geography, landscapes, archaeology, anthropology, history, architecture, agriculture, industry, trade, poverty, wealth, urbanization, housing, transport, mural paintings, music, dance, education, pollution, migration, family life; SEAN SPRAGUE COLLECTION of Third World photographs covering life and activities in developing countries

Access and conditions Open to the public by appt (tel), Mon-Fri 9–5. All material available for editorial reproduction and for advertising. Colour material loaned free of charge for two weeks (print fees charged). Reproduction rights, holding and service fees charged. Staff will undertake some research; fees charged to commercial users. Most material copyright.

132 • MIDDLE EAST CENTRE

St Antony's College, Oxford OX2 6JF
Tel (0865) 59651

Enquiries to Gillian Grant, Archivist

Items About 100,000: b/w original and copy photographs, lantern slides, glass negatives, colour transparencies (35mm), postcards, colour photographic prints, original cartoons, unprinted film negatives, illustrated maps, illustrated books, stereographs

Dates of photographs 1860 to c. 1960

Subjects Political history, archaeology and anthropology of the Middle East, including the Arabian Peninsula, Palestine and Jordan, Syria and Lebanon, Iraq, Turkey, Kurdistan, Central Asia, Iran, Afghanistan, Sudan, Egypt, Eritrea, North Africa (Libya, Morocco, etc.) and comprising over 33 separate collections including architecture, development of major towns and cities, portraits of rulers, historic meetings, official events, military history, industrial development, education, medical services, missionary work, social, religious and cultural life of the region, the British at work and play, transport (railways, ships, aircraft, roads), police, schools, aerial views, landscapes, townscapes, Mecca pilgrimage (1912)

Access and conditions Open to qualified researchers by appt (write), closed during university vacations. Some material available for editorial reproduction but not for advertising. B/w prints and duplicate colour transparencies available for a fee. Photocopies available. Reproduction rights fees charged. Card catalogue and brochure available; G. M. Grant, ed., *Historical Photographs of the Middle East.*

133 • MIDDLE EAST PHOTOGRAPHIC ARCHIVE

MEED House, 21 John Street, London WC1N 2BP
Tel (01) 404 5513   Telex 27165 MEEDAR

Enquiries to Helen Finney, Manager

Items 200,000: colour transparencies (35mm), b/w original photographs

Dates of subject matter Prehistory to present

Dates of photographs Contemporary

Subjects Comprehensive coverage of life in the Middle East and also some coverage of India, Africa and South-east Asia including archaeology, landscape, agriculture, wildlife, towns, cities, villages, architecture, crafts, art, festivals, markets, religion, industry and construction, banking, communications, hospitals, hotels, portraits; special collections include Alistair Duncan's coverage of Jerusalem and the West Bank, and Anthony Hutt's photographs of ancient architecture in USSR, Indonesia, Malaysia, Pakistan, India and Thailand

Access and conditions Open to qualified researchers by appt (tel), Mon-Fri 9.30–5.30. All material available for editorial reproduction and for advertising. B/w and colour material loaned free of charge for one month. Reproduction rights, holding and service fees charged. Staff of three will undertake some research. All material copyright.

134 • ARCHIE MILES

Bentleys, West Street, Kingham, Oxfordshire
OX7 6YQ
Tel (060871) 500

Enquiries to Archie Miles

Items About 100,000: colour transparencies (35mm), b/w original photographs, daguerreotypes and ambrotypes, cartes-de-visite, cabinet photographs

Dates of subject matter Prehistory to present

Dates of photographs 1850–1900; 1972 to present

Subjects Castles, cathedrals, churches, farms and farming, landscapes, cottages, shops, celebrations, hotels (interiors and exteriors), flowers (wild and garden), transport (road, rail, sea, air), maritime England including boats, beaches, fishing, lifeboats, ships, shipbuilding and maritime history, people, animals; in Yorkshire, Lancashire, Nottinghamshire, Derbyshire, Gloucestershire, Oxfordshire, Dorset, Devon, Cornwall, Hampshire, Home Counties, Scotland and Wales; Ireland including west country scenics, shops, bars, travel, Connemara flowers; Trinidad and Tobago, beaches, rain forest, flora and fauna; HISTORY OF PHOTOGRAPHY COLLECTION: royalty, politicians, authors, scientists, music hall, sports, children, tradesmen, costume, landscape, military, freemasons, gypsies, humour, coal-pit lasses, a ghost

Access and conditions Open to the public by appt (tel), Mon-Fri 9–5. All material available for editorial reproduction and for advertising. B/w and colour material loaned free of charge for one month. Reproduction rights and holding fees charged. Staff will undertake research.

135 • MILLBROOK HOUSE LIMITED

90 Hagley Road, Edgbaston, Birmingham
B16 8YH
Tel (021) 454 1308

Enquiries to Pat Whitehouse or Christine Brook

Items About 170,000: b/w original and copy photographs, colour transparencies (35mm, 5″ × 4″)

Dates of subject matter 1843 to present

Dates of photographs 1900 to present

Subjects Railways worldwide with special coverage of railways in Africa, South America, South-east Asia and China; worldwide geography with special emphasis on China and archaeology; *Illustrated London News* 1843 to 1880

Access and conditions Open to qualified researchers by appt (write). All material available for editorial reproduction and for advertising. B/w and colour material loaned free of charge for six weeks (print fees charged). Photocopies available. Reproduction rights, holding and service fees charged; service fees deductible from use fees. Staff of three will undertake some research. Most material copyright. Computer catalogue in preparation.

136 • THE MITCHELL LIBRARY

North Street, Glasgow G3 7DN
Tel (041) 221 7030 Telex 778732

Department of Arts and Recreation

Enquiries to Departmental Librarian

Items About 2000: b/w original photographs, original cartoons, press cuttings

Dates of subject matter 1850 to 1931

Dates of photographs 1899 to 1931

Subjects SIR THOMAS LIPTON COLLECTION of watercolours of 1901 America's Cup race; WILLIAM SIMPSON COLLECTION relating to the Crimean War, and countries visited by 19th-century war correspondent including Russia, India, Greece, Turkey; coverage of Tzar Alexander's wedding

Access and conditions Open to the public, Mon-Fri 9.30–9, Sat 9.30–5. All material available for editorial reproduction and for advertising. No loans; b/w prints and colour transparencies available for a fee. Reproduction rights fees charged. Staff of two will undertake some research.

Department of Rare Books and Manuscripts

Enquiries to Departmental Librarian

Items Illustrated books, lantern slides

Dates of subject matter *c.* 1800 to *c.* 1910

Subjects Illustrated books with emphasis on natural history especially ornithology and British topography; lantern slides include Scottish landscapes, Glasgow, the Glasgow Clarion Club (Labour movement), and the Paris Exhibition

Access and conditions Open to the public, Mon-Fri 9.30–9, Sat 9.30–5. All material available for editorial reproduction and for advertising. No loans; b/w prints available for a fee; material may be copied by outside photographers. Photocopies available. Reproduction rights fees charged. Staff of three will undertake some research.

Department of Social Sciences

Enquiries to Daniel McCallum, Departmental Librarian

Items 200: b/w original photographs, postcards, posters, illustrated books

Dates of subject matter 19th century to present

Dates of photographs 1880 to present

Subjects Scottish Regimental history, earliest material relating to the Afghan Campaign in 1880; trade unions; postcard collection of ships worldwide *c.* 1900

Access and conditions Open to the public, Mon-Fri 9.30–9, Sat 9.30–5. All material available for editorial reproduction and for advertising. No loans; b/w prints and duplicate colour transparencies available for a fee. Reproduction rights fees charged. Staff will undertake some research. Some material copyright.

137 • COLIN MOLYNEUX

58 Bryn Siriol, Ty-Isaf, Caerphilly, Mid Glamorgan CF8 2AJ
Tel (0222) 866469

Enquiries to Colin or Helen Molyneux

Items About 40,000: colour transparencies (35mm, 7 × 6 cm)

Dates of subject matter Prehistory to present

Dates of photographs 1930 to present

Subjects Landscape and general coverage of the British Isles with extensive coverage of Aberdeen, Bristol, Birmingham, Cardiff, Devon, Dyfed, Glamorgan, Gwynedd, Powys, Yorkshire; agriculture, industrial landscapes, crafts, transport, human interaction, markets, natural history

Access and conditions Open to qualified researchers by appt (tel), Mon-Fri 9–5. All material available for editorial reproduction and for advertising. Colour material loaned free of charge for one month. Reproduction rights, holding and service fees charged; service fees deductible from use fees. Staff will undertake research. All material copyright. Catalogue in preparation.

138 • KEITH MONEY

Carbrooke Hall Farm, Thetford, Norfolk 1P25 6TG
Tel (095383) 424

Enquiries to Keith Money

Items 20,000: b/w original and copy photographs, colour transparencies (2¼″), colour photographic prints, postcards, posters, illustrated books

Dates of photographs 1959 to present

Subjects Old-fashioned roses, including breeds from Napoleonic times to 1920, *Rosa gallica*, China roses, *Rosa centifolia*, hybrid teas, Bourbon roses, etc.; horses and showjumping (1959–65), international riders; British life and landscape (1957–1965); Kenya and the Masai, aerial photographs; World War I recruitment posters; Royal Ballet (1963 to 1970), British ballet, rehearsal and performance photographs

Access and conditions Not open; written requests only. All material available for editorial reproduction and for advertising. B/w and colour material loaned free of charge for four weeks. Photocopies available. Reproduction rights and holding fees charged. Staff will undertake some research. Partial catalogue.

139 • MONITOR PRESS FEATURES

17 Old Street, London EC1V 9HL
Tel (01) 253 7071 Telex 24718

Enquiries to David Willis

Items Over 250,000: b/w original photographs,
colour transparencies (35mm, 5″ × 4″)

Dates of subject matter 1959 to present

Dates of photographs 1959 to present

Subjects Portraits of personalities including show
business, politics, sports, industry; geography,
agriculture, natural history, transport, human
interaction

Access and conditions Open to qualified
researchers by appt (tel), Mon-Fri 9–5. All material
available for editorial reproduction and for
advertising. B/w material loaned by arrangement
(print fee charged); colour material loaned free of
charge for one month. Reproduction rights, holding
and service fees charged; service fees deductible
from use fees. Research undertaken. All material
copyright.

TONY MORRISON *see* SOUTH AMERICAN
PICTURES

140 • MAGGIE MURRAY

72 Mildmay Road, London N1 4NG
Tel (01) 249 3132

Enquiries to Maggie Murray

Items 18,000: b/w original photographs, colour
transparencies (35mm)

Dates of subject matter 1960 to present

Dates of photographs 1960 to present

Subjects Social problems, social change,
economics in England, feminist and socialist issues
and events, demonstrations, education, housing,
status of women, childcare, child development,
peace movement; Africa (extensive coverage)
including Egypt, Ethiopia, Ghana, Kenya, Mali,
Rwanda, Senegal, Somalia, Sudan, Tanzania,
Uganda, Upper Volta and especially development
issues and situation of women; USSR, India,
Middle East, Western Europe including Greece
especially development issues and the situation of
women

Access and conditions Open to qualified
researchers by appt (tel), Mon-Fri 9–5. All material
available for editorial reproduction and for
advertising with some restrictions. B/w and colour
material loaned free of charge for one month.
Reproduction rights, service and holding fees
charged. Staff will undertake research.

141 • DAVID MUSCROFT PHOTOGRAPHY

Alpha House, 10 Carver Street, Sheffield,
Yorkshire S1 4FS
Tel (0742) 28547

Enquiries to David Muscroft or Trevor Smith

Items About 62,000: b/w original photographs,
colour transparencies (35mm, 7 × 6 cm), colour
photographic prints, b/w copy photographs

Dates of photographs 1870 to present

Subjects News coverage from 1975, feature
photography including animals, human interest
and humour; posed models; travel coverage of
California, New Orleans, Bermuda, St Lucia,
Barbados, South Germany, Paris, Morocco and the
Seychelles; industry in the UK; personalities
including sporting, political, royal, and show
business personalities; sports coverage including
darts, golf, horse-racing, American football, white-
water canoeing; FALKLANDS PICTORIAL COLLECTION
includes old photographic coverage of the Islands
including settlements, sailing ships, whaling,
portraits, and contemporary coverage; SNOOKER
PHOTOGRAPHY includes all aspects of the game
including players, venues, action shots

Access and conditions Open to qualified
researchers, Mon-Fri 9–5. All material available
for editorial reproduction and for advertising. B/w
and colour material loaned by arrangement.
Reproduction rights fees charged. Staff of three will
undertake research. Most material copyright.

142 • NAAS LIMITED

49 Goodge Street, London W1P 1FB
Tel (01) 580 7448

Enquiries to Michael Evans, Manager

Items 30,000: b/w original and copy photographs,
colour transparencies (35mm, 5″ × 4″)

Dates of subject matter Prehistory to present

Dates of photographs *c.* 1973 to present

Subjects Geography and current events in Asia, Africa and the Middle East: Afghanistan, rebel fighters and leaders, refugees; China, historical sites, people, landscapes; India, holy places, market places, people; Iran, Ayatollah Khomeini, demonstrations, mosques, the poor; Egypt, architecture, streetscenes, Luxor, Gourna, Aswan, Cairo, Giza; Morocco, traditional scenes, people, market places, calligraphy, design, crafts; Gulf States, Oman, United Arab Emirates, Bahrain, Qatar, development, people, desert scenes, falcons, pearl traders, modern buildings, camels, dhows, immigrant workers; Somalia – Sudan, refugees from Somalia, Ethiopia and Eritrea, refugee camps (extensive coverage); Saudi Arabia, all aspects of pilgrimage, Mecca, Medina, people, architecture, old buildings, heads of state, development; USSR, Samarkand, market places, Tashkent, buildings, people; Africa, Kenya, Mali, Senegal, Niger, Nigeria, Mauritania, the west coast; Turkey, mosques, people; Iraq, Syria, Jordan, Lebanon, Yemen; Islamic Press Agency Picture Library

Access and conditions Open to qualified researchers by appt (tel), Mon-Fri 9.30–6. All material available for editorial reproduction and for advertising. B/w and colour material loaned free of charge for one month. Reproduction rights, service and holding fees charged. Staff of four will undertake research; search fee for large projects.

143 • EDMUND NÄGELE

Hermes Lodge, Bredon's Norton, Tewkesbury, Gloucestershire GH20 7EZ
Tel (0684) 72400

Enquiries to Edmund Nägele

Items About 5000: colour transparencies (7 × 6 cm, 7″ × 5″)

Dates of photographs 1979 to present

Subjects Geographic and travel coverage of UK, Europe, Canada, USA including Hawaii; atmospheric shots; posed models; vintage cars; aerial coverage of UK and Europe

Access and conditions Open to qualified researchers by appt (tel). All material available for editorial reproduction and for advertising. Colour material loaned free of charge for one month. Reproduction rights, holding and service fees charged. Staff will undertake some research. Photographer available for assignment. All material copyright.

144 • THE NATIONAL TRUST

Photographic Library, 36 Queen Anne's Gate, London SW1H 9AS
Tel (01) 222 9251

Enquiries to Martin Trelawny, Librarian

Items About 23,000: b/w original photographs, colour transparencies (35mm, 6 × 6 cm, 5″ × 4″)

Dates of subject matter Prehistory to present

Dates of photographs 1890s to present

Subjects Properties in the care of the National Trust including stately homes, medieval houses, castles, cottages, farms, windmills, ancient monuments, industrial archaeology, follies, gardens; landscapes, coastal areas, wildlife, natural history; fine art, furniture, silverware, glassware, ceramics, musical instruments, tapestries, needlework, armour

Access and conditions Open to qualified researchers by appt (write). All material available for editorial reproduction and for advertising. B/w and colour material loaned free of charge for one month; material may be copied by outside photographers. Reproduction rights, holding and service fees charged; service fees deductible from use fees. Staff of three will undertake some research. Most material copyright.

145 • THE NATIONAL TRUST FOR SCOTLAND

5 Charlotte Square, Edinburgh EH2 4DU
Tel (031) 226 5922 Telex 727955

Enquiries to Jean Gowans, Photographic Librarian

Items About 40,000: b/w original photographs, colour transparencies (35mm, 5″ × 4″), glass negatives, unprinted film negatives, b/w copy photographs, colour photographic prints, architectural drawings

Dates of subject matter Prehistory to present

Dates of photographs 1897 to present

Subjects Properties and areas in the care of the National Trust for Scotland including castles and great houses, smaller dwellings and buildings of historic interest, gardens, areas of countryside including Falls of Glomach and part of Glen Coe, and islands; special collections include ARCHIVE OF ST KILDA and the BUTE COLLECTION

Access and conditions Open to qualified researchers by appt (tel), Mon-Fri 9–5.30. Most material available for editorial reproduction and for advertising. B/w and colour material loaned free of charge for one month; material may be copied by outside photographers. Photocopies available. Reproduction rights fees charged. Staff will undertake limited research. Most material copyright.

146 • NETWORK PHOTOGRAPHERS

Unit 228, Highbury Workshops, 22 Highbury Grove, London N5 1HJ
Tel (01) 226 2592

Enquiries to Library

Items 50,000: b/w original photographs, colour transparencies (35mm)

Dates of photographs 1980 to present

Subjects Social documentary coverage of Great Britain and Northern Ireland including health, education, housing, industry, politics, transport, sport and leisure, performing and visual arts; some overseas coverage including Central America, Africa, Saudi Arabia, USSR, China

Access and conditions Open to qualified researchers by appt, Mon-Fri 9–5. All material available for editorial reproduction and for advertising. B/w material loaned free of charge for one month; duplicate colour transparencies available for a fee. Photocopies available. Reproduction rights and service fees charged. Staff will undertake limited research. All material copyright.

147 • PETER NEWARK'S WESTERN AMERICANA

3 Barton Buildings, Queen Square, Bath, Avon BA1 2JR
Tel (0225) 334213

Enquiries to Peter Newark

Items 250,000: b/w copy photographs, b/w original photographs, colour transparencies (35mm, 5″ × 4″), colour photographic prints, old fine art prints, stereographs

Dates of subject matter 15th century to present

Dates of photographs 1850 to present

Subjects All aspects of the American west including natural history, wildlife, Indian life and culture, exploration, settlement, wars, weaponry, cowboys and cattle trade, mining, agriculture, timber industry, fur trade, towns and cities, justice, personalities; paintings and illustrations by George Catlin, Karl Bodmer, Frederic Remington, Charles Russell, Charles Schreyvogel and Rufus Zogbaum; USA history including discovery, colonial America, slavery, the revolution, military history, aviation, space flight, political life, transport, writers and artists, gangsters, prizefighters; world history including ancient civilizations, medieval warfare, monarchy worldwide, Elizabethan England, English Civil War, Napoleonic Wars, Crimean War, British in India, Japanese and Chinese history, Russian history including the Revolution, French history to World War I, Victorian and Edwardian personalities, British political life, World Wars I and II

Access and conditions Open to qualified researchers by appt. All material available for editorial reproduction and for advertising. B/w and colour material loaned free of charge for two months. Photocopies available. Reproduction rights and holding fees charged; service fees charged only when no material is used. Staff will undertake some research. 50% of material copyright. Printed catalogue available.

148 • NEWSLINK AFRICA LTD

Suite No 411, London International Press Centre, 76 Shoe Lane, Fleet Street, London EC4A 3JB
Tel (01) 353 0186   Telex 23862 PRESCENT G

Enquiries to Director

Items About 10,000: b/w original photographs, b/w copy photographs, colour transparencies (35mm), colour photographic prints, glass negatives, postcards, press cuttings

Dates of subject matter 1969 to present

Subjects Comprehensive coverage of Africa including geography, natural history, wildlife, anthropology, cities, towns, villages, architecture, social change, politics, demonstrations, ecology, poverty, agriculture, industry including mining, textiles and manufacturing industries, transport, education, religion, music, sport, family life, social groups, accidents, drought, floods, the media, portraits

Access and conditions Open to qualified researchers by appt, Mon–Fri 9–5. All material available for editorial reproduction; advertising use by special arrangement only. B/w and colour material loaned free of charge for 30 days (print fees charged). Reproduction rights, holding and service fees charged. Staff will undertake some research. All material copyright. Catalogue in preparation.

149 • NORTH OF ENGLAND NEWSPAPERS

Priestgate, Darlington, County Durham DL1 1NF
Tel (0325) 460177

Enquiries to Photosales

Items About 40,000: b/w original photographs, b/w copy photographs

Dates of photographs 1960 to present

Subjects News coverage of north-east England including personalities and localities appearing in *The Northern Echo* and the *Evening Despatch*

Access and conditions Not open; telephone and postal requests only. All material available for editorial reproduction and for advertising. No loans; b/w prints available for a fee. Photocopies available. Reproduction rights fees charged. All material copyright.

150 • NORTH WEST COUNTIES PRESS LTD

4 Manor Street, Bolton, Lancashire BL1 1TU
Tel (0204) 25477

Enquiries to Andrea Berry or Les Williamson

Items Over 500,000: unprinted film negatives, colour transparencies (35mm)

Dates of photographs 1968 to present

Subjects Local news coverage including political leaders and personalities at Blackpool Conferences; all major international sports events including the Olympic Games, Winter Olympics, Commonwealth Games, international soccer, Rugby League, international swimming, ice-dancing, ice-skating, golf, tennis including Wimbledon, showjumping; political figures and demonstrations in the UK; special collection of Victorian lantern slides showing church mission work in Canada

Access and conditions Open to qualified researchers by appt (tel), Mon–Fri 9–5. All material available for editorial reproduction and for advertising. B/w and colour material loaned free of charge for one month. Photocopies available. Reproduction rights, holding and service fees charged. Staff will undertake some research for a fee. All material copyright.

151 • NORTHERN IRELAND INFORMATION SERVICE

Stormont Castle, Belfast BT4 3ST
Tel (0232) 63011 Telex 74163

Enquiries to Christine McCamley

Items About 2000: b/w original photographs, colour transparencies (35mm), colour photographic prints

Subjects Life in Ulster including agriculture, industry, education, communications, employment, health and social services, energy, security, sport and recreation, landscapes, historic buildings

Access and conditions Open to qualified researchers by appt (tel), Mon–Fri 9–5. All material available for editorial reproduction; advertising use by special arrangement only. B/w prints and duplicate colour transparencies available for a fee. No reproduction rights fees charged. Staff of two will undertake some research. All material copyright.

152 • NORTHERN IRELAND TOURIST BOARD

River House, 48 High Street, Belfast BT1 2DS
Tel (0232) 231221

Enquiries to Betty Wilson, Photographic Librarian

Items 38,000: b/w original photographs, colour transparencies (35mm, 2¼″)

Dates of subject matter Prehistory to present

Dates of photographs 1970 to present

Subjects General tourist and travel coverage of Northern Ireland including landscapes, towns, villages, resorts, wildlife, ancient monuments, sports, parks, arts and crafts, hotels, farmhouses

Access and conditions Open to the public by appt (tel), Mon–Fri 9–5. All material available for editorial reproduction and for advertising. B/w and colour material loaned free of charge for one month. Reproduction rights and holding fees charged. Staff will undertake some research. All material copyright.

153 • NORTHERN PICTURE LIBRARY

Unit 2, Bentinck Street Industrial Estate, Ellesmere Street, Manchester M15 4LN
Tel (061) 834 1255

Enquiries to Everley Hartley

Items 55,000: colour transparencies (35mm, 5″ × 4″)

Dates of subject matter BC to present

Dates of photographs 1950 to present

Subjects Worldwide geography, landscapes, architecture, urban landscapes, wildlife, natural history, sport including winter sport, posed models, industrial archaeology, people at work

Access and conditions Open to qualified researchers by appt (tel), Mon-Fri 9–5. All material available for editorial reproduction and for advertising (some restrictions). B/w and colour material loaned free of charge for one month. Reproduction rights and service fees charged. Staff will undertake research. All material copyright. Card catalogue available.

154 • OPENEYE PHOTO AGENCY

15 Culverland Road, Exeter EX4 6JJ
Tel (0392) 77221

Enquiries to Chris Wormald

Items About 2000: colour transparencies (35mm, 120mm), b/w original photographs

Dates of subject matter 1965 to present

Dates of photographs 1965 to present

Subjects Alternative lifestyles including festivals, fairs, rock concerts, folk music and dancing, communes and communities, peace movement

Access and conditions Open to qualified researchers by appt (tel), Mon-Fri 8.30–6. All material available for editorial reproduction and

for advertising. B/w and colour material loaned free of charge for two months. Reproduction rights, holding and service fees charged; service fees deductible from use fees. Photographer available for assignment. Staff of two will undertake research for a fee. All material copyright.

155 • ORPIX

The Powerhouse, Alpha Place, Flood Street, London SW3 5SZ
Tel (01) 351 7541 Telex 892781 RALLON G

Enquiries to Emma Van Gruisen

Items 10,000: colour transparencies (35mm, 2¼″), b/w original photographs, unprinted film negatives

Dates of subject matter 1600 to present

Dates of photographs 1975 to present

Subjects Expeditions and wilderness subjects including Operation Drake, Operation Raleigh, Batting, Black River; young people sailing, in jungle environments, trekking, assisting in local communities and in scientific research; ships and vessels including brigantines, storms, inflatable craft, river-running, local dug-outs, wireless operators, STOL planes, helicopters and supplies, Goodyear airship; scientific research including marine biology, jungle camps, rain forest study, aerial walkways, batting, archaeology, medical research; camps including communications, food, expedition supplies, medical tents, accommodation; geology and geography including volcanoes, deserts, rain forests, erosion, slash and burn techniques, deforestation, forest fires; people including Indonesians, Marshall Bennet Islanders, Papua New Guinea mud-men, Papua New Guinea Highlanders, Bahamians, Cuna Indians, Oaxaca Indians; natural history, flora and fauna, snakes, frogs, bats, underwater photography including diving on coral, Blue Holes, sunsets, seascapes, markets; Caribbean islands including Grand Bahamas, New Providence, Cat Island, South Andros, Turks and Caicos, British Virgin Islands, St Thomas, US Virgin Islands, St Vincent; Central America including Honduras, Panama, Costa Rica; South America including Ecuador, Chile, Peru, Galapagos Islands; South Pacific Islands including Fiji, Marshall Bennet Islands; Papua New Guinea, Sulawesi, Indonesian Islands, Brunei, Sarawak;

India, Arctic, Iran, Seychelles, Kenya, South Africa, Namibia, Spain, West Germany, UK

Access and conditions Open to qualified researchers by appt (tel), Mon-Fri 9–6. All material available for editorial reproduction and for advertising. B/w and colour material loaned free of charge for one month. Reproduction rights and holding fees charged. Staff will undertake research; negotiable fee for large projects.

156 • CHRISTINE OSBORNE

MIDDLE EAST PICTURES AND PUBLICITY

53A Crimsworth Road, London SW8 4RJ
Tel (01) 720 6951

Enquiries to Christine Osborne

Items 30,000: colour transparencies (35mm), b/w original photographs, postcards, press cuttings, illustrated books

Dates of photographs 1965 to present

Subjects All aspects of life in Muslim and developing countries including geography, architecture, archaeology, agriculture, crafts, costume, markets, food, women at work, education, religion, transport, sports and leisure, human interaction; countries covered include Bahrain, Egypt, Iran, Iraq, Jordan, Kuwait, Lebanon, Malaysia, Morocco, Oman, Pakistan, Qatar, Senegal, Gambia, Sierra Leone, Sudan, Tunisia, Turkey, United Arab Emirates, North Yemen (Muslim coverage); Bali, Burma, Hong Kong, India, Macao, Nepal, Singapore, Taiwan and Thailand; Ethiopia, Gambia, Kenya, Senegal, Zimbabwe; Pacific area including Australia, New Zealand, Fiji, Tonga, New Caledonia and Dependencies, Hawaii and Polynesia

Access and conditions Open to the public by appt (tel). All material available for editorial reproduction and for advertising. B/w and colour material loaned free of charge for 30 days. Photocopies available. Reproduction rights, service and holding fees charged; service fees deductible from use fees. Research undertaken. All material copyright. Printed catalogue available.

157 • RON OULDS COLOUR LIBRARY

Walkmill, Dolau, Llandrindod Wells, Powys
LD1 5TL
Tel (059 787) 266

Enquiries to Ron or Dorothy Oulds

Items Over 100,000: b/w original photographs, colour transparencies (35mm, 7 × 6 cm, 5″ × 4″), unprinted film negatives, glass negatives

Dates of photographs c. 1948 to present

Subjects News coverage of life and events in the West Sussex area for local, regional and national press; human interaction, landscape and architectural coverage of UK

Access and conditions Open to qualified researchers (tel but first-time users write), Mon-Fri 9–5. All material available for editorial reproduction and for advertising. B/w prints loaned free of charge for one month (print fees charged); colour material loaned free of charge for one month. Reproduction rights, holding and service fees charged. Research undertaken for a fee. Photographer available for assignment. All material copyright. Catalogue in preparation.

158 • TOM PARKER COLOUR LIBRARY

1 Mansion House, Main Street, Burton, Carnforth, Lancashire LA6 1LQ
Tel (0524) 781995

Enquiries to Tom Parker

Items 20,000: colour transparencies (35mm, 2¼″, 5″ × 4″)

Dates of photographs 1950 to present

Subjects Landscapes in the UK including rivers, lakes, mountains, agriculture, gardens, shipping, fishing, houses; some European coverage; close-up shots of wheatfields and flowers

Access and conditions Open to qualified researchers by appt (tel), Mon-Fri 9–5. All material available for editorial reproduction and for advertising. Colour material loaned for a fee. Reproduction rights, holding and service fees charged; service fees deductible from use fees. Research undertaken; fee charged if no material is used. All material copyright.

159 • ANN AND BURY PEERLESS

22 King's Avenue, Minnis Bay, Birchington-on-
Sea, Kent CT7 9QL
Tel (0843) 41428

Enquiries to Ann or Bury Peerless

Items 10,000: colour transparencies (35mm)

Dates of subject matter BC to present

Dates of photographs 1963 to present

Subjects World religions including Hinduism,
Buddhism, Judaism, Christianity, Islam, Sikhism;
geographical coverage of India, Pakistan,
Bangladesh, Sri Lanka, Egypt, Uganda, Kenya
including agriculture, art and architecture; Indian
history (manuscripts, sculpture, archaeology)

Access and conditions Open to qualified
researchers by appt (tel), Mon-Fri 9–5. All material
available for editorial reproduction and for
advertising. Colour material loaned by
arrangement. Reproduction rights fees charged.
Research undertaken. All material copyright.

160 • PETER PHIPP PHOTO LIBRARY

Studio 11A, 79 Bedford Gardens, London W8 7EG
Tel (01) 727 0100, 221 4179

Enquiries to Peter Phipp

Items Over 4000: colour transparencies (35mm,
2¼″)

Dates of photographs 1970 to present

Subjects Travel industry including cities,
beaches, resorts worldwide; posed models including
children

Access and conditions Open to qualified
researchers by appt (tel). All material available for
editorial reproduction and for advertising (some
restrictions). Colour material loaned free of charge
for four weeks. Photocopies and Polaroids
available. Reproduction rights and holding fees
charged. Research undertaken. Photographer
available for assignment. All material copyright.

161 • PHOTO CO-OP

61 Webbs Road, London SW11 6RX
Tel (01) 228 8949

Enquiries to Chris Boot, Administrator

Items About 6000: b/w original photographs,
colour transparencies (35mm)

Dates of photographs 1980 to present

Subjects Social documentary issues with
emphasis on London including women and feminist
issues, children and childcare, peace movement,
co-operatives, community centres, community arts
projects, education, health, social service, housing
and homelessness, transport, unemployment,
youth, voluntary and funded organizations, trade
unions; some coverage of health and women in
USA and India

Access and conditions Open to the public by appt
(tel), Mon-Fri 2–6. All material available for
editorial reproduction and for advertising (some
restrictions). B/w and colour material loaned free of
charge for one month. Photocopies available.
Reproduction rights fees charged. Staff of seven
will undertake some research for a fee.
Photographers available for assignment. All
material copyright. Duplicated catalogue available.

162 • PHOTO LIBRARY INTERNATIONAL

St Michaels Hall, Bennett Road, Leeds LS6 3HN
Tel (0532) 789321 Telex 55293 CHAMCOM G/PL

Enquiries to Librarian

Items 75,000 colour transparencies (35mm,
5″ × 4″)

Dates of subject matter Prehistory to present

Dates of photographs 1975 to present

Subjects Geography worldwide, landscapes,
climatic conditions, cloudscapes, the seasons, wild
and domestic animals, archaeology, architecture,
industry, science, technology, health, education,
social groups, human interaction, babies, children,
transport, space, entertainment, leisure, sports,
crafts

Access and conditions Open to qualified
researchers by appt (tel), Mon-Fri 9–5. All material
available for editorial reproduction and for
advertising. Colour material loaned free of charge
for one month. Reproduction rights, holding and
service fees charged; service fees deductible from
use fees. Staff of four will undertake some research.
Most material copyright. Card catalogue available.

163 • THE PHOTO SOURCE

Incorporating COLOUR LIBRARY
INTERNATIONAL, KEYSTONE PRESS
AGENCY, CENTRAL PRESS LTD, FOX
PHOTOS LTD

Unit C1, Enterprise Business Estate, 2 Mill
Harbour, London E14 9TE
Tel (01) 987 1212 Telex 888258

Enquiries to Sheldon Marshal, Managing
Director

Items 9½ million: b/w original and copy
photographs, colour transparencies (35mm, 5″ × 4″,
larger), glass negatives

Dates of subject matter Prehistory to present

Dates of photographs 1900 to present

Subjects CENTRAL PRESS COLLECTION:
comprehensive sports collection, especially cricket;
modern history, personalities and royalty;
KEYSTONE COLLECTION: world history, events, wars,
personalities, royalty, geography, natural history,
science, art, disasters (earthquakes, volcanoes),
b/w from turn of the century, colour from 1960; FOX
COLLECTION: pre-war personalities, geography,
royalty, war, sport, fashion, World War II, special
collection of transport and especially trains;
COLOUR LIBRARY INTERNATIONAL COLLECTION:
travel, especially USA and Canada, industry,
transport, architecture, antiques, children and
families, couples, posed models, animals

Access and conditions Open to qualified
researchers by appt (tel), Mon–Fri 9.30–5.30. All
material available for editorial reproduction and
for advertising. B/w and colour material loaned free
of charge for one month. Photocopies available.
Reproduction rights, service and holding fees
charged. Staff of 48 will undertake some research.

164 • PHOTOFILE INTERNATIONAL LTD

17 Victoria Grove, London W8 5RW
Tel (01) 584 6738 Telex 8956130

Enquiries to Sandra Schadeberg

Items 20,000: colour transparencies (35mm,
5″ × 4″)

Dates of subject matter Present

Dates of photographs 1970 to present

Subjects People, situations, sunsets, rivers,
mountains, animals, food, seasons, industrial,
corporate and design images

Access and conditions Open to qualified
researchers by appt, Mon–Fri 10–6. All material
available for editorial reproduction and for
advertising (all pictures have model release).
Colour material loaned for one month.
Reproduction rights, service and holding fees
charged. Staff will undertake research.

165 • THE PHOTOGRAPHERS LIBRARY

81A Endell Street, London WC2H 9AJ
Tel (01) 836 5591

Enquiries to Karen McCunnall or Shan Cowell

Items 50,000: colour transparencies (35mm,
7 × 6 cm, 2¼″)

Dates of subject matter Contemporary

Dates of photographs 1981 to present

Subjects Worldwide geography and travel,
landscapes, sport, leisure, food; agriculture,
industry, commerce, transport, technology, health-
care; babies, children, families, human interaction,
posed models

Access and conditions Open to qualified
researchers by appt (write), Mon–Fri 9–5. All
material available for editorial reproduction and
for advertising. Colour material loaned free of
charge for 28 days. Reproduction rights, holding
and service fees charged. Staff of four will
undertake some research. All material copyright.

166 • PHOTON PHOTO LIBRARY

20 Store Street, London WC1 7DH
Tel (01) 580 8878

Enquiries to Siri de Normanville

Items About 30,000: colour transparencies
(35mm, 7 × 6 cm, 5″ × 4″), b/w original
photographs

Dates of photographs 1930s to present

Subjects Worldwide geography, travel,
landscapes, skies, sunsets, waterscapes;
underwater marine life, tropical agriculture,
plants, trees, flowers, animals, birds; architecture,
industry, human interaction, children; art

photography; special collection of Wolfgang Suschitzky's social documentary photographs worldwide

Access and conditions Open to the public by appt (tel), Mon-Fri 9.30–6. All material available for editorial reproduction and for advertising. B/w and colour material loaned free of charge for one month. Photocopies available. Reproduction rights, holding and service fees charged; service fees deductible from use fees. All material copyright. Card catalogue available.

167 • PICKTHALL PICTURE LIBRARY

34 Down View Close, Yapton, Sussex BN18 0LD
Tel (0243) 552839

Enquiries to Barry Pickthall

Items 60,000: b/w original photographs, colour transparencies (35mm, 6 × 6 cm)

Dates of subject matter 1970 to present

Dates of photographs 1970 to present

Subjects Sailing, windsurfing and waterscenes; international sailing events including Admiral's Cup and America's Cup, BOC and Whitbread round the world race classics; waterfalls worldwide, rivers, brooks, seaside and coastal scenes; wildlife and waterfowl, natural history worldwide; country scenes including farms, fields, woodlands, cottages; travel coverage of Africa, Canada, China, France, Greece, Holland, Hong Kong, India, Indonesia, Iran, Malaya, Singapore, South America, Spain, UK, USA

Access and conditions Open to qualified researchers by appt (tel), Mon-Fri 9–5. All material available for editorial reproduction and for advertising. B/w and colour material loaned free of charge for one month. Reproduction rights, holding and service fees charged; search fees deductible from use fee. Staff will undertake some research. All material copyright. Printed catalogue available.

168 • PICTOR INTERNATIONAL LTD

Twyman House, 31-39 Camden Road, London NW1 9LR
Tel (01) 482 0478 Telex 21497 PICTOR G

Enquiries to Picture Librarian

Items About 500,000: colour transparencies (35mm, 7 × 6 cm, 9 × 6 cm)

Dates of photographs 1960s to present

Subjects Geography worldwide, tourism and travel, wild and domestic animals, landscapes, climatic conditions, seasons, pollution, human interaction, social groups and family groups, babies, children; architecture, transport, agriculture, industry, medicine, science, technology, leisure, entertainment, sports, festivals

Access and conditions Open to qualified researchers by appt, Mon-Fri 9–5.30. All material available for editorial reproduction and for advertising. Colour material loaned free of charge for two weeks. Reproduction rights and holding fees charged; service fees charged only when no material is used. Staff will undertake some research. All material copyright. Printed catalogue available.

169 • PICTORIAL NOSTALGIA LIBRARY

291 Pickhurst Rise, West Wickham, Kent BR4 0AH
Tel (01) 777 8331

Enquiries to Peter Nolan Lawrence

Items 75,000: b/w original photographs, colour transparencies (35mm), postcards, greetings cards, press cuttings, art reproductions, original cartoons, ephemera

Dates of subject matter 830 to 1920

Dates of photographs 1850s to present

Subjects Nostalgia of social change in the period between 1830 and 1920 including babies, children, eccentrics, beauties, actresses, portraits, romance, music, the seaside, patriotism, royalty; aviation, motoring, cycling, shipping, boating; architecture, landscapes, politics, servants, agriculture, religion, advertising, fashion, cosmetics, food

Access and conditions Not open; telephone and postal requests only. All material available for editorial reproduction and for advertising. Colour transparencies loaned free of charge for one month; material may be copied by outside photographers. Photocopies available. Reproduction rights, holding and service fees charged; service fees deductible from use fees. Staff will undertaken some research for a fee. Some material copyright.

170 • PICTORIAL PRESS LTD

Photo Library, Woodbridge House, 30 Aylesbury
Street, London EC1R 0BL
Tel (01) 253 4023 Telex 24744 CASLONG

Enquiries to Librarian

Items Two million: b/w original photographs, b/w
copy photographs, colour transparencies (35mm,
5″ × 4″), glass negatives

Dates of subject matter 1800 to present

Dates of photographs 1880 to present

Subjects Historical and military coverage
including Court of Imperial China in early 20th
century, Russia pre-1914, the Crimean and the
American Civil Wars; World War I including
material from Turkey, Russia and East Africa;
pre-1939 material including the Brazilian navy,
Swiss and Swedish armies, Sino-Japanese War;
World War II including history of the Nazi Party;
USSR including troop training, nursing, battle
scenes, women fighter pilots, submarines, industry,
agriculture, education; North African landings;
concentration camps; Japanese army and
government leaders; Australian fighter and
bomber squadrons at UK bases, USA war
production, civil defence, relocation of Japanese
citizens, propaganda cartoons, German occupation
of Czechoslovakia, partisans in Yugoslavia;
liberation of Holland, German surrender signings,
Yalta Conference; portraits of USSR generals,
USA service chiefs and politicians, military
aircraft, London bomb damage; military aircraft;
popular music of all types from the 1940s to the
present including about 2000 artists with detailed
coverage of the Beatles, Rolling Stones, Who and
David Bowie; teenagers and teenager culture,
fashion and activities from 1950s to present;
personalities including film stars from early cinema
to late 1970s, royalty worldwide (mostly 20th
century), political and military leaders including
material relating to Jesuits, Hungarian literary
figures of 19th century, US leaders, Kennedy
family, UK politicians and civil servants of the
1940s and 1950s, politicians and trade unionists of
the 1980s, eastern European politicians in the late
1940s and early 1950s; miscellaneous coverage
including Dr Adenauer, Lord Altrincham, Fred
Astaire, Christiaan Barnard, Enid Blyton,
Salvador Dali, John Dulles, Sinclair Lewis, Paul
Robeson, Albert Schweitzer and Sir Henry Wood;
transport with special emphasis on motor cars from
1920s to present; posed female models; special
collection on all aspects of childhood development
and education; medicine including hospital scenes

Access and conditions Open to qualified
researchers by appt, Mon-Fri 9.30–5.30. All
material available for editorial reproduction and
for advertising. B/w and colour material loaned free
of charge for one month (print fees charged).
Photocopies available. Reproduction rights, holding
and service fees charged. Staff of three will
undertake some research. Most material copyright.

171 • PICTURE INDEX

Hope Lodge, 41 Hassocks Road, Hurstpierpoint,
Sussex BN6 9QL
Tel (0273) 832365

Enquiries to Guy Gravett

Items About 250,000: b/w original photographs,
colour transparencies (35mm)

Dates of photographs 1951 to present

Subjects Glyndebourne Festival opera
productions from 1951 to present; châteaux,
vineyards and wine production in France,
Germany, Italy, Spain and Portugal

Access and conditions Not open; telephone and
postal requests only. All material available for
editorial reproduction and for advertising (some
restrictions). B/w prints loaned free of charge for
one month (print fees charged). Reproduction
rights and holding fees charged; service fees
charged only when no material is used. Staff will
undertake some research. All material copyright.

172 • THE PICTURE LIBRARY

Studio 21, Liddell Road, Maygrove Road, London
NW6 2EW
Tel (01) 328 5582/3

Enquiries to Nicola Shrimpton

Items 10,000: colour transparencies (35mm, 2¼″,
5″ × 4″)

Subjects Sports, including hang-gliding,
ballooning, wind-surfing, surfing, power boats,
water-skiing, skiing, ice-hockey, hockey, golf,
running, roller-skating, cricket, cross-country,
cycling, fox-hunting, motor racing, hot rods; people
including babies, mothers and children, children,
men and women, couples, families, crowds, posed
models; personalities including Royal Family;
animals including insects, fish, birds, swans, dogs,

cats, farm animals, zoo animals; weather including sunsets, seascapes, skyscapes and clouds, ice and snow, water; gardens, trees, flowers; agriculture, farming; architecture including churches, houses, cottages, exteriors and interiors, bridges; transport including roads, cars, HGVs, ships and boats, sea planes, aircraft, helicopters, rockets, trains, tanks; geography including mountains, moons; entertainment including ballet, concerts, circuses, fine art, statues; festivals including Christmas, carnivals; business and industry, oil rigs, construction; medicine; education; world travel, especially USA and London, including scenics, landscapes, beaches; food and drink, fires, chimneys, flags, abstracts

Access and conditions Open to qualified researchers by appt (tel), Mon-Fri 9–5.30. All material available for editorial reproduction and for advertising. Colour material loaned free of charge for two weeks. Reproduction rights, holding and service fees charged; service fees deductible from use fees. Staff will undertake research. Card catalogue.

173 • PICTUREBANK PHOTO LIBRARY LTD

Imperial House, Lower Teddington Road, Kingston upon Thames KT1 4EP
Tel (01) 943 2356, 943 2998 Telex 928017

Enquiries to Lorraine Robertson

Items Over 15,000: colour transparencies (35mm, 7 × 6 cm, 2¼", 5" × 4")

Dates of photographs 1979 to present

Subjects Worldwide geography, UK landscapes, posed models, family groups, children, couples; action sports; travel including hotels, resorts, tourists in Europe, the USA and the Caribbean; domestic and farm animals; climatic conditions, sunsets, atmospheric shots; fine art

Access and conditions Open to qualified researchers by appt (write). All material available for editorial reproduction and for advertising. Colour material loaned free of charge for one month. Reproduction rights, holding and service fees charged. Staff will undertake some research; negotiable research fee charged. Most material copyright.

174 • PICTUREPOINT

Hurst House, 157-169 Walton Road, East Molesey, Surrey KT8 0DX
Tel (01) 941 4520

Enquiries to Assistant Librarian

Items 750,000: colour transparencies (35mm, 6 × 6 cm, 7 × 6 cm, 5" × 4")

Dates of photographs 1940s to present

Subjects Geography worldwide, archaeology, landscapes, aerial views, agriculture, pollution, climatic conditions, geology, wild and domestic animals, gardens, flowers, fruit, fungi, trees and timber; children, posed models, human interaction, beauty and health, festivals, food, fireworks; transport, technology, science, industry, weaponry, mining, printing, shipping, oil and gas, computers, textiles, whaling

Access and conditions Open to qualified researchers by appt (tel), Mon-Fri 9–5. All material available for editorial reproduction and for advertising. Colour material loaned free of charge for one month. Reproduction rights, holding and service fees charged. Staff will undertake some research; negotiable research fees charged. All material copyright.

175 • PIXFEATURES

5 Latimer Road, Barnet, Hertfordshire EN5 5NU
Tel (01) 449 9946

Enquiries to Peter or Valerie Wickman

Items About 300,000: b/w original photographs, b/w copy photographs, colour transparencies (35mm), glass negatives

Dates of photographs 1905 to present

Subjects News photographs (contemporary and historical) mainly of British subjects up to 1968 and worldwide subjects from 1968 to the present; worldwide scenery, politics, events, World War II, South Africa, good selection on terrorism, personalities; representatives for *Stern* magazine photographs

Access and conditions Not open; telephone and mail requests only. All material available for editorial reproduction; some for advertising. B/w and colour material loaned free of charge for three weeks. Photocopies available. Reproduction rights, service and holding fees charged. Staff will undertake research.

176 • AXEL POIGNANT PHOTO LIBRARY

17 Oakcroft Road, London SE13 7ED
Tel (01) 852 3931

Enquiries to Roslyn Poignant

Items About 50,000: b/w original photographs, colour transparencies (35mm, 2¼″, 2¼″ × 3¼″), glass negatives, lantern slides, old fine art prints, unprinted film negatives, illustrated books

Dates of subject matter BC to present

Dates of photographs 1870 to present

Subjects Anthropology and ethnography, natural history and geography of Australasia, Mexico, Malaysia; Sicily including customs, festivals, folklore, crafts, agriculture; Galicia; Viking and pre-Viking sites in Scandinavia and the UK; deafness and hard of hearing in the UK

Access and conditions Open to qualified researchers by appt (tel). Most material available for editorial reproduction and for advertising. B/w and colour material loaned free of charge for one month. Reproduction rights and holding fees charged; service fees charged only when no material is used. Staff will undertake some research; negotiable research fee charged. Most material copyright.

177 • POPPERFOTO

24 Bride Lane, Fleet Street, London EC4Y 8DR
Tel (01) 353 9665/6 Telex 8814206 POPPER G

Enquiries to M. J. Hollingshead, Chief Librarian

Items Over three million: b/w original and copy photographs, colour transparencies (35mm, 5″ × 4″, larger), unprinted film negatives, glass negatives

Dates of subject matter Prehistory to present

Dates of photographs 1870 to present

Subjects World news, politics, personalities including Royalty, wars (especially World War II), British social history, sport, entertainment, world geography, industry, agriculture, anthropology, science and technology, inventions and discoveries, accidents and disasters, crime, police, transport (road, air, rail, sea), natural history, architecture; HERBERT PONTING COLLECTION: Capt. Scott's Antarctic expedition 1910–1912; CONWAY PICTURE LIBRARY, NAUTICAL PHOTO LIBRARY; material from United Press International, Planet News, Exclusive News Agency

Access and conditions Open to qualified researchers, Mon-Fri 9.30–5.30. All material available for editorial reproduction and for advertising. B/w and colour material loaned free of charge for 90 days. Reproduction rights, service and holding fees charged. Staff will undertake research.

178 • POWER PIX INTERNATIONAL PICTURE LIBRARY

35 North Street, Tillingham, Southminster, Essex CM0 7TR
Tel (062187) 614 Telex 995411

Enquiries to Dennis Power

Items Over 60,000: colour transparencies (35mm, 6 × 6 cm, 7 × 6 cm, 5″ × 4″)

Dates of photographs 1970 to present

Subjects Travel both in the UK and overseas, landscapes, architecture, historical monuments, agriculture, natural history including animals, birds (especially East African), fish, insects, flowers, trees, fungi; gardens; climatic conditions including sunsets, sunrises, clouds, storms, lightning, marine life especially on Great Barrier Reef in Australia; sports and hobbies including water sports, windsurfing, sub-aqua diving, water-skiing, yachting, flying, parachuting, ballooning, fishing, craft-work; family groups including children; posed models; transport including vintage cars, steam engines, railway engines, trains, buses; aircraft both military and civil worldwide; construction industry including motorways and buildings; personalities and portraits

Access and conditions Open to qualified researchers by appt (tel). All material available for editorial reproduction and for advertising. Colour material loaned free of charge for one month. Reproduction rights fees charged. Staff will undertake some research. All material copyright.

179 • FIONA PRAGOFF

9 Lancashire Court, New Bond Street, London W1Y 9AD
Tel (01) 491 8609, 723 3693

Enquiries to Fiona Pragoff

Items 10,000: colour transparencies (35mm, 120mm), b/w original photographs

Dates of photographs 1975 to present

Subjects Children and babies including portraits, groups, family shots, with adults, twins; children playing, learning, exercising, sleeping, eating, at school, at parties; general travel coverage of US (New England, New York), Portugal, Malta, UK including landscapes, sunsets, rainbows

Access and conditions Open to qualified researchers by appt (tel), Mon-Fri 9–5.30. All material available for editorial reproduction and for advertising. B/w and colour material loaned free of charge by arrangement. Reproduction rights fees charged; holding fees charged by arrangement. Staff of two will undertake some research. All material copyright. Subject list available.

180 • THE PRESS ASSOCIATION LTD

Photographic Library, 85 Fleet Street, London
EC4P 4BE
Tel (01) 353 7440

Enquiries to Picture Librarian

Items Over two million: b/w original photographs, colour transparencies (35mm), glass negatives, unprinted film negatives

Dates of photographs *c*. 1900 to present

Subjects National and international news coverage updated daily; pictures can also be supplied from any of the major European news pictures agencies; special collections include the CENTRAL NEWS LIBRARY from *c*. 1900 to 1940 and the LONDON NEWS AGENCY

Access and conditions Open to qualified researchers by appt (tel), Mon-Fri 9–5.30. All material available for editorial reproduction and for advertising. No loans; b/w prints and duplicate colour transparencies available for a fee. Reproduction rights and service fees charged. Staff will undertake research for a fee. All material copyright.

181 • PRESS FEATURES SYNDICATE

95 Kipling Avenue, Goring-by Sea, West Sussex
BN12 6LJ
Tel (0903) 41907

Enquiries to Church Semple

Items About 500,000: b/w original photographs, colour transparencies (35mm)

Dates of subject matter 1969 to present

Dates of photographs 1969 to present

Subjects News feature coverage including crime, film and television personalities, human interest, children; mainly UK coverage but some Japanese and American material

Access and conditions Open to qualified researchers by appt (write). All material available for editorial reproduction and for advertising. B/w and colour material loaned free of charge for two months. Reproduction rights fees charged. Staff of two will undertake some research. All material copyright.

182 • PUBLIC RECORD OFFICE

Ruskin Avenue, Kew, Richmond, Surrey
TW9 4DU
Tel (01) 876 3444

Enquiries to Search Department

Items Number unknown: b/w original photographs, b/w copy photographs, glass negatives, daguerreotypes, postcards, original cartoons, illustrated maps, posters, greetings cards, architectural drawings

Dates of subject matter Late 18th century to present

Dates of photographs Mid-19th century to present

Subjects Photographic record of the activities of central government and administration including work of individual departments such as Foreign Office, War Office, Ministry of Information, Colonial Office, Board of Trade; large collection relating to history and development of railways in the UK, the armed forces (Royal Navy, Army and Royal Air Force); important collection relating to the Festival of Britain 1951; complete set of Ministry of Information posters during World War II; the photographic collection is scattered throughout the archives

Access and conditions Open to the public, Mon-Fri 9.30–5. Most material available for editorial reproduction and for advertising. No loans; b/w prints and duplicate colour transparencies available for a fee. Photocopies available. Reproduction rights fees charged. Most material copyright. Card and typescript catalogues available.

183 • PUBLIC RECORD OFFICE OF NORTHERN IRELAND

66 Balmoral Avenue, Belfast BT9 6NY
Tel (0232) 661621

Enquiries to Director

Items About 100,000: b/w original photographs, glass negatives, illustrated maps, b/w copy photographs, colour transparencies (35mm), posters

Dates of subject matter 1350 to 1970s

Dates of photographs 1850 to 1970s

Subjects Northern Ireland including political events and political figures, visits by royalty, transport, architecture, World War II, agriculture, industry (especially linen), social history; Crimean War, travel coverage of Western Canada during the 1870s

Access and conditions Open to the public, Mon-Fri 9.30–4.45. All material available for editorial reproduction and for advertising. No loans; b/w prints and duplicate colour transparencies available for a fee; material may be copied by outside photographers. Photocopies available. Reproduction rights fees charged. Staff will undertake limited research. Most material copyright.

184 • RAYMONDS NEWS AND PHOTO AGENCY LTD

Old Hall, St Peter's Churchyard, Derby DE1 1NN
Tel (0332) 40404

Enquiries to Managing Director

Items Over 60,000: b/w original photographs, colour transparencies (35mm)

Dates of subject matter 1950 to present

Dates of photographs 1950 to present

Subjects News coverage in Derbyshire, Staffordshire, Nottinghamshire and Leicestershire including sport (football, cricket, horse-racing), industry (Burton Brewery, Rolls Royce Motor Company, British Rail works, coalmining), customs, ceremonies

Access and conditions Open to the public by appt (tel), Mon-Sat 9–6. All material available for editorial reproduction and for advertising. B/w prints and duplicate colour transparencies available for a fee. Reproduction rights and service fees charged. Staff of four will undertake research for a fee. Photographers available for assignments. All material copyright. Card catalogue available.

185 • REAL PICTURES

Camera House, 3 Broad Street, Kidderminster, Worcestershire DY10 2NH
Tel (0562) 752582

Enquiries to Trevor Haywood

Items About 120,000: b/w original photographs, colour transparencies (35mm, 2¼″)

Dates of photographs 1960 to present

Subjects Geography, natural history and tourism of the British Isles including Stratford-upon-Avon (Shakespearean sites, houses, gardens, etc.), Warwick, Kenilworth, Charlcote Park; the Lake District including Borrowdale, Derwentwater, Buttermere, Wastwater, major fells and valleys; horses, especially Shire horses and also showjumping, eventing, driving, Princess Anne and Captain Mark Phillips; wine and beer making including ingredients, chemicals, equipment, step-by-step pictures, finished beer and wine displays; farmyard animals, British flora and fauna, household pets, Acton Scott Working Farm Museum, birds of prey, kestrels, buzzards, owls, hawks; steam trains, Severn Valley Railway at Bewdley, Arley, Bridgenorth and Kidderminster; classic cars, modern petrol engines, cars and motor cycles, fairs and fairgrounds, steam engines; midland towns and counties including Worcestershire, Herefordshire, Shropshire, stately homes, cathedrals, abbeys; Yugoslavia including comprehensive recent material on holiday and cultural themes

Access and conditions Open to mail and telephone requests. All material available for editorial reproduction and for advertising. B/w and colour material loaned free of charge for one month. Reproduction rights and service fees charged. Staff of three will undertake research. All material copyright.

186 • REFLECTIONS OF A BYGONE AGE

27 Walton Drive, Keyworth, Nottingham
NG12 5HT
Tel (06077) 4087

Enquiries to Brian Lund

Items 50,000 postcards

Dates of subject matter 1900 to 1939

Dates of photographs 1900 to 1939

Subjects General coverage up to outbreak of World War II with emphasis on pre-World War I material including Edwardian social and political humour, Edwardian landscape artists, World War I propaganda, railway stations, shipping, horse-drawn and motor transport, sport, social history, entertainment, theatre

Access and conditions Open to qualified researchers by appt (write). All material available for editorial reproduction and for advertising. B/w material loaned free of charge for one month; b/w prints and duplicate colour transparencies available for a fee. Photocopies available. Reproduction rights fees charged. Research undertaken. Some material copyright.

187 • RENTASNAP PHOTO LIBRARY

51 Herbert Road, Nottingham NGS 1BS
Tel (0602) 604680

Enquiries to Helen or John Birdsall

Items 500: b/w original photographs

Dates of photographs 1980 to present

Subjects Contemporary social documentary coverage with emphasis on Nottingham but including housing, youth, unemployment, the Peace Movement, CND, anti-nuclear protestors at Greenham Common and other anti-nuclear movements and demonstrations

Access and conditions Open to the public, Mon-Fri 10–5. All material available for editorial reproduction and for advertising. B/w material loaned free of charge for one month. Photocopies available. Reproduction rights, holding and service fees charged. Staff will undertake research. Printed catalogue available.

188 • REPORT AND INTERNATIONAL FREELANCE LIBRARY LTD

411 Oxford Street, London W1R 1FG
Tel (01) 493 7737, 493 7507

Enquiries to Helen Warby

Items Over one million: b/w original photographs, b/w copy photographs, colour transparencies (35mm), glass negatives, press cuttings

Dates of photographs 1950 to present

Subjects Social change in post-World War II Britain with emphasis on urban decay, politics, demonstrations, trade union movement, industry, education, theatre, music, personalities; special collections include fringe theatre, new music, North and South Vietnam, Biafra, Nicaragua, Peace Movement

Access and conditions Open to qualifed researchers by appt (tel). All material available for editorial reproduction but not for advertising. Colour material loaned for a fee; b/w prints and duplicate colour transparencies available for a fee. Reproduction rights, holding and service fees charged. Staff of three will undertake some research. All material copyright. Catalogue in preparation.

189 • REX FEATURES LIMITED

18 Vine Hill, London EC1R 5DX
Tel (01) 278 7294, 278 3362 Telex 24224

Enquiries to B/w or Colour Library

Items Over three million: b/w original photographs, b/w copy photographs, colour transparencies (35mm, 5″ × 4″)

Dates of subject matter 1955 to present

Dates of photographs 1955 to present

Subjects Comprehensive national and international news coverage, politics, personalities, show business, rock and pop music, art, medicine, science; special emphasis on current affairs, off-beat and amusing pictures, celebrities, royalty (British and foreign); London agents for SIPA

Access and conditions Open to qualified researchers by appt (tel). B/w and colour material loaned free of charge for one month (print fees charged). Photocopies available. Reproduction rights, holding and service fees charged; service fees may be deductible from use fees. Staff of five will undertake some research; negotiable research fees charged. All material copyright. Catalogue in preparation.

190 • DAVID RICHARDSON

39 Chester Street, Coventry CV1 3DH
Tel (0203) 24447, (04427) 6473

Enquiries to David Richardson

Items 50,000: b/w original photographs, colour transparencies (35mm)

Dates of subject matter 1976 to present

Dates of photographs 1976 to present

Subjects Multi-racial communities in the UK including West Indian, European, Sikh, Hindu, Muslim and Irish communities mainly in Coventry and Wolverhampton covering housing, work, leisure, religion, sport and education; all major Sikh, Hindu, Muslim, Jewish and Christian religious festivals; rites of passage including birth and naming ceremonies, baptisms, confirmations, weddings and funerals; gypsies in the UK including site conditions, baptisms, weddings and funerals; David Richardson has access to large private collection of Indian religious documents, books and manuscripts dating from c. 1500

Access and conditions Open to qualified researchers by appt (tel), Mon-Fri 9–5. All material available for editorial reproduction and for advertising. B/w and colour material loaned free of charge by arrangement (print fee charged). Photocopies available. Reproduction rights and service fees charged. Research undertaken. Photographer available for assignment. All material copyright.

191 • PETER ROBERTS

15 The Comyns, Bushey Heath, Hertfordshire WD2 1HN
Tel (01) 950 3958

Enquiries to Peter Roberts

Items 30,000: b/w original photographs, colour transparencies (35mm, 7 × 6 cm), unprinted film negatives, posters, press cuttings

Dates of subject matter 11th century to present

Dates of photographs 1883 to present

Subjects Motor cars with emphasis on vintage models; horses and ponies as domestic animals including care, grooming, exercise, training, riding instruction, showjumping; travel coverage of castles in Britain, France, Germany, Austria and Switzerland

Access and conditions Open to qualified researchers by appt (tel), Mon-Fri 9–5. All material available for editorial reproduction and for advertising. B/w and colour material loaned free of charge for three months. Reproduction rights fees charged. All material copyright.

192 • ROYAL COMMONWEALTH SOCIETY LIBRARY

18 Northumberland Avenue, London WC2N 5BJ
Tel (01) 930 6733

Enquiries to Photographic Cataloguer

Items Over 60,000: b/w original photographs, postcards, lantern slides, illustrated books

Dates of photographs 1850s to present

Subjects Imperial and commonwealth history including events, personalities, military campaigns, architecture, landscapes, ethnography, agriculture, industries, trade, communications, social and leisure activities; special collections include the QUEEN MARY COLLECTION covering royal visits to India in early 20th century; ROYAL COLONIAL INSTITUTE COLLECTION of members' portraits; BRITISH ASSOCIATION OF MALAYSIA COLLECTION; the FISHER COLLECTION; individual photographers include Samuel Bourne, W. L. H. Skeen & Co, G. R. Lambert & Co, W. E. Fry, William D. Young, A. C. Gomes, Lisk-Carew Bros

Access and conditions Open to the public by appt (tel). All material available for editorial reproduction and for advertising. No loans; b/w prints available for a fee. Reproduction rights and service fees charged. Staff will undertake limited research. All material copyright. Card and printed catalogues available.

193 • S & G PICTURE LIBRARY

68 Exmouth Market, London EC1 4RA
Tel (01) 278 1223 Telex 21120 REF 1317

Enquiries to Nick Pearce, Librarian

Items 1,785,000: glass negatives, unprinted film negatives, b/w original photographs, colour transparencies (35mm, 5" × 4"), colour photographic prints

Dates of subject matter 1900 to present

Dates of photographs 1900 to present

Subjects Sporting fixtures and events in the UK both amateur and professional from 1910 including exclusive collection of cricket matches at Headingly and Lords and Rugby at Twickenham; British Royal Family from 1900 including coverage of overseas tours; politics from 1920 including government ministers, politicians, conferences, political events; crimes and convicted criminals from 1920, law courts; entertainment including actors, actresses and musicians with special emphasis on rock music in the 1960s and 1970s; S & G includes the collections of Sport and General, Barratts Photo Press, Fleet Street News Agency and London News Service

Access and conditions Open to qualified researchers by appt (tel but first-time users write), Mon-Fri 9.30–5.30. All material available for editorial reproduction and for advertising (model releases not supplied). B/w and colour material loaned free of charge for one month; b/w prints and duplicate colour transparencies available for a fee. Photocopies and Polaroids available. Reproduction rights, holding and service fees charged. Staff of five will undertake some research for a fee. Photographers available for assignment. Most material copyright.

194 • SAGA SCENE

A division of SAGA HOLIDAYS plc

Enbrook House, Sandgate, Folkestone, Kent CT20 3SG
Tel (0303) 47533 Telex 966331

Enquiries to Caroline Butterfield, Photographic Service Manager

Items 20,000: colour transparencies (35mm, 5" × 4")

Dates of subject matter 1979 to present

Dates of photographs 1979 to present

Subjects Older people on holiday in the UK and overseas including Spain, Canary Islands, Portugal, Austria, Yugoslavia, Greece, Israel and USA; activities covered include rambling, dancing, golf, bridge, whist, swimming; travel on aircraft, ships (including cruises), trains and coaches

Access and conditions Open to qualified researchers by appt (write), Mon-Fri 9–5. All material available for editorial reproduction and for advertising. Colour material loaned free of charge for one month; duplicate colour

transparencies available for a fee. Reproduction rights, service and holding fees charged; service fees deductible from use fees. Staff will undertake limited research for a fee. All material copyright.

195 • ST ANDREWS UNIVERSITY LIBRARY

North Street, St Andrews, Fife KY16 9TR
Tel (0334) 76161 ext 514

Enquiries to Robert Smart, Keeper of Manuscripts

Items Over 300,000: b/w original photographs, glass negatives, unprinted film negatives, lantern slides, b/w copy photographs, colour transparencies (35mm), postcards, original cartoons, illustrated maps, old fine art prints, 20th-century fine art prints, art reproductions, posters, greetings cards, architectural drawings, press cuttings, illustrated books

Dates of subject matter Mid-19th century to present

Dates of photographs Mid-19th century to present

Subjects VALENTINE AND SONS LTD COLLECTION including landscape coverage of the British Isles 1878–1967; GEORGE COWIE COLLECTION of local news coverage of St Andrews with special emphasis on golf, 1929–1982; David Jack architectural survey of St Andrews, 1977; HENRIETTA GILMOUR COLLECTION, 1890–1912, covering riding, hunting, shooting, fishing, society balls; DONALD MACCULLOCH COLLECTION of West Highland landscape, 1930–1955; J. E. A. STEGGALL COLLECTION of amateur travel coverage of Scotland, 1886–1925

Access and conditions Open to the public by appt (write), Mon-Fri 9–5. All material available for editorial reproduction and for advertising. B/w prints and duplicate colour transparencies available for a fee. Photocopies available. Reproduction rights fees charged. Most material copyright. Subject lists available.

196 • SCHOOL OF SCOTTISH STUDIES

University of Edinburgh, Photographic Archive, 27 George Square, Edinburgh EH8 9LD
Tel (031) 667 1011 ext 6691/2

Enquiries to John MacQueen, Director

Items About 10,000: b/w original and copy photographs, colour transparencies (35mm), glass negatives, lantern slides, postcards

Dates of subject matter *c.* 1750 to present

Dates of photographs *c.* 1900 to present

Subjects Traditional crafts and practices in rural and urban Scottish society with special emphasis on the Highlands and Islands; basket-making, weaving, net-making, seasonal customs such as making corn dollies at harvest-time; portraits; special collections include the DR WERNER KISSLING COLLECTION of life in the Western Isles from the 1930s to 1950s, and the JOHN LEVY COLLECTION covering India, Nepal, China and Japan, and Islamic culture in North Africa during the 1950s and 1960s

Access and conditions Open to the public, Mon-Fri 10–4. Most material available for editorial reproduction and for advertising. No loans; b/w prints and duplicate colour transparencies available for a fee. Reproduction rights and service fees charged. Staff will undertake some research. Most material copyright. Card catalogue available.

197 • SCOPE PICTURE AGENCY

Delta House, Bark Street, Bolton, Lancashire BL1 2AT
Tel (0204) 31719

Enquiries to Eric Whitehead

Items 16,000: b/w original photographs, colour transparencies (35mm, 5″ × 4″), colour photographic prints, glass negatives

Dates of photographs 1940 to present

Subjects Sports, especially snooker, indoor bowling and sports personalities; North of England including people and places; general English life including rural scenes, villages, people at work, village fêtes, town fairs, school garden parties, morris dancing, clog dancing; worldwide geography, tourism, landscapes, mountaineering; politicians

Access and conditions Open to qualified researchers by appt, Mon-Sat 9–5. All material available for editorial reproduction and for advertising. B/w and colour material loaned free of charge for three months. Reproduction rights and holding fees charged. Staff of three will undertake research. Card catalogue.

198 • *THE SCOTSMAN* PUBLICATIONS LTD

20 North Bridge, Edinburgh EH1 1YT
Tel (031) 225 2468 ext 438 Telex 72255 & 727600

Enquiries to Bill Brady, Retail Unit Supervisor

Items Three million: unprinted film negatives, b/w original and copy photographs, colour transparencies (35mm, 5″ × 4″) glass negatives, press cuttings

Dates of subject matter *c.* 1880 to present

Dates of photographs *c.* 1880 to present

Subjects TOPIX COLLECTION (1920–1979): (includes the files of the *Graphic Photo Union* and the *Kemsley Picture Agency* as well as the *Times Newspapers Ltd* and material from Roy Thomson's regional newspapers) world news, personalities, sports, royalty, World War I, French occupation of the Ruhr in 1923, Spanish Civil War, World War II, British political history, entertainment, transport, science and invention, education, accidents, social change, medicine, industry, strikes, trades unions; *SCOTSMAN* and *EVENING NEWS* COLLECTION: national and international news with emphasis on Scotland, personalities, pop stars, politicians, industry, mining, oil, micro-chip technology, agriculture (old and new), fishing, nuclear power stations (Sellafield, Hunterston, etc.), news events, miners' strike, launching of the Queen Mary, sports (1970 Commonwealth Games, windsurfing, football, etc.), Edinburgh Festivals (1947 to present), Edinburgh townscapes, Scottish landscapes, ship-building

Access and conditions Open to qualified researchers, Mon-Fri 9.30–5.30. All material available for editorial reproduction and for advertising. B/w and colour material loaned free of charge for two weeks (longer by arrangement). B/w prints available for a fee. Reproduction rights and service fees charged. Staff of five will undertake research.

199 • SCOTTISH PICTURE LIBRARY IN LONDON

67 Fishponds Road, London SW17 7LH
Tel (01) 672 6399

Enquiries to Nicholas Gentilli

Items Over 10,000: colour transparencies (35mm)

Dates of photographs 1980 to present

Subjects All aspects of contemporary life in Scotland including wildlife, landscapes, aerial coverage, cities, towns, villages, agriculture, architecture, industry, crafts, transport (all types), sport, leisure, entertainment, food, family and social groups, human interaction, babies, children; special collections on mountains and peaks, and Duchess of Westminster's hunting estate

Access and conditions Open to qualified researchers by appt (first-time users write), Mon-Fri 9–5. All material available for editorial reproduction and for advertising. Colour material loaned free of charge for one month. Reproduction rights, holding and service fees charged; service fees deductible from use fees. Research undertaken for a fee. Photographers available for assignment. All material copyright.

200 • SCOTTISH TOURIST BOARD

23 Ravelston Terrace, Edinburgh EH4 3EU
Tel (031) 332 2433 Telex 72272

Enquiries to Moira Campbell, Photo Librarian

Items 85,000: colour transparencies (35mm, 2¼"), b/w original photographs

Dates of subject matter Prehistory to present

Dates of photographs 1972 to present

Subjects Scotland – all areas including landscapes, wildlife, cities and towns, leisure, entertainment, sport, theatre, opera, Edinburgh Festival, industries and crafts (glass-blowing, pottery, leather work, whisky distilleries, ski-manufacture, textiles), transport, architecture, castles, tourist accommodation, caravans and camping, conferences

Access and conditions Open to the public by appt (tel), Mon-Fri 9–5.30. All material available for editorial reproduction and for advertising. B/w material loaned free of charge for seven days; colour material loaned free of charge for one month; b/w prints and duplicate colour transparencies available for a fee. Reproduction rights and service fees charged. Staff will undertake limited research. All material copyright.

SEAPHOT LIMITED see PLANET EARTH PICTURES

201 • SEFTON PHOTO LIBRARY

30 Mason Street, Manchester M4 4EY
Tel (061) 834 9423

Enquiries to Sefton Samuels

Items 50,000: colour transparencies (35mm, 7 × 6 cm, 2¼"), b/w original photographs

Dates of subject matter c. 1880 to present

Dates of photographs c. 1880 to present

Subjects Comprehensive collection including animals, birds, flowers, trees, environment, seasons, climatic conditions, sunrise, sunset; children, family groups, posed models; agriculture, technology and industry including construction, oil rigs and refineries, collieries, power stations; transport including aircraft, boats, railways; sport, leisure, humour, musicians; personalities especially leading north-western personalities such as Sir Bernard Lovell, Cyril Smith, James Anderton, L. S. Lowry, Theodore Major, Lord Winstanley and Sir Matt Busby; increasing overseas coverage including Africa, Australia, Canada, Belgium, China, Denmark, France, Greece, Holland, Hong Kong, India, Italy, Luxembourg, Maldives, Monaco, Morocco, Nepal, Pakistan, Portugal, Seychelles, Spain, Switzerland, Sri Lanka, Thailand, Tunisia, USA and the West Indies; special collection of Victorian and Edwardian material covering social conditions, architecture, transport and costume; special collection of famous musicians both classical and jazz including Sir John Barbirolli, Sir Adrian Boult, Daniel Barenboim, Carlo-Mariah Giulini, Itzak Perlman, Louis Armstrong, Duke Ellington, Count Basie, Sidney Bechet, Phil Seaman and Benny Goodman

Access and conditions Open to qualified researchers by appt (tel), Mon-Fri 9.30–6. All material available for editorial reproduction and for advertising. B/w and colour material loaned free of charge for one month. Reproduction rights, holding and service fees charged. Staff of three will undertake some research. All material copyright. Printed subject list available.

202 • BRIAN AND SALLY SHUEL

13 Woodberry Crescent, London N10 1PJ
Tel (01) 883 2531

Enquiries to Brian and Sally Shuel

Items Over 115,000: b/w original photographs,

colour transparencies (35mm), old fine art prints, unprinted film negatives

Dates of subject matter Prehistory to present

Dates of photographs 1960 to present

Subjects Traditional customs throughout the British Isles including seasonal and annual events, folk dances, games, plays, legal customs, church services such as the Clown Service, well-dressing; coverage of some 400 bridges in UK from prehistoric structures to modern Humber Bridge; general travel coverage

Access and conditions Open to qualified researchers by appt (tel). All material available for editorial reproduction and for advertising. B/w and colour material loaned free of charge for three months. Photocopies available. Reproduction rights and service fees charged. Staff will undertake some research. All material copyright. Catalogue in preparation.

203 • JOHN SIMS

11A Parkhill Road, London NW3 2YH
Tel (01) 586 0780

Enquiries to John Sims

Items Over 25,000: colour transparencies (35mm), b/w original photographs, colour photographic prints, art reproductions

Dates of subject matter Prehistory to present

Dates of photographs 1977 to present

Subjects Geography mainly of the UK and southern Europe, but also including Spain, Switzerland, Greece, France, Italy, USA (eastern seaboard, South Carolina, Georgia, Kentucky, Smoky Mountains, New York State); abstracts, architecture (modern and classical) especially in London, Paris, Milan, cemeteries, construction, energy and power, farming, fairgrounds, flora, horticulture (indoor and house plants, shrubs, parks, gardens), infra-red photography, landscapes, mannequins, markets, rocks and natural forms, seasons, shipping and haulage, shops and stores, skies, clouds and sunsets, transport, trees, woods and forests, water, weather

Access and conditions Open to qualified researchers by appt (tel), Mon-Fri 9–6. All material available for editorial reproduction and for advertising. B/w and colour material loaned free of charge for one month. Reproduction rights, service and holding fees charged; service fees deductible from use fees. Staff will undertake research.

204 • EDWIN SMITH PHOTOGRAPHS

The Coach House, Windmill Hill, Saffron Walden, Essex CB10 1RK
Tel (0799) 23373

Enquiries to Olive Smith

Items 80,000: b/w original photographs, colour transparencies ($5'' \times 4''$)

Dates of subject matter Prehistory to 1971

Dates of photographs 1935 to 1971

Subjects Landscape and detailed architectural coverage of the British Isles and Italy including churches, houses, gardens, vernacular architecture; coverage of France, Germany, Greece, Spain, the Netherlands and Scandinavia; early material (1935–1950) includes special collection of fairgrounds and circuses, London streets and shops of the 1930s, portraits, fashion photography for *Vogue* magazine, complete record of John Gielgud's performances in *King Lear* and *Othello* at the Old Vic in 1940, miners from Ashington Colliery in Newcastle at work and home in 1936; some coverage of British Museum material

Access and conditions Not open; telephone and postal requests only. All material available for editorial reproduction but not for advertising. B/w and colour material loaned free of charge for three months. Reproduction rights and holding fees charged. Research undertaken. Compulsory credit line. All material copyright.

205 • SOUTH AMERICAN PICTURES

Tony Morrison, 48 Station Road, Woodbridge, Suffolk IP12 4AT
Tel (03943) 3963 Telex 987271

Enquiries to Marion Morrison

Items Over 50,000: colour transparencies (35mm), b/w original photographs, b/w copy photographs, postcards, illustrated maps, old fine art prints, art reproductions, unprinted film negatives, posters, press cuttings, illustrated books

Dates of subject matter Prehistory to present

Dates of photographs 1961 to present

Subjects South America (south of Panama) but some coverage of Mexico and West Indies including all aspects of contemporary life (excluding politicians and personalities), landscapes, the environment, natural history, geology, ecology, ecosystems and anthropology, natural resources, cities, towns; special collection of material including religion and native medicine, tourism and transport, music and the arts; salvage of *SS Great Britain* in the Falkland Islands, the Nasca Lines of Peru, Amazon rainforest, steam and modern railways; some coverage of Iran, Jordan, village life in India and the River Danube; growing collection of contemporary East Anglian life and environment

Access and conditions Open to qualified researchers by appt, Mon-Fri 9–5. All material available for editorial reproduction and for advertising. B/w and colour material loaned free of charge for two months; b/w prints and duplicate colour transparencies available for a fee. Photocopies available. Reproduction rights fees charged; holding and service fees charged by arrangement; service fees deductible from use fees. Staff of three will undertake research; negotiable research fee charged. Almost all material copyright. Computer lists available.

206 • SPECTRUM COLOUR LIBBRARY

146 Oxford Street, London W1N 9DL
Tel (01) 637 1587, 637 2108, 637 3682

Enquiries to Keith Jones

Items Over eight million: b/w original photographs, colour transparencies (35mm, 5″ × 4″, 10″ × 8″), lantern slides

Dates of subject matter Prehistory to present

Dates of photographs 1945 to present

Subjects Comprehensive collection covering worldwide geography including Arctic and Antarctic regions, natural history including birds, fish, insects, reptiles, flowers, fruit, vegetables, plants, trees, cacti, fungi, domestic and wild animals; agriculture, horticulture, geology, industry, medicine, computers, trade, business, weaponry; environment including pollution, deserts, British landscapes, seascapes, beaches, seasons, sunset and sunrise, climatic conditons; babies, children, family groups; sports including winter sports, ballooning, cycling, potholing, fishing and watersports; architecture, cottages, houses, castles, churches, hotels, inns; abstracts, fairgrounds, circuses, food and cookery, houseplants, travel, ships, boats, aircraft, railways, motor transport including roads and motorways; special collections include the FORMAT PHOTO LIBRARY, A.C.K. WARE LIBRARY, WILDLIFE PHOTO

LIBRARY, ANNE CUMBERS COLLECTION of cats, dogs and horses, BAVARIA VERLAG LIBRARY of worldwide travel and sport.

Access and conditions Open to qualified researchers by appt (tel), Mon-Fri 9.30–5.30. All material available for editorial reproduction and for advertising. B/w and colour material loaned free of charge for 30 days. Photocopies available. Reproduction rights and holding fees charged; service fees charged only when no material is used. Staff of five will undertake research. All material copyright. Card catalogue available.

207 • FRANK SPOONER PICTURES

Room 805/6, Africa House, 64-78 Kingsway, London WC2B 6AY
Tel (01) 405 9943/4/5 Telex 21251 TICKG

Enquiries to Picture Librarian

Items About 500,000: colour transparencies (35mm), b/w original photographs

Dates of subject matter 1956 to present

Dates of photographs 1956 to present

Subjects National and international news coverage with emphasis on events since 1976 and including political leaders and events, current affairs, economy, demonstrations, industry, science and technology, British and European royal families, social events, sports, travel, fashion, cinema, theatre; international coverage includes Central America, Peru, Chile, South Africa, Iranian Revoluton, Israel and occupied territories, Iran-Iraq War, Civil War in Chad, Libya, Lebanon, Northern Ireland, Zimbabwe; Frank Spooner acts as London agent for Gamma Press Images, Paris, Liaison Incorporated, New York, Mega Productions, Los Angeles

Access and conditions Open to qualified researchers by appt (tel), Mon-Fri 9.30–6. All material available for editorial reproduction and for advertising. B/w and colour material loaned free of charge for one month. Photocopies available. Reproduction rights, service and holding fees charged. Staff of five will undertake research. All material copyright. Computer catalogue available.

SPORTS AND GENERAL *see* S & G

208 • STOCKPHOTOS

8 Charing Cross Road, London WC2 0HG
Tel (01) 240 7361 Telex 894839 TIBG

Enquiries to Katherine Sharp, Librarian

Items 75,000: colour transparencies (35mm,
5″ × 4″)

Dates of subject matter Prehistory to present

Dates of photographs 1977 to present

Subjects Geography worldwide, detailed coverage
of New York and London, abstracts, interiors,
religion, medicine, motor and air transport,
industry (including oil, construction, space
research and computers), agriculture; leisure
activities including eating, drinking, parties,
gambling, discotheques; sports including keep-fit,
fishing, swimming, sailing, windsurfing, water-
skiing, surfing, golf, cycling, hang-gliding, hiking,
tennis, climbing; babies, children singly and in
groups, with animals, family groups, posed models
indoors and outdoors, romantic situations,
weddings; the environment worldwide, climatic
conditions, the seasons, landscapes and seascapes
including water and waterfalls, lakes, rivers,
volcanoes, mountains, woods, trees, flowers,
deserts, beaches; wild, domestic and farm animals,
birds, insects, reptiles, marine life

Access and conditions Open to qualified
researchers by appt (tel), Mon-Fri 9.30–5.30. All
material available for editorial reproduction and
for advertising (some restrictions on small amount
of material without model release). Colour
transparencies loaned free of charge for 30 working
days. Reproduction rights and service fees charged.
Staff of three will undertake research. All material
copyright. Printed catalogue available.

209 • TONY STONE WORLDWIDE

28 Finchley Road, London NW8 6ES
Tel (01) 586 7671 Telex 21824

Enquiries to Felicity Townson, Sales Manager

Items About 500,000: colour transparencies
(35mm, 5″ × 4″, 7″ × 5″, 10″ × 8″)

Dates of photographs Contemporary

Subjects Worldwide coverage, abstracts,
agriculture, aviation, babies, business and finance,
children, couples, cats, dog, families, food and
drink, flowers, posed models, wildlife, industry,
technology, computer graphics, sport, transport,

people and places, landscapes, seascapes, skies,
graphic abstracts

Access and conditions Open to qualified
researchers by appt (tel), Mon-Fri 9.15–5.15. All
material available for editorial reproduction and
for advertising. Colour material loaned free of
charge; period negotiable. Reproduction rights,
service and holding fees charged. Staff of 45 will
undertake research. Colour brochure available.

210 • JESSICA STRANG

86 Cambridge Gardens, London W10 6HS
Tel (01) 969 7292

Enquiries to Jessica Strang

Items About 20,000: colour transparencies
(35mm)

Dates of photographs Early 1970s to present

Subjects Architecture and architectural details in
London including ceramics, tiles, commercial signs,
murals, pavement art, shop fronts, people and
animals in architecture; architecture overseas with
emphasis on pattern, colour, embellishment,
fantasy decoration, stained glass windows, in Italy,
Sicily, Corsica, Spain, Malaysia, Singapore,
Thailand, Burma, Indonesia, Australia, USA
(emphasis on New York and Washington); interior
design with detailed coverage of contemporary
room design, use of fabric and paint finishes,
domestic artefacts, themes; window boxes,
doorways, porches, gateways, conservatories,
patios, balconies, greenhouses, gardens formal and
informal; use of buildiing materials (stone, brick,
wood); people in living and working environments

Access and conditions Open to the public by
appt (tel). All material available for editorial
reproduction and for advertising. Reproduction
rights, holding and service fees charged; service
fees deductible from use fee; rental fee charged if
material unused. All material copyright. Card
catalogue available.

211 • SYNDICATION INTERNATIONAL

4-12 Dorrington Street, London EC1N 7TB
Tel (01) 831 6751/8

Enquiries to Picture Librarian

Items About one million: b/w original

photographs, b/w copy photographs, colour transparencies (35mm, 5″ × 4″), glass negatives, original cartoons

Dates of subject matter 1900 to present

Dates of photographs 1900 to present

Subjects Material from *Mirror* Group Newspapers and IPC women's and juveniles' magazines; emphasis on news events, personalities, royalty, sport, entertainment, fashion and beauty; special collections include the JAMES BARR COLLECTION of educational and geographical material; comic strips and cartoons

Access and conditions Open to qualified researchers by appt (first-time users write), Mon-Fri 9.30–5.30. All material available for editorial reproduction and for advertising (some restrictions). B/w and colour material loaned free of charge for one month (print fees charged). Reproduction rights, holding and service fees charged. Staff will undertake some research; negotiable research fee charged. All material copyright.

212 • PATRICK THURSTON COLOUR LIBRARY

10 Willis Road, Cambridge CB1 2AQ
Tel (01) 359 2153, (0223) 352547

Enquiries to Patrick Thurston

Items 6000: colour transparencies (35mm)

Dates of subject matter Prehistory to present

Dates of photographs 1960 to present

Subjects General coverage of Britain including landscapes, climatic conditions, monuments, museums, towns, villages, bridges, canals, castles, cathedrals, public houses, transport, customs, recreation; overseas coverage includes Amsterdam, Bangkok, Eire, Elba, Rome, Tokyo, Venice and Vienna

Access and conditions Open to qualifed researchers by appt (tel), Mon-Fri 9–6. All material available for editorial reproduction and for advertising. Colour material loaned free of charge for one month. Reproduction rights and service fees charged. Staff of two will undertake research. Photographer available for assignment. All material copyright. Card catalogue available.

213 • TIMES NEWSPAPERS LIMITED

The Times, The Sunday Times and *The Sunday Times Magazine*

PO Box 7, 200 Gray's Inn Road, London WC1X 8EZ
Tel (01) 837 1234 Telex 264971

Enquiries to Photosales for b/w material, Syndication Department for colour material

Items About five million: b/w original photographs, colour transparencies (35mm, 5″ × 4″)

Dates of subject matter 1922 to present

Dates of photographs 1922 to present

Subjects National and international news coverage including political, social and sports events and personalities; special collections include TOPIX PHOTOGRAPHS 1914–1974, GRAPHIC PHOTO UNION, KEMSLEY, *daily sketch* and SUNDAY GRAPHIC

Access and conditions Open to the public by appt (write), Mon-Fri 10.30–5. Most material available for editorial reproduction and for advertising. Colour material loaned for a fee; b/w prints available for a fee. Reproduction rights and holding fees charged. Staff will undertake some research; negotiable research fee charged. All material copyright. Card catalogue available.

214 • TOPHAM PICTURE LIBRARY

P.O. Box 33, Edenbridge, Kent TN8 5PB
Tel (034286) 313 Telex 95351 ANSWERBACK TOPHAM G

Enquiries to Joanna Smith

Items Three million: b/w original photographs, b/w negatives, colour transparencies (35mm, 2¼″, 5″ × 4″, larger), original cartoons, glass negatives, woodcuts and engravings, postcards, colour photographic prints, illustrated books

Dates of subject matter Prehistory to present

Dates of photographs 1850 to present

Subjects Worldwide news events and features, politics, social and political history, trade union movement, union leaders, industries, world geography, military history, agriculture and rural life, urban development, transport (road, rail, air, sea), crime, entertainment, personalities, fashion, sport, natural history, Royalty, religion, League of Nations, World War I, Sino-Japanese War, World

War II and UK homefront; English social history, Edwardian life; world history (engravings). The central JOHN TOPHAM COLLECTION (1927–1965) has been supplemented by acquisition of material from the files of the news agencies United Press International (UPI), Planet News, Acme, International News Photos (INP) and INI; photographs syndicated by the Press Association (PA), Associated Press (AP) and Universal Pictorial Press (UPP) are available from Topham to book publishers 30 days after release date; other collections include COUNCIL FOR THE PROTECTION OF RURAL ENGLAND (CPRE) 1930–1935, PICTUREPOINT b/w 1945–1965, JOHN MARKHAM/NATURE CONSERVANCY 1935–1972, Francis Frith and other Victorian and Edwardian photographers 1850–1914, Harold Bastin 1900–1960, Bruce Coleman b/w 1960 to present, *Geographical Magazine* 1966–1975, Alfieri b/w 1914–1940, Central News (incorporating Exclusive News Agency) 1900–1935, *Private Eye* cartoons 1962 to present

Access and conditions Open to qualified researchers by appt (tel), Mon-Sat 8am–10pm. All material available for editorial reproduction and for advertising. B/w and colour material loaned free of charge; loan period from 14 days to 60 days (book publishers only). Photocopies available. Reproduction rights, service and holding fees charged. Staff of nine will undertake research. Card and printed catalogues.

215 • TESSA TRAEGER

7 Rossetti Studios, 72 Flood Street, London
SW3 5TF
Tel (01) 352 3641

Enquiries to Kate Gadsby

Items 7000: colour transparencies (35mm, 5″ × 4″)

Dates of photographs 1970 to present

Subjects Gardens including herb, water, formal, cottage and large gardens; food; landscapes in UK; travel in Europe and Far East with emphasis on France and Italy including restaurants and food; flower collages, children's fashion

Access and conditions Open to the public by appt (tel). All material available for editorial reproduction and for advertising. Colour material loaned free of charge for one month. Reproduction rights, holding and service fees charged. Staff will undertake limited research. All material copyright.

216 • TRANSWORLD FEATURE SYNDICATE (UK) LTD

Tubs Hill House, Sevenoaks, Kent TN13 1BL
Tel (0732) 458204 Telex 95677

Enquiries to Shirley Wergan, Picture Manager

Items 350,000: colour transparencies (35mm)

Dates of subject matter 1970 to present

Dates of photographs 1970 to present

Subjects Magazine material covering fashion, beauty, fitness, health, children, babies, romance, with special emphasis on material from *Elle*, *McCalls*, *Vital* and magazines published by Mondadori and Rizzoli; also material from English *Parents*, French *Parents*, *20 Ans* and *Jacinte*; stills from contemporary American television with emphasis on material from Shooting Star Agency, California; British television actors and actresses; material from Yorkshire Television and *TV Times*

Access and conditions Open to qualified researchers by appt (first-time users write), Mon-Fri 8.30–5.30. Colour material loaned free of charge for three weeks. Reproduction rights, service and search fees charged. Staff of four will undertake research. All material copyright.

217 • TRAVEL PHOTO INTERNATIONAL

8 Delph Common Road, Aughton, Ormskirk, Lancashire L39 5DW
Tel (0695) 423720

Enquiries to Vivienne Crimes

Items 90,000: colour transparencies (35mm, 7 × 6 cm, 2¼″)

Dates of subject matter BC to present

Dates of photographs 1975 to present

Subjects Landscape, worldwide geography, architecture, travel, human interaction, archaeology, agriculture, geology, sunsets, clouds, flowers and fruit

Access and conditions Open to the public by appt (tel). All material available for editorial reproduction and for advertising. Colour material loaned free of charge for 28 days. Reproduction rights and holding fees charged; service fees charged only when no material is used. Staff will undertake some research. All material copyright. Duplicated catalogue available.

218 • TROPIX PHOTOGRAPHIC LIBRARY

156 Meols Parade, Meols, Wirral, Merseyside
L47 6AN
Tel (051) 632 1698

Enquiries to Veronica Birley, Director

Items Over 25,000: colour transparencies (35mm),
b/w original photographs

Dates of subject matter BC to present

Dates of photographs 19th century to present

Subjects All aspects of life in the tropical, sub-
tropical and developing regions of the world
including Argentina, Afghanistan, Bangladesh,
Belize, Benin, Brazil, Cameroon, Cayman Islands,
Chile, Colombia, Egypt, Ethiopia, Ghana, India,
Israel, Ivory Coast, Jordan, Kenya, Libya,
Malaysia, Maldives, Morocco, Nigeria, Papua New
Guinea, Philippines, Saharan region, St Lucia,
Sierra Leone, Soviet Central Asia, Sri Lanka,
Sudan, Tanzania, Thailand, Togo, Tunisia, Turkey,
United Arab Emirates, Upper Volta, Zimbabwe:
urban, rural and desert dwelling peoples, social and
family groups, festivals, religion, clothing and
costume, crafts, painting and sculpture, music,
musical instruments, dancing, food and drink;
architecture, housing (apartments, colonial, high-
rise, labour camps, mud huts, shanty and slum,
tents, urban sprawl); education and adult literacy,
agriculture, livestock, machinery, tools, sprays,
crop pests, industry and trade (fishing, textiles,
timber, cottage industries, tourism, bazaars,
supermarkets, street traders), docks, transport
(aircraft, train, boat, bus, lorry, car, cycle, dhow,
handcart, rickshaw); climatic conditions, flora and
fauna including coverage of Mediterranean flora,
habitats (mountains, deserts, marshes, semi-
deserts, salt rivers), conservation including erosion
and control, land use, deforestation, afforestation;
research biologists working in medicine and
agriculture; pollution (urban, water supplies, open
sewers, refuse); alternative and intermediate
technologies including natural sources of energy;
catchment, conservation, storage and use of water;
medicine and health care including traditional
medicine, health centres and dispensaries,
hospitals, mother and baby clinics, immunisation,
hygiene, nutrition and health education; medical
workers including doctors, nurses, medical
auxiliaries, laboratory technicians, medical
researchers; tropical diseases, cases, parasites,
disease vectors, research and control; small
collection of photographs of life in West Africa
c. 1900

Access and conditions Open to qualified
researchers by appt (write), Mon-Fri 9–5. All
material available for editorial reproduction and
for advertising. B/w and colour material loaned free
of charge for one month. Reproduction rights,
holding and service fees charged. Staff will
undertake research; fees charged for large projects.
Photographers available for assignment. All
material copyright. Computer lists available.

219 • TURNER'S TRAVELS

7 Rosewood Avenue, Burnham-on-Sea, Somerset
TA8 1HD
Tel (0278) 783519

Enquiries to Michael Turner

Items About 3000: colour transparencies (35mm),
illustrated maps

Dates of photographs 1982 to present

Subjects Travel coverage of Egypt, Thailand,
Mexico, Panama, Costa Rica, Nicaragua,
Honduras, El Salvador, Guatemala including
lifestyles, poverty and human interaction; special
coverage of places visited by Sir Francis Drake

Access and conditions Open to the public by
appt (write). All material available for editorial
reproduction and for advertising. Colour material
loaned free of charge for eight weeks. Reproduction
rights, service and holding fees charged. Staff will
undertake some research. All material copyright.
Subject list available.

220 • THE TWO AND A QUARTER SQUARE GLAMOR LIBRARY LTD

112-116 Park Hill Road, Harborne, Birmingham
B17 9HD
Tel (021) 426 1600

Enquiries to Peter Donnelly, Director

Items 1200: colour transparencies (2¼″)

Dates of subject matter 1978 to present

Dates of photographs 1978 to present

Subjects Posed models in variety of settings

Access and conditions Open to qualified
researchers by appt (tel), Mon-Fri 9.–5.30. All
material available for editorial reproduction and
for advertising. Colour material loaned free of
charge for ten days; duplicate colour

transparencies available for a fee. Reproduction rights fees charged. Staff of four will undertake some research. All material copyright.

221 • UNIVERSAL FEATURES

9 Paradise Close, Eastbourne, East Sussex
BN20 8BT
Tel (0323) 28760

Enquiries to John Hamilton, Picture Editor

Items 500,000: b/w original photographs, b/w copy photographs, colour transparencies (35mm)

Dates of photographs 1969 to present

Subjects Personalities including sports, television and film personalities; coverage of crime in UK, USA, Germany and Scandinavia with emphasis on unusual crime; at-home photo-stories of famous people; red-light districts and night-clubs in most major cities worldwide

Access and conditions Open to qualified researchers by appt (write). All material available for editorial reproduction and for advertising. B/w and colour material loaned free of charge for three months. Photocopies available. Reproduction rights, holding and service fees charged. Staff will undertake limited research. Most material copyright.

222 • UNIVERSAL PICTORIAL PRESS & AGENCY LTD

30-34 New Bridge Street, London EC4V 6BN
Tel (01) 248 6730   Telex 8952718 UNIPIX G

Enquiries to Jo Banks, Librarian

Items 700,000: b/w negatives, colour transparencies (35mm, 6 × 6 cm)

Dates of photographs 1944 to present

Subjects UK news and features including personalities, royalty, politics, trade unionism, civil service, education, public and professional organizations, business, law, religion, diplomacy, military, writing, journalism, arts, ballet, opera, music, theatre, television, cinema, pop music, football, Rugby, cricket, tennis, athletics, swimming, golf, boxing, skating, motor-car and cycle-racing, horse-racing, showjumping, architecture and landscapes, mostly UK; some overseas material

Access and conditions Open to qualified researchers by appt (tel), Mon-Fri 9–5.30. All material available for editorial reproduction, but not for advertising. B/w material loaned free of charge (period negotiable); colour loaned for a rental fee. B/w prints and duplicate colour transparencies available for a fee. Reproduction rights and service fees charged. Staff of 34 will undertake research.

223 • UNIVERSITY COLLEGE OF NORTH WALES

Department of Manuscripts

Arts Library, College Road, Bangor, Gwynedd
LL57 2DG
Tel (0248) 351151   Telex 61100

Enquiries to Tomos Roberts

Items About 1500: b/w original and copy photographs, postcards, glass negatives, architectural drawings, colour transparencies (35mm), lantern slides, colour photographic prints

Dates of subject matter c.1284 to present

Dates of photographs c. 1870 to present

Subjects North Wales local history, especially architecture and including castles, churches, country houses and other buildings; Welsh religious, literary and educational personalities; glass negatives by F. H. May of Pwllheli (commercial photographer), views of North Wales towns and villages 1920–1930; officers, staff and students of UCNW Bangor 1884–1984; postcards of European towns and cities collected by J. R. and Anne Williams c. 1923–1936

Access and conditions Open to the public, Mon-Fri 9–1, 2–5. All material available for editorial reproduction. Material must be copied by outside photographers. No reproduction rights fees charged. Staff will undertake limited research.

224 • UNIVERSITY OF READING

The Library, Whiteknights, Reading, Berkshire
RG6 2AE
Tel (0734) 874331

Enquiries to Dr J. A. Edwards, Keeper of Archives and Manuscripts

Items About 2000: b/w original and copy

photographs, colour transparencies (35mm), colour photographic prints, glass negatives, illustrated books, old fine art prints, posters, lantern slides, postcards, original cartoons, illustrated maps, art reproductions, unprinted film negatives, architectural drawings

Dates of subject matter *c.* 1700 to 1960

Dates of photographs Early 20th century to present

Subjects Archival material including photographs relating to the University, Huntley and Palmer biscuit factory, the Astor family; historical agricultural photographs; productions of Samuel Beckett's plays; watercolours and drawings by Eleanor Watkins between 1914 and 1939 mainly of botanical subjects but also of people in Malaya and South Africa

Access and conditions Open to the public by appt (write), Mon-Fri 9–5. Most material available for editorial reproduction and for advertising. No loans; b/w prints and duplicate colour transparencies available for a fee. Photocopies available. Reproduction rights fees charged. Staff will undertake limited research. Most material copyright.

225 • UNIVERSITY OF SALFORD ARCHIVES

Photographic Archive, Clifford Whitworth University Library, The Crescent, Salford, Greater Manchester M5 4WT
Tel (061) 736 5843

Enquiries to J. C. P. Blunden-Ellis

Items 1400: b/w original and copy photographs, colour transparencies (35mm), glass negatives, fine art prints, unprinted film negatives, posters, press cuttings and tearsheets

Dates of subject matter *c.* 1800 to present

Dates of photographs 1890 to present

Subjects WEIR COLLECTION: railways, especially signalling and the School of Signalling, some scenes of stations and steam trains (*c.* 1900–1915), locomotives; SALFORD FILM COLLECTION, *The Changing Face of Salford*, industrial archaeology, industrial scenes, buildings; WALTER GREENWOOD COLLECTION: (Salford novelist) portraits, press cuttings, announcements, notices, posters, tickets; STANLEY HOUGHTON COLLECTION: (Salford author) first-night photographs of his play, *Hindle Wakes*;

SALFORD UNIVERSITY COLLECTION: buildings, laboratories and classrooms dating back to 1890s; photo of L. S. Lowry at work in the School of Art

Access and conditions Open to qualified researchers by appt (write). All material available for editorial reproduction and for advertising. B/w and colour material loaned; material may be copied by outside photographers. Photocopies available for a fee. No reproduction rights fees charged. Staff will undertake limited research.

226 • UNIVERSITY OF WARWICK LIBRARY

Modern Records Centre, Coventry, Warwickshire CV4 7AL
Tel (0203) 24011 ext 2014

Enquiries to Richard Storey, Archivist

Items About 1500: b/w original and copy photographs, lantern slides, postcards, posters, ephemera

Dates of subject matter 19th and 20th centuries

Dates of photographs 1900 to present

Subjects Maurice Edelman (wartime service and as MP), comedian Robb Wilton (portraits and performances), Sir Leslie Scott (Lord Justice of Appeal, MP, barrister), Lady Allen of Hurtwood (landscape architect, campaigner for children's welfare); China, civil disturbances (1920s); Germany (1936) including Olympic Games, decorations; Germany (1946) including visit by Victor Gollancz; adventure playgrounds for children and other play facilities (1960s); toy-making by firemen (World War II); trade union conferences, group portraits; motor-cycle shows, cycle publicity; British prisons

Access and conditions Open to the public by appt, Mon-Fri 9–5. Some material available for editorial reproduction but not for advertising. No loans: b/w prints available for a fee. Material may be copied by outside photographers. No reproduction rights fees charged. Staff of three will undertake some research (30 minues per query). Printed catalogue.

227 • VIDOCQ PHOTO LIBRARY

9 Vicarage Street, Frome, Somerset BA11 1TX
Tel (0373) 64548

Enquiries to Joan Bishop, Picture Researcher

Items 250,000: b/w original photographs, b/w copy photographs, colour transparencies (35mm, 5″ × 4″), glass negatives

Dates of subject matter Prehistory to present

Dates of photographs 1930 to present

Subjects Geography (worldwide coverage) with emphasis on Sri Lanka, the Far East, Africa, Yugoslavia, Greenland and Iceland; agriculture, aircraft, architecture, custom-built and vintage cars, railways, education, flora and fauna (including some Caribbean coverage), insects including butterflies and moths (some electron micrographs), inland waterways, industrial waste disposal, sports including cycling and horse-racing, yachts, theatre; special collection of Yorkshire in the 1930s and 1940s

Access and conditions Open by appt, Mon-Fri 9–6. All material available for editorial reproduction and for advertising. B/w and colour material loaned free of charge for 60 days. Reproduction rights, holding and service fees charged; service fees deductible from use fees. Most material is held by individual photographers for whom Vidocq act as agents and consignments are called in according to clients' requirements. All material copyright.

228 • VIEWFINDER COLOUR PHOTO LIBRARY

The Production House, 147A St Michaels Hill, Cotham, Bristol BS2 8DB
Tel (0272) 731729

Enquiries to Sarah Boait, Proprietor

Items 15,000: colour transparencies (35mm, 5″ × 4″)

Dates of subject matter Prehistory to present

Dates of photographs 1974 to present

Subjects Geography including Europe and UK, USA, Middle East, Hong Kong, Nepal and India; detailed coverage of south-west England and South Wales including landscapes, seascapes, climatic conditions, the seasons, natural history, wild and domestic animals and birds, social groups, agriculture, industry, transport; social documentary features on Welsh miners, steelworkers, police training, Northern Ireland, Eton College; special effects and creative pictorials

Access and conditions Open to qualified

researchers by appt (tel), Mon-Fri 9–6. All material available for editorial reproduction and for advertising. Colour material loaned free of charge for one month. Reproduction rights, holding and service fees charged. Staff will undertake research. Photographers available for assignment. All material copyright.

229 • VISION INTERNATIONAL

30 Museum Street, London WC1A 1LH
Tel (01) 636 9516 Telex 23539 VISION G

Enquiries to Susan Pinkus or David Alexander, Directors

Items 500,000: b/w original photographs, b/w copy photographs, colour transparencies (35mm, 5″ × 4″, 10″ × 8″), glass negatives, old fine art prints, 20th-century fine art prints

Dates of subject matter Prehistory to present

Dates of photographs 1890 to present

Subjects Worldwide geography and travel, pregnancy, birth and child development to adolescence, health and medicine, industry, computer technology, agriculture, plants and gardens, natural history and wildlife, architecture, sport, fine art, religion, family life, transport including railways, landscapes, underwater photography; special collections include the DONALD MCLEISH COLLECTION, the CNRI FRENCH MEDICAL COLLECTION (including photomicrographs) and Scala fine art material

Access and conditions Open to qualified researchers by appt (tel), Mon-Fri 9.30–5.30. All material available for editorial reproduction and for advertising (some restrictions). B/w and colour material loaned free of charge for one month; b/w prints available for a fee. Photocopies and Polaroids available. Reproduction rights, holding and service fees charged; service fees deductible from use fees. Staff of four will undertake some research. Photographers available for assignment. All material copyright.

230 • VISNEWS SLIDE SERVICE

Cumberland Avenue, Park Royal, London NW10 7EH
Tel (01) 965 7733 Telex 22678

Enquiries to Pauline McElhatton, Head of Slide Service

Items 60,000: colour transparencies (35mm), illustrative maps

Dates of subject matter 1910 to present

Dates of photographs 1972 to present

Subjects News coverage of international political personalities including heads of state, government ministers, international delegates, ambassadors, heads of international organizations; international locations including capital cities, monuments, important buildings, government centres, airports, military headquarters, banks, religious centres; aircraft, military hardware, spacecraft and satellites; sports personalities; stills available from contemporary news action pictures recorded on film and videotape; stills available from Gaumont Graphic, Empire News Bulletin, Gaumont British News, Universal News and British Paramount News newsreels giving worldwide coverage of all significant political and social events since the beginning of the century

Access and conditions Open to the public by appt (tel), Mon-Fri 9–6. All material available for editorial reproduction and for advertising. Colour material loaned free of charge for one month; duplicate colour transparencies available for a fee. Reproduction rights, holding and service fees charged; service fees deductible from use fees. Staff of three will undertake some research; fees charged for large projects. All material copyright. Computer list in preparation.

231 • VISTACOLOUR

70 Southway, London N20 8DB
Tel (01) 445 3000

Enquiries to Peter Brown

Items 12,000: colour transparencies (2¼", 2¼" × 3¼")

Dates of subject matter 1970 to present

Dates of photographs 1970 to present

Subjects Tourists and tourism worldwide with emphasis on the Mediterranean and the Caribbean but also including India, Sri Lanka and Kenya

Access and conditions Open to qualified researchers by appt (tel), Mon-Fri 9.–5.30. All

material available for editorial reproduction and for advertising. Colour material loaned free of charge for three months. Reproduction rights fees charged. Staff of two will undertake research. Photographers available for assignment. All material copyright.

232 • V S PICTURE LIBRARY

V S Studios, Chelsea Wharf, 15 Lots Road, London SW10 0QH
Tel (01) 351 2592

Enquiries to Katherine Vibert or Ian Stokes

Items 20,000: colour transparencies (35mm, 7 × 6 cm), b/w original photographs, pin-registered sequences (35mm)

Dates of subject matter BC to present

Dates of photographs 1970 to present

Subjects Travel coverage of Belgium, Botswana, Greece, Holland, Norway, Portugal, South Africa (including mining industry), Spain, USA, West Germany; British landscapes, industry, transport, emergency services in action (fire, ambulance and police), social, working and family groups; sports including parachuting, motor racing, sailing, rowing, snooker, skateboarding; detailed coverage of London including landscapes, historic monuments, inner-city poverty, theatres, clubs, parks; male and female posed models, city illuminations, public houses, restaurants (interiors, exteriors, food), house interiors, hotels, stores, community centres; rivers, skies, sunsets, sunrises, moonrises, seashores, natural history (including flowers, lichens, grasses, fungi), trees worldwide; Plymouth landscapes; fashion and beauty; pin-register sequences include flowers opening, dice and coins spinning, sunsets, sunrises, moonrises, waterdrops, snooker balls, flames, traffic, fibre optical effects, rotating globe, night illuminations, industrial machinery in action

Access and conditions Open to the public by appt (tel), Mon-Fri 9–6. All material available for editorial reproduction and for advertising. B/w and colour material loaned free of charge for one month; b/w prints and duplicate colour transparencies available for a fee. Staff will undertake research. Reproduction rights and holding fees charged. All material copyright. Printed subject list available.

233 • WALES EXPRESS SERIES

Express House, Lord Street, Wrexham, Clwyd
LL11 1LR
Tel (0978) 350101

Enquiries to David Robinson, Editor

Items About 2000: unprinted film negatives,
b/w original photographs

Dates of subject matter 1980 to present

Dates of photographs 1980 to present

Subjects News coverage in north-east Wales
including political and cultural events, industry
(coalmining), sport

Access and conditions Open to the public by
appt (tel), Mon-Thurs 9–5, Fri 9–4. All material
available for editorial reproduction and for
advertising. B/w material loaned by arrangement
(print fee charged). Photocopies available.
Reproduction rights fees charged. Staff of two will
undertake some research. All material copyright.
Computer catalogue available.

234 • WALES TOURIST BOARD

Brunel House, 2 Fitzalan Road, Cardiff CF2 1VY
Tel (0222) 499909 Telex 497269

Enquiries to Siân Nelson

Items 37,000: colour transparencies (35mm,
5″ × 4″, larger), b/w photographs

Dates of photographs 1976 to present

Subjects Wales, including activities, sports,
entertainment, events, theatre, music, bridges and
viaducts, castles, houses, historic sites, museums
and art galleries, churches and chapels, crafts,
customs and traditions, coracles, food, markets,
industrial sites, rivers, waterfalls, lakes,
mountains, parks, towns, villages, transport (road,
airports, marinas, railways, narrow-gauge
railways), tourist attractions, accommodation

Access and conditions Open to the public by
appt (tel). All material available for editorial
reproduction and for advertising. B/w prints loaned
free of charge for one month; original colour
transparencies loaned for a deposit or
duplicated for a fee. No reproduction rights fees
charged. Staff will undertake some research.

235 • BRUCE WARLAND COLLECTION

9 Paradise Close, Eastbourne, East Sussex
BN20 8BT
Tel (0323) 28760

Enquiries to John Hamilton

Items About 600,000: colour transparencies
(35mm, 2¼″, 5″ × 4″), b/w original photographs

Dates of photographs 1965 to present

Subjects Posed models (pin-ups, glamour, nudes)
from Bruce Warland Ltd (1965 to 1974); posed
models photographed for Probe Publications Ltd
(five monthly magazines) from 1970 to present; UK
representatives for similar material from US and
Germany (1980 to present)

Access and conditions Open to qualified
researchers by appt (write), Mon-Fri 9–5. All
material available for editorial reproduction and
for advertising; all material fully model-released.
B/w and colour material loaned free of charge for
three months. Photocopies available. Reproduction
rights, service and holding fees charged. Staff will
undertake research.

236 • SIMON WARNER

Whitestone Farm, Stanbury, Keighley, West
Yorkshire BD22 0JW
Tel (0535) 44644

Enquiries to Simon Warner

Items 16,000: b/w unprinted film negatives, colour
transparencies (35mm, 7 × 6 cm)

Dates of subject matter BC to present

Dates of photographs 1967 to present

Subjects General coverage of Britain with special
emphasis on Yorkshire including the Dales, North
York Moors, South Pennines and coastal area
covering natural history, conservation, upland
farming, country life, landscapes, architecture,
tourism, industry; North Wales especially
Snowdonia region

Access and conditions Open to qualified
researchers by appt (tel), Mon-Fri 9–5. All material
available for editorial reproduction and for
advertising. B/w contact prints and colour material
loaned free of charge for two months; b/w
reproduction-quality prints and duplicate colour
transparencies available for a fee. Reproduction
rights and service fees charged; service fees
deductible from use fees. Staff will undertake

research. Photographer available for assignment. All material copyright.

237 • JOHN WATNEY PHOTO LIBRARY

43 Gertrude Street, London SW10 0JQ
Tel (01) 352 0949

Enquiries to Patsy Watney

Items About 50,000: colour transparencies (35mm, 2¼"), b/w original photographs, b/w copy photographs, illustrated books

Dates of subject matter Prehistory to present

Dates of photographs 1970 to present

Subjects Medical photography including photomicrographs and electronmicrographs; geography of the British Isles including Northern Ireland and Eire, North Wales, Highlands and Islands, West Country and south-east coast; some travel coverage of France, Finland (excluding Lapland), Greece, Poland and the Sinai area of the Red Sea; Royal Marine Commandos on exercises in the United Kingdom, Arctic and the Mediterranean; steamboats and steam vehicles; general coverage of miscellanea such as herbs, manufacture of glass eyeballs, snuff and screws, a sawmill in action, wine-tasting, graveyards; special collection of b/w prints of etchings, engravings and woodcuts of historical and medical subjects

Access and conditions Open to qualified researchers by appt (tel), Mon-Fri 9.30–6. All material available for editorial reproduction and for advertising. B/w and colour material loaned free of charge for one month. Reproduction rights and holding fees charged. Staff will undertake research. 98% of material copyright. Catalogue in preparation.

238 • WEIDENFELD (PUBLISHERS) LTD

91 Clapham High Street, London SW4 7TA
Tel (01) 622 9933

Enquiries to Simon Cobley, Archivist

Items About 180,000: b/w original and copy photographs, colour transparencies (35mm, 5" × 4", 10" × 8")

Dates of subject matter BC to present

Dates of photographs 1900 to present

Subjects Landscapes, gardens, flowers, architecture, historical houses, furniture, domestic life, food, portraits of historical figures including politicians, explorers, aristocrats, scientists, novelists, poets; naval warfare, Jewish history, kings and queens of England, historical fashion, books and manuscripts, religion, psychology, music, art including some Oriental coverage

Access and conditions Open to qualified researchers by appt (tel), Mon-Fri 9.30–5.30. All material available for editorial reproduction; advertising use by special arrangement only. B/w and colour material loaned free of charge for six months. Photocopies available. Reproduction rights fees charged; holding fees charged if material not used. Most material copyright.

239 • WESTWARD HO ADVENTURE HOLIDAYS LTD

10 Belgrave Road, London SW13 9NS
Tel (01) 741 1494

Enquiries to Sir Ranulph Fiennes

Items 8000: colour transparencies (35mm), b/w original photographs, colour photographic prints, press cuttings

Dates of photographs 1968 to present

Subjects Voyages of exploration and discovery incuding the White Nile by hovercraft (1968), people, ruins, deserts; the Jostedalsbre Glacier (Norway) including parachute drop to top of glacier and survey of glaciers on the east of Jostedalsbre; Dhofar (Oman) war (1968–1970) and later comparative journeys (1971, 1972, 1979, 1984); British Columbia, first journey by river through BC from the Yukon to the US including South Nahanni River, Liard River, Hiland River, Kechika and Tochieka (Fox) Rivers, Fraser River, Parsnip River, Pack and Crooked Rivers, Peace Bennett Dam, landscapes, animals, rubber boats in rapids; Greenland (Thule District), sledge journey into interior and along coast; North Pole, journey towards pole for five months (1978) on foot, in open snow, etc.; Transglobe Expedition, journey around earth's polar axis, Antarctic and Arctic Oceans, Northwest Passage, Northern Canada, Sahara, Pacific Ocean (north to south), Atlantic Ocean (south to north), Campbell Island and its fauna, Ellesmere Island, wintering in both polar continents and reaching both poles, animals, flora, birds, local people, terrain, ice formations, sand dunes, African rain forest

Access and conditions Open to qualified researchers by appt. All material available for editorial reproduction and for advertising. User must collect material and arrange for duplicate prints or transparencies to be made. Reproduction rights and service fees charged. Staff will undertake some research. All material copyright.

240 • WHITE AND REED

12A Castle Street, Reading, Berkshire RG1 7RD
Tel (0734) 56628

Enquiries to David White or Richard Reed, Partners

Items More than 6000: b/w original photographs, colour transparencies (35mm)

Dates of subject matter 1950 to present

Dates of photographs 1950 to present

Subjects Coverage of news events including personalities and sport from the Thames Valley area between Swindon, Oxford, Basingstoke and Heathrow; special collection of animal pictures

Access and conditions Open to qualified researchers by appt (write), Mon-Fri 9–5. All material available for editorial reproduction and for advertising. No loans; b/w prints and duplicate colour transparencies available for a fee. Photocopies available. Reproduction rights fees charged. Staff will undertake research. All material copyright.

241 • LIAM WHITE PHOTOGRAPHY

296 South Lambeth Road, London SW8 1UJ
Tel (01) 627 4406

Enquiries to Liam White

Items 12,000: colour transparencies (35mm), b/w original photographs

Dates of subject matter Prehistory to present

Dates of photographs 1974 to present

Subjects General coverage including education and agriculture but with special emphasis on development and aid agencies in Kenya, Tanzania, Rwanda, Sudan, Zambia, Lesotho, Guatemala, Honduras, Philippines, and Hong Kong; portraits of British writers, historians, academics and politicians; leisure and pleasure in England

including morris dancing, brass bands, picnics, fêtes, re-enactment of Civil War battles; London including tourist sites, shops, parks, canals, pageantry, public and private art galleries, concert halls and concerts; some coverage of Scotland, Wales, France and New York City including the St Patrick's Day Parade and Irish pubs in the city; special collection on the Roman Catholic Church worldwide covering missionary activity, major events and personalities since 1974

Access and conditions Open to qualified researchers by appt (tel), Mon-Fri 9–6. All material available for editorial reproduction and for advertising. B/w and colour material loaned free of charge for one month; b/w prints and duplicate colour transparencies available for a fee. Photocopies available. Reproduction rights, holding and service fees charged; service fees deductible from use fees. Staff will undertake research. Photographer available for assignment. All material copyright. Printed list available.

242 • DEREK G. WIDDICOMBE

Oldfield, High Street, Clayton West, Huddersfield, West Yorkshire HD8 9NS
Tel (0484) 862638

Enquiries to Derek Widdicombe

Items 70,000: colour transparencies (35mm, 2¼″, 2¼″ × 3¼″), b/w original photographs, unprinted film negatives

Dates of subject matter BC to present

Dates of photographs 1953 to present

Subjects Coverage of the UK including geology, landscapes (lakes, mountains, rivers, forests, coastlines), climatic conditions, the seasons, natural history, wildlife, pollution, national parks, archaeology, monuments, architecture, National Trust properties, palaces, churches, chapels, houses, hotels, inns, oasthouses, tithe barns, almshouses, civic buildings, museums and art galleries, agriculture, agricultural shows, auctions, markets; industries including construction, mining, quarrying, energy, paper mills, woollen mills, horticulture; festivals, leisure, theatre, music, art, sport, education, transport, religion; babies, children, old people; special collections include Noel Habgood's landscape photographs and Colin Westwood's architectural photographs

Access and conditions Open to qualified researchers by appt (tel), Mon-Fri 9–5. All material available for editorial reproduction and for advertising. B/w and colour material loaned free of charge for one month. Reproduction rights, holding and service fees charged; service fees deductible from use fees. Staff will undertake research; negotiable research fee charged. All material copyright. Subject index available.

243 • JANINE WIEDEL PHOTO LIBRARY

6 Stirling Road, London SW9 9EE
Tel (01) 737 0007

Enquiries to Janine Wiedel

Items 10,000: b/w original photographs, colour transparencies (35mm)

Dates of photographs 1965 to present

Subjects Industry including factories and places of work, steel mills, coal mines, chain makers, drop forges, Stoke-on-Trent potteries, Birmingham jewellery quarter, offices; people at work including factory workers, lathe and machine operators, production line workers, shop workers, craft workers, farmers; schools and education including West Indians, teachers and students, an inner London comprehensive school, the Yehudi Menuhin Violin School, school for the deaf, schools for the mentally subnormal, free schools, semi-free schools (Kirkdale), New York store-front projects (Harlem), Bedford-Stuyvesant Museum School (Brooklyn, NY); peoples including Eskimos, Iranians, Irish tinkers, gypsies, West Indians, Indians, etc.; social issues including unemployment, the homeless, immigrant groups, marches and demonstrations, English festivities; medicine including pregnancy and childbirth, operating room, midwifery, nurses and doctors; recreation including bingo, dancing, pubs, mime and theatre artists, hang gliding, horse-races, skiing; USA including New York streets, Wall Street area, schools, Harlem nursery school, Vermont snow scenes, San Francisco streets, California, Black Panther movement, Berkeley Peoples' Park riot (1969), Yosemite National Park, Bicentennial (Boston area), New England; portraits including Henry Moore, Edward Steichen, Ned O'Gorman, Gordon Wasson, Salvador Dali, Stephan Grapelli; represented by Black Star in New York

Access and conditions Open to qualified researchers by appt (tel), Mon-Fri 9–6. All material available for editorial reproduction and for advertising. B/w material loaned free of charge for three months; colour for one month. Reproduction rights, service and holding fees charged. Staff will undertake research.

244 • THOMAS A. WILKIE CO. LTD

41-2 Drummond Road, Guildford, Surrey GU1 4NX
Tel (0483) 573810

Enquiries to Thomas Wilkie, Managing Director

Items Over 100,000: b/w original photographs, b/w copy photographs, colour transparencies (35mm, 7 × 6 cm, 5″ × 4″), glass negatives

Dates of subject matter 1831 to present

Dates of photographs 1860 to present

Subjects All aspects of agriculture in the UK (including factory farming) since the 1950s covering breeds of cattle, sheep, pigs, poultry, crops, machinery, buildings, and landscapes; French agriculture since 1980; general travel coverage of France, Holland and Spain, winter sports in Austria (skiing and toboganning), mountaineering in Snowdonia, Cornwall and the Swiss Alps and 1950–1970; UK sports coverage of the 1950s and 1960s; wine production in France, Germany, Austria and Spain including vineyards, bottling plants, and finished products; local history of Guildford since 1831 including landscapes, architecture, social history and portraits

Access and conditions Open to qualified researchers by appt (write), Mon-Thurs 8.30–5.30. All material available for editorial reproduction and for advertising. B/w material loaned free of charge for 14 days; colour transparencies loaned free of charge for 30 days; b/w prints and duplicate colour transparencies available for a fee. Reproduction rights, holding and service fees charged; service fees deductible from use fees. Staff of three will undertake some research; negotiable research fee charged. Photographers available for assignment. All material copyright. Printed catalogue available free of charge.

245 • ANDY WILLIAMS PHOTO LIBRARY

3 Levylsdene, Merrow, Guildford, Surrey GU1 2RS
Tel (0483) 572778

SYNDICATION INTERNATIONAL
presents

THE PICTUREGOER LIBRARY

AN ALL STAR CAST
from
40 GOLDEN YEARS OF FILM-MAKING

CONTACT: S.I. LIBRARY   4-12 DORRINGTON STREET   LONDON EC1N 7TB

TEL: DAYTIME: 01-831 6751 ex. 53 or 51
NIGHTLINE: 01-831 6758

Enquiries to Andy Williams

Items 20,000: colour transparencies (6 × 7 cm, 5″ × 4″)

Dates of subject matter 1960 to present

Dates of photographs 1960 to present

Subjects General landscape and architectural coverage of Great Britain and Northern Ireland including churches, cathedrals, historic houses, cottages, old inns, harbours, sunsets, atomspheric pictures; special section on London scenes including tourist and historic locations; general travel, architectural and landscape coverage of Austria, Belgium, Eire, France, Hong Kong, Majorca, Netherlands, Switzerland and West Germany

Access and conditions Open to qualified researchers by appt (tel). All material available for editorial reproduction and for advertising. Colour transparencies loaned free of charge for 28 days. Reproduction rights, holding and service fees charged. Staff of three will undertake research. Photographer available for assignment. All material copyright. Card catalogue of London pictures available.

246 • D. C. WILLIAMSON

Basement, 68A Redcliffe Square, London SW10 9BN
Tel (01) 373 2160

Enquiries to David Williamson, Proprietor

Items 20,000: colour transparencies (35mm, 5″ × 4″), b/w original photographs

Dates of subject matter BC to present

Dates of photographs 1964 to present

Subjects General travel coverage of Eastern Europe including Armenia, Azerbaijan, Bulgaria, Czechoslovakia, Georgia, Hungary, Lithuania, Mongolia, Poland, Romania, Siberia, Uzbekistan, Yugoslavia: landscapes, cities, tourist resorts, historical buildings and monuments, some industrial material including locomotive manufacture and servicing and chemical equipment in Yugoslavia, food processing in Hungary; also general travel coverage of Austria, Belgium, Channel Islands, England and Wales, France, West Germany, Greece, Malta, Netherlands, Malaysia, Singapore, Thailand

Access and conditions Open to qualified researchers by appt (write). All material available

for editorial reproduction and for advertising. B/w and colour material loaned free of charge for four weeks; b/w prints and duplicate colour transparencies available for a fee. Reproduction rights, service and holding fees charged; service fees deductible from use fees. Staff will undertake some research. Photographers available for assignment. All material copyright. Computer subject lists available.

247 • VAL WILMER

10 Sydner Road, London N16 7UG
Tel (01) 249 1205

Enquiries to Val Wilmer

Items 40,000: b/w original photographs, colour transparencies (35mm), b/w copy photographs, posters, ephemera

Dates of subject matter 1920 to present

Dates of photographs 1960 to present

Subjects Black and popular western music with special emphasis on black performers, locations and cultural settings, and including jazz, gospel, blues, soul, rock, reggae in the USA, Europe and Africa; British rock bands and artists of the 1960s; English, Irish, Moroccan, Turkish, West African folk music; political and social coverage of black culture in the USA, and Afro-Caribbean and Asian culture in the UK; general travel coverage of Morocco, Gambia, Sierra Leone, Liberia, Ghana, Nigeria, Niger, Togo, Benin; women's movement, gay and lesbian cultural and political events in Britain since 1970

Access and conditions Open to qualified researchers by appt (tel), Mon-Fri 9–5. All material available for editorial reproduction and for advertising. B/w and colour material loaned free of charge for one month; b/w prints and duplicate colour transparencies available for a fee. Reproduction rights, holding and service fees charged. Staff will undertake some research. Photographer available for assignment. All material copyright.

248 • REECE WINSTONE

23 Hyland Grove, Bristol BS9 3NR
Tel (0272) 503646

Enquiries to Reece Winstone

Items 50,000: b/w original and copy photographs

Dates of photographs 1840 to present

Subjects Bath and Bristol including architecture, streets, historical monuments, transport; landscape coverage of the British Isles including human interaction, customs

Access and conditions Not open; telephone and postal requests only. All material available for editorial reproduction and for advertising. B/w material loaned free of charge for one month. Reproduction rights fees charged. All material copyright.

249 • TIMOTHY WOODCOCK PHOTOGRAPHY

82 Sirdar Road, London N22 6RD
Tel (01) 889 7459, 889 5455

Enquiries to Timothy Woodcock

Items 15,000: b/w original photographs, colour transparencies (35mm, 5″ × 4″)

Dates of subject matter BC to present

Dates of photographs 1976 to present

Subjects Geographical coverage of the UK, landscapes, architecture of England and Wales including interior shots; children up to 10 years old at home, at school, engaged in various activities; East African wildlife; photographic techniques including use of different lenses, focus, lighting, darkroom techniques

Access and conditions Open to qualified researchers by appt (tel), Mon-Fri 9–5. All material available for editorial reproduction and for advertising. B/w and colour material loaned free of charge for three months. Reproduction rights fees charged. Staff of three will undertake some research. Photographer available for assignment. All material copyright.

250 • JOHN WOODHOUSE COLLECTION

32 Cherrywood Gardens, Nottingham NG3 6LQ
Tel (0602) 504211

Enquiries to John Woodhouse

Items About 7500: b/w original photographs, colour transparencies (35mm), postcards, unprinted film negatives

Dates of photographs 1958 to present

Subjects Mountaineering, adventure sports including ballooning, land yachting, canoeing, hang-gliding, windsurfing, parachuting, pot-holing; comprehensive sports coverage; miscellaneous coverage including accidents, babies, children, churches, ducks, dogs, fairs, fellrunning, ladies, charity football, floods, fogs, hurdling, power stations, sheep, steam engines, toll houses, Vale of Belvoir, youth hostels

Access and conditions Open to the public by appt (tel), Mon-Fri 9–5. All material available for editorial reproduction and for advertising. B/w and colour material loaned free of charge for two months. Reproduction rights fees charged. Research undertaken. Photographer available for assignment. All material copyright.

251 • WOODMANSTERNE PUBLICATIONS LTD

Watford Business Park, Watford, Hertfordshire WD1 8RD
Tel (0923) 28236, 45788

Enquiries to Ruth Powell, Picture Librarian

Items Over 30,000: colour transparencies (35mm, 5″ × 4″, 2¼″ × 3¼″)

Dates of subject matter BC to present

Dates of photographs 1950 to present

Subjects All aspects of life in England, Scotland and Wales: architecture with emphasis on cathedrals and stately homes (coverage of all major cathedrals, National Trust and National Trust for Scotland properties both interior and exterior); landscape, archaeology, geological features, seasonal scenes, animals, birds, insects and spiders, parks and gardens, urban landscapes; the Royal Family, costume, arms and armour, opera and ballet, art exhibits from more than 25 museums and galleries in the UK, sculpture, jewellery, illuminated manuscripts, rare books, textiles, ceramics, metal work; African birds; space exploration including spacecraft and satellites, moon landings, lunar landscapes; transport including aircraft, motor transport, locomotives, ships and boats including hovercrafts; travel coverage of Austria, Bali, Denmark, Finland, France, Germany, Holy Land, India, Iran, Italy, Java, Mali, Nepal, Norway, Peru, Scandinavia, Singapore, Sweden, Switzerland, Turkey;

volcanoes and volcanic activity in Italy, Hawaii, Chile, Peru, Ecuador, Mexico, USA, Iceland, Africa, Canary Islands

Access and conditions Open to the public by appt (tel), Mon-Fri 9–5.30. All material available for editorial reproduction and for advertising. Colour material loaned free of charge for one month. Reproduction rights, holding and service fees charged. Staff of two will undertake some research; fees charged for large projects. Woodmansterne owns copyright to 95% of collection; in other cases copyright clearance is the responsibility of user. Printed subject lists available.

252 • WOOLVERTON COLOUR LIBRARY

Eardisland, Leominster, Herefordshire HR6 9BD
Tel (05447) 584

Enquiries to John or Patricia Woolverton

Items About 10,000: colour transparencies (7 × 6 cm, 5″ × 4″)

Dates of subject matter BC to present

Dates of photographs 1950 to present

Subjects Landscape and architectural coverage of the UK, France, Holland, Belgium, Germany, Switzerland, Austria and Italy including natural history, the seasons, geography

Access and conditions Open to qualified researchers by appt (tel). All material available for editorial reproduction and for advertising. Colour material loaned free of charge for 28 days. Reproduction rights and holding fees charged. Staff will undertake research. All material copyright.

253 • GEORGE WRIGHT

Mountover Farm, Rampisham, Dorchester, Dorset DT2 0PL
Tel (093583) 333

Enquiries to George Wright

Items 15,000: colour transparencies (35mm)

Dates of subject matter BC to present

Dates of photographs 1975 to present

Subjects Prehistoric sites, cathedrals, churches, cities, towns, villages, historic houses and gardens,

landscapes, museums and collections, social groups, regional cookery in England; special section on gardens and gardening; some coverage of material from Museum of Labour History; Middle Eastern coverage including Bahrain, Djibouti, North Yemen, Syria, Turkey; general travel coverage including regional cooking of India, Nepal, Spain, France, Italy, West Germany and Eire

Access and conditions Open to qualified researchers by appt (write), Mon-Fri 9–5. All material available for editorial reproduction and for advertising. Colour material loaned free of charge for one month. Reproduction rights, holding and service fees charged; service fees deductible from use fees. Research undertaken for a fee. Photographers available for assignment. All material copyright.

254 • GEORGE YOUNG PHOTOGRAPHERS

74 Kempock Street, Gourock, Strathclyde PA19 1ND
Tel (0475) 33261/2

Enquiries to Susan Rae

Items 10,000: colour transparencies (35mm, 5″ × 4″), b/w original photographs

Dates of subject matter BC to present

Dates of photographs 1950 to present

Subjects Landscape and scenic pictures of Scotland (including Islands); villages, towns, cities, ancient monuments, transport, human interaction; some coverage of Majorca, Algarve, Ibiza, Austria and Italy

Access and conditions Open to qualified researchers by appt (write), Mon-Fri 9–5.30. All material available for editorial reproduction and for advertising. Colour material loaned free of charge for one month; b/w prints available for a fee. Reproduction rights, holding and service fees charged. Staff will undertake some research for a fee. Photographers available for assignment. All material copyright.

255 • ZEAL PHOTOGRAPHS

Sainfoin, Little Croft Road, Goring, Reading, Berkshire RG8 9ER
Tel (0491) 872227

Enquiries to Gordon Carlisle, Manager

Items 40,000: colour transparencies (35mm, 2¼″), b/w original photographs

Dates of subject matter 1950 to present

Dates of photographs 1950 to present

Subjects Field sports, mainly shooting and fishing in the United Kingdom including game birds and animals, all aspects of gamekeeping, sportsmen and women in action, guns and gundogs, grouse moors, landscapes, rivers, lakes, salmon, trout, fishing tackle; country sports, crafts and pastimes, horse trials, polo matches, gymkhanas, fairs, flower arranging; agriculture, harvesting, farm animals, machinery; forestry; some general European landscape and travel coverage including Andorra, Corfu, Corsica, Crete, France, Greece, Ireland, Portugal, Spain, Yugoslavia; winter sports in Austria, France and Switzerland

Access and conditions Open to the public by appt (tel), Mon-Fri 9–5. All material available for editorial reproduction and for advertising. B/w and colour material loaned free of charge for one month; b/w prints and duplicate colour transparencies available for a fee. Reproduction rights fees charged. Staff will undertake research. All material copyright.

256 • ZEFA PICTURE LIBRARY (UK) LTD

20 Conduit Place, London W2 1HZ
Tel (01) 262 0101

Enquiries to Jackie Townsend, Library Manager

Items 600,000: colour transparencies (35mm, 2¼″, 5″ × 4″, 10″ × 8″)

Dates of subject matter BC to present

Dates of photographs 1950 to present

Subjects Comprehensive contemporary collection including worldwide geography, climatic conditions and phenomena, landscapes, wild and domestic animals, birds, fish, crustacea, insects, natural history, agriculture, human social groups and activities, architecture, industry and industrial processes, computers, crafts, skills, occupations, professions, sports including winter sports, religions, communication, road, rail, sea and air transport, medicine, engineering, science, technology, tourism, leisure, music, art

Access and conditions Open to qualified researchers by appt (tel), Mon-Fri 9.30–5.30. All material available for editorial reproduction and for advertising. Colour material loaned free of charge for 15 days; duplicate colour transparencies available for a fee. Reproduction rights, holding and service fees charged; service fees deductible from use fees. Staff of five will undertake some research. All material copyright.

257 • ZOOM PHOTO SYNDICATION LTD

171A Gloucester Avenue, London NW1 8LA
Tel (01) 722 8823

Enquiries to Derek Burton

Items Four million: b/w original and copy photographs

Dates of photographs 1910 to 1957

Subjects History of past events, personalities, sports, transport, fashion, accidents, geography, royalty, show business, aviation (including Lindbergh's flight), natural history, World War I, Ethiopian-Italian War, World War II, Sino-Japanese War, Korean War, Russia between the wars, natural phenomena (earthquakes, volcanoes), religion, inventions, cities (especially London, New York, Berlin, Hamburg)

Access and conditions Open to qualified researchers by appt (tel), Mon-Fri 9–5. All material available for editorial reproduction and for advertising. B/w material loaned free of charge for one week. Reproduction rights, service and holding fees charged. Staff of four will undertake research. Catalogue in preparation.

Aerial Photography Collections

258 • AERIAL ARCHAEOLOGY AIR PHOTOGRAPHS COLLECTION

Aerial Archaeology Publications, 15 Colin McLean Road, East Dereham, Norfolk NR19 2RY
Tel (0362) 2271

Enquiries to Derek A. Edwards, Editor, Aerial Archaeology Publications

Items About 9000: b/w original photographs, colour transparencies (35mm), colour photographic prints

Dates of subject matter *c.* 3000 BC to present

Dates of photographs 1974 to present

Subjects Aerial photography; archaeological sites and historic monuments, churches, country houses in eastern England; counties of Norfolk and Suffolk

Access and conditions Open to qualified researchers by appt (write). All material available for editorial reproduction; advertising use by special arrangement only. No loans; b/w prints and duplicate colour transparencies must be ordered. Photocopies available. Print, duplicate and reproduction rights fees charged. Staff will undertake some research; research fee negotiable for larger projects. All material copyright. Duplicated catalogue available based on National Grid Reference.

259 • AEROFILMS LTD

Gate Studios, Station Road, Boreham Wood, Hertfordshire WD6 1EJ
Tel (01) 207 0666

Enquiries to Peter D. O'Connell, Chief Librarian

Items About 800,000: b/w original and copy photographs, colour transparencies (5″ × 4″, larger), colour photographic prints, glass negatives, postcards, stereographs, stereo pairs and mosaics, index plots of vertical photography

Dates of subject matter BC to present

Dates of photographs 1919 to present

Subjects Aerial photography both oblique and vertical with emphasis on the United Kingdom but including Europe, Africa, the Middle East and the Americas; complete vertical coverage of about 25% of England; Hunting Survey (i.e., vertical survey photography of complete counties) of Essex and Hertfordshire (1980) and Bedfordshire and Greater London (1981); remote sensing photography; Sir Alan Cobham trail-blazing and with his flying circus; old aircraft; Falkland Islands Dependency Antarctic Survey (FIDAS) 1955–1956 (b/w only); MILL COLLECTION of 19th-century streetscenes and people, mostly in London

Access and conditions Open to the public, Mon-Thurs 9–5.30, Fri 9–4.30. All material available for editorial reproduction and for advertising. Loans to approved users only; b/w prints and duplicate colour transparencies available for a fee. Photocopies available. Reproduction rights fees charged; service and/or research fees charged only when no material is used. Staff of four will undertake some research in response to specific requests; map references must be provided with boundaries marked if single sites are required. All material copyright. Printed catalogue available: *The Aerofilms Book of Aerial Photography*, 3rd edition, 1971, from Aerofilms.

260 • ASTRAL AERIAL SURVEYS LTD

108 Chiswick High Road, London W4 1PU
Tel (01) 944 4115

Enquiries to D. A. Cresswell

Items 12,000: colour photographic prints, colour transparencies (35mm, 2¼″, 5″ × 4″)

Dates of subject matter Roman times to present

Dates of photographs 1983 to present

Subjects Oblique aerial views of London, especially the City and the West End

Access and conditions Open to the public by appt (tel), Mon-Sat 9.15–1, 2–5.45. All material available for editorial reproduction and for advertising. No loans; b/w prints, colour prints and duplicate colour transparencies available for a fee. Reproduction rights fees charged. Staff will undertake limited research.

261 • NOTTINGHAMSHIRE COUNTY COUNCIL

Aerial Photography Library, Planning and Transport Department, Trent Bridge House, Fox Road, West Bridgford, Nottingham NG2 6BJ
Tel (0602) 824824 ext 309   Telex 37485

Enquiries to Senior Administrative Officer

Items About 5000: b/w original photographs

Dates of photographs 1945 to present

Subjects Vertical aerial coverage of Nottinghamshire

Access and conditions Open to the public by appt (tel), Mon–Fri 9–5. All material available for editorial reproduction; advertising use by special arrangement only. B/w prints available for a fee. Photocopies available. All material copyright.

262 • SEALAND AERIAL PHOTOGRAPHY

Goodwood Airfield, Goodwood, Nr. Chichester, West Sussex PO18 0PH
Tel (0243) 781025

Enquiries to Kim Smith

Items 50,000: colour photographic prints, colour transparencies (35mm, 2¼″, 5″ × 4″), b/w original photographs, unprinted film negatives

Dates of photographs 1972 to present

Subjects Aerial photographs (mostly oblique but some vertical) including general views of most towns and cities in England, industrial estates, heavy industrial complexes, factories, oil refineries, chemical works; construction including buildings, motorways, sea defences, dams; schools, cathedrals, castles and stately homes, ancient monuments and chalk figures, sports stadiums including football, tennis, athletics and rugby, scenic shots of coastal resorts and villages, shipping, safari parks, quarries and gravel pits, mining complexes, geographical and geological subjects including coastal features, river development, communications patterns, etc.; vertical photographs are mostly quarries and town centres

Access and conditions Open to qualified researchers by appt (tel), Mon–Fri 9.30–5.30. All material available for editorial reproduction and for advertising. Photocopies available. B/w prints available for a fee; colour material loaned free of charge for three weeks. Reproduction rights, service and holding fees charged. Staff will undertake research. Computer print-out catalogue.

263 • UNIVERSITY OF CAMBRIDGE

Collection of Air Photographs

The Mond Building, Free School Lane, Cambridge CB2 3RF
Tel (0223) 358389

Enquiries to David Wilson, Curator of Aerial Photography

Items 355,000: b/w original photographs, colour transparencies (35mm, 70mm, 5″ × 5″)

Dates of photographs 1945 to present

Subjects Aerial coverage of the British Isles showing agriculture, crop trials, soil mapping, soil erosion, geomorphology, geological mapping, quaternary geology, forestry, plant and animal ecology, conservation, archaeology (prehistoric to industrial), landscape, architecture, settlement, land use; some coverage of Denmark and the Netherlands

Access and conditions Open to the public by appt (tel). All material available for editorial reproduction and for advertising. No loans; b/w prints and duplicate colour transparencies available for a fee. Photocopies available. Reproduction rights fees charged. Staff will undertake some research; fees charged for large projects. All material copyright. Card catalogue available.

264 • UNIVERSITY OF KEELE

Air Photo Library, Staffordshire ST5 5BG
Tel (0782) 621111

Enquiries to Sheila Walton, Curator

Items 5,500,000: b/w original photographs

Dates of photographs 1939 to 1945

Subjects Aerial coverage of Western Europe during World War II including parts of former German-occupied countries and north shore of Mediterranean; good coverage of both rural and urban areas; *no* coverage of any territory now belonging to member nations of Warsaw Pact nor of the UK

Access and conditions Open to the public by appt (write). All material available for editorial reproduction and for advertising. No loans; b/w prints available for a fee. Reproduction rights fees charged. Staff will undertake research for a fee. All material copyright.

265 • WEST AIR PHOTOGRAPHY

23 Cecil Road, Weston-super-Mare, Avon
BS23 2NG
Tel (0934) 21333

Enquiries to Simon White, Manager

Items 150,000: b/w original photographs, colour photographic prints, colour transparencies (35mm)

Dates of subject matter BC to present

Dates of photographs 1965 to present

Subjects Oblique aerial coverage of south-western England and southern Wales, both rural and urban: geographical features, towns, villages, industrial complexes (including the Milford Haven oil refinery), ports and offshore shipping activity in Avon, Cornwall, Devon, Gloucestershire, Somerset, West, Mid and South Glamorgan, Gwent and the southern parts of Dyfed and Powys

Access and conditions Open to the public by appt (tel), Mon-Fri 9–5. All material available for editorial reproduction and for advertising. B/w and colour material loaned free of charge for three weeks; b/w and colour prints available for a fee. Reproduction rights and service fees charged. Staff will undertake some research. Photographers available for assignment. All material copyright.

Local History & Geography

266 • ABERDEEN CENTRAL LIBRARY

Local Studies Photographic Collection

Rosemount Viaduct, Aberdeen AB9 1GU
Tel (0224) 634622

Enquiries to Peter Grant, City Librarian

Items About 7000: b/w original and copy photographs, lantern slides, colour transparencies (35mm), postcards, colour photographic prints, glass negatives

Dates of subject matter Prehistory to present

Dates of photographs 1850s to present

Subjects Aberdeen and Aberdeenshire including scenes of city life, streets and markets, industry (fishing, farming, paper mills), portraits of local people both formal and at work; photographs by the firm of George Washington Wilson (mid-19th to early 20th century) of Scotland, England, South Africa and Australia

Access and conditions Open to the public, Mon-Fri 9–8, Sat 9–5. All material available for editorial reproduction and for advertising. No loans; b/w prints and duplicate colour transparencies available for a fee. Photocopies available. Reproduction rights and service fees charged. Staff will undertake limited research and mail photocopies. Card catalogue in preparation.

267 • ABERDEEN JOURNALS LTD

Press and Journal and *Evening Express* Picture Library, Lang Stracht, Mastrick, Aberdeen AB9 8AF
Tel (0224) 690222 Telex 73133

Enquiries to T. M. Forsyth, Librarian

Items About 100,000: b/w original and copy photographs, glass negatives, cuttings and tearsheets

Dates of subject matter *c.* 1945 to present; some earlier

Dates of photographs 1870 to present

Subjects Aberdeen and environs, Scotland, industry, sport, towns, local and Scottish personalities

Access and conditions Open to the public by appt (tel), Mon-Fri 9–4.30. All material available for editorial reproduction and for advertising. B/w material loaned by arrangement; prints available for a fee. Reproduction rights fees charged. Staff will undertake very limited research in answer to specific requests.

268 • ABERGAVENNY MUSEUM

Castle Street, Abergavenny, Gwent NP7 5EY
Tel (0873) 4282

Enquiries to Anna Tucker

Items 500: b/w original and copy photographs, postcards, illustrated maps, fine art prints

Dates of subject matter 1870 to present

Dates of photographs 1870 to present

Subjects Abergavenny and surrounding areas in Gwent, with special emphasis on buildings, streetscenes, recreation and sports; family photographs

Access and conditions Open to the public by appt (tel); 1 Mar–31 Oct Mon-Sat 11–1, 2–5, Sun 2.30–5; 1 Nov–28 Feb Mon-Sat 11–1, 2–4. All material available for editorial reproduction and for advertising. No loans; b/w prints and duplicate transparencies available for a fee. Material may be copied by outside photographers. Reproduction rights fees charged. Some material out of copyright. Card catalogue.

269 • ABERYSTWYTH PUBLIC LIBRARY

Local History Collection

Corporation Street, Aberystwyth, Dyfed
SY23 3BU
Tel (0970) 617464

Enquiries to D. Geraint Lewis, Area Librarian

Items 15,000: b/w original and copy photographs, colour transparencies (35mm, 5″ × 4″, larger), colour photographic prints, glass negatives, postcards, illustrated maps, unprinted film negatives, press cuttings and tearsheets, illustrated books, b/w slides

Dates of subject matter 13th century to present

Dates of photographs 1860 to present

Subjects Ceredigion and especially Aberystwyth local history including rural life, farming, industry (lead mining, ship building), maritime activities, transportation (railways, buses, cars, vans), commerce, architecture (schools, churches, chapels), festivities (coronations, carnivals, eisteddfods), personalities, local government, councils

Access and conditions Open to the public, Mon-Fri 9.30–5, Sat 9.30–1. Some material available for editorial reproduction; for advertising by special arrangement. B/w and colour material loaned (if library has duplicates); b/w prints and duplicate colour transparencies available for a fee. Photocopies available. No reproduction rights fees charged. Staff will undertake limited research. Card catalogue available.

270 • ABINGDON MUSEUM

The County Hall, Market Place, Abingdon, Oxfordshire OX14 3JE
Tel (0235) 23703

Enquiries to Nancy Stebbing, Curator

Items 1000: b/w original and copy photographs, posters

Dates of subject matter Prehistory to present

Dates of photographs 1860 to present

Subjects Local history of Abingdon and surrounding villages including landscapes, archaeology, architecture, streets, houses, shops, transport, industry, crafts, social history, portraits, local events

Access and conditions Open to the public by appt (tel), Mon-Fri 2–5. All material available for editorial reproduction and for advertising. No loans; b/w prints and duplicate colour transparencies available for a fee. Photocopies available. Reproduction rights fees charged. Staff will undertake limited research. All material copyright. Card catalogue in preparation.

271 • ABINGTON MUSEUM

Abington Park, Northampton NN1 5LW
Tel (0604) 31454

Enquiries to Judith Hodgkinson, Keeper of Social History

Items Over 5000: glass negatives, lantern slides, b/w original photographs, postcards, stereographs, daguerreotypes, b/w copy photographs, greetings cards, illustrated books

Dates of subject matter Mostly 1890–1920

Dates of photographs 1890–1920

Subjects Northamptonshire local and social history; public houses 1890–1910; towns and villages, architecture, local personalities and families

Access and conditions Open to the public by appt, Mon-Fri 9–12.30, 2–5. All material available for editorial reproduction but not for advertising. No loans; b/w prints can be ordered. Material may be copied by outside photographers. No reproduction rights fees. Staff will undertake limited research. Card catalogue.

272 • ALFRETON LIBRARY

Severn Square, Alfreton, Derbyshire DE5 7BJ
Tel (0773) 833199

Enquiries to Jan Colombo, Group Librarian

Items About 230: b/w copy photographs, colour photographic prints

Dates of subject matter 1900 to present

Dates of photographs 20th century

Subjects Local history of Somercotes, Leabrooks, Riddings, Swanwick, South Normanton, South Wingfield including people and places, industries, mining, historic buildings; recent town centre development in Alfreton

Access and conditions Open to the public, Mon-Fri 10–7, Sat 9.30–4. All material available for editorial reproduction and for advertising. No loans; material may be copied by outside photographers. Reproduction rights fees charged. Staff will undertake limited research. Copyright clearance is responsibility of user. Card catalogue available.

273 • ANGUS DISTRICT COUNCIL

Libraries and Museums Services, County Buildings, Forfar DD8 3LG
Tel (0307) 65101

Enquiries to Director of Museums and Libraries

Items About 18,500: b/w original photographs, lantern slides, glass negatives, colour transparencies (35mm), stereographs, colour photographic prints, unprinted film negatives, daguerreotypes, b/w copy photographs, postcards

Dates of subject matter 2000 BC to present

Dates of photographs Mid-nineteenth century to present

Subjects Angus District, including streets and buildings, local personalities, events, military, archaeology, agriculture, countryside, sea and seashore, harbours, fishing and whaling, business (services and retail), bridges, railways, schools, industry, recreation; late nineteenth-century agriculture and rural life, fishing, industry and engineering; Arbroath engineering industry (glass negatives) and personalities; Angus Town Councils and personalities; lantern slides by W. C. Orkney; photos by the Brechin Photographic Society including J. D. Ross; glass negatives (mainly land and seascapes) by D. Watterson; prints by J. Valentine (Dundee) and George Washington Wilson (Aberdeen); work by local commercial photographers and glass negatives from local newspaper collections; museum specimens, displays, historic sites, natural sciences including geology and biology; includes photographic collections of ARBROATH LIBRARY, ARBROATH MUSEUM, BRECHIN LIBRARY AND MUSEUM, CARNOUSTIE LIBRARY, FORFAR LIBRARY AND MUSEUM, MONTROSE MUSEUM, MONTROSE LIBRARY

Access and conditions Open to qualified researchers by appt, Mon-Fri 9–5. All material available for editorial reproduction and for advertising with written permission of the Director of Libraries and Museums. No loans; b/w prints

and duplicate colour transparencies available for a fee. Photocopies available. Reproduction rights fees charged. Staff will undertake some research.

274 • ARGYLL AND BUTE DISTRICT LIBRARY

Hunter Street, Kirn, Dunoon, Argyll PA23 8JR
Tel (0369) 3735

Enquiries to Andrew Ewan, District Librarian

Items 5000: glass negatives, b/w original photographs, postcards

Dates of subject matter Mid-19th century to present

Dates of photographs c. 1900–1939

Subjects Argyll and Bute district, buildings, transport, piers, views, landscapes

Access and conditions Open to qualified researchers by appt (write), Mon-Fri 9–5. Some material available for editorial reproduction and for advertising with the permission of Council. No loans; b/w prints available for a fee. No reproduction rights fees. Staff will undertake limited research.

275 • ARNOLD LIBRARY

Front Street, Arnold, Nottingham NG5 7EE
Tel (0602) 202247

Enquiries to K. M. Negus

Items About 1900: b/w copy photographs, colour transparencies (35mm), colour photographic prints

Dates of subject matter 12th century to present

Dates of photographs c. 1870 to present

Subjects Arnold old and new, including people, buildings, events, sports (football, cricket), school photographs, choirs, transportation, factories, aerial photographs (vertical and oblique), streetscenes, landscapes and scenic views

Access and conditions Open to the public, Mon-Fri 9–8, but Wed 9.30–1, Sat 9–1. All material available for editorial reproduction and for advertising. B/w material loaned free of charge for three weeks; b/w prints available. Duplicate colour transparencies available for a fee. Photocopies and Polaroids available. No reproduction rights fees charged. Staff will undertake limited research.

276 • ASHFORD LIBRARY

Local Studies Collection

Church Road, Ashford, Kent TN23 1QX
Tel (0233) 20649, 35526

Enquiries to D. R. Mole, Group Librarian

Items 1600: b/w copy and original photographs, colour photographic prints, colour transparencies (35mm), postcards, lantern slides, original cartoons

Dates of subject matter AD 43 to present

Dates of photographs 1880 to present

Subjects Ashford district including life and activities with emphasis on towns and villages, architecture (timber-framed houses, tithe barns), scenics (including a World War I tank), transportation (horse-drawn vehicles, automobiles), industry including The British Wheel Works (largest wheelwrights in the UK) and their ambulances and stretchers (the Ashford litter), personalities, farming (Ashford Market, osier beds, hop farming), windmills, fire-fighting including the Ashford Volunteer Fire Brigade (oldest in the country), recreation, sport, education, archaeology

Access and conditions Open to the public, Mon-Tues 9.30–6, Wed 9.30–5, Thurs-Fri 9.30–7, Sat 9–5. All material available for editorial reproduction and for advertising. No loans; b/w prints and duplicate colour transparencies available for a fee. Photocopies available. No reproduction rights or service fees charged. Staff will undertake limited research (up to 30 minutes). Compulsory credit line. Some copyright material requires written permission of copyright holder.

277 • ATHELSTAN MUSEUM

Town Hall, Cross Hayes, Malmesbury, Wiltshire SN16 9BZ
Tel (06662) 2143

Enquiries to Roberta Prince, Custodian

Items About 400: b/w copy and original photographs, old fine art prints, postcards, posters, illustrated books, engineering drawings

Dates of subject matter 1860 to present

Dates of photographs 1860 to present

Subjects Local history of Malmesbury and surrounding area with special emphasis on branch line of Great Western Railway including construction, and iron foundry including engineering drawings

Access and conditions Open to the public, Tues-Sat 11–1, 2–4 (summer), Wed, Fri & Sat 2–4 (winter). Some material available for editorial reproduction and for advertising; some for private research only. No loans; b/w prints available for a fee. Reproduction rights fees charged. Staff will undertake limited research. Most material copyright. Card catalogue in preparation.

278 • BARNET LIBRARY

Ravensfield House, The Burroughs, London NW4 4BQ
Tel (01) 202 5625

Enquiries to David Ruddon, Borough Librarian

Items About 11,000: b/w original and copy photographs, colour transparencies (35mm), glass negatives, postcards, illustrated maps, posters, greetings cards

Dates of subject matter c. 1850 to present

Dates of photographs Late 19th century to present

Subjects London Borough of Barnet including the former Boroughs of Hendon and Finchley, local history including people, buildings, recreation, sports, transport, railways, trams, horse-drawn vehicles, early aircraft at the London Aerodrome

Access and conditions Open to the public by appt (write), Mon Thurs Fri 9–1, Tues Wed Sat 9–5.30. Most material available for editorial reproduction and for advertising. B/w prints and duplicate colour transparencies available for a fee. Photocopies available. No reproduction rights fees charged. Staff will undertake some research. Card catalogue.

279 • BATH REFERENCE LIBRARY

18 Queen Square, Bath BA1 2HP
Tel (0225) 28144

Enquiries to M. Joyce

Items About 7500: b/w original and copy photographs, colour transparencies (35mm), postcards, illustrated maps, fine art prints, posters, illustrated books

Dates of subject matter Roman times to present

Dates of photographs 1920 to present; some mid-19th century

Subjects Bath and environs including history, architecture, streets, transport, events, portraits of local personalities

Access and conditions Open to the public, Mon-Fri 9.30–7.30, Sat 9.30–5. Some material available for editorial reproduction, but not for advertising. No loans; b/w prints available. Material may be copied by outside photographers. Photocopies available. Reproduction rights and service fees charged. Staff will undertake limited research. Catalogue of fine art prints available: *Images of Bath*, ed. James Lees-Milne and David Ford, St Helena Press, Richmond, Surrey, 1982.

280 • THE BEAFORD ARCHIVE

The Beaford Centre, Beaford, Winkleigh, Devon EX19 8LU
Tel (08053) 201, 202

Enquiries to Archive Assistant

Items Over 55,000: b/w original and copy photographs

Dates of photographs 1850 to present

Subjects Old Archive: history of the North Devon area from 1850–1950 including country life and activities, agriculture, hunting, shooting, fishing, estate work, forestry, clay getting; commercial life, markets and shops; villages and village activities including fêtes, fairs, celebrations, customs, outings and seaside outings; advent of railway, motor car and mechanised farming; portraits both studio and outdoor; some small towns (Barnstaple, Okehampton, South Molton): New Archive: (since 1972 by James Ravilious; 1971–72 by Roger Deakin) North Devon area, chiefly but not exclusively within a ten-mile radius of the village of Dolton; village and country life, work and entertainment; surviving customs and recent innovations; traditional crafts and new ways

Access and conditions Open to the public by appt. All material available for editorial reproduction and for advertising at the discretion of the Archive. No loans; b/w prints and duplicate colour transparencies available for a fee. Photocopies available. Reproduction rights fees and research fees charged. Staff of three will undertake research. Card catalogue available.

281 • BEAMISH NORTH OF ENGLAND OPEN AIR MUSEUM

Beamish Hall, Stanley, County Durham DH9 OR9
Tel (0207) 231811

Enquiries to Rosemary E. Allan, Keeper of Social History

Items 100,000: b/w copy and original photographs, colour transparencies (35mm, 5″ × 4″), glass negatives, daguerreotypes, lantern slides, postcards, fine art prints, unprinted film negatives, stereographs, posters, greetings cards, illustrated books

Dates of subject matter Middle Ages to present

Dates of photographs 1850 to 1984

Subjects Social history in the Counties of Cleveland, Durham, Northumberland, Tyne and Wear with special emphasis on agriculture, coalmining, leadmining, engineering, domestic exteriors and interiors, streetscenes, North Eastern topography, shop exteriors and interiors, schools, transport, customs and traditions; glass negatives from the files of the *Durham Advertiser* and prints from the *Evening World* (Jarrow) newspapers; photographs by James Fenton, Francis Frith, Rev. J. W. Pattison, J. W. Bee, Dr. W. C. Fothergill, Daisy Edis, William Bainbridge and Sinclair

Access and conditions Open to qualified researchers by appt (tel), Tues-Thurs 9–5. Most material available for editorial reproduction and for advertising. B/w prints and duplicate colour transparencies available for a fee. Photocopies available. Reproduction rights fees charged. Staff will undertake limited research. Card catalogue.

282 • BEDFORDSHIRE COUNTY COUNCIL LEISURE SERVICES

County Hall, Bedford, Bedfordshire MK42 9AP
Tel (0234) 56181

Enquiries to Director, Leisure Services Dept.

County Hall Library Collection

Items 2200: b/w original and copy negatives, colour transparencies (35mm), glass negatives

Dates of photographs *c.* 1900 to present

Subjects Bedfordshire geography and topography, agriculture and local industries

Luton Central Library (Reference Division)

Items 2000: b/w original and copy photographs, glass negatives, postcards

Dates of photographs 1860 to present

Subjects Luton and environs especially buildings and streetscenes, trades, transport, local personalities; photographs by Frederick Thurston

Luton Central Library (Slide Loan Collection)

Items 1300: colour transparencies (35mm)

Dates of subject matter 1300 to present

Dates of photographs 1970 to present

Subjects Local history of Luton, Bedford and many neighbouring towns, streetscenes, architecture (almshouses, castles, banks, bridges, churches, cinemas, hotels, pubs), industries (lace-making, hat manufacture, mineral water bottling, Vauxhall Motors, SKF Ltd, Commer Cars), transport, railways, farms, schools and colleges, dairies, parks, stately homes, straw plaiting, Eleanor Cross at Waltham Cross.

Access and conditions Open to the public; tel for details. Most material available for editorial reproduction and for advertising. Some material loaned; b/w prints and duplicate colour transparencies available for a fee. No reproduction rights fees. Staff will undertake limited research. Printed catalogue available.

283 • BERKSHIRE COUNTY LIBRARY

Central Library, Abbey Square, Reading, Berkshire RG1 3BG
Tel (0734) 875444

Enquiries to Local Studies Librarian

Items About 3000: b/w original photographs, postcards, old fine art prints

Dates of subject matter *c.*1750 to present

Dates of photographs 1880 to present

Subjects Local history of Reading and surrounding area including landscapes, architecture, streetscenes, social history, road and rail transport, industry including biscuit-making, brewing, bulbs and seeds; Hocktide ceremony at Hungerford; Reading University, local schools

Access and conditions Open to the public, Mon Wed Sat 9.30–5, Tues Thurs Fri 9.30–7. Most

material available for editorial reproduction and for advertising. No loans; b/w prints available for a fee; material may be copied by outside photographers. Photocopies available. Reproduction rights and service fees charged. Staff will undertake limited research. Some material copyright. Card catalogue in preparation.

284 • BERKSHIRE RECORD OFFICE

Shire Hall, Shinfield Park, Reading, Berkshire RG2 9XS
Tel (0734) 875444 ext 3182

Enquiries to Adam Green, County Archivist

Items 2000: b/w original photographs, glass negatives, lantern slides, illustrated maps, architectural drawings

Dates of subject matter Prehistory to 1950s

Dates of photographs 1880 to 1950

Subjects Berkshire geography and topography, architecture both secular and ecclesiastical; group and individual portraits of local personalites

Access and conditions Open to the public by appt (tel), Mon 2–5, Tues & Wed 9–5, Thurs 9–9, Fri 9–4.30. Some material available for editorial reproduction subject to copyright restrictions. B/w prints available for a fee. Photocopies available. Reproduction rights fees charged. Staff will undertake limited research. Copyright clearance is responsibility of user.

285 • BEWDLEY MUSEUM

The Shambles, Load Street, Bewdley, Worcestershire DY12 2AE
Tel (0299) 403573

Enquiries to Charles Fogg, Curator

Items 1200: original and copy photographs, colour transparencies (35mm), colour photographic prints, postcards, unprinted film negatives, glass negatives, fine art prints, illustrated maps, cuttings and tearsheets

Dates of subject matter *c.* 1500 to 1900

Dates of photographs *c.* 1900 to present

Subjects Crafts and industries of the Bewdley area including forestry, hauling, charcoal burning, besom-making, bark-peeling, basket-making, brass-founding, rope-making; topography of Bewdley, the River Severn and the Telford bridge

Access and conditions Open to the public by appt (tel), Mon-Fri 9–5. All material available for editorial reproduction and for advertising. No loans; b/w prints available for a fee. Photocopies available. Reproduction rights fees charged. Staff will undertake limited research. Card catalogue available.

286 • BEXLEY LIBRARIES AND MUSEUMS SERVICE

Hall Place, Bourne Road, Bexley, Kent DA5 1PQ
Tel (0322) 526574

Enquiries to Mick Scott, Reference Librarian

Items 9500: b/w original photographs, colour transparencies (35mm), glass negatives, lantern slides, postcards, illustrated maps

Dates of photographs 1860 to present

Subjects London Borough of Bexley including work, industry, schools, buildings, streetscenes, people, costume, churches

Access and conditions Open to the public, Mon-Sat 9–5. Some material available for editorial reproduction and for advertising. B/w prints and duplicate transparencies available for a fee. Photocopies available. Reproduction rights and service fees charged. Staff will undertake some research. Card catalogue.

287 • BIGGAR MUSEUM TRUST

Moat Park, Biggar, Strathclyde ML12 6DT
Tel (0899) 21050

Enquiries to Brian Lambie

Items About 13,500: b/w original and copy photgraphs, colour transparencies (35mm), glass negatives, daguerreotypes, lantern slides, postcards, stereographs, posters, greetings cards, illustrated books

Dates of subject matter 17th century to present

Dates of photographs 1843 to present

Subjects Local history including trades, agriculture, village and borough life, sport, demolished houses; John Buchan (Lord Tweedsmuir), writer and politician, all aspects of

his career, forebears, books, films; Albion Motors (1899–c. 1970), complete photo archive of large commercial motor manufacturer

Access and conditions Open to the public by appt. All material available for editorial reproduction and for advertising. No loans; b/w prints and colour transparencies available for a fee. Reproduction rights fees charged. Staff will undertake some research.

288 • THE BINGHAM LIBRARY

The Waterloo, Cirencester, Gloucestershire GL7 2PZ
Tel (0285) 3582

Enquiries to Alan Welsford, Librarian

Items About 4000: b/w original photographs, glass negatives, lantern slides, illustrated maps, fine art prints

Dates of subject matter Roman time to present

Dates of photographs 19th century

Subjects THOMAS COLLECTION: topographic photographs of the Cotswolds c. 1912 to 1950, villages, architecture; COX COLLECTION: small portraits of local personalities, tradesmen, farmers; topography of Cirencester and environs

Access and conditions Open to the public by appt (tel), Mon 10–5, Tues Thurs Fri 10–7, Wed 10–1. All material available for editorial reproduction and for advertising. No loans; b/w prints available for a fee; material may be copied by outside photographers. Photocopies available. Reproduction rights and service fees charged. Staff will undertake limited research.

289 • BIRMINGHAM PUBLIC LIBRARIES

Central Library, Chamberlain Square, Birmingham B3 3HQ
Telex 337655 BIRLIB G

Fine Arts Department

Tel (021) 235 4547

Enquiries to Derek Fontaine, Head of Dept

Items Over 2000: posters, greetings cards, Victorian colour prints, illustrated books

Dates of subject matter Prehistory to present

Subjects British 19th- and 20th-century Christmas and valentine cards; Victorian scrapbooks and colour prints; contemporary posters advertising art exhibitions since 1975

Access and conditions Open to the public, Mon-Fri 9–8, Sat 9–5. All material available for editorial reproducton and for advertising; copyrighted material must be cleared with owner of copyright. No loans; b/w prints and colour transparencies available for a fee. Photocopies available. Reproduction rights fees charged. Staff will undertake limited research.

Local Studies Department

Tel (021) 235 4220

Enquiries to Patrick Baird, Head of Dept

Items Over 250,000: b/w original and copy photographs, colour transparencies (35mm), colour photographic prints, glass negatives, daguerreotypes, lantern slides, postcards, illustrated maps, fine art prints, art reproductions, unprinted film negatives, architectural drawings, illustrated books

Dates of subject matter 1651 to present

Dates of photographs 1857 to present; a few earlier

Subjects History of Birmingham and Warwickshire from 1651 to the present including the following special collections: Warwickshire Photographic Survey detailing most aspects of life and views of buildings (1857–1950); the Improvement Scheme showing slum housing in Birmingham prior to demolition c. 1870; slum housing in Birmingham c. 1905; Victorian schools and children c. 1898 to 1902; engravings, etc., of Birmingham c. 1651 to 1970; munitions workers (1914); Black Country workers, women workers (1905); World War II blitz collection (1940 to 1942); trams (c. 1880 to 1953)

Access and conditions Open to the public, Mon-Fri 9–6, Sat 9–5. All material available for editorial reproduction and for advertising; copyrighted material must be cleared with owner of copyright. No loans; b/w prints and duplicate colour transparencies available for a fee. Photocopies available. Reproduction rights fees charged. Staff will undertake limited research.

Visual Aids Collection

Tel (021) 235 4306

Enquiries to Keith W. Heyes, Head of Dept

Items 365,000: cuttings and tearsheets (mounted), posters, colour transparencies (35mm)

Dates of subject matter Prehistory to present

Dates of cuttings c. 1920 to present, some earlier

Subjects Cutting file: 350,000 mounted illustrations on all subjects about 40% of which are identified as to source; colour transparencies: Birmingham and its history

Access and conditions Open to the public, Mon-Fri 9–6, Sat 9–5. All material available for editorial reproduction and for advertising; copyrighted material must be cleared with copyright owner. Cuttings: 100 may be borrowed at a time for four weeks and can be renewed. B/w and colour material loaned free of charge for 28 days; b/w prints available for a fee. Material may be copied by outside photographers. No reproduction rights fees. Staff will undertake limited research. Card and printed catalogues available.

290 • BISHOPSGATE INSTITUTE

230 Bishopsgate, London EC2M 4QH
Tel (01) 247 6844

Enquiries to David Webb, Librarian

Items 5000: b/w original and copy photographs, lantern slides, postcards, illustrated maps, fine art prints, illustrated books

Dates of subject matter c. 1600 to present

Dates of photographs c. 1870 to present

Subjects London topography including photographs by C. Mathews of the City and Spitalfields (1912), by John Todd of the City (c. 1909–1913); complete set of photographs by the Society for Photographing Relics of Old London (1875–1886); interiors and exteriors of City churches by Salmon (1870–1880)

Access and conditions Open to the public by appt, Mon-Fri 9.30–5.30. All material available for editorial reproduction and for advertising. No loans; b/w prints available for a fee. Material may be copied by outside photographers. Photocopies available. Reproduction rights fees charged at the discretion of the Librarian. Staff will undertake some research.

291 • BLACK COUNTRY SOCIETY

8 Coxcroft Avenue, Quarry Bank, West Midlands
DY5 2ED

Enquiries to David Whyley

Items About 3000: b/w original and copy
photographs, colour transparencies (35mm), colour
photographic prints, glass negatives, lantern
slides, postcards, unprinted film negatives,
illustrated books, fine art prints

Dates of subject matter 11th century to present

Dates of photographs 1850 to present

Subjects Black Country local history including
life and activities, industry, mining, steel-making,
chain-making, social history, railways, public
houses, canals, streetscenes, towns and villages
past and present, personalities, sports

Access and conditions Open to qualified
researchers by appt (write). Some material
available for editorial reproduction and for
advertising. No loans; b/w prints and duplicate
colour transparencies available for a fee.
Photocopies available. Reproduction rights fees
charged. Staff will undertake research.

292 • BLACKBURN DISTRICT LIBRARY

Town Hall Street, Blackburn, Lancashire
BB2 1AH
Tel (0254) 661221

Enquiries to The Reference Librarian

Items 7000: b/w original and copy photographs,
colour photographic prints, postcards

Dates of subject matter 3000 BC to present

Dates of photographs 1854 to present

Subjects Blackburn and district, especially the
old County Borough, with emphasis on
architecture, transport, industry, textiles, people

Access and conditions Open to the public by
appt, Mon-Wed 9.30–8, Thurs-Fri 9.30–5, Sat
9.30–4. Some material available for editorial
reproduction with approval of Lancashire Library
Headquarters. No loans; b/w prints available for a
fee. Photocopies available. Staff will undertake
limited research.

293 • BLACKPOOL CENTRAL LIBRARY

Queen Street, Blackpool, Lancashire FY1 1PX
Tel (0253) 23977

Enquiries to James Burkitt, District Librarian

Items 2500: b/w original photographs, glass
negatives, postcards

Dates of subject matter *c*. 1850 to present

Dates of photographs 1860 to present

Subjects Blackpool and district of Fylde and Wyre
local history including architecture, roads, and
streets, police, fire brigade, sports, swimming,
bathing, beaches, conferences, Royal visits; some
photographs by Francis Frith

Access and conditions Open to the public, Mon-
Fri 10–7 (closed Wed after 1), Sat 10–5. All
material available for editorial reproduction; some
restrictions on advertising use. No loans; b/w prints
available for a fee. Reproduction rights fees
charged at the discretion of the Librarian. Staff will
undertake limited research. Card catalogue
available.

294 • BODMIN TOWN MUSEUM

c/o Town Council, Shire House, Bodmin, Cornwall
PL31 1NR
Tel (0208) 5516

Enquiries to Leslie E. Long

Items About 3500: b/w original photographs and
copy photographs

Subjects Bodmin and environs social history and
topography including coastal and inland scenery,
architecture, events, people, Royal visits, schools
and school groups, potters and pottery shows, china
clay cookers, tin mines; G. W. F. ELLIS COLLECTION
(1939 to 1970s) of Cornish scenes

Access and conditions Open to the public May –
Oct; by appt only (write) Nov – Apr. Some material
available for editorial reproduction and for
advertising. Material may be copied by outside
photographers. Copyright for material in the Ellis
collection is held by the Cornwall Local Studies
Centre, Redruth Library, Clinton Road, Redruth,
Cornwall; the Ellis negatives are also held by
Redruth Library.

295 • BOLSOVER LIBRARY

Church Street, Bolsover, Derbyshire S44 6TZ
Tel (0246) 823179

Enquiries to Bernard Haigh, Group Librarian

Items 300: b/w copy prints

Dates of subject matter 17th century to present

Dates of photographs *c.* 1860 to *c.* 1955

Subjects Local history of Bolsover, Creswell,
Swinebrook and Langwith areas of Derbyshire
including life and activities, buildings, mines and
mining villages

Access and conditions Open to the public by
appt, Mon Tues Fri 9–7, Wed Thurs 9–5.30, Sat
9.30–4. All material available for editorial
reproduction but not for advertising. No loans; b/w
prints available for a fee. Reproducton rights fees
charged. Staff will undertake limited research.

296 • BOLTON CENTRAL REFERENCE LIBRARY

Le Mans Crescent, Bolton Lancashire BL1 1SE
Tel (0204) 22311 ext 351

Enquiries to Barry Mills, Local Studies Librarian

Items About 4200: b/w original and copy
photographs, colour transparencies (35mm,
$5'' \times 4''$, $10'' \times 8''$), glass negatives, postcards,
engravings

Dates of subject matter 1651 to present

Dates of photographs 1870 to present

Subjects Bolton Metropolitan Borough and
former Turton Urban District to the north
including streetscenes, general and aerial views,
landscapes and townscapes, mills and mill
architecture, transport (canals, railways, Horwich
Locomotive Works), architecture (churches,
historic buildings including Hall-i-th-wood,
Smithills Hall and Turton Tower, public buildings,
Town Hall and Libraries), coalmining (especially
Pretoria Pit Disaster, 1910), civil event and royal
visits

Access and conditions Open to the public, Mon
Tues Thurs Fri 9–5.30, Wed 9–1, Sat 9–5. Some
material available for editorial reproduction but
not for advertising. No loans; material may be
copied by outside photographers. Photocopies
available. Reproduction rights fees charged. Card
catalogue available.

297 • BOOTLE LIBRARY

220 Stanley Road, Bootle, Merseyside L20 3EN
Tel (051) 933 4508

Enquiries to J. Jenkins

Items About 10,000: b/w copy and original
photographs, colour transparencies (35mm), colour
photographic prints, glass negatives, lantern
slides, postcards, unprinted film negatives

Dates of subject matter Late 19th century to
present

Dates of photographs Late 19th century to
present

Subjects Local history of Bootle, Southport and
Crosby and surrounding area including geology,
landscapes, architecture, housing, churches, docks
and shipping, streetscenes, transport, education,
hospitals, local events and civil ceremonies, fire
service, police force, royal visits, coastal activities,
sport, social history, portraits

Access and conditions Open to the public, Mon
& Tues 10–5, Wed & Fri 10–8, Thurs & Sat 10–1.
Material held at three locations but the main
access point is Bootle Library. Most material
available for editorial reproduction and for
advertising (some restrictions). No loans; b/w
prints and duplicate colour transparencies
available for a fee; material may be copied by
outside photographers. Photocopies available.
Reproduction rights fees charged. Staff will
undertake limited research. Most material
copyright. Card catalogue available.

298 • BOSTON LIBRARY

County Hall, Boston, Lincolnshire PE21 6LX
Tel (0205) 67123

Enquiries to Stephen Moore, Area Librarian

Items About 600: b/w original and copy
photographs, postcards, fine art prints, colour
transparencies (35mm), colour photographic
prints, greetings cards, press cuttings and
tearsheets, illustrated books

Dates of subject matter Prehistory to present

Dates of photographs *c.* 1890 to present

Subjects Lincolnshire and especially Boston and
environs, local history, fens and drainage,
architecture, transport especially docks and
shipping, local industries, agriculture,

personalities; Pilgrim Fathers, places associated with them in the 17th century, modern memorial, villages they came from in Lincolnshire (e.g. John Cotton was vicar of St. Botolph's near Boston), some drawings and early book illustrations

Access and conditions Open to the public by appt (tel), Mon-Fri 9.30–6.30, Sat 9.30–12.30. Some material available for editorial reproduction and for advertising. B/w prints and duplicate colour transparencies available for a fee. Photocopies available. Reproduction rights fees charged. Staff will undertake limited research.

299 • BOTANIC GARDENS MUSEUM

Churchtown, Southport, Merseyside PRN 7NB
Tel (0704) 27547

Enquiries to Stephen Paul Forshaw, Acting Curator

Items 6000: b/w original and copy photographs, colour transparencies (35mm), postcards, unprinted film negatives, glass negatives, illustrated maps, posters, lantern slides

Dates of subject matter 1800 to present

Dates of photographs 1850 to present

Subjects Photograph collection: local history including Southport and environs, Vulcan Motor Works, manufacturers, streetscenes, seascapes, promenade, local events, personalities, lifeboats, wrecks, fire brigade, architecture, shrimping industry, special collection on Captain Scott and Antarctic Expedition; postcard collection: Southport and environs including parks, streetscenes, promenade, seascapes, pier, fairground and amusements, personalities, humour, and also Lancashire, Merseyside, Lake District, Isle of Man, Wales, Scotland, Ireland, Europe, humour, Victoriana, oddities; prints, posters, etc. of urban landscapes and streetscenes, local personalities, shore scenes, events, lifeboats, wrecks, parks, landscapes, cartoons

Access and conditions Open to the public by appt (write), Tues-Sat 10–6 (May-Sept), Tues-Sat 10–5 (Oct to Apr). Some material available for editorial reproduction and for advertising. B/w and colour material loaned free of charge for three months. B/w prints and duplicate colour transparencies available for a fee. Reproduction rights and service fees charged. Staff will undertake limited research. Card catalogue available.

300 • BRADFORD PUBLIC LIBRARY

Local Studies Department

Prince's Way, Bradford, West Yorkshire BD1 1NN
Tel (0274) 753661/2

Enquiries to The Chief Librarian

Items About 5000: b/w original and copy photographs, glass negatives, postcards, illustrated maps, colour transparencies (35mm), colour photographic prints

Dates of subject matter Early 19th century to present

Dates of photographs *c.* 1860 to present

Subjects Bradford Metropolitan District history, architecture, personalities, transport, industry, streetscenes including buildings, housing, Town Hall, Wool Exchange, chapels, parks, pubs

Access and conditions Open to the public by appt (tel), Mon-Fri 9–8, Sat 9–5. Some material available for editorial reproduction and for advertising. B/w prints and duplicate transparencies available for a fee. Reproduction rights fees charged. Staff will undertake limited research. Card catalogue available.

301 • BRIGHTON REFERENCE LIBRARY

Church Street, Brighton, East Sussex BN1 1UE
Tel (0273) 601197

Enquiries to Illustrations Team Librarian

Items Over 22,000: b/w original and copy photographs, glass negatives, daguerreotypes, lantern slides, postcards, fine art prints, unprinted film negatives, posters, greetings cards, illustrated books, ephemera

Dates of subject matter 1800 to present

Dates of photographs 1850 to present

Subjects Brighton and Sussex history, especially church and vernacular architecture of Sussex; 19th-century agriculture; the seaside including bathing, bathing machines, holidays by the sea; the railway especially London to Brighton line, Southern Railways including locomotives, stations, lines; Brighton during World War I and II (photographs and posters); every town, village and hamlet in East and West Sussex, especially architecture and country houses; British 19th-century social life and leisure; general coverage of World War II; the following special collections:

SUSSEX SURVEY PHOTOGRAPHS, *HERALD NEWSPAPER* photographs stent railway photographs, simmons photographs, madgwick railway photographs

Access and conditions Open to the public by appt (tel), Mon-Fri 10–7 (closed Wed), Sat 10–4. All material available for editorial reproduction and for advertising. B/w prints and colour transparencies available for a fee by arrangement with outside photographer. Photocopies available. No reproduction rights fees. Staff will undertake research and mail photocopies. Compulsory credit line. Partial catalogue available.

302 • BRISTOL CENTRAL LIBRARY

Local Studies Department

College Green, Bristol BS1 5TL
Tel (0272) 276121

Enquiries to Geoffrey Langley, County Reference Librarian

Items About 6000: b/w original photographs, colour transparencies (35mm), b/w copy photographs, postcards, posters, cuttings and tearsheets, illustrated books

Dates of subject matter Medieval to present

Dates of photographs *c.* 1860 to present

Subjects Bristol and adjacent areas of Somerset including history, topography and architecture; aerial photographs, chiefly oblique

Access and conditions Open to the public by appt (tel). Some material available for editorial reproduction and for advertising. B/w material loaned by special arrangement; colour loaned to local groups only. Photocopies available. Reproduction rights fees charged. Staff will undertake limited research only. Copyright clearance is responsibility of user.

303 • BROMLEY LIBRARY

Local Studies Department

Central Library, High Street, Bromley, Kent BR1 1EX
Tel (01) 460 9955 Telex 896712 BROLIB G

Enquiries to P. C. Turner, Assistant Local History Librarian

Items About 6000: b/w original and copy photographs, colour transparencies (35mm), colour photographic prints, glass negatives, daguerreotypes, lantern slides, postcards, illustrated maps, unprinted film negatives, stereographs, posters, architectural drawings, 19th-century engravings

Dates of subject matter 1800 to present

Dates of photographs 1850 to present

Subjects London Borough of Bromley and environs (including former boroughs of Beckenham, Penge, Chislehurst and Orpington), aerial photographs, agriculture, architecture (domestic, civil and ecclesiastic), railways, streetscenes, shops, transport, portraits, ALAN WARWICK COLLECTION on the Crystal Palace (35mm)

Access and conditions Open to the public, Tues & Thurs 9.30–8, Wed & Fri 9.30–6, Sat 9.30–5 (closed Mon). All material available for editorial reproduction and for advertising subject to copyright restrictions. B/w prints available for a fee. Colour transparencies loaned. Photocopies available. Reproduction rights fees charged. Staff will undertake some research. Copyright clearance is responsibility of user. Kalamazoo strip catalogue available.

304 • BRUCE CASTLE MUSEUM

Haringey Local History Collections

Lordship Lane, London N17 8NU
Tel (01) 808 8772

Enquiries to Claire F. Tarjan

Items About 7000: b/w original and copy photographs, colour transparencies (35mm), glass negatives, lantern slides, fine art prints, architectural drawings

Dates of subject matter *c.* 1600 to present

Dates of photographs *c.* 1850 to present

Subjects London Borough of Haringey (including former boroughs of Tottenham, Hornsey and Wood Green) including history, housing, streetscenes, agricultural life, industry, transport, people, social activities, sports, services, institutions, SHADBOLT COLLECTION of Hornsey in the 1850s; BRITISH POSTAL HISTORY COLLECTION (photographs and prints); the MUSEUM OF THE MIDDLESEX REGIMENT COLLECTION including prints and photographs of regimental history

Access and conditions Open to the public by appt (tel), weekday afternoons. All material available for editorial reproduction and for advertising. No loans; b/w prints and duplicate colour transparencies available for a fee. Material may be copied by outside photographers. Photocopies available. Reproduction rights fees charged. Staff will undertake some research.

305 • BUCKINGHAMSHIRE COUNTY LIBRARY

Buckinghamshire Collection

Walton Street, Aylesbury, Bucks HP20 1UU
Tel (0296) 5000 ext 250 Telex 83101

Enquiries to Librarian, Buckinghamshire Collection

Items About 11,000: b/w original and copy photographs, colour photographic prints, colour transparencies (35mm), postcards, illustrated maps, fine art prints, posters, greetings cards, cuttings and tearsheets, illustrated books, ephemera

Dates of subject matter Prehistory to present

Dates of photographs 19th century to present

Subjects Buckinghamshire history and topography (especially aerial photographs) including archaeology, architecture, churches, transport, education, agriculture, geology, industry, crafts, heraldry

Access and conditions Open to the public, Mon 9–5, Tues-Fri 9–8, Sat 9–7. All material available for editorial reproduction and for advertising subject to copyright restrictions. No loans; material may be copied by outside photographers. Photocopies available. No reproduction rights fees. Staff will undertake some research. Copyright clearance is responsibility of user.

306 • BURNLEY DISTRICT LIBRARY

Local Studies Section

Grimshaw Street, Burnley, Lancashire BB11 2BD
Tel (0282) 37115

Enquiries to Raymond Pickles, District Librarian

Items 11,000: b/w original and copy photographs, colour transparencies (35mm), glass negatives, lantern slides, postcards, posters, architectural drawings, illustrated books

Dates of subject matter c. 1850 to present

Dates of photographs c. 1880 to present

Subjects Burnley and north-east Lancashire including architecture, industry, transport, sport, education, religious life, portraits of local personalities, cotton mills, shops, pubs, schools, chapels, coalmining (miners, pitheads), textile engineering; excavations and artefacts from Bronze Age burial site

Access and conditions Open to the public by appt (tel), Mon Wed Thurs 9.30–7, Tues 9.30–1, Fri 9.30–5, Sat 9.30–1, 2–4. Some material available for editorial reproduction and for advertising. B/w material loaned free of charge for one month. Photocopies available. Reproduction rights fees charged at the discretion of the copyright holder. Staff will undertake limited research.

307 • BURY CENTRAL LIBRARY

Local Studies Section

Manchester Road, Bury, Lancashire BL9 0DR
Tel (061) 764 8625

Enquiries to Rita Hirst, Reference Librarian

Items 4500: b/w original and copy photographs, colour transparencies (5″ × 4″, larger), postcards, glass negatives

Dates of subject matter 1830s to present

Dates of photographs 1855 to present

Subjects Bury and environs local history and topography, architecture (shops, houses), transport (trams, buses, trains), streetscenes, celebrations, people (Robert Peel, John Kay), industry (cotton mills, paper mills, slipper making mills, engineering works)

Access and conditions Open to the public, Mon & Tues 9–5.30, Wed-Fri 9–7.30, Sat 9–4.30. All material available for editorial reproduction and for advertising. No loans; b/w prints available for a fee. Photocopies available. Reproduction rights fees charged at the Librarian's discretion. Staff will undertake research. Partial card catalogue available.

308 • CALDERDALE CENTRAL LIBRARY

Photographic Collections

Northgate House, Northgate, Halifax, West Yorkshire HX1 1UN
Tel (0422) 57257 ext 2628

Enquiries to Michael Corbett, Librarian

Items About 18,600: b/w original photographs, colour photographic prints, postcards, art reproductions, lantern slides, original cartoons, colour transparencies (35mm), fine art prints, illustrated maps

Dates of subject matter 17th century to present

Dates of photographs 1920 to present

Subjects Calderdale Photographic Survey: old buildings in Calderdale and especially in Halifax, streets; HORSFALL TURNER COLLECTION: local history of Calderdale including architecture, streetscenes, ceremonies including Pace Egg Play performed at Easter, Rush Bearing Ceremony in which bundles of rushes in ornamental carts are pulled by young men in costume, morris dances

Access and conditions Open to the public, Wed 10–12, Mon-Fri 10–8, Sat 10–5. Some material available for editorial reproduction and for advertising subject to copyright clearance. No loans; material may be copied by outside photographers. Photocopies available. No reproduction rights fees charged. Staff will undertake limited research.

309 • CAMBRIDGE ANTIQUARIAN SOCIETY

Cambridgeshire Photographic Record, Central Library, 7 Lion Yard, Cambridge CB2 3QD
Tel (0223) 65252 Telex 817266

Enquiries to Michael Petty, Local Studies Librarian

Items About 15,000: b/w original photographs, glass negatives, postcards, unprinted film negatives, lantern slides

Dates of subject matter 16th century to *c.* 1965

Dates of photographs 1890s to 1960s

Subjects Cambridge (streets, town, colleges and university), Cambridgeshire villages, cottages, farm buildings, windmills; photographs of the fenlands by D. G. Reid

Access and conditions Open to the public, Mon-Fri 9.30–5.30, Sat 9–5. All material available for editorial reproduction and for advertising. B/w prints and duplicate colour transparencies available for a fee. Photocopies available. Reproduction rights and service fees charged. Staff will undertake very limited research. Card catalogue available.

310 • CAMBRIDGE AND COUNTY FOLK MUSEUM

Castle Street, Cambridge CB3 0AQ
Tel (0223) 355159

Enquiries to Tom Doig, Curator

Items 25,000: b/w original photographs, colour transparencies (35mm, 10″ × 8″), original children's drawings (19th century), menu cards, printed inn signs, glass negatives, daguerreotypes, lantern slides, postcards, original cartoons, illustrated maps, fine art prints, stereographs, posters, greetings cards, illustrated books

Dates of subject matter 1700 to 1950

Dates of photographs 1850 to present

Subjects Cambridge town, county and university views and personalities, old and antique household objects, fenland life, early children's toys, surgeon's and dentist's tools, inn signs, perambulators, doll's houses, Noah's arks, lace making tools

Access and conditions Open to the public by appt (write), Tues-Sat 10.30–5. All material available for editorial reproduction and for advertising. B/w and colour material loaned; b/w prints available for a fee. Reproduction rights fees charged at the Curator's discretion. Staff will undertake up to one hour of research free of charge; fee charged subsequently per hour.

311 • CAMBRIDGESHIRE CENTRAL LIBRARY

Cambridgeshire Collection

7 Lion Yard, Cambridge CB2 3QD
Tel (0223) 65252 Telex 817266

Enquiries to Michael Petty, Local Studies Librarian

Items 100,000: b/w original and copy photographs, colour transparencies (35mm), glass negatives, lantern slides, postcards, illustrated maps, fine art prints, unprinted film negatives, posters, illustrated books

Dates of subject matter 1574 to present

Dates of photographs 1860 to present

Subjects Cambridge, Cambridgeshire and Isle of Ely including the fenlands, villages (especially Burwell, Bottisham and Whaddon) and village life, transport (especially buses), streetscenes, colleges, schools, churches, shops, police, fire brigade, events

Access and conditions Open to the public, Mon-Fri 9.30–5.30, Sat 9–5. Most material available for editorial reproduction and for advertising. B/w and colour material loaned; b/w prints and duplicate colour transparencies available for a fee. Photocopies available. Reproduction rights fees charged; service fees negotiable. Staff will undertake limited research. Card catalogue available.

312 • CAMBRIDGESHIRE COUNTY RECORD OFFICE

Shire Hall, Castle Street, Cambridge CB3 0AP
Tel (0223) 317281

Enquiries to Michael Farrar, County Archivist

Items About 2500: b/w original and copy photographs, colour transparencies (35mm), colour photographic prints, glass negatives, lantern slides, postcards, original cartoons, illustrated maps, prints, unprinted film negatives, posters, greetings cards, architectural drawings, illustrated books

Dates of subject matter c. 1100 to present

Dates of photographs 1890 to 1975

Subjects Cambridgeshire and Isle of Ely local history, including architecture (old buildings, churches, schools), transport, landscape, families, aerial photographs (vertical and oblique), dovecots, mazes, windmills; libraries and library equipment in England and abroad; county photographs by Francis Frith

Access and conditions Open to the public, Mon-Thurs 9–12.45, 1.45–5.15, Fri 9–12.45, 1.45–4.15. All material available for editorial reproduction subject to copyright clearance. No loans; b/w prints and duplicate colour transparencies available for a fee. Photocopies available. Reproduction rights fees charged. Staff will undertake some research. Card catalogue available.

313 • CARDIFF CENTRAL LIBRARY

The Hayes, Cardiff, South Glamorgan CF1 2QU
Tel (0222) 382116

Enquiries to R. Ieuan Edwards, County Librarian

Items About 13,000: b/w original and copy photographs, fine art prints, postcards

Dates of subject matter Late 18th century to present

Dates of photographs c. 1860 to present

Subjects Local history of the three counties of Glamorgan (especially Cardiff and Gwent) filed (for both Cardiff and for towns and villages) by street names, but including architecture (churches, shops, chapels, houses, public buildings), transport, coalmining, docks area, scenery

Access and conditions Open to the public by appt (tel), Mon-Fri 9.30–8, Sat 9.30–5.30. Most material available for editorial reproduction but not for advertising. No loans; b/w prints available for a fee. Material may be photographed by outside photographer. Photocopies available. Reproduction rights fees charged. Staff of two will undertake very limited research and mail photocopies in answer to written requests.

314 • CHARD AND DISTRICT MUSEUM

Godworthy House, High Street, Chard, Somerset TA20 1LL
Tel (04606) 3762

Enquiries to Marjorie Edwards, Administrator

Items About 300: posters, postcards, b/w original and copy photographs, greetings cards

Dates of subject matter 19th century to present

Dates of photographs c. 1870s to 1920

Subjects Posters: 19th-century posters relating to Chard and environs including sale notices of local properties, legal notices, anti-Catholic and other religious posters, election addresses; photographs: Chard in the 19th century, shops, industry, patients wearing appliances supplied by James Gillingham (local manufacturer of artificial appliances); paper-lace valentine cards

Access and conditions Open to the public by appt (tel). All material available for editorial reproduction and for advertising. B/w prints and colour transparencies available for a fee. Reproduction rights fees charged. Staff will undertake some research. Compulsory credit line.

315 • CHELTENHAM CENTRAL LIBRARY

Clarence Street, Cheltenham, Gloucestershire
GL50 3JT
Tel (0242) 582269

Enquiries to Eileen Loder or Roger Beacham

Items About 3500: b/w original photographs, postcards

Dates of subject matter 1820 to present

Dates of photographs 1880 to present

Subjects Cheltenham and environs history and topography, architecture, streetscenes, views of Cheltenham, scenes throughout UK and portraits by local photographer Hugo van Wadenoyen (1892–1959); National Buildings Record views of Cheltenham (1943)

Access and conditions Open to the public by appt (tel), Mon-Fri 9.30–7, Sat 9.30–1. Most material available for editorial reproduction and for advertising. B/w prints available for a fee. Photocopies available. Reproduction rights fees charged. Staff will undertake some research. Compulsory credit line.

316 • CHERTSEY MUSEUM

The Cedars, 33 Windsor Street, Chertsey, Surrey
KT16 8AT
Tel (09328) 65764

Enquiries to Paul Larkin, Assistant Curator

Items About 3000: b/w original and copy photographs, colour transparencies (35mm), colour photographic prints, glass negatives, daguerreotypes, postcards, original cartoons, illustrated maps, fine art prints, art reproductions, unprinted film negatives, stereographs, posters, greetings cards, architectural drawings, cuttings and tearsheets, illustrated books

Dates of subject matter *c.* 800 to present

Dates of photographs 1850 to present, some earlier

Subjects Borough of Runnymede (emphasis on south-eastern half and towns of Chertsey, Thorpe, Ottershaw, and Addlestone) history and topography, architecture, streetscenes, industry (especially iron foundry and aircraft propellor works), portraits and groups; items in museum collection, e.g. archaeology, clocks, dolls, silver, costume; 18th- and 19th-century costumes and accessories, fashion plates (very full set) 1800 to 1900

Access and conditions Open to the public by appt (tel), Tues & Thurs 2–5, Wed Fri Sat 10–1, 2–5. All material available for editorial reproduction and for advertising. B/w prints available for a fee; colour transparencies loaned. No reproduction rights fees. Staff will undertake limited research. Card catalogue available. Compulsory credit line.

317 • CHESHIRE RECORD OFFICE

Duke Street, Chester CH1 1RP
Tel (0244) 602574

Enquiries to F. I. Dunn, County Archivist

Items B/w original and copy photographs, colour transparencies (35mm), colour photographic prints, glass negatives, lantern slides, postcards, illustrated maps, fine art prints, unprinted film negatives, posters, architectural drawings, illustrated books

Subjects Cheshire local history

Access and conditions Open to the public by appt (tel), Mon-Fri 9.45–4.30. Some material available for editorial reproduction and for advertising with permisssion of the Archivist. B/w prints and duplicate colour transparencies available for a fee. Photocopies available. Material may be copied by outside photographers. Reproduction rights and service fees charged. Staff will undertake some research for a fee. Card and printed catalogues available.

318 • CHESTER CITY RECORD OFFICE

Town Hall, Chester, Cheshire CH1 2HJ
Tel (0244) 40144 ext 2108

Enquiries to Annette M. Kennett, City Archivist

Items About 500: b/w original and copy photographs, colour transparencies (35mm), colour photographic prints, postcards, illustrated maps, fine art prints, unprinted film negatives, architectural drawings, illustrated books

Dates of subject matter *c.* 1820 to present

Dates of photographs *c.* 1900 to present

Subjects Chester and environs including architecture (churches, houses, shops), streetscenes, local transport, the River Dee, local events and personalities, people, royal visits

Access and conditions Open to the public weekdays 9–1, 2–5, Tues & Fri until 9. Most material available for editorial reproduction, but not for advertising. No loans; b/w prints and duplicate colour transparencies available for a fee. Reproduction rights fees charged. Staff of two will undertake limited research only.

319 • CHESTER LIBRARY

Northgate Street, Chester, Cheshire CH1 2EF
Tel (0244) 312935

Enquiries to V. Green, Librarian, Reference Section

Items 17,000: b/w photographs, glass negatives, postcards, illustrated maps, fine art prints, posters, illustrated books

Dates of subject matter 19th and 20th centuries

Dates of photographs 1960 to present

Dates of fine art 19th century to present

Subjects LOCAL HISTORY COLLECTION: 19th-century prints of Chester and environs; CHESTER PHOTOGRAPHIC SURVEY COLLECTION: Chester life and activities, buildings, streets, shops, businesses, transport, industry, architecture, churches, chapels

Access and conditions Open to the public, Mon Tues Thurs Fri 9.30–8, Wed 9.30–5, Sat 9.30–1. Most material available for editorial reproduction and for advertising with the Librarian's permission. B/w material loaned free of charge. Material may be copied by outside photographers. Fees negotiable. Staff will undertake some research in response to written requests. Partial card catalogue.

320 • CHESTERFIELD CENTRAL LIBRARY

New Beetwell Street, Chesterfield, Derbyshire S40 1QN
Tel (0246) 209292/3/4/5

Enquiries to John Lilley, Local Studies Librarian

Items 7319: b/w original and copy photographs, postcards, lantern slides, colour transparencies

(35mm, 5″ × 4″, larger), colour photographic prints, glass negatives, fine art prints, original cartoons, illustrated maps

Dates of subject matter Prehistory to present

Dates of photographs 1880s to present

Subjects Local history of north Derbyshire and especially Chesterfield and environs including life and activities, architecture, general views, aerial views, industry, personalities, well dressings, buildings, streets, churches, theatres, sport, fire brigade, playbills, special occasions, transport including a collection on railways and George Stephenson in Derbyshire, Chatsworth House, Haddon Hall, Hardwick Hall, industrial relics

Access and conditions Open to the public Mon-Fri 9.30–7, Sat 9.30–4. Most material available for editorial reproduction and for advertising. No loans; b/w prints and duplicate colour transparencies available for a fee. Photocopies available. Material may be copied by outside photographers. Reproduction rights fees charged. Staff will undertake limited research.

321 • CHETHAM'S LIBRARY

Long Millgate, Manchester M3 1SB
Tel (061) 834 7961

Enquiries to Michael Powell, Librarian

Items 2300: b/w original and copy photographs, colour transparencies (35mm), glass negatives, lantern slides, postcards, original cartoons, illustrated maps, fine art prints, posters, greetings cards, architectural drawings, cuttings and tearsheets, illustrated books

Dates of subject matter Prehistory to 1900

Dates of photographs 1890s to 1900

Subjects North-west England, especially Manchester, including streetscenes, buildings, local characters and events, archaeological sites and remains, theatre bills, political posters, customs

Access and conditions Open to the public Mon-Fri 9.30–12.30, 1.30–4.30, Sat 9.30–12.30 by appt. All material available for editorial reproduction and for advertising. No loans; b/w prints and duplicate colour transparencies available for a fee. Photocopies available. Reproduction rights and service fees charged. Staff will undertake some research. Card catalogue available.

322 • CHORLEY DISTRICT LIBRARY

Avondale Road, Chorley, Lancashire PR7 2EH

(From March 1986: Chorley District Central
Library, Union Street, Chorley, Lancashire
PR7 1EF)
Tel (02572) 77222/3

Enquiries to Duncan Farquhar, District
Librarian

Items 2700: b/w original and copy photographs,
lantern slides, postcards, unprinted film negatives,
architectural drawings, illustrated books

Dates of subject matter Prehistory to present

Dates of photographs c. 1860 to present

Subjects Chorley district history including
archaeology, architecture, buildings and
environments threatened by redevelopment,
special events including Royal Visits, cotton mills,
canals, police service

Access and conditions Open to the public, Mon
Tues Wed Fri 10–7, Thurs 10–1, Sat 9.30–12.15,
1.30–4.30. Some material available for editorial
reproduction and for advertising. B/w prints
available for a fee. Photocopies available.
Reproduction rights fees charged. Staff will
undertake some research.

323 • CLIFFE CASTLE ART GALLERY AND MUSEUM

Cliffe Castle, Spring Gardens Lane, Keighley, West
Yorkshire BD20 6LH
Tel (0535) 64184

Enquiries to Anne Ward, Principal Keeper

Items About 2000: b/w original photographs,
lantern slides, postcards, posters, stereographs,
glass negatives, greetings cards

Dates of subject matter 1850 to 1950

Dates of photographs Late 19th century

Subjects Yorkshire especially Keighley and
environs, architecture, landscapes, townscapes,
personalities, local history; photographs by Alex
Keighley; alpine photographs by Alfred Holmes

Access and conditions Open to qualified
researchers by appt (write), Mon-Fri 10–4.30. All
material available for editorial reproduction but
not for advertising. No loans; material may be
copied by outside photographer. Photocopies
available. Reproduction rights fees charged.

324 • CLWYD RECORD OFFICE

Old Rectory, Hawarden, Deeside, Clwyd CH5 3NR
Tel (0244) 532364

Enquiries to Geoffrey Veysey, County Archivist

Items About 9000: b/w original and copy
photographs, fine art prints, postcards, glass
negatives, colour photographic prints, illustrated
maps, posters, greetings cards, architectural
drawings, illustrated books, watercolours

Dates of subject matter Romano-British to
present

Dates of photographs 1860s to present

Dates of fine art late 18th and early 19th century

Subjects Clwyd local history including general
views of towns and villages, architecture (interiors
and exteriors), monuments and antiquities,
archaeological finds (pottery, metal implements,
etc.), groups of people (schools, churches and
chapels, sports, organizations), local personalities
including W. E. Gladstone and family, events
(return of Boer War volunteers, railway accidents,
Whit Monday processions, eisteddfods),
communications, transport (horse-drawn vehicles,
early motor cars, railways), people at work
(farming, smithies, factory workers), places of work
(collieries, lead mines, quarries, etc.); photographs
by Francis Frith of local towns; shipping
photograph albums of J. Crichton & Co. Ltd,
Saltney; railway photographs of R. J. Dean

Access and conditions Open to the public by
appt (tel), Mon-Fri 8.45–4.45. Some material
available for editorial reproduction and for
advertising. No loans; b/w prints and duplicate
colour transparencies available for a fee.
Reproduction rights fees charged. Staff will
undertake limited research. Printed catalogue of
topographical prints available.

325 • CLYDEBANK CENTRAL LIBRARY

Dumbarton Road, Clydebank G81 1XH
Tel (041) 952 1416, 952 8765

Enquiries to Patricia Malcolm, Local History
Librarian

Items 10,000: b/w original and copy photographs,
colour transparencies (35mm), colour photographic
prints, glass negatives, lantern slides, postcards,
illustrated maps, unprinted film negatives, posters,
architectural drawings, press cuttings and
tearsheets

Dates of subject matter 1800s to present

Dates of photographs 1850s to present

Subjects Clydebank local history, streets, shops, people, local events, shipyards, ship construction, launching and launching ceremonies including the *Queen Mary*, the *Queen Elizabeth*, the *Queen Elizabeth II*; ALEX HOLMES COLLECTION: local contemporary photojournalism; SINGER COLLECTION: the Singer factory, employees, working environment, machine models and parts, workers' outings, picnics

Access and conditions Open to the public by appt (tel). Most material available for editorial reproduction but not for advertising. No loans; b/w prints and duplicate colour transparencies available for a fee. No reproduction rights fees. Staff will undertake some research. Card catalogue available.

326 • COLCHESTER AND ESSEX MUSEUM

Museum Resource Centre, 14 Ryegate Road, Colchester, Essex CO1 1YG
Tel (0206) 712481/2

Enquiries to David T-D. Clarke, Curator

Items About 10,000: b/w original and copy photographs, colour transparencies (35mm), glass negatives, daguerreotypes, lantern slides, postcards, original cartoons, illustrated maps, unprinted film negatives, architectural drawings, press cuttings and tearsheets

Dates of subject matter Prehistory to present

Dates of photographs *c.* 1860 to present

Subjects Essex, especially Colchester and district, including archaeological sites and finds, historic buildings, personalities, natural history, local events and activities, portraits

Access and conditions Open to the public by appt (write), Mon-Fri 10–5. All material available for editorial reproduction and for advertising. No loans; b/w prints and duplicate transparencies available for a fee. Photocopies available. Reproduction rights and service fees charged. Staff will undertake limited research.

327 • COLCHESTER LIBRARY

Local Studies Department

Trinity Square, Colchester CO1 1JR
Tel (0206) 562243

Enquiries to Local Studies Librarian

Items Over 11,000: b/w original and copy photographs, colour transparencies (35mm), postcards, illustrated books, fine art prints, posters, colour photographic prints, greetings cards, architectural drawings, illustrated maps, press cuttings and tearsheets

Dates of subject matter 100 BC to present

Dates of photographs 1859 to present

Subjects Essex local history, especially Colchester and north-east Essex, including towns, villages, architecture, scenery, transport, trains, horses, vehicles, trams, buses, ships, yachts, boats, farming, industry, local personalities

Access and conditions Open to the public by appt, Mon-Fri 9–8, Thurs 9–5. All material available for editorial reproduction and for advertising subject to copyright clearance. No loans; b/w prints and duplicate colour transparencies available for a fee. Photocopies available. No reproduction rights fees. Staff will undertake limited research.

328 • COLNE LIBRARY

Pendle District Photographic Collection

Market Street, Colne, Lancashire BB8 0AP
Tel (0282) 865045, 865495

Enquiries to Peter Wightman, Acting District Librarian

Items 18,000: b/w original and copy photographs, glass negatives, unprinted film negatives, lantern slides, colour transparencies (35mm), colour photographic prints, illustrated maps

Dates of subject matter Prehistory to present

Dates of photographs *c.* 1870 to present

Subjects The Pendle District of Lancashire including the following villages: Nelson, Colne, Trawden, Wycoller, Foulridge, Earby, Salterforth, Blacko, Barnoldswick, Brogden, Bracewell, Barrowford, Roughlee, Barley, Newchurch, Higham, Reedley, Fence, Brierfield and also Burnley District, Ribble Valley District, Yorkshire;

material further classified under the following headings: natural history, geography and topography, architecture and planning, history, genealogy and biography, religion and religious denominations, agriculture, industry and commerce, retailing, commercial trading, communications, road-passenger transport, bridges, railways, administration, Council, health and welfare, public utilities, parks and recreation, welfare and youth services, public protections, education, cultural and recreational activities, music, sport, customs and traditions and containing such specific items as, for example, Deerstones (iron age wall), Penny's dyeworks, organ grinder, Green Fair, clog dancer, fossilized fern, Stanley Mills Handbell Ringers, Royal Morris Dancers, Amos Pickles' bakery van, Wycoller Hall, phantom horse rider, cock fighting, postman on bicycle, medieval lead-smelting works, canal barge, Rushbearing Queen crowning ceremony, Top Withens

Access and conditions Open to the public, Mon & Wed 9.30–7, Tues 9.30–12, Thurs & Fri 12–5, Sat 9.30–4.30. Most material available for editorial reproduction and for advertising. B/w prints available for a fee. Photocopies available. Reproduction rights fees charged. Staff will undertake limited research. Superbly detailed catalogue available, *Colne Library Publication No. 6, 1981*.

329 • COLWYN AREA LIBRARY

Local History Collection

Woodland Road West, Colwyn Bay, Clwyd LL29 7DH
Tel (0492) 2358 Telex 61533

Enquiries to Kathryn M. Guest, Reference Librarian

Items About 1000: b/w original and copy photographs

Dates of subject matter *c.* 1870 to present
Dates of photographs *c.* 1870 to present

Subjects Colwyn Bay and Rhos on Sea including architecture, transport, streetscenes, seaside, piers, personalities, people, aerial views

Access and conditions Open to the public by appt (tel), Mon-Fri 10–6, Wed 10–6, Sat 9.30–12.30. Most material available for editorial reproduction but not for advertising. B/w prints

available for a fee. Photocopies available. No reproduction rights fees. Staff will undertake limited research. Compulsory credit line.

330 • COOKWORTHY MUSEUM

The Old Grammar School, Fore Street, Kingsbridge, Devon TQ7 1AW
Tel (0548) 3235

Enquiries to Kathy Tanner

Items About 2500: b/w original and copy photographs, postcards, colour transparencies (35mm), greetings cards, architectural drawings

Dates of subject matter *c.* 1600 to 1950

Dates of photographs *c.* 1860 to 1950

Subjects South Devon, especially old Kingsbridge rural district life and activities including fishing, farming, celebrations, buildings, transport, trade, personalities, wrecks, Salcombe-built vessels

Access and conditions Open to qualified researchers by appt (write), Mon-Fri 9–5. Some material available for editorial reproduction, but not for advertising. B/w material loaned free of charge for one month; b/w prints available for a fee. Duplicate colour transparencies available for a fee. Reproduction rights and holding fees charged. Staff will undertake limited research.

331 • CORNWALL COUNTY LIBRARY

County Local Studies Library, 2–4 Clinton Road, Redruth, Cornwall TR15 2QE
Tel (0209) 216760

Enquiries to Terry Knight

Items About 200,000: unprinted film negatives, glass negatives, b/w copy photographs, posters, postcards

Dates of subject matter 3000 BC to present

Dates of photographs 1850s to present

Subjects Cornwall, history, topography, antiquities, customs, architecture, industry, railways, transport, mining, leisure and tourism, aerial views; GEORGE ELLIS COLLECTION (95,000 glass negatives, 1939 to 1981), Bodmin and vicinity local history including agricultural shows, community events (May Queens, etc.), royal visits, portraits, weddings, photojournalism

Access and conditions Open to qualified researchers by appt, Tues-Thurs 9.30–12.30, 1.30–5, Fri 9.30–12.30, 1.30–7, Sat 9.30–12.30. Most material available for editorial reproduction and for advertising (subject to copyright clearance in some cases). No loans; b/w prints available for a fee. Photocopies available. Reproduction rights fees charged. Staff of two will undertake limited research.

332 • COTSWOLD DISTRICT COUNCIL MUSEUMS SERVICE

Corinium Museum, Park Street, Cirencester, Gloucester GL7 2BX
Tel (0285) 5611

Enquiries to David Viner, Curator of Museums

Items About 2000: b/w original and copy photographs, colour transparencies (35mm), postcards, glass negatives, lantern slides, architectural drawings, fine art prints

Dates of subject matter 1st century AD to present

Dates of photographs *c.* 1875 to present

Subjects CORINIUM MUSEUM COLLECTION: archaeology of Romano-British town of Corinium, sculptures, mosaics, and archaeological finds and structures from excavations, coins, full-scale reconstructions; Cotswold prehistory, long barrows, etc.; Cirencester Abbey; wool trade; COTSWOLD COUNTRYSIDE COLLECTION, Northleach: social history of the area especially agricultural history, processes and techniques; transport history, horse-drawn vehicles, farm wagons, road vehicles, railways; Cirencester, especially architectural developments in the town, buildings, social history, personalities, commerce; access to THAMES & SEVERN CANAL COLLECTION

Access and conditions Open to qualified researchers by appt, 31 Oct to 1 Apr closed Mon, Tues-Sat 10–5; 2 Apr to 30 Oct Mon-Sat 10–5.30. All material available for editorial reproduction and for advertising. B/w material loaned free of charge for three months; colour transparencies duplicated for a fee. Photocopies available. Reproduction rights fees charged. Staff will undertake some research.

333 • *COVENTRY EVENING TELEGRAPH*

Corporation Street, Coventry, Warwickshire CV1 1FP
Tel (0203) 25588

Enquiries to Keith Draper, Chief Librarian

Items 100,000: b/w original photographs

Dates of photographs 1945 to present

Subjects Local news photography including local views and streetscenes, motor vehicles, news features, World War II air raid damage in Coventry

Access and conditions Open to qualified researchers by appt (tel). Most material available for editorial reproduction and for advertising. B/w prints available for a fee. Photocopies available. Reproduction rights fees charged. Staff of six will undertake limited research.

334 • THE CRAVEN MUSEUM

Town Hall, High Street, Skipton, North Yorkshire BD23 1AH
Tel (0756) 4079

Enquiries to Jane Mansergh, Curator

Items About 2000: fine art prints, b/w original and copy photgraphs, lantern slides, glass negatives, postcards, architectural drawings, greetings cards

Dates of subject matter 14th century to present

Dates of photographs *c.* 1860 to 1970s

Subjects Skipton and the Craven area including history, architecture (domestic and ecclesiastical), Bolton Abbey, Skipton Castle, Holy Trinity Church, Barden Tower, Gordale Scar, landscapes and townscapes, shops, personalities

Access and conditions Open to the public by appt, Apr-Sept Mon-Fri 11–5 (closed Tues), Sat 10–12, 1–5, Sun 2–5, Oct-Mar Mon-Fri 2–5 (closed Tues), Sat 10–12, 1.30–4.30. All material available for editorial reproduction and for advertising, subject to copyright clearance. No loans; material may be copied by outside photographers. No reproduction rights fees charged. Staff will undertake some research. Compulsory credit line. Partial card catalogue available.

335 • CREWE PUBLIC LIBRARY

Prince Albert Street, Crewe, Cheshire CW1 2DH
Tel (0270) 211123

Enquiries to Geoffrey R. Pimlett, Principal
Librarian

Items 1500: b/w original and copy photographs,
postcards, unprinted film negatives

Dates of subject matter 1880 to present

Dates of photographs 1900 to 1980

Subjects Crewe local history, architecture,
railways, town centre redevelopment, railway
workers' housing, railway engineering works, Rolls
Royce Motors factory; ALBERT HUNN COLLECTION:
buildings in Crewe before the major demolition in
the 1960s

Access and conditions Open to the public by
appt, Mon Tues Thurs Fri 9–7, Wed 9–5, Sat 9–1.
All material available for editorial reproduction
and for advertising. B/w material loaned free of
charge; b/w prints and duplicate colour
transparencies available for a fee. Reproduction
rights fees charged. Staff will undertake limited
research. Publication available: Howard Curran,
Michael Gilsenan, Bernard Own and Joy Owen,
Change at Crewe, Crewe Public Libraries, 1984.

336 • CROYDON PUBLIC LIBRARY

Surrey and Croydon Photographic Collection

Katharine Street, Croydon, Surrey CR9 1ET
Tel (01) 688 3627

Enquiries to Martin A. Hayes, Local History
Librarian

Items About 10,000: b/w original and copy
photographs

Dates of subject matter 15th century to present

Dates of photographs 1870 to present

Subjects Local history of Croydon and Surrey
including architecture (Palace of Archbishops of
Canterbury, 16th-century Whitgift almshouses,
medieval parish church of St John the Baptist),
sports including old football ground of Crystal
Palace, markets, fairs, festivals including electing
the Mayor and beating the bounds, suffragettes,
rural scenes (parks, estates), lavender and mint

growing in late 19th and early 20th century in
Mitcham area, industry (snuff mills, gunpowder
mills and corn mills along the River Wandle),
bell-making firm of Gillett and Johnstone,
streetscenes, horse-drawn and electric trams
(1879–1950), cars, pennyfarthings, steam and
electric railway trains, shops

Access and conditions Open to the public by
appt (tel), Mon 9.30–7, Tues-Fri 9.30–6, Sat 9–5.
Most material available for editorial reproduction
and for advertising. No loans; b/w prints available
for a fee. Photocopies available. Reproduction
rights fees charged. Staff will undertake some
research.

337 • CUMBRIA COUNTY COUNCIL RECORD OFFICE

The Castle, Carlisle, Cumbria CA3 8UR
Tel (0228) 23456 ext 316

Enquiries to Bruce Jones, County Archivist

Items About 3000: b/w original and copy
photographs, colour transparencies (35mm), glass
negatives, postcards, original cartoons, illustrated
maps, posters, greetings cards, architectural
drawings

Dates of subject matter *c.* 1600 to present

Dates of photographs *c.* 1860 to present

Subjects Cumbria local history and especially the
old county of Cumberland

Access and conditions Open to the public, Mon-
Fri 9–5. Most material available for editorial
reproduction and for advertising. B/w prints and
duplicate colour transparencies available for a fee.
Reproduction rights fees charged at the Archivist's
discretion. Staff will undertake limited research.
Photocopies available.

338 • CUMNOCK AND DOON VALLEY DISTRICT LIBRARY

Bank Glen, Cumnock KA18 1PH
Tel (0290) 22024

Enquiries to I. C. Crawford, District Librarian

Items B/w original and copy photographs, colour
transparencies (35mm, 5″ × 4″), glass negatives,

lantern slides, illustrated maps, stereographs, architectural drawings, press cuttings, illustrated books

Dates of photographs 1880 to present

Subjects Ayrshire local history especially Cumnock and Doon Valley district, life and activities including mining communities, towns and villages, transport, railways, miners' houses, mines and pits, men in working clothes, farms, architecture, churches, shops, celebrations

Access and conditions Open to the public by appt (tel). Some material available for editorial reproduction and for advertising. No loans; b/w prints available for a fee. Photocopies available. No reproduction rights fees charged. Staff will undertake some research and mail photocopies. Compulsory credit line.

339 • DARLINGTON BRANCH LIBRARY

Crown Street, Darlington, County Durham
DL1 1NB
Tel (0325) 469858

Enquiries to John Mallam, Divisional Librarian

Items About 10,750: b/w original and copy photographs, colour transparencies (35mm, 5″ × 4″, larger), colour photographic prints, glass negatives, postcards, unprinted film negatives, posters, architectural drawings, illustrated books

Dates of subject matter 1800 to present

Dates of photographs c. 1850 to present

Subjects Darlington and environs and parts of County Durham and north Yorkshire local history including architecture (shops, businesses, schools, housing), streetscenes; transport including trams (horse-drawn and electric), trolley buses, modern buses, railways; industries and works outings (picnics), events, people, school children, group photos

Access and conditions Open to the public, Mon-Fri 9–1, 2.15–7, Sat 9–1, 2.15–5. All material available for editorial reproduction and for advertising subject to copyright clearance. No loans; b/w prints and duplicate colour transparencies available for a fee. Photocopies available. Service fees charged. Compulsory credit line. Staff of three will undertake limited research for out-of-town users. Card catalogue available.

340 • DARLINGTON MUSEUM

Tubwell Row, Darlington, County Durham
DL1 1PD
Tel (0325) 463795

Enquiries to Alan Suddes, Assistant Curator

Items About 2000: b/w original and copy photographs, postcards, colour transparencies (35mm), lantern slides, posters, greetings cards

Dates of subject matter 1800s to present

Dates of photographs 1890s to present

Subjects Darlington and environs local history especially from the 19th century to the present including streetscenes, shops; RAILWAY COLLECTION: industrial and other locomotives of the British Isles, railway history in the Darlington area, including original watercolour *Opening of the S & D Railway, 1825* by John Dobbin, posters from international railway companies, railway ephemera

Access and conditions Open to the public by appt, Mon-Wed & Fri 10–1, 2–6, Thurs 10–1, Sat 10–1, 2–5.30. All material available for editorial reproduction and for advertising. Some b/w material loaned; b/w prints and duplicate transparencies available for a fee. Photocopies available. Reproduction rights fees charged for commercial use. Staff will undertake limited research.

341 • DARTFORD CENTRAL LIBRARY

Central Park, Dartford, Kent DA1 1EU
Tel (0322) 21133/4

Enquiries to Geoff Beetles, Reference and Information Librarian

Items About 10,000: b/w original and copy photographs, colour photographic prints, glass negatives, lantern slides, postcards, fine art prints, posters, greetings cards, architectural drawings, cuttings and tearsheets, illustrated books

Dates of subject matter Prehistory to present

Dates of photographs 1880s to present

Subjects Dartford and environs and north-west Kent, history of Dartford and vicinity; E. C. YOUENS COLLECTION (glass negatives)

Access and conditions Open to the public by appt, Mon-Sat, closed Wed afternoons. All material available for editorial reproduction and for advertising subject to copyright clearance. B/w material not loaded; b/w prints available for a fee. Reproduction rights fees charged. Staff will undertake some research. Card catalogue.

342 • DARTINGTON RURAL ARCHIVE

Dartington Hall, Totnes, Devon TQ9 6JE
Tel (0803) 812168

Enquiries to Moira Mellor

Items Over 4000: b/w transparencies (35mm), unprinted film negatives, b/w copy photographs

Dates of subject matter 15th century to 1930

Dates of photographs 1850 to 1930

Subjects South Devon (area contained by South Hams & Teignbridge District Councils and Torbay) and southern half of Dartmoor local history including village, market town and rural life, agriculture, transport, trades and crafts, architecture, portraits, schools, clothing, portraits, interiors, royal visits, recreation and leisure activities (sports, fairs, tea parties, fêtes, picnics, etc.); indexed by village and town with subject cross reference

Access and conditions Open to the public by appt (tel 10–5 weekdays), Wed 2–4 and by special arrangement. Most material available for editorial reproduction and for advertising. No loans; b/w prints available for a fee. Photocopies available. Reproduction rights fees charged. Staff will undertake some research. Card catalogue available.

343 • DARTMOOR NATIONAL PARK AUTHORITY

Parke, Haytor Road, Bovey Tracey, Devon TQ13 9JQ
Tel (0626) 832093

Enquiries to John W. H. Weir, Information Officer

Items 15,000: colour transparencies (35mm), b/w original photographs, original cartoons, illustrated maps, postcards, illustrated books, posters, greetings cards

Dates of subject matter 4000 BC to present

Dates of photographs 1974 to present

Subjects Dartmoor National Park including

access, agriculture, archaeology, buildings, departments, education, geology, industrial archaeology, industry, interpretation and information, landscape, military, natural history, recreation, sport, social history, transport, communications, water, weather, works, ground services

Access and conditions Open to qualified researchers by appt (write). All material available for editorial reproduction and for advertising. B/w and colour material loaned free of charge for one month. Photocopies available. Reproduction rights and service fees charged. Staff of two will undertake some research. Compulsory credit line. Card catalogue available.

344 • DERBY CENTRAL LIBRARY

Derby Local Studies Department

25B Irongate, Derby, Derbyshire DE1 3GL
Tel (0332) 31111 ext 2184

Enquiries to Local Studies Librarian

Items About 5000: b/w original and copy photographs, glass negatives, original cartoons, posters, colour photographic prints, illustrated books

Dates of subject matter c. 1800 to present

Dates of photographs 1840s to present

Subjects Derbyshire local history with emphasis on Derby and the southern part of the county including architecture, transport (buses, trams), customs including well dressing, portraits, topographical photographs by Richard Keene (19th-century local photographer), aerial views

Access and conditions Open to the public, Mon Tues 9–7, Wed-Fri 9–5, Sat 9.30–4. All material available for editorial reproduction and for advertising. No loans; b/w prints available for a fee. Photocopies available. Material may be copied by outside photographers. Reproduction rights fees charged. Staff will undertake limited research. Copyright clearance is responsibility of user.

345 • DEVON CENTRAL LIBRARY

Westcountry Studies Library, Castle Street, Exeter, Devon EX4 3PQ
Tel (0392) 53422

Enquiries to Ian Maxted, Westcountry Studies Librarian

Items 60,000: glass negatives, lantern slides, b/w original and copy photographs, unprinted film negatives, posters, fine art prints, postcards, colour transparencies (35mm), colour photographic prints, illustrated maps, original cartoons, illustrated books, press cuttings and tearsheets

Dates of subject matter Prehistory to present

Dates of photographs 1860 to present

Subjects Devon and south-west England especially architecture (major public buildings, churches, large private houses, country houses), landscape, coastal scenes; social life, industries, shipping, agriculture, portraits; JOHN STUBB COLLECTION (local photographer 1865–1917) of church architecture; A. W. SEARLEY COLLECTION (local photographer 1860–1942) of world geography and travel; special collection on Napoleon (about 350 items)

Access and conditions Open to the public by appt (tel), Mon Tues Thurs Fri 9.30–8, Wed 9.30–6, Sat 9.30–4. Most material available for editorial reproduction and for advertising. No loans; b/w prints and duplicate colour transparencies available for a fee. Photocopies available. Reproduction rights fees charged. Staff of four will undertake very limited research only.

346 • DEVON RECORD OFFICE

Castle Street, Exeter, Devon EX4 3PU
Tel (0392) 53509

Enquiries to M. M. Rowe, County Archivist

Items About 4000: b/w original and copy photographs, unprinted film negatives, glass negatives, daguerreotypes, lantern slides, postcards, illustrated maps, architectural drawings

Dates of subject matter Prehistory to present

Dates of photographs Mid-19th century to present

Subjects COPELAND COLLECTION (c. 1920–1930): Devon houses and churches including exteriors, interiors, towers, porches, doorways, fonts, pulpits, Devon stone crosses, Devon church houses; CHAPMAN COLLECTION: photographs by B. Chapman and Son, commercial photographers of Dawlish including Devon topography, churches, houses, inns (1890–1960), Princetown Prison mutiny (1932); miscellaneous collection:

topography of Devon, some of other counties, some overseas

Access and conditions Open to the public by appt (tel), Mon-Thur 9.30–5, Fri 9.30–4. Some material available for editorial reproduction. B/w prints available for a fee by arrangement with local photographers. Photocopies available. Reproduction rights fees charged. Staff will undertake limited research. Catalogue available.

347 • DEWEY MUSEUM

c/o Warminster Library, Three Horse Shoes Mall, Warminster, Wiltshire BA12 9BT
Tel (0985) 216022

Enquiries to Jack Field, Honorary Curator, Trinity Cottage, 16 Vicarage Street, Warminster BA12 8JE. Tel (0985) 215640

Items About 600: b/w original photographs, b/w copy photographs, colour photographic prints, postcards, old fine art prints, architectural drawings

Dates of subject matter BC to present

Dates of photographs 1860 to present

Subjects Local history of Warminster and surrounding area including geology, architecture, streetscenes, festivals, social history

Access and conditions Open to the public by appt, Mon-Fri 10–5, Sat 10–12.30. Some material available for editorial reproduction and for advertising; some for private research only. No loans; b/w prints available for a fee. Reproduction rights fees charged. Staff will undertake limited research. Some material copyright. Card catalogue in preparation.

348 • IAN DEWHIRST

14 Raglan Avenue, Fell Lane, Keighley, West Yorkshire BD22 6BJ

Items About 1000: b/w copy negatives, glass negatives, postcards, b/w original photographs

Dates of subject matter c. 1800 to present

Dates of photographs c. 1850 to present

Subjects Yorkshire and the Keighley district, streetscenes, transport, social conditions, architecture, trades and crafts, recreation

Access and conditions Not open; written requests only. All material available for editorial reproduction and for advertising. B/w prints available for a fee. No reproduction rights fees charged. Staff will undertake some research.

349 • DICK INSTITUTE

Elmbank Avenue, Kilmarnock, Strathclyde KA1 3BU
Tel (0563) 26401

Enquiries to James Hunter, Curator

Items Over 12,000: b/w original and copy photographs, colour transparencies (35mm, 5″ × 4″), colour photographic prints, lantern slides, glass negatives, daguerreotypes, postcards, original cartoons, illustrated maps, fine art prints, art reproductions, unprinted film negatives, greetings cards, architectural drawings, illustrated books

Dates of subject matter Prehistory to present

Dates of photographs 1845 to present

Subjects Ayrshire local history, streetscenes, farming, ships, railways, mansions, castles, portraits; Scottish landscapes and portrait paintings; book illustrations by William Bell Scott; paintings by Sir Lawrence Alma Tadema and Frederic Lord Leighton; 16th- and 17th-century decorative arts; musical instruments, arms and armour, textile design

Access and conditions Open to qualified researchers by appt, Mon-Fri 9–5. All material available for editorial reproduction and for advertising. B/w and colour material loaned free of charge for one month. B/w prints and duplicate colour transparencies available for a fee. Photocopies available. Reproduction rights fees charged. Staff will undertake some research.

350 • DORSET COUNTY LIBRARY

Local Studies Collection

Colliton Park, Dorchester, Dorset DT1 1XJ
Tel (0305) 63131

Enquiries to Local Studies Librarian

Items 12,000: colour transparencies (35mm), b/w original and copy photographs, postcards, illustrated books, glass negatives, illustrated maps,

fine art prints, press cuttings and tearsheets, unprinted film negatives, posters, greetings cards

Dates of subject matter Prehistory to present

Dates of photographs 1850s to present

Subjects Dorset topography, archaeology and ancient monuments including Maiden Castle, Cerne Giant, Roman Ring, tumuli; architecture, farming, railways, portraits of local people, most towns and villages of Dorset including aerial views; local authors including John Cowper Powys and Theodore Francis Powys; HARDY COLLECTION including plays, films, local places connected with the novels, portraits of Thomas Hardy and his family

Access and conditions Open to the public, Mon Tues Wed Fri 9.30–7, Thurs 9.30–5, Sat 9–1. Some material available for editorial reproduction and for advertising. B/w prints available for a fee; colour transparencies loaned or duplicated for a fee. Photocopies available. Reproduction rights fees charged. Staff will undertake some research. Compulsory credit line.

351 • DORSET NATURAL HISTORY AND ARCHAEOLOGICAL SOCIETY

Dorset County Museum, Dorchester, Dorset DT1 1XA
Tel (0305) 62735

Enquiries to Roger Peers

Items About 32,000: b/w original and copy photographs, colour transparencies (35mm, 5″ × 4″, larger), colour photographic prints, glass negatives, daguerreotypes, lantern slides, postcards, original cartoons, illustrated maps, fine art prints, art reproductions, unprinted film negatives, posters, greetings cards, architectural drawings, press cuttings and tearsheets, illustrated books

Dates of subject matter Prehistory to present

Dates of photographs 1859 to present

Subjects Dorset archaeology, history and topography, natural history, geology, rural crafts, mills, barns, hill forts, every country house, cottage and farm, literary figures including Thomas Hardy (including his family and his circle), William Barnes, Sylvia Townsend Warner, John Fowles

Access and conditions Open to qualified researchers by appt (write), Mon-Fri 10–5, Sat 10–1, 2–5. Most material available for editorial reproduction and for advertising subject to copyright clearance. No loans; b/w prints and duplicate colour transparencies available for a fee. Photocopies available. Reproduction cutting rights fees charged. Staff will undertake some research. Card catalogue.

352 • DOVER LIBRARY

Maison Dieu House, Dover, Kent CT16 4DW
Tel (0304) 204241

Enquiries to Christine Harwood, Senior Assistant Librarian

Items About 700: b/w original and copy photographs, colour photographic prints, postcards, fine art prints, illustrated books, art reproductions

Dates of subject matter 12th century to present

Dates of photographs 1850s to present

Subjects Dover local history including streetscenes, architecture, business, transportation (shipping, railways), scenics and townscapes, some aerial views, Dover Castle

Access and conditions Open to the public by appt, Mon Tues Thurs 9.30–6, Wed 9.30–1, Fri 9.30–7, Sat 9.30–5. Some material available for editorial reproduction and for advertising. No loans; b/w prints and duplicate colour transparencies available for a fee. Reproducton rights fees charged. Staff will undertake limited research.

353 • DOVER MUSEUM

Ladywell, Dover, Kent CT16 1DQ
Tel (0304) 201066

Enquiries to Curator

Items Over 4000: b/w original and copy photographs, fine art prints, postcards, lantern slides, colour photographic prints, glass negatives, unprinted film negatives, illustrated maps, architectural drawings, press cuttings and tearsheets

Dates of subject matter AD 43 to 1976

Dates of photographs 1850 to 1976

Subjects Local history of the town and port of Dover with emphasis on architecture, civic occasions including Cinque Port ceremonies,

Channel crossings (air, sea, canoe, swimming), scenic views, transport (trams, trains, ships), industries; special subjects: Dover Castle, the Western Heights, the military

Access and conditions Open to the public (write), Mon-Fri 10–4.45 (closed Wed). All material available for editorial reproduction and for advertising, subject to copyright clearance. No loans; b/w prints and duplicate colour transparencies available for a fee. Photocopies available. Reproduction rights fees charged. Staff will undertake some research and mail photocopies.

354 • DUCHY OF CORNWALL

10 Buckingham Gate, London SW1E 6LA
Tel (01) 834 7346

Enquiries to John W. Y. Higgs, Secretary and Keeper of the Records

Items About 6000: b/w original photographs, colour photographic prints, illustrated maps, fine art prints, illustrated books, colour transparencies (5″ × 4″)

Dates of subject matter 14th century to present

Dates of photographs 1850 to present

Subjects Landed interests of the Duchy of Cornwall including farms, the Isles of Scilly, Dartmoor; visits to the estates by HRH the Prince of Wales, Duke of Cornwall, and by the Princess of Wales; visits by the Queen, members of the Royal Family and previous Dukes of Cornwall

Access and conditions Open to the public by appt (write), Mon-Fri 9.30–5. Some material available for editorial reproduction with the Secretary's approval, but not for advertising. B/w and colour material loaned free of charge. Reproduction rights fees charged. Staff of two will undertake some research. Printed catalogue available.

355 • DUDLEY PUBLIC LIBRARIES

Archives and Local History Department

St James's Road, Dudley, West Midlands DY1 1HR
Tel (0384) 55433 exts 5514, 5526 Telex 339831

Enquiries to Hilary Atkins, Archivist and Local History Librarian

Items About 15,000: b/w original and copy photographs, colour transparencies (35mm, 5″ × 4″), colour photographic prints, glass negatives, postcards, posters, press cuttings and tearsheets, illustrated books, lantern slides, illustrated maps, architectural drawings

Dates of subject matter 13th century to present

Dates of photographs *c*. 1860 to present

Subjects Local history of the Metropolitan Borough of Dudley including Dudley, Dudley Castle, Stourbridge, Halesowen, Brierley Hill, Kingswinford, Sedgley, Cosely; local buildings and streets (systematic survey of streets in parts of Dudley 1955–1965), industries including coal, limestone and clay mining, glassmaking (hand-blown crystal), iron and steelmaking, chain and nail making, engineering, canals, portraits of local people; some aerial views; coverage of Black Country; T. W. KING COLLECTION of canal photographs (1923–1961)

Access and conditions Open to the public, Mon Wed Fri 9–1, 2–5, Tues & Thurs 2–7. All material available for editorial reproduction and for advertising, subject to copyright clearance. No loans; b/w prints and duplicate colour transparencies available for a fee. Photocopies available. Reproduction rights fees charged. Staff of three will undertake very limited research only. Card catalogue available.

356 • DUMBARTON PUBLIC LIBRARY

Strathleven Place, Dumbarton G82 1BD
Tel (0389) 63129

Enquiries to Arthur Jones, Librarian

Items About 6000: b/w original and copy photographs, colour transparencies (35mm), glass negatives, lantern slides, postcards, illustrated maps, unprinted film negatives, architectural drawings, press cuttings and tearsheets, illustrated books

Dates of subject matter Prehistory to present

Dates of photographs 1860s to present

Subjects Dumbartonshire and especially Dumbarton local history, life and activities, towns and villages, industries (especially shipbuilding and associated industries), transport, architecture, streetscenes, personalities

Access and conditions Open to the public by appt (tel), Mon Tues Thurs 10–8, Wed Fri Sat 10–5.

All material available for editorial reproduction and for advertising subject to copyright clearance. B/w prints and duplicate colour transparencies available for a fee. Photocopies available. No reproduction rights fees charged. Staff will undertake some research. Copyright clearance responsibility of user. Card catalogue.

357 • DUMFRIES MUSEUM

The Observatory, Dumfries, DG2 7SW
Tel (0387) 53374

Enquiries to David Lockwood, Curator of Museums

Items 2000: b/w original and copy photographs, colour transparencies (35mm, 5″ × 4″, larger), colour photographic prints, glass negatives, daguerreotypes, lantern slides, postcards, original cartoons, illustrated maps, fine art prints, stereographs, posters, greetings cards, architectural drawings, press cuttings and tearsheets, illustrated books

Dates of subject matter Prehistory to present

Dates of photographs 1850 to present

Subjects Local history of Dumfriesshire, Kirkcudbrightshire and Wigtownshire, but especially Dumfries, landscapes and townscapes, streets, houses and rural dwellings, transport including shipping, railways, horse-drawn vehicles and automobiles, demolitions, constructions, events, occupations, local people, festivals, museum objects and staff

Access and conditions Open to the public by appt (tel), Mon-Fri 9–1, 2–5. Most material available for editorial reproduction and for advertising by special arrangement. No loans; b/w prints and duplicate colour transparencies available for a fee. Photocopies available. Reproduction rights fees charged at the Curator's discretion. Staff will undertake limited research.

358 • DUNDEE CENTRAL LIBRARY

The Wellgate, Dundee, Tayside DD1 1DB
Tel (0382) 23141 ext 318

Enquiries to John B. Ramage, Chief Librarian

Items About 22,500: glass negatives, b/w original and copy photographs, lantern slides, posters, postcards, colour transparencies (35mm), colour photographic prints, fine art prints, architectural drawings, press cuttings and tearsheets, illustrated books

Dates of subject matter 14th century to present

Dates of photographs 1870s to present

Subjects Dundee and environs local history including streetscenes, industry, education, buildings, shops, markets, social scenes, harbour, ships, public utilities, volunteer forces, bridges, transport

Access and condtions Open to the public by appt (tel), Mon Tues Fri Sat 9.30–5, Wed Thurs 9.30–7. All material available for editorial reproduction; some restriction on advertising use. B/w prints loaned or available for a fee. Reproduction rights fees charged. Staff of six will undertake limited research. Copyright clearance responsibility of user. Card catalogue available.

359 • DUNDEE DISTRICT ARCHIVE AND RECORD CENTRE

City Chambers, City Square, Dundee, Tayside DD1 2BY
Tel (0382) 23141 ext 4494

Enquiries to Archivist

Items About 2000: b/w original and copy photographs, glass negatives, lantern slides, press cuttings

Dates of photographs c. 1860 to present

Subjects Demolition of slum property, civil engineering works (c. 1900 to c. 1950), interior and exterior slum photographs (c. 1920 to c. 1955). constructon and maintenance of water reservoirs (c. 1900 to c. 1950), construction and maintenance of electricity generating stations and early hydroelectric schemes (c. 1910 to c. 1940), gas generating plant, domestic appliances, coke-filling equipment (c. 1913 to c. 1940)

Access and conditions Open to to the public by appt (tel), Mon-Fri 9.15–4.45. All material available for editorial reproduction and for advertising. No loans; b/w prints available for a fee. Material may be copied by outside photographers. Photocopies available. Reproduction rights fees charged.

360 • DUNFERMLINE CENTRAL LIBRARY

Local History Collection

Abbot Street, Dunfermline, Fife KY12 7NW
Tel (0383) 723661

Enquiries to James K. Sharp, Director

Items About 6000: b/w original and copy photographs, colour transparencies (35mm), colour photographic prints, postcards, glass negatives, posters, stereographs, architectural drawings

Dates of subject matter 16th century to present

Dates of photographs 1860s to present

Subjects Local history of west Fife and especially Dunfermline including buildings, streets, transport, industry, portraits

Access and conditions Open to the public by appt, Mon Tues Thur Fri 10–1, 2–7, Wed 10–1, Sat 10–1, 2–5. All material available for editorial reproduction but not for advertising. No loans; material may be copied by outside photographers. Photocopies available. Reproduction rights fees charged. Staff will undertake limited research. Copyright clearance is responsibility of user.

361 • DURHAM COUNTY LIBRARY

Durham Local Collection

Branch Library, South Street, Durham DH1 4QS
Tel (0385) 64003

Enquiries to James Main, Divisional Librarian

Items About 2500: b/w original photgraphs, fine art prints, glass negatives, postcards, illustrated maps, posters, architectural drawings, illustrated books

Dates of subject matter c. 1800 to present

Dates of photographs c. 1860 to present

Subjects Durham County and City local history especially villages and towns, industry, architecture, portraits, coalmining

Access and conditions Open to the public, Mon-Fri 9–1, 2–5, Sat 9–1. All material available for editorial reproduction and for advertising subject to copyright clearance. No loans; b/w prints available for a fee. Photocopies available. Reproduction rights fees charged. Staff will undertake some research.

362 • DYFED ARCHIVES

Carmarthenshire Record Office, County Hall, Carmarthen, Dyfed SA31 1JP
Tel (0267) 233333 ext 4182

Enquiries to Susan Beckley, Archivist-in-Charge

Items About 500: b/w original photographs, fine art prints, postcards, posters, greetings cards, colour transparencies (35mm)

Dates of subject matter 18th to 20th century

Dates of photographs 1870 to present

Dates of fine art 1780s to 1900

Subjects Former county of Carmarthenshire local history including castles (Newcastle, Dynevor Castle, Kidwelly Castle, Carreg-Cennen Castle, etc.), local churches and chapels, streetscenes, schools, farming, weaving; CASTELL GORFOD COLLECTION of 18th-century engravings of all parts of Wales; National Eisteddfod

Access and conditions Open to the public, Mon-Thurs 9–4.45, Fri 9–4.15. All material available for editorial reproduction and for advertising subject to copyright clearance. No loans; photocopies available. Material may be copied by outside photographers; negatives must be returned to the Archives. Reproduction rights fees charged. Staff of two will undertake limited research.

363 • DYFED COUNTY COUNCIL

Cultural Service Department

County Library, Dew Street, Haverfordwest, Dyfed SA61 1SU
Tel (0437) 4591

Enquiries to Joan Evans, Assistant Librarian

Items 4080: colour transparencies (35mm), fine art prints, postcards, illustrated maps, b/w original and copy photographs, posters, colour photographic prints

Dates of subject matter 17th century to present

Dates of photographs 1870 to present

Subjects Architecture (domestic, shops, castles), streetscenes, towns including Milford Haven, Broad Haven, Fishguard, good collection on Tenby and old bathing machines, harbours, fishing boats, agriculture (hay-making), schools, people in old Welsh costume (some photos, mostly illustrations), personalities (Lloyd George speaking, Mrs

Emmeline Pankhurst visiting), local carnival (Portfield fun fair held in October), cromlechs (standing stones)

Access and conditions Open to the public by appt (tel), Mon Wed Thurs 9.30–5, Tues & Fri 9.30–7, Sat 9.30–1. Most material available for editorial reproduction and for advertising subject to the Librarian's approval. Some b/w and colour material loaned; b/w prints and duplicate colour transparencies available for a fee. No reproduction rights fees. Photocopies available. Staff will undertake some research. Card catalogue available.

364 • EAST LOTHIAN DISTRICT LIBRARY

Library Headquarters, Lodge Street, Haddington, East Lothian EH41 3DX
Tel (062082) 4161 ext 346

Enquiries to Brian M. Gall, District Librarian

Items 750: b/w original and copy photographs, colour photographic prints, postcards, illustrated maps, posters, architectural drawings, press cuttings and tearsheets

Dates of subject matter 13th century to present

Dates of photographs 19th and 20th century

Subjects East Lothian, especially the towns of Prestonpans, Haddington, North Berwick and Dunbar, local history, streetscenes and architecture, life and activities, local personalities (historical and recent), fishing, harbours, farming, the seaside, group pictures of local societies and institutions

Access and conditions Open to the public Mon 2–6, Tues 10–1, Thurs & Fri 2–5. All material available for editorial reproducton and for advertising subject to copyright clearance. Photocopies available. B/w prints and colour transparencies available for a fee. Material may be copied by outside photographers. Reproduction rights fees charged. Staff will undertake limited research in response to out-of-town requests. Copyright clearance responsibility of user. Card catalogue.

365 • EAST PRESTON AND KINGSTON PRESERVATION SOCIETY

40 Sea Road, East Preston, West Sussex BN16 1JP

Enquiries to Richard Preston

Items 100: unprinted film negatives, b/w original and copy photographs, postcards

Dates of subject matter 16th century to 1940

Dates of photographs 1900 to 1940

Subjects Local history of East Preston and Kingston and environs, especially farming, architecture, landscapes, people and social life

Access and conditions Open to qualified researchers by appt (write). All material available for editorial reproduction and for advertising with the Society's permission. B/w prints available for a fee. Staff will undertake limited research.

366 • EAST SUSSEX RECORD OFFICE

The Maltings, Castle Precincts, Lewes, East Sussex BN7 1YT
Tel (0273) 475400 ext 12/356

Enquiries to Roger Davey, County Records Office

Items Over 2500: b/w original and copy photographs, glass negatives, postcards, original cartoons, illustrated maps, fine art prints, posters, architectural drawings

Dates of subject matter 12th century to present

Dates of photographs *c.* 1880 to present

Subjects East Sussex local people and scenes, especially buildings; large collection of building plans from boroughs and district councils

Access and conditions Open to the public Mon-Thurs 8.45–4.45, Fri 8.45–4.15. All material available for editorial reproduction and for advertising subject to depositor's permission. No loans; b/w prints available for a fee. Photocopies available. No reproduction rights fees charged. Staff will undertake limited research. Partial catalogues available arranged by parish.

367 • ECCLES CENTRAL LIBRARY

City of Salford Cultural Services Department

Church Street, Eccles M30 0EP
Tel (061) 789 1430, 789 7331

Enquiries to Local History Librarian

Items About 10,000: b/w copy and original photographs, colour transparencies (35mm), colour photographic prints, glass negatives, lantern slides, postcards, old fine art prints, illustrated books

Dates of subject matter 18th century to present

Dates of photographs 1880 to present

Subjects Local history of Eccles, Barton, Winton, Patricroft, Monton and Worsley including architecture, education, industry (heavy engineering), Bridgewater and Manchester Ship Canal, personalities, social history; emphasis on streetscenes; special collection of material relating to James Nasmyth, Scottish machinist and inventor of steam hammer including sketched drawings, illustrated books, his life and work, photographs of items manufactured by his firm, steam locomotives

Access and conditions Open to the public, Mon Tues Thurs Fri 9–7, Wed 9–5, Sat 9–1. Most material available for editorial reproduction and for advertising. No loans; b/w prints and duplicate colour transparencies available for a fee; material may be copied by outside photographers. Photocopies available. Reproduction rights fees charged. Staff will undertake limited research. Some material copyright. Card catalogue available.

368 • EDINBURGH CITY CENTRAL LIBRARY

1 George IV Bridge, Edinburgh EH1 1EG
Tel (031) 225 5584

Edinburgh Room

Enquiries to Antony P. Shearman, City Librarian, ext 223

Items About 44,000: b/w original and copy photographs, lantern slides, fine art prints, colour transparencies (35mm), colour negatives, press cuttings and tearsheets, illustrated books, postcards, architectural drawings, stereographs, illustrated maps

Dates of subject matter 15th century to present
Dates of photographs 1840s to present

Dates of fine art 16th century to present

Subjects Local history topography of Edinburgh, especially architectural detail and costume; calotypes by D. O. Hill and Robert Adamson and also by Dr Thomas Keith (1840s and 1850s, streets and buildings); JAMES SKENE COLLECTION of watercolour drawings of Edinburgh streetscenes and buildings, general views, etc., mostly 1817–1819; panoramic, aerial and bird's-eye views; transport including horse-drawn vehicles, railways, trams, buses; Firth of Forth steam ferries, ships built at Henry Robb shipyard at Leith; city social life including prints of city characters, late 18th- and early 19th-century portraits by John Kay and Benjamin Crombie's portraits and caricatures of local people, *Modern Athenians* (1837–1847); caricatures in watercolour by Ned Holt; cinema exteriors; special categories in 35mm colour transparencies include wild flowers of Edinburgh, 19th-century costume, early 20th-century school interiors, Edinburgh zoo

Access and conditions Open to qualified researchers by appt (tel), Mon-Fri 9–9, Sat 9–1, (material from safe, Mon-Fri 2–4). Some material available for editorial reproduction and for advertising. B/w prints and duplicate colour transparencies available for a fee. Photocopies available. Access/service fee charged. Staff will undertake some research.

Scottish Department

Enquiries to Margaret Burgess, Librarian in Charge, ext 237

Items About 20,000: colour transparencies (35mm), lantern slides, b/w original and copy photographs, fine art prints, glass negatives, press cuttings and tearsheets, stereographs, illustrated maps, illustrated books

Dates of subject matter Prehistory to present

Dates of photographs *c.* 1850 to present

Subjects Scotland excluding Edinburgh, topographical prints and drawings indexed by subject, artist and engraver; photographs by Dr Thomas Keith (1850s), DR ISABEL F. GRANT COLLECTION on Highland folk-life at the turn of the century and including housing (interiors and exteriors), crafts including pottery, weaving, spinning, carding, dyeing, thatching, rope-making; peat-cutting, fishing, net-making, fishing boats, farming including hand ploughing, harvesting, sowing, shoeing ponies, people washing clothes in streams, Highland funerals, pipers

Access and conditons Open to the public by appt (tel), Mon-Fri 9–9, Sat 9–1. Some material available for editorial reproduction and for advertising. B/w prints and duplicate colour transparencies available for a fee. Photocopies available. Reproduction rights fees charged. Staff

will undertake limited research. Card catalogue available.

369 • PASSMORE EDWARDS MUSEUM

Romford Road, Stratford, London E15 4LZ
Tel (01) 519 4296

Enquiries to Pat M. Wilkinson, Principal Assistant Curator

Items *c.* 23,000: b/w original and copy photographs, glass negatives, postcards, lantern slides, greetings cards, daguerreotypes, fine art prints, illustrated maps, posters, architectural drawings, illustrated books, press cuttings and tearsheets

Dates of subject matter *c.* 500 BC to *c.* 1950

Dates of photographs mainly 1930–1939

Subjects Essex local history including buildings, churches, townscapes and landscapes, historical sites, special emphasis on Becontree Hundred, systematic photographs of river areas in Newham; personalities file including the Fry family and other Essex families and *Vanity Fair* caricatures of Essex MPs (*c.* 1895–1905)

Access and conditions Open to the public by appt (write), Mon-Fri 10–6, Sat 10–1, 2–5. Some material available for editorial reproduction and for advertising. No loans; b/w prints available for a fee. Reproduction rights and service fees charged. Staff will undertake some research.

370 • ELGIN LIBRARY

Local Studies Collection

Grant Lodge, Cooper Park, Elgin IV30 1HS
Tel (0343) 2746

Enquiries to Mike Seton, Principal Librarian

Items 13,880: b/w copy and original photographs, colour transparencies (35mm), colour photographic prints, glass negatives, postcards, posters, illustrated books

Dates of subject matter *c.* 1800 to present

Dates of photographs 1900 to present

Subjects Local history of Moray district with emphasis on towns, architecture, streetscenes; landscapes, agriculture, distilleries, fisheries and fishing boats, portraits, transport, social history

Access and conditions Open to the public by appt (tel), Mon-Fri 10–8, Sat 10–12. Most material available for editorial reproduction and for advertising. No loans; b/w prints and duplicate colour transparencies available for a fee. Photocopies available. Reproduction rights fees charged. Staff will undertake limited research. Most material copyright. Card catalogue available.

371 • ELLESMERE PORT CENTRAL LIBRARY

Civic Way, Ellesmere Port, South Wirral, Cheshire L65 0BG
Tel (051) 355 8101   Telex 627348

Enquiries to Bob Hunt, Local History Librarian

Items About 1000: b/w original and copy photographs, colour transparencies (35mm)

Dates of subject matter 1860s to present

Dates of photographs *c.* 1900 to date

Subjects Ellesmere Port industrial and social history, transport with emphasis on canal history including Manchester Ship Canal, petrochemical industry, docks, ships and shipping, architecture, streetscenes, festivals, local pantomime society, sports

Access and conditions Open to the public by appt (tel), Mon-Fri 9–5. All material available for editorial reproduction and for advertising, subject to copyright clearance. B/w prints available for a fee; colour transparencies loaned or duplicated. Photocopies available. Reproduction rights fees charged. Staff will undertake some research. Catalogue available.

372 • ENFIELD LOCAL HISTORY UNIT

Southgate Town Hall, Green Lanes, London N13 4XD
Tel (01) 886 6555

Enquiries to Graham Dallin, Local History Officer

Items About 15,000: b/w original and copy photographs, glass negatives, postcards

Dates of subject matter *c.* 1650 to present

Dates of photographs 1868 to present

Subjects Enfield, Edmonton and Southgate local history especially architecture, streetscenes, World War II bomb damage; Royal Small Arms Factory, Enfield, including celebration at end of Boer War (1902), general views of factory, some pictures of actual weapons; transport history including railways, especially Great Northern and Great Eastern Railways, good views of locomotives, railway stations, signal boxes; tramways including tracks being laid in Enfield in 1909; early views of Edmonton (1892–1930), glass plates by first town librarian, Dr Farnborough, distinguished amateur photographer

Access and conditions Open to to the public by appt (tel), Mon-Sat 9.–5, closed first Sat in month. Most material available for editorial reproduction and for advertising. No loans; b/w prints available for a fee. Material may be copied by outside photographers. Photocopies available. Staff will undertake some research and supply photocopies.

373 • ESSEX RECORD OFFICE

Chelmsford Branch

County Hall, Chelmsford, Essex CM1 1LX
Tel (0245) 267222 ext 2104

Enquiries to Victor Gray, County Archivist

Items 17,500: postcards, b/w original and copy photographs

Dates of photographs *c.* 1865 to present

Subjects FREDERICK SPALDING COLLECTION: (1865–1945) photographs by three generations of family high-street photographers: Chelmsford and environs including topography, agriculture, churches, houses, landscapes, villages, architecture, cars, lorries, tractors, agricultural machinery, streetscenes, water mills, windmills; FRITH COLLECTION: 600 photographs of Essex (1890–1940) by Francis Frith and his sons; general collection: local history of Chelmsford and environs (*c.* 1870 to present) and 300 b/w photographs of Essex windmills; postcard collection: (10,000 postcards) Essex topography filed by parish including agriculture, ecclesiology, blacksmiths, bridges, elections, fires, fishing, floods, groups, harbours and quays, hospitals, hotels and restaurants, humour, inns, libraries, markets, military forces, music and musicians, pageants, pumps, sport (cricket, golf, hunting, quoits, race courses, recreation grounds, swimming, tennis, yachting), rivers, fords and weirs, schools, ships and shipbuilding, shops and shopkeepers, steam engines, stocks and whipping posts, thatch, theatres, transport (bicycles, boats, buses, canals, ferries, motoring, railways, trams), water supplies, mills (tide, water, wind), war and war memorials, workhouses; many postcards of Chelmsford by Spalding

Access and conditions Open to the public by appt (write), Mon 10–8.45, Tues-Thurs 9.15–5.15, Fri 9.15–4.15. All material available for editorial reproduction and for advertising. No loans; b/w prints available for a fee. Reproduction rights fees charged. Staff will undertake limited research. Card catalogue available.

Southend Branch

c/o Central Library, Victoria Avenue, Southend-on-Sea, Essex SS2 6EX
Tel (0702) 612621

Items 10,000: b/w original photographs, glass negatives, postcards, posters, architectural drawings, illustrated books

Dates of subject matter 1381 to present

Dates of photographs *c*. 1860 to present

Subjects Local history of Southend-on-Sea and environs north to the River Crouch and west to Basildon including piers, sea-front (beaches, esplanades, etc.), public works, public transport (including tramways, railways), streetscenes, village scenes, vernacular architecture, ecclesiastical architecture, schools, road accidents

Access and conditions Open to the public by appt (tel). Most material available for editorial reproduction and for advertising. B/w prints available for a fee. Reproduction rights fees charged. Card catalogue.

374 • EVESHAM LIBRARY

Public Hall, Market Place, Evesham, Hereford and Worcester WR11 4RW
Tel (0386) 2291, 41348

Enquiries to Keith Barber, Librarian

Items Over 400: b/w original photographs, glass negatives, postcards, fine art prints, architectural drawings, cuttings and tearsheets

Dates of subject matter 14th century to present

Dates of photographs 1885 to present

Subjects General collection: Vale of Evesham, villages and hamlets, town of Evesham,

streetscenes, events, architecture, aerial photographs of Evesham and some of the surrounding villages; WARD COLLECTION (*c.* 1885–1910): Evesham and environs, architecture including cottages and vernacular buildings, churches, remains of Abbey, some Georgian buildings

Access and conditions Open to the public, Mon-Fri 9.30–5.30 (closed Wed), Sat 9.30–4. Most material available for editorial reproduction and for advertising subject to copyright clearance. No loans; material may be copied by outside photographer. Photocopies available. Reproduction rights fees charged at the Librarian's discretion. Staff will undertake limited research. Copyright clearance is responsibility of user.

375 • FALCONER MUSEUM

Tolbooth Street, Forres, Moray IV36 0PH
Tel (0309) 73701

Enquiries to District Curator

Items About 800: colour transparencies (35mm), b/w original photographs, b/w copy photographs, postcards, old fine art prints, greetings cards, illustrated books

Dates of subject matter Late 18th century to present

Dates of photographs 1870 to present

Subjects Local history including landscapes, architecture, streetscenes, social history, portraits; mounted wildlife specimens including local mammals, fish and insects

Access and conditions Open to the public by appt (tel), Mon-Fri 10–4.30. All material available for editorial reproduction; advertising use by special arrangement only. Colour material loaned free of charge by arrangement; b/w prints available for a fee; material may be copied by outside photographers. Staff will undertake research. Most material copyright. Card catalogue available.

376 • FERMANAGH COUNTY MUSEUM

Castle Barracks, Enniskillen, County Fermanagh, Northern Ireland BT74
Tel (0365) 25050 ext 68

Enquiries to Helen Hicky, Museum Curator

Items 5000: colour transparencies (35mm, 5″ × 4″), b/w original and copy photographs, fine art prints, illustrated maps, postcards

Dates of subject matter Prehistory to present

Dates of photographs *c*. 1900 to present

Subjects County Fermanagh local history, including archaeology, megalithic tombs, crosses, pagan idols, churches, hill forts, castles, crannogs, standing stones, quernstones, leather, beads, bronze, etc.; towns and villages including streetscenes, general views, public buildings, street furniture; local events, transport, military, maps, people; architecture including town architecture, schools, bridges, houses, rural buildings, industrial buildings, mills; folklife including objects, crafts, weaving, basket making, creel making (woven willow material), straw work, straw costumes, turf cutting, farming, blacksmiths, leisure activity; natural history, landscapes and lakescapes, flora, animals; museum collection: unusual collection of stone carvings from iron age to 19th century and including religious idols

Access and conditions Open to the public by appt (tel), Mon-Fri 9–5. Some material available for editorial reproduction and for advertising. No loans; b/w prints and duplicate colour transparencies available for a fee. Photocopies available. Reproduction rights fees charged. Staff of two will undertake some research. Card catalogue.

377 • FIRST GARDEN CITY MUSEUM

296 Norton Way South, Letchworth Garden City, Hertfordshire SG6 1SU
Tel (04626) 3149

Enquiries to Doreen Cadwallader

Items About 3000: b/w original and copy photographs, colour transparencies (35mm, larger), colour photographic prints, glass negatives, lantern slides, postcards, original cartoons, illustrated maps, posters, greetings cards, architectural drawings, press cuttings and tearsheets, illustrated books

Dates of subject matter 1898 to present

Dates of photographs *c*. 1898 to present

Subjects Letchworth Garden City history, streetscenes, industry, social amenities, farming, aerial views, housing, transport, public utility services, entertainment

Access and conditions Open to the public, Mon-Fri 2–4.30, mornings by appt, Sat 10–1, 2–4. Most material available for editorial reproduction and for advertising. No loans; b/w prints available for a fee. Material may be copied by outside photographers. Reproduction rights fees charged. Staff will undertake some research.

378 • FOLKESTONE CENTRAL LIBRARY

Local History Collection

Grace Hill, Folkestone, Kent CT20 1HD
Tel (0303) 57583

Enquiries to Brian Boreham, Reference and Local History Librarian

Items About 10,000: b/w original and copy photographs, colour photographic prints, glass negatives, postcards, illustrated maps, fine art prints, posters, greetings cards, architectural drawings, press cuttings and tearsheets, illustrated books, drawings

Dates of subject matter 300 AD to present

Dates of photographs *c*. 1850 to present

Subjects Folkestone, Hythe, Romney Marsh, Lyminge and Elham local history including life and activities, architecture, scenics, transport including shipping, ferries and colliers, railways, horse-drawn vehicles and trams; businesses, personalities, trades, farms, hotels, archaeological sites and finds; scenic and novelty postcards; miscellaneous material on other parts of Kent

Access and conditions Open to the public by appt (tel), Mon & Thurs 9–6, Tues & Fri 9–7, Wed 9–1, Sat 9–5. Some material available for editorial reproduction but not for advertising. B/w prints and duplicate colour transparencies available for a fee. Photocopies available. Reproduction rights fees charged. Staff will undertake limited research.

379 • THE FOSTER COLLECTION

38 Greenfield Road, Little Sutton, South Wirral L66 1QR
Tel (051) 339 2023

Enquiries to H. J. Foster

Items About 1600: unprinted film negatives, glass

negatives, b/w original and copy photographs, colour transparencies (35mm), illustrated books

Dates of subject matter 19th century to 1970s

Dates of photographs 1960s to 1970s

Subjects Birkenhead and surrounding area with emphasis on architecture and redevelopment including railway stations, markets, shopping centre, theatres, streetscenes.

Access and conditions Open to qualified researchers by appt (tel). All material available for editorial reproduction and for advertising. B/w prints available for a fee; colour transparencies loaned for a fee. Reproduction rights and service fees charged. Staff will undertake some research for a fee. All material copyright. Catalogue available.

380 • GAINSBOROUGH LIBRARY

Cobden Street, Gainsborough, Lincolnshire
DN21 2NS
Tel (0427) 4780

Enquiries to Area Librarian

Items About 1400: b/w original and copy photographs, colour transparencies (35mm), glass negatives, postcards, colour photographic prints, fine art prints, posters

Dates of subject matter *c.* 1300 to present

Dates of photographs 1850 to present

Subjects Gainsborough local history including streets and buildings, aerial views, personalities, railways, rural scenes, Lincolnshire towns and villages; CARTER COLLECTION including shipping on the River Trent (especially early paddle-steamers), sailing barges on the River Trent and associated canals, especially Thames barges, Humber Keels and Humber sloops, aegre (tidal bore) on the River Trent, ships and barges built at Watson's Shipyard, Gainsborough; BROCKLEHURST COLLECTION: b/w photographs of Gainsborough *c.* 1900 and scenes on the river Trent

Access and conditions Open to the public, Mon-Fri 9.30–7, Sat 9.30–12.30. All material available for editorial reproduction and for advertising. No loans; b/w prints available for a fee. Photocopies available. Reproduction rights fees charged. Staff will undertake some research. Card catalogue.

381 • GATESHEAD CENTRAL LIBRARY

Local Studies Photograph Collection

Prince Consort Road, Gateshead, Tyne and Wear
NE8 4LN
Tel (0632) 77348 Telex 537379

Enquiries to Tom Marshall, Local Studies Librarian

Items 15,000: b/w original and copy photographs, colour transparencies (35mm), colour photographic prints, glass negatives, postcards, unprinted film negatives, posters, press cuttings and tearsheets

Dates of subject matter 13th century to present

Dates of photographs 1870 to present

Subjects Gateshead local history including architecture, scenics, bridges, River Tyne, transport, trade and industry, personalities, events, cinemas, shops, public houses, public buildings

Access and conditions Open to the public, Mon Tues Thurs Fri 9–7.30, Wed 9–5. All material available for editorial reproduction and for advertising. No loans; b/w prints and duplicate colour transparencies available for a fee. Material may be copied by outside photographers. Photocopies available. No reproduction rights fees charged. Staff will undertake some research and mail photocopies. Compulsory credit line.

382 • GILLINGHAM CENTRAL LIBRARY

High Street, Gillingham, Kent ME1 1BE
Tel (0634) 51066/7

Enquiries to Stephen Robinson, Group Librarian

Items About 2600: b/w original and copy photographs, lantern slides, fine art prints, colour photographic prints, illustrated maps, colour transparencies (35mm)

Dates of subject matter *c.* 1600 to present

Dates of photographs 1890 to present

Subjects Local history of Gillingham and some Medway towns including the Jezreelites, agriculture, brick making, cement industry, education, transport, shopping; special collections on Louis Brennan (inventor of monorail), James McCudden VC (World War I fighter pilot) and Will Adam (b. 1564), first Englishman in Japan and founder of the Japanese navy

Access and conditions Open to the public, Mon Tues Thurs Fri 9.30–7.30, Wed & Sat 9.30–1, 2–5. Some material available for editorial reproduction and for advertising. No loans; b/w prints available for a fee. Material may be copied by outside photographers. Photocopies available. Reproduction rights fees charged. Staff will undertake limited research.

383 • GLOSSOP LIBRARY

Victoria Hall, Glossop, Derbyshire SK13 9DQ
Tel (04574) 2616

Enquiries to Librarian

Items About 250: b/w original and copy photographs, colour transparencies (35mm), lantern slides, postcards

Dates of subject matter 1850 to present

Dates of photographs 1900 to present

Subjects Glossop local history including scenic views, events, housing, industry, mills (cotton, calico printing, paper), transport, trams

Access and conditions Open to to the public, Mon Wed Thurs Fri 10–7.30, Tues 10–5, Sat 9.30–4. Most material available for editorial reproduction and for advertising subject to copyright clearance. No loans; b/w prints and duplicate transparencies available for a fee. Reproduction rights fees charged for material to which Library holds copyright. Staff will undertake limited research. Copyright clearance is responsibility of user.

384 • GLOUCESTER CITY MUSEUM AND ART GALLERY

Brunswick Road, Gloucester, Gloucestershire
GL1 1HP
Tel (0452) 24131

Enquiries to John Rhodes, Curator

Items About 1700: b/w original photographs, colour transparencies (35mm, 5″ × 4″), fine art prints, illustrated maps, paintings and drawings

Dates of subject matter Prehistory to present

Dates of photographs 1900 to present

Subjects Local history and archaeology including Gloucester prison (*c*. 1900) and local excavations from 1956 to the present; 18th- and early 19th-

century furniture, silver and porcelain; exceptionally fine collection of barometers

Access and conditions Open to the public by appt (tel), Mon-Fri 10–5. All material available for editorial reproduction and for advertising. B/w prints available for a fee; colour transparencies loaned for a rental fee. Reproduction rights and service fees charged. Staff will undertake some research and mail consignments. Card catalogue available.

385 • GLOUCESTER COUNTY LIBRARY

Brunswick Road, Gloucester GL1 1HT
Tel (0452) 20020, 20684   Telex 43513

Enquiries to Jill Voyce

Items 15,000: b/w original and copy photographs, colour transparencies (35mm), lantern slides, glass negatives, postcards, unprinted film negatives, press cuttings and tearsheets, illustrated books

Dates of subject matter Prehistory to present

Dates of photographs *c*. 1870 to present

Subjects Gloucestershire history and topography, architecture, streetscenes, landscapes and townscapes, transport, schools, sports, industry, agriculture, churches, folk customs, trades and traditional pursuits, personalities born in or associated with the county

Access and conditions Open to the public by appt (tel), Mon Tues Thurs 9–8, Wed Fri 9–5, Sat 9–1. Most material available for editorial reproduction and for advertising subject to copyright clearance. No loans; b/w and colour material copied for a fee. Photocopies available. Reproduction rights and service fees charged. Staff will undertake some research. Printed catalogues available.

386 • GLOUCESTERSHIRE COUNTY RECORD OFFICE

Worcester Street, Gloucester GL1 3DW
Tel (0452) 425295

Enquiries to David Smith, County Archivist

Items Over 10,000: b/w original and copy photographs, unprinted film negatives, glass negatives, postcards, colour transparencies (35mm), illustrated maps, fine art prints, architectural drawings, press cuttings and tearsheets, lantern slides, original cartoons, stereographs, posters, greetings cards, illustrated books, colour photographic prints

Dates of subject matter 17th to 20th century

Dates of photographs *c.* 1850 to present

Subjects Gloucestershire towns, villages and countryside scenes, churches and tombstones (general and detailed shots, 1960s–1980s), Gloucestershire families and personalities, country houses, schools, public buildings, services including police; Cotswold Publishing Co. (glass and film negatives) postcard views of Gloucestershire and other locations in British Isles; Henry Fox Talbot: Chess Players (2), York (1); River Severn, canals (Gloucester-Berkeley, Stroudwater, Thames & Severn); local industries and trades including Forest of Dean coalmining, Stroud Valley mills, Severn fishing, Cotswold farm buildings, shop frontages and markets; military subjects including the Royal Gloucestershire Hussars in the Middle East 1914–1918; aircraft designed by the Gloster Aircraft Co. *c.* 1920–1956

Access and conditions Open to the public by appt, Mon-Fri 9–1, 2–5, Thurs to 8. Some material available for editorial reproduction and for advertising. B/w prints and duplicate colour transparencies available for a fee. Photocopies available. Service fees charged; no reproduction rights fees. Staff will undertake research for a fee. Card catalogue available.

387 • GRANGE MUSEUM OF LOCAL HISTORY

Neasden Lane, London NW10 1QB
Tel (01) 452 8311

Enquiries to Local History Librarian

Items About 6000: b/w original and copy photographs, colour transparencies, glass negatives, lantern slides, postcards, illustrated maps, fine art prints, posters, architectural drawings, original cartoons, colour photographic prints, illustrated books

Dates of subject matter *c.* 1750 to present

Dates of photographs 1870 to present

Subjects Local history of the area covered by the London Borough of Brent (formerly Willesden, Wembley and Kingsbury), topography including streets, housing, schools, pubs, hospitals; transport, industry, civic and other events, fire

service, local personalities; St Mary's parish church, Willesden, and St Andrew's Church, Kingsbury (prints and paintings); WEMBLEY HISTORY SOCIETY COLLECTION of photographs of British Empire Exhibition (1924–1925)

Access and conditions Open to the public by appt (tel), Mon-Fri 12–5 (Wed 12–8), Sat 10–5. Most material available for editorial reproduction; for advertising at the Librarian's discretion. No loans; b/w prints available for a fee. Material may be copied by outside photographers. Reproduction rights fees charged. Staff will undertake limited research only.

388 • GRANTHAM LIBRARY

Isaac Newton Centre, Grantham, Lincolnshire NG31 0EE
Tel (0476) 63926

Enquiries to Cheryl Broughton or Gillian Doodson

Items About 500: b/w original and copy photographs, colour transparencies (35mm), glass negatives, postcards, posters, greetings cards, architectural drawings, press cuttings and tearsheets, illustrated books

Dates of subject matter *c.* 1850 to present

Dates of photographs 1880 to present

Subjects *Day by Day* (Grantham in World War II) by Walter Lee; streets, houses and places in Grantham *c.* 1890 and later, some now destroyed; aerial photographs of Grantham and district; railways and railway ephemera (timetables, maps); sports and pastimes, topography of surrounding villages, industries in and near Grantham; Isaac Newton Exhibition photographs

Access and conditions Open to the public by appt (tel). All material available for editorial reproduction and for advertising subject to copyright clearance. No loans; b/w prints and colour transparencies available for a fee. Photocopies available. Reproduction rights fees charged. Staff will undertake some research and mail prints. Card catalogue.

389 • GRAVESEND CENTRAL LIBRARY

Windmill Street, Gravesend, Kent DA12 1AQ
Tel (0474) 65600, 52758

Enquiries to Christophe Bull and Colin Crook

Items 8000: b/w copy and original photographs, colour photographic prints, glass negatives, lantern slides, postcards, illustrated maps, fine art prints, art reproductions, posters, greetings cards, architectural drawings, press cuttings, illustrated books

Dates of subject matter Prehistory to present

Dates of photographs *c.* 1850 to present

Subjects Local history of Gravesend and Northfleet and the parishes of Chalk, Cobham, Denton, Higham, Ifield, Luddesdowne, Meopham, Nurstead, and Storme; some material on parishes of Cliffe, Southfleet, Swanscombe, Greenhithe, Ash, Ridley and Trottiscliffe; cement industry, factories, workers, kilns, ship building, agriculture, paper mills

Access and conditions Open to the public by appt, Mon-Fri 9–5 (Wed closed after 1), Sat 9.30–5. All material available for editorial reproduction and for advertising. B/w prints and duplicate colour transparencies available for a fee. Photocopies available. Reproduction rights fees charged. Staff will undertake some research. Card catalogue.

390 • GREATER LONDON COUNCIL PRINT COLLECTION

Greater London Record Office and History Library, 40 Northampton Road, London EC1R 0HB
Tel (01) 633 7193 Telex 919443

Enquiries to John F. C. Phillips, Curator of Maps and Prints

Items About 40,000: fine art prints (engravings, etc.), watercolours, illustrated maps, postcards, art reproductions, posters, architectural drawings, press cuttings and tearsheets

Dates of subject matter *c.* 1550 to present

Subjects London and former county of Middlesex history and topography, major buildings and streets, the River Thames, panoramas and bird's eye views, architecture, education, entertainment, manufacturing, poverty, prisons, shops, sport, street lighting, street traders, transport (water, road, rail), water supply; comprehensive supply of maps

Access and conditions Open to the public by appt (tel), Tues-Fri 10–4.45, closed Mondays and last two weeks in October. All material available for editorial reproduction and for advertising. No loans; b/w prints available for a fee. Photocopies available. Staff will undertake limited research in answer to specific inquiries.

391 • GREATER LONDON COUNCIL PHOTOGRAPH LIBRARY

Greater London Council, 40 Northampton Road, London EC1R 0HB
Tel (01) 633 6759 Telex 919443

Enquiries to Christopher Denvir, Assistant, Greater London Photograph Library

Items 350,000: b/w original and copy photographs, colour photographic prints, colour transparencies (35mm), glass negatives, postcards, illustrated maps, fine art prints, unprinted film negatives, illustrated books

Dates of subject matter *c.* 1600 to present

Dates of photographs *c.* 1860 to present

Subjects Greater London history and topography with emphasis on former LCC area, fire stations, housing conditions, Festival of Britain, schools, housing estates, theatres, cinemas, public houses, hospitals, architecture including interiors of important buildings; WHIFFEN COLLECTION: London 1920 to 1940; TYSSEN GEE COLLECTION: City of London 1950 to 1960; AVERY COLLECTION: London 1950 to 1960

Access and conditions Open to the public, Tues-Fri 10–4.45. Some material available for editorial reproduction and for advertising. B/w material loaned free of charge for one month; b/w prints available for a fee; colour transparencies duplicated for a fee. Photocopies available. Reproduction rights fees charged. Staff will undertake limited research. Card catalogue available.

392 • GREENWICH LOCAL HISTORY LIBRARY

Woodlands, 90 Mycenae Road, London SE3 7SE
Tel (01) 858 4631

Enquiries to Julian Watson, Local History Librarian

Items 10,000: b/w original and copy photographs, colour transparencies (35mm), colour photographic prints, glass negatives, lantern slides, postcards, original cartoons, illustrated maps, fine art prints, posters, architectural drawings, press cuttings and tearsheets, watercolours and drawings, illustrated books

Dates of subject matter 1520 to present

Dates of photographs *c*. 1850 to present

Subjects History of the London Borough of Greenwich including Greenwich, Woolwich, Eltham, Deptford, Blackheath, Kidbrooke, Plumstead, Charlton, Abbey Wood, Thamesmead; Royal Greenwich Observatory, Greenwich Park, National Maritime Museum, Queen's House, Royal Naval College, Woolwich Arsenal, Woolwich Dockyards, Royal Artillery Barracks, Charlton House, Eltham Palace, *Cutty Sark*; SPURGEON COLLECTION: street life in Greenwich in the 1880s; A. R. MARTIN COLLECTION: comprehensive survey of Greenwich, Blackheath, Charlton and Kidbrooke *c*. 1921–1939; collection of 350 English watercolours and drawings (17th century)

Access and conditions Open to the public, Mon Tues Thurs 9–8, Sat 9–5, closed Wed & Fri. Most material available for editorial reproduction and for advertising. B/w prints available for a fee or loaned for one month. Colour transparencies available for a fee. Photocopies available. Staff will undertake limited research. Reproduction rights fees charged. Card catalogue; printed catalogues for watercolours, drawings and recent acquisitions.

393 • GRIMSBY CENTRAL LIBRARY

Town Hall Square, Grimsby, Humberside
DN31 1HG
Tel (0472) 53123/4

Enquiries to Derek Wattam, Group Reference Services Officer

Items 15,000: b/w original and copy photographs, postcards, posters

Dates of subject matter 13th century to present

Dates of photographs 1850 to present

Subjects Local history of South Humberside and the former county of Lincolnshire, with emphasis on the Grimsby and Cleethorpes areas, architecture; significant coverage of the deep-sea fishing industry, fishing boats, trawlers, dock scenes, seaside scenes

Access and conditions Open to the public by appt (tel), Mon-Fri 9–8, Sat 9–4. All material available for editorial reproduction subject to

copyright clearance, but not for advertising. No loans; b/w prints available for a fee. No reproduction rights fees charged. Staff will do very limited research only, checking files in response to specific requests. Compulsory credit line.

394 • GUILDFORD LIBRARY

Local Studies Library, 77 North Street, Guildford, Surrey GU1 4AL
Tel (0483) 34054

Enquiries to John Janaway, Senior Librarian

Items Over 4000: illustrated books, postcards, b/w original photographs, b/w copy photographs, engravings, glass negatives, colour photographic prints, colour transparencies (35mm), stereographs, architectural drawings, press cuttings

Dates of subject matter BC to present

Dates of photographs 1853 to present

Subjects Local history of Surrey including landscapes, towns, villages, architecture, transport (horse-drawn and motor), streetscenes, social history, portraits, agriculture and industry

Access and conditions Open to the public, Mon & Fri 10–8, Tues & Thurs 10–5, Wed 10–1, Sat 9.30–4. All material available for editorial reproduction and for advertising. No loans; b/w prints and duplicate colour transparencies available for a fee; material may be copied by outside photographers. Photocopies available. Reproduction rights fees charged. Staff of four will undertake limited research. Most material copyright. Card catalogue available.

395 • GUILDHALL ART GALLERY

c/o Guildhall Library, Aldermanbury, London EC2P 2EJ
Tel (01) 606 3030 ext 2856

Enquiries to Vivien Knight, Assistant Keeper

Items 1700: b/w original photographs

Dates of subject matter 16th to 20th century

Dates of photographs 1920s to present

Subjects Topography of London, portraits of Lord Mayors, Victorian genre painting, landscapes, works by Millais, Rossetti, Hunt and minor associates of the Pre-Raphaelites, City of London ceremonies, sculpture and portrait busts

Access and conditions Open to qualified researchers by appt (tel), Mon-Fri 9.15–5. All material available for editorial reproduction and for advertising. B/w prints available for a fee. Colour material available through Bridgeman Art Library (q.v.). Reproduction rights fees charged. Partial printed catalogue available.

396 • GUILDHALL LIBRARY PRINT ROOM

Aldermanbury, London EC2P 2EJ
Tel (01) 606 3030 ext 2864

Enquiries to Ralph Hyde, Keeper of Prints and Maps

Items 100,000: fine art prints, b/w original photographs, ephemera, posters, colour transparencies (35mm), postcards, original cartoons, architectural drawings, colour photographic prints, illustrated books

Dates of subject matter 15th century to present

Dates of photographs c. 1855 to present

Subjects London and environs with emphasis on the City of London, topography, social history, economics, maps, portraits, ephemera; PHILIP NORMAN COLLECTION of illustrations of London inns, taverns and coffee houses; CROSS COLLECTION: photographs of World War II air raid damage; CIVIC ENTERTAINMENTS COLLECTION: City of London banquet menus and invitation cards; FIRE PROTECTION ASSOCIATION COLLECTION: fires and firefighting worldwide; WORSHIPFUL COMPANY OF MAKERS OF PLAYING CARDS COLLECTION: historic playing cards; WILLSHIRE COLLECTION: Old Master prints; LONDON THEATRE BILLS AND PROGRAMMES COLLECTION: including circuses and other shows; WORSHIPFUL COMPANY OF CLOCKMAKERS COLLECTION: clocks and clockmaking; LONDON TRADE CARDS AND BILLS COLLECTION; ST PAUL'S CATHEDRAL COLLECTION OF PRINTS AND DRAWINGS including prints of the Cathedral (interiors and exteriors), some views of surrounding areas, and a collection of diagrams possibly from Christopher Wren's office to do with construction of the Cathedral

Access and conditions Open to the public by appt (tel), Mon-Fri 9.30–5. All material available for editorial reproduction and for advertising. B/w prints available for a fee; colour material available

through Bridgeman Art Library (q.v.). Reproduction rights fees charged. Staff will undertake limited research. Card catalogue available; printed catalogue available of selected prints and drawings.

397 • GUNNERSBURY PARK MUSEUM

Gunnersbury Park, London W3 8LQ
Tel (01) 992 1612

Enquiries to Ann Balfour Paul, Curator

Items 5000: b/w original photographs, fine art prints, colour transparencies (35mm, 5″ × 4″), colour photographic prints, glass negatives, daguerreotypes, lantern slides, postcards, illustrated maps, art reproductions, unprinted film negatives, stereographs, posters, greetings cards, architectural drawings, press cuttings and tearsheets, illustrated books

Dates of subject matter 17th century to 20th century

Dates of photographs c. 1850 to present

Subjects Local history of the London Boroughs of Ealing and Hounslow and environs, emphasis on Ealing, Acton, Brentford, Chiswick; rural landscapes, villages, towns, architecture, ordinary and famous people, trades, industries, laundries, transport, civic life, sports, leisure, military and naval subjects, education, elections, churches

Access and conditions Open to the public by appt (tel), Mon-Fri 9–5.15 (museum hours, afternoons only, Mar-Oct 1–5, Nov-Feb 1–4). Most material available for editorial reproduction and for advertising with some restrictons. B/w and colour material loaned free of charge for four weeks. Photocopies available. Reproduction rights fees charged. Staff will undertake some research.

398 • GWENT COUNTY LIBRARY

Local History Collection

Central Library, John Frost Square, Newport, Gwent NPT 1PA
Tel (0633) 211376

Enquiries to Brenda Strong, Reference Librarian

Items About 3000: b/w original and copy photographs, postcards, illustrated maps, fine art prints, posters, greetings cards, illustrated books

Dates of subject matter 17th century to present

Dates of photographs 19th century to present

Subjects Gwent local history, topography, views of buildings, places, Newport docks, transporter bridge, aerial views of Newport, early maps of Monmouthshire (e.g. Speeds, Saxton), Chartist prints, broadsides (1839), portraits of local personalities

Access and conditions Open to the public, Mon-Wed 9.30–6, Thurs 9.30–5, Fri 9.30–7, Sat 9.30–4. All material available for editorial reproduction and for advertising. No loans; b/w prints available for a fee. Photocopies available. No reproduction rights fees. Staff will undertake research in response to telephone or written requests, time permitting.

399 • GWYNEDD ARCHIVES SERVICE

Photographic Collection

County Offices, Caernarfon, Gwynedd LL55 1SH
Tel (0286) 4121

Enquiries to Bryn R. Parry, County Archivist

Items 100,000: b/w original and copy photographs, glass negatives, unprinted film negatives, colour transparencies (35mm, 5″ × 4″, larger), colour photographic prints, daguerreotypes, lantern slides, postcards, original cartoons, stereographs, illustrated maps, fine art prints, posters, greetings cards, architectural drawings, press cuttings and tearsheets, illustrated books

Dates of subject matter 1100 to present

Dates of photographs 1860 to present

Subjects History of former county of Caernarfonshire and especially transport history (shipping, yachting, railways); industry including slate quarrying, dressing and transportation; local government (officers, functions), education, agriculture, tourism and mountaineering, topography of town and country, law and order (especially the Beaumaris Gaol Museum), maritime subjects; World War II (material from C.O.I.); seal hunting in Canada (colour); David Lloyd George; collections of photographs by Francis Frith, W. A. Pound, John Wickend, Griffith Jones, R. W. Tomlinson, Ivor Jones, Guy Hughes, Harold Coulter, and Francis Bedford

Access and conditions Open to the public, Mon Tues Thurs Fri 9–5, Wed 9–7. Most material available for editorial reproduction and for advertising (some restrictions). No loans; b/w prints and duplicate colour transparencies available for a fee. Photocopies available. Reproduction rights fees charged. Staff will undertake some research. Card catalogue.

400 • HACKNEY LIBRARY

Rose Lipman Library, De Beauvoir Road, London N1 5SQ
Tel (01) 241 2886

Enquiries to Jon Newman, Archives Assistant

Items 12,000: b/w original and copy photographs, colour transparencies (35mm), glass negatives, lantern slides, postcards, fine art prints, architectural drawings, stereographs, press cuttings and tearsheets

Dates of subject matter 1700 to present

Dates of photographs 1860 to present

Subjects London Borough of Hackney (including former Boroughs of Shoreditch, Hackney and Stoke Newington) local history including topography, architecture, streetscenes, large houses, churches, theatres, schools and other institutions; some interior views; local government including housing, public health and leisure, local industry, transport, portraits and family albums

Access and conditions Open to the public by appt (tel), Mon 10–8, Tues-Fri 10–5.30, Sat 10–5 (closed 1–2). Some material available for editorial reproduction and for advertising. No loans; b/w prints and duplicate colour transparencies available for a fee. Photocopies available. Reproduction rights fees charged. Staff will undertake limited research. Card catalogue.

401 • HALE CIVIC SOCIETY

Photographic Collection

Hale Library, Leigh Road, Hale, Altrincham, Cheshire WA15 9BG
Tel (061) 941 2102, 928 2509

Enquiries to Branch Librarian

Items About 1300: b/w original and copy photographs, glass negatives, postcards, lantern slides

Dates of subject matter 17th century to present

Dates of photographs 1880 to present

Subjects Local history of Hale including topography, architecture, people

Access and conditions Open to the public, Mon & Fri 10–5, Tues & Thurs 10–7.30, Sat 10–4, closed Wed. All material available for editorial reproduction and for advertising. No loans; b/w prints available for a fee. Photocopies available. Reproduction rights fees charged. Staff will undertake some research. Printed catalogue.

402 • HAMILTON DISTRICT MUSEUM

129 Muir Street, Hamilton, Strathclyde ML3 6BJ
Tel (0698) 283981

Enquiries to Terry MacKenzie, Museum Curator

Items About 8000: b/w original and copy photographs, colour transparencies (35mm), lantern slides, glass negatives, postcards, fine art prints, posters, greetings cards, architectural drawings, daguerreotypes

Dates of subject matter Prehistory to present

Dates of photographs *c.* 1850 to present

Subjects Local history of Hamilton and Lanarkshire including domestic life, streetscenes, leisure activities (e.g. children at play), Victorian funfair, Sunday-school outings, buildings, local government, personalities, transport including railways, automobiles, trams and horse-drawn vehicles, industry including mining and engineering, agriculture; glass negatives by A. H. Allen (*c.* 1860 to 1914) including farming, fishing, people at work, Lanarkshire views, portraits

Access and conditions Open to the public by appt (write), Mon-Sat 10–5. All material available for editorial reproduction and for advertising. No loans; b/w prints available for a fee. No reproduction rights fees charged. Staff will undertake some research. Compulsory credit line. Card catalogue available.

403 • HAMMERMSITH AND FULHAM PUBLIC LIBRARIES

Hammersmith Local History Collection

Central Library, Shepherds Bush Road, London W6 7AT
Tel (01) 748 6032 ext 15

Enquiries to Elizabeth A. Aquilina, Local History Librarian

Items 19,000: b/w original photographs, colour transparencies (35mm), glass negatives, lantern slides, colour photographic prints, fine art prints, postcards, original cartoons, posters, greetings cards, architectural drawings, press cuttings and tearsheets, illustrated books, watercolours

Dates of subject matter 17th century to present

Dates of photographs *c.* 1860 to present

Subjects Hammersmith local history, life and activities, architecture, transport, streetscenes; watercolours by E. A. Phipson showing Hammersmith *c.* 1900–1910

Access and conditions Open to the public by appt (tel), Mon Tues Thurs 9.15–8, Fri 9.15–5, Sat 9.15–1, 2–5. Some material available for editorial reproduction and for advertising. No loans; b/w prints and duplicate colour transparencies available for a fee. Photocopies available. No reproduction rights fees charged. Staff will undertake limited research.

Fulham Local History Collection

Fulham Library, 598 Fulham Road, London SW6 5NX
Tel (01) 736 1127

Enquiries to Christine M. Bayliss

Items 17,000: b/w original and copy photographs, lantern slides, glass negatives, colour photographic prints, fine art prints, watercolours

Dates of subject matter 18th century to present

Dates of photographs *c.* 1860 to present

Subjects Fulham local history including life and activities, architecture, transport, streetscenes; CECIL FRENCH BEQUEST: oil paintings and watercolours by Sir Edward Burne-Jones, Frederic Lord Leighton, Albert Moore, William Shackleton, Sir Lawrence Alma-Tadema, S. W. Waterhouse, G. F. Watts, and others

Access and conditions Open to the public by appt (tel), Mon Tues Thurs 9.15–8, Fri 9.15–5, Sat 9.15–1, 2–5. Some material available for editorial reproduction and for advertising. No loans; b/w prints and duplicate colour transparencies available for a fee. Photocopies available. No reproduction rights fees charged. Staff will undertake limited research.

404 • HAMPSHIRE COUNTY MUSEUM SERVICE

Chilcomb House, Chilcomb Lane, Bar End,
Winchester, Hampshire SO23 8RD
Tel (0962) 66242

Enquiries to Janet Grant, Director

Items About 5000: b/w original and copy
photographs, colour transparencies (35mm), glass
negatives, daguerreotypes, lantern slides,
postcards, original cartoons, illustrated maps, fine
art prints, art reproductions, stereographs,
greetings cards, illustrated books

Dates of subject matter Prehistory to present

Dates of photographs *c.* 1870 to present

Dates of fine art 17th century to present

Subjects Hampshire history, topography,
agriculture, social history, archaeology, costume,
personalities; items in museum collections,
decorative arts, fine arts (oil paintings,
watercolours, prints) textiles, natural history,
geology, social and industrial history, agricultural
history, metal work.

Access and conditions Open to the public by
appt, Mon-Fri 8–5. All materials available for
editorial reproduction and for advertising. B/w
prints and colour transparencies available for a fee,
but may take up to six months to deliver prints.
Photocopies available. Reproduction rights fees
charged. Staff will undertake limited research.

405 • HAMPSHIRE RECORD OFFICE

20 Southgate Street, Winchester, Hampshire
SO23 9EF
Tel (0962) 63153

Enquiries to Rosemary Dunhill, County
Archivist

Items About 4700: b/w original and copy
photographs, colour photographic prints, colour
transparencies (35mm), glass negatives, lantern
slides, postcards, illustrated maps, posters,
greetings cards, architecture drawings, illustrated
books, press cuttings and tearsheets

Dates of subject matter Prehistory to present

Dates of photographs *c.* 1850 to present

Subjects Hampshire life and history, people,
places and events, rural and urban life, industry,
agriculture, business, schools, churches,
transport, important occasions, celebrations,

landscapes, townscapes, architecture, local
organizations; FRANCIS FRITH COLLECTION: master
prints from which postcards were issued (*c.* 1870 to
c. 1930), including Beaulieu Place (exteriors and
Hall), large collection on Bournemouth (1890s to
1920s) especially the pier, horse-drawn cabs,
paddle steamers, sands, beach scenes, Durley
Chine, Boscombe, Boscombe Chine, Christchurch
(exteriors and interiors), Priory Church, Shelley's
monument, Farnborough including Royal Aircraft
Establishment, New Forest, Romsey Abbey,
Broadlands, Winchester including College and
College chapel, Cathedral, Chawton Manor (Jane
Austen's house); miscellaneous collection including
200 drawings by John Chute of alterations done to
stately home The Vyne (*c.* 1750–1770s), drawings
of Strawberry Hill, Twickenham, sketches of
Florence Nightingale by her cousin Joanna
Bonham Carter, watercolours by local Hampshire
artists, prints of stately homes, parks and rivers of
the county, 17th and 18th century

Access and conditions Open to the public, Mon-
Thurs 9–4.45, Fri 9–4.15. Most material available
for editorial reproduction and for advertising. No
loans; b/w prints and colour transparencies
available for a fee. Photocopies available.
Reproduction rights fees charged. Staff will
undertake limited research. Card catalogue.

406 • HAMPSTEAD GARDEN SUBURB ARCHIVES TRUST

c/o The Institute, Central Square, London
NW11 7BN

Enquiries to Brigid Crafton Green

Items About 900: b/w original and copy
photographs, colour transparencies (35mm), colour
photographic prints, glass negatives, lantern
slides, postcards, posters, architectural drawings,
illustrated books

Dates of photographs *c.* 1890 to present

Subjects History of Hampstead Garden Suburb
including pre-development views, personalities
connected with its development including the
founder, Dame Henrietta Barnett and her life in
Whitechapel; streetscenes, public buildings, formal
occasions (e.g. opening of buildings), leisure
activities (e.g. garden and gardening, amateur
dramatics), children in the Suburb, recent events

Access and conditions Open to the public by
appt (write). Most material available for editorial

reproduction and for advertising with the Trust's permission. No loans; material may be copied by outside photographers. No reproduction rights fees charged. Staff will undertake limited research. Compulsory credit line.

407 • THE HARBOROUGH MUSEUM
Collection of Market Harborough Historical Society Museum Trust

Council Offices, Adam and Eve Street, Market Harborough, Leicestershire LE16 7LT
Tel (0858) 32468

Enquiries to Samuel P. Mullins, Keeper

Items About 1500: b/w original and copy photographs, glass negatives, postcards, calotypes, daguerreotypes, fine art prints

Dates of subject matter 100 BC to present

Dates of photographs 1855 to present

Subjects South Leicestershire and north-west Northamptonshire, especially Market Harborough, including life and activities with emphasis on townscapes, trade and industries, community activities; REV. WILLIAM LAW COLLECTION (c. 1955–6) including calotypes by early photographer of local scenes and his Victorian vicarage, The Coombes, at Marston Trussell

Access and conditions Open to the public by appt, Mon-Fri 10–4.30. All material available for editorial reproduction and for advertising. B/w prints available for a fee. Photocopies available. Reproduction rights fees charged. Staff will undertake limited research.

408 • HARLOW NEW TOWN RECORD CENTRE
Information Services Department

Harlow Council, Town Hall, Harlow, Essex CM20 1HJ
Tel (0279) 446711

Enquiries to Jackie Storey, Information Assistant

Items About 7000: b/w original and copy photographs, colour transparencies (35mm), colour photographic prints, postcards

Dates of subject matter 1900 to present

Dates of photographs 1900 to present

Subjects Local history of new town of Harlow, construction since 1947 including houses, industry (Standard Telecommunications, Cossor Electronics, BP), aerial views, landscapes, churches, schools, pubs, leisure facilities, hospitals, medical facilities, sculpture (about 30 pieces) including works by Rodin, Elizabeth Frink, Henry Moore, Barbara Hepworth and others, some views of Old Harlow and preserved buildings

Access and conditions Open to the public by appt (write), Mon-Fri 9–4.30. All material available for editorial reproduction and for advertising by arrangement. B/w and colour material loaned free of charge for one month; b/w prints and duplicate colour transparencies available for a fee. Reproduction right fees charged. Staff will undertake some research.

409 • HARROGATE LIBRARY

Central Library, Victoria Avenue, Harrogate HG1 1EG
Tel (0423) 502744

Enquiries to George Capel, Divisional Organizer, Reference and Information Services

Items Over 7000: b/w original photographs, postcards, b/w copy photographs, glass negatives, lantern slides

Dates of subject matter c. 1800 to present

Dates of photographs late 19th century to present

Subjects Local history of Harrogate and surrounding area including landscapes, architecture, streetscenes, social history, transport

Access and conditions Open to the public by appt (tel), Mon Tues Wed Fri 9–7, Thurs 9–5, Sat 9–1. Most material available for editorial reproduction and for advertising. B/w material loaned free of charge for one month (print fees charged); material may be copied by outside photographers. Photocopies available. Reproduction rights fees charged. Staff will undertake limited research. Most material copyright.

410 • HARROW REFERENCE LIBRARY

Harrow Local Collection

PO Box 4, Civic Centre, Station Road, Harrow,
Middlesex HA1 2UU
Tel (01) 863 5611 ext 2056

Enquiries to Robert Thomson

Items 7350: b/w original and copy photographs,
colour transparencies (35mm), fine art prints,
lantern slides, glass negatives, colour photographic
prints, illustrated books

Dates of subject matter *c.* 1780 to present

Dates of photographs 1860 to present

Subjects History and topography of London
Borough of Harrow and environs, including
architecture, streetscenes, landscapes and
townscapes, especially of Harrow Hill, Harrow
School, Pinner, Stanmore, Bentley Priory, Canons
(18th-century house), churches, especially St
Lawrence Whitchurch and St Mary's Church,
Harrow Hill; transportation, including GEORGE
KERLEY PHOTOGRAPHIC COLLECTION of the
Metropolitan Railway, and also Harrow area,
Harrow and Wealdstone railway disaster of 1952;
aerial photographs of Borough of Harrow;
personalities; PINNER LOCAL HISTORY SOCIETY
COLLECTION (about 1400 items): photographic
record of the area covered by the 1864 Pinner
parish and including a street-by-street survey
(1972), detailed coverage of some houses, and some
local events

Access and conditions Open to the public by
appt (tel), Mon-Fri 9–8, Sat 9–5, closed Wed. Most
material available for editorial reproduction and
for advertising. B/w and colour material loaned free
of charge for one month. Material may be copied by
outside photographers. Photocopies available. No
reproduction rights fees charged. Staff will
undertake limited research. Card catalogue.

411 • HASTINGS OLD TOWN HALL MUSEUM OF LOCAL HISTORY

High Street, Hastings, East Sussex TN34 1ET
Tel (0424) 435952

Enquiries to Victoria Williams, Curator

Items 300: b/w original and copy photographs,
colour transparencies (35mm)

Dates of subject matter 4th century AD to
present

Dates of photographs 1850 to present

Subjects Local history of Hastings area including
the fishing industry, the Cinque Ports, seaside
entertainments and souvenirs, personalities (Logie
Baird, Titus Oates, Grey Owl, Robert Tressell,
Rider Haggard)

Access and conditions Open to the public by
appt (tel), Easter-Sept Mon-Sat 10–1, 2–5, Oct-
Easter Sun 3–5. Most material available for
editorial reproduction and for advertising. No
loans; b/w prints and duplicate colour
transparencies available for a fee. Photocopies
available. Reproduction rights fees charged. Staff
will undertake limited research. Card catalogue
available.

412 • HAVERING CENTRAL REFERENCE LIBRARY

St Edwards Way, Romford, Essex RM1 3AR
Tel (7008) (from London 70) 46040 ext 3169

Enquiries to Brian Evans, Reference Librarian

Items About 2500: b/w original and copy
photographs, colour transparencies (35mm), fine
art prints, drawings, watercolours

Dates of subject matter 17th century to present

Dates of photographs 1850 to present

Subjects London Borough of Havering including
former Urban District of Hornchurch and Borough
of Romford, local history, local churches, mansions,
schools, industries, streets, transport, portraits;
Essex County local history (prints and
photographs); drawings and watercolours by local
artist Alfred Bamford (late 19th century)

Access and conditions Open to the public by
appt, Mon-Fri 9.30–8, Sat 9.30–5. Most material
available for editorial reproduction and for
advertising by special arrangement. No loans; b/w
prints and duplicate colour transparencies
available for a fee. Photocopies available.
Reproduction rights fees charged. Staff will
undertake limited research. Card catalogue.

413 • HAWICK MUSEUM

Wilton Lodge Park, Hawick TD9 7JL
Tel (0450) 73457

Enquiries to Rosemary Jones, District Museums Curator

Items About 6000: b/w original photographs, b/w copy photographs, lantern slides, postcards

Dates of subject matter BC to present

Dates of photographs 1870s to present

Dates of fine art 1850 to present

Subjects Local history of Hawick and surrounding area including landscapes, agriculture (sheep farming), industries with special emphasis on knitwear and hosiery, craftsmen such as wheelwrights and cobblers, commercial activity, social history, local events and personalities; oil paintings and watercolours by Scottish artists including F. C. B. Cadell, William Johnstone, William McTaggart and Sir William MacTaggart

Access and conditions Open to the public, Apr-Sept Mon-Sat 10–12, 2–4, Sun 2–5, Oct-Mar Mon-Fri 10–12, 1–4, Sun 2–4, closed Sat. All material available for editorial reproduction and for advertising. B/w material loaned free of charge for three weeks (print fees charged); material may be copied by outside photographers. Photocopies available. No reproduction rights fees charged. Staff of two will undertake limited research. Some material copyright. Card catalogue available.

414 • HEREFORD LIBRARY

Broad Street, Hereford HR4 9AU
Tel (0432) 272456

Enquiries to Robin Hill, Senior Librarian

Items About 10,000: glass negatives, b/w original photographs, lantern slides, postcards, fine art prints, press cuttings and tearsheets, colour photographic prints, illustrated maps, watercolours and drawings

Dates of subject matter Prehistory to present

Dates of photographs c. 1860 to present

Subjects Hereford and Herefordshire local history including architecture, especially churches; rural industries including hop-growing, apples and pears, cider-making, agriculture; streetscenes and general views of Hereford, market towns and countryside of Herefordshire; ALFRED WATKINS COLLECTION (1890–1935) of photographs including many illustrating the theory of ley-lines; aerial photographs of Hereford and other towns and Ministry of Defence survey of the county (c. 1948–

1952); portraits of local personalities; F. C. MORGAN COLLECTION (1925–1950s): Hereford local history (see list above); WALKER PILLEY COLLECTION: Herefordshire history 16th century to c. 1914, including illustrated books and albums of photographs, mostly topographical; fine art prints of Herefordshire topography 17th century and later

Access and conditions Open to the public, Tues Wed 9.30–6, Thurs 9.30–5, Fri 9.30–8, Sat 9.30–4. All material available for editorial reproduction and for advertising. B/w prints available for a fee. Photocopies available. Material may be copied by outside photographers. No reproduction rights fees charged. Staff will undertake limited research.

415 • HEREFORD AND WORCESTER RECORD OFFICE

Hereford Branch

County Record Office, The Old Barracks, Harold Street, Hereford HR1 2QX
Tel (0432) 265441

Enquiries to Assistant County Archivist

Items About 5000: b/w original and copy photographs, glass negatives, postcards, illustrated maps, posters, architectural drawings

Dates of photographs c. 1860 to present

Subjects Life and activities in the former county of Hereford including landscape and architectural coverage, social history, trade, industry, transport

Access and conditions Open to the public by appt (tel). Most material available for editorial reproduction and for advertising. No loans; b/w prints available for a fee; material may be copied by outside photographers. Photocopies available. Reproduction rights and service fees charged. Staff will undertake limited research. Copyright clearance is responsibility of user.

Worcester Branch

County Record Office, County Hall, Spetchley Road, Worcester WR5 2NP
Tel (0905) 353366 ext 3613

Enquiries to Head of Record Services

Items About 60,000: b/w original and copy photographs, glass negatives, postcards, illustrated maps, posters, architectural drawings

Dates of subject matter 1860 to present

Dates of photographs 1860 to present

Subjects Life and activities in the former county of Worcestershire including extensive architectural coverage; social history, education, transport, industry, commerce

Access and conditions Open to the public by appt (tel), Mon-Fri 9–5. Most material available for editorial reproduction and for advertising. No loans; b/w prints available for a fee; material may be copied by outside photographers. Photocopies available. Reproduction rights and service fees charged. Staff will undertake limited research. Most material copyright; copyright clearance is responsibility of user.

416 • HERITAGE CENTRE MUSEUM AND ART GALLERY

Fairfield West, Kingston upon Thames, Surrey KT1 2PS
Tel (01) 546 5386

Enquiries to Colin A. Cornish, Local History Officer

Items 5500: b/w original and copy photographs, colour transparencies (5″ × 4″), colour photographic prints, glass negatives, lantern slides, postcards, illustrated maps, fine art prints, art reproductions, unprinted film negatives, posters, greetings cards, press cuttings and tearsheets, ephemera

Dates of subject matter 1700 to present

Dates of photographs *c.* 1870 to present

Subjects Local history of Surrey and Thames Valley, especially the London Borough of Kingston upon Thames including New Malden, Old Malden, Surbiton, Chessington, Hook and Coombe and including topography, architecture, transport, industry, personalities, schools, sport, theatre; 19th- and 20th-century watercolours and oil paintings by local artists; photographic prints from the Kingston Photographic Society (New Kingston Camera Club) photographic survey 1894–1910; ephemera collection including broadsides (public notices)

Access and conditions Open to the public, Mon-Sat 10–5. Some material available for editorial reproduction and for advertising. B/w material loaned free of charge for one month. Photocopies

available. Material may be copied by outside photographers. Reproduction rights fees and service fees charged. Staff will undertake limited research only. Card catalogue.

417 • HERTFORDSHIRE RECORD OFFICE

County Hall, Hertford SG13 8DE
Tel (0992) 54242 ext 413

Enquiries to Peter Walne, County Archivist

Items About 30,000: b/w original and copy photographs, colour transparencies (35mm), glass negatives, lantern slides, postcards, illustrated maps, architectural drawings, press cuttings and tearsheets, fine art prints

Dates of subject matter *c.* 1300 to present

Dates of photographs *c.* 1860 to present

Subjects Hertfordshire local history, topography, architecture (ecclesiastical and secular), streetscenes, transport, dress (costume), personalities, people, maps of estates with ground plans of buildings, decorative title cartouches and other pictorial material; memorial brasses; extra-illustrated copies of county histories (18th- and 19th-century) with additional watercolour drawings and illustrations; COUNTY VIEWS COLLECTION of engravings, prints and photographs; F. H. STINGEMORE COLLECTION (glass negatives) of county topography; BUCKLER COLLECTION of topographical drawings and of houses and churches, *c.* 1830; OLDFIELD COLLECTION of topographical drawings *c.* 1790

Access and conditions Open to the public by appt (write), Mon-Thurs 9.15–5.15, Fri 9.15–4.30. All material available for editorial reproduction and for advertising. B/w prints and duplicate colour transparencies available for a fee. Photocopies available. Reproduction rights fees charged. Staff will undertake limited research.

418 • HIGHLAND REGIONAL COUNCIL

Library Service Reference Collection

31A Harbour Road, Inverness, Highland IV1 1UA
Tel (0463) 235713

Enquiries to Peter Reynolds, Senior Librarian (Reference)

Items About 1000: b/w original photographs, postcards, glass negatives

Dates of subject matter 14th century to present

Dates of photographs 1900 to present

Subjects Scottish Highlands, especially buildings, scenes of Highland life, aerial views

Access and conditions Open to the public by appt, Mon-Fri 9–5. All material available for editorial reproduction and for advertising subject to copyright clearance. B/w material loaned free of charge for two weeks. Photocopies available. Material may be copied by outside photographers. No reproduction rights fees charged. Staff will undertake some research. Card catalogue.

419 • HITCHIN MUSEUM AND ART GALLERY

Paynes Park, Hitchin, Hertfordshire SG5 1EQ
Tel (0462) 34476

Enquiries to Alan Fleck, Curator

Items 71,200: b/w original and copy photographs, colour transparencies (35mm), glass negatives, unprinted film negatives, postcards, lantern slides, architectural drawings, greetings cards, stereographs, daguerreotypes, press cuttings and tearsheets, fine art prints, watercolours

Dates of subject matter 900 to present

Dates of photographs 1850 to 1960

Subjects Local history of Hertfordshire and especially Hitchin, Letchworth, Baldock, Stevenage, Luton, Cambridge, Peterborough, Barnet including agriculture (ploughing, reaping, rick-building, etc), industry (tanning, straw-plaiting, lavender distillation, bacon manufacture), churches, education, events including Hitchin coronation and jubilee celebrations (1887–1902), transport (horse-drawn and internal combustion); local photojournalism (negatives) from the *Hertfordshire Pictorial* and *Hitchin Comet* newspapers

Access and conditions Open to the public by appt (tel), Mon-Sat 10–5. All material available for editorial reproduction and for advertising. No loans; b/w prints and duplicate colour transparencies available for a fee. Reproduction rights fees charged. Staff will undertake some research. Card catalogue available.

420 • HOUNSLOW PUBLIC LIBRARY

Local Studies Department

Treaty Road, Hounslow, Middlesex TW3 1DR
Tel (01) 570 7510

Enquiries to Andrea Cameron, Local Studies Librarian

Items About 15,000: b/w original and copy photographs, colour transparencies (35mm), colour photographic prints, glass negatives, lantern slides, postcards, illustrated maps, fine art prints, art reproductions, posters, greetings cards, architectural drawings, press cuttings and tearsheets, illustrated books

Dates of subject matter 17th century to present

Dates of photographs 1850 to present

Subjects London Borough of Hounslow including Chiswick, Brentford, Isleworth, Osterley, Hounslow, Heston, Cranford, Bedfont, Feltham and Hanworth, local history including buildings, people, transport, farming, market gardening, mills, fire brigades, education; LAYTON COLLECTION: topographical prints, photographs and maps covering the whole of England, but especially London and Middlesex

Access and conditions Open to the public by appt (tel), Mon-Wed 9–8, Thurs 9–1, Fri-Sat 9–5. Some material available for editorial reproduction but not for advertising. No loans; b/w prints and duplicate colour transparencies available for a fee. Photocopies available. Reproduction rights fees charged. Staff will undertake some research. Card catalogue.

421 • HULL LOCAL STUDIES LIBRARY

Central Library, Albion Street, Kingston upon Hull HU1 3TS
Tel (0482) 224040 ext 221

Enquiries to Jill Crowther, Local Studies Librarian

Items About 10,000: b/w original and copy photographs, postcards, glass negatives, illustrated maps, colour photographic prints, lantern slides, posters, greetings cards, architectural drawings, illustrated books

Dates of subject matter *c.* 1300 to present

Dates of photographs *c.* 1870 to present

Subjects Hull and the former East Riding of Yorkshire; emphasis on Hull, scenic views, streetscenes, transport, docks, shipping; Hull and Barnsley Railway; housing conditions *c.* 1890–1930

Access and conditions Open to the public, Mon-Fri 9.30–8, Sat 9–4.30. All material available for editorial reproduction and for advertising. No loans; b/w prints available for a fee; colour transparencies and duplicates available for a fee. Photocopies available. No reproduction rights fees charged. Staff will undertake limited research. Compulsory credit line.

422 • THE ISCA COLLECTION

5 Abbey Road, Exeter, Devon EX4 7BG
Tel (0392) 38699

Enquiries to Peter Thomas

Items Over 40,000: b/w original and copy photographs, glass negatives, daguerreotypes, lantern slides, postcards, original cartoons, stereographs, illustrated books

Dates of subject matter 1850 to present

Dates of photographs *c.* 1860 to present

Subjects History of the city of Exeter in photographs and old postcards, special collection of the Exe estuary including conservation, ornithology, flora and fauna, historical material; history of photography and photographic apparatus

Access and conditions Not open; telephone or mail requests only. Most material available for editorial reproduction and for advertising. B/w prints available for a fee; colour transparencies loaned for a fee. Reproduction rights fees charged. Staff will undertake research.

423 • THE JERSEY MUSEUM – SOCIÉTÉ JERSIAISE

9 Pier Road, St Helier, Jersey, Channel Islands
Tel (0534) 75940

Enquiries to Martyn Brown, Director

Items About 10,000: b/w original and copy photographs, colour transparencies (35mm, 5″ × 4″), colour photographic prints, glass negatives, daguerreotypes, lantern slides, postcards, original cartoons, illustrated maps, fine art prints, art reproductions, unprinted film negatives, stereographs, posters, greetings cards,

architectural drawings, press cuttings and tearsheets, illustrated books

Dates of subject matter 17th century to present

Dates of photographs *c.* 1850 to present

Subjects Local history of Jersey and the Channel Islands including shipping, agriculture, transport, military, German occupation during World War II , architecture, flora, local industries, railways, personalities, archaeology, geology, celebrations, royal visits

Access and conditions Open to qualified researchers by appt (write), Mon-Sat 10–5. All material available for editorial reproduction and for advertising. B/w prints and duplicate colour transparencies available for a fee. Photocopies available. Reproduction rights and service fees charged. Staff will undertake some research. Card catalogue.

424 • KEIGHLEY AREA LIBRARY

North Street, Keighley, West Yorkshire BD21 3SX
Tel (0535) 67024

Enquiries to Ian Dewhirst, Reference Librarian

Items About 1000: b/w original and copy photographs, glass negatives, postcards

Dates of subject matter *c.* 1800 to present

Dates of photographs *c.* 1860 to present

Subjects History and topography of Keighley and environs, including Haworth, streetscenes, transport, social conditions, local personalities, public buildings, housing, demolition and reconstruction, aerial views, local events

Access and conditions Open to the public, Mon Wed Thurs Fri 9.30–7, Tues 9.30–12, Sat 9.30–5. Some material available for editorial reproduction and for advertising. No loans; material may be copied by outside photographers. No reproduction rights fees charged. Staff will undertake some research.

425 • KENT ARCHIVES OFFICE

County Hall, Maidstone, Kent ME14 1XQ
Tel (0622) 671411 ext 3312

Enquiries to Kathleen Topping

Items Numbers unknown: b/w original and copy

photographs, glass negatives, postcards, original cartoons, illustrated maps, fine art prints, posters, greetings cards, architectural drawings, illustrated books, ephemera

Dates of subject matter 18th to 20th centuries

Dates of photographs 1880s to present

Subjects Kent history, topography, architecture, ceremonies; late 19th- and early 20th-century family collections including: BRABOURNE COLLECTION: Lord Brabourne and his family, some material from India; HARDING OF PENSHURST COLLECTION: Harding family, some material from India; STANHOPE OF CHEVENING COLLECTION: Stanhope family, Kentish material; CORNWALLIS-MANN COLLECTION: prominent Kentish family; ROYAL WEST KENT REGIMENT COLLECTION: military groups, ceremonies, portraits

Access and conditions Open to the public by appt (tel), Mon-Thurs 9–5. Some material available for editorial reproduction and for advertising at the discretion of the archivist. No loans; b/w prints and duplicate colour transparencies available for a fee. Photocopies available. Reproduction rights fees charged. Staff will undertake limited research.

426 • KENT COUNTY LIBRARY

Maidstone Branch
Local Studies Collection

Springfield, Maidstone, Kent ME14 2LH
Tel (0622) 671411 ext 3244

Enquiries to Christine Dunn, County Local Studies Librarian

Items About 23,000: b/w original and copy photographs, colour transparencies (35mm), glass negatives, postcards, fine art prints, illustrated books, lantern slides

Dates of subject matter Prehistory to present

Dates of photographs *c.* 1850 to present

Subjects Kent including most towns and villages, local history and topography, seaside, churches, architecture (especially country houses); collections of photographs by Francis Frith, W. H. Boyer of Sandwich and F. Hodges of Brenchley (note: illustrations are filed by place name)

Access and conditions Open to the public by appt (tel), Mon-Fri 9–6, Sat 9–4. Some material available for editorial reproduction and for

advertising. No loans; b/w prints and duplicate colour transparencies available for a fee. Photocopies available. Reproduction rights fees charged. Staff will undertake limited research.

Margate Branch
Picture Collection

Central Library, Cecil Square, Margate, Kent CT9 1RE
Tel (0843) 223626, 2292895

Enquiries to John Brazier, Art and Exhibitions Officer

Items About 11,500: b/w original photographs, fine art prints, drawings, postcards, watercolours, stereographs, illustrated maps, ephemera, illustrated books

Dates of subject matter Prehistory to present

Dates of photographs *c.* 1850 to present

Dates of fine art 17th century to present

Subjects Margate local history including seaside activities, and personalities, ships and shipwrecks, transport, scenery, architecture, religion; Royal Sea Bathing Hospital, Theatre Royal, fire, floods, storms, entertainment; Isle of Thanet local history including Broadstairs, Kingsgate, St Peter's, Ramsgate, St Lawrence, Minster, Monkton, Acol, Sarre, St Nicholas, Shuart, Birchington, Westgate, Cliftonville, Reculver, Richborough, Cinque Ports – history, topography, personalities; topographical record of Kent and Kentish life in 19th and early 20th centuries including fishing industry (especially at Ramsgate), agriculture, markets and farm sales, streetscenes, transport; paintings, drawings and prints by Thomas Hennell and others

Access and conditions Open to the public by appt (tel), Mon-Fri 9.30–5.30. Most materials available for editorial reproduction and for advertising. No loans; b/w prints available for a fee. Photocopies available. Reproduction rights fees charged. Staff will undertake some research. Card catalogue.

427 • KIDDERMINSTER LIBRARY

Market Street, Kidderminster, Hereford and Worcester DY10 1AD
Tel (0562) 752832

Enquiries to Rex Clark, Assistant County Librarian

Items About 6000: b/w original and copy photographs, colour transparencies (35mm), colour photographic prints, lantern slides, postcards, posters, architectural drawings, illustrated books

Dates of subject matter 1850 to present

Dates of photographs *c*. 1850 to present

Subjects North-western Worcestershire, especially Wyre Forest, including architecture, industry (especially carpet manufacturing), transport (road, rail, trams, horse-drawn), streetscenes

Access and conditions Open to the public by appt (tel), Mon Tues Thurs-Sat 9.30–4. Some material available for editorial reproduction and for advertising. No loans; material may be copied by outside photographers. Reproduction rights fees may be charged by owners of copyright, but not by Library. Staff will undertake some research and mail photocopies.

428 • KING'S LYNN CENTRAL LIBRARY

Local Studies Collection

London Road, King's Lynn, Norfolk PE30 5EZ
Tel (0553) 772568, 761393

Enquiries to Raymond Wilson, Divisional Librarian

Items 30,000: b/w original and copy photographs, glass negatives, lantern slides, postcards, colour photographic prints, unprinted film negatives

Dates of subject matter *c*. 1300 to present

Dates of photographs 1880 to present

Subjects King's Lynn and environs local history, including streets, hotels, buildings, churches, schools, Council, industries, sports, societies, army, RAF, port and shipping, docks, tugs, lightships, ferries, World Wars I and II, hospitals, west Norfolk villages, archaeology, libraries, museums, fires, fleets, slum clearance, newspapers, markets, marts, fairs, circuses, bus services, theatres, people, monasteries; TAYLOR AND BOWSKILL COLLECTIONS of Victorian and Edwardian photographs of local streetscenes, shops, events, civic occasions, fires, churches, regattas, river views etc.; BENSTEAD MAGIC LANTERN SLIDE COLLECTION comprising local views, Indian scenes, British Army in India *c*. 1904, children's nursery slides, fairy tales, Peter Pan, etc.; aerial

photographs (1928 to present) including King's Lynn river views, shopping centre, industrial estates, west Norfolk villages and seaside resorts

Access and conditions Open to the public by appt (tel), Tues-Fri 10–7, Mon & Sat 10–5. All material available for editorial reproduction and for advertising. B/w prints and duplicate colour transparencies available for a fee. Photocopies available. Reproduction rights and service fees charged. Staff will undertake limited research. Card catalogue.

429 • KINGSTON UPON HULL CITY COUNCIL RECORD OFFICE

79 Lowgate, Kingston upon Hull HU1 2AA
Tel (0482) 222015/6

Enquiries to Geoffrey Oxley, City Archivist

British Transport Docks Board (Humber Ports) Collection

Items About 150: b/w original photographs

Dates of subject matter 1400 to 1970

Dates of photographs 1935 to 1970

Subjects Docks and adjacent areas of the city, ships, dock vehicles and equipment; Royal visits

Town Clerk's Collection

Items About 400: b/w original photogaphs, colour photographic prints

Dates of subject matter 1400 to 1960

Dates of photographs 1900 to 1960

Subjects Docks, roads, railways, local views

Environmental Health Collection

Items About 50: b/w original photographs

Dates of subject matter 1860 to 1980

Dates of photographs 1920 to 1980

Subjects Buildings unfit for human habitation, condemned meat; communal air raid shelters (1939–1945)

Department of Industrial Development Collection

Items 200: b/w original photographs, colour transparencies (35mm)

Dates of subject matter 1400 to 1980

Dates of photographs 1930 to 1980

Subjects Streets and buildings in Hull, industrial development, civic events, aerial photographs

Rosedowns Collection

Items 200: b/w original photographs

Dates of subject matter 1900 to 1970

Dates of photographs 1900 to 1980

Subjects Plant, staff and products of engineering company making processing machinery for food industries

City Engineers Collection

Items 75,000: b/w original and copy photographs, glass negatives

Dates of subject matter 1800 to 1980

Dates of photographs 1930 to 1980

Subjects Hull buildings, engineering works

Brigham and Cowan Collection

Items 75: b/w original photographs

Dates of subject matter 1800 to 1914

Dates of photographs 1900 to 1914

Subjects Damaged ships, mostly in the Central Dry Dock, Humber St, Hull

Milburn Collection

Items 65: b/w original photographs

Dates of subject matter 1870 to 1914

Dates of photographs 1900 to 1914

Subjects Annual camps of the 1st Battalion 2nd Northumbrian Royal Field Artillery and 2nd East Yorkshire RGA (1904–1909); motoring (1903–1908), Mr Milburn and friends

Alec-Smith Collection

Items About 150: b/w original photographs

Dates of subject matter 1900 to 1960

Dates of photographs 1930 to 1960

Subjects Timber trade; Alec-Smith family, timber merchants, who imported timber from Scandinavia and elsewhere and sold it from their yard at the docks

Other material:

Items Over 100,000: architectural drawings, b/w original photographs, postcards, original cartoons, illustrated maps, posters

Dates of subject matter 1400 to 1980

Dates of photographs 1850 to 1980

Subjects Local people and places, buildings, streetscenes, personalities

Access and conditions Open to the public by appt (tel), Mon-Thurs 8.30–5, Fri 8.30–4.30. All material available for editorial reproduction and for advertising. B/w prints and duplicate colour transparencies available for a fee. Photocopies available. Reproduction rights fees charged. Staff of three will undertake some research.

430 • KIRKCALDY CENTRAL LIBRARY

Local History Collection

War Memorial Grounds, Kirkcaldy, Fife KY1 1YK
Tel (0592) 260707

Enquiries to Janet Klak

Items 7000: b/w original and copy photographs, colour transparencies (35mm), postcards

Dates of subject matter 12th century to present

Dates of photographs 1860 to present

Subjects Kirkcaldy and district local history, social history, topography, architecture including castles (especially Ravenscraig Castle), streetscenes, transport including horse-drawn trams, buses and cars, schools, church and club groups, works outings; industries including linoleum, linen and mining, factory interiors and exteriors

Access and conditions Open to the public, Mon-Thurs 10–7, Fri-Sat 10–5. Some material available for editorial reproduction and for advertising. No loans; b/w prints available for a fee, colour transparencies photographed to order. Photocopies available. No reproduction rights fees. Staff will undertake some research.

431 • KIRKCALDY MUSEUM AND ART GALLERY

War Memorial Gardens, Kirkcaldy, Fife KY1 1YG
Tel (0592) 260732

Enquiries to Andrew Kerr, Curator

Items 4000: b/w original and copy photographs, colour transparencies (35mm), glass negatives, lantern slides, stereographs, postcards

Dates of subject matter 1700 to 1980

Dates of photographs 1870 to 1980

Subjects Local history and topography of Kirkcaldy and environs and Fife including industries, fishing, engineering, pottery, mining, commerce; 19th- and 20th-century Scottish art, especially work by William McTaggart and S. J. Peploe

Access and conditions Open to the public by appt (tel), Mon-Fri 11–5. Most material available for editorial reproduction and for advertising. B/w prints and duplicate colour transparencies available for a fee. Photocopies available. Reproduction rights fees charged. Staff will undertake limited research. Card catalogue.

432 • KIRKLEES LIBRARY AND ART GALLERY

Local Studies Library, Alexandra Walk, Huddersfield, West Yorkshire HD1 2SU
Tel (0484) 513808

Enquiries to Jane Helliwell

Items 30,000: postcards, b/w original and copy photographs, glass negatives, lantern slides, colour transparencies (35mm), colour photographic prints, stereographs

Dates of subject matter 1800 to present

Dates of photographs 1870 to present

Subjects Postcards (20,600) of local manufacturer, Banforth, including comic seaside pictures, sentimental greeting cards, World Wars I and II, local scenes (streets, transport, buildings); Kay & Stewart woollen mill (1902) including all aspects of its work from dyes to posed foremen

Access and conditions Open to the public by appt (tel), Mon-Fri 9–8, Sat 9–4. Most material available for reproduction and for advertising, some subject to copyright clearance. No loans; b/w prints and duplicate colour transparencies available for a fee. Photocopies available. Reproduction rights and service fees charged. Staff will undertake some research. Copyright clearance responsibility of user.

433 • KNOWLSEY CENTRAL LIBRARY

Local Studies Collection

Derby Road, Huyton, Merseyside L36 9UJ
Tel (051) 443 3734

Enquiries to Local Studies Librarian

Items About 3300: b/w original and copy photographs, colour transparencies (35mm, 5″ × 4″), postcards, posters

Dates of subject matter 1850 to present

Dates of photographs 1860 to present

Subjects Local history of Knowlsey and environs including Cronton, Halewood, Huyton, Kirkby, Prescot, Roby, Simonswood, Tarbock, Whiston; life and activities, architecture, services, transport, businesses, chemical and paper industries, factory buildings, industrial estates, personalities, recreation, royal visits, schools, sports, agriculture, some aerial views

Access and conditions Open to the public, Mon-Fri 9–5. Some material available for editorial reproduction but not for advertising. No loans; b/w prints and duplicate transparencies available for a fee. Photocopies available. No reproduction rights fees charged. Staff will undertake some research.

434 • KYLE AND CARRICK DISTRICT LIBRARY AND MUSEUM SERVICE

Carnegie Library, 12 Main Street, Ayr, Strathclyde KA8 8ED
Tel (0292) 269141

Enquiries to Reference Library

Items About 5000: b/w original and copy photographs, colour transparencies (35mm), colour photographic prints, glass negatives, lantern slides, postcards, illustrated maps, fine art prints, stereographs, architectural drawings

Dates of subject matter c. 1700 to present

Dates of photographs 1875 to present

Subjects LIBRARY COLLECTION: local topography, aerial photographs, streetscenes, architecture including vernacular houses, country houses and castles especially Culzean Castle, harbours, fish-net making, schools, farming, local events; MUSEUM COLLECTION: oil paintings by the Scottish Colourists (Fergusson, Peploe) late 19th and early 20th century; works by the Glasgow Boys, Edward Hornel, George Henry, J. Christie, and others;

MACLAURIN COLLECTION: paintings, sculpture and etchings by R. B. Kitaj, Henry Moore, John Hoyland, Robert Colquhoun and others

Access and conditions Open to the public by appt, Mon-Fri 9–7.30. Some material available for editorial reproduction but not for advertising. Library: B/w and colour loaned for two months. Service fees charged. No reproduction rights fees. Compulsory credit line. Staff will undertake some research in response to written requests. Museum: No loans; b/w prints and duplicate colour transparencies available for a fee. Reproduction rights fees charged. Staff will undertake research in response to written requests.

435 • LAMBETH ARCHIVES DEPARTMENT

Minet Library, 52 Knatchbull Road, London SE5 9QY
Tel (01) 733 3279

Enquiries to Pamela Hatfield, Borough Archivist

Items 10,000: b/w original and copy photographs, fine art prints, watercolours, illustrated books, architectural drawings, postcards, press cuttings and tearsheets, illustrated maps

Dates of subject matter *c*. 1700 to present (a few earlier)

Dates of photographs *c*. 1860 to present

Subjects Surrey (including those areas now in Greater London) and London Borough of Lambeth in particular; topography, architecture, transport including trams and horse-drawn vehicles, personalities, industry, housing, shops and markets, theatres and playbills, Vauxhall Gardens, Crystal Palace (Norwood), social life; Henry Petrie watercolours of Surrey churches (*c*. 1800); photographs by Delamotte of the construction of the Crystal Palace

Access and conditions Open to the public by appt (tel), Mon-Fri 9.30–5, closed Wed. Some material available for editorial reproduction and for advertising. Photocopies available. Material may be copied by outside photographers. No reproduction rights fees. Compulsory credit line. Staff will undertake limited research. Card catalogue.

436 • PETER GERARD LAWS

21 Lidden Road, Penzance, Cornwall TR18 4PG
Tel (0736) 3544

Enquiries to Peter Gerard Laws

Items 15,000: colour transparencies (35mm), postcards, unprinted film negatives, glass negatives, lantern slides, colour photographic prints

Dates of subject matter 1850 to present

Dates of photographs 1850 to present

Subjects Industrial archaeology in Cornwall, including mining, railways, maritime, china clay, fishing; the National Trust in Devon and Cornwall; the Scilly Isles; railway history; Cornish churches, lighthouses; Isambard Kingdom Brunel and his family

Access and conditions Open to qualified researchers by appt (write), Mon-Fri 9–5. All material available for editorial reproduction but not for advertising. B/w and colour material loaned free of charge. Reproduction rights fees charged. Staff will undertake research. Compulsory credit line.

437 • LEICESTERSHIRE RECORD OFFICE

57 New Walk, Leicester LE1 7JB
Tel (0533) 554100 ext 238

Enquiries to County Archivist

Items About 10,000: b/w original and copy photographs, colour photographic prints, colour transparencies (35mm), glass negatives, lantern slides, postcards, illustrated maps, unprinted film negatives, architectural drawings

Dates of subject matter *c*. 1880 to present

Dates of photographs *c*. 1880 to present

Subjects Leicestershire topography; NEWTON COLLECTION recording the building of the Great Central Railway (1892–1900); BRUSH COLLECTION of railway rolling stock, trolley buses, trams and buses built by Brush Electrical Engineering Co. (1882–1955); HERBERT MORRIS COLLECTION: cranes (1900–1950), photographs of listed buildings (1965–1970)

Access and conditions Open to the public by appt (write), Mon-Thurs 9.15–5, Fri 9.15–4.45, Sat 9.15–12.15. All material available for editorial reproduction and for advertising. B/w prints available for a fee. Photocopies available. Reproduction rights fees charged. Staff will undertake limited research. Card catalogue.

438 • LEWISHAM LOCAL HISTORY CENTRE

The Manor House, Old Road, London SE13 5SY
Tel (01) 852 5050

Enquiries to Librarian

Items About 32,000: b/w original and copy photographs, postcards, unprinted film negatives, fine art prints, colour transparencies (35mm), colour photographic prints, glass negatives, daguerreotypes, lantern slides, original cartoons, illustrated maps, art reproductions, posters, greetings cards, architectural drawings, press cuttings and tearsheets, illustrated books

Dates of subject matter 19th century to present

Dates of photographs *c.* 1850 to present

Subjects London Borough of Lewisham including Deptford and western part of Blackheath, local history including public buildings, businesses, personalities, rivers, streams, canals, road and rail transport, mills, inns, education, sport and recreation, wars (local impact)

Access and conditions Open to the public, Mon Fri Sat 9.30–5, Tues Thurs 9.30–8, closed daily 1–2 and Wed. Some material available for editorial reproduction but not for advertising. No loans; b/w prints and duplicate colour transparencies available for a fee payable in advance. Photocopies available. Reproduction rights fees charged. Staff will undertake limited research. Compulsory credit line. Card catalogue.

439 • LINCOLN CENTRAL LIBRARY

Local Studies Collection

Free School Lane, Lincoln LN2 1EZ
Tel (0522) 33541

Enquiries to Reference Library

Items About 13,500: b/w original and copy photographs, colour transparencies (35mm), glass negatives, lantern slides, illustrated maps, posters, architectural drawings, illustrated books

Dates of subject matter *c.* AD 100 to present

Dates of photographs *c.* 1850 to present

Subjects Lincoln and Lincolnshire topography, especially Lincoln Cathedral; topographical drawings by J. C. Nattes of churches, manor houses, etc.; TENNYSON COLLECTION: 1500 photographs of Tennyson, his family and friends including some by Julia Margaret Cameron

Access and conditions Open to the public by appt, Mon Tues Thurs Fri 9–7, Wed 9–1, Sat 9–12.30. Some material available for editorial reproduction and for advertising. No loans; b/w prints and duplicate colour transparencies available for a fee. Photocopies available. Reproduction rights fees charged. Staff will undertake limited research. Card catalogue; printed catalogue of Tennyson material.

440 • LINCOLNSHIRE ARCHIVES OFFICE

The Castle, Lincoln LN1 3AB
Tel (0522) 25158

Enquiries to Dr G. A. Knight, Principal Archivist

Items B/w original and copy photographs, colour transparencies (35mm, 5″ × 4″), colour photographic prints, glass negatives, postcards, illustrated books

Dates of subject matter 11th century to present

Dates of photographs *c.* 1850 to present

Subjects Lincolnshire local history including architecture, streetscenes, landscape, rural life, agriculture, social conditions, windmills, irrigation, illustrated diaries, large collection of enclosure awards

Access and conditions Open to the public by appt, Mon-Fri 9.15–4.45. Most material available for editorial reproduction and for advertising. B/w prints and duplicate colour transparencies available for a fee. Photocopies available. Reproduction rights and service fees charged. Staff will undertake limited research.

441 • LINDSAY INSTITUTE

Hope Street, Lanark, Strathclyde ML11 7LZ
Tel (0555) 61331

Enquiries to Gordon W. Kane, Head of Accessions

Items About 350: b/w original photographs, lantern slides, postcards, posters

Dates of subject matter 18th century to present

Dates of photographs c. 1900 to present

Subjects Clydesdale and district including social history, geography, history and culture; ancient local festival of Lanimers including various Lanimer Queens and their courts; scenes of New Lanark, Robert Owen's settlement; posters: sports meetings, horse-racing, Lanimer Day celebrations, circuses, fairs, public notices

Access and conditions Open to the public by appt (tel), Mon-Fri 10–7.30. All material available for editorial reproduction and for advertising use with the Librarian's approval. No loans; b/w prints available for a fee. Material may be copied by outside photographers. No reproduction rights fees charged. Staff will undertake limited research. Compulsory credit line.

442 • LIVERPOOL CITY LIBRARIES

Record Office and Local History Department

William Brown Street, Liverpool L3 8EW
Tel (051) 207 2147

Enquiries to Archivist

Items 100,000: b/w original and copy photographs, glass negatives, lantern slides, postcards, illustrated maps, fine art prints, unprinted film negatives, posters, architectural drawings, press cuttings and tearsheets, illustrated books, watercolours (4000)

Dates of subject matter c. 1650 to present

Dates of photographs c. 1890 to present

Subjects Lancashire and Cheshire local history, especially Liverpool, and including topography, biography, streets and districts, docks, housing, theatres and cinemas, parks and gardens, transport, industry; E. CHAMBRÉ HARDMAN COLLECTION: work of local photographer since 1926 including society portraits as well as coverage of shipping, Liverpool; watercolour collection: works commissioned since 1852, topographical views, streets, buildings, local subjects

Access and conditions Open to the public, Mon-Fri 9–9. All material available for editorial reproduction and for advertising. No loans; b/w prints and duplicate colour transparencies available. Reproduction rights fees charged. Staff will undertake limited research.

443 • LLANELLI BOROUGH LIBRARY

Llanelli Local Illustrations Collection

Public Library, Vaughan Street, Llanelli, Dyfed SA15 3AS
Tel (05542) 3538

Enquiries to Reference Librarian

Items 4000: b/w original and copy photographs, colour transparencies (35mm, 5″ × 4″), colour photographic prints, postcards, unprinted film negatives, architectural drawings, illustrated books

Dates of subject matter 1750 to present

Dates of photographs 1880 to present

Subjects Llanelli and district local history, including industrial history of Llanelli tinplate manufacturing; streetscenes, houses, people, portraits, topography, townscapes and landscapes

Access and conditions Open to the public, Mon-Fri 9.30–7, Sat 9.30–6. Some material available for editorial reproduction. B/w and colour material available for a fee. Material may be copied by outside photographers. Photocopies available. No reproduction rights fees charged. Staff will undertake some research.

LONDON *see* GREATER LONDON

444 • LONG EATON LIBRARY

Tamworth Road, Long Eaton, Nottingham NG10 1JG
Tel (0602) 735426

Enquiries to Ruth Fern, Group Librarian

Items About 4000: b/w original and copy photographs, postcards

Dates of subject matter Late 19th century to present

Dates of photographs 1900 to present

Subjects Long Eaton and Sawley local history, streetscenes, buildings, lace factories, floods, visiting Royalty, opening of Library (material indexed according to street names)

Access and conditions Open to the public Mon Wed Thurs Fri 1.30–7, Tues 9.30–12.30, Sat 9.30–4. All material available for editorial reproduction but not for advertising. No loans; b/w prints available for a fee. Material may be copied by outside photographers. No reproduction rights fees. Staff will undertake limited research. Copyright clearance responsibility of user.

445 • LUDLOW MUSEUM

Old Street, Ludlow, Shropshire SY8 1NW
Tel (0584) 3857

Enquiries to John Norton

Items About 1700: b/w original and copy photographs, glass negatives, daguerreotypes, lantern slides, postcards, illustrated maps, fine art prints, greetings cards, architectural drawings

Dates of subject matter 1650 to present

Dates of photographs 1850 to present

Subjects History of Ludlow and environs including historic buildings, rural landscapes, people at work, trades and professions, sporting events including hunting, shooting, football, cricket, etc., local civic occasions, farming, mining and quarrying, school groups, Victorian shop fronts, etc.

Access and conditions Open to the public by appt, Mon-Fri 9–5. Most material available for editorial reproduction and for advertising. No loans; material may be copied by outside photographer (museum can arrange). No reproduction rights fees charged. Staff will undertake limited research. Card catalogue.

446 • LYNN MUSEUM

Market Street, King's Lynn, Norfolk PE30 1NL
Tel (0553) 775001

Enquiries to Curator

Items About 2000: b/w original and copy photographs, colour transparencies (35mm), glass negatives, lantern slides, postcards, stereographs, greetings cards, architectural drawings

Dates of subject matter 17th century to present

Dates of photographs 19th century to present

Subjects History of Lynn and west Norfolk, including early 20th-century photographic survey of Lynn, topographical paintings and drawings; pencil sketches, watercolours and oil paintings by Henry Baines (1820–1894) and Walter Dexter (1876–1958); engravings by Henry Bell (1647–1711)

Access and conditions Open to the public by appt (write), Mon-Sat 10–5. Some material available for editorial reproduction but not for advertising. B/w prints available for a fee; colour loaned for a rental fee. Reproduction rights fees charged. Staff will undertake limited research.

447 • MAIDENHEAD CENTRAL LIBRARY

Local History Collection

St Ives Road, Maidenhead, Berkshire SL6 1QU
Tel (0628) 25657

Enquiries to Patricia Curtis, Principal Librarian

Items About 500: b/w original and copy photographs, glass negatives, lantern slides, postcards, illustrated maps, old fine art prints, 20th-century fine art prints, posters, architectural drawings, illustrated books

Dates of subject matter *c.* 1895 to present

Dates of photographs *c.* 1895 to present

Subjects Local history of Maidenhead and surrounding area including landscapes, streetscenes, architecture, portraits, social history, transport

Access and conditions Open to the public by appt (write), Mon-Fri 9.30–7, Sat 9–1. All material available for editorial reproduction and for advertising. No loans; material may be copied by outside photographers. Photocopies available. Reproduction rights fees charged. Staff will undertake some research. All material copyright.

448 • MAIDSTONE MUSEUMS AND ART GALLERY

The Kent County Photographic Record and Survey

St Faith's Street, Maidstone, Kent ME14 1LH
Tel (0622) 54497

Enquiries to R. A. Stutely, Technical Assistant

Items About 3000: b/w original photographs, glass negatives, postcards, lantern slides, illustrated maps, b/w copy photographs, daguerreotypes, fine art prints

Dates of subject matter 1100 to present

Dates of photographs 1860 to present

Subjects Local history of Kent and especially Maidstone, emphasis on architecture, old street scenes, local industry, agriculture (hop picking), churches, local personalities

Access and conditions Open to the public by appt (tel), Mon-Fri 10–5. Most material available for editorial reproduction and for advertising. No loans; material may be copied by outside photographers. Photocopies available. Reproduction rights fees charged for commercial use. Staff will undertake some research.

449 • MALMESBURY CIVIC TRUST

Malmesbury Library, Cross Hayes, Malmesbury, Wiltshire SN16 9BG
Tel (06662) 3611

Enquiries to Anthony Newton, Librarian

Items About 600: b/w original photographs

Dates of photographs 1963 to 1964

Subjects Photo survey of the fronts of buildings in Malmesbury (almost complete), back views of some and also general views, villages and architecture in the rural district of Malmesbury

Access and conditions Open to the public by appt (tel), Mon 2–8, Tues 10–5, Wed 10–8, Thurs closed, Fri 10–8, Sat 9.30–1. All material available for editorial reproduction and for advertising. B/w prints loaned. No reproduction rights fees. Staff will undertake very limited research.

450 • MALVERN LIBRARY

Local History Collection

Graham Road, Malvern, Hereford and Worcester WR14 2HW
Tel (06845) 61223

Enquiries to Librarian

Items About 1200: b/w original and copy photographs, glass negatives, postcards, original cartoons, illustrated maps

Dates of subject matter 18th century to present

Dates of photographs *c*. 1850 to present

Subjects Malvern local history, landscapes especially of the Malvern Hills, townscapes, buildings, 19th-century portraits of local personalities

Access and conditions Open to qualified researchers by appt (tel), Mon 9.30–5.30, Tues 9.30–8, closed Wed, Thurs-Fri 9.30–5.30, Sat 9.30–4. Some material available for editorial reproduction and for advertising. B/w prints available for a fee. Reproduction rights fees charged. Staff will undertake some research. Card catalogue.

451 • MANCHESTER CENTRAL LIBRARY

Local History Library, St Peter's Square, Manchester M2 5PD
Tel (061) 236 9422 ext 265   Telex 667149, 669475

Enquiries to Assistant Librarian, Local History Room

Items 130,000: b/w original and copy photographs, glass negatives, lantern slides, postcards, colour photographic prints, illustrated maps, posters, cuttings and tearsheets, sketches and watercolours, illustrated books

Dates of subject matter 18th century to present

Dates of photographs 1870 to present

Dates of fine art 18th century to present

Subjects Manchester life and history, topography and streetscenes, surrounding towns and villages in south Lancashire and north Cheshire, architecture, events (e.g., Peterloo massacre), transport (Liverpool-Manchester Railway, Manchester Ship Canal, other local canals), churches, housing, theatres and cinemas, public houses, old halls, Manchester Town Hall, textile industry, education (schools, colleges), industrial revolution (mills, factories, warehouses, etc.), portraits, buildings, police, World War II (in Manchester); *News Chronicle* photographs; special collections include first Photographic Survey Record of Manchester (*c*. 1892–1901), the BARRITT COLLECTION of sketches of 18th-century Manchester, the JAMES COLLECTION of late 18th - and early 19th-century prints, the PHILIPS COLLECTION of views (old halls and castles) of Lancashire and Cheshire, the PHIPSON COLLECTION of watercolours (local halls, churches, inns, etc.), the RALSTON COLLECTION on early 19th-century and Regency Manchester, the RIMMER COLLECTION of pen-and-ink sketches of scenes in Lancashire, Cheshire and Wales, the WARDLEY/MUDD COLLECTION of 19th-century photographs of central Manchester, the GREENWOOD COLLECTION of drawings of Manchester and environs

Access and conditions Open by appt, Mon-Fri 9.30–4.30. Some material available for editorial reproduction and for advertising. No loans; b/w prints and duplicate colour transparencies available for a fee. Photocopies available. Reproduction rights fees charged. Compulsory credit line. Staff will undertake some research. Card catalogue available.

452 • MANCHESTER POLYTECHNIC

Manchester Studies Archive of Family Photographs

Cavendish House, Cavendish Street, Manchester M15 6BG
Tel (061) 228 6171 ext 2551

Enquiries to Audrey Linkman, Research Fellow

Items About 50,000: b/w 35mm negatives

Dates of subject matter 1860 to 1950

Dates of photographs 1860 to 1950

Subjects Greater Manchester including the cotton towns of north-east Lancashire and areas bordering on Cheshire and Derbyshire, emphasis on ordinary working people, life and activities of the region; practices and conventions of high-street professional photographers and amateur photographers; studio portraits of babies and children, men, women, families, barmitzvahs, confirmations, in Sunday best, working clothes, fancy dress, etc.; interiors of working-class homes, factories and mills (c. 1900); streetscenes including portraits of children and family groups outside their own homes, shops, pubs, outdoor traders and outside workmen, special street activities such as processions, pageants, street parties; schools including class groups outside in school yard and inside the classroom, sports teams, drill teams, special school activities such as Empire Day, May Day, school plays; work, especially the cotton industry but also engineering and others, groups inside and out, mills and factories, works outings, celebrations; leisure and celebrations, especially holidays, outings to all north-west resorts and particularly Blackpool, special occasions, sports, music hall, cinema, youth organizations including Girl Guides, Boys Brigade; extensive collection on Manchester's Jewish community and other Jewish communities throughout Britain

Access and conditions Open to the public by appt (tel), Mon-Thurs 9–6, Fri 9–5. All material available for editorial reproduction and for advertising subject to the consent of the original donor. B/w prints available for a fee. Reproduction rights fees charged at the discretion of the copyright holder. Staff will undertake some research; fee for large projects. Card catalogue, subject index and depositor index with detailed information about donors' families.

453 • MARYLEBONE LIBRARY

Archives and Local History Department

Marylebone Road, London NW1 5PS
Tel (01) 828 8070 ext 4030

Enquiries to R. A. Bowden, Archivist

Items About 30,000: b/w original and copy photographs, colour transparencies, fine art prints, glass negatives, lantern slides, postcards, illustrated maps, unprinted film negatives, posters, architectural drawings, original cartoons, greetings cards, press cuttings and tearsheets, illustrated books

Dates of subject matter 17th century to present

Dates of photographs c. 1890 to present

Subjects Former London boroughs of Paddington and St Marylebone, history, topography and social life, especially good material for Regent's Park; ASHBRIDGE COLLECTION of the history of St Marylebone (17th to 19th centuries) including outstanding prints, drawings, maps, watercolours, press cuttings

Access and conditions Open to the public, Mon-Fri 9.30–7, Sat 9.30–1, 2–5. All material available for editorial reproduction and for advertising. B/w prints available for a fee; colour transparencies loaned free of charge for three weeks. Material may be copied by outside photographers. Photocopies available of some material. Reproduction rights fees charged. Staff will undertake some research; limit of one hour per inquiry. Printed and card catalogues; Ann Cox-Johnson, *Handlist to the Ashbridge Collection,* 1959.

454 • THE TOM HARRISSON MASS-OBSERVATION ARCHIVE

The Library, University of Sussex, Brighton, East Sussex BN1 1QL
Tel (0273) 606755 ext 1054

Enquiries to Dorothy Sheridan, Archivist

Items About 800: b/w original and copy photographs, postcards, unprinted film negatives, posters, ephemera (leaflets, booklets, tickets, brochures, drawings, newspaper cuttings, etc.)

Dates of subject matter 1937 to 1950

Dates of photographs 1937 to 1945

Subjects WORKTOWN PROJECT 1937–1940: Blackpool and Bolton, including (Bolton) streetscenes, traffic signs, pedestrians, road accident, funeral procession, children playing, window shopping, groups of people outside churches, schools, pubs, etc., children at dance classes, graffiti, interiors of churches, chapels, pubs, political meetings, cinema; (Blackpool) holiday scenes, the beach, prom, side shows, stalls, slot machines, coaches, signs and billboards, people going into polling booths, children's games, sports events, pigeon fanciers; all photographs by Humphrey Spender; RETURN TO WORKTOWN 1959: same subject matter, but more restricted collection; photographs by Michael Wickham

Access and conditions Open to the public by appt (write), Mon-Thurs 9.15–5.15. All material available for editorial reproduction and for advertising, subject to copyright clearance. B/w prints available for a fee. Photocopies available. Reproduction rights and service fees charged. Staff will undertake some research.

455 • MATLOCK LIBRARY

County Offices, Matlock, Derbyshire DE4 3AG
Tel (0629) 3411 ext 6840

Enquiries to Jean Radford, Local Studies Librarian

Items 4000: b/w original and copy photographs, colour photographic prints, glass negatives, postcards, fine art prints

Dates of subject matter 18th century to present

Dates of photographs Late 19th century to present

Subjects Derbyshire local history, life and activities, transport (trams, buses, railway), local architecture, streetscenes, sports, portraits

Access and conditions Open to the public, Mon-Fri 9–5, Sat (by appt) 9.30–1. Most material available for editorial reproduction and for advertising. No loans; material may be copied by outside photographers. Photocopies available.

Reproduction rights fees charged. Staff will undertake limited research. Copyright clearance is responsibility of user. Card catalogue in preparation.

456 • MERE MUSEUM

c/o Mere Library, Barton Lane, Mere, Warminster, Wiltshire BA12 6JA
Tel (0747) 860546

Enquiries to David Longbourne, Honorary Curator

Items 800: b/w original photogaphs, postcards, old fine art prints, posters

Dates of subject matter Mid-19th century

Dates of photographs Mid-19th century

Subjects Local history of Mere and surrounding area including landscapes, natural history, architecture, agriculture

Access and conditions Open to the public, Mon Wed Thurs and Fri 2–5, 6–8, Tues 10–1, 2–5. Most material available for editorial reproduction and for advertising. No loans; b/w prints available for a fee. Staff will undertake limited research. Most material copyright. Computer list in preparation.

457 • MERTHYR TYDFIL PUBLIC LIBRARY

Local History Photographic Collction

High Street, Merthyr Tydfil, Mid Glamorgan CF47 8AF
Tel (0685) 3057

Enquiries to Arts Officer

Items About 4500: b/w copy photographs, b/w original photographs, colour photographic prints, colour transparencies (35mm), glass negatives, postcards, architectural drawings, illustrated books

Dates of subject matter Early 19th century to present

Dates of photographs Mid-19th century to present

Subjects Local history of Merthyr Tydfil and surrounding area including landscapes, villages, architecture, industry, religion, social history, portraits

Access and conditions Open to the public by appt (tel), Mon-Fri 9–6.30, Sat 9–12. Most material available for editorial reproduction; advertising use by special arrangement only. No loans; b/w prints and duplicate colour transparencies available for a fee; material may be copied by outside photographers. Photocopies available. Reproduction rights fees charged. Staff will undertake limited research. Most material copyright.

458 • METROPOLITAN BOROUGH OF NORTH TYNESIDE

Libraries and Arts Department

Local Studies Centre, Old Central Library, Howard Street, North Shields, Tyne and Wear NE30 1LY
Tel (0632) 582811 ext 17   Telex 53134

Enquiries to Principal Librarian, Local Studies

Items About 10,000: b/w copy photographs, b/w original photographs, colour transparencies (35mm), colour photographic prints, glass negatives, lantern slides, postcards, illustrated books, posters, architectural drawings, press cuttings

Dates of subject matter 1400 to present

Dates of photographs 1900 to 1939

Subjects Local history of North Tyneside including streetscenes, portraits, housing, transport, industry (foundries, fish works), works outings, social history

Access and conditions Open to the public, Mon Wed Thurs Fri 9–5, Tues 9–7. Most material available for editorial reproduction and for advertising. Colour material loaned free of charge for one month; b/w prints and duplicate colour transparencies available for a fee. Photocopies available. No reproduction rights fees charged. Staff of two will undertake some research. Some material copyright. Card catalogue available.

459 • MID GLAMORGAN COUNTY LIBRARY

Local Studies Collection

Coed Parc, Park Street, Bridgend, Mid Glamorgan CF31 4BA
Tel (0656) 57451

Enquiries to County Librarian

Items 6000: b/w original photographs, b/w copy photographs, glass negatives, postcards, illustrated maps

Dates of subject matter 1750 to present

Dates of photographs 1880 to present

Subjects Local history of the Mid Glamorgan area with special emphasis on Ogwr Taff Ely and Rhymney District including Bridgend, Pontypridd and Portcawl: life and activities including landscapes, architecture, transport (horse-drawn vehicles, buses, trams, canal transport, railways), industry, business, mining, strikes, social history, personalities

Access and conditions Open to the public, Mon-Fri 9–5. All material available for editorial reproduction and for advertising. B/w material loaned by arrangement; b/w prints available for a fee; material may be copied by outside photographers. Photocopies available. Staff will undertake limited research. Compulsory credit line. Most material copyright.

460 • MITCHAM LIBRARY

Local Studies Collection

London Road, Mitcham, Surry CR4 2YR
Tel (01) 648 4070

Enquiries to Michael Harkin, Reference Librarian

Items 500: b/w original and copy photographs, lantern slides, postcards

Dates of subject matter c. 1800 to present

Dates of photographs c. 1900 to present

Subjects Mitcham local history, especially buildings and streetscenes, cricket, aerial photographs of All England Lawn Tennis Club at Wimbledon

Access and conditions Open to the public by appt (tel), Mon Tues Thurs Fri 9–7, Wed 9–1, Sat 9–5. All material available for editorial reproduction and for advertising. No loans; b/w prints available for a fee. Photocopies available. Reproduction rights fees charged. Staff will undertake some research.

461 • THE MITCHELL LIBRARY

Local Studies Collection

The Glasgow Room, North Street, Glasgow
G3 7DN
Tel (041) 221 7030

Enquiries to Departmental Librarian, Local
Studies Collection

Items About 8000: b/w copy and original
photographs, colour transparencies (35mm), glass
negatives, illustrated books, postcards, lantern
slides

Dates of subject matter *c.* 1820s to present

Dates of photographs 1890s to present

Subjects Local history of Glasgow including
architecture, housing, churches, schools, hospitals,
streetscenes, transport, industry (heavy
engineering, locomotives, iron foundries,
shipbuilding), social history, markets, crafts,
portraits

Access and conditions Open to the public, Mon-
Fri 9.30–9, Sat 9.30–5. All material available for
editorial reproduction and for advertising. No
loans; b/w prints and duplicate colour
transparencies available for a fee. Photocopies
available. Reproduction rights fees charged. Staff
will undertake some research. Some material
copyright.

462 • MORAY DISTRICT RECORD OFFICE

Tolbooth, Forres, Moray IV36 0AB
Tel (0309) 73617

Enquiries to Dr D. A. Iredale, District Archivist

Items 145,000: architectural drawings, unprinted
film negatives, b/w copy photographs, b/w original
photographs, colour photographic prints, posters,
postcards, greetings cards, glass negatives

Dates of subject matter Prehistory to present

Dates of photographs 1855 to present

Subjects Local history of Moray and area and also
material on Aberdeenshire, Inverness-shire and
the Scottish borders including architecture,
housing, public buildings, schools, churches,
harbours, fishermen, distilleries, gas works, farms
and farm buildings, workshops, shops; some travel
coverage of Germany, Italy, India and Ireland
1910–1912; special collection of architectural
drawings by C. E. Doig, Alex and William Reid and

John and William Wittet; drawings and
photographs by Hugh Falconer and Peter Anson

Access and conditions Open to the public by
appt (tel), Mon-Fri 9–4.30. Most material available
for editorial reproduction and for advertising. No
loans; b/w prints and duplicate colour
transparencies available for a fee; material may be
copied by outside photographers. Photocopies
available. No reproduction rights fees charged.
Some material copyright. Card catalogue available.

463 • MORDEN LIBRARY

Local Studies Collection

Morden Road, London SW19 3DA
Tel (01) 542 2842

Enquiries to Richard Alexander, Reference
Librarian

Items 750: b/w original and copy photographs,
postcards

Dates of subject matter *c.* 1650 to present

Dates of photographs *c.* 1920 to present

Subjects Local history of the parishes of Merton
and Morden, especially buildings and streetscenes

Access and conditions Open to the public by
appt (tel), Mon Tues Thurs Fri 9–7, Wed 9–1, Sat
9–5. All material available for editorial
reproduction and for advertising. No loans; b/w
prints and duplicate colour transparencies
available for a fee. Reproduction rights fees
charged. Photocopies available. Staff will
undertake limited research.

464 • MOTHERWELL DISTRICT LIBRARIES

33 Hamilton Road, Motherwell, Strathclyde
ML1 3BZ
Tel (0698) 51311

Enquiries to District Librarian

Items About 3000: b/w copy photographs, colour
transparencies (35mm), b/w original photographs,
colour photographic prints, postcards, unprinted
film negatives

Dates of photographs 1890 to present

Subjects Local history of Motherwell and
surrounding area including landscapes,

architecture, housing, churches, schools, streetscenes, transport, social history, portraits; industry including mining c. 1900, iron and steel works, coachbuilders (Stewarts of Wishaw building buses, lorries and vans from 1920s, and Scotts of Bellshill building horse-drawn carts and vans from 1920s), confectionery; special collections include the HURST NELSON WAGONS AND ROLLING STOCK COLLECTION, and a street survey 1967–8

Access and conditions Open to the public by appt (tel), Mon-Fri 9–5. All material available for editorial reproduction and for advertising. No loans; b/w prints and duplicate colour transparencies available for a fee. Photocopies available. Reproduction rights fees charged. Staff will undertake very limited research. Most material copyright.

465 • MUSEUM OF EAST ANGLIAN LIFE

Crowe Street, Stowmarket, Suffolk IP14 1DL
Tel (0449) 612229

Enquiries to Curator

Items 6000: b/w original photographs, b/w copy photographs, glass negatives, postcards, colour transparencies (35mm)

Dates of subject matter Mid-19th century to present

Dates of photographs 1860 to present

Subjects Agriculture from the late 19th century in East Anglia covering rural crafts and industries including wheelwrights, blacksmiths, hurdle-makers, builders; crops and livestock; sea and coastal fisheries; reconstructed Museum buildings; production and processing of milk and butter; mills and milling; transport especially carts and waggons; towns, villages, portraits; FISONS FERTILIZERS COLLECTION and RANSOMES COLLECTION of glass negatives (manufacturers of agricultural machinery)

Access and conditions Open to the public by appt (write), Mon-Fri 9–5. All material available for editorial reproduction and for advertising. No loans; b/w prints and duplicate colour transparencies available for a fee. Reproduction rights and service fees charged. Staff will undertake limited research. Compulsory credit line. Most material copyright. Card catalogue available.

466 • MUSEUM OF LAKELAND LIFE AND INDUSTRY

Abbot Hall, Kendal, Cumbria LA9 5AL
Tel (0539) 22464

Enquiries to M. E. Burkett, Director

Items About 35,000: Glass negatives, b/w original photographs, colour transparencies (35mm), lantern slides, postcards, fine art prints, greetings cards, original cartoons, b/w copy photographs, unprinted film negatives

Dates of subject matter 3000 BC to present

Dates of photographs c. 1870 to present

Subjects Social and economic history of the Lake District, urban and rural, including buildings, villages and towns; farming and agriculture, tools, ploughing, harrowing, reaping, binding, cutting, working and loading hay, cutting and loading bracken, hedging, ditching, dry-stone walling, sheep and shepherds including clipping, dipping, lambing, digging out of snow, foddering in snow, going to market; cattle, poultry, damson-picking, agricultural shows, peat-cutting; coppice trades and woodland industries including charcoal burners and their huts, charcoal pit-stead, bobbin mills (exterior and interior), implements and machinery related to bobbin-turning, swill-making and swill-makers' workshops, clogging and shoe-making, weaving and the woollen trade, hoop makers; slate-quarrying, mining, pre-World War II factories, laundry equipment; Lake District oak furniture (mid-17th to early-18th century), hooked rugs; Appleby Horse-Fair including gypsies, caravans, horses and ponies; sports including rock climbing, pioneer climbers and climbs of the Fell and Rock Climbing Club of the English Lake District photographed by Abrahams of Keswick (glass negatives) and published in Alan Hankinson, *A Camera on the Crags,* Heinemann, 1975; Cumberland and Westmoreland style wrestling, fishing, fell races, guide races, Grasmere and Ambleside sports, hound and sheepdog trials, hunting including meets of fox hounds and otter hounds, posed groups, groups at kills, etc.; transportation including Lake transport, Windermere ferry (c. 1880–1960, steam and diesel, with horse-drawn coaches and carts and early motor vehicles), rowing boats, sailing boats, yachts including Windermere Class c. 1880–1960, steam boats and launches, steamers on Windermere and Ullswater, the Gondola on Coniston; horse-drawn transport including carts, coaches, landaus, charabancs, private and public, on passes, outside hotels; motor vehicles including early motorcars, buses and motorcycles parked or *en route,* breakdowns, garages; bicycles, steam and traction engines including steam rollers; trains; the Great Freeze including Windermere, Derwentwater, skaters, ice yachts, horse-drawn sleighs, snow scenes, giant icicles; posed portrait studies (mainly 1880–1900); landscapes and pictorial views; rushbearing; glass negatives by Stanley Davies, a Windermere furniture-maker c. 1925 to c. 1960, of each piece he designed, and by the following: the Abrahams of Keswick (additional fees payable to the Fell & Rock Climbing Club of Great Britain for use of their material on deposit at this museum), Mason of Ambleside, Herbert Bell of Ambleside (c. 1900), Herbert & Son of Windermere (c. 1870–1890), the Rev. Kemble of Wray (1900–1915), Joseph Hardman of Kendal (c. 1920–1960), Walmsley of Ambleside (c. 1890), J. Jameson of Penrith (1935–1936), D. and D. S. Potts (1890–1990)

Access and conditions Open by appt (write) to qualified researchers, Mon-Fri 10.30–5. All material available for editorial reproduction and for advertising. B/w prints available for a fee; colour material loaned for a rental fee (duplicate transparencies also available for a fee). Material may be copied by outside photographers. Photocopies available. Reproduction rights, service and holding fees charged. Staff will undertake limited research for specific requests; fees charged for large projects. Museum owns copyright to part of collection; in other cases copyright clearance is responsibility of user.

467 • MUSEUM OF LONDON

150 London Wall, London EC2Y 5HN
Tel (01) 600 3699

Enquiries to Irene Shaw, Photographic Records Officer

Items About 50,000: b/w original photographs, b/w copy photographs, colour transparencies (35mm, 5″ × 4″), glass negatives, daguerreotypes, lantern slides, postcards, original cartoons, illustrated maps, old fine art prints, 20th-century fine art prints, posters, greetings cards, architectural drawings, press cuttings, illustrated books

Dates of subject matter Prehistory to present

Dates of photographs 1840s to present

Subjects All aspects of the history of London and environs including archaeology, landscapes, architecture, coinage, costume, domestic life, special events, transport, political and social life; special collections include the PAVLOVA COLLECTION, the PORT OF LONDON AUTHORITY COLLECTION and suffragette material

Access and conditions Open to the public by appt, Mon-Fri 9–5. All material available for editorial reproduction and for advertising. No loans; b/w prints and duplicate colour transparencies available for a fee. Photocopies available. Reproduction rights fees charged. Staff will undertake limited research. Most material copyright.

468 • NATIONAL LIBRARY OF SCOTLAND

George IV Bridge, Edinburgh EH1 1EW
Tel (031) 226 4531 Telex 72638 NLSEDI G

Enquiries to Librarian

Items Over one million: b/w original photographs, b/w copy photographs, colour transparencies (35mm, 5″ × 4″), colour photographic prints, glass negatives, lantern slides, postcards, original cartoons, illustrated maps, old fine art prints, 20th-century fine art prints, art reproductions, unprinted film negatives, stereographs, posters, greetings cards, architectural drawings, press cuttings, illustrated books, drawings, illuminated manuscripts

Dates of subject matter Prehistory to present

Dates of photographs 1843 to present

Subjects All aspects of Scottish history and culture; special collections include the GRAHAM BROWN MOUNTAINEERING COLLECTION, the FANNY BULLOCK WORKMAN HIMALAYAN TRAVEL COLLECTION, F. E. MACDONALD COLLECTION of town planning in Scotland and Europe 1960s to 1980s, ALEXANDER CAIN COLLECTION of Scottish scenes 1930s to 1960s; photographers include D. O. Hill, R. Adamson, William Carrick, William Notman, James Valentine, George Washington Wilson, Thomas Anna, Archibald Burns, Alexander A. Inglis, Robert Macpherson, George Piazzi Smyth, John Thomson, Samuel Bourne, Roger Fenton

Access and conditions Open to the public by appt, Mon-Fri 9–5. Most material available for editorial reproduction and for advertising. No loans; b/w prints and duplicate colour transparencies available for a fee. Photocopies available. Reproduction rights and service fees charged. Staff will undertake limited research. Card and printed catalogues available.

469 • NATIONAL LIBRARY OF WALES

Department of Pictures and Maps

Aberystwyth, Dyfed SY23 3BU
Tel (0970) 3816 Telex 35165

Enquiries to Keeper of Pictures and Maps

Items About one million: b/w original and copy photographs, illustrated maps, glass negatives, unprinted film negatives, postcards, fine art prints, colour transparencies (35mm), colour photographic prints, lantern slides, daguerreotypes, original cartoons, illustrated books, stereographs, art reproductions, posters, greetings cards, architectural drawings, press cuttings, illustrated books

Dates of subject matter *c.* 1650 to present

Dates of photographs *c.* 1850 to present

Subjects Welsh history, topography, portraits, customs, costumes, architecture, history, music, religion, natural history; special collection of late 18th- and early 19th-century watercolours; views and portraits in all media; drawings by John Warwick Smith, Thomas Rowlandson, Moses Griffith, Samuel Hieronymus Grimm; works by modern artists Kyffin Williams, John Pelts; large collection of engravings, lithographs, etc.

Access and conditions Open to the public by appt, Mon-Fri 9.30–6, Sat 9.30–5. Most material available for editorial reproduction and for advertising. B/w prints and duplicate colour transparencies available for a fee. Photocopies available. Reproduction rights fees charged. Staff will undertake limited research. Card catalogue.

470 • NATIONAL MUSEUM OF ANTIQUITIES OF SCOTLAND

Country Life Section

Queen Street, Edinburgh EH2 1JD
Tel (031) 557 3550

Enquiries to Gavin Sprott, Assistant Keeper

Items About 110,000: unprinted film negatives, b/w original and copy photographs, glass negatives, lantern slides, colour transparencies (35mm), colour photographic prints, postcards, architectural drawings

Dates of photographs *c.* 1860 to present

Subjects Life in the Scottish countryside including farming, trades, skills, social and domestic life, buildings, transport, communications, fishing, sea-faring

Access and conditions Open to the public by appt (tel), Mon-Fri 9.30–5.30. Some material available for editorial reproduction but not for advertising. B/w and colour prints available for a fee. Reproduction rights and service fees charged. Staff will answer questions and advise, but cannot undertake research.

471 • NEWARK DISTRICT COUNCIL MUSEUM

Appletongate, Newark, Nottinghamshire
NG24 1JY
Tel (0636) 702358

Enquiries to Curator

Items 40,000: unprinted film negatives, glass negatives, architectural drawings, b/w original photographs, maps, lantern slides, colour transparencies (35mm), b/w copy photographs, postcards

Dates of subject matter Prehistory to present

Dates of photographs 1875 to present

Subjects Local history of Newark including landscapes, architecture, social history, education, transport, agriculture, industry, trades, portraits; special collection of material from the *Newark Advertiser,* and archives from W. H. Nicholson & Sons Ltd, agricultural engineers.

Access and conditions Open to the public by appt (write), Mon-Fri 9–5. All material available for editorial reproduction and for advertising. No loans; b/w prints available for a fee. Photocopies available. Reproduction rights fees charged. Most material copyright.

472 • NEWARKE HOUSES MUSEUM

Photographic Collection

The Newarke, Leicester LE2 7B1
Tel (0533) 554100

Enquiries to Jane Legget, Keeper of Leicestershire History

Items 43,300: b/w original and copy photographs, colour transparencies (5″ × 4″, larger), colour photographic prints, daguerreotypes, lantern slides, postcards, original cartoons, stereographs, posters, greetings cards, architectural drawings, press cuttings and tearsheets, illustrated books, photograph albums, cartes-de-visite, advertisements, ephemera

Dates of subject matter 1485 to present

Dates of photographs *c.* 1850 to present

Subjects Leicestershire, especially Leicester but including all villages and towns in the county; occupations, especially clockmaking, clocks, watches, sundials and also agriculture (ploughing, stock-raising, horses), blacksmiths, boot- and shoe-making, bottling, brewing, building, fell-mongering, hosiery, shopkeeping (general, butcher, chemist, cutler, hardware, ironmonger, grocer, tobacconist, street traders), Swithland slate, thatching, wheelwright; civic life including public health, fire service, security, law and order, Royal Family, postal history, religion, institutions (Friendly Societies, Boy Scouts, suffragettes); military history, arms and armour, firearms and accessories, Leicestershire Regiment, Leicestershire Volunteers, Leicestershire Yeomanry, World Wars I and II, army medical hospitals; cultural life, theatres, music halls, cinema, clubs, sports, toys and games, newspapers, tobacco and snuff; folk customs; local events, processions, hunger marches, pageants, celebrations; local personalities (Daniel Lambert, Mary Linwood, etc.); domestic life, wartime Leicester, post-war Leicester, civil defence, household articles (vacuum cleaners), lighting and heating, furnishings, water supply, sanitation, laundry, gardening, crafts, lace, tatting, sewing machines, needlework, kitchens, vernacular architecture; BRITISH COUNCIL COLLECTION of life in Leicester (1945); HEAWOOD COLLECTION: work of local photographer, postcards of streetscenes, markets, hunting, Melton Mowbray at the turn of the century; MORRIS COLLECTION: international expert on bells, pictures of bells and bell-ringing from all over the world and especially Leicestershire churches; HILL COLLECTION: local scenes (1900–1925); STEWART COLLECTION: photographs by local doctor (1890–1910), local scenes

Access and conditions Open to the public by appt (tel), Mon-Thurs 10–5.30. Most material available for editorial reproduction and for advertising with the Keeper's approval. B/w prints available for a fee; colour transparencies loaned for a rental fee. Photocopies available. Reproduction rights and service fees charged. Staff will undertake some research.

473 • NEWCASTLE UNDER LYME PUBLIC LIBRARY

Local History Photographic Collection

Ironmarket, Newcastle under Lyme, Staffordshire ST5 1AT
Tel (0782) 618125

Enquiries to Area Reference Librarian

Items About 4000: b/w copy photographs, b/w original photographs, colour transparencies (35mm), colour photographic prints, postcards

Dates of photographs *c.* 1870 to present

Subjects Local history of North Staffordshire, Newcastle-under-Lyme and Stoke-on-Trent including landscapes (including aerial shots), architecture, churches, public houses, housing, industries (including mining and iron founding), public services, social history, education, transport, leisure, sport and entertainment

Access and conditions Open to the public, Mon Wed Fri 9–7, Tues & Thurs 9–5, Sat 9–1. Most material available for editorial reproduction; advertising use by special arrangement only. No loans; b/w prints and duplicate colour transparencies available for a fee. Staff will undertake limited research. Most material copyright. Card catalogue available.

474 • NEWCASTLE UPON TYNE CENTRAL LIBRARY

Local Studies Department Illustrations Collection

Princess Square, Newcastle upon Tyne NE99 1MC
Tel (0632) 610691   Telex 53373 LINCLE G

Enquiries to Local Studies Librarian

Items Over 100,000: b/w original photographs, b/w copy photographs, glass negatives, postcards, lantern slides, colour transparencies (35mm), posters, colour photographic prints, theatre playbills, architectural drawings, illustrated maps

Dates of subject matter AD 120 to present

Dates of photographs *c.* 1854 to present

Subjects Local history of Northumberland, Durham, Tyne and Wear with special emphasis on Newcastle and including landscapes, architecture, streetscenes, transport, shops, housing (especially sub-standard housing in the 1930s and 1960s), education, social history, portraits, industry including engineering and coalmining; ships under construction and completed by Armstrong, Mitchell & Whitworth between 1890 and 1914; special collection of theatre playbills from Theatre Royal, Newcastle and other local theatres; other special collections include the KNOPF COLLECTION of portraits c. 1910 to 1920s; AUTY-HASTINGS COLLECTION of the north-east especially Newcastle between c. 1890 and 1910; THOMPSON COLLECTION of Newcastle between c. 1910 and 1930; Lowry lantern slides of Northumberland and Durham c. 1900 to 1910; SIGNEY COLLECTION of Newcastle streets and buildings c. 1962 to 1972; FENWICK COLLECTION of mainly rural Northumberland 1929 to 1957; official coverage of the North East Coast Exhibition of 1929

Access and conditions Open to the public, Mon-Thurs 9–9, Fri & Sat 9–5. Most material available for editorial reproduction and for advertising. No loans; b/w prints and colour transparencies available for a fee. Photocopies available. Reproduction rights fees charged. Staff will undertake some research. Some material copyright.

475 • NORFOLK RURAL LIFE MUSEUM

Beech House, Gressenhall, Dereham, Norfolk
NR20 4DR
Tel (0362) 860563

Enquiries to Bridget Yates

Items 2000: b/w copy photographs, b/w original photographs, glass negatives, trade catalogues and leaflets

Dates of subject matter c. 1860 to present

Dates of photographs c. 1870 to present

Subjects Rural life in Norfolk including agriculture, buildings, crafts, trades, domestic life; special collection of trade catalogues and leaflets from 1860 onwards illustrating kitchen equipment, stoves, ranges, building materials, trade tools, argicultural implements, vehicles, garden furniture, sports and recreational equipment

Access and conditions Open to the public by appt (tel), Mon-Fri 9–5. Most material available for editorial reproduction and for advertising. No loans; b/w prints available for a fee. Reproduction rights fees charged. Staff will undertake limited research. All material copyright.

476 • NORRIS LIBRARY AND MUSEUM

The Broadway, St Ives, Huntingdon,
Cambridgeshire PE17 4BX
Tel (0480) 65101

Enquiries to Curator

Items About 10,000: b/w original photographs, postcards, posters, b/w copy photographs, colour transparencies (35mm), colour photographic prints, illustrated books

Dates of subject matter BC to present

Dates of photographs c. 1880 to present

Subjects Local history of Huntingdonshire including landscapes, archaeology, towns, villages, architecture, historic monuments, agriculture, transport; special collection of photographs by Sidney Inskip Ladds

Access and conditions Open to the public by appt (write). All material available for editorial reproduction and for advertising. No loans; b/w prints and duplicate colour transparencies available for a fee. Material may be copied by outside photographers. Some material copyright.

477 • NORTH EAST FIFE DISTRICT LIBRARY

Local History Collection

County Buildings, St Catherine Street, Cupar, Fife
KY15 4TA
Tel (0334) 53722

Enquiries to Ian Copland, District Librarian

Items 2000: b/w original photographs, b/w copy photographs, colour transparencies (35mm), colour photographic prints, lantern slides, postcards, illustrated books

Dates of subject matter 15th century to present

Dates of photographs 1856 to present

Subjects Local history of north-east Fife with special emphasis on St Andrews, Cupar and East Fife fishing communities including architecture, housing, shops, markets, harbours, streetscenes, social history

Access and conditions Open to the public by appt (tel), Mon Tues Wed Fri 10–7, Thurs Sat 10–5. Most material available for editorial reproduction and for advertising. B/w and colour material loaned free of charge for three weeks; material may be copied by outside photographers. Photocopies available. Reproduction rights fee sometimes charged. Staff will undertake limited research. Most material copyright.

478 • NORTH YORKSHIRE COUNTY LIBRARY

Bertram Unné Collection

County Library Headquarters, 21 Grammar School Lane, Northallerton, North Yorkshire DL6 1DF
Tel (0609) 6271

Enquiries to County Librarian

Items About 30,000: b/w original photographs, unprinted film negatives, press cuttings, glass negatives

Dates of subject matter BC to 1975

Dates of photographs c. 1945 to 1975

Subjects Yorkshire since 1945 including landscape with special emphasis on North and West Ridings; architecture including churches, abbeys (including Fountains Abbey) and stately homes with comprehensive coverage of Harrogate and York; agriculture; rural industries including pottery-, rope- and cheese-making; rural life including markets, shows, hunting, riding and fishing

Access and conditions Open to the public by appt, Mon-Fri 9–5. All material available for editorial reproduction and for advertising. B/w material loaned by arrangement; material may be copied by outside photographers. Photocopies available. Reproduction rights and service fees charged. Staff will undertake some research. All material copyright. Card catalogue available.

479 • NORTHAMPTONSHIRE RECORD OFFICE

Delapre Abbey, Northampton NN4 9AW
Tel (0604) 62129

Enquiries to County Archivist

Items 20,000: b/w original and copy photographs, colour transparencies (35mm), glass negatives, lantern slides, postcards, illustrated maps, old prints, posters, greetings cards, architectural drawings, press cuttings

Dates of subject matter AD 600 to present

Dates of photographs 1850 to present

Dates of fine art 1600 onwards

Subjects Northamptonshire historical buildings, views, scenes, personalities, groups, transport, factory interiors and products

Access and conditions Open to the public by appt (tel), Mon-Fri 9.30–5.30. Most material available for editorial reproduction and for advertising, subject to conditions stipulated by depositors. B/w and colour prints available for a fee. Photocopies available. Reproduction rights fees charged. Staff will undertake very limited research. Catalogue available.

480 • NORWICH CENTRAL LIBRARY

Photographic Collection

Local Studies Department, Bethel Street, Norwich, Norfolk NR2 1NJ
Tel (0603) 611277

Enquiries to County Local Studies Librarian

Items About 30,000: b/w copy photographs, b/w original photographs, colour transparencies (35mm), press cuttings, posters, lantern slides, postcards, old fine art prints, glass negatives

Dates of subject matter Prehistory to present

Dates of photographs 1845 to present

Subjects Local history of Norfolk with emphasis on Norwich including towns, villages, landscapes, architecture, industry (shoe-manufacturing, printing, flour-milling, brush-making, brick-making, sweet-manufacturing, sugar-refining), transport, agriculture, crafts including thatching, sport, leisure, social history, portraits; special collections include photographs by P. H. Emerson, Christopher Davies, John Payne Jennings and Thomas Damant Eaton

Access and conditions Open to the public, Mon-Fri 9–5. Most material available for editorial reproduction and for advertising. No loans; b/w prints available for a fee; material may be copied by outside photographers. Reproduction rights fees charged. Staff will undertake limited research. Some material copyright. Card catalogue available.

481 • NOTTINGHAM CENTRAL LIBRARY

Local Studies Illustrations Collection

Angel Row, Nottingham NG1 6HP
Tel (0602) 412121 ext 48 Telex 37662

Enquiries to Local Studies Librarian

Items About 100,000: b/w original photographs,
b/w copy photographs, colour transparencies
(35mm), postcards, colour photographic prints,
glass negatives, lantern slides, illustrated maps,
old fine art prints, posters, greetings cards, press
cuttings, illustrated books

Dates of subject matter Prehistory to present

Dates of photographs *c.* 1858 to present

Subjects Local history of Nottingham and
surrounding area including landscapes,
architecture, transport, housing (especially before
slum clearance), streetscenes, education, social
history, industry; special collections include
photographs by Joseph Byron, Samuel Bourne,
H.E. Bird, S. W. A. Newton; special sections on the
lives of Lord Byron, D. H. Lawrence and Alan
Sillitoe

Access and conditions Open to the public, Mon-
Fri 9–8, Sat 9–1. Most material available for
editorial reproduction and for advertising. B/w
prints and duplicate colour transparencies
available for a fee; material may be copied by
outside photographers. Photocopies available.
Reproduction rights fees charged. Staff will
undertake limited research. Most material
copyright.

482 • OLD MILL HOUSE MUSEUM

Local History Photographic Collection

Mill Green, Hatfield, Hertfordshire AL9 5PD
Tel (07072) (from London 30) 71362

Enquiries to Christine Johnstone, Curator

Items About 200: b/w original photographs, b/w
copy photographs, postcards, posters

Dates of photographs 1860 to present

Subjects Local history of Welwyn Garden City
and Hatfield including landscapes, architecture,
social history, streetscenes, education, water mills
and powered flight

Access and conditions Open to the public by
appt (write), Tues-Fri 10–5, Sat 2–5. All material

available for editorial reproduction; advertising use
by special arrangement only. No loans; b/w prints
available for a fee; material may be copied by
outside photographers. Reproduction rights and
service fees charged; service fees deductible from
use fees. Staff will undertake some research. Some
material copyright.

483 • OPEN EYE GALLERY

90-92 Whitechapel, Liverpool L1 6EN
Tel (051) 709 9460

Enquiries to Neil Burgess, Director

Items About 5000: b/w original photographs,
colour photographic prints, b/w copy photographs,
unprinted film negatives

Dates of subject matter 1870 to present

Dates of photographs 1870 to present

Subjects Merseyside, including social history, the
1941 Blitz, housing, theatre, parks, mental health,
portraits, personalities, human interaction;
photographers include Herbert Barraud, Martin
Parr, Graham Smith, Martin Roberts, Joel
Meyerovitz, E. Chambré Hardman, Mike
Beddington, John Stoddart, Harry Hammond,
George Blair, Bill Watmough

Access and conditions Open to qualified
researchers by appt, Mon-Sat 9.30–5.30. Most
material available for editorial reproduction;
advertising by special arrangement only. B/w
material loaned free of charge by arrangement.
Reproduction rights and service fees charged. Staff
will undertake limited research. Most material
copyright; copyright clearance is responsibility of
user.

484 • OXFORDSHIRE COUNTY LIBRARIES

Local History Collections

Central Library, Westgate, Oxford OX1 1DJ
Tel (0865) 815749

Enquiries to Leonard White, County Librarian

Items About 75,000: b/w original photographs,
b/w copy photographs, glass negatives, colour
transparencies (35mm), old fine art prints, colour
photographic prints, 20th-century fine art prints,
lantern slides, illustrated maps, illustrated books,
postcards, posters

Dates of subject matter 17th century to present

Dates of photographs *c.* 1860 to present

Subjects Local history of Oxfordshire with emphasis on Oxford and communities along the course of the Thames; landscapes, towns and villages, architecture, agriculture, industry, leisure, personalities; special collections include the work of Henry Taunt, 1842–1922

Access and conditions Open to the public by appt (tel). All material available for editorial reproduction and for advertising. No loans; b/w prints available for a fee; material may be copied by outside photographers. Reproduction rights fees charged. Staff will undertake limited research. Most material copyright.

485 • OXON AND BUCKS NEWS-PHOTO AGENCY

11 Suffolk House, 263 Banbury Road, Oxford OX2 7HN
Tel (0865) 512575 Telex 837474

Enquiries to News Desk or Picture Desk

Items 10,000: b/w original photographs

Dates of photographs 1982 to present

Subjects Local news coverage of events (including sporting events) in Oxfordshire

Access and conditions Not open; telephone and postal requests only. All material available for editorial reproduction and for advertising. B/w prints available for a fee. Reproduction rights fees charged. Staff will undertake some research. All material copyright.

486 • THE PEMBROKESHIRE RECORD OFFICE

The Castle, Haverfordwest, Dyfed JA61 2EF
Tel (0437) 3707

Enquiries to John Owen, Archivist

Items 500: b/w original photographs, b/w copy photographs, glass negatives, postcards, illustrated maps, posters, greetings cards, architectural drawings, illustrated books

Dates of subject matter 11th century to present

Dates of photographs *c.* 1870 to present

Subjects Local history in the former county of Pembroke including landscapes, architecture, streetscenes, social history, transport, shipping, education, portraits

Access and conditions Open to the public, Mon–Thurs 9–4.45, Fri 9–4.15. Some material available for editorial reproduction but not for advertising. No loans; material may be copied by outside photographers. Photocopies available. No reproduction rights fees charged. Staff will undertake limited research. Most material copyright; copyright clearance is responsibility of user. Card catalogue available.

487 • PERTH MUSEUM AND ART GALLERY

George Street, Perth PH1 5LB
Tel (0738) 32488

Enquiries to James Blair, Curator

Items Over 100,000: b/w original photographs, b/w copy photographs, colour transparencies (5″ × 4″), glass negatives, daguerreotypes, lantern slides, postcards, original cartoons, illustrated maps, old fine art prints, 20th-century fine art prints, art reproductions, unprinted film negatives, stereographs, posters, greetings cards, architectural drawings, illustrated books

Dates of subject matter Prehistory to present

Dates of photographs 1860 to 1950

Subjects Local history of Perth and surrounding area including social history, streetscenes, country houses, commerce, industry (especially the linen industry), ceremonies, events, portraits; Perth silver including work by Robert Keay the elder, Robert Keay the younger and Robert Jairdine; paintings by Scottish artists including works by D. Y. Cameron, T. B. Blacklock, Horatio McCulloch; European paintings from the 16th to 18th centuries; special collections include glass negative collections of Jackson, Wood and Couper

Access and conditions Open to the public by appt, Mon-Sat 10–5. Most material available for editorial reproduction and adveritising. B/w prints available for a fee; colour material loaned for a fee. Reproduction rights fees charged. Staff will undertake limited research. Most material copyright. Card and printed catalogues available.

488 • PETERBOROUGH CENTRAL LIBRARY

Local Studies Collection

Broadway, Peterborough, Cambridgeshire
PE1 1RX
Tel (0733) 48343   Telex 32634

Enquiries to   Local Studies Librarian

Items   About 1000: b/w original and copy photographs, colour transparencies (35mm), glass negatives, postcards, illustrated maps, fine art prints, unprinted film negatives, posters, illustrated books

Dates of subject matter   17th century to present

Dates of photographs   c. 1870 to present

Subjects   Peterborough and environs including daily life and activities, architecture, Peterborough Cathedral, landscapes, transport, personalities; some material from adjacent parts of Northamptonshire, Huntingdonshire, Cambridgeshire, Lincolnshire and Rutland; engravings of the Roman site Durobrivae and 19th-century excavations

Access and conditions   Open by appt (tel) to the public, Mon Wed Fri 10–7, Thurs 10–5, Sat 9.30–5. All material available for editorial reproduction and for advertising subject to copyright clearance. No loans; b/w prints and duplicate colour transparencies available for a fee. Photocopies available. Reproduction rights fees charged. Staff will undertake some research.

489 • PETERHEAD ARBUTHNOT MUSEUM

St Peter Street, Peterhead, Grampian AB4 6QD
Tel (0779) 77778

Enquiries to   Research Cataloguer

Items   About 5000: b/w original photographs, b/w copy photographs, glass negatives, lantern slides, postcards, 20th-century fine art prints, illustrated books

Dates of subject matter   15th century to present

Dates of photographs   c. 1880 to present

Subjects   Local history of Peterhead and surrounding area including landscapes, architecture, streetscenes, housing, portraits, with special emphasis on fishing industry

Access and conditions   Open to the public by appt (write), Mon-Sat 10–5. Most material available for editorial reproduction; advertising use by special arrangement only. No loans; b/w prints available for a fee. Staff will undertake limited research. Compulsory credit line. Most material copyright. Catalogue in preparation.

490 • PLYMOUTH CENTRAL LIBRARY

Drake Circus, Plymouth, Devon PL4 8AL
Tel (0752) 264676

Enquiries to   John R. Elliott, Area Librarian (West)

Local History Collection

Items   13,500: b/w original and copy photographs, colour transparencies (35mm), postcards, glass negatives, fine art prints

Dates of subject matter   17th century to present

Dates of photographs   1880 to present

Subjects   Devon and Cornwall and especially Plymouth local history including villages and towns, Scilly Isles, streetscenes, aerial views, Plymouth blitz and reconstruction, the Citadel, the Hoe (Victorian and Edwardian strollers), the Barbican and Fish Market, the Pier, public buildings (churches, Town Hall), large industries (Wrigley's, Farley's), portraits including Drake and Raleigh

Access and conditions   Open to the public, Mon-Fri 9–9, Sat 9–4. Some material available for editorial reproduction and for advertising subject to copyright clearance. No loans; b/w prints and duplicate colour transparencies available for a fee. Photocopies available. Reproduction rights fees charged.

491 • POOLE MUSEUM SERVICE

The Guildhall, Market Street, Poole, Dorset
BH15 1NP
Tel (0202) 67151 ext 3550

Enquiries to   Annette Downing, Museum Officer

Items   About 18,000: b/w original photographs, b/w copy photographs, colour transparencies (35mm, 5″ × 4″), colour photographic prints

Dates of subject matter   15th century to present

Dates of photographs   c. 1850 to present

Dates of fine art 18th century to present

Subjects Local history of Poole including landscapes, architecture, streetscenes, social history, transport, with special emphasis on activities of the port; oil paintings and watercolours including works by B. F. and H. K. Gribble

Access and conditions Open to the public by appt, Mon-Fri 10–5. All material available for editorial reproduction; advertising use by special arrangement only. No loans; b/w prints and duplicate colour transparencies available for a fee. Reproduction rights fees charged. Most material copyright.

492 • PORTSMOUTH CITY MUSEUM AND ART GALLERY

Local History Collection

Museum Road, Old Portsmouth, Hampshire PO1 2LJ
Tel (0705) 827261 ext 63

Enquiries to Alastair Penfold, Keeper of Local History

Items About 3500: postcards, b/w original photographs, colour transparencies (35mm), glass negatives, b/w copy photographs, illustrated maps, architectural drawings, posters, oil paintings, watercolours, engravings, prints

Dates of subject matter 1680 to present

Dates of photographs 1865 to prsent

Subjects Local history of Portsmouth and surrounding area with emphasis on system of fortifications between 16th and 19th centuries; development of the town, architecture, streetscenes, social history, transport including road, rail, sea and air; effects of Naval Dockyard on town, Army and Naval buildings, garrison life in Portsmouth

Access and conditions Open to the public by appt (write), Mon-Fri 9–5. All material available for editorial reproduction but not for advertising. No loans; b/w prints and duplicate colour transparencies available for a fee; material may be copied by outside photographers. Photocopies available. Reproduction rights and service fees charged. Staff will undertake limited research. Compulsory credit line. Most material copyright. Card catalogue available.

493 • PORTSMOUTH CITY RECORDS OFFICE

3 Museum Road, Portsmouth, Hampshire PO1 2LE
Tel (0705) 829765

Enquiries to Sarah Peacock, City Records Officer

Items About 5000: b/w original photographs, glass negatives, unprinted film negatives, postcards

Dates of subject matter 19th century to present

Dates of photographs 19th century to present

Subjects Local history and topography of Portsmouth and immediate surrounding district including buildings, streets, churches, Portsmouth docks, women working in the docks in World War I, local people and events, processions

Access and conditions Open to the public, Mon Tues Wed 9.30–12.30, 2–5, Thurs 9.30–12.30, 2–7, Fri 9.30–12.30, 2–4. Some material available for editorial reproduction subject to copyright clearance by user. No loans; b/w prints available for a fee. Material may be copied by outside photographers. Reproduction rights fees charged.

494 • PRESTON DISTRICT CENTRAL LIBRARY

Local Studies Collection

Market Square, Preston, Lancashire PR1 2PP
Tel (0772) 53191

Enquiries to District Librarian

Items About 2000: b/w original photographs, b/w copy photographs, postcards, lantern slides

Dates of subject matter 19th century to present

Dates of photographs 1850 to present

Subjects Local history of Preston and surrounding area including landscapes, architecture, streetscenes, social history, transport, royal visits and local events

Access and conditions Open to the public by appt (tel), Mon-Fri 9–5. All material available for editorial reproduction; advertising use by special arrangement only. No loans; b/w prints available for a fee; material may be copied by outside photographers. Photocopies available. Reproduction rights fees charged. Compulsory credit line. Some material copyright. Card catalogue available.

495 • PRIAULX LIBRARY

Candie Road, St Peter Port, Guernsey, Channel Islands
Tel (0481) 21998

Enquiries to Librarian

Items About 5000: b/w original and copy photographs, colour photographic prints, glass negatives, postcards, original cartoons, old fine art prints, art reproductions, posters, architectural drawings, press cuttings, illustrated books

Dates of subject matter Prehistory to present

Dates of photographs Mid-19th century to present

Subjects All aspects of the history of the Channel Islands including landscapes, portraits of residents (including writers and artists working there), houses, harbours, local events and activities, social history, transport

Access and conditions Open to the public by appt (write), Mon-Sat 10–5. All material available for editorial reproduction; advertising use by special arrangement only. No loans; material may be copied by outside photographers. Photocopies available. Reproduction rights fees charged. Staff will undertake limited research. Some material copyright. Card catalogue available.

496 • RAMSGATE LIBRARY

Local History Collection

Guildford Lawn, Ramsgate, Kent CT11 9AY
Tel (0843) 593532

Enquiries to Iris Huckstep, Branch Librarian

Items Over 600: b/w original photographs, press cuttings, postcards, lantern slides

Dates of subject matter 1100 to present

Dates of photographs 1860 to present

Subjects Local history of Ramsgate and surrounding area including landscapes, architecture, industry (mostly light engineering), tourism, fishing, transport (ships, hovercraft, aircraft, trains), port development, portraits, local events, social history

Access and conditions Open to the public, Mon Tues Wed 9.30–6, Thurs & Sat 9.30–5, Fri 9.30–8. Most material available for editorial reproduction and for advertising. No loans; b/w prints available for a fee. Photocopies available. Reproduction

rights fees charged by arrangement. Staff will undertake some research. Most material copyright.

497 • RAWTENSTALL DISTRICT LIBRARY

Queen's Square, Rawtenstall, Rossendale, Lancashire BB4 6QU
Tel (0706) 227911/2

Enquiries to J. D. McLaney, District Librarian

Items 4500: b/w original and copy photographs, unprinted film negatives, lantern slides, glass negatives, colour transparencies (35mm), postcards, posters, greetings cards, architectural drawings, press cuttings and tearsheets, printing blocks, illustrated books

Dates of photographs 1850 to present

Subjects Rossendale local history including Bacup, Haslingden, Rawtenstall, Whitworth, Ramsbottom, Baxenden, Dunnockshaw, e.g. museums, churches, libraries, town halls, fire stations, schools and colleges, hospitals, mills (textile and footwear), streets and roads, landscapes and townscapes, mines and quarries, councillors and mayors, processions and festivals, sports, plays, concerts, choirs, transport (trams, trolley buses, motor buses, trains, bicycles)

Access and conditions Open to the public, Mon-Fri 9.30–5 (closed Wed at 1), Sat 9.30–4. Some material available for editorial reproduction and for advertising. No loans; b/w prints and duplicate colour transparencies available for a fee. Photocopies available. Reproduction rights fees charged. Staff will undertake some research and mail photocopies.

498 • REDBRIDGE CENTRAL LIBRARY

Local History Collection

112B High Road, Ilford, Essex IG1 1BY
Tel (01) 478 4319

Enquiries to Peter Wright

Items About 10,000; b/w original photographs, b/w copy photographs, art reproductions, glass negatives, lantern slides, colour transparencies (35mm), postcards, colour photographic prints, architectural drawings, posters

Dates of subject matter 1860 to present

Dates of photographs 1860 to present

Subjects Local history and development of Borough of Redbridge as commuter suburb and including Ilford, Wanstead and Woodford: architecture, houses, churches, schools, streetscenes, area during World Wars; farms and large houses

Access and conditions Open to the public by appt (tel), Mon-Fri 9–8, Sat 9–4. Most material available for editorial reproduction and for advertising. B/w and colour material loaned free of charge for two months; material may be copied by outside photographers. Photocopies available. No reproduction rights fees charged. Staff will undertake limited research. Compulsory credit line. Some material copyright. Duplicated catalogue available.

499 • REDDITCH LIBRARY

15 Market Place, Redditch, Hereford and Worcester B98 8AR
Tel (0527) 63291

Enquiries to S. Harvey, Area Librarian

Items About 3000: b/w copy photographs, postcards, colour transparencies (35mm)

Dates of subject matter c. 1900 to present

Dates of photographs c. 1900 to present

Subjects Streetscenes, churches, social life, buildings (government and commercial), transport, hospitals, houses, industries, factories, needlemaking including 30 prints of needle-making processes c. 1877

Access and conditions Open to the public by appt (tel), Mon-Fri 9–5. Some material available for editorial reproduction but not for advertising. B/w material loaned free of charge; period negotiable. Photocopies available. No reproduction rights frees charged.

500 • RENFREW DISTRICT COUNCIL MUSEUMS AND ART GALLERIES SERVICE

Local History Photographic Collection

High Street, Paisley, Strathclyde PA1 2BA
Tel (041) 889 3151

Enquiries to David Shearer, Chief Curator

Items About 5000: b/w original photographs, b/w copy photographs, colour transparencies (35mm, 5″ × 4″), glass negatives, daguerreotypes, lantern slides, postcards, original cartoons, illustrated maps, stereographs, architectural drawings, illustrated books

Dates of subject matter Prehistory to present

Dates of photographs c. 1860 to present

Subjects Local history of Renfrew with special emphasis on Paisley including landscapes, architecture, transport (trams, railways and horse-drawn vehicles), industries including local shipbuilding, Paisley shawl, cotton thread, tools, woodworking machines; social history, personalities

Access and conditions Open to the public by appt (write), Mon-Fri 10–5. All material available for editorial reproduction and for advertising (some restrictions). B/w and colour material loaned free of charge by arrangement (print fees charged); material may be copied by outside photographers. Photocopies available. Reproduction rights fees may be charged. Staff will undertake limited research. Some material copyright.

501 • RENFREW DISTRICT LIBRARIES SERVICE

Marchfield Avenue, Paisley, Strathclyde PA3 2RJ
Tel (041) 887 3672

Enquiries to K. Hinshalwood, Local History Librarian

Items About 1000: b/w original photographs, b/w copy photographs, colour transparencies (35mm), colour photographic prints, postcards, posters, architectural drawings, press cuttings, illustrated books

Dates of subject matter 1800 to present

Dates of photographs 1975 to present

Subjects Urban development in Paisley especially threatened buildings, demolition in progress, construction and renovation; ephemera including funeral invitations and political and religious handbills

Access and conditions Open to the public by appt (tel). All material available for editorial reproduction but not for advertising. No loans; b/w prints and colour transparencies available for a fee. Photocopies available. No reproduction rights fees charged. Staff will undertake some research. Compulsory credit line. Most material copyright. Card catalogue available.

502 • ROCHDALE CENTRAL LIBRARY

Local Studies Collection

Esplanade, Rochdale, Lancashire OL16 1AQ
Tel (0706) 47474 ext 423

Enquiries to John Cole, Local Studies Librarian

Items 16,000: b/w copy photographs, b/w original photographs, posters, glass negatives, lantern slides, original cartoons, illustrated maps, daguerreotypes

Dates of subject matter 18th century to present

Dates of photographs 1850 to present

Subjects Local history of Rochdale, Middleton, Heywood, Littleborough, Milnrow and Wardle including a large number of streetscenes, transport (steam and electric trams, horse-drawn vehicles, early motor vehicles, local railway, omnibuses); commercial activity, woollen industry, cotton mills including many interiors, police force, fire brigade; reservoirs, building construction including the Town Hall and local bridges; special collections include the JOHN JACKSON COLLECTION of local landscapes (1860–1885), travel photographs of Australia, China, Japan, Egypt and Italy in early 1870s, and collection of local theatre bills and political posters

Access and conditions Open to the public, Mon Tues Thurs Fri 9.30–8, Wed 9.30–5, Sat 9.30–4. Some material available for editorial reproduction and for advertising. Staff will undertake limited research. No loans; b/w prints available for a fee. Photocopies available. Reproduction rights fees charged. Some material copyright.

503 • ROCHESTER GUILDHALL MUSEUM

High Street, Rochester, Kent ME1 1QU
Tel (0634) 48717

Enquiries to Michael Moad, Museum Curator

Items About 9500: glass negatives, b/w original and copy photographs, posters, lantern slides, fine art prints, architectural drawings, postcards, colour transparencies (35mm), unprinted film negatives, daguerreotypes, illustrated books

Dates of subject matter c. AD 150 to present

Dates of photographs 1850 to present

Subjects Topography of Rochester, Chatham, Cobham, Wrotham, Gravesend; Rochester streetscenes, architecture including 17th-century Guildhall, Castle Keep, Cathedral; portraits by Sir Godfrey Kneller and others of William of Orange, Queen Anne, Joseph Williamson; Michael Dahl portrait of Sir Cloudesly Shovell; items in museum collection including ship models, Roman artefacts, costumes, arms and armour

Access and conditions Open to the public by appt, Mon-Sat 10–12.30, 2–5.30. Most material available for editorial reproduction and for advertising subject to the Committee's approval. No loans; b/w prints and duplicate colour transparencies available for a fee. Photocopies available. Reproduction rights fees may be charged or donation requested.

504 • RUTLAND COUNTY MUSEUM

Catmos Street, Oakham LE15 6HW
Tel (0572) 3654

Enquiries to Keeper

Items About 1000: b/w original photographs, b/w copy photographs, colour transparencies (35mm), glass negatives, postcards, lantern slides

Dates of subject matter Prehistory to present

Dates of photographs Mid-19th century to present

Subjects Local history of the former county of Rutland including archaeology, landscapes, agriculture (craft tools, farm wagons and agricultural implements), industry, trades, social history, portraits

Access and conditions Open to the public by appt (write). Most material available for editorial reproduction and for advertising. No loans; b/w prints and duplicate colour transparencies available for a fee; material may be copied by outside photographers. Reproduction rights fees charged.

505 • SAFFRON WALDEN MUSEUM

Museum Street, Saffron Walden, Essex CB10 1JL
Tel (0799) 22494

Enquiries to Curator

Items About 7000: b/w original photographs, colour transparencies (35mm, 5″ × 4″), old fine art prints, lantern slides, postcards, art reproductions, glass negatives, greetings cards, ambrotypes, watercolours, oil paintings

Dates of subject matter Prehistory to present

Dates of photographs 1855 to present

Subjects Local history of Saffron Walden and north-west Essex including landscapes, architecture, churches, windmills, houses, social history, portraits; print of first Eddystone lighthouse by Henry Winstanley; some Cruickshank cartoons

Access and conditions Open to the public by appt (write). Some material available for editorial reproduction but not for advertising. No loans; b/w prints available for a fee; material may be copied by outside photographers. Photocopies available. Reproduction rights fees charged. Staff will undertake limited research. Some material copyright. Card catalogue in preparation.

506 • ST ALBANS CENTRAL LIBRARY

Victoria Street, St Albans, Hertfordshire AL1 3JQ
Tel (0727) 60000

Enquiries to Heather Adams, Chief Librarian

Items 5000: b/w original photographs, colour transparencies (35mm), postcards, old fine art prints, b/w copy photographs, colour photographic prints, glass negatives, original cartoons, illustrated books

Dates of subject matter BC to present

Dates of photographs 1880 to present

Subjects Local history of St Albans including architecture, social history, transport, industry, trades; good coverage of the Cathedral; special collections include the Kent Slides (19th-century glass negatives) and the Buckingham Cartoons (19th-century local political cartoons)

Access and conditions Open to the public by appt, Mon Tues Wed Fri 9.30–7, Thurs & Sat 9.30–1. All material available for editorial reproduction and for advertising. No loans; b/w prints and duplicate colour transparencies available for a fee; material may be copied by outside photographers. Photocopies available. Reproduction rights fees charged. Staff will undertake research. Some material copyright. Card catalogue available.

507 • ST HELEN'S CENTRAL LIBRARY

Gamble Institute, Victoria Square, St Helen's, Merseyside WA10 1DY
Tel (0744) 24061 ext 2234

Enquiries to Vivien Hainsworth or Susan Mills

Items About 11,000: b/w original photographs, b/w copy photographs, glass negatives, lantern slides, postcards, illustrated maps, old fine art prints, posters, architectural drawings

Dates of subject matter 1868 to present

Dates of photographs c. 1870 to present

Subjects Local history of St Helen's covering the development of the area as an industrial town and including landscapes, architecture, aerial shots, streetscenes, transport (rail, horse-drawn and motor vehicles, trams), markets, parks, parades, industry including Pilkingtons and Beechams, mining, slum clearance and redevelopment, police, fire brigade, youth organizations, sport, family groups

Access and conditions Open to the public, Mon-Fri 9–5, Sat 9–1. All material available for editorial reproduction and for advertising (some restrictions). No loans; b/w prints available for a fee. Photocopies available. Reproduction rights fees charged. Staff of two will undertake limited research. Compulsory credit line. Most material copyright. Card catalogue available.

508 • SALFORD LOCAL HISTORY LIBRARY

Peel Park, The Crescent, Salford, Greater Manchester M5 4WU
Tel (061) 736 3353

Enquiries to Local History Librarian

Items About 10,000: b/w copy photographs, b/w original photographs, colour transparencies (35mm), colour photographic prints, lantern slides, postcards

Dates of subject matter 19th century to present

Dates of photographs c. 1880 to present

Subjects All aspects of life in Salford with emphasis on last 20 years including general and aerial views, floods, architecture, churches, markets, transport (railways, Manchester Ship Canal, buses, trams), industry (heavy and light engineering, mills), shops, sports, customs, social history, portraits of local people; collection includes some photographs by Samuel Coulthurst

Access and conditions Open to the public, Mon Wed Thurs 9–5, Tues & Fri 9–7, Sat 9–1. Most material available for editorial reproduction and for advertising. No loans; b/w prints and duplicate colour transparencies available for a fee; material may be copied by outside photographers. Photocopies available. Reproduction rights fees charged. Staff of four will undertake limited research. Most material copyright. Card catalogue available.

509 • SALFORD MUSEUM

Social History Collections

Peel Park, The Crescent, Salford, Greater Manchester M5 4WU
Tel (061) 872 0251

Enquiries to Evelyn Vigeon, Keeper of Social History and Antiquities

Items About 5000: b/w original photographs, b/w copy photographs, lantern slides, glass negatives, daguerreotypes, stereographs, greetings cards

Dates of subject matter *c*. 1500 to present

Dates of photographs *c*. 1860 to present

Subjects Local history of Salford and area with emphasis on social history and working life; World War I timber yard and sawmill; special collections include old advertising material and work of early photographers including A. Brothers and James Mudd; portraits of local people

Access and conditions Open to qualified researchers by appt. Some material available for editorial reproduction and for advertising. B/w prints and duplicate colour transparencies available for a fee. Reproduction rights fees charged. Staff will undertake limited research. Most material copyright. Card catalogue in preparation.

510 • SCARBOROUGH LIBRARY

Central Library, Vernon Road, Scarborough, North Yorkshire YO11 2NN
Tel (0723) 364285

Enquiries to Divisional Organizer, Reference and Information Services

Items About 400: b/w copy photographs, illustrated books, old fine art prints, postcards, b/w original photographs, press cuttings, glass negatives, lantern slides

Dates of subject matter Prehistory to present

Dates of photographs *c*. 1860 to present

Subjects Local history of Scarborough and north-east Yorkshire including landscapes, towns, villages, coastal views, social history, architecture, transport, shipping, fishing, trade, education, portraits

Access and conditions Open to the public by appt (tel), Mon-Thurs 10–5.30, Fri 10–7, Sat 10–4. Most material available for editorial reproduction and for advertising. No loans; b/w prints available for a fee; material may be copied by outside photographers. Photocopies available. Reproduction rights fees charged. Staff will undertake some research. Some material copyright.

511 • SCOLTON MANOR MUSEUM

Spittal, Haverfordwest, Dyfed SA62 5QL
Tel (043782) 328

Enquiries to Curator

Items Over 5000: b/w original and copy photographs, colour transparencies (35mm, 5″ × 4″, larger), colour photographic prints, unprinted film negatives, lantern slides, posters, glass negatives, daguerreotypes, postcards, fine art prints, greetings cards, architectural drawings, press cuttings and tearsheets, illustrated books

Dates of subject matter 6000 BC to present

Dates of photographs 1850 to present

Subjects Local history of former county of Pembrokeshire including archaeology (artefacts, sites), social history, domestic life, industrial history, maritime traditions, natural history, topography and landscapes

Access and conditions Open to qualified researchers by appt (write), Oct-Mar Mon-Fri 11–4, Apr-Sept Mon-Fri 10–5.30. Most material available for editorial reproduction and for advertising. No loans; b/w prints and duplicate colour transparencies available for a fee. Material may be copied by outside photographers. Photocopies available. Reproduction rights fees charged. Staff will undertake some research; fee charged for long projects. Compulsory credit line. Partial card catalogue.

512 • SCOTTISH RECORD OFFICE

HM General Register House, Edinburgh EH1 3YY
Tel (031) 556 6585 ext 282

Enquiries to Officer in charge of the Search Room

Items Unknown number: b/w original and copy photographs, colour transparencies (35mm), glass negatives, lantern slides, postcards, illustrated maps, unprinted film negatives, posters, greetings cards, architectural drawings, technical drawings

Dates of subject matter 17th century to present

Dates of photographs 1850 to present

Dates of drawings Late 17th century to present

Subjects Main photographic collections include the W. E. BOYD COLLECTION of British railway locomotives between 1880 and 1960; shipbuilding on the Clyde and Tay and Forth between late 19th and mid-20th century including JOHN BROWN COLLECTION, ROBB CALEDON LTD COLLECTION and BURNTISLAND AND LEITH COLLECTION; general and electrical engineering between 1880 and 1950 including the WEST END ENGINE WORKS COLLECTION and PARSONS PEEBLES LTD COLLECTION; architectural drawings of public, commercial, ecclesiastical, estate and domestic buildings in Scotland from late 17th century to present

Access and conditions Open to the public (appt preferred), Mon-Fri 9–4.45. All material available for editorial reproduction but not for advertising. No loans; b/w prints and colour transparencies available for a fee. Reproduction rights fees charged. Staff will undertake some research. Some material copyright.

513 • SCUNTHORPE BOROUGH MUSEUM AND ART GALLERY

Local History Photographic Collection

Oswald Road, Scunthorpe DN15 7BD
Tel (0724) 843533

Enquiries to John Goldsmith, Keeper of Local History

Items About 5000: b/w original photographs, b/w copy photographs, colour transparencies (35mm), postcards, glass negatives, lantern slides, stereographs, greetings cards

Dates of subject matter Medieval to present

Dates of photographs 1867 to present

Subjects Local history of Scunthorpe and north-west Lincolnshire including landscapes, architecture, agriculture, industry (special section on iron and steel industries), rural crafts including wheelwrights and blacksmiths, social history, local events; special collection of photographs by J. W. Hall of Winterton of local landscapes and portraits in the 1860s and 1870s; contemporary surveys of area

Access and conditions Open to the public by appt (write), Mon-Fri 10–5. Most material available for editorial reproduction; advertising use by special arrangement only. No loans; b/w prints and duplicate colour transparencies available for a fee. Photocopies available. Reproduction rights fees charged. Most material copyright. Duplicated catalogue available.

514 • SEVENOAKS LIBRARY

Local Studies Collection

The Drive, Sevenoaks, Kent TN13 3AB
Tel: (0732) 453118, 452384

Enquiries to Heather Painter, Reference Librarian

Items About 5000: b/w original photographs, b/w copy photographs, postcards, old fine art prints, 20th-century fine art prints, press cuttings, illustrated books, colour photographic prints, posters

Dates of subject matter 1200 to present

Dates of photographs Late 19th century to present

Subjects Local history of Sevenoaks and surrounding area including landscapes, architecture, churches, schools, public houses, large houses and estate including Penshurst Place, Knole House and Hever Castle; transport, light industry, social history, portraits of local people

Access and conditions Open to the public, Mon Tues Wed Fri 9.30–5.30, Thurs 9.30–7, Sat 9–5. Most material available for editorial reproduction and for advertising. No loans; b/w prints available for a fee; material may be copied by outside photographers. Photocopies available. No reproduction rights fees charged. Staff of two will undertake limited research. 50% material copyright. Card catalogue available.

515 • SHEERNESS LIBRARY

44 Trinity Road, Sheerness, Kent ME12 2PS
Tel (0795) 662618

Enquiries to Joy Pritchard, Group Librarian

Items 800: b/w original and copy photographs, postcards, illustrated maps, art reproductions, architectural drawings, illustrated books

Dates of subject matter 1350 to present

Dates of photographs 1900 to present

Subjects Isle of Sheppey local history, landscape, everyday life, streets, shops, housing, dockyard, historic buildings, Kingsferry Bridge, tourism

Access and conditions Open to the public, Mon Tues Fri 9.30–6, Thurs 9.30–7, Sat 9.30–4, closed Wed. Some material available for editorial reproduction and for advertising. No loans; b/w prints and colour transparencies available for a fee. Material may be copied by outside photographers. Reproduction rights fees charged. Staff will undertake limited research only. Card catalogue.

516 • SHEFFIELD CITY MUSEUMS

Picture Collection

Weston Park, Sheffield, South Yorkshire S10 2TP
Tel (0742) 27226

Enquiries to Philip Broomhead, Director

Items About 2000: watercolours, oil paintings, lithographs, drawings, etchings, b/w original photographs, glass negatives, lantern slides, colour transparencies (35mm), b/w copy photographs, colour photographic prints, postcards, original cartoons, illustrated maps, stereographs, posters, greetings cards, architectural drawings, illustrated books

Dates of subject matter 1500 to present

Dates of photographs 1864 to present

Subjects Collection of oil paintings and watercolours by local artists including works by William Ibbit and S. Parker; original artwork for cutlery and silversmith design and 19th-century foundry work; local history of Sheffield and surrounding area including landscapes, architecture, social history, transport, industry including the steel industry, portraits, local events such as opening of Sheffield Town Hall by Queen Victoria and coverage of 1864 flood by James Mudd and Theophilus Smith

Access and conditions Open to the public by appt (write), Mon-Fri 10–5. All material available for editorial reproduction and for advertising. No loans; b/w prints and duplicate colour transparencies available for a fee; material may be copied by outside photographers. Photocopies of certain items available. Reproduction rights fees charged; service fees sometimes charged. Staff will undertake very limited reseach. Most material copyright. Card catalogue available.

517 • SHEPTON MALLET SOCIETY AND SHEPTON MALLET AMENITY TRUST LTD

Barron Down House, Shepton Mallet, Somerset BA4 5QH
Tel (0749) 3525

Enquiries to Fred Davis, 25 Allyn Saxon Drive, Shepton Mallet, Somerset BA4 5QH

Items About 2500: colour transparencies (35mm), b/w copy photographs, b/w original photographs, colour photographic prints, postcards, illustrated maps, posters, greetings cards, press cuttings, illustrated books

Dates of subject matter 1830 to present

Dates of photographs 1880 to present

Subjects Local history of Shepton Mallet and surrounding area covering landscapes, architecture, local personalities, families, leisure including travelling circuses, local trades and industries including stone-quarrying, the woollen industry (weavers' cottages, managers' houses, local mills), brewing, agriculture, fire-fighting equipment

Access and conditions Open to qualified researchers by appt (write). All material available for editorial reproduction and for advertising. B/w material loaned free of charge for two months; b/w prints and duplicate colour transparencies available for a fee; material may be copied by outside photographers. Reproduction rights fees charged. Staff of two will undertake some research; negotiable research fee charged. 50% of material copyright.

518 • SHROPSHIRE LIBRARIES

Local Studies Department

Castle Gates, Shrewsbury, Shropshire SY1 2AS
Tel (0743) 61058

Enquiries to Local Studies Librarian

Items 20,000: b/w original photographs, colour
photographic prints, colour transparencies
(35mm), glass negatives, postcards, illustrated
maps, old fine art prints, 20th-century fine art
prints, stereographs

Dates of subject matter Prehistory to present

Dates of photographs 1842 to present

Subjects Local history of Shropshire with special
emphasis on Shrewsbury, Ludlow and Bridgnorth
and including landscapes, archaeology,
architecture, industry (coalmining, iron foundries,
building of railway carriages in the 1880s),
agriculture, transport; negatives from the
Shropshire Newspaper Group acquired two years
after publication; detailed 1980 survey of shops,
hospitals, churches, chapels and other buildings

Access and conditions Open to the public by
appt (tel), Mon & Wed 9.30–5.30, Tues & Fri
9.30–7.30, Sat 9.30–5, closed Thurs. Some material
available for editorial reproduction but not for
advertising. No loans; b/w prints available for a fee;
material may be copied by outside photographers.
Photocopies available. Staff will undertake limited
research. Most material copyright.

519 • BILL SMITH

344 Grace Way, Stevenage, Hertfordshire
SG1 5AP
Tel (0438) 312874

Enquiries to Martha Snowden

Items 23,000: b/w original photographs, colour
transparencies (35mm)

Dates of photographs 1965 to present

Subjects Hertfordshire, especially north
Hertfordshire, people, news, crafts, industries,
topography; English traditional dances including
clog and morris dancing

Access and conditions Open to qualified
researchers by appt (tel). All material available for
editorial reproduction; some for advertising. B/w
material loaned free of charge for one month;
colour for two weeks. Reproduction rights, service
and holding fees charged. Staff will undertake
some research. All material copyright.

520 • SNOWDONIA NATIONAL PARK

National Park Office, Penrhyndeudraeth,
Gwynedd LL48 6LS
Tel (0766) 770274

Enquiries to National Park Officer

Items About 5000: colour transparencies (35mm)

Dates of subject matter Prehistory to date

Dates of photographs 1950s to present

Subjects Area covered by Snowdonia National
Park including landscapes, geology, botany and
wildlife; recreational activities including sailing,
canoeing, rowing, windsurfing, fishing, climbing,
walking; mountain rescue; industrial archaeology
including remains of lead and slate mines;
agriculture, forestry, hydroelectric power and
atomic power stations; Snowdon railway, picnic
sites, tree-planting schemes, footpath restoration

Access and conditions Open to qualified
researcher by appt (tel), Mon-Fri 9–5. Most
material available for editorial reproduction but
not for advertising. Colour material loaned free of
charge for two months; duplicate colour
transparencies available for a fee. Reproduction
rights fees charged. Staff of two will undertake
some research. Compulsory credit line. All material
copyright. Card catalogue available.

521 • SOLIHULL CENTRAL LIBRARY

Local History Collection

Homer Road, Solihull, Warwickshire B91 3RG
Tel (021) 705 4917/8/9 ext 477

Enquiries to Sue Bates, Local History Librarian

Items About 5000: b/w original and copy
photographs, colour transparencies (35mm), colour
photographic prints, glass negatives, postcards,
illustrated maps, unprinted film negatives,
illustrated books

Dates of subject matter Prehistory to present

Dates of photographs c. 1850 to present

Subjects Local history of the Metropolitan
Borough of Solihull (including Castle Bromwich,
Kingshurst, Chelmsley Wood, Elmdon, Bickenhill,
Manston Green, Hampton-in-Arden, Meriden,
Knowle, Temple Balsall, Balsall Common,
Chadwick End, Olton, Shirley, Hockley Heath,
Bentley Heath, Dorridge and Solihull),
architecture, transport, farming, people,
streetscenes, business and industry; some material
from Birmingham, Coleshill, Redditch

Access and conditions Open to the public, Mon Tues 9.30–5.30, Wed closed, Thurs & Fri 9.30–8, Sat 9.30–5. Some material available for editorial reproduction and for advertising. B/w and colour prints available for a fee. Photocopies available. Reproduction rights fees charged. Card catalogue.

522 • SOMERSET COUNTY COUNCIL LIBRARY SERVICE

Local History Library, The Castle, Castle Green, Taunton, Somerset TA1 4AD
Tel (0823) 88871

Enquiries to David Bromwich, Librarian

Items 17,000: glass negatives, lantern slides, postcards, architectural drawings, postcards, b/w original photographs, b/w copy photographs

Dates of subject matter BC to present

Dates of photographs 1860s to present

Subjects Local history of Somerset and South Avon including landscapes, architecture especially church exteriors, interiors and details, public buildings and country houses, towns, villages, streetscenes, social history, transport, local crafts and trades including basket-making, peat-cutting, cider-making, cheese-making, teazle-growing for use in cloth-making process, iron-mining, slate- and stone-quarrying, strawberry-growing; customs include wassailing, the Minehead hobby horse, harvest-home processions and church services

Access and conditions Open to the public, Tues-Fri 9.30–12.30 & 2–5.30, Sat 9.30–12.30, 2–4. All material available for editorial reproduction but not for advertising. No loans; b/w prints available for a fee; material may be copied by outside photographers. Photocopies available for a fee. Reproduction rights fees charged. Staff will undertake some research. Most material copyright. Card catalogue available.

523 • SOMERSET RECORD OFFICE

Obridge Road, Taunton, Somerset TA2 7PU
Tel (0823) 78805, 87600

Enquiries to County Archivist

Items 5000: b/w original photographs, glass negatives, postcards, illustrated maps, architectural drawings, ephemera

Dates of subject matter 705 to present

Dates of photographs Mid-19th century to present

Subjects Local history of Somerset (former county area prior to 1974 boundary changes) including landscapes, archaeology, architecture, social history, agriculture, industry, shipping, transport; architectural plans of schools, churches, vicarages, estate cottages and buildings and also Pittsburgh Eastern Penitentiary and Dauphin County prisons in USA, 1821–1822; collection of water-finder's photographs in Africa c. 1910

Access and conditions Open to the public by appt (write), Mon-Thurs 9–4.50, Fri 9–4.20, Sat 9.15–12.15. All material available for editorial reproduction and for advertising. No loans; material may be copied by outside photographers. Photocopies available. Reproduction rights fees charged for commercial use. Staff will undertake limited research. Some material copyright. Card catalogue available.

524 • SOUTH TYNESIDE CENTRAL LIBRARY

Local History Department

Prince Georg Square, South Shields, Tyne and Wear NE33 2PE
Tel (0632) 568841 ext 270

Enquiries to T. Graham, Head of Culture and Leisure Department

Items Over 20,000: b/w original and copy photographs, posters, glass negatives, postcards, lantern slides, colour photographic prints, greetings cards, illustrated maps

Dates of subject matter c. 1790 to present

Dates of photographs 1855 to present

Dates of posters 1790 to 1880

Subjects South Tyneside including South Shields, Jarrow, Hebburn, East and West Boldon, Boldon Colliery, Whitburn and Cleadon; streets, buildings, ships, the Jarrow March, local personalities, industries, etc.; PARRY COLLECTION: work by local commercial photographer (c. 1900–1945); CLEET COLLECTION and FLAGG COLLECTION: South Shields slum clearance in the 1930s; KELLY COLLECTION: posters from South Shields (c. 1790 to 1880) on local elections, entertainment, theatre

Access and conditions Open to the public, Mon-Fri 9.30–5.30. Most material available for editorial reproduction and for advertising subject to copyright clearance. No loans; b/w prints and duplicate colour transparencies available for a fee. Photocopies available. No reproduction rights fees charged. Staff will undertake some research and mail photocopies. Card catalogue.

525 • SOUTH YORKSHIRE COUNTY RECORD OFFICE

Cultural Activities Centre, Ellin Street, Sheffield, South Yorkshire S1 4PL
Tel (0742) 29191 ext 33, 34

Enquiries to C. M. Short, County Archivist

Items About 1000: b/w original and copy photographs, colour transparencies (35mm), glass negatives, daguerreotypes, lantern slides, postcards, illustrated maps, unprinted film negatives, stereographs, posters, architectural drawings

Dates of photographs 1850 to present

Subjects South Yorkshire local history

Access and conditions Open to the public by appt, Mon-Thurs 9–5, Fri 9–4. Some material available for editorial reproduction and for advertising subject to copyright clearance. B/w prints and duplicate colour transparencies available for a fee. Photocopies available. Reproduction rights fees charged. Staff will undertake limited research; 30 minutes per enquiry. Card catalogue.

526 • SOUTHAMPTON CITY RECORD OFFICE

Civic Centre, Southampton SO9 4XR
Tel (0703) 223855 ext 2251

Enquiries to City Archivist

Items About 10,000: b/w original photographs, b/w copy photographs, colour transparencies (35mm, 5″ × 4″), colour photographic prints, glass negatives, lantern slides, postcards, stereographs, greetings cards, architectural drawings, press cuttings, illustrated books

Dates of subject matter 13th century to present

Dates of photographs 1860 to present

Subjects Life of Southampton and the surrounding area over the past 150 years with special emphasis on buildings and streets; coverage of city life during World Wars I and II including embarkation of troops and special ferries for the wounded during World War I and surveys of bomb damage during World War II

Access and conditions Open to the public, Mon-Fri, 9–1, 1.30–5. Most material available for editorial reproduction; advertising use by special arrangement only. B/w prints and duplicate colour transparencies available for a fee; material may be copied by outside photographers. Photocopies available. Service fees charged; reproduction rights fees sometimes charged. Most material copyright. Card catalogue.

527 • SOUTHERN NEWSPAPERS plc

Echo Library, 45 Above Bar, Southampton SO9 7BA
Tel (0703) 34134 Telex 47388

Enquiries to Peter Ashton, Librarian

Items Over one million: b/w original photographs, b/w copy photographs, glass negatives, postcards, lantern slides, press cuttings

Dates of subject matter 1880s to present

Dates of photographs 1880s to present

Subjects News coverage of Southampton and surrounding area covering events, personalities, sports; local history of Southampton and surrounding area covering social history, industry, transport; photographs from the files of the Press Association, Monitor, Camera Press, Universal Pictorial Press, ASP and Sportsfotos

Access and conditions Open to the public by appt (write), Mon-Sat 9–5. Most material available for editorial reproduction and for advertising. B/w prints available for a fee. Photocopies available. Reproduction rights and service fees charged. Staff of four will undertake some research for a fee. Southern Newspapers own copyright to 50% of collection; in other cases copyright clearance is responsibility of user.

528 • SOUTHWARK LIBRARIES

Local Studies Library, 211 Borough High Street, London SE1 1JA
Tel (01) 403 3507

Enquiries to Bernard Nurse, Local Studies Librarian

Items About 25,000: b/w original photographs, glass negatives, colour transparencies (35mm), postcards, illustrated maps, b/w copy photographs, old fine art prints, posters, illustrated books, lantern slides, colour photographic prints, 20th-century fine art prints, architectural drawings, daguerreotypes

Dates of subject matter BC to present

Dates of photographs 1846 to present

Subjects Local history of Southwark including Bermondsey, Rotherhithe, Walworth, Peckham, Camberwell, Dulwich covering architecture, streetscenes, housing, churches, schools, public houses, Surrey docks, industry (food-processing, beer- and vinegar-brewing, leather-tanning), local government, transport (shipping, railways, horse-drawn and motor vehicles), personalities, World War II bomb damage, rebuilding

Access and conditions Open to the public by appt (tel), Mon & Thurs 9.30–8, Tues & Fri 9.30–5, Sat 9.30–1, closed Wed. Most material available for editorial reproduction and for advertising. Some b/w material loaned free of charge for one month; material may be copied by outside photographers. Photocopies available. Reproduction rights fees charged. Staff will undertake some research. Compulsory credit line. Some material copyright.

529 • STAVELEY LIBRARY

Hall Lane, Staveley, Chesterfield, Derbyshire S40 3TP
Tel (0246) 472448

Enquiries to Mandy Hicken, Group Librarian

Items 250: b/w original and copy photographs

Dates of subject matter 18th century to present

Dates of photographs 1880s to present

Subjects Staveley local history including streetscenes, architecture (old churches, Neverthorpe Grammar School, Staveley Hall), railway works, school groups, personalities including Sir Josiah Court (early researcher into industrial diseases)

Access and conditions Open to the public, Mon Tues Thurs Fri 9–7, Wed 9–5.30. Some material available for editorial reproduction and for advertising. B/w prints available for a fee. Photocopies available. No reproduction rights fees charged. Staff will undertake limited research.

530 • STOCKPORT LIBRARIES REFERENCE AND INFORMATION SERVICE

Central Library, Wellington Road South, Stockport SK1 3RS
Tel (061) 480 2966, 480 3038, 480 7297 Telex 667184

Enquiries to David Reid, Senior Reference Librarian

Items 25,000: b/w original photographs, b/w copy photographs, glass negatives, lantern slides, postcards, original cartoons, illustrated maps, old fine art prints, 20th-century fine art prints, art reproductions, unprinted film negatives, stereographs, posters, greetings cards, architectural drawings, press cuttings, illustrated books

Dates of subject matter 17th century to present

Dates of photographs c. 1880 to present

Subjects Local history of Stockport and surrounding area including landscapes, architecture, streetscenes, social history, family groups, transport, trade and industry including hat-making and cotton

Access and conditions Open to the public by appt (write), Mon-Fri 9–8, Sat 9–12. All material available for editorial reproduction and for advertising. No loans; b/w prints available for a fee; material may be copied by outside photographers. Photocopies available. Reproduction rights fees charged. Staff of two will undertake limited research. Most material copyright. Card catalogue available.

531 • STRATFORD REFERENCE LIBRARY

The Local Studies Library, Water Lane, London E15 4NJ
Tel (01) 534 4545 ext 5661/2

Enquiries to Howard Bloch, Local Studies Librarian

Items 25,250: b/w original and copy photographs, b/w transparencies, glass negatives, colour transparencies (35mm), postcards, illustrated maps

Dates of subject matter Prehistory to present

Dates of photographs 1880 to present

Subjects Former Boroughs of East Ham and West Ham, local history, commercial life, education, schools, health and welfare, leisure activities including festivals and street parades, maps, parks, people, public buildings, public houses, religious organizations including churches and chapels, streetscenes, houses, great houses, transport, World Wars I and II including local views of bomb damage

Access and conditions Open to the public by appt (tel), Mon Tues Thurs Fri 9.30–7, Wed & Sat 9.30–5. Some material available for editorial reproduction and for advertising. No loans; b/w prints and duplicate colour transparencies available for a fee. Photocopies available. Reproduction rights fees charged. Staff will undertake some research. Card catalogue.

532 • STRATHKELVIN DISTRICT LIBRARIES

Local Studies Collection

The William Patrick Library, Camphill Avenue, Kirkintilloch, Glasgow G66 1DW
Tel (041) 776 1328

Enquiries to Don Martin, Principal Assistant

Items About 12,000: colour transparencies (35mm), b/w original photographs, b/w copy photographs, colour photographic prints, glass negatives, lantern slides, postcards, unprinted film negatives, architectural drawings, press cuttings

Dates of subject matter AD 142 to present

Dates of photographs *c.* 1850 to present

Subjects Local history of Strathkelvin and district with special emphasis on the towns of Kirkintilloch and Bishopsbriggs and villages of Auchinloch, Cadder, Campsie Glen, Chryston, Gartcosh, Milton of Campsie, Muirhead, Moodiesburn, Torrance and Twechar including landscapes, architecture, archaeology (the Antonine Wall), agriculture, industry (iron foundries, coalmining, coachbuilding of motor vehicles and lorries, Hay and McGregor boatyards), transport including railways and the Forth and Clyde Canal, social history, education, personalities

Access and conditions Open to the public by appt (tel), 9.45–5. All material available for editorial reproduction but not for advertising. No loans; b/w prints and duplicate colour transparencies available for a fee. Photocopies available. No reproduction rights fees charged.

Staff of two will undertake limited research. Some material copyright; in small number of cases copyright clearance is the responsibility of user. Subject lists available.

533 • STRATHKELVIN DISTRICT MUSEUMS

The Cross, Kirkintilloch, Glasgow G66 1PW
Tel (041) 775 1185

Enquiries to Susan Selwyn, Curator

Items About 800: b/w original photographs, colour transparencies (35mm), glass negatives

Dates of subject matter BC to present

Dates of photographs 1880 to present

Subjects Local history of Strathkelvin and surrounding area including archaeology (Antonine Wall), landscapes, architecture, social history, industry (shipyards, iron foundries), trade, Forth and Clyde Canal, transport

Access and conditions Open to the public by appt (tel), Mon-Sat 9–5. All material available for editorial reproduction; advertising use by special arrangement only. No loans; b/w prints and duplicate colour transparencies available for a fee; material may be copied by outside photographers. Photocopies available. No reproduction rights fees charged. Staff of two will undertake some research. Compulsory credit line. Most material copyright.

534 • SUFFOLK RECORD OFFICE

County Hall, Ipswich, Suffolk IP4 2JS
Tel (0473) 55801

Enquiries to Amanda Arrowsmith, County Archivist

Items About 40,000: glass negatives, b/w copy photographs, postcards

Dates of subject matter 15th century to present

Dates of photographs 1860 to present

Subjects Local history of Suffolk with special emphasis on Ipswich from 1860 to 1890 including social history, architecture (some medieval houses), landscapes, agriculture, trade and industry, crafts including rush-weaving and basket-making, customs, fêtes, transport including railways, passenger and fishing boats in Ipswich docks, motor and horse-drawn vehicles; special collections include the VICK COLLECTION of views and portraits of Ipswich people 1860 to 1890, the COWELL COLLECTION of landscapes, the BURROWS COLLECTION of rural scenes, the GIRLING COLLECTION of landscapes and fishing boats in Lowestoft

Access and conditions Open to the public by appt (tel), Mon-Thurs 9–5, Fri 9–4. All material available for editorial reproduction; advertising use by special arrangement only. No loans; b/w prints and colour transparencies available for a fee. Photocopies available. Reproduction rights fees charged. Staff of four will undertake some research. Some material copyright. Card and duplicated catalogues available.

535 • SUNDERLAND CENTRAL LIBRARY

Local Studies Library, Borough Road, Sunderland, Tyne and Wear SR1 1PR
Tel (0783) 41235/8 Telex 922488 BUREAU G REF SLI

Enquiries to Philip Hall

Items About 7500: b/w original and copy photographs, colour transparencies (35mm), postcards, glass negatives, illustrated books, illustrated maps

Dates of subject matter Prehistory to present

Dates of photographs 1880 to present

Subjects Durham county and Sunderland history and topography, including shipping and ship-building, transport (railways, early motor cars), towns, streets, local architecture, sports and leisure, market, wedding groups

Access and conditions Open to the public, Mon-Thurs 9.30–7.30, Fri 9.30–5, Sat 9.30–4. Some material available for editorial reproduction and for advertising. No loans; b/w prints and duplicate colour transparencies available for a fee. Staff will undertake limited research. Copyright clearance is responsibility of user. Card catalogue available.

536 • SURREY COUNTY COUNCIL

County Planning Department

Conservation and Archaeology Section, County Hall, Kingston upon Thames, Surrey KT1 2DT
Tel (01) 546 1050 ext 3665

Enquiries to County Planning Officer

Items About 25,000: b/w original photographs, glass negatives, b/w copy photographs

Dates of subject matter 1300 to present

Dates of photographs 1950 to present

Subjects Grades 1 and 2 listed buildings within the county with main emphasis on pre-Victorian and timber-framed structures

Access and conditions Open to the public by appt (write). All material available for editorial reproduction and for advertising. No loans; b/w prints available for a fee. Photocopies available. Reproduction rights and service fees charged. Staff will undertake limited research. All material copyright. Card catalogue available.

537 • SURREY RECORD OFFICE

County Hall, Kingston upon Thames, Surrey KT1 2DN
Tel (01) 546 1050 ext 3561

Enquiries to County Archivist

Items Over 5000: b/w original photographs, glass negatives, daguerreotypes, postcards, illustrated maps, old fine art prints, architectural drawings, illustrated books, engravings, estate, enclosure and tithe maps

Dates of subject matter *c.* 1200 to present

Dates of photographs *c.* 1880 to present

Subjects Local history of the present administrative county of Surrey including landscapes, architecture, transport, industry, crafts, social history, urban development, portraits; special collections include the HESTAIR DENNIS COLLECTION showing public service vehicles manufactured by the company between 1900 and 1950; PALMERS OF MERTON COLLECTION showing small iron items manufactured by the firm; ROYAL PHILANTHROPIC SOCIETY COLLECTIONS of destitute children; 1890s photographs of inmates of lunatic asylum; 1930s coverage of shanty town developments

Access and conditions Open to the public by appt (tel). Most material available for editorial reproduction but not for advertising. No loans; b/w prints available for a fee. Photocopies available. Reproduction rights fees charged. Staff will undertake very limited research. Most material copyright. Card catalogue available.

538 • SWANSEA CITY ARCHIVES

Guildhall, Swansea SA1 4PE
Tel (0792) 50821 ext 2115, 2122

Enquiries to Dr J. R. Alban, City Archivist

Items About 30,000: colour transparencies
(35mm, 5″ × 4″, larger), b/w original and copy
photographs, colour photographic prints, postcards,
architectural drawings, illustrated maps, posters,
glass negatives, lantern slides, original cartoons,
fine art prints, unprinted film negatives, greetings
cards, press cuttings, illustrated books

Dates of subject matter *c.* 1750 to present

Dates of photographs *c.* 1850 to present

Subjects Swansea and environs local history,
topography, industry (collieries, tin plate, copper
works, docks)

Access and conditions Open to the public by
appt (tel), Tues & Wed 9.30–12.45, 2.15–4.30.
Some material available for editorial reproduction
but not for advertising. No loans; b/w prints and
duplicate colour transparencies available for a fee.
Reproduction rights and service fees charged. Staff
will undertake limited research. Card catalogue.

539 • SWINTON CENTRAL LIBRARY

Local History Library, Chorley Road, Swinton,
Lancashire M27 2AF
Tel (061) 793 3560/1

Enquiries to Janet McFarland, Librarian

Items About 9000: b/w copy photographs, b/w
original photographs, colour transparencies
(35mm), colour photographic prints, lantern slides,
postcards, illustrated books

Dates of subject matter 18th century to present

Dates of photographs 1880 to present

Subjects Local history of Swinton, Pendlebury,
Clifton and Warley covering all aspects of life and
activities including landscapes, architecture,
streetscenes, social history, education, industry
(light engineering), sport, portraits, family life

Access and conditions Open to the public, Mon
Tues Wed Fri 9–7, Thurs 9–5, Sat 9–1. Most
material available for editorial reproduction and
for advertising. No loans; b/w prints and duplicate
colour transparencies available for a fee; material
may be copied by outside photographers.
Photocopies available. Reproduction rights fees
charged. Staff will undertake limited research.
Some material copyright. Card catalogue available.

540 • TAMESIDE LOCAL STUDIES LIBRARY

Stalybridge Library, Trinity Street, Stalybridge,
Cheshire SK15 2BN
Tel (061) 338 2708, 338 3831

Enquiries to Alice Lock, Local History Librarian

Items About 15,000: b/w original and copy
photographs, unprinted film negatives, lantern
slides, colour transparencies (35mm), postcards,
fine art prints, oil paintings, watercolours,
drawings

Dates of photographs *c.* 1880 to present

Subjects Tameside area (including Ashton-
under-Lyne, Audenshaw, Denton, Droylsden,
Dukinfield, Hyde, Longdendale, Mossley,
Stalybridge), architecture, streetscenes, people,
industry, cotton industry, leisure, families,
transport, events, local government

Access and conditions Open to the public, Mon-
Fri 9–7.30 (closed Thur), Sat 9–4. Some material
available for editorial reproduction and for
advertising. No loans; b/w prints and duplicate
colour transparencies available for a fee.
Photocopies available. Material may be copied by
outside photographers. Reproduction rights fees
charged. Staff will undertake research for specific
requests. Copyright clearance is responsibility of
user. Card catalogue.

541 • TIVERTON MUSEUM SOCIETY

Tiverton Museum, St Andrew Street, Tiverton,
Devon EX16 6PH
Tel (0884) 256295

Enquiries to Honorary Curator

Items About 4000: b/w original photographs, b/w
copy photographs, glass negatives, lantern slides,
original cartoons, posters

Dates of subject matter 1700 to present

Dates of photographs 1850 to present

Subjects Local history of Tiverton and mid-Devon
including landscapes, architecture, villages,
churches, public houses, transport (including
construction of railway in 1880s), industry
including breweries and manufacture of Heathcote
lace, crafts, agriculture, Tiverton Hunt (fox and
stag hounds), social history, portraits of local
people

Access and conditions Open to the public, Mon-

Sat 10.30–4.30. All material available for editorial reproduction and for advertising by special arrangement only. No loans; b/w prints available for a fee. Photocopies of some items available. Reproduction rights, service and hire fees for non-copyright material charged. Staff will undertake limited research; negotiable research fee charged. Most material copyright. Card catalogue available.

542 • TORQUAY CENTRAL LIBRARY

Lymington Road, Torquay, Devon TQ1 3DT
Tel (0803) 211251

Enquiries to Peter J. Bottrill, Area Librarian

Items About 4000: b/w original and copy photographs, colour transparencies (35mm, 5″ × 4″, larger), colour photographic prints, postcards, glass negatives, press cuttings and tearsheets, illustrated books

Dates of subject matter Prehistory to present

Dates of photographs 1850 to present

Subjects Local history of south Devon and especially Torbay including streetscenes, harbour, trawlers, yachts, tramways, landscapes, beach scenes, ships, bathing machines, local personalities, piers, sea walls (construction), cliff railways, fisheries, floods

Access and conditions Open to the public, Mon Tues Wed Fri 9–7, Thurs 9–6, Sat 9–5. All material available for editorial reproduction and for advertising, some material subject to copyright clearance. No loans; b/w prints and duplicate colour transparencies available for a fee. Photocopies available. Reproduction rights fees charged. Staff will undertake limited research, time permitting.

543 • TORQUAY MUSEUM

529 Babbacombe Road, Torquay, Devon TQ1 1HG
Tel (0803) 23975

Enquiries to Mrs E. L. White, Honorary Curator, 20 Trumlands Road, Torquay, Devon

Items About 30,000: b/w original photographs, b/w copy photographs, lantern slides, postcards, old fine art prints, stereographs, press cuttings, lithographs

Dates of subject matter 1750 to present

Dates of photographs 1850 to present

Subjects Local history of Devon with special emphasis on Torbay and South Devon including landscapes, streetscenes, towns and villages, architecture, churches, public houses, industry including terracotta potteries, transport (railways, horse-drawn vehicles, trams), portraits of local people, some news events, maritime life of Torbay; special collection of local natural history

Access and conditions Open to qualified researchers by appt (write). All material available for editorial reproduction by special arrangement only but not for exhibition or advertising use. B/w prints and duplicate colour transparencies available for a fee by arrangement. Reproduction and service fees charged. Limited research undertaken. Compulsory credit line. Most material copyright. Card catalogue in preparation.

544 • THE TOTNES MUSEUM

70 Fore Street, Totnes, Devon TQ9 5RE
Tel (0803) 863821

Enquiries to William Bennett, Custodian

Items About 1400: b/w original and copy photographs, fine art prints, postcards, lantern slides, greetings cards, illustrated books, daguerreotypes, architectural drawings

Dates of subject matter Early 17th century to present

Dates of photographs 1850 to 1950

Subjects Totnes and environs local history including river commerce, steamers on the River Dart, warehouses (1850), pleasure steamers Totnes to Dartmouth, architecture dating from 16th century including museum building (1575), bank (1585), World War I photographs of Devon regiments, posters of Jubilees, Queen Victoria's coronation, silver, golden and diamond Jubilees and local celebrations, subsequent Royal Jubilees (Edward VII, George V, George VI, Elizabeth II); Elizabethan house during and after reconstruction, Victorian birthday, Christmas and valentine cards

Access and conditions Open to the public by appt (write), Apr 1–Oct 31 Mon-Fri 10.30–1, 2–5. All material available for editorial reproduction and for advertising. No loans; b/w prints and colour transparencies available for a fee. Reproduction rights and service fees charged.

545 • TOWER HAMLETS CENTRAL LIBRARY

Local History Library Picture Collection

277 Bancroft Road, London E1 4DQ
Tel (01) 980 4366 ext 47

Enquiries to Local History Librarian

Items About 20,000: b/w original and copy photographs, colour transparencies (35mm), posters, glass negatives, fine art prints, colour photographic prints, lantern slides, postcards, original cartoons, illustrated maps, illustrated books, architectural drawings, greetings cards, press cuttings and tearsheets

Dates of subject matter *c.* 1100 to present

Dates of photographs 19th century to present

Subjects HUGUENOT/SPITALFIELDS WEAVERS COLLECTION including press cuttings, some 19th-century illustrations and photographs; WHIFFIN COLLECTION: work by local Poplar photographer including social history, streets, people, civic ceremonies, buildings (1920–1950); SHIPPING COLLECTION: East and West India Docks, ships, ship-building, 19th-century firms operating at the Docks, related illustrations and press cuttings; general collection: Limehouse, Mile End, Tower of London, St Katherine's Dock, Spitalfields, Bethnal Green, Whitechapel, Shadwell, Wapping, St George's-in-the-East, Isle of Dogs, Bow, Bromley, Poplar, including places of worship, parks, buildings, streets, aerial views, entertainments, personalities, social life and conditions, industries, poverty, public services, markets, political and non-political demonstrations, suffragettes, battle of Cable Street, Siege of Sidney Street, transport, dock strikes, urban farms, ethnic minorities.

Access and conditions Open to the public by appt (tel), Mon Tues Thurs Fri 9–8, Wed & Sat 9–5. Some material available for editorial reproduction but not for advertising. B/w and colour material loaned free of charge for three weeks. Photocopies available. Reproduction rights fees charged. Staff will undertake some research. Card catalogue.

546 • TRAFFORD LIBRARY SERVICE

Libraries Department

PO Box 20, Tatton Road, Sale, Greater Manchester M33 1YS
Tel (061) 973 2253

Enquiries to John Watters, Borough Librarian

Items 3000: b/w original photographs, b/w copy photographs, colour photographic prints, colour transparencies (35mm), glass negatives, postcards, illustrated maps, old fine art prints, 20th-century fine art prints, art reproductions, unprinted film negatives, posters, architectural drawings, press cuttings, illustrated books, ephemera

Dates of subject matter 1880s to present

Dates of photographs 1880s to present

Subjects Local history of Trafford and surrounding area including landscapes, villages, architecture, social history, transport, leisure, industry (Ford Motor Company Factory, electrical company), portraits; material relating to the Manchester Ship Canal and the Trafford Park Industrial Estate

Access and conditions Open to the public, Mon-Fri 8.30–4.30. All material available for editorial reproduction and for advertising. No loans; b/w prints and duplicate colour transparencies available for a fee. Photocopies available. No reproduction rights fees charged; service fees charged for commercial use. Staff will undertake limited research. Most material copyright.

547 • ULSTER FOLK AND TRANSPORT MUSEUM

Cultra Manor, Holywood, Co. Down BT18 0EU
Tel (02317) 5411

Enquiries to Kenneth Anderson

Items About 100,000: b/w original and copy photographs, colour transparencies (35mm, 5″ × 4″), glass negatives, daguerreotypes, lantern slides, postcards, unprinted film negatives, stereographs

Dates of subject matter 17th century to present

Dates of photographs 1850 to present

Subjects Aspects of life in Ulster including agricultural, industrial and domestic architecture, furniture, domestic utensils, costume, agriculture, crafts; road, rail, sea and air transport; trade, socio-political and religious groups, folklore, music, sports and pastimes; W. A. GREEN COLLECTION of landscapes and agriculture in Ulster, also coverage of linen industry *c.* 1910 to 1930

Access and conditions Open to qualified researchers by appt (write). All material available for editorial reproduction but not for advertising.

Colour material loaned for a fee; b/w prints available for a fee. Reproduction rights and service fees charged; service fees deductible from use fees. Staff will undertake limited research; negotiable research fee charged. Most material copyright. Card catalogue available.

548 • ULSTER MUSEUM

Department of Local History, Numismatics and Industrial Archaeology

Botanic Gardens, Belfast BT9 5AB
Tel (0232) 668251/5

Enquiries to Librarian, Department of Local History

Items About 16,000: glass negatives, lantern slides, unprinted film negatives, colour transparencies (35mm, 5″ × 4″), b/w original photographs, postcards, illustrated maps, posters, greetings cards

Dates of subject matter c. 1600 to present

Dates of photographs c. 1860 to present

Subjects Local history of Ulster with emphasis on Belfast including landscapes, ancient and historical monuments, architecture, industry (linen, shipbuilding), transport, education, social history, portraits; military uniforms, insignia, flags, banners, weapons of the Irish armed forces and police force; coins, medals, clocks, watches; special collections include the ROBERT WELCH PHOTOGRAPHIC COLLECTION of landscapes, geology, botany, zoology and folk life in Northern Ireland, 1880 to 1930s, and the ALEXANDER HOGG PHOTOGRAPHIC COLLECTION including Belfast streetscenes, industrial and social life and portraits of local people, 1900 to 1940

Access and conditions Open to the public by appt (tel), Mon-Fri 10–5. All material available for editorial reproduction and for advertising. B/w material loaned free of charge by arrangement; colour material loaned for a fee (print fees charged); material may be copied by outside photographers. Photocopies available. Reproduction rights, holding and service fees charged. Staff will undertake limited research. Some material copyright. Card catalogue available and printed catalogue to Welch Collection, Brian S. Turner, *A list of the photographs in the R. J. Welch Collection in the Ulster Museum,* 2 Vols, 1979, 1983.

549 • UNIVERSITY OF DURHAM

The University Library (Special Collections)

Palace Green Section, Palace Green, Durham DH1 3EH
Tel (0385) 64466

Enquiries to E. M. Rainey, Keeper of Rare Books

Items About 3000: b/w original photographs, glass negatives, b/w copy photographs, colour transparencies (35mm, 5″ × 4″, larger), colour photographic prints, stereographs, topographical prints and maps

Dates of subject matter 17th century to present

Dates of photographs 1850s to present

Subjects History and development of Durham University and local history of the county and city of Durham; 17th-century topographical prints of Durham Cathedral; J. R. AND D. EDIS COLLECTION of b/w negatives including some coverage of Cathedral and general local history including landscapes, architecture, social history, portraits; C. W. GIBBY PHOTOGRAPHIC NEGATIVE COLLECTION of Durham 1930s to 1950s; A. A. MACFARLANE-GRIEVE COLLECTION of Durham University 1912 to 1930s

Access and conditions Open to qualified researchers by appt (write), Mon-Fri 9–5. Most material available for editorial reproduction and for advertising. No loans; b/w prints and duplicate colour transparencies available for a fee. Staff will undertake some research. All material copyright.

550 • UNIVERSITY OF NOTTINGHAM LIBRARY

Manuscripts Department

Nottingham NG7 2RD
Tel (0602) 506101 ext 3440

Enquiries to Keeper of Manuscripts

Items About 20,000: b/w original photographs, b/w copy photographs, colour transparencies (35mm, 5″ × 4″), colour photographic prints, glass negatives, daguerreotypes, lantern slides, postcards, illustrated maps, old fine art prints, posters, architectural drawings, illustrated books, illuminated manuscripts

Dates of subject matter 1000 to present

Dates of photographs 1854 to present

Subjects Family, estate, ecclesiastical,

commercial and trade union manuscript material from the 12th century; photographic collections relating to the local history of Nottingham and surrounding area including landscapes, social history, portraits, industry; RAY-WILLOUGHBY COLLECTION of natural history; special collection relating to cotton-growing and processing worldwide 1920–1977; hand-drawn and printed maps, architectural drawings; coverage of the Crimea, Turkey, Greece and Hong Kong, photographers include Evans, Robertson, Bemrose and Walker; material relating to the University of Nottingham including portraits; Russian war posters and British posters of World War II

Access and conditions Open to the public by appt (write). Most material available for editorial reproduction and for advertising (some restrictions). No loans; b/w prints and duplicate colour transparencies available for a fee. Photocopies availble. Reproduction rights and service fees charged. Some material copyright.

551 • UNIVERSITY OF SOUTHAMPTON LIBRARY

Cope Collection

Highfield, Southampton SO9 5NH
Tel (0703) 559122 ext 3335 Telex 47661

Enquiries to G. Hampson, Sub-Librarian, Special Collections

Items About 4500: old fine art prints, illustrated books, b/w original and copy photographs, glass negatives, lantern slides, postcards, illustrated books

Dates of subject matter 1600 to present

Dates of photographs *c.* 1860 to present

Subjects Local history and topography of Hampshire and the Isle of Wight including villages, towns, events, personalities, transport, houses, streetscenes

Access and conditions Open to the public by appt (tel). All material available for editorial reproduction and for advertising at the Librarian's discretion. No loans; b/w prints and duplicate colour transparencies available for a fee; material may be copied by outside photographers. Photocopies available. Reproduction rights and service fees charged. All material copyright. Catalogue available.

552 • UXBRIDGE LIBRARY

22 High Street, Uxbridge, Middlesex UB8 1JN
Tel (0895) 50600 Telex 934224
(Note: The Library is moving in 1987.)

Enquiries to Local History Librarian

Items Over 6000: b/w original and copy photographs, colour photographic prints, glass negatives, daguerreotypes, postcards, original cartoons, illustrated maps, posters, greetings cards, architectural drawings, press cuttings and tearsheets, illustrated books, ephemera

Dates of subject matter Prehistory to present

Dates of photographs 1850s to present

Subjects Local history and topography of the London Borough of Hillingdon, parts of west Middlesex, London, the south east and Buckinghamshire, especially Uxbridge, Ruislip, Eastcote, Northwood, Yiewsley, West Drayton, Hayes, Harlington and including general scenes, streetscenes, houses, pubs, education, churches, social life, trades, sport; the Uxbridge Panorama (*c.* 1800) showing the frontages of both sides of Uxbridge High Street; paintings and prints of local subjects; the Mills Family Album; Ellen Terry and Gordon Craig, theatrical portraits, illustrated books; Gillray's *A Middlesex Election*

Access and conditions Open to the public by appt (tel), Mon-Fri 9.30–8, Sat 9.30–5. All material available for editorial reproduction but not for advertising. B/w material loaned free of charge for one month. Material may be copied by outside photographers. Photocopies available. No reproduction rights fees charged. Staff will undertake some research. Compulsory credit line.

553 • VALE AND DOWNLAND MUSEUM CENTRE

The Old Surgery, Church Street, Wantage, Oxfordshire OX12 8BL
Tel (02357) 66838

Enquiries to Nancy Stebbing, Curator

Items About 750: b/w original photographs, b/w copy photographs, colour transparencies (35mm), postcards, glass negatives, daguerreotypes, lantern slides, lithographs, etchings, woodcuts

Dates of subject matter Prehistory to present

Dates of photographs 1850 to present

Subjects Local history of Wantage and villages in Vale of White Horse including landscapes, architecture, churches, schools, farms, streetscenes, archaeology; industry including iron works, milling, brickworks, breweries; transport including railway stations, Wiltshire and Berkshire Canal, Wantage tramway; social history, portraits; some aerial coverage of archaeological sites

Access and conditions Open to the public by appt (write), Tues-Sat 10.30–4.30, Sun 2–5. All material available for editorial reproduction and for advertising. B/w prints and duplicate colour transparencies available for a fee. Photocopies available. Reproduction rights fees charged. Staff will undertake limited research. Some material copyright. Card catalogue available.

554 • WALSALL LIBRARY AND MUSEUM SERVICES

Local History and Archives Service, Central Library, Lichfield Street, Walsall, West Midlands WS1 1TR
Tel (0922) 21244 ext 3111

Enquiries to Marilyn Lewis, Archivist

Items About 5000: b/w copy photographs, b/w original photographs, unprinted film negatives, architectural drawings, glass negatives, lantern slides, posters, postcards

Dates of subject matter 19th century to present

Dates of photographs 1850 to present

Subjects Local history of Walsall and surrounding area including architecture, streetscenes, social history, transport (canals, railways, buses), trade, industry including foundries and saddlers' workshops

Access and conditions Open to the public by appt (tel), Mon-Fri 9.30–7, Sat 9.30–5. All material available for editorial research and for advertising. No loans; b/w prints and duplicate colour transparencies available for a fee; material may be copied by outside photographers. Photocopies available. Reproduction rights fees charged. Staff will undertake limited research. Most material available. Card catalogue available.

555 • WARRINGTON LIBRARY

Local History Collection

Museum Street, Warrington, Cheshire WA1 1JB
Tel (0925) 571232

Enquiries to David Rogers, Principal Librarian

Items 16,000: b/w original and copy photographs, postcards, illustrated books, posters, colour transparencies (35mm), old fine art prints, glass negatives, press cuttings, architectural drawings, 20th-century fine art prints, daguerreotypes, colour photographic prints

Dates of subject matter 18th century to present

Dates of photographs 1850 to present

Subjects Local history of Warrington and area between Newton-le-Willows, Budsworth, Penketh and Glazebrook including landscapes, towns, villages, architecture, public houses, social history, transport, industry (wire-making, soap-manufacture, tanning), cottage industries including pin-making and fustian-cutting (a few interiors); detailed photographic survey of Warrington town centre development 1973–1981; special collections of political posters from general and by-elections, theatre playbills, Frith negatives and prints of Warrington and area

Access and conditions Open to the public, Mon-Wed & Fri 9–7.30, Thurs 9–5, Sat 9–1. All material available for editorial reproduction and for advertising. No loans; b/w prints and duplicate colour transparencies available for a fee; material may be copied by outside photographers. Photocopies available. Reproduction rights fees charged. Staff will undertake limited research. Compulsory credit line. Some material copyright. Card catalogue.

556 • WARWICKSHIRE COUNTY RECORD OFFICE

Priory Park, Cape Road, Warwick CV34 4JS
Tel (0926) 493431 ext 2508

Enquiries to Michael Farr, County Archivist

Items About 20,000: postcards, b/w original photographs, b/w copy photographs, glass negatives, lantern slides, stereographs, architectural drawings, illustrated books, colour transparencies (35mm)

Dates of subject matter 11th century to present

Dates of photographs 1850 to present

Subjects Local history collection covering the county of Warwickshire (including those parts transferred to the West Midlands in 1974 but excluding Coventry) and concentrating on pre-1940 material: landscapes, towns, villages, streetscenes, social history, churches, country houses, cottages, dwellings, transport, agriculture, industry, factories, trades, workshops, including some interior and coverage of silk-ribbon weaving and hatmaking, large collection of horse-drawn and motorized vehicles such as water-carts and street-cleaning trucks manufactured by local firm for public authority use, family albums of landed Warwickshire families.

Access and conditions Open to the public, Mon-Fri 9–1, 2–5.30, Sat 9–12.30. All material available for editorial reproduction; advertising use by special arrangement only. No loans; b/w prints and colour transparencies available for a fee; material may be copied by outside photographers. Photocopies available. Reproduction rights fees charged. Staff will undertake limited research, visit by user is usually necessary. Some material copyright. Card catalogue.

557 • WARWICKSHIRE MUSEUM SERVICE

Market Place, Warwick CV34 4SA
Tel (0926) 493431

Enquiries to Curator

Items About 50,000: b/w original photographs, b/w copy photographs, colour transparencies (35mm), lantern slides, unprinted film negatives, postcards, stereographs, ambrotypes, tintypes, autochrome glass colour transparencies

Dates of subject matter BC to present

Dates of photographs 1850 to present

Subjects Local history of Warwickshire including towns and villages, streetscenes, churches, public houses, social history, transport, industry especially stone quarrying; part of photographic archive of Eagle Engineering commercial vehicle body manufacturers; survey of Atherstone houses for the local health inspector; 1930 survey of county roads; special collection of lantern slides of museum items (1900–1925) covering worldwide geology, biology, social history and costume

Access and conditions Open to the public by appt (tel), Mon-Sat 10–5.30. Some material available for editorial reproduction and for advertising. No loans; b/w prints and duplicate colour transparencies available for a fee. Reproduction rights and service fees charged. Staff will undertake limited research. Some material copyright.

558 • WATT LIBRARY

9 Union Street, Greenock, Strathclyde PA16 8JH
Tel (0475) 20186

Enquiries to Reference Services Assistant

Items About 6000: b/w original and copy photographs, colour transparencies (35mm), colour photographic prints, glass negatives, lantern slides, postcards, original cartoons, illustrated maps, posters, architectural drawings

Dates of subject matter *c.* 1850 to present

Dates of photographs 1850 to present

Subjects Local history of Gourock, Greenock, Port Glasgow, Kilmacolm, Innerkip and Wemyss Bay including streetscenes, harbours, Provosts, aerial photographs, World War II bomb damage, industries, schools, housing, transport

Access and conditions Open to the public, Mon & Thurs 2–5, 6–8, Tues & Fri 10–12.30, 2–5, Wed & Sat 10–1. Some material available for editorial reproduction, but not for advertising. No loans; Library will arrange for material to be copied by outside photographer. Reproduction rights fees charged at the discretion of the copyright holder. Staff will undertake some research.

559 • WELHOLME GALLERIES

Welholme Road, Great Grimsby, South Humberside DN32 9LP
Tel (0472) 59161 ext 101

Enquiries to Janet Tierney, Curator

Items About 30,000: b/w copy photographs, lantern slides, glass negatives, unprinted film negatives, b/w original photographs, colour transparencies (35mm), postcards, stereographs, greetings cards, colour photographic prints, daguerreotypes, posters, illustrated maps

Dates of subject matter 1750 to present

Dates of photographs 1850 to present

Subjects Town and country life in Lincolnshire

covering craftsmen, industry, folk life, agricultural activities, buildings (including substantial coverage of windmills, watermills, country houses and religious buildings), studio portraits, people at work, social and cultural events including ox-roasts and maypole dancing, inland waterways, transport, fishing; special collections include the work of several 19th-century photographers such as Nainby of Alford, Turner of Saxilby and Collis of Cleethorpes; fine art collections include the SKELTON COLLECTION of watercolours and sketches of Grimsby and surrounding area between 1800 and 1930; the DOUGHTY COLLECTION of 18th- and 19th-century marine paintings; artists represented include Carmichael, Tudgay, Whitcombe, Mitchell

Access and conditions Open to the public by appt (tel), Tues-Sat 10–5. All material available for editorial reproduction and for advertising. B/w and colour material loaned free of charge by arrangement; b/w prints and duplicate colour transparencies available for a fee; material may be copied by outside photographers. Photocopies available. Reproduction rights fees charged. Staff will undertake some research. All material copyright.

560 • WELLS MUSEUM

8 Cathedral Green, Wells, Somerset BA5 2UE
Tel (0749) 73477

Enquiries to Honorary Curator

Items About 3000: glass negatives, colour transparencies (35mm), b/w original photographs, lantern slides, old fine art prints, postcards, illustrations

Dates of subject matter BC to present

Dates of photographs 1870 to present

Subjects PHILLIPS COLLECTION of glass negatives covering local history (except Wells Cathedral); DR REID AND DR PARKER COLLECTIONS covering landscape and architecture of Somerset; HARRY SAVORY COLLECTION of Mendip Hill and caves; John Hassall's illustrations of cave and prehistoric scenes; engravings of local landscapes from 18th to 20th centuries

Access and conditions Open to the public by appt (write). All material available for editorial reproduction and for advertising (some restrictions). No loans; b/w prints and duplicate colour transparencies available for a fee.

Reproduction rights fees charged. Staff will undertake limited research. Most material copyright. Card catalogue available.

561 • WELSH FOLK MUSEUM

St Fagan's, Cardiff CF5 6XB
Tel (0222) 569441 ext 237

Enquiries to Archivist

Items 100,000: b/w original photographs, b/w copy photographs, colour transparencies (35mm, 2¼", 5" ×4"), colour photographic prints, glass negatives, daguerreotypes, lantern slides, postcards, stereographs, posters, greetings cards, architectural drawings

Dates of subject matter *c.* 1870 to present

Dates of photographs *c.* 1890 to present

Subjects Social history of Wales covering domestic, corporate and cultural life including agriculture, rural crafts (woodworking, textiles, basketry, blacksmithing), industries including the woollen industry, vernacular architecture and folklore

Access and conditions Open to the public by appt (tel), Mon-Fri 9.30–4.30. All material available for editorial reproduction but not for advertising. B/w prints available for a fee; colour transparencies loaned for a fee. Photocopies available. Reproduction rights fees charged. Staff of three will undertake research. Compulsory credit line. Some material copyright. Card catalogue available.

562 • WELWYN HATFIELD MUSEUM SERVICE

Old Mill House Museum, Mill Green, Hatfield, Hertfordshire AL9 5PD
Tel (07072) 71362

Enquiries to Christine Johnstone, Curator

Items About 1300: b/w copy photographs, b/w original photographs, colour transparencies (35mm), postcards, colour photographic prints, daguerreotypes

Dates of subject matter AD 300 to present

Dates of photographs 1800 to present

Subjects Local and social history of Hatfield, Welwyn Garden City, Welwyn New Town and surrounding villages covering urban views, architecture with special emphasis on churches and schools, Hatfield House, horse-drawn private transport, motorized private and public transport, railways, shops, agriculture, industry including watermills, food processing and British Aerospace

Access and conditions Open to the public by appt (tel), Tues-Fri 10–5. All material available for editorial reproduction; advertising use by special arrangement only. No loans; b/w prints and duplicate colour transparencies available for a fee; material may be copied by outside photographers. Reproduction rights and service fees charged; service fees deductible from use fees. Staff will undertake some research; fees charged for large projects. Compulsory credit line. Most material copyright. Duplicated catalogue available.

563 • WEST DEVON RECORD OFFICE

Unit 3, Clare Place, Coxside, Plymouth, Devon
PL4 0JW
Tel (0752) 264685

Enquiries to Elizabeth Stuart, Senior Assistant Archivist

Items B/w copy photographs, b/w original photographs, architectural drawings

Dates of photographs 1890s to present

Subjects Local history of Plymouth and West Devon including landscapes, architecture, social history, personalities, transport, agriculture, trades; special collections include photographs of woodcarvings from Devon churches; bombardment of Antwerp and the Dardanelles Campaign 1914–1915; Plymouth and Devonport during the Blitz by Fred Crisp, 1940–1941; architectural plans relating to manor of Stoke Damerel, 1831–1951

Access and conditions All material available for editorial reproduction and for advertising by special arrangement only. No loans; b/w prints available for a fee; material may be copied by outside photographers. Photocopies available for a fee. Reproduction rights fees charged by arrangement. Staff of five will undertake limited research. Most material copyright. Card catalogue available.

564 • WEST YORKSHIRE ARCHIVES SERVICE

Leeds District Archives, Chapeltown Road, Sheepscar, Leeds LS7 3AP
Tel (0532) 628339

Enquiries to District Archivist

Items About 200,000: architectural drawings, b/w original photographs, lantern slides, glass negatives, b/w copy photographs, unprinted film negatives, illustrated maps, postcards

Dates of subject matter 16th century to present

Dates of photographs 1860 to present

Subjects Local history including coverage of slum-clearance areas c. 1960s; architectural plans submitted for building approval 1867–1948; GREENWOOD & BATLEY (ENGINEERS) LTD PHOTOGRAPHIC COLLECTION including experimental machinery c. 1840–1929; JONES OF HAWORTH COLLECTION including family photographs and buildings in Cambrideshire, Norfolk, Warwickshire, Yorkshire and the USA between 1890 and 1910; Kitson family photographs; Photopress Press Agency files 1960–1979; BARRAN COLLECTION of postcards of UK and Europe between 1900 and 1970; YORKSHIRE WATER AUTHORITY COLLECTION of reservoir construction for Leeds Corporation in the early 20th century; BAXENDALE KAYLL LTD COLLECTION of stained glass designs; Harvey and Whiting family photographs c. 1860–1930

Access and conditions Open to the public by appt (write). Most material available for editorial reproduction and for advertising. No loans; b/w prints and duplicate colour transparencies available for a fee; material may be copied by outside photographers. Photocopies available. Reproduction rights fees charged. Staff will undertake limited research. Most material copyright.

565 • WEYBRIDGE MUSEUM

Church Street, Weybridge, Surrey KT13 8DE
Tel (0932) 43573

Enquiries to Avril Lansdell, Curator

Items About 5000: b/w original and copy photographs, oil paintings, watercolours, prints, drawings

Dates of subject matter 1800 to present

Dates of photographs 1860s to present

Subjects Photographic collection: Elmbridge Borough local history, including villages of Claygate, Cobham, East Molesey, Esher, Hersham, Hinchley Wood, Long Ditton, Oatlands, Oxshott, Stoke D'Abernon, Thames Ditton, Walton-on-Thames, West Molesey, Weybridge; people at work, sports teams, bands, schools, fire brigades, pageants, local events, industry, transport, agriculture, shop keepers, small industries including saddlery, boat-building, propellor making; Fine art collection: topographic collection of the towns and villages listed above

Access and conditions Open to qualified researchers by appt (tel), Mon-Fri 10–1, 2–5. Most material available for editorial reproduction but not for advertising. B/w prints available for a fee; colour material may be copied by outside photographers. Photocopies available. Reproduction rights fees charged. Card catalogue.

566 • WIGAN RECORD OFFICE

Town Hall, Leigh, Lancashire WN7 2DY
Tel (0942) 672421 ext 220

Enquiries to Borough Archivist

Items About 15,000: b/w original photographs, colour transparencies ($10'' \times 8''$, $5'' \times 4''$), b/w copy photographs, glass negatives, lantern slides, postcards, original cartoons, illustrated maps, old fine art prints, stereographs, posters, greetings cards, architectural drawings, press cuttings, illustrated books

Dates of subject matter 17th century to present

Dates of photographs 1850 to present

Subjects Wigan Metropolitan Borough with emphasis on Wigan and Leigh including all aspects of life and activities with special emphasis on coalmining and other occupations of heavily industrialized area; shops, public houses, streetscenes, landscapes; WILLIAM WICKHAM COLLECTION of late Victorian photographs including underground photography, social history, Wigan people, 1893 coal strike; architecture and city development

Access and conditions Open to the public by appt (tel), Mon-Fri 10–4. All material available for editorial reproduction and for advertising. No loans; b/w prints and duplicate colour transparencies available for a fee. Photocopies available. Reproduction rights fees charged. Staff of two will undertake limited research. Some material copyright. Card catalogue available.

567 • WILLIAMSON ART GALLERY AND MUSEUM

Photographic Collection

Slatey Road, Birkenhead, Wirral, Merseyside L43 4UE
Tel (051) 652 4177

Enquiries to Clifford Thornton, Curator

Items About 15,000: glass negatives, lantern slides, b/w original photographs, old fine art prints, original cartoons

Dates of subject matter BC to present

Dates of photographs 1890 to present

Subjects Archive of the Cammell Laird Shipbuilders at Birkenhead: construction of merchant and naval vessels for the United Kingdom and overseas including submarines and destroyers in World War I, general views of the yard, slipways, docks, labour force, shipyard machines, workshops including smithy, foundry, boiler shop, engine shop, laboratory, gas plant, power station; local history of Birkenhead, Bromborough, Eastham, Heswall, Wallasey and West Kirby on the Wirral peninsula covering agriculture, industry, topography, shipping, social history; CHRISTOPHER SYMES COLLECTION of Bromoils comprising genre scenes of France and Italy in the early 20th century

Access and conditions Open to the public by appt (tel), Mon-Fri 10–4. All material available for editorial reproduction and for advertising. No loans; b/w prints and duplicate colour transparencies available for a fee. Photocopies and Polaroids available for a fee. Reproduction rights fees charged. Staff will undertake some research. Compulsory credit line. Most material copyright. Card catalogue to photographic collection; printed catalogue to Cammell Laird collection.

568 • WILTSHIRE ARCHAEOLOGICAL AND NATURAL HISTORY SOCIETY

The Museum, 41 Long Street, Devizes, Wiltshire SN10 1NS
Tel (0380) 77369

Enquiries to Pamela Colman, Librarian

Items 30,000: b/w original photographs, b/w copy photographs, colour photographic prints, postcards, original cartoons, illustrated maps, old fine art prints, unprinted film negatives, posters, architectural drawings, press cuttings, illustrated books, watercolours, drawings, engraved portraits

Dates of subject matter Prehistory to present

Dates of photographs 1850 to present

Subjects Local history of Wiltshire including archaeology, landscapes, towns and villages, architecture, trades, agriculture, education, transport, festivals, portraits; special collection of drawings by John Buckler, Robert Kemm, John Britton, George Cattermole, Samuel Prout, William Bartlett, John Nash

Access and conditions Open to the public by appt (write), Tues-Sat 11–5. All material available for editorial reproduction and for advertising. No loans; b/w prints and duplicate colour transparencies available for a fee. Reproduction rights fees charged. Staff will undertake research; negotiable research fee charged. Most material copyright.

569 • WILTSHIRE LIBRARY AND MUSEUM SERVICE

Bythesea Road, Trowbridge, Wiltshire BA14 8BS
Tel (02214) 3641 Telex 44297

Enquiries to John Chandler, Local Studies Officer

Items About 40,000: b/w original photographs, b/w copy photographs, glass negatives, colour transparencies (35mm), colour photographic prints, postcards

Dates of subject matter BC to present

Dates of photographs 1860s to present

Subjects Local history collection covering the county of Wiltshire and including rural and urban landscapes, agriculture, towns, villages, churches, public houses, country houses, cottages, transport, industry (especially Bath stone), railway engineering, fire brigades; special collections include the WILTSHIRE TIMES newspaper collection from 1930s to 1960s and the BROOK COLLECTION of railway material

Access and conditions Open to the public, Mon-Fri 9–5. Some material available for editorial reproduction and for advertising; some for private research only. No loans; b/w prints and duplicate colour transparencies available for a fee. Photocopies available for a fee. Reproduction rights fees sometimes charged depending on use of

material. Staff will undertake limited research. Some material copyright. Computer list in preparation.

570 • WIMBLEDON LIBRARY

Local Studies Collection

Wimbledon Hill Road, London SW19 7NB
Tel (01) 946 1136

Enquiries to Reference Librarian

Items 2000: b/w original and copy photographs, colour photographic prints, colour transparencies (35mm), postcards

Dates of subject matter Late 18th century to present

Dates of photographs 19th century to present

Dates of fine art *c.* 1790 to 1900

Subjects Wimbledon local history, especially buildings and streetscenes; Surrey local history, especially old Surrey and London south of the Thames, buildings, streetscenes

Access and conditions Open to the public by appt (tel), Mon Tues Thurs Fri 9–7, Wed & Sat 9–5. All material available for editorial reproduction and for advertising. No loans; b/w and colour material available for a fee. Photocopies available. Reproduction rights fees charged. Staff will undertake limited research.

571 • WINCHESTER LIBRARY

Local Studies Collection

Jewry Street, Winchester, Hampshire SO23 8RX
Tel (0962) 60644 ext 69 Telex 47121

Enquiries to P. E. Stevens

Items Over 6100: b/w original and copy photographs, colour transparencies (35mm), postcards, glass negatives, fine art prints, lantern slides, unprinted film negatives

Dates of subject matter Prehistory to present

Dates of photographs 1880 to 1980

Subjects Hampshire with emphasis on Winchester, general views of towns, villages and countryside, landscapes, streetscenes; architecture including castles, churches, chapels, abbeys and ruins; vernacular architecture including cottages, barns, walls, granaries on staddle-stones, gables, flintwalls, thatch; industrial buildings and features including breweries, brickworks, canal-locks, docks, foundries, garages, laundries, power-stations, post offices, shops, cinemas, etc.; street furniture including milestones, lamp-posts, pillar-boxes, horse-troughs, water-pumps, telegraph poles, war memorials, boundary markers, etc.; transport including bicycles, boats, cars, delivery vans, ferries, fire-engines, railways, roads, etc.; events including carnivals, processions, bands, accidents, Maundy presentations, May Day, mayor-making, military and naval occasions, floods, snow, etc.; people including portraits and groups, Mayors, clergy, royalty, MPs, children, families, soldiers, firemen, etc.; monumental inscriptions including plaques, memorials, notices and advertisements; archaeological features including burial mounds, field systems, Roman roads, etc.

Access and conditions Open to the public by appt (tel), Mon Tues Wed Fri 10–7, Thurs 10–1, Sat 10–4. Most material available for editorial reproduction and for advertising. B/w prints available for a fee; colour transparencies loaned for one month and duplicates available for a fee. Reproduction rights fees charged. Staff will undertake some research and mail photocopies. Card catalogue available.

572 • WINDERMERE NAUTICAL TRUST

Rayrigg Road, Windermere, Cumbria LA23 1BN
Tel (09662) 5565

Enquiries to Nigel Dalziel, Curator

Items About 10,000: b/w original and copy photographs, colour transparencies (35mm), glass negatives, postcards, architectural drawings

Dates of subject matter 1860 to present

Dates of photographs 1860 to present

Subjects Social and nautical history of Windermere including general landscapes, important houses around the lake, steam launches, steamboats, motorboars, yachts, rowing boats, winter sports on the lake, ice boats, ice scenes, ice-skating; tourists and day trippers, railways; 19th-century studio portraits of Bowness people

Access and conditions Open to qualified researchers by appt (write), Mon-Sat 10–5. All material available for editorial reproduction and for advertising. No loans; b/w prints and duplicate colour transparencies available for a fee.

Photocopies available. Reproduction rights and service fees charged. Staff will undertake some research. Compulsory credit line. Card catalogue.

573 • WOLVERHAMPTON PUBLIC LIBRARIES

Central Library, Snow Hill, Wolverhampton, West Midlands WV1 3AX
Tel (0902) 773824

Enquiries to Christine West, Reference Librarian

Items About 9000: b/w original and copy photographs, colour transparencies (35mm), colour photographic prints, glass negatives, lantern slides, postcards, original cartoons, illustrated maps, unprinted film negatives, stereographs, posters, greetings cards, architectural drawings, press cuttings, illustrated books

Dates of subject matter c. 17th century to present

Dates of photographs c. 1850 to present

Subjects Local history of Wolverhampton including landscapes, architecture, streetscenes, social history, transport, industry including Bilston Steelworks, Chubb Locks, Courtaulds, Goodyear Tyres, Manders Paints, Norton Villiers, car manufacture, festivals and fairs, portraits

Access and conditions Open to the public, Mon-Fri 10–7, Sat 10–5. All material available for editorial reproduction and for advertising. No loans; b/w prints and duplicate colour transparencies available for a fee. Photocopies available. Reproduction rights fees charged. Staff of seven will undertake some research. Most material copyright. Card catalogue available.

574 • ALEXANDER WOOD MEMORIAL LIBRARY

39-41 Princes Street, Ardrossan, Strathclyde KA22 8BT
Tel (0294) 69137

Enquiries to Karen Adamson, Assistant Librarian, Local History

Items About 300: b/w original and copy photographs, postcards, colour photographic prints, daguerreotypes, illustrated maps, fine art prints, architectural drawings, press cuttings and tearsheets, illustrated books, ephemera

Dates of subject matter 1800 to present

Dates of photographs 1880 to 1930, some 1980s

Subjects Cunningham district local history, especially towns (19th century), streets, shops, local events (unveiling war memorials, processions), portraits, ships and shipping, Nobel's Explosives Company of Stevenston; ephemera of local interest, election notices, playbills, etc.; ALEXANDER WOOD MEMORIAL COLLECTION: photographs, etchings, unframed paintings

Access and conditions Open to the public, Mon-Fri 9–5. All material available for editorial reproduction but not for advertising. No loans; material may be copied by outside photographers (library will arrange this if requested). Photocopies available. No reproduction rights fees charged. Staff will undertake some research and mail photocopies or photographic prints. Card catalogue.

575 • WOODSPRING CENTRAL LIBRARY

Weston-super-Mare Collection

The Boulevard, Weston-super-Mare BS23 1PL
Tel (0934) 24133, 20373

Enquiries to Librarian-in-charge

Items About 400: b/w copy and original photographs, postcards, glass negatives, illustrated maps

Dates of subject matter c. 1840 to present

Dates of photographs c. 1954 to present

Subjects Weston-super-Mare, Worle and local villages including Bleadon, Hutton, Locking and Congresbury with emphasis on architecture, scenics, transportation (including Great Western Railway and Weston, Clevedon and Portishead Light Railway, trams and donkeys), tourism, business, industry, personalities

Access and conditions Open to the public, Mon-Fri 9.30–8, Sat 9.30–5. Some material available for editorial reproduction, but not for advertising. No loans; b/w prints available for a fee. Photocopies available. Reproduction rights fees charged. Staff will undertake up to one hour's research for non-Avon County residents.

576 • WORCESTER CITY LIBRARY

Foregate Street, Worcester WR1 1DT
Tel (0905) 353366 ext 3813

Enquiries to Paul Ellis, Reference and Local Studies Librarian

Items 7000: b/w original photographs, colour transparencies (35mm), glass negatives, colour photographic prints, lantern slides

Dates of photographs 1890 to present

Subjects Worcester City and County of Hereford and Worcester topography, architecture, transportation, life and activities, streetscenes, sports, schools, country villages, people

Access and conditions Open to the public by appt (tel), Mon 9.30–7, Tues & Wed 9.30–5.30, closed Thurs, Fri 9.30–7, Sat 9.30–4. All material available for editorial reproduction and for advertising. B/w prints and duplicate colour transparencies available for a fee. Photocopies available. Reproduction rights fees charged. Staff will undertake limited research.

577 • WORCESTER CITY MUSEUM SERVICES

Photographic Collection

City Museum and Art Gallery, Foregate Street, Worcester WR1 1DT
Tel (0905) 25371

Enquiries to Curator

Items 5000: b/w original photographs, b/w copyright photographs, colour transparencies (35mm), colour photographic prints, glass negatives, daguerreotypes, lantern slides, postcards, original cartoons, illustrated maps, old fine art prints, 20th-century fine art prints, stereographs, posters, greetings cards, architectural drawings, press cuttings, illustrated books

Dates of subject matter 1500 to present

Dates of photographs 1850 to present

Dates of fine art 1650 to present

Subjects Local history of the city of Worcester and surrounding area covering all aspects of social, domestic and working life including trade and industry, agriculture and hop cultivation, local streets and buildings, horse-drawn transport, motor transport, railways, local personalities;

photographs from the Worcester Regiment and Yeomanry collections

Access and conditions Open to the public by appt (tel), Mon-Fri 9.30–6, closed Thurs, Sat 9.30–5. All material available for editorial reproduction and for advertising. B/w prints and duplicate colour transparencies available for a fee; some colour material loaned free of charge for one month; material may be copied by outside photographers. Photocopies available. Reproduction rights fees charged. Staff will undertake limited research. Worcester City Museums Service owns copyright to 50% of collection; in other cases copyright clearance is the responsibility of user.

578 • YELDE HALL MUSEUM

Market Place, Chippenham, Wiltshire SN15 3HL
Tel (0249) 651488

Enquiries to Bimp Simpkins, Honorary Curator

Items About 300: b/w original photographs, b/w copy photographs, postcards, posters

Dates of subject matter 1860s to present

Dates of photographs 1860s to present

Subjects Local history with special emphasis on football and cricket clubs and the firm of Westinghouse (manufacturers of signal boxes and braking systems for railways) including interiors of factory and a signal box in action in India

Access and conditions Open to the public, summer Mon-Sat 10–12, 2–4.30. Some material

available for editorial reproduction and for advertising; some for private research only. No loans; b/w prints available for a fee. Reproduction rights fees charged. Staff will undertake limited research. Most material copyright. Card catalogue in preparation.

579 • YORK CENTRAL LIBRARY

Museum Street, York YO1 2DS
Tel (0904) 55631 ext 36

Enquiries to Assistant County Librarian

Items 9000: b/w copy photographs, b/w original photographs, glass negatives, lantern slides, illustrated maps, architectural drawings

Dates of subject matter 1st century to present

Dates of photographs *c.* 1850 to present

Subjects Local history of North Yorkshire with special emphasis on York and Selby including landscapes (some aerial photographs), archaeology, architecture, streetscenes, social history

Access and conditions Open to the public by appt (write). Most material available for editorial reproduction and for advertising. B/w and colour material loaned free of charge for one month; b/w prints and duplicate colour transparencies available for a fee; material may be copied by outside photographers. Photocopies available. Reproduction rights and service fees charged. Staff will undertake limited research. Most material copyright.

Foreign History & Geography

580 • ANGLO-CHINESE EDUCATIONAL INSTITUTE

152 Camden High Street, London NW1 0NE
Tel (01) 485 8241

Enquiries to Alan Paterson

Items About 7000: b/w original photographs, colour photographic prints

Dates of subject matter Prehistory to present

Dates of photographs 1965 to present

Subjects China including archaeology, agriculture (fruits, vegetables, nuts, beans, tea, coffee, seaweed, sugar, animal husbandry, fishing, sea-farming, tobacco, latex, cotton, silk, sizal, jute, state farms, communes), architecture, arts and crafts, handicrafts, children, education, energy (coal, gas, oil, hydroeleric power), entertainments (song, dance, music, film, theatre, literature and writers, story-telling, opera, acrobatics, juggling, ballet), environment, lifestyle, foreign policy, health (acupuncture, welfare, recreation), history, historic sites (Long March, Great Wall), industry, armed forces, minority nationalities from Tibet, Inner Mongolia, Korea, and in Yunnan, Guizhou, Guangxi, Guangzhou, Kansu, and Hainan Island and including also the following groups: Uighur, Kazakh, Tajik, Khalkas, Olunchun, Hui, Li, Miao, Nahsi, Tung, Wa, Tai, Yi, Penglung, She (Fukien), Kelas; political history (Mao Zedong, Zhou Enlai, Cultural Revolution), science and technology, sport (Asian Games, archery, athletics, gymnastics, shooting, calisthenics, cycling, stadiums and spectators, tug-of-war, wu shu, fencing, sword play, ball games, watersports, winter sports, mountaineering), trade, transportation, women

Access and conditions Open to the public by appt (tel), Mon-Fri 9–5. All material available for editorial reproduction and for advertising. B/w material loaned free of charge for one month. Material may be copied by outside photographers by special arrangement. Photocopies available. Reproduction rights and service fees charged. Staff will undertake some research.

581 • BERMUDA DEPARTMENT OF TOURISM

9/10 Savile Row, London W1X 2BL
Tel (01) 734 8813 Telex 22853

Enquiries to Sheelagh Greene

Items 3500: colour transparencies (35mm), b/w original photographs

Dates of photographs 1979 to present

Subjects Bermuda including beaches, aerial views, landscapes, fishing, golf, tennis, transport, flowers and trees, tourists, buildings, gardens, historical sites, hotels

Access and conditions Open to qualified researchers by appt (tel), Mon-Fri 9–5. All material available for editorial reproduction and for advertising. B/w and colour material loaned free of charge. Staff will undertake some research. All material copyright.

582 • BRITAIN/ISRAEL PUBLIC AFFAIRS COMMITTEE

126-134 Baker Street, London W1M 1FH
Tel (01) 486 4141

Enquiries to Deborah Richardson

Items 26,000: b/w original and copy photographs, colour transparencies (35mm)

Dates of subject matter BC to present

Dates of photographs 1920s to present

Subjects Israel including archaeology, history, agriculture (irrigation, land reclamation, etc.), forests, natural resources and energy, science and technology, industry, architecture, cities (Haifa, Tel Aviv, Jerusalem, etc.), towns, kibbutzim, religions, schools, universities, sports, sights, people (including immigrants from other countries), events, government (Prime Ministers, members, buildings), personalities (athletes, artists)

Access and conditions Open to qualified researchers by appt (tel), Mon-Thurs 9.30–5, Fri 9.30–12. All material available for editorial reproduction and for advertising. B/w prints available for a fee; colour material loaned. Photocopies available. Reproduction rights and service fees charged for colour only; service fee deductible from use fee. Staff will undertake limited research, time permitting.

583 • W. CHINQUE

Photographs from Xinhua News Agency

76 Chancery Lane, London WC2A 1AA
Tel (01) 242 9217

Enquiries to W. Chinque

Items In London 20,000: b/w original and copy photographs, colour photographic prints, colour transparencies (35mm, 5″ × 4″)

Dates of subject matter Prehistory to present

Dates of photographs Mid-19th century to present

Subjects All aspects of life in China including geography, history, industry, agriculture, politics, economics, education and welfare; some material held in London but bulk of collection in Beijing and can be ordered

Access and conditions Open to qualified researchers by appt (write), Mon-Fri 10–4. All material available for editorial reproduction and for advertising. B/w and colour material loaned for a fee but reproduction and fees must be by prior agreement. Reproduction rights fees charged. Staff of two will undertake some research. Photographers available for assignment. All material copyright.

584 • FINNISH TOURIST BOARD

66 Haymarket, London SW1Y 4RF
Tel (01) 839 4048

Enquiries to Rita Müller, Marketing Executive

Items 2500: colour transparencies (35mm), b/w original photographs

Dates of photographs 1960 to present

Subjects Finland tourism, including towns, cities, accommodation, events, people, Helsinki and Lapland in winter and summer, ferries, lakes, winter sports including winter fishing and reindeer safaris, all summer sports including watersports, windsurfing, canoeing, cycling, hiking, hotels, holiday villages, natural history and wildlife, folk costumes, annual festivals, Christmas including Father Christmas, Christmas in the Arctic Circle, in a hut and with reindeer, shopping, design including textiles, jewellery, furniture and ceramics; special collection on museums and churches

Access and conditions Open to qualified researchers, Mon-Fri 9.15–12, 1–5.15. Some material available for editorial reproduction but not for advertising. B/w and colour material loaned free of charge for one month. No reproduction rights fees. Staff will undertake some research.

585 • FOOD AND WINE FROM FRANCE

Nuffield House, 41 Piccadilly, London W1V 9AJ
Tel (01) 439 8371   Telex 263144

Enquiries to Katharine Wales

Items About 300: colour transparencies (35mm), b/w original photographs

Dates of photographs 1977 to present

Subjects Wines and wine-making including vines, grape varieties, wine regions of France, cellars, vinification, bottling; cheeses including methods of manufacture; French charcuterie and pâtés; fresh fruit and vegetables grown in France (b/w only)

Access and conditions Open to qualified researchers by appt (tel), Mon-Fri 9–5.30. All material available for editorial reproduction and for advertising. B/w and colour material loaned free of charge for one month. No reproduction rights fees charged. Staff will undertake limited research.

586 • FRENCH PICTURE LIBRARY

26A Denbigh Place, London SW1V 2HA
Tel (01) 834 3007

Enquiries to Barrie Smith

Items 7000: colour transparencies (35mm, 6 × 6 cm), b/w original photographs, postcards

Dates of photographs 1975 to present

Subjects France, including travel, people, winter sports and skiing, ice-skating, cross-country skiing, snow-surfing, hang-gliding on skis, hot-air ballooning; châteaux all over France, especially along the Loire, Cher and Indre rivers; agriculture including vineyards and wine-making, food, sunflowers, maize, cheese, markets, restaurants, shops, churches, cathedrals, monuments, crafts, general views

Access and conditions Open to qualiified researchers by appt (tel). All material available for editorial reproduction and for advertising. B/w and colour material loaned free of charge for one month. Reproduction rights and holding fees charged. Staff will undertake some research.

587 • HONG KONG GOVERNMENT OFFICE

Photograph Collection

6 Grafton Street, London W1X 3LB
Tel (01) 499 9821 ext 221   Telex 05128 404

Enquiries to Ursula Price, Librarian

Items B/w photographs

Dates of photographs Contemporary

Subjects Contemporary Hong Kong including general views, industry, New Territories, agriculture, portraits of government officials

Access and conditions Open to qualified researchers, Mon-Fri 9.30–1, 2–5.30. All material available for editorial reproduction and for advertising. B/w material loaned free of charge. Colour material may be obtainable from Hong Kong in some cases. No reproduction rights fees charged. Staff will undertake some research.

588 • DENIS HUGHES-GILBEY PICTURE LIBRARY

Broad Oak, Sturminster Newton, Dorset DT10 2HG
Tel (0258) 72498, after summer 1986 (01) 402 5048

Enquiries to Ann Hughes-Gilbey

Items 10,000: colour transparencies (35mm, 2¼")

Dates of photographs 1972 to present

Subjects Regions of France (not Paris), especially food and wine – cultivation of food, all stages of preparation and cooking, French regional dishes and their recipes in their home settings; French

cheeses (cow, goat, ewe) from dairy and shop to platter including manufacture in farms and small co-ops (e.g. Roquefort and its 'magic caves'); fruit, vegetables and gardeners; livestock, cereals and farmers; fish and fishermen; rearing of geese for *foie gras;* picking, drying, shelling and pressing of walnuts; pigs and dogs searching for truffles; markets, shops, shop-fronts, interesting signs; wine areas, great and small, including growing, grafting, pruning and pressing, spraying and harvesting, ageing and bottling, extensive coverage of champagne, beaujolais and the châteaux of Bordeaux; spirits including cognac, fruit eaux-de-vie, *marc* made by travelling distillers; related trades and crafts (such as *tonnellerie*) in many regions; artisans and craftsmen including potters, weavers, ochre workers, coopers, chairmakers, tobacco growers, blacksmiths, lacemakers, basketweavers, *sabotiers,* cooks, *vignerons,* bakers, cheesemakers; castles and cathedrals, country cottages, streetscenes, rural views, *calvaries* and *coiffes* of Brittany, shopping, picnicking, eating and drinking, postmen, shepherds, chefs and children, scything, fishing, ploughing and haymaking; similar but small collections for India (Rajasthan, Bombay), Nepal, Italy (Lazio province), southern Portugal

Access and conditions Open to qualified researchers by appt (tel), Mon-Sat 9–6.30. All material available for editorial reproduction and for advertising. Colour material loaned free of charge for one month. Reproduction rights, service and holding fees charged; service fee deductible from use fee. Staff will carry out research.

589 • INDIA OFFICE LIBRARY AND RECORDS

British Library, 197 Blackfriars Road, London SE1 8NG
Tel (01) 928 9531

Enquiries to Head of Prints and Drawings Section

Items 184,000: b/w original and copy photographs, colour transparencies (35mm), glass negatives, daguerreotypes, lantern slides, fine art prints, illustrated books

Dates of photographs 1850 to 1940

Subjects India including topography, architecture and social history, mostly of the British in India; scenes of daily life, work, industry, streetscenes, private life, events, portraits of personalities, private and public figures, family groups, both Indians and British in India

Access and conditions Open to the public by appt (tel), Mon-Fri 9.30–5. All material available for editorial reproduction but not for advertising. B/w prints and duplicate colour transparencies available for a fee. Reproduction rights fees charged. Staff will undertake limited research only.

590 • JAPAN INFORMATION CENTRE

Photographic Library, Japanese Embassy, 9 Grosvenor Square, London W1X 9LB
Tel (01) 493 6030

Enquiries to Photographic Librarian

Items About 500: b/w original photographs, colour transparencies (35mm, 5″ × 4″), postcards, posters, illustrated books

Dates of subject matter AD 500 to present

Dates of photographs 1865 to present

Subjects Japan including personalities, politicians, the Imperial family, industry, technology, science, overseas aid, transport (aviation, shipping, railroads, roads, bridges), cities, agriculture, horticulture, sericulture, fishing industry, cultured pearls, animals, traditional music, dance, theatre, Ikebana, tea ceremony, architecture, gardens, landscapes, education, general life (homes, social welfare), state events, topical photographs from JIJI Press; some pre-war photographs

Access and conditions Open to the public by appt (tel), Mon-Fri 10–12.30, 2.30–5. All material available for editorial reproduction and for advertising with a few restrictions. B/w and colour material loaned free of charge for one month. No reproduction rights fees charged.

591 • THE DAVID KING COLLECTION

90 St Paul's Road, London N1 2QP
Tel (01) 226 0149

Enquiries to David King

Items 175,000: b/w original and copy photographs, colour transparencies (35mm, 2¼″, 5″ × 4″), colour photographic prints, lantern slides, postcards, original cartoons, illustrated maps, fine art prints,

art reproductions, posters, architectural drawings, press cuttings and tearsheets, illustrated books, ephemera, badges, caricatures, journals, magazines

Dates of subject matter *c*. 1900 to present

Dates of photographs *c*. 1900 to present

Subjects History of Russia and the Soviet Union from 1900 until the fall of Khrushchev; comprehensive documentation of the lives of Lenin, Trotsky and Stalin with accurate captions; the Tzars, Russo-Japanese War (1904), 1905 Revolution, 1905 caricature magazines, World War I, February and October Revolutions of 1917, Civil Wars and Wars of Intervention, famine of 1920, Bolshevik leaders, struggle for power in the 1920s, Stalinist leaders, Five-Year Plans, industrialization, collectivization, Stalin cult, Moscow trials, great purges, labour camps of the 1930s, religion, women, children, health, education, sport, international communist movement, Red Army, Great Patriotic War 1941-1945, de-Stalinization under Khrushchev in the 1950s; special collections on Soviet artists and designers including El Lissitsky, Alexander Rodchenko, Gustav Klutsis and others, agitprop and proletcult, Socialist Realism, sculpture and paintings, architecture, film, theatre, literature, music, posters, graphic design; special collections on China since 1949 and Mao Zedong, Eastern Europe since 1945, Marx and Engels, the Weimar Republic in Germany (including work by John Heartfield and George Grosz), the IWW (Industrial Workers of the World) (Wobblies) and American labour struggles (1890s to present); special collection on the Spanish Civil War

Access and conditions Open to qualified researchers by appt, Mon-Fri 10–6. All material available for editorial reproduction but not for advertising. B/w prints and duplicate colour transparencies available for a fee, but must be returned. Photocopies available. Reproduction rights fees charged. Staff will undertake research; negotiable fee for long projects.

592 • LUXEMBOURG EMBASSY

Information Section, 27 Wilton Crescent, London SW1X 8SD
Tel (01) 235 6961 Telex 28120 AMBLUX G

Enquiries to Information Section

Items About 50: b/w original photographs, posters

Dates of photographs 1960 to present

Subjects Luxembourg countryside, views, towns, castles, cities including the new EEC area, industry including steel, viticulture, synthetics, tyres; Luxembourg Royal Family and government ministers

Access and conditions Open to the public by appt (tel), Mon-Fri 10–12, 3–5. All material available for editorial reproduction and for advertising with the Embassy's approval. B/w material loaned free of charge for two weeks. No reproduction rights fees charged. Staff will undertake some research.

593 • NOVOSTI PRESS AGENCY

3 Rosary Gardens, London SW7 4NW
Tel (01) 373 8421

Enquiries to Photo Librarian

Items 250,000: b/w original and copy photographs, colour transparencies (35mm, 5″ × 4″), original cartoons, art reproductions, posters, illustrated books

Dates of subject matter BC to present

Dates of photographs 1860 to present

Subjects All aspects of life in USSR including landscapes, cities, towns, villages, agriculture, industry, historical monuments, architecture, science and technology, education, social services, armed forces, leisure, sport, art (including material from galleries such as the Hermitage and Tretyakov), music, theatre, ballet; lives, society and customs of nationalities within the Soviet Union from Siberia and the Soviet Far East to Central Asian Republics and European Russia; archive material includes coverage of pre-revolutionary Russia, Great October Revolution, the Civil War, Five-Year Plans and World War II

Access and conditions Open to qualified researchers by appt (tel). All material available for editorial reproduction and for advertising. B/w and colour material loaned free of charge for two months (print fees charged). Photocopies available. Reproduction rights, holding and service fees charged; service fees deductible from use fees. Staff will undertake research. All material copyright. Card catalogue in preparation.

594 • THE POLISH LIBRARY

Photographic Collection

Polish Social and Cultural Association,
238-246 King Street, London W6 0RF
Tel (01) 741 0474

Enquiries to Librarian

Items Over 40,000: b/w copy and original photographs, illustrated books, posters, postcards, original cartoons, colour photographic prints

Dates of subject matter Prehistory to present

Dates of photographs 1925 to present

Subjects Poland 1918–1938 including politics, economy, industry, education, architecture, landscapes, social history, literature, the arts, folklore; Polish royalty, politicians, personalities; Poland during World War II including the occupation, prisoners of war in Germany and the USSR, internees, refugees, Polish government in exile, Polish armed forces; Polish communities abroad in the USA, UK, Germany and Italy; Poland after 1945 including architecture, industry, political life, the arts, crafts

Access and conditions Open to qualified researchers by appt (write). Most material available for editorial reproduction; advertising use by special arrangement only. B/w material loaned free of charge for two weeks; material may be copied by outside photographers. Photocopies available. Reproduction rights and service fees charged. Staff will undertake limited research.

595 • SEYCHELLES TOURIST BOARD

PO Box 4PE, 50 Conduit Street, London W1A 4PE
Tel (01) 439 9699

Enquiries to Sue Rosser

Items 1000: colour transparencies (35mm, 5″ × 4″), b/w photographs

Dates of photographs 1975 to present

Subjects Seychelles scenery, beaches, people, buildings, transport, flora, fauna, hotels, watersports, sunsets

Access and conditions Open to qualified researchers by appt (tel), Mon-Fri 9.30–5.30. All material available for editorial reproduction and for advertising. B/w material loaned free of charge for one month; colour for three months. No reproduction rights fees charged.

596 • SOCIETY FOR CULTURAL RELATIONS WITH THE USSR

Elsie Timbey Collection

320 Brixton Road, London SW9 6AB
Tel (01) 274 2282

Enquiries to Roxane Permar or Beryl Graham, Librarians

Items 30,000: b/w original and copy photographs, colour transparencies (35mm), colour photographic prints, glass negatives, lantern slides, postcards, illustrated maps, old fine art prints, 20th-century fine art prints, art reproductions, posters, greetings cards, press cuttings, illustrated maps

Dates of subject matter Prehistory to present

Dates of photographs 1850 to present

Subjects Social, cultural and economic development of the USSR: medical and health care including industrial, maternity and paediatric care, institutes, hospitals, clinics, medical congresses, wartime conditions; architecture, historic buildings and monuments, contemporary architecture, urban housing, prefabricated housing, war damage; agriculture, crops, livestock including poultry, cultivation, irrigation, machinery, collective and state farming; light and heavy industry, fishing, forestry, food-processing, meat-packing, dairy, sugar, wine production, textiles, ceramics, rubber, car production, iron and steel, mining (iron ore, copper, coal, gold, diamonds), oil, gas, chemicals, hydroelectricity, atomic power; space research and flights, Soviet and international scientists, animals in space, cosmonauts; folk art from the 18th and 19th centuries, lace-work, embroidery, carvings, rugs, toys; fine art including paintings, frescoes and murals, icons, portraits, sculpture, industrial art, manuscripts, graphic art, engravings, posters, cartoons; museum collections including the Tretyakov Gallery, Hermitage, Russian Museum, Pushkin Museum, Shevchenko State Museum, Institute of the North and Byelorussian State Art Museum; music including concerts, composers and *conservatoires;* ballet (individual companies and dancers); theatre, costumes, set design, programmes, children's theatre, gypsy theatre, puppet theatre, individual productions from the 1940s onwards in Moscow and elsewhere; opera productions from the 1950s onwards; cinema stills; portraits of Russian and Soviet writers; folk dancers and choirs, musical instruments, ensembles from various Republics; geography including the Arctic regions; festivals, demonstrations, politicians, elections, congresses, co-operatives, international affairs, family life, festivals, weddings, holidays, leisure, furniture, transport, science, libraries, bookshops, military exercises, trade unions, religion; life during World War II including the armed forces, women in wartime, war with Japan, demobilization, reconstruction, anniversaries of liberation of Byelorussia and Ukraine

Access and conditions Open to the public by appt (write), Tues Wed Thurs 10–5. All material available for editorial reproduction and for advertising. B/w and colour material loaned free of charge for one month; b/w prints and duplicate colour transparencies available for a fee. Photocopies available. Reproduction rights fees charged. Staff of three will undertake some research; fees charged for large projects. All material copyright. Card catalogue available.

597 • SOUTH AFRICA TOURISM BOARD

Regency House, 1-4 Warwick Street, London W1R 5WB
Tel (01) 439 9661 ext 22 Telex 298946

Enquiries to Rose Tilly or Jock Webster

Items Over 5000: b/w original and copy photographs, colour transparencies (35mm, 120mm, 5″ × 4″), illustrated maps

Dates of subject matter 17th century to present

Dates of photographs 1974 to present

Subjects Tourist coverage of South Africa including landscapes, aerials, wildlife, towns, cities, transport, education, industry (including gold and diamond mines), crafts, ceremonies, sport, health spas, theatre, museums, historic buildings, monuments

Access and conditions Open to qualified researchers by appt (tel), Mon-Fri 9–5.30. All material available for editorial reproduction and for advertising. B/w and colour material loaned free of charge for two months. Photocopies available. No reproduction rights fees charged. Staff will undertake research. All material copyright.

598 • AVA VARGUS

12 Station Road, Hampton, Middlesex TW12 2BX
Tel (01) 941 5850

Enquiries to Ava Vargus

Items About 2000: colour transparencies (35mm), b/w original photographs, 20th-century fine art prints, unprinted film negatives

Dates of subject matter 16th century to present

Dates of photographs 1980 to present

Subjects Tarahumara people of the Sierra Madre in Chihuahua, northern Mexico: culture and lifestyle including housing, crafts, agriculture (corn-growing, cattle- and chicken-raising), costume, rituals, festivals; coverage of archaeological site at Casas Grandes

Access and conditions Open to qualified researchers by appt (tel), Mon-Fri 9–6. All material available for editorial reproduction by special arrangement only. B/w material loaned free of charge for two months; colour material loaned free of charge for one month. Reproduction rights fees charged. Some research undertaken; fees charged for large projects. All material copyright.

599 • WEIMAR ARCHIVE

8-9 The Incline, Coalport, Telford, Shropshire
TF8 7HR
Tel (0952) 580500

Enquiries to Simon Taylor, Director

Items About 1000: b/w original and copy photographs, colour transparencies (35mm), original cartoons, postcards, unprinted film negatives, leaflets, posters

Dates of subject matter 1800–1945

Dates of photographs 1860–1945

Subjects German history from 1800 covering political and social events, personalities, background conditions, art, cinema, theatre with special emphasis on the Weimar republic and working-class parties, trade unions, neo-Fascism and the rise of Hitler; collection of colour posters relating to political parties 1919–1933; documentary archive of Nazi propaganda and resistance movements

Access and conditions Open to qualified researchers by appt (write), Mon-Fri 9–5. All material available for editorial reproduction and for advertising by special arrangement only. B/w

material loaned free of charge for one month; colour material loaned free of charge for one week; b/w prints and duplicate colour transparencies available for a fee. Photocopies available. Reproduction rights, service and holding fees charged; service fees deductible from use fees. Staff of two will undertake some research; fees charged for large projects. Some material copyright.

600 • WIENER LIBRARY LTD

4 Devonshire Street, London W1N 2BH
Tel (01) 636 7247

Enquiries to Alexandra Wiessler, Researcher

Items About 2000: b/w original photographs, unprinted film negatives, illustrated books, b/w copy photographs, colour transparencies (35mm), postcards, original cartoons, press cuttings, cigarette cards, illustrated maps, art reproductions, posters, greetings cards

Dates of subject matter 1919 to present

Dates of photographs 1933 to present

Subjects Jewish life in Germany and other European countries since the Weimar Republic with the main emphasis on the rise of Fascism, the Third Reich and World War II including Jews as citizens, anti-Semitism, discrimination, persecution, migration, refugees, Jews in Nazi-occupied Europe, concentration camps, ghettos, synagogues, war and war crimes trials, memorials, Jews since 1945, fascism and racism in different countries

Access and conditions Open to qualified reseachers by appt (write), Mon-Fri 10–5. All material available for editorial reproduction and for advertising by special arrangement only. No loans; b/w prints and duplicate colour transparencies available for a fee; material may be copied by outside photographers. Photocopies available. Reproduction rights and service fees charged. Staff of four will undertake some research. The Wiener Library owns copyright to 30% of collection; in other cases copyright clearance is the responsibility of user. Card catalogue and duplicated catalogue available.

Military History

601 • ARMY MUSEUMS OGILBY TRUST

Connaught Barracks, Duke of Connaught's Road,
Aldershot, Hampshire GU11 2LR
Tel (0252) 24431 ext 2102

Enquiries to Major J. M. A. Tamplin T. D.

Items About 60,000: b/w original photographs,
b/w copy photographs, glass negatives, postcards,
colour photographic prints, colour transparencies
(35mm), fine art prints, greetings cards, press
cuttings and tearsheets, illustrated books

Dates of subject matter 1660 to present

Dates of photographs 1860 to present

Subjects The British Army including military
costume, dress, weapons, battlescenes,
personalities; British Army Auxiliary Forces;
British Empire, Commonwealth and foreign armies

Access and conditions Open to qualified
researchers by appt (write), Mon-Fri 9.30–4.30. All
material available for editorial reproduction but
not for advertising. No loans; b/w prints and
duplicate colour transparencies available for a fee.
Photocopies available. Reproduction rights and
service fees charged. Staff of three will undertake
some research. Compulsory credit line.

602 • THE AUCKLAND COLLECTION

60 High Street, Sandridge, Nr St Albans,
Hertfordshire AL4 9BZ
Tel (0727) (from London 56) 55128

Enquiries to Reg Auckland

Items 10,000: aerial (b/w and colour), propaganda
leaflets, postcards, posters

Dates of subject matter 1914 to present

Subjects Original leaflets, postcards, newspapers,
news-sheets, magazines (both miniature and
large), instructions, warnings, utility articles, etc.,
dropped in time of war, civil war, civil disturbance
and the like by aircraft, balloon, shell, rocket,
grenade, and V1; propaganda

Access and conditions Open to qualified
researchers by appt (write). All material available
for editorial reproduction and for advertising.
Colour and b/w material loaned by arrangement;
material may be copied by outside photographers.
Photocopies available. Reproduction rights fees
charged. Owner will undertake research for a fee.

603 • BLANDFORD PRESS LTD

Link House, West Street, Poole, Dorset BH15 1LU
Tel (0202) 671171   Telex 418304

Enquiries to Lynne Roberts, Chairman

Items About 3000: artwork, original cartoons

Dates of subject matter 1700 to 1945

Dates of artwork 1960 to present

Subjects World military history including
uniforms, badges and insignia, aircraft, ships,
tanks and other fighting vehicles, flags,
submarines; motor cars, costumes, trains

Access and conditions Not open: mail requests
only. All material available for editorial
reproduction and for advertising (with occasional
restrictions). Some film is available, otherwise b/w
prints and colour transparencies can be made for a
fee. Material loaned free of charge for one month.
Reproduction rights fees charged. Staff will
undertake limited research. All material copyright.

604 • THE BORDER REGIMENT AND KING'S OWN ROYAL BORDER REGIMENT MUSEUM

Queen Mary's Tower, The Castle, Carlisle,
Cumbria CA3 8UR
Tel (0228) 32774

Enquiries to Curator

Items About 1500: b/w original photographs,

colour transparencies (35mm), colour photographic prints, glass negatives, daguerreotypes, postcards, posters, prints, paintings

Dates of subject matter 18th century to present

Dates of photographs 1860 to present

Subjects Military history including soldiers on parade, on exercises, at home, abroad, at war, in groups, on recreation; military uniforms past and present (battle dress, full dress); tattoos (e.g. Leeds 1937–38, Aldershot 1924); miniature portraits of soldiers during the Napoleonic wars (1801 to 1830); soldiers going out to the north-west frontier of India; portraits of soldiers (1890s to World War I); Boer War (several albums); World War I, private album of photographs from Gallipoli; World War II, private album of photographs of Chindits in Burma, air drops, wounded, etc.; soldiers in Northern Ireland (south Armagh, Belfast), group photos (1980); museum collection: tinned rations, diaries, banners from the Boer War; relics from the Indian Mutiny including a baby's bonnet; beadwork, pin cushions and petit point made by soldiers posted to India (19th century); Chinese drum, war maps, other items from the Opium War; Russian prayer book, weapons and musical instruments from the Crimean War; silver cups, candelabra, medals and decorations from various campaigns, landscapes in the United Kingdom, Middle East, Europe, Africa

Access and conditions Open to qualified researchers by appt (write). All material available for editorial reproduction and for advertising. B/w and colour material loaned free of charge for one month. Photocopies available. Staff will undertake limited research. Donation expected in lieu of fees.

605 • THE GORDON HIGHLANDERS' MUSEUM

Regimental Headquarters, The Gordon Highlanders, Viewfield Road, Aberdeen AB1 7XH
Tel (0224) 38174

Enquiries to Regimental Secretary

Items 500: b/w original photographs, glass negatives, postcards, greetings cards, illustrated books

Dates of subject matter 1794 to present

Dates of photographs 1856 to present

Subjects The regimental life of the Gordon Highlanders from 1850 to the present

Access and conditions Open to the public by appt (tel), Wed & Sun 2–5 and by appt. All material available for editorial reproduction and for advertising with the Regiment's permission. No loans; b/w prints available for a fee. Reproduction rights fees charged. Staff will undertake limited research only. Catalogue available.

606 • ROBERT HUNT LIBRARY

22 Bedfordbury, London WC2N 4BT
Tel (01) 379 6711

Enquiries to Graham Mason

Items About 500,000: b/w copy and original photographs, colour transparencies (35mm, 5″ × 4″), colour photographic prints, postcards, art reproductions, unprinted film negatives, stereographs, posters, illustrated books

Dates of subject matter 1500 to 1980

Dates of photographs 1900 to 1980

Subjects Military history including 19th-century conflicts, World Wars I and II, Spanish Civil War, post-World War II colonial conflicts, Korean War, Middle East Wars, Vietnam War; 19th- and 20th-century social history; film stars, posed models

Access and conditions Open to qualified researchers by appt (tel), Mon-Fri 9.30–5.30. All material available for editorial reproduction and for advertising. B/w and colour material loaned free of charge for three months. Photocopies available. Reproduction rights, service and holding fees charged; service fees deductible from use fees. Staff will undertake some research. Copyright clearance responsibility of user.

607 • IMPERIAL WAR MUSEUM

Lambeth Road, London SE1 6HZ
Tel (01) 735 8922

Department of Photographs

Enquiries to Jane Carmichael, Keeper of Department of Photographs

Items About five million: b/w original and copy photographs, colour transparencies (35mm, 5″ × 4″), colour photographic prints, glass negatives, stereographs

Dates of photographs 1900 to present

Subjects All aspects of wars involving Britain and the Commonwealth countries from World War I onwards, but especially World Wars I and II; operations of the Army, Navy and Air Force, all aspects of civilian war effort; Commonwealth activities, especially Australia, New Zealand and Canada; some coverage of other allied and opponents' forces and civilian populations; history of military campaigns, especially the Western Front in World War I and the Middle East and northern Europe in World War II, as well as naval and aerial conflicts; technical aspects such as army equipment and the development of various types of aircraft and ships and their production; post-1945 material includes predominantly army material and covers the Korean War and emergencies in Malaya, Kenya, Cyprus, Northern Ireland and the Falklands; photographic collections of the following people have also been acquired: Field Marshal Sir Francis Festing, Field Marshal Sir Gerald Templer, Admiral Sir William Whitworth, Air Marshal Sir Victor Goddard, Wing Commander T. R. Cave-Brown-Cave, Major General D. Lloyd-Owen, Florence Farmborough; Colonel T. E. Lawrence's collection relating to his career in Egypt and Palestine in 1914–1918 was acquired in 1935 and has been supplemented by photographs taken by members of the Imperial Camel Corps who worked with Lawrence; collections include work by photographers James Jarché, Horace Nicholls, Sir Cecil Beaton and others

Access and conditions Open to the public by appt (tel), Mon-Fri 10-5. All material available for editorial reproduction and for advertising. Colour transparencies loaned for a rental fee; b/w prints available for a fee. Photocopies available. Reproduction rights fees charged. Staff of 23 will undertake some research in answer to specific requests.

Art, Medallion and Poster Collections

Department of Art

Enquiries to Angela Weight, Keeper of Department of Art

Items About 70,000: posters, fine art prints, postcards, colour transparencies (5″ × 4″), medallions, original cartoons

Dates of subject matter 1914 to present

Subjects Art collection: paintings, drawings and sculpture illustrating major theatres of war and the home front in World Wars I and II, some of Commonwealth armed forces; print collection: mostly World War I, majority French, some German and British work, including the BUTE COLLECTION of French patriotic and satirical prints; poster collection: examples from all belligerent nations in both World Wars, recruiting, charities, war loans, civilian effort

Access and conditions Open to the public by appt (tel); Art Reference Room Tues Wed Fri 10–4.30; Public Galleries Mon-Sat 10–5.50, Sun 2–5.50. Some material available for editorial reproduction and for advertising with the approval of the Keeper of Art. Colour transparencies loaned for a rental fee; b/w prints available for a fee. Reproduction rights fees charged.

608 • INSTITUTION OF ROYAL ENGINEERS

Royal Engineers Corps Library, Brompton Barracks, Chatham, Kent ME4 4UG
Tel (0634) 44555

Enquiries to Major J. T. Hancock, Librarian

Items About 50,000: b/w original photographs, glass negatives, architectural drawings, lantern slides, postcards, fine art prints

Dates of subject matter 1700 to present

Dates of photographs 1856 to present

Subjects Military engineering in both war and peace; units of the Corps of Royal Engineers, their work, equipment and activities; personalities, places, buildings, hobbies and life in the army both on and off duty; private albums showing places, people, architecture, etc., at the worldwide stations at which the Corps served or visited and including everything from trenches to castles, from peasants to royalty, from dart games to big-game shooting; photographic record of the North American Boundary Commission, the Abyssinian Campaign, the construction of the Kensington Science Museum (note: School of Military Engineering formed a photographic instruction department in 1856 and as a result the quality of the 19th-century photography is very high)

Access and conditions Open to the public by appt, Mon Wed Fri 9–12.30, 1.30–4.40, Tues & Thurs 9–12.30, 1.30–4. All material available for editorial reproduction and for advertising. No loans; library will photograph items and supply user with undeveloped film for a fee. Photocopies available. Reproduction rights fees charged. Staff will undertake limited research only.

609 • KING'S OWN SCOTTISH BORDERERS REGIMENT

The Barracks, Berwick on Tweed,
Northumberland TD15 1DQ
Tel (0289) 307426

Enquiries to Regimental Secretary

Items About 2000: b/w original and copy photographs, colour transparencies (35mm, 5″ × 4″, larger), colour photographic prints, glass negatives, daguerreotypes, postcards, original cartoons, illustrated maps, fine art prints, stereographs, posters, greetings cards, illustrated books

Dates of subject matter 1689 to present

Dates of photographs 1840 to present

Subjects Regimental history, watercolours, photo albums, uniforms, trophies

Access and conditions Open to the public by appt (write), Mon-Fri 9.30–5. All material available for editorial reproduction but not for advertising. No loans; b/w prints and duplicate colour transparencies available for a fee. Photocopies available. Reproduction rights and service fees charged. Staff will undertake some research.

610 • MAC CLANCY COLLECTION LIMITED

9 Duck Lane, London W1V 1FL
Tel (01) 439 6450

Enquiries to John Mac Clancy

Items About 20,000: b/w original and copy photographs, colour transparencies (35mm, 5″ × 4″)

Dates of subject matter 1640 to present

Dates of photographs Late 19th century to present

Subjects Military history including Napoleonic Wars, Crimean War, Boer War, Russo-Japanese and Sino-Japanese Wars, World War I, Russian Revolution, World War II and the Spanish Civil War; history of aviation, military and civil; contemporary NATO and Soviet armaments; 18th- and 19th-century social history; 17th-, 18th- and 19th-century flora and fauna

Access and conditions Open to the public by appt (first-time users write), Mon-Fri 10–6. All material available for editorial reproduction and for advertising (some restrictions). B/w and colour

material loaned free of charge for one month. Photocopies available. Reproduction rights and holding fees charged; service fees charged only when no material is used. Staff of three will undertake some research. Most material copyright.

611 • MILITARY ARCHIVE AND RESEARCH SERVICES

2 The New Buildings, Braceborough, Nr Stamford, Lincolnshire PE9 4NT
Tel (077836) 637

Enquiries to Diane Moore

Items About 40,000: b/w original and copy photographs, colour transparencies (35mm, 5″ × 4″), colour photographic prints, lantern slides

Dates of subject matter 1500 to present

Dates of photographs 1900 to present

Subjects Major wars and battles, military transport, missiles, weapons and equipment; special emphasis on modern and historic combat aircraft, armoured fighting vehicles and warships; civic aircraft, railways, submersibles, oil exploration and production; modern and historic motor vehicles and railways; portraits of personalities

Access and conditions Open to qualified researchers by appt (write), Mon-Fri 9–5. All material available for editorial reproduction and for advertising. B/w and colour material loaned free of charge for 12 weeks. Photocopies available for a fee. Reproduction rights, holding and service fees charged; service fees deductible from use fees. Staff of four will undertake research. Some material copyright.

612 • NATIONAL ARMY MUSEUM

Royal Hospital Road, London SW3 4HT
Tel (01) 730 0717 ext 24

Enquiries to Keeper of Records

Items 300,000: b/w original and copy photographs, colour transparencies (35mm, 5″ × 4″), glass negatives, daguerreotypes, lantern slides, postcards, original cartoons, illustrated maps, old fine art prints, 20th-century fine art prints, art reproduction, unprinted film negatives, stereographs, posters, greetings cards, architectural drawings, press cuttings, illustrated books, paintings, drawings, ephemera

Dates of subject matter 1485 to present

Dates of photographs 1845 to present

Subjects History of the British Army (mostly pre-1914), the Indian Army and Colonial Forces (to independence) including uniforms, weapons, medals and trophies

Access and conditions Open to holders of reader's ticket (available on application), Tues-Sat 10–4.30. Most material available for editorial reproduction and for advertising. B/w prints and duplicate colour transparencies available for a fee. Photocopies available. Most material copyright. Card catalogue available.

613 • PHOTOPRESS

1 Gifford Terrace Road, Hyde Park, Plymouth, Devon PL1 2JR
Tel (0752) 27699

Enquiries to David Reynolds, Director

Items Over 10,000: colour transparencies (35mm), colour photographic prints, b/w copy photographs, b/w original photographs

Dates of subject matter 1960 to present

Dates of photographs 1960 to present

Subjects British armed forces including the navy, army and airforce; coverage of Borneo, Aden, Northern Ireland and the Falklands; modern infantry weapons and armour, military exercises in Europe and Britain; ships and submarines, tanks and armoured vehicles, aircraft

Access and conditions Open to qualified researchers by appt (write), Mon-Fri 9–5. All material available for editorial reproduction and for advertising (some restrictions). B/w and colour material loaned free of charge for 28 days; material may be copied by outside photographers. Photocopies available. Reproduction rights, holding and service fees charged. Staff will undertake some research. All material copyright. Printed catalogue available.

614 • PLYMOUTH CENTRAL LIBRARY

Naval History Collection

Drake Circus, Plymouth, Devon PL4 8AL
Tel (0752) 264677

Enquiries to John R. Elliott, Area Librarian (West)

Items About 8000: b/w original and copy photographs, colour photographic prints

Dates of subject matter 16th century to present

Dates of photographs 1880s to present

Subjects Warships, especially those of the Royal Navy; personnel in uniform, some French and American ships, views of the Royal Dockyards from the River Tamar

Access and conditions Open to the public, Mon-Fri 9–9, Sat 9–4. Some material available for editorial reproduction and for advertising subject to copyright clearance. No loans; b/w prints and duplicate colour transparencies available for a fee. Photocopies available. Reproduction rights fees charged.

615 • ROYAL AIR FORCE MUSEUM

Aerodrome Road, London NW9 5LL
Tel (01) 205 2266

Enquiries to Reginald Mack, Senior Assistant, Photographic Section

Items Over 500,000: b/w original photographs, illustrated maps, illustrated books, b/w copy photographs, colour transparencies (35mm, $5'' \times 4''$), unprinted film negatives, glass negatives, architectural drawings, posters, colour photographic prints, old fine art prints, 20th-century fine art prints, lantern slides, postcards, original cartoons, cuttings

Dates of subject matter BC to present

Dates of photographs 1903 to present

Dates of fine art 18th-century to present

Subjects Aviation history and the continuing development of aircraft worldwide both military and civil with special emphasis on the history of the RAF covering not only aircraft but also airfields, personnel, weaponry, radar and radio equipment, air-sea rescue, armoured cars, lorries, ambulances, powered cranes, fire engines; categories of aircraft include airliners, helicopters, autogyros, trainers, transports, bombers, fighters, sea planes, gliders, airships, balloons; special collections include the CHARLES E. BROWN COLLECTION covering civil and military aircraft, Royal Naval vessels and society portraits of the 1920s and 1930s; also the archives of British Airways and its predecessors (Imperial Airways, BOAC and BEA) prior to 1973

Access and conditions Open to persons over 10 years of age by appt (tel), Mon-Fri 9–5. All material available for editorial reproduction and for advertising. No loans; b/w prints and duplicate colour transparencies available for a fee. Photocopies available for a fee. Reproduction rights fees charged (payable in advance by non-UK users). Staff of three will undertake some research. Compulsory credit line. The Royal Air Force Museums owns copyright to some 15% of the collection; in other cases copyright clearance is the responsibility of the user. Card catalogue in preparation.

616 • THE ROYAL HAMPSHIRE REGIMENT AND MEMORIAL GARDEN

Serle's House, Southgate Street, Winchester, Hampshire SO23 9EG
Tel (0962) 61781 ext 261

Enquiries to Curator

Items About 2000: glass negatives, lantern slides, postcards, original cartoons, illustrated maps, old fine art prints, 20th-century fine art prints, art reproductions, unprinted film negatives, posters, greetings cards, architectural drawings, illustrated books

Dates of subject matter *c.* 1864 to present

Dates of photographs *c.* 1860 to present

Subjects Worldwide coverage of battalions of the Regiment in both wartime and peacetime including uniforms, orders, decorations; competitive sport including hockey, football, cricket; individual portraits of officers and men

Access and conditions Open to the public by appt (write), Mon-Fri 10–4. All material available for editorial reproduction but not for advertising. No loans; material may be copied by outside photographers. No reproduction rights fees charged but donation to Museum requested. Staff will undertake limited research. Compulsory credit line. Most material copyright. Partial index available.

617 • ROYAL MARINES MUSEUM

Royal Marines Eastney, Southsea, Hampshire
PO4 9PX
Tel (0705) 822351 ext 6135 or 6186

Enquiries to Director

Items Over 60,000: b/w original photographs, colour transparencies (35mm, 5″ × 4″), b/w copy photographs, colour photographic prints, glass negatives, daguerreotypes, old fine art prints, posters, illustrated maps, original cartoons, architectural drawings, greetings cards, postcards

Dates of subject matter 1664 to present

Dates of photographs 1890 to present

Subjects Military and social history of the Royal Marines from their establishment in 1664 including uniforms, campaign medals, living conditions, Royal Marines band, ceremonial

Access and conditions Open to the public by appt (write), Mon-Fri 10–4.30, Sat and Sun 10–12.30. All material available for editorial reproduction and for advertising. No loans; material may be copied by outside photographers. Photocopies available. Reproduction rights fees charged. Staff of three will undertake limited research. Most material copyright.

618 • SARPEDON PRESS SERVICES

First Floor, 3 Lawson Road, Southsea, Hampshire
PO5 1SD
Tel (0705) 833470

Enquiries to Sarah Gregg

Items 5000: b/w original photographs, colour transparencies (35mm)

Dates of subject matter AD 67 to present

Dates of photographs 1900 to present

Subjects British Military activity in India and the Middle East between 1900 and 1930; SOLENT STRONGHOLD COLLECTION of fortifications and heritage sites including medieval defence structures, castles, historic ships; fishing fleet at Portsmouth

Access and conditions Open to qualified researchers by appt (write), Mon-Fri 9–5. All material available for editorial reproduction and for advertising. B/w and colour material loaned free of charge by arrangement (print fees charged). Photocopies available. Reproduction rights, holding and service fees charged. Staff of two will undertake research. All material copyright. Printed catalogue available.

619 • TANGMERE MILITARY AVIATION MUSEUM

Tangmere Airfield, PO Box 50, Chichester,
West Sussex PO20 6ER
Tel (0243) 775223

Enquiries to Andy Saunders, Curator

Items About 3000: b/w copy and original
photographs, postcards, illustrated maps

Dates of subject matter 1914 to present

Dates of photographs 1914 to present

Subjects History of RAF Tangmere from 1916;
air combat in World War II with special emphasis
on Battle of Britain 1940; portraits of RAF pilots;
crashed German aircraft from World War II;
general aviation history

Access and conditions Open to qualified
researchers by appt (write). Most material
available for editorial reproduction; advertising use
by special arrangement only. B/w prints available
for a fee. Photocopies available. Reproduction
rights and service fees charged; service fees
deductible from use fees. Staff will undertake some
research. Most material copyright.

620 • THE TANK MUSEUM

Bovington Camp, Wareham, Dorset BH20 6JG
Tel (0929) 462721 exts 463, 329

Enquiries to David Fletcher, Librarian

Items About 10,000: b/w original and copy
photographs, colour transparencies (35mm), glass
negatives, lantern slides, colour photographic
prints, postcards, posters

Dates of subject matter 1900 to present

Dates of photographs 1900 to present

Subjects Comprehensive collection of armoured
fighting vehicles both wheeled and tracked as types
and in action; collection concentrates on British
vehicles but material from many other countries is
included, mainly Germany, France, Italy, Japan,
USA and USSR; associated vehicles including cars,
lorries, motorcycles, tractors, landrovers, jeeps;
collection of photographs of British troops in India
between World Wars I and II

Access and conditions Open to the public by
appt (tel), Mon-Fri 10–5. All material available for
editorial reproduction and for advertising (some
restrictions on contemporary material). No loans;
b/w prints and duplicate colour transparencies
available for a fee; material may be copied by
outside photographers. Photocopies available.
Reproduction rights and service fees charged. Staff
of two will undertake limited research; fees
charged for large projects.

621 • C & S TAYLOR

3 North Avenue, Eastbourne, East Sussex
BN20 8NB

Enquiries to Clive Taylor

Items 15,000: b/w original photographs

Dates of subject matter 1970 to present

Dates of photographs 1970 to present

Subjects British and British-built warships from
1970, both surface and aerial coverage; some detail
of weapons and fittings

Access and conditions Open to the public by
appt (write). All material available for editorial
reproduction and for advertising. B/w material
loaned free of charge by arrangement. Photocopies
available. Reproduction rights fees charged.
Research undertaken. Photographer available for
assignment. All material copyright.

622 • US NAVY PUBLIC AFFAIRS OFFICE

PO Box 13, 7 North Audley Street, London
W1Y 1WJ
Tel (01) 409 4414

Enquiries to Richard Fox, Petty Officer 1st Class

Items 350: b/w photographs, colour
transparencies (35mm)

Dates of photographs Current

Subjects US Navy ships (Atlantic Command) and
US Navy aircraft

Access and conditions Not open; mail requests
only. All material available for editorial
reproduction but not for advertising. B/w and
colour material available free of charge. No
reproduction rights fees charged. Staff will
undertake limited research.

Natural History, Anthropology & Archaeology

623 • ANCIENT ART AND ARCHITECTURE COLLECTION

RONALD SHERIDAN'S PHOTO LIBRARY

6 Kenton Road, Harrow-on-the-Hill, Middlesex
HA1 2BL
Tel (01) 422 1214 Telex 268048

Enquiries to Ronald Sheridan

Items 150,000: colour transparencies (35mm, 7 × 6 cm, 2¼", 5" × 4"), b/w original photographs, b/w copy photographs

Dates of subject matter 25,000 BC to 19th century AD

Dates of photographs Modern

Subjects Worldwide coverage of historical, ancient and prehistoric subjects, human civilizations, arts, archaeology, history, religions and beliefs, architecture; emphasis on classical civilizations of the Mediterranean and Middle East including Mesopotamia, Babylon, Phoenicia, Egypt, the Holy Land, Greece, Rome, Persia, countries of Islam; British and European art and history; India, Far East, Pre-Columbian North and South America, Viking and Celtic cultures

Access and conditions Open to qualified researchers by appt (tel), Mon-Fri 9–5. All material available for editorial reproduction and for advertising. B/w material loaned free of charge for two months; colour loaned free of charge for one month. Photocopies available. Reproduction rights and holding fees charged; service fees charged only when no material is used. Staff of four will undertake research. All material copyright. Computer-printed catalogue available.

HEATHER ANGEL *see* BIOFOTOS

624 • ANIMAL PHOTOGRAPHY LTD

4 Marylebone Mews, New Cavendish Street,
London W1M 7LF
Tel (01) 935 0503

Enquiries to Sally Anne Thompson

Items 50,000: colour transparencies (35mm, 2¼"), b/w original photographs, stereographs

Dates of photographs 1956 to present

Subjects Animals (domestic, farmyard and wild) including horses (most breeds and usually photographed in country of origin, activities, dressage, showjumping, eventing, grooming, etc.), dogs (most breeds and activities connected with dogs), cats (better-known breeds and common cats in action), East African wild animals, animals and birds of the Galapagos Islands, British sheep (most varieties), small animals (rats, mice, gerbils, hamsters, guinea pigs)

Access and conditions Open to qualified researchers by appt (tel), Mon-Fri 9–5.30. All material available for editorial reproduction and for advertising. B/w and colour material loaned free of charge for one month. Reproduction rights fees charged; service and holding fees occasionally charged. Staff will undertake some research. Photographers available for assignment. All material copyright.

625 • ANIMALS UNLIMITED

25 Hollies Road, London W5 4UU
Tel (01) 568 4960

Enquiries to Paddy Cutts

Items 40,000: colour transparencies (35mm, 7 × 6cm), b/w original photographs, colour photographic prints

Dates of photographs 1975 to present

Subjects Domestic, farm and zoo animals including cats, dogs, horses, birds, mice, rats, gerbils, hamsters, guinea pigs; special collection of rare English farm animals, especially those protected and preserved by the Rare Breeds Trust; entertainment including live rock concerts, theatre, ballet, musicals, etc.

Access and conditions Open to the public by appt (tel), Mon-Fri 9.30–5.30. All material available for editorial reproduction and for advertising. B/w and colour material loaned free of charge for one month. Reproduction rights, holding and service fees charged; service fees deductible from use fees. Staff will undertake research.

626 • AQUILA PHOTOGRAPHICS

PO Box 1, Studley, Warwickshire B80 7JG
Tel (052785) 2357

Enquiries to Alan Richards

Items 50,000: colour transparencies (35mm, 5″ × 4″), b/w original photographs

Dates of photographs 1974 to present

Subjects Natural history (worldwide coverage) including liverworts, lichens, mosses, flowers, trees, insects, butterflies, amphibians, reptiles, birds and mammals; ecology, environmental subjects, geography, agriculture. Birds are a special subject; professional ornithological expertise is provided as required.

Access and conditions Open to qualified researchers by appt, Mon-Fri 9–5. All material available for editorial reproduction and for advertising. B/w and colour material loaned free of charge for one month. Reproduction rights, service and holding fees charged; service fees deductible from use fees. Staff of three will undertake research in the collection and send consignments to users.

627 • ARDEA LONDON LTD

35 Brodrick Road, London SW17 7DX
Tel (01) 672 2067, 672 8787
Telex 896691 TLXIRG (prefix ARDEA)

Enquiries to Su Gooders

Items Over 150,000: colour transparencies (35mm, 5″ × 4″), b/w original photographs, fine art prints

Dates of photographs 1970 to present

Subjects Natural history including worldwide coverage of insects, birds, fish, amphibians, reptiles, mammals and plants usually in natural habitat and also domestic animals; geography including deserts, tropical rain forests, polar regions, geology, conservation, ecology, pollution, evolution, forestry, oceans and seas, underwater photos, weather; agriculture including farming, rural life, canals, cheesemaking; archaeology and anthropology including primitive cultures, Aborigines; scenic and geographic coverage of the following countries: Afghanistan, Africa (Botswana, Egypt, Ethiopia, Kenya, Madagascar, South Africa), North and South America, Antarctica, Atlantic Islands, Argentina, Australia, Bangladesh, Canada, China, France, Greece (including Crete and Corfu), Iceland, India, Italy, Mediterranean islands (including Corsica, Cyprus and Majorca), Nepal, Norway, Papua New Guinea, Saudi Arabia, Spain, Sri Lanka, Turkey, UK; small archive of British historical prints (18th and 19th century) illustrating the South Sea Bubble, fashion, railways, political cartoons, social history, animals, birds and plants

Access and conditions Open to qualified researchers by appt (tel). All material available for editorial reproduction and for advertising. B/w and colour material loaned free of charge for four weeks. Reproduction rights, service and holding fees charged. Staff of four will undertake research.

628 • ROBERT ARNOLD

5 Dunhallin, Waternish, Dunvegan, Isle of Skye IV55 8GH
Tel (047083) 270

Enquiries to Robert Arnold

Items 2000: Colour transparencies (35mm)

Dates of photographs 1979 to present

Subjects Marine animals of the Hebrides, mainly invertebrates; underwater photography

Access and conditions Open to qualified researchers by appt. All material available for editorial reproduction and for advertising. Colour transparencies loaned free of charge for one month. Reproduction rights, service and holding fees charged. Staff will undertake some research. All material copyright. Additional material with Seaphot (q.v.).

629 • A-Z BOTANICAL COLLECTION LTD

Holmwood House, Mid Holmwood, Dorking, Surrey
RH5 4HE
Tel (0306) 888130

Enquiries to Mark MacAndrew

Items About 86,000: colour transparencies (2¼",
35mm, 5" × 4"), b/w original and copy photographs

Dates of photographs 1966 to present

Subjects Agriculture including ploughing,
harvesting, spraying, crops, herbs, fruit and
vegetables, heath fires; horticulture including sets
on propagation, pruning, potting, planting out,
Spalding, Kew and Wisley Gardens; gardens and
garden features including town, country, cottage,
rock, formal and miniature gardens, statues, steps,
seats, pergola, stately homes; flowers including
flower heads and whole plants, beds and borders,
tubs, urns, window boxes, hothouse and pot-grown
plants; wild flowers and weeds including single
plants, close-ups and long shots, scenics, fields of
poppies, seed dispersal; grasses including growing
plants and studio close-ups; flower arrangements
both simple vases and elaborate compositions;
house plants including ferns, desert plants, tropical
plants, bonsai, cacti, displays, home and
greenhouse settings; shrubs including close-ups of
flowers, foliage, berries, whole subject, scenic
borders, hedges; trees including sets of fruit,
flower, foliage, seed, bole and bark, whole subject,
timber, woods, forest, arboreta, tree damage,
annular rings; fungi, mushrooms, algae, lichens;
pests and diseases including aphids, galls, leaf
miners, Dutch Elm disease, black spot, mildew;
mood pictures

Access and conditions Open to qualified
researchers by appt. All material available for
editorial reproduction and for advertising, but not
for slide shows or lectures (except commercial a/v).
B/w and colour material loaned free of charge for
one month. Reproduction rights, service and
holding fees charged; service fees deductible from
use fees. Staff of three will undertake research. All
material copyright.

630 • B & B PHOTOGRAPHS

Dodds, Clifford Chambers, Stratford-upon-Avon,
Warwickshire CV37 8HX
Tel (0789) 204636

Enquiries to Dr Stefan T. Buczacki

Items 25,000: colour transparencies (35mm), b/w
original and copy photographs, unprinted film
negatives, illustrated books

Dates of photographs 1960 to present

Subjects Horticulture and gardening, especially
the pests, diseases and disorders of plants;
biogeography and crops of Japan, Korea, Malawi,
Southern Africa, Florida, California, Seychelles,
the Mediterranean lands; natural history,
especially British plant life; biological education
(e.g. micrographs, anatomy, skeletons, plant
physiology); British habitats

Access and conditions Not open; telephone
requests only. All material available for editorial
reproduction and for advertising. B/w and colour
material loaned free of charge for one month.
Photocopies available. Reproduction rights and
holding fees charged. Staff will undertake some
research. All material copyright.

631 • BECKETT PICTURE AGENCY

Bramley Cottage, Stanhoe, King's Lynn, Norfolk
PE31 8QF
Tel (04858) 225

Enquiries to Gillian Beckett

Items About 26,000: colour transparencies
(35mm)

Dates of photographs 1959 to present

Subjects Horticulture including individual
garden plants, flowers, fruit and foliage, whole
plants and details, garden features, historic and
famous gardens, gardening techniques, pests and
diseases; landscape and topography including
features of geographical and historical interest,
glacial features, prehistoric sites, past land uses,
planned landscapes, building materials, rural
buildings, cottages, barns, windmills, etc., with
emphasis on East Anglian examples; natural
history including natural habitats, woodland,
grassland, fens, coasts, plants and flowers in
habitats and in detail, some insects (no birds or
mammals); geography and natural history of Great
Britain and some material from Europe, Turkey,
New Zealand, Chile, Japan, USA, Atlantic and
Pacific Islands

Access and conditions Open to qualified
researchers by appt. All material available for
editorial reproduction and for advertising. Colour

material loaned free of charge for four months. Reproduction rights fees charged. Staff will undertake research. Card catalogue.

632 • BIOFOTOS

Highways, 6 Vicarage Hill, Farnham, Surrey GU9 8HJ
Tel (0252) 716700 Telex 858623 TELBUR G REF BIOFOTOS

Enquiries to Heather Angel

Items 255,000: colour transparencies (35mm, 6 × 6cm), b/w original photographs

Dates of photographs 1970 to present

Subjects World wildlife, natural history, landscape, underwater photography, geography, geology, gardens and gardening; abstracts, African animals, amphibians, animal behaviour, aquatic life, arid regions, atmospheric photographs, birds, camouflage, carnivorous plants, cliffs, close-ups, coastlines, conservation, coral reefs, courtship, deserts, designs in nature, ecology, environment, ferns, field clues, fieldwork, fish, flowers, forests, fossils, freshwater habitats, freshwater life, fungi, glaciation, grasses, habitats, insects, invertebrates, leaves, lichens, liverworts, mammals, marine habitats, marine life, marsupials, molluscs, mosses, natural phenomena, orchids, patterns, pests, photographic techniques, photomicrographs, pollution, pond life, ponds, reptiles, rivers, rocks, sea, seashore, seashore life, seaweeds, shells, spiders, sunrise, sunset, textures, topography, tracks and signs, trees, tropical fish, tropical rain forest, urban wildlife, vulcanism, warning coloration, water, weather, wetlands, wild flowers, wildlife, woodlands; and in the following regions: Africa, Antarctica, Arizona, Australia, Britain, California, East Africa, Galapagos, Hawaii, Kashmir, Madagascar, New Zealand, South Africa, Seychelles, South America, Sri Lanka, China, Iceland

Access and conditions Open to qualified researchers by appt, Mon-Fri 9–5.30. All material available for editorial reproduction and for advertising. B/w and colour material loaned free of charge for one month. Photocopies available. Reproduction rights and holding fees charged; service fees charged only when no material is used. Staff of six will undertake research. Subject catalogue available.

633 • BIOPHOTO ASSOCIATES

The Cottage, Rigton Hill, North Rigton, Leeds, West Yorkshire LS17 0DJ
Tel (0532) 431751 ext 6573, evenings and weekends (0423) 74348

Enquiries to Gordon F. Leedale

Items Over 25,000: colour transparencies (35mm, 5″ × 4″, larger), b/w original photographs, colour photographic prints

Dates of photographs 1970 to present

Subjects Biology and medicine, especially microscopy, light microscopy of small organisms, parts of larger organisms, plant anatomy, animal histology, plant and animal organs, tissues and cells; scanning electron microscopy of whole plants and animals, parts of organisms in close-up, surface details; transmission electron microscopy of shadowed and sectioned material for highly-magnified details of plant and animal organs, cells, organelles and inclusions; human biology, anatomy, morphology, diseases, operations, disease symptoms, X-rays, hospitals, scientific instruments, microscopes, etc.; natural history including portraits of viruses, bacteria, algae, fungi, protozoa and all plant and animal groups including lichens, mosses, liverworts, lycopods, horsetails, ferns, cycads, conifers, flowering plants, sponges, coelenterates, mesozoans, worms, molluscs, crustaceans, insects, spiders, echinoderms, fishes, amphibians, reptiles, birds and mammals including man; biological topics including gardening, horticulture, farming, agriculture, industry, biotechnology, laboratories, ecology, habitats, populations, geographic regions, geology, rocks, crystals, minerals, fossils

Access and conditions Open to qualified researchers by appt (tel). All material available for editorial reproduction and for advertising. B/w and colour material loaned free of charge for one month. Reproduction rights, service and holding fees charged. Staff will undertake research. All material copyright.

634 • SDEUARD C. BISSERÔT

40 Nugent Road, Bournemouth, Dorset BH6 4ET
Tel (0202) 425028

Enquiries to Sdeuard C. Bisserôt

Items 15,000: colour transparencies (2¼″, 35mm), b/w original photographs, glass negatives

Dates of photographs 1945 to present

Subjects Natural history including amphibians, reptiles, bats (special subject), birds, domestic animals, fish (salt and freshwater), wild flowers, fruits and seeds, fungi, people, galls, mammals, spiders, trees, snails and slugs, marine life, habitats, pollution, weather; landscapes and scenics from Borneo, Canary Islands, Ecuador, Morocco, Norway, Seychelles, Singapore, Spain, Portugal, Yugoslavia, United Kingdom

Access and conditions Open to the public by appt, Mon-Fri 9–6. All material available for editorial reproduction and for advertising. B/w and colour material loaned free of charge for 90 days. Reproduction rights and holding fees charged. Staff will undertake research. Photographer available for assignment. All material copyright.

635 • JANET & COLIN BORD PHOTOGRAPH LIBRARY

Melangell House, Princes Street, Montgomery, Powys SY15 6PY
Tel (068681) 405

Enquiries to Janet Bord

Items 50,000: b/w original photographs, colour transparencies (35mm, 6 × 6cm)

Dates of subject matter 4000 BC to present

Dates of photographs 1970 to present

Subjects Archaeology and antiquities of the United Kingdom and Eire, especially prehistoric sites, Roman sites, crosses, carvings, churches; rural Britain especially villages, landscape, farms, nature; Wales, especially history, buildings, landscape, folklore and customs

Access and conditions Open to qualified researchers by appt. All material available for editorial reproduction and for advertising. B/w and colour material loaned free of charge for three months. Reproduction rights fees charged. Staff will undertake research. All material copyright. Card catalogue.

636 • BOTANICAL PICTURES

15 Rutland Street, London SW7 1EJ
Tel (01) 589 7890

Enquiries to Linda Burgess

Items About 10,000: colour transparencies (35mm)

Dates of photographs 1980 to present

Subjects Gardens and gardening including cottage gardens, window gardens, town gardens, container gardens, herb gardens, famous gardens, conservatories, vegetables, extensive collection of UK cultivated plants filed alphabetically

Access and conditions Open to qualified researchers by appt, Mon-Fri 9.30–5.30. All material available for editorial reproduction and for advertising. Colour material loaned free of charge for two weeks. Reproduction rights, service and holding fees charged. Staff will undertake research. All material copyright.

637 • PAT BRINDLEY

11 Victoria Terrace, Cheltenham, Gloucestershire GL52 6BN
Tel (0242) 33927

Enquiries to Pat Brindley

Items 51,000: colour transparencies (2¼″), unprinted film negatives

Dates of photographs 1960 to present

Subjects Horticulture including garden flowers, alpines, heaths and heathers, shrubs and trees; gardens and garden scenes, greenhouses and conservatories, propagation, practical gardening; house plants in house settings and portraits including cacti and succulents; vegetables and vegetable gardens, displays of vegetables; garden fruits and soft fruits

Access and conditions Open to qualified researchers by appt (tel). All material available for editorial reproduction and for advertising. B/w and colour material loaned free of charge for three months. Reproduction rights, service and holding fees charged. Staff will undertake research. All material copyright.

638 • BRITISH MUSEUM (NATURAL HISTORY)

Cromwell Road, London SW7 5BD
Tel (01) 589 6323

General Library

Enquiries to Susan Goodman, ext 382

Items 8000: b/w original and copy photographs, architectural drawings, postcards, colour transparencies (35mm, 5″ × 4″), glass negatives, lantern slides, colour photographic prints, drawings and water colours

Dates of subject matter 16th century to present

Dates of photographs 1850 to present

Subjects Natural history, topography, expeditions, portraits of naturalists; British Museum (Natural History) building, galleries and exhibitions, staff, specimens

Botany Library

Enquiries to Judith Diment, ext 421

Items About 370,000: fine art prints, original drawings, watercolours, illustrated books, colour transparencies (35mm, 5″ × 4″), b/w original photographs, glass negatives, postcards, posters, lantern slides, greetings cards

Dates of subject matter 16th century to present

Dates of photographs 1850 to present

Subjects Botany including the J. REEVES COLLECTION (19th century) of Chinese plants, a 19th-century collection of Indian plants by native artists, an 18th-century collection of Australian and Pacific plants from Captain Cook's voyages, the G. D. EHRET COLLECTION (18th century), the F. BAUER COLLECTION (19th century) THE F. H. ROUND COLLECTION, the A. H. CHURCH COLLECTION, the C. DALBY COLLECTION, the M. STONES COLLECTION, the K. WEST COLLECTION (all 20th century)

Entomology Library

Enquiries to Pamela Gilbert, ext 306

Items 3000: b/w original and copy photographs, colour transparencies (35mm), original drawings, glass negatives, lantern slides, illustrated books

Dates of subject matter 16th century to present

Dates of photographs 1850 to present

Subjects Insects, especially butterflies and moths, portraits of entomologists; PAGDEN COLLECTION: nests of bees and wasps; P. CRAMER COLLECTION; H. C. DOLLMAN COLLECTION; A. J. E. TERZI COLLECTION

Mineral Library

Enquiries to Eileen Brunton, ext 530

Items About 4400: colour transparencies (35mm, 5″ × 4″), b/w original and copy photographs, glass negatives, lantern slides, original drawings, postcards, colour photographic prints

Dates of subject matter 16th century to present

Dates of photographs 1850 to present

Subjects Minerals, rocks, gems; *Challenger* Expedition (19th century); portraits of mineralogists

Palaeontology Library

Enquiries to Ann Lum, ext 207

Items About 11,000: drawings, lantern slides, b/w original photographs, illustrated books, colour transparencies (35mm, 5″ × 4″), colour photographic prints, posters, architectural drawings

Dates of subject matter 16th century to present

Dates of photographs 1850 to present

Subjects Geology, stratigraphy, tectonics, palaeontology, anthropology, fossils, dinosaurs, geological expeditions, portraits of geologists, M. WILSON COLLECTION, N. PARKER COLLECTION

Zoology Library

Enquiries to Ann Datta, ext 272

Items 208,000: drawings and watercolours, b/w original photographs, colour transparencies (35mm, 5″ × 4″), lantern slides, posters, illustrated books

Dates of subject matter 16th century to present

Dates of photographs 1850 to present

Subjects Zoology, animals (except insects and birds), behaviour of animals, physiology of animals; CAPTAIN COOK COLLECTION: Australian and Pacific animals (18th and 19th centuries); F. C. SELONS COLLECTION: South African animals (lantern slides)

Access and conditions Open to qualified researchers by appt (tel), Mon-Fri 10–4.30. Most material available for editorial reproduction and for advertising. No loans; b/w prints and duplicate colour transparencies available for a fee. Photocopies available. Reproduction rights fees charged. Staff will undertake very limited research. Some material out of copyright; in other cases copyright clearance is responsibility of user. Partial card catalogue available.

Zoological Museum

Tring Library, Akeman Street, Tring,
Hertfordshire HP23 6AP
Tel (044) 282 4181

Enquiries to Anne Vale

Items 65,000: illustrated books, b/w original
photographs, original drawings and watercolours,
lantern slides, glass negatives, colour photographic
prints, colour transparencies (35mm, 5″ × 4″),
postcards

Subjects Ornithology including birds, behaviour
of birds, habitat of birds, portraits of ornithologists,
Tring Museum

Access and conditions Open to qualified
researchers by appt (tel), Mon-Fri 10–1, 2–4.30.
Most material available for editorial reproduction
and for advertising. No loans; b/w prints and
duplicate colour transparencies available.
Photocopies available. Reproduction rights fees
charged. Staff will undertake very limited
research. Some material out of copyright; in other
cases copyright clearance is responsibility of user.
Partial card catalogue available.

639 • KEVIN CARLSON

Path Cottage, Hickling, Norwich, Norfolk
NR12 0YJ
Tel (069261) 360

Enquiries to Dr Kevin Carlson

Items 10,000: colour transparencies (35mm), b/w
original photographs, glass negatives

Dates of photographs 1947 to present

Subjects Natural history including insects,
amphibians and reptiles (Europe, birds in natural
habitats (Europe), Africa, South America, Canada,
Australia) and mammals (mainly African); flowers,
trees, etc. (mainly European but some from
countries as listed above); landscapes, habitats,
miscellaneous wild life (e.g. tracks and signs)

Access and conditions Open to qualified
researchers by appt (tel), Mon-Fri 9.30–5.30. All
material available for editorial reproduction and
for advertising. B/w prints available for a fee.
Colour material loaned free of charge for three
months. Reproduction rights and holding fees
charged. Staff will undertake research.

640 • BRUCE COLEMAN LTD

17 Windsor Street, Uxbridge, Middlesex UB8 1AB
Tel (0895) 57094 Telex 429093

Enquiries to Jill Geary, Librarian

Items 400,000: colour transparencies (35mm,
6 × 6cm, 5″ × 4″)

Dates of photographs 1960 to present

Subjects Natural history, invertebrates, insects,
fish, amphibians, reptiles, mammals, exceptional
and comprehensive ornithology collection
especially penguins and caged birds, special
collection of domestic animals (cats, dogs, horses),
polar and desert wildlife, wildlife of North America
and especially National Parks, collection of animal
camouflage, especially insects; wildlife research
(tracking, whales), animal exploitation (hunting,
trapping); WORLD WILDLIFE FUND INTERNATIONAL
COLLECTION; horticulture, especially roses, orchids,
edible and inedible fungi; agriculture; world
geography including Africa, South America and
South-east Asia, ecology, environment,
conservation, landscapes, meteorology, geology
(fossils, caves, volcanoes); special collections on
Thailand and Greece; NASA photos

Access and conditions Open to qualified
researchers by appt (tel), Mon-Fri 9–5. All material
available for editorial reproduction and for
advertising. Colour material loaned free of charge
for one month. Reproduction rights and holding
fees charged; service fees charged only when no
material is used. Staff of 10 will undertake
research.

641 • ROBERT J. CORBIN

107 Kenilworth Avenue, London SW19 7LP
Tel (01) 946 7546

Enquiries to Robert J. Corbin

Items 45,000: b/w original photographs, colour
transparencies (2¼″)

Dates of photographs 1964 to present

Subjects Horticulture including portraits of
flowers, vegetables, trees, shrubs, lawn weeds,
vines and fruiting plants, greenhouse culture,
small domestic gardens including window boxes
and tubs, pests and diseases (England); practical
strip series showing 'how to' and including
budding, grafting, pruning, soil cultivation, sowing,
lawn care, fertilizing, garden maintenance, garden
machinery; London parks, National Trust Property

ACE PHOTO AGENCY

01-629 0303

22 MADDOX STREET, LONDON W1R 9PG   TELEX: 266801 MEXCO G

BRITAIN ON VIEW
Photographic Library

THAMES TOWER BLACK'S ROAD HAMMERSMITH LONDON W6 9EL

Britain On View Photographic Library houses the most comprehensive pictorial record of the traveller's Britain.

It contains more than 200,000 original colour transparencies and a similar number of black and white photographs covering England, Scotland, Wales and Northern Ireland. Coast and countryside, towns and villages, historic buildings and famous landmarks are all depicted.

There is extensive coverage of London, pageantry and specialised subjects such as theatre, pubs, restaurants, sports and pastimes festivals, old customs, shopping and characters from many walks of life.

The photographic library is open between 11am and 4pm (by appointment).

For further information regarding reproduction fees etc contact Jill Moore, Chief Photographic Librarian.

Telephone number 01-846 9000.

BTA Official Photographic Library ETB

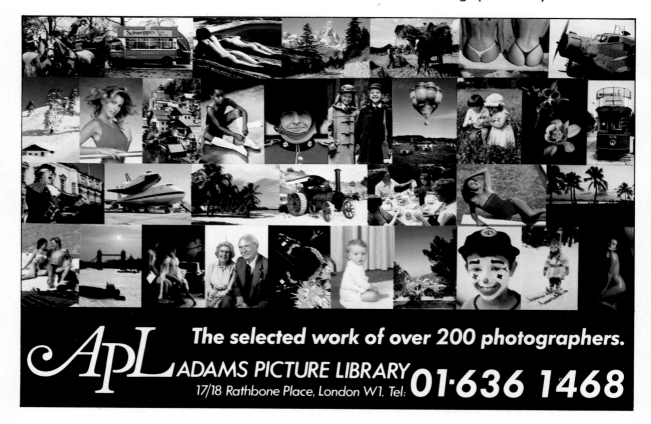

gardens (Kew Gardens, Hampton Court, Sissinghurst, Blickling Hall, Wisley, etc.); parks in Australia, Canada, New Zealand; horticulture in South China, Versailles gardens, Keukenhof (Holland), gardens of Emperor's Palace, Tokyo

Access and conditions Open to qualified researchers by appt (tel), Mon-Fri 9–5. All material available for editorial reproduction and for advertising. B/w and colour material loaned free of charge for one month. Reproduction rights, service and holding fees charged. Staff will undertake some research. All material copyright.

642 • HORACE DOBBS UNDERWATER PHOTOGRAPHIC SERVICES

Dolphin Parklands, North Ferriby, Humberside HU14 3ET
Tel (0482) 632650

Enquiries to Dr Horace Dobbs

Items 5000: colour transparencies (35mm), b/w original photographs

Dates of subject matter 1500 BC to present

Dates of photographs 1950 to present

Subjects Bottle-nosed dolphins, killer whales; underwater photography in the Philippines, the Red Sea, the Galapagos Islands, the Indian Ocean, and in British waters; natural history of the Galapagos Islands

Access and conditions Open to qualified researchers by appt (write). All material available for editorial reproduction and for advertising. B/w and colour material loaned free of charge for one month. Reproduction rights and service fees charged; service fee deductible from use fee. Staff will undertake some research. All material copyright.

643 • VALERIE FINNIS

The Dower House, Boughton House, Kettering, Northamptonshire NN14 1BJ
Tel (0536) 82279

Enquiries to Valerie Finnis

Items 50,000: b/w original and copy photographs, colour transparencies (2¼″), lantern slides

Dates of photographs 1965 to present

Subjects Gardens in England, Scotland and Ireland, flowers and plants of all descriptions, fruit and vegetables, floral arrangements

Access and conditions Open to qualified researchers by appt (write). All material available for editorial reproduction and for advertising. Colour material loaned free of charge for one month. Reproduction rights, service and holding fees charged; service fees deductible from use fees. Staff will undertake some research.

644 • FLORACOLOUR

21 Oakleigh Road, Hillingdon, Uxbridge, Middlesex UB10 9EL
Tel (0895) 51831

Enquiries to H. C. W. Shaw

Items 15,000: colour transparencies (35mm)

Dates of subject matter Prehistory to present

Dates of photographs 1960 to present

Subjects Gardens in England, Europe, Canada, Madeira; flowers and flower shows (specialist and general); stately homes; travel in Russia, Austria, Venice, Italy, Sicily, French Riviera, Madeira, Crete; transport museums, zoos, planes, flower arrangements, miniature railways, period costumes, model villages, Portmeirion, church interiors, river trip to Greenwich

Access and conditions Open to the public by appt (write) three days a week. All material available for editorial reproduction and for advertising. No loans; duplicate colour transparencies available for a fee. Reproduction rights fees charged. Staff will undertake some research. Printed catalogue.

645 • RON AND CHRISTINE FOORD COLOUR PICTURE LIBRARY

155B City Way, Rochester, Kent ME1 2BE
Tel (0634) 47348

Enquiries to Ron or Christine Foord

Items 35,000: colour transparencies (35mm)

Dates of photographs 1960 to present

Subjects Natural history especially plants and insects; British wildflowers (over 1000 species) including close-ups, whole plant and habitat shots,

European wildflowers especially wild orchids and alpine flowers, garden plants including flower close-ups and whole plant, shrubs, trees, hedges and topiary, algae, mosses, lichen, fungi; cacti and succulents (greenhouse grown) in flower, seeding, etc.; miniature trees in containers, bonzai; pests and diseases of plants, including galls, fasciation mildew, black spot; insects, especially British, photographed alive in the wild, including butterflies and moths, flies, ichneumon and hover flies, dragon and damsel flies, aphids, bugs, beetles, bees, wasps, ants, woodlice, spiders, grasshoppers, groundhoppers, crickets, cockroaches; geography and landscape of Britain, Austria and Liechtenstein including churches, houses, castles, farms, roads, bridges, rivers, clouds, cromlechs, etc.; geology and mineralogy; some birds, mammals, reptiles and amphibians; some material from the Burren (County Clare), especially wildflowers

Access and conditions Open to qualified researchers by appt (tel), Mon-Fri 9–7. All material available for editorial reproduction and for advertising. Colour material loaned free of charge. Reproduction rights fees charged. Staff will undertake some research. All material copyright.

646 • WERNER FORMAN ARCHIVE LTD

36 Camden Square, London NW1 9XA
Tel (01) 267 1034

Enquiries to Barbara Heller

Items 35,000: colour transparencies (2¼″, larger), b/w original photographs

Dates of subject matter 6000 BC to early 20th century

Dates of photographs 1950 to present

Subjects Art and culture of ancient civilizations in the Near and Far East and primitive societies of the world including archaeological sites and landscapes; the Vikings, ancient Mexico, ancient Egypt, Assyria, ancient Greece, China, Moghul and Hindu India, Indonesia, the Middle East, Oceania, Orkney Islands, Canary Islands, Soviet Central Asia; rare collections of oriental and primitive jewellery, sex and fertility magic, the Exotic White Man collection (white man as depicted in the art of Africa, Asia and the Americas), Tibetan and Nepalese Lamaistic bronzes, Dogon art, Vietnamese art, Korean art, masks, tapestries and embroideries, Persian and

Indian miniatures including the Genghis Khan miniatures, Scythian treasure in the Hermitage museum

Access and conditions Open to qualified researchers by appt (tel), Mon-Fri 9.30–5.30. All material available for editorial reproduction and for advertising. B/w and colour material loaned free of charge for two months. Photocopies available. Reproduction rights fees and holding fees charged; service fee charged only when no material is used. Staff will undertake research. Computer catalogue and cross-index in preparation.

647 • MICHAEL GIBSON

Westlands, Oakcroft Road, West Byfleet, Surrey KT14 6JH
Tel (09323) 42470

Enquiries to Michael Gibson

Items Over 1000: colour transparencies (35mm)

Dates of photographs 1960 to present

Subjects Roses, including the latest varieties added year by year, old garden and species roses including *Rosa X dupontii, Rosa moyesii, Rosa gallica versecolor, Rosa Mundi,* Damask, St Nicholas, *Trigintepetala*

Access and conditions Open to qualified researchers by appt, Mon-Fri 9–5. All material available for editorial reproduction and for advertising. Colour material loaned free of charge for three months. Reproduction rights and holding fees charged. Staff will undertake some research.

648 • DEREK GOULD

8 Woodcut, Penenden Heath, Maidstone, Kent ME14 2EQ
Tel (0622) 59711

Enquiries to Derek Gould

Items About 12,000: colour transparencies (35mm)

Dates of photographs 1980 to present

Subjects Horticulture including shrubs, conifers, climbing plants, perennials, rockery plants, alpines, roses, bulbs, corms, tubers, heathers, grasses, annuals, water and bog plants, indoor and greenhouse plants, garden views, garden ornaments, beds and borders, wildlife in the garden, container gardening

Access and conditions Open to qualified researchers by appt, Mon-Fri 9–6. All material available for editorial reproduction and for advertising. Colour material loaned free of charge for three months. Reproduction rights fees charged. Staff will undertake research. All material copyright. Computer print-out catalogue available.

649 • IRIS HARDWICK LIBRARY OF PHOTOGRAPHS

13 Duck Street, Cerne Abbas, Dorset DT2 7LA
Tel (03003) 502

Enquiries to Kay Sanecki

Items 45,000: colour transparencies (35mm, 2¼″), b/w original photographs

Dates of photographs 1960 to present

Subjects Horticulture and garden history including plant portraits, vegetables, herbs and herb gardens, fruit, kitchen gardens, garden features (terraces, steps, water gardens, greenhouses, statuary, sundials, containers), trees and shrubs, house plants, wild flowers, small gardens, gardens open to the public, cottages and cottage gardens, garden design; special collection of South American plants; countryside of England and Wales

Access and conditions Open to qualified researchers by appt (tel), Mon-Fri 9–5. All material available for editorial reproduction and for advertising. B/w and colour material loaned free of charge for one month. Reproduction rights, service and holding fees charged. Staff will undertake research.

650 • HORNIMAN MUSEUM AND LIBRARY

London Road, London SE23 3PQ
Tel (01) 699 2339

Enquiries to David Boston, Director

Items 1000: b/w original photographs

Dates of subject matter Prehistory to present

Dates of photographs 1900 to present

Subjects Anthropology, especially articles of daily use from all periods and from all over the world; musicology, especially musical instruments from all periods and from all over the world; CARSE COLLECTION (18th to 20th centuries) of wind instruments of Western music, ethnic musical instruments; natural history, mounted specimens; mask-making techniques from Cross River State, Nigeria

Access and conditions Open to the public by appt (tel), Mon-Sat 10.30–6, Sun 2–6. All material available for editorial reproduction and for advertising at the Curator's discretion. No loans; b/w prints available for a fee. Material may be copied by outside photographers. Reproduction rights fees charged. Staff will undertake some research.

651 • ERIC AND DAVID HOSKING

20 Crouch Hall Road, London N8 8HX
Tel (01) 340 7703

Enquiries to David Hosking

Items 220,000: colour transparencies (35mm, 5″ × 4″, larger), b/w original photographs

Dates of photographs 1929 to present

Subjects Natural history, birds, mammals, reptiles, amphibians, insects and plants worldwide; marine biology including seaweeds, invertebrates, fishes, sea shore, aquarium tanks, through the microscope, plankton spreads, single organisms, development sets, British and North European species and some from the Mediterranean, California and Florida

Access and conditions Open to qualified researchers by appt (tel), Mon-Sat 9–7. All material available for editorial reproduction and for advertising. B/w and colour material loaned free of charge for one month. Reproduction rights, service and holding fees charged. Staff will undertake research. Card catalogue.

652 • ANTHONY AND ALYSON HUXLEY

50 Villiers Avenue, Surbiton, Surrey KT5 8BD
Tel (01) 399 1479

Enquiries to Anthony Huxley

Items About 20,000: colour transparencies (35mm, 6 × 6cm)

Dates of subject matter 6000 BC to present

Dates of photographs 1960 to present

Subjects Horticulture, wild flowers and plants in close-up and as complete plants, habitats (jungle, mountains, etc.) and landscape associated with flora in each country; geography and general subjects including archaeological sites in Europe (especially alpine flora and wild orchids), Greece and Turkey (comprehensive coverage including flora and archaeology), Morocco, Lebanon, Syria, Jordan, Kashmir, western Himalayas, East Africa, South Africa, Malaysia, Ecuador, southern Mexico, USA, western Canada, China

Access and conditions Open to qualified researchers by appt, Mon-Fri 9.30–5.30. All material available for editorial reproduction and for advertising. Colour material loaned free of charge for two months. Reproduction rights and holding fees charged. Staff will undertake research.

653 • ILEX NATURAL HISTORY

Downsview, 39 Highfield Crescent, Brighton, East Sussex BN1 8JD
Tel (0273) 507512

Enquiries to Patricia Haddon

Items About 3000: colour transparencies (35mm), postcards

Dates of subject matter 1910 to present

Dates of photographs 1960 to present

Subjects Botany including flowering plants, shrubs, trees, grasses, fungi, ferns, mosses, liverworts and lichens (from the UK, Europe, Turkey, Malta, Iceland, Caribbean), plant habitats (British, European, Caribbean, Icelandic) and general countryside, landscapes and villages; conservation techniques and nature reserve management; marine life including fish, invertebrates, algae, marine habitats; entomology including butterflies, moths, insects and related species; ornithology including wildfowl and British birds; British mammals, reptiles and amphibians; national and local nature reserves and RSPB reserves; postcards: British resorts, tea gardens, scenic views (all *c.* 1910)

Access and conditions Open to qualified researchers by appt (tel), daily after 4 p.m. All material available for editorial reproduction and for advertising. Colour material loaned free of charge for one month. B/w prints (postcard collection) can be ordered. Reproduction rights and holding fees charged. Staff will undertake research.

654 • E. A. JANES PHOTOGRAPHIC

10 Boxwell Road, Berkhamsted, Hertfordshire HP4 3EY
Tel (04427) 71342

Enquiries to Ernie Janes

Items 30,000: b/w original photographs, colour transparencies (35mm)

Dates of photographs 1970 to present

Subjects Natural history of the British Isles including birds, mammals, flowers, landscapes, farming, domestic pets; country crafts and people

Access and conditions Open to qualified researchers by appt (tel). All material available for editorial reproduction and for advertising. B/w and colour material loaned free of charge for three months. Reproduction rights and holding fees charged; service fees charged only when no material is used. Staff will undertake research.

655 • THE FRANK LANE AGENCY

19 Dors Close, London NW9 7NT
Tel (01) 205 9486

Enquiries to Jean Lane

Items 80,000: colour transparencies (35mm, 5″ × 4″), b/w original photographs

Dates of photographs 1945 to present

Subjects Natural history with emphasis on animals in their natural habitat and including insects, fish, amphibians, reptiles, birds and mammals; special collection of birds and of fish and underwater photography; animal behaviour, bullfights, plants and flowers, fungi, moths and butterflies, urban wildlife, tracks, zoos and zoo animals, canyons, deserts, erosion, estuaries, mountains, pollution, prairies, rivers and streams, salt and soda pans, sea and seashore, seasons, swamps, trees, tundra, waterfalls; weather and natural phenomena including aurora borealis, avalanches, blizzards, clouds, dew, drought, dust storms, earthquakes, eclipses, floods, fog, frost, geysers, glaciers, hail, hurricanes, ice and icebergs, jet trails, lightning, meteors, meteorites, mirages, mist, moon, permafrost, rain, rainbows and icebows, snow, solar heat, sun, sunrise, sunset, tornadoes, volcanoes, waterspouts, winds, special collection on Alaska and Alaska earthquake; farms and farming, harvesting, burning, haying, turf-cutting, dry-stone-walling, thatching, scarecrows

Access and conditions Open to qualified researchers by appt (tel), Mon-Fri 8–6. All material available for editorial reproduction and for advertising. B/w and colour material loaned free of charge for one month. Reproduction rights, service and holding fees charged. Staff will undertake research; negotiable fee for large projects.

656 • LEAGUE AGAINST CRUEL SPORTS LTD

Anti-Bloodsport File, 83-87 Union Street, London SE1 1SG
Tel (01) 407 0979, 403 4396

Enquiries to Michael Huskisson, Public Relations Officer

Items 5000: b/w original photographs, colour transparencies (35mm), unprinted film negatives, illustrated books

Dates of photographs 1965 to present

Subjects All hound sports, fox-hunting, stag-hunting, hare-hunting, hare-coursing, mink-hunting, otter-hunting; rare photographs of kills, evidence of hunt malpractices, artifical fox earths, foxes being tipped from sacks, general hunting scenes, evidence of hunt havoc, cats killed or injured by hounds

Access and conditions Open to qualified researchers by appt (write), Mon-Fri 9.30–7. All material available for editorial reproduction and for advertising consonant with the League's purposes. B/w and colour material loaned free of charge for purposes of selection; for publication user must make copy print or duplicate transparency and return original. Photocopies available. Reproduction rights fees charged. Staff will undertake research.

657 • LONDON SCIENTIFIC FILMS

57-59 Rochester Place, London NW1 9JU
Tel (01) 482 2239 Telex 21736 GOWER G

Enquiries to Dr Nick Taylor

Items Over 50,000: b/w original photographs, colour transparencies (35mm)

Dates of photographs 1974 to present

Subjects Natural history and science with emphasis on macro-photography of animals and plants, medical photography and photomicroscopy of a vast range of organisms and structures

Access and conditions Open to qualified researchers by appt (tel), Mon-Fri 9.30–5.30. All material available for editorial reproduction and for advertising. B/w and colour material loaned free of charge for one month. Photocopies available. Reproduction rights and service fees charged. Staff of three will undertake research. Subject catalogue.

658 • *MARY ROSE* TRUST

Old Bond Store, 48 Warblington Street, Portsmouth, Hampshire PO1 2ET
Tel (0705) 839766 or 750521

Enquiries to Arthur Rogers, Press Office

Items 4000: b/w original photographs, colour transparencies (35mm)

Dates of subject matter Mid-16th century to present

Dates of photographs 1979 to present

Subjects All aspects of the work involved in raising the *Mary Rose* including underwater archaeology, history of the project, recovery of the ship, Tudor artefacts

Access and conditions Open to qualified researchers by appt (write). Most material available for editorial reproduction and for advertising by special arrangement only. B/w and colour material loaned free of charge by arrangement (print fees charged). Photocopies and Polaroids available for a fee. Reproduction rights and service fees charged. Staff will undertake limited research. All material copyright.

659 • TANIA MIDGLEY

14A Bolton Gardens, London SW5 0AL
Tel (01) 373 7223

Enquiries to Tania Midgley

Items About 30,000: colour transparencies
(35mm)

Dates of photographs 1972 to present

Subjects All types of gardens in the UK from
stately homes to cottage gardens including
planning and design, trees, shrubs, flowering
plants, close-ups; some Italian and French
coverage

Access and conditions Open to qualified
researchers by appt (tel). All material available for
editorial reproduction and for advertising. Colour
material loaned free of charge for one month.
Reproduction rights fees charged; service fees
charged when no material is used. Some research
undertaken. All material copyright.

660 • PATRICK MORRIS
PHOTOGRAPHICS

West Mains, London Road, Ascot, Berkshire
SL5 7DG
Tel: (0990) 21001

Enquiries to Patrick Morris

Items About 35,000: colour transparencies
(35mm), illustrated books, x-rays of biological
subjects

Dates of subject matter Prehistory to present

Dates of photographs 1965 to present

Subjects Worldwide natural history including
plants (details of seeds and structure), animals,
invertebrates, fish, birds, mammals (anatomical
details, bones, teeth), fossils, dinosaurs, habitats,
ecology; geography including places, scenery,
people, major buildings, crops, Papua New Guinea,
USA (most states), Australia, East Africa
(including Ethiopia), Falkland Islands, Pribilof
Islands, Alaska, Sri Lanka, Malaysia, Hong Kong,
UK, Europe, Tunisia, Israel; geology including
fossils, glaciers, geothermals; man and
environment including pollution, farming, mining,
domestic animals, erosion, exploitation of plants
and animals, forestry, logging, worldwide
examples, National Parks and Nature Reserves,
conservation, habitats, deserts, forests and their
ecology and use by man; history including major

buildings and places especially in US and UK;
taxidermy, comprehensive collection of old and new
methods and specimens

Access and conditions Open to qualified
researchers by appt (tel), Mon-Fri 9.30–5.30. All
material available for editorial reproduction and
for advertising. Colour material loaned free of
charge for one month. Reproduction rights and
holding fees charged. Staff of three will undertake
research in answer to specific requests.

661 • TONY MOTT

72 Roding Road, London E5 0DW
Tel (01) 985 9538

Enquiries to Tony Mott

Items 15,000: colour transparencies (35mm), b/w
original photographs

Dates of subject matter 15th century to present

Dates of photographs 1970 to present

Subjects Historic houses and gardens of Britain
and Europe both private and public including
garden buildings, garden sculpture and fountains,
architecture; and in France, East and West
Germany, USSR, Italy

Access and conditions Open to qualified
researchers by appt. All material available for
editorial reproduction and for advertising. B/w and
colour material loaned free of charge for one
month. Reproduction rights fees charged. Staff will
undertake research.

662 • MUSEUM OF ANTIQUITIES OF
THE UNIVERSITY OF
NEWCASTLE UPON TYNE

Department of Archaeology

The Quadrangle, The University, Newcastle upon
Tyne NE1 7RU
Tel (0632) 328511 ext 3846

Enquiries to L. Allason-Jones, Senior Technician

Items About 20,000: b/w original photographs,
colour transparencies (35mm), b/w copy
photographs, lantern slides, glass negatives,
unprinted film negatives, architectural drawings

Dates of subject matter 6000 BC to present

Dates of photographs c. 1850 to present

Subjects 19th- and 20th-century photographs relating to sites and excavations on Hadrian's Wall; aerial coverage of Northumberland including Hadrian's Wall, prehistoric settlements, medieval and industrial archaeology; objects in site museums

Access and conditions Open to the public by appt (write), Mon–Fri 9–5. All material available for editorial reproduction; advertising use by special arrangement only. No loans; b/w prints and duplicate colour transparencies available for a fee; material may be copied by outside photographers. Photocopies available. Reproduction rights and service fees charged. Staff will undertake limited research. All material copyright. Card catalogue available.

663 • NATIONAL ANTI-VIVISECTION SOCIETY LTD

51 Harley Street, London W1N 1DD
Tel (01) 580 4034, 641 0612

Enquiries to General Secretary

Items 130: b/w original photographs, b/w colour photographic prints

Dates of photographs 1980 to present

Subjects Animals awaiting or undergoing experiments in countries including USA, Mexico, Spain, Japan and China

Access and conditions Open to qualified researchers by appt (tel). All material available for editorial reproduction and for advertising. B/w material loaned by arrangement. Photocopies available. No reproduction rights fees charged but donation to work of Society appreciated. Staff will undertake some research. All material copyright.

664 • NATURAL HISTORY AND ARCHAEOLOGY PHOTOGRAPHS

17 Oakfield Road, Harpenden, Hertfordshire AL5 2NJ
Tel (05827) 5856

Enquiries to John B. Free

Items 20,000: colour transparencies (35mm)

Dates of subject matter BC to present

Dates of photographs 1960 to present

Subjects Archaeology in Greece, India, Japan, Malta, Mexico, Sicily, Tunisia and the UK; general geographical coverage of India, Japan, Nepal, Mexico and Oman; UK agriculture; wild and domestic mammals and birds; invertebrates including slugs, snails, spiders, millipedes, centipedes and worms; insects including ants, termites, wasps, butterflies, moths, grasshoppers, stick insects, earwigs, silkmoths and silk production, hover flies, ladybirds, beetles, lacewings, locusts, weevils, aphids, blowflies, beetles, cockroaches, cotton stainers, special collections include bees (honeybees, bumblebees, solitary bees) and beekeeping worldwide; tropical agriculture

Access and conditions Open to qualified researchers by appt (tel), Mon–Fri 9–5. All material available for editorial reproduction and for advertising. Colour material loaned free of charge for one month. Reproduction rights and service fees charged; service fees deductible from use fees. All material copyright.

665 • NATURAL HISTORY PHOTOGRAPHIC AGENCY

Little Tye, 57 High Street, Ardingly, Sussex RH17 6TB
Tel (0444) 892514

Enquiries to Tim Harris

Items 30,000: colour transparencies (35mm, 5″ × 4″), b/w original photographs

Dates of subject matter 1970 to present

Subjects Natural history including landscapes, ecology, the environment, mammals, birds, reptiles, amphibians, fish, marine life, insects, plants; special collections of African wildlife, and the Bushmen, and high-speed photographs of insects, birds and bats

Access and conditions Open to qualified researchers by appt, Mon–Fri 9–5. All material available for editorial reproduction and for advertising. B/w and colour material loaned free of charge for two months. Reproduction rights, holding and service fees charged. Staff will undertake some research. All material copyright.

666 • NATURAL SCIENCE PHOTOGRAPHS

33 Woodland Drive, Watford, Hertfordshire
WD1 3BY
Tel (0923) 45265

Enquiries to Peter Ward

Items About 250,000: colour transparencies
(35mm, 2¼″)

Dates of photographs 1960 to present

Subjects Natural history worldwide including
mammals, birds, reptiles, amphibia, fish,
invertebrates (both terrestrial and aquatic);
horticulture, fungi, plants and trees (wild and
cultivated) with special emphasis on British
botany; ethnography, geography, geology, climatic
conditions, ecology, conservation, habitats,
landscapes, agriculture, farming, farm animals;
prehistoric animal reconstructions; special section
on animal behaviour; freshwater angling in the
UK; Australasia, London representatives for the
Archives of the Queensland Museum (Australia)

Access and conditions Open to qualified
researchers by appt, Mon-Fri 9–5. All material
available for editorial reproduction and for
advertising. Colour material loaned free of charge
for one month (six to eight weeks for overseas
clients). Reproduction rights, holding and service
fees charged; service fees deductible from use fees.
Staff will undertake some research. Photographers
available for assignment. All material copyright.
Catalogue in preparation.

667 • NATURE PHOTOGRAPHERS LTD

149 Ash Hill Road, Ash Vale, Aldershot,
Hampshire GU12 5DW
Tel (0483) 811569, (0252) 27901

Enquiries to Frank Blackburn

Items 120,000: colour transparencies (35mm,
6 × 6cm), b/w original photographs

Dates of photographs c. 1965 to present

Subjects Natural history worldwide including
landscapes, climatic conditions, pollution,
conservation, geology, birds, mammals, insects,
fish, marine life, reptiles, amphibians, wild and
cultivated flowers, horticulture, agriculture,
gardens, fungi, trees; photographers represented
include Baron Hugo van Lawick, S. Bisserôt, E. A.
Janes, Brinsley Burbidge, F. V. Blackburn, Andy

Callow, Owen Newman, Kevin Carlson, Michael
Gore, Don Smith, D. Scott, Andrew Cleave, Paul
Sterry

Access and conditions Open to qualified
researchers by appt (tel), Mon-Fri 9–5. All material
available for editorial reproduction and for
advertising. B/w and colour material loaned free of
charge for 28 days. Reproduction rights, holding
and service fees charged; service fees deductible
from use fees. Staff will undertake some research.
All material copyright.

668 • MAURICE NIMMO

Pen y Cefn, Hayscastle Cross, Haverfordwest,
Dyfed SA62 5NY
Tel (0348) 840382

Enquiries to Maurice Nimmo

Items 12,000: colour transparencies (35mm, 2¼″,
3¼″ × 2¼″, 5″ × 4″), b/w original photographs,
glass negatives, colour photographic prints

Dates of subject matter Prehistory to present

Dates of photographs 1930 to present

Subjects Natural history of England and Wales
(excluding animals and birds) including
landscapes, seascapes, coastal scenes, climatic
conditions, sunrises, sunsets, ice and snow scenes,
lightning, heath fires, erosion; trees, shrubs,
wildflowers, garden flowers, damage to trees by
wind, fungi and insects; lichens, fungi, grasses;
prehistoric flints, cromlechs, clapper bridges and
pack-horse bridges

Access and conditions Open to qualified
researchers by appt (write). All material available
for editorial reproduction and for advertising. B/w
material loaned free of charge for two months;
colour material loaned free of charge for one
month. Reproduction rights and holding fees
charged. Research undertaken. All material
copyright.

669 • NORFOLK ARCHAEOLOGICAL UNIT

Union House, Gressenhall, East Dereham, Norfolk
NR20 4DR
Tel (0362) 860528 ext 4

Enquiries to Derek Edwards

Items 20,000: b/w original photographs, colour transparencies (35mm), postcards, colour photographic prints

Dates of subject matter BC to present

Dates of photographs 1974 to present

Subjects Aerial coverage of archaeological sites, historic sites, churches, country houses and mansions in Norfolk and edge of adjacent counties

Access and conditions Open to qualified researchers by appt, Mon-Fri 9–5. Some material available for editorial reproduction; advertising use by special arrangement only. No loans; b/w prints and duplicate colour transparencies available for a fee. Photocopies available. Reproduction rights fees charged. Staff will undertake research for a fee. All material copyright. Card catalogue available.

670 • OXFORD SCIENTIFIC FILMS LTD

Long Hanborough, Oxford OX7 2LD
Tel (0993) 883311

Enquiries to Picture Library

Items 250,000: colour transparencies (35mm, 5″ × 4″), b/w original photographs

Dates of photographs 1970 to present

Subjects Natural history, wildlife and biology including animals, plants, micro-organisms (portraits, behaviour, life-histories); macro-photography, photomicrography, electron micrography; time-lapse, high-speed, special effects photography; histology, embryology; ecology, conservation, pollution, anthropology, ethnology, agriculture, pets, meteorology, geography, geology

Access and conditions Open to qualified researchers by appt (tel but first-time users write), Mon-Fri 8.45–5.30). All material available for editorial reproduction and for advertising. B/w and colour material loaned free of charge for six weeks. Reproduction rights and holding fees charged; service fees charged only when no material is used. Staff will undertake limited research. All material copyright.

671 • PEOPLE'S DISPENSARY FOR SICK ANIMALS

PDSA House, South Street, Dorking, Surrey RH4 2LB
Tel (0306) 888291

Enquiries to Information Department Manager

Items 15,000: b/w original photographs, press cuttings, colour transparencies (35mm), glass negatives

Dates of subject matter 1928 to present

Dates of photographs 1928 to present

Subjects History and work of the PDSA including treatment and care of animals by veterinary officers, veterinary surgeries, operating theatres, waiting rooms; X-ray photographs showing unusual abdominal finds; charitable fund-raising events with personalities from theatre, cinema and radio

Access and conditions Open to qualified researchers by appt (tel), Mon-Fri 9–5. Most material available for editorial reproduction and for advertising. B/w and colour material loaned free of charge by arrangement; material may be copied by outside photographers. Photocopies available. No reproduction rights fees charged.

672 • PHOTORESOURCES

The Orchard, Marley Lane, Kingston, Canterbury, Kent CT4 6JH
Tel (0227) 830075

Enquiries to M. Dixon

Items 40,000: colour transparencies (35mm, 6 × 6cm, 9 × 6cm, 5″ × 4″), b/w original photographs, colour photographic prints, illustrated books

Dates of subject matter 300,000 BC (Lower Palaeolithic) to present

Dates of photographs 1970 to present

Subjects Archaeology, ancient art, art, ethnology, history, mythology, world religions and museum objects from the following cultures: African, American Indian, Anglo-Saxon, Assyrian, Babylonian, Biblical, Ancient Breton, Bronze Age, Buddhist, Byzantine, Canaanite, Celtic, Central American, Chalcolithic, Chinese, Christian, Copper Age, Cretan, Dacian, Danish, Egyptian, Eskimo, Etruscan, Greek, Hindu, Hittite, Indian, Irish, Iron Age, Islamic, Japanese, La Tene, Luristan, Maltese, Medieval European, Megalithic,

Melanesian, Mesolithic, Mesopotamian, Mexican, Minoan, Moghul, Neolithic, Nigerian, Norman, Norse, Norwegian, Oceanic, Ordos, Palaeolithic, Parthian, Peruvian, Phoenician, Pictish, Polynesian, Punic, Roman, Romanesque, Romanian, Sassanian, Saxon, Scandinavian, Scythian, Siberian, Siculo-Norman, South American, Stone Age, Sumerian, Swedish, Victorian, Viking and including bronzes, coins, dinosaurs, fossils, gods and goddesses, gold (ancient), horses in art, ivories, jewellery (ancient), metalwork (ancient), mosaics, painting (ancient), pottery, tapestries, warfare (ancient), Steppe art

Access and conditions Open to qualified researchers by appt. All material available for editorial reproduction and for advertising. B/w prints available for a fee; colour transparencies loaned free of charge for one month. Photocopies available. Reproduction rights, service and holding fees charged. Staff of two will undertake some research. All material copyright.

673 • PHOTOS HORTICULTURAL PICTURE LIBRARY

169 Valley Road, Ipswich, Suffolk IP1 4PJ
Tel (0473) 53041

Enquiries to Michael Warren

Items 50,000: colour transparencies (35mm, 2¼″, 5″ × 4″)

Dates of photographs 1970s to present

Subjects Horticulture and gardens in the UK with some coverage of France and Italy including pests, diseases, trees, fruit, vegetables, herbs, greenhouses, borders and tubs, house plants, pruning, potting, planting out, step-by-step garden work

Access and conditions Open to qualified researchers by appt (tel), Mon-Fri 9–5. All material available for editorial reproduction and for advertising. Colour material loaned free of charge for one month. Reproduction rights and holding fees charged. Staff will undertake research. All material copyright.

674 • PITT RIVERS MUSEUM

University of Oxford Photographic Archive Collections, South Park Road, Oxford OX1 3AH
Tel (0865) 512541 ext 602

Enquiries to Elizabeth Edwards

Items About 50,000: b/w original photographs, glass negatives, lantern slides, unprinted film negatives, postcards, stereographs

Dates of subject matter 19th century to present

Dates of photographs 1850 to present

Subjects Ethnography and anthropology worldwide including material culture, daily life, ritual, music, dance, weapons

Access and conditions Open to qualified researchers by appt (write). Most material available for editorial reproduction and for advertising. B/w material loaned free of charge for four months (print fees charged). Reproduction rights fees charged. Staff will undertake some research; negotiable research fee charged.

675 • PLANET EARTH PICTURES

4 Harcourt Street, London W1H 1DS
Tel (01) 262 4427/8 Telex 28221 REDFOT G

23 Burlington Road, Bristol BS6 6TJ
Tel (0272) 741206

Enquiries to Gillian Lythgoe, Managing Director

Items 70,000: colour transparencies (35mm, 6 × 6cm, 7 × 6cm), b/w original photographs

Dates of subject matter Prehistory to present

Dates of photographs 1965 to present

Subjects Animals and plants worldwide, their habitats, behaviour and ecology, including mammals, fish, reptiles, insects and other invertebrates covering such diverse species as acorn worms, alder flies, antelope, beetles, bower birds, buffalo, caddis flies, cat fish, coelacanth, cuttlefish, eagles, electric fish, elephants, frogs, giraffes, grasshoppers, herons, impala, kangaroos, lice, lions, manatees, millipedes, newts, owls, parrots, piranha fish, platypus, possums, rhinoceros, salamander, scorpions, sea slugs, sloths, squid, storks, surgeon fish, swans, toads, toucans, turtles, vultures, wasps, weaver birds, wildebeest, woodpeckers and zebra; plant life include aquatic plants, bromeliads, cacti, cereals, clubmoss, conifers, deciduous trees, epiphytes, ferns, forest flowers, fruit, fungi, grains, grasses, herbs, lichens, mosses, mountain plants, vegetables, xerophytes; the environment and resources including geology and biology worldwide; comprehensive collection of underwater and surface marine photography including algae, amphora, aquaculture, archaeology, beaches, boats, breakwaters, coastlines, conservation, caves, cliffs, coral reefs, divers and diving, docks, exploration, fish farming, fishing, ice, icebergs, life-saving, oceanographic research, oil production, photogrammetry, plankton, rock pools, sailing, salvage, scientific research, sand dunes, seashores, seismic profiling, submersibles, sunken cities, shipwrecks, storms, sunrise, sunset, surfing, tides, trawling, watersports, whaling (marine animals and plants are listed under wildlife)

Access and conditions Open to qualified researchers by appt (tel), Mon-Fri 9–5. All material available for editorial reproduction and for advertising. B/w and colour material loaned free of charge for one month. Reproduction rights and service fees charged. Staff of two will undertake some research; fees charged for large projects. All material copyright. Printed catalogue available.

676 • PREMAPHOTOS WILDLIFE

2 Willoughby Close, King's Coughton, Alcester, Warwickshire B49 5QJ
Tel (0789) 762938

Enquiries to Jean Preston-Mafham, Picture Librarian

Items 38,000: colour transparencies (35mm)

Dates of photographs 1975 to present

Subjects Natural history including algae, seaweeds, liverworts, mosses, ferns, flowering plants, cacti, trees, fruits, seeds, lichens, fungi; marine life, arachnids, insects, butterflies and moths, beetles and weevils; fish, amphibians, reptiles, birds and mammals; habitats in the UK, Australia, Borneo, Ecuador, Kenya, Malaysia, Mexico, Peru, South Africa, Trinidad and the USA; landscapes and agriculture

Access and conditions Open to qualified researchers by appt (tel), Mon-Fri 9–5. All material available for editorial reproduction and for advertising. Colour material loaned free of charge for two months. Reproduction rights fees charged; holding fees charged when material is held for more than two months and not used. Staff will undertake some research. All material copyright. Card catalogue available.

677 • PRESS-TIGE PICTURE LTD

3 Newmarket Road, Cringleford, Norwich, Norfolk NR4 6UE
Tel (0603) 54345

Enquiries to Tony Tilford

Items 50,000: colour transparencies (35mm), b/w original photographs

Dates of photographs 1965 to present

Subjects Natural history, European geography, landscapes, agriculture, wildlife with special emphasis on European mammals, birds worldwide especially passerines, moths and bats in flight; portraits of people from different countries; high-speed, macro- and micro-photography

Access and conditions Open to qualified researchers by appt (write). All material available for editorial reproduction and for advertising. B/w material loaned free of charge by arrangement; colour material loaned free of charge for 30 days. Photocopies available for a fee. Reproduction rights, holding and service fees charged. Staff will undertake some research. Photographers available for assignment. All material copyright.

678 • RIDA PHOTO LIBRARY

The Triangle, Kingston upon Thames, Surrey KT1 3RU
Tel (01) 942 8632

Enquiries to David Bayliss

Items 10,000: colour transparencies (35mm, 2¼″, 5″ × 4″), b/w original photographs

Dates of subject matter Prehistory to present

Dates of photographs 1965 to present

Subjects Geology and geography including fossils of all major groups throughout geological history, minerals, rock types, applications in jewellery and decorative ware; field geology and geography including faults, folds, dykes, sills, lava flows, landforms and features caused by volcanic, glacial, river, marine and aeolian action, vegetation, climatic conditions, lakes, rivers, seas, soils; economic geography including mining and quarrying, brick-making, oil-rigs, agriculture, fishing, forestry and irrigation; civil engineering, communications and transport including dams, bridges, aqueducts, rivers, canals, power stations, factories, trains, ships, aircraft, road transport;

anthropology including fossil man from Olduvai Gorge, Kenya and early tools; urban and rural life of indigenous communities worldwide; natural history including wild flowers, grasses, sedges, rushes, horsetails, ferns, mosses, trees and shrubs with emphasis on British species; fungi, algae; wild and domestic animals in Europe and African game reserves; birds of Great Britain; some coverage of reptiles, insects, rivers and marine life; vintage cars and motorcycles, watches from 1820s to present, architecture of Roman world

Access and conditions Open to qualified researchers by appt (tel), Mon-Fri 9–5. B/w and colour material loaned free of charge for one month. Photocopies available. Reproduction rights, holding and service fees charged; service fees deductible from use fees. Staff of two will undertake some research. All material copyright. Card catalogue available.

679 • ROYAL ANTHROPOLOGICAL INSTITUTE OF GREAT BRITAIN AND IRELAND

Photographic Collection

56 Queen Anne Street, London W1M 9LA
Tel (01) 486 6832

Enquiries to Christopher Pinnery, Photo Librarian

Items About 40,000: b/w original and copy photographs, colour transparencies (5″ × 4″), glass negatives, lantern slides, postcards, daguerreotypes, art reproductions, stereographs

Dates of subject matter c. 2000 BC to AD 1945

Dates of photographs c. 1850 to 1945

Subjects Social and physical anthropology and ethnography worldwide with emphasis on Africa but also including coverage of South-east Asia and China; anthropological studies, portraits; special collections include the MILLS COLLECTION on the Pacific and Far East; British Association Racial Commission; E. H. Mann on Nicobar and Andaman Islands; Emil Torday on Zaire; Neverovsky on Angola; A. I. Richards on Zimbabwe; Max Gluckman on Zambia; I. Schapera on Botswana; C. G. Seligman of Sri Lanka; 19th century observers including travellers and colonial administrators

Access and conditions Open to the public by appt (tel), Mon-Fri 10–5. All material available for editorial reproduction; advertising use by special arrangement only. B/w material loaned free of charge for four months (print fees charged). Photocopies available. Reproduction rights and holding fees charged. Staff will undertake limited research. Some material copyright. Card catalogue available.

680 • ROYAL COMMISSION ON ANCIENT AND HISTORICAL MONUMENTS OF SCOTLAND

National Monuments Record of Scotland, 6-7 Coates Place, Edinburgh EH3 7HF
Tel (031) 225 5994

Enquiries to Curator

Items 250,000: b/w original and copy photographs, colour transparencies (35mm), glass negatives, lantern slides, postcards, illustrated maps, unprinted film negatives, stereographs, greetings cards, architectural drawings, press cuttings, illustrated books

Dates of subject matter BC to present

Dates of photographs 1850 to present

Subjects Ancient and historical monuments in Scotland including archaeological sites, ecclesiastical, domestic and industrial architecture; special collections include photographic negatives of B. C. Clayton, John Forbes White and Erskine Beveridge; architectural drawings including collection from the London office of William Burn, the National Art Survey Drawings, and the SIR ROBERT LORIMER COLLECTION

Access and conditions Open to the public, Mon-Fri 9.30–5.30. Most material available for editorial reproduction and for advertising. No loans; b/w prints available for a fee. Photocopies available. Reproduction rights fees charged. Staff will undertake some research. Most material copyright.

681 • ROYAL COMMISSION ON ANCIENT AND HISTORICAL MONUMENTS IN WALES

National Monuments Record for Wales, Edleston House, Queen's Road, Aberystwyth, Dyfed SY23 2HP
Tel (0970) 4381/2

Enquiries to Curator

Items About 130,000: b/w original and copy photographs, colour transparencies (35mm), colour photographic prints, architectural drawings, glass negatives, postcards, art reproductions, manuscript material

Dates of subject matter BC to present

Dates of photographs 1940s to present

Subjects Ancient and historic monuments in Wales including earthworks, castles, abbeys, churches, houses and industrial structures; collection incorporates the former National Buildings Record

Access and conditions Open to the public by appt, Mon-Fri 9.30–4.30. Most material available for editorial reproduction and for advertising. No loans; b/w prints and duplicate colour transparencies available for a fee. Photocopies available. Reproduction rights fees charged. Staff will undertake limited research. Most material copyright. Card catalogue available.

682 • ROYAL COMMISSION ON HISTORICAL MONUMENTS (ENGLAND)

National Monuments Record, Fortress House, 23 Savile Row Row, London W1X 1AB
Tel (01) 734 6010

Enquiries to Alan Aberg (Archaeology), Stephen Croad (Architecture), John Hampton (Air Photographs)

Items Three million: b/w original and copy photographs, colour photographic prints, colour transparencies (35mm, 5″ × 4″, 8″ × 6″), glass negatives, lantern slides, postcards, unprinted film negatives, architectural drawings

Dates of subject matter Prehistory to c. 1940

Dates of photographs 1840s to present

Subjects Archaeological sites, ancient monuments and historic buildings in England including aerial coverage

Access and conditions Open to the public, Mon-Fri 10–5.30; aerial photographs open by appt (tel). Most material available for editorial reproduction and for advertising. No loans; b/w prints and duplicate colour transparencies available for a fee. Photocopies available. Reproduction rights fees charged. Most material copyright.

683 • THE ROYAL SOCIETY FOR THE PROTECTION OF BIRDS

Photographic Library, The Lodge, Sandy, Bedfordshire SG19 2DL
Tel (0767) 80551 ext 2035

Enquiries to Chris Sargeant, Film Unit

Items About 19,000: b/w original photographs, colour transparencies (35mm, 2¼″), lantern slides, glass negatives

Dates of subject matter 1940 to present

Dates of photographs 1940 to present

Subjects Birds of the British Isles and Europe in flight and in habitat

Access and conditions Open to the public by appt (tel), Mon-Fri 9–5.15. All material available for editorial reproduction and for advertising. B/w and colour material loaned free of charge for 30 days. Reproduction rights, holding and service fees charged. Staff of two will undertake some research for a fee. All material copyright.

684 • ST ALBANS MUSEUM SERVICE

Verulamium and City Museums, St Michaels, St Albans, Hertfordshire AL3 4SW
Tel (0727) 59919, 54659

Enquiries to James Brown, Keeper of Photographic Services

Items About 10,000: b/w original and copy photographs, colour transparencies (35mm, 5″ × 4″), colour photographic prints, glass negatives, lantern slides, unprinted film negatives

Dates of subject matter Prehistory to present

Dates of photographs 1860 to present

Subjects VERULAMIUM MUSEUM: archaeology, late Iron Age material excavated in St Albans area; Roman pottery, glass metalwork, mosaics, statuettes, painted wall plaster; medieval pottery and metalwork; CITY MUSEUM: SALAMAN COLLECTION of craft tools with emphasis on woodworking trades, reconstructed workshops, antique ceramics, glass, treen, silver, metalwork, dolls, children's toys and games, costumes and furniture; collection of geological samples; collection of British butterflies; local history of St Albans and surrounding area including landscapes, architecture, transport, industry, crafts, social history, portraits, family photograph albums

Access and conditions Open to qualified

researchers by appt (tel), Mon-Fri 9–5.15. All material available for editorial reproduction and for advertising. B/w and colour material loaned free of charge for one month; b/w prints and duplicate colour transparencies available for a fee. Photocopies available. Reproduction rights, holding and service fees charged. Staff will undertake some research. Most material copyright.

685 • KENNETH SCOWEN

The White House, Headley Grove, Headley, Nr Epsom, Surrey KT18 6NR
Tel (0372) 377292

Enquiries to Kenneth Scowen

Items About 25,000: colour transparencies (35mm, 5″ × 4″), b/w original photographs, unprinted film negatives

Dates of photographs 1953 to present

Subjects Landscape coverage of countryside throughout the British Isles; gardens and horticulture in the British Isles including public and private gardens, flowers, shrubs, trees, borders, vegetables

Access and conditions Open to qualified researchers by appt (write), Mon-Fri 9–5.30. All material available for editorial reproduction and for advertising. B/w and colour material loaned free of charge for 14 days. Reproduction rights, holding and service fees charged. Staff will undertake some research for a fee. All material copyright.

SEAPHOT *see* PLANET EARTH PICTURES

686 • MICK SHARP

Eithinog, Waun, Penisarwaun, Caernarfon, Gwynedd LL55 3PW
Tel (0286) 872425

Enquiries to Mick Sharp

Items 1400: colour transparencies (35mm), b/w original photographs

Dates of subject matter Prehistory to present

Dates of photographs 1974 to present

Subjects Archaeology in the British Isles and some coverage of Brittany including techniques, excavations and finds; field monuments, megalithic tombs and other prehistoric burial chambers, henges, stone circles, standing stones, rows, avenues and settings, megalithic art and cup-and-ring marks in the British Isles and Brittany; prehistoric settlements and defended sites in Britain especially in Scotland; Roman and Dark Ages sites in Britain; early Christian monuments and settlements, churches with archaeological interest and unusual sites; deserted settlements in the Western Isles, vernacular architecture in Britain and Brittany; castles and historic houses in Britain; landscape views of Britain with emphasis on Isle of Skye; archaeological monuments and courtyard houses in Iraq

Access and conditions Open to qualified researchers by appt. All material available for editorial reproduction; advertising use by special arrangement only. B/w and colour material loaned free of charge for one month. Photocopies available. Reproduction rights and holding fees charged. Research undertaken; Mick Sharp has access to other specialist archaeological collections. All material copyright. Printed subject lists available.

687 • DONALD SMITH COLLECTION

Kingfishers Old House, Riverside, Bramerton, Norfolk NR14 7EG
Tel (05088) 621

Enquiries to Donald Smith

Items 5000: colour transparencies (35mm)

Dates of subject matter 18th century to present

Dates of photographs 1950 to present

Subjects Horticulture in the UK including flowering plants, fruit and fruiting plants, shrubs, trees, lawns, ground cover, gardens (including coverage of historic houses); gardeners at work, equipment, glasshouses, protected cultivation, pests and diseases, weed control

Access and conditions Open to qualified researchers by appt, Mon-Fri 9–5. All material available for editorial reproduction and for advertising. Colour material loaned free of charge for two months. Reproduction rights and holding fees charged. Staff will undertake some research. All material copyright.

688 • PETER STILES PICTURE LIBRARY

10 Selden Road, Worthing, Sussex BN11 2LL
Tel (0903) 39337

Enquiries to Peter Stiles

Items 3000: colour transparencies (35mm, 2¼″), colour photographic prints

Dates of subject matter 1970 to present

Dates of photographs 1970 to present

Subjects Natural history and botany including insects, reptiles, tropical fish, fungi, cacti and succulents, flowers, ferns, shrubs, rock plants and alpines, bromeliads; horticulture including rock gardens, garden pools, propagation, construction sequences (re-potting, turfing, building rock gardens); general landscape and travel coverage of Great Britain including the Lake District, Cornwall, Scotland, London

Access and conditions Open to the public by appt (write). All material available for editorial reproduction and for advertising. Colour material loaned free of charge for two weeks. Reproduction rights and holding fees charged. Research undertaken; negotiable research fee charged. Photographer available for assignment. All material copyright. Typed catalogue available.

689 • SURVIVAL ANGLIA LTD

Brook House, 113 Park Lane, London W1Y 4DX
Tel (01) 408 2288 Telex 299689

Enquiries to Sue Harrison, Stills Library Manager

Items 70,000: colour transparencies (35mm), b/w original photographs

Dates of photographs 1960 to present

Subjects Mammals and birds worldwide; reptiles, amphibians, invertebrates, fish; trees, flowers, fungi; conservation work, scenics, African and South American tribes

Access and conditions Open to qualified researchers by appt (tel), Mon-Fri 9.30–5.30. All material available for editorial reproduction and for advertising. B/w and colour material loaned free of charge for six weeks; duplicate colour transparencies available for a fee. Reproduction rights fees charged. Staff of two will undertake research. All material copyright. Card catalogue.

690 • UNIVERSITY MUSEUM OF ARCHAEOLOGY AND ANTHROPOLOGY

Downing Street, Cambridge CB2 3DZ
Tel (0223) 359714

Enquiries to Dr David W. Phillipson, Curator

Items About 20,000: b/w original and copy photographs, colour transparencies (35mm, 5″ × 4″), glass negatives, lantern slides

Dates of subject matter Prehistory to present

Dates of photographs 1880 to present

Subjects Prehistoric archaeology and anthropology worldwide; HADDON COLLECTION of early 20th-century b/w photographs forms nucleus of collection

Access and conditions Open to qualified researchers by appt (write). Some material available for editorial reproduction; advertising use by special arrangement only. No loans; b/w prints and duplicate colour transparencies available for a fee. Reproduction rights fees charged. Some material copyright.

691 • UNIVERSITY OF READING

The Ure Museum of Greek Archaeology

Department of Classics

The University, Reading, Berkshire RG6 2AA
Tel (0734) 875123 ext 358 or 269

Enquiries to Jane F. Gardner

Items About 2500: b/w original photographs, unprinted film negatives, glass negatives, colour transparencies (35mm)

Dates of subject matter Egyptian pre-dynastic to c. 200 BC

Dates of photographs c. 1950 to present

Subjects Egyptian antiquities, Greek vases and figurines, Greek and Roman lamps, archaeology

Access and conditions Open to qualified researchers by appt (write), Mon-Fri 9–5. All material available for editorial reproduction and for advertising. No loans; b/w prints and duplicate colour transparencies available for a fee. No reproduction rights fees charged. Staff will undertake some research. Compulsory credit line. All material copyright.

692 • THE WILDFOWL TRUST

Slimbridge, Gloucestershire GL2 7BT
Tel (045389) 333

Enquiries to Joe Blossom

Items 10,000: colour transparencies (35mm), b/w
original photographs

Dates of photographs 1946 to present

Subjects Ducks, geese, swans and flamingos
worldwide

Access and conditions Open to qualified
researchers by appt. Some material available for
editorial reproduction and for advertising. Colour
material loaned free of charge for one month.
Reproduction rights and holding fees charged. Staff
will undertake limited research. All material
copyright.

693 • WILDLIFE AND COUNTRY PHOTOS LTD

55 The Street, Newnham, Sittingbourne, Kent
ME9 0LN
Tel (079589) 411

Enquiries to Brian Hawkes

Items 350,000: colour transparencies (35mm), b/w
original photographs, colour photographic prints

Dates of subject matter 3000 BC to present

Dates of photographs 1950 to present

Subjects Natural history including insects,
spiders, amphibians, reptiles, snakes, land birds,
sea birds, mammals, sea mammals, domestic and
farm animals, horses, wild animals, bats, plants
including lichens, fungi, flowers, orchids, fruit,
bushes, shrubs, trees; environmental problems,
ecology, conservation, pollution; agriculture
including forestry, farming, crops, country scenes;
seasons, weather, snow and ice, icebergs;
geography (especially England and Wales)
including landscapes, mountains, volcanoes,
deserts, seashores, ponds, rivers, lakes, erosion,
Alpine scenes, parks, National Parks, nature
reserves; transport (land, sea, air) including
lighthouses, railways, locomotives; architecture
including castles, churches, cathedrals, abbeys;
industry and industrial archaeology, quarries, pits,
harbours; travel and topography; London;
education and schools; cities, villages and towns,
urban problems, rubbish and dumps, street
furniture, postboxes; people, children

Access and conditions Open to qualified
researchers by appt (tel), Mon-Fri 9–6. All material
available for editorial reproduction and for
advertising. B/w and colour material loaned free of
charge for three months. Reproduction rights and
holding fees charged. Staff will undertake
research.

694 • WILDLIFE AND COUNTRYSIDE PHOTOGRAPHIC

Petley Farm, Marley Lane, Battle, East Sussex
TN33 0RE
Tel (042487) 677

Enquiries to James Good

Items 18,000: colour transparencies (35mm), b/w
original photographs

Dates of photographs 1950 to present

Subjects Natural history, insects, reptiles, birds
including eggs and nests, animals, special
collection of British and European deer, fungi, wild
flowers, trees, shrubs, garden flowers, orchids,
fishing, hunting, shooting, country scenes

Access and conditions Open to qualified
researchers by appt (write). All material available
for editorial reproduction and for advertising. B/w
and colour material loaned free of charge for three
months. Reproduction rights and holding fees
charged. Staff will undertake research.

695 • WILDLIFE MATTERS PHOTOGRAPHIC LIBRARY

Marlham, Henley Down, Catsfield, East Sussex
TN33 9BN
Tel (042483) 566

Enquiries to John Feltwell

Items About 10,000: colour transparencies
(35mm), b/w original photographs

Dates of photographs 1978 to present

Subjects Wild flowers, herbal and medicinal
plants, gardens and garden flowers, trees,
European and tropical honey-bees, butterflies,
moths, entomology; ecology and conservation,
nature reserves, hedgerows, ancient meadows,
woods, heaths, indicator species, amenities, urban
conservation, motorway biology, habitats and
habitat loss, effects of man and agriculture on

<u>Whatever you're looking for...</u>

Pictor probably have just the picture you need in
stock. We have every type of subject in formats from
35mm to 10" x 8". So the next time you're looking
for a picture, get on the phone to Pictor.
That's what we're here for.

Pictor
International
LONDON PARIS MILAN MUNICH

Twyman House, 31-39 Camden Road, London NW1 9LR. Telephone: 01-482 0478

countryside, fruits, fungi, lichens, grasses, molluscs, amphibia, reptiles, birds especially waterfowl; special emphasis on flora and fauna of the Mediterranean and south-east England, European limestone flora and Burren in western Ireland; aerial coverage of nature reserves in southern England; rainforest ecology of South-east Asia

Access and conditions Open to qualified researchers by appt, Mon-Fri 9–5. All material available for editorial reproduction and for advertising. B/w and colour material loaned free of charge for six weeks; material may be copied by outside photographers. Reproduction rights fees charged. Research undertaken for a fee. All material copyright. Computer list available.

696 • WILTSHIRE LIBRARY AND MUSEUM SERVICE

Sites and Monuments Record, Bythesea Road, Trowbridge, Wiltshire BA14 8BS
Tel (02214) 3641 Telex 44297

Enquiries to Roy Canham, Field Archaeological Officer

Items 3500: b/w original photographs, colour transparencies (35mm), colour photographic prints

Dates of subject matter BC to present

Dates of photographs 1975 to present

Subjects Archaeology of Wiltshire from prehistoric times mainly by aerial coverage of sites and including Stonehenge, Silbury Hill, Avebury, Figsbury Ring, shrunken villages and track waves

Access and conditions Open to qualified researchers by appt (tel), Mon-Fri 9–5. All material available for editorial reproduction and for advertising. No loans; b/w prints and duplicate colour transparencies available for a fee. No reproduction rights fees charges. Staff of four will undertake limited research. All material copyright. Card catalogue in preparation.

697 • WORLD WILDLIFE FUND – UNITED KINGDOM

Photographic Library, 11-13 Ockford Road, Godalming, Surrey GU7 1QU
Tel (04868) 20551 Telex 859602

Enquiries to Jane Atkinson, Conservation Department

Items About 3000: b/w original photographs, colour transparencies (35mm), b/w copy photographs, line drawings

Dates of subject matter 1961 to present

Dates of photographs 1961 to present

Subjects Worldwide conservation of mammals, reptiles, amphibians, fish, birds, insects including butterflies, crustaceans, molluscs, aquatic life with special emphasis on endangered species; flowering plants in the UK and worldwide with special emphasis on the rainforests, destruction of tropical forests in South America and Africa, conservation projects undertaken by the Fund both in the UK and overseas, individuals (e.g. Duke of Edinburgh, David Bellamy and David Attenborough) connected with the Fund; environment destruction, animals products and trophies, hunting and poaching, tourism, Fund symbols and promotions

Access and conditions Not open; telephone and mail requests only. Most material available for editorial reproduction and for advertising; some for private research only. B/w and colour material loaned free of charge for one month. Photocopies available. Reproduction rights, holding and service fees charged; service fees deductible from use fees. Staff of two will undertake some research. Most material copyright. Printed catalogue in preparation.

698 • WORLDWIDE BUTTERFLIES LTD & LULLINGSTONE SILK FARM

Compton House, Nr Sherborne, Dorset DT9 4QN
Tel (0935) 74608

Enquiries to Robert Goodden, Director

Items 10,000: colour transparencies (35mm, 6 × 6cm, 2¼″), b/w original photographs

Dates of photographs c. 1960 to present

Subjects Butterflies and butterfly farm, including rare early stages of lepidoptera both exotic and European; large collection of *Saturniidae* (silkworms), *Papilionidae* and *Nymphalidae;* all species of British butterflies; silk farm, all stages in life cycle of silk worm, rearing in progress, reeling the silk; interesting genetic strains of larvae, different-coloured cocoons, unique chocolate race of *Bombyx mori* (normally white)

Access and conditions Not open; postal requests

only. Most material available for editorial reproduction and for advertising. Colour transparencies loaned free of charge for from two to four weeks. Reproduction rights fees charged. Staff will undertake some research.

699 • YORK ARCHAEOLOGICAL TRUST FOR EXCAVATION AND RESEARCH LTD

47 Aldwark, York YO1 2BX
Tel (0904) 643211 Telex 57623 JORVIK G

Enquiries to Dominic Tweddle, Assistant Director

Items About 20,000: b/w original photographs, colour transparencies (35mm, 60 × 45mm, 120mm)

Dates of subject matter AD 71 to present

Dates of photographs 1972 to present

Subjects Excavations in York since 1972, the conservation of archaeological material; special emphasis on Viking material (about 40% of collection), including reconstructed Viking street scenes and artefacts from Jorvik Viking Centre; Viking-age sites, sculptures and finds in Yorkshire; historic buildings of York, including buildings now demolished and buildings in the course of restoration

Access and conditions Open to qualified researchers by appt (write), Mon-Fri 9–4.30. All material available for editorial reproduction and for advertising. Colour transparencies loaned for a fee; b/w prints and duplicate colour transparencies available for a fee. Photocopies available for a fee. Reproduction rights and holding fees charged. Staff of two will undertake limited research. All material copyright.

700 • YORKSHIRE ARCHAEOLOGICAL SOCIETY

23 Clarendon Road, Leeds LS2 9NZ
Tel (0532) 457910

Enquiries to Pamela Campion, Librarian

Items 6500: b/w original and copy photographs, glass negatives, lantern slides, postcards, original cartoons, illustrated maps, old fine art prints, 20th-century fine art prints, posters, broadsheets, architectural drawings, illustrated books

Dates of subject matter BC to present

Dates of photographs 1870 to 1955

Subjects Archaeological history of Yorkshire including landscape and architecture, digs and artefacts; special collection of church fonts and doorways

Access and conditions Open to the public by appt, Mon Thurs Fri 9.30–5, Tues & Wed 2–8.30. All material available for editorial reproduction and for advertising by special arrangement only. No loans; material may be copied by outside photographers. Photocopies available. No reproduction rights fees charged. Staff will undertake limited research. Compulsory credit line. Most material copyright. Card catalogue in preparation.

701 • THE ZOOLOGICAL SOCIETY OF LONDON

Regent's Park, London NW1 4RY
Tel (01) 722 3333

The Library

Enquiries to Reginald Fish, Librarian

Items About 18,000: glass negatives, lantern slides, postcards, old fine art prints, press cuttings, illustrated books

Dates of subject matter 1870 to 1970

Dates of photographs 1870 to 1970

Subjects Mammals, birds, reptiles, fish, insects and other invertebrates in the collection of the London Zoo; coverage of veterinary care, zoo buildings, general views, personnel, visitors

Access and conditions Open to the public by appt (tel), Mon-Fri 9.30–5.30. All material available for editorial reproduction and for advertising. B/w prints available for a fee. Reproduction rights and service fees charged. Staff will undertake very limited research. Most material copyright.

Photographic Section

Enquiries to Michael Lyster, Photographer

Items About 45,000: unprinted film negatives, colour transparencies (35mm), b/w original photographs

Dates of subject matter 1960 to present

Dates of photographs 1960 to present

Subjects All animals (mammals, birds, reptiles, fish, insects and other invertebrates) in the collections of the London and Whipsnade Zoos including general views, buildings, feeding and caring for animals, keepers, visitors, some veterinary coverage

Access and conditions Open to the public by appt (tel), Mon-Fri 9.30–5.30. All material available for editorial reproduction and for advertising. B/w and colour material loaned free of charge for one month. Reproduction rights and holding fees charged; service fees charged sometimes. Staff will undertake very limited research. All material copyright.

Religion

702 • BRITISH AND FOREIGN BIBLE SOCIETY

Stonehill Green, Westlea, Swindon, Wiltshire
SN5 7DG
Tel (0793) 486381

Enquiries to Information Officer

Items About 13,000: colour transparencies
(35mm, 5″ × 4″), b/w original and copy
photographs, colour photographic prints, glass
negatives, postcards, unprinted film negatives,
cuttings and tearsheets, illustrated books

Dates of subject matter AD 380 to present

Dates of photographs 20th century

Subjects Activities of the Society in the UK and
abroad (especially Asia and Africa) including
printing and distribution of the Bible by vans,
shops, stalls, bicycles etc., to individual groups,
crowds; Bible Society staff in the UK and abroad,
past presidents; Bible House activities including
translating, conferences, celebrations, training
classes, literacy outreach, sponsored walks, action
groups, fund raising; Bible reading in the UK and
abroad, literacy and new readers; world geography,
natural history, towns, rural scenes, people at
work, church activities, historical buildings and
monuments

Access and conditions Open to the public by
appt, Mon-Fri 9.30–4.30. Some material available
for editorial reproduction and for advertising. B/w
and colour material loaned free of charge.
Photocopies available. Reproduction rights fees
charged; other fees negotiable. Staff will undertake
some research.

703 • THE BUDDHIST SOCIETY PHOTOGRAPHIC ARCHIVES

58 Eccleston Square, London SW1V 1PH
Tel (01) 834 5858

Enquiries to John Snelling, General Secretary

Items About 1000: b/w original photographs,
colour transparencies (35mm), colour photographic
prints, glass negatives, lantern slides, postcards,
fine art prints, unprinted film negatives, posters,
greetings cards, illustrated books, original prints
and drawings

Dates of subject matter 2500 BC to present

Dates of photographs c. 1890 to present

Subjects Buddhism and especially the history of
Western Buddhism, including images of the
Buddha and Buddhist monks, temples,
monasteries, monuments, ceremonies, festivals,
meetings; Buddhist iconography (paintings, wall
hangings, statues, *objets d'art*, etc); distinguished
Buddhists including Christmas Humphreys QC;
pictures from Buddhist countries including Tibet,
Burma, Sri Lanka, Thailand, Japan, China, Nepal,
India, etc.; historic events in the recent history of
Buddhism

Access and conditions Open to qualified
researchers by appt (write), Mon-Fri 9–5. Some
material available for editorial reproduction. Some
material loaned; in other cases b/w prints and
duplicate colour transparencies available for a fee.
Reproduction rights fees charged. Staff will
undertake limited research.

704 • CHRISTIAN AID

PO Box No 1, London SW9 8BH
Tel (01) 733 5500 Telex 916504 CHRAID G

Enquiries to Joseph Cabon (b/w), Nan Fromer
(colour)

Dates of photographs 1978 to present

Subjects Worldwide coverage of Third World
development including agriculture, health
(community-based medicine, clinics, nutrition),
industry (large complexes, village crafts),
education (training, technical co-operation,
literacy), refugees and displaced persons (war,
unemployment, natural disasters), tourism and its

effects on the Third World, urban environments (housing, building, markets and street vendors, people at work), water (drilling, pumps, wells, irrigation, conservation)

Access and conditions Open to the public by appt, Mon-Fri 9.30–5.30. Most material available for editorial reproduction but not for advertising. B/w material loaned free of charge for one month; colour transparencies loaned for a rental fee. Reproduction rights and holding fees charged. Staff will undertake some research.

705 • CHURCH MISSIONARY SOCIETY

Photograph Bureau and Slide Library, 157 Waterloo Road, London SE1 8UU
Tel (01) 928 8681

Enquiries to Jean Woods, Librarian

Items 30,000: colour transparencies (35mm), b/w original photographs

Dates of subject matter *c.* 1300 to present

Dates of photographs 1960 to present

Subjects Missionary work in Africa and Asia (30 countries) including medical care, development, teaching and church work, agriculture, education, local customs and scenery

Access and conditions Open to qualified researchers by appt (tel), Mon-Fri 9.30–5. Some material available for editorial reproduction and for advertising. B/w and colour material loaned free of charge for one month; duplicate colour transparencies available for a fee. Material may be copied by outside photographers. Reproduction rights fees charged. Card catalogue available.

706 • COUNCIL FOR THE CARE OF CHURCHES

83 London Wall, London EC2M 5NA
Tel (01) 638 0971

Enquiries to David Williams, Librarian

Items About 170,000: b/w original and copy photographs, colour transparencies (35mm), postcards, cuttings and tearsheets

Dates of subject matter 7th century to present

Dates of photographs Late 19th century to present

Subjects Ecclesiastical art and architecture with special reference to the buildings and furnishings of Anglican churches and cathedrals, including churchyards; conservation of church furnishings; contemporary arts and crafts in churches; National Survey of English Churches initiated during World War II

Access and conditions Open to the public by appt (tel), Mon-Fri 9.30–1, 2–5. Some material available for editorial reproduction but not for advertising. B/w and colour material loaned. Photocopies available. Reproduction rights fees charged. Staff of two will undertake some research for out-of-town requests.

707 • THE DEAN AND CHAPTER LIBRARY

The College, Durham DH1 3EH
Tel (0385) 62489

Enquiries to Roger C. Norris, Deputy Chapter Librarian

Items Over 3000: colour transparencies (35mm), glass negatives, postcards, b/w original and copy photographs, lantern slides, illustrated maps, unprinted film negatives, illustrated books, fine art prints

Dates of subject matter 6th century to present

Dates of photographs 1860 to present

Dates of fine art 17th to 19th centuries

Subjects Durham cathedral, its buildings, treasures, antiquities, personalities; Durham County churches; THOMAS ROMANS COLLECTION: archaeology, Roman and Saxon remains

Access and conditions Open to the public by appt (write), Mon-Fri 9–1, 2.15–5, closed in August. Some material available for editorial reproduction but not for advertising. No loans; b/w prints and duplicate transparencies available for a fee. Photocopies available. Reproduction rights and service fees charged. Staff will undertake limited research in response to specific requests. Card catalogue available.

708 • KEITH ELLIS COLLECTION

38 Colne Avenue, West Drayton, Middlesex UB7 7AL
Tel (0895) 448997

Enquiries to Keith Ellis

Items 10,000: b/w original negatives, colour transparencies (35mm, 2¼″), colour negatives

Dates of subject matter 14th century to present

Dates of photographs 1964 to present

Subjects Christian life including church buildings and furnishings, worship, festivals including Christmas, Easter, harvest, etc., customs; mission and outreach including evangelical campaigns by Billy Graham, Luis Palau and others; youth work in churches; portraits of Christian leaders and supporters; historical material relating to John and Charles Wesley, including ceramics, jugs and plates, personal effects including wig, umbrella and glasses, buildings and chapels and the New Room in Bristol; British Royal Family; customs associated with the City of London; natural history, especially flowers, and some landscapes and views around the UK

Access and conditions Open to qualified researchers by appt (tel), Mon-Fri 9–5. All material available for editorial reproduction and for advertising. B/w and colour material loaned free of charge for a negotiable period. Reproduction rights and holding fees charged. Staff will undertake research. All material copyright.

709 • HEREFORD CATHEDRAL LIBRARY

The Cathedral, Hereford HR1 2NG
Tel (0432) 58403, 273537

Enquiries to Penelope E. Morgan, Honorary Librarian

Items About 2400: glass negatives, lantern slides, b/w original photographs, architectural drawings, illustrated maps, fine art prints

Dates of subject matter 12th century to present

Dates of photographs 1925 to 1978

Subjects Hereford Cathedral including interiors and exteriors, chancel, nave, details of sculpture, all bosses in ceilings and vaulting, capitals, some stained glass, general views and details of exterior; prints of the cathedral (1970 & 1820 views), portraits of past and present Bishops, Deans, Prebendaries, etc.; watercolour of Vicar's cloister by J. M. W. Turner; details from illuminated manuscripts (earliest: 8th-century Gospels); incunabula including two Caxtons

Access and conditions Open to qualified researchers by appt (tel), Tues-Thurs 10–12.30 and by special appt. Some material available for editorial reproduction, but not for advertising. No loans; b/w prints available for a fee. Reproduction rights fees charged. Staff will undertake very limited research in response to out-of-town requests.

710 • IPA PICTURE LIBRARY

Crown House, Crown Lane, East Burnham, Nr Slough, Buckinghamshire SL2 3SG
Tel (02814) 5177   Telex 847031 ARABIA G

Enquiries to Hibah Griffin

Items 10,000: colour transparencies (35mm, larger), b/w original photographs

Dates of photographs 1980 to present

Subjects Islam and the Arab world including religion, culture and civilization; contemporary Muslim world, personalities in the news, economic development, banking, industry, education, health, agriculture, communications, architecture, traditional crafts, religious festivals and observances; Muslims at work, recreation, learning and worship; special coverage of the Hadj (pilgrimage), including aerial views; Muslim countries and minorities worldwide.

Access and conditions Open to the public by appt (tel), Mon-Fri 9.30–5.30. All material available for editorial reproduction and for advertising. B/w and colour material loaned free of charge for four weeks. Photocopies available. Reproduction rights and handling fees charged, handling fee deductible from use fee. Staff of three will undertake research.

711 • THE JEWISH MUSEUM

Woburn House, Upper Woburn Place, London WC1H 0EP
Tel (01) 388 4525

Enquiries to Edgar Samuel, Director

Items B/w photographs, oil paintings, prints and drawings

Dates of subject matter AD 800 to 1910

Subjects Paintings, prints and drawings (18th-and early 19th-century) of Jewish social history, portraits of rabbis in England. Note: prints and drawings are currently in storage and inaccessible, but may become available again in a few years. Items in the museum collection may be photographed by outside photographers by arrangement.

Access and conditions Open to the public by appt (tel), Tues-Thurs 10–4, Fri & Sun 10–12.45. Some material available for editorial reproduction. No loans; material may be photographed by outside photographers. Reproduction rights fees charged.

712 • KESTON COLLEGE

Heathfield Road, Keston, Kent BR2 6BA
Tel (0689) (from London 66) 50116

Enquiries to Jillian Hewitt, Photo Archivist

Items 2000: b/w original and copy photographs, colour transparencies (35mm), colour photographic prints, illustrated maps, art reproductions, posters, greetings cards

Dates of photographs 1915 to present

Subjects Religious life in communist countries, especially the Soviet Union and also Czechoslovakia, Poland, Romania, Bulgaria, Yugoslavia, China and Albania and filed by religious denomination and then by individuals: religious life, buildings; photographs of Soviet labour camps, prisons and psychiatric hospitals where religious believers have been incarcerated; religious groups represented include Russian Orthodox, Roman Catholic, Baptist, Pentecostal, Seventh-Day Adventist, Georgian Orthodox and Uniate; some photos are of *samizdat* nature, i.e. they were unofficially circulated, e.g. picture prayer cards about imprisoned believers circulated by Baptists in the Soviet Union

Access and conditions Open to qualified researchers by appt (write), Mon-Fri 9–5. Some material available for editorial reproduction but not for advertising. B/w and colour material loaned free of charge for one month. B/w prints and duplicate colour transparencies available for a fee. Reproduction rights and service fees charged. Staff will undertake limited research. Compulsory credit line.

713 • METROPOLITAN CATHEDRAL OF CHRIST THE KING

Cathedral House, Mount Pleasant, Liverpool
L3 5TQ
Tel (051) 709 9222

Enquiries to Administrator

Items About 1000: b/w original photographs, colour transparencies (35mm), colour photographic prints, glass negatives, architectural drawings, press cuttings and tearsheets

Dates of subject matter 1930 to present

Dates of photographs 1930 to present

Subjects Construction of the cathedral; crypt designed by Sir Edwin Lutyens (1930); cathedral as a whole designed by Sir Frederick Gibberd (1960); historic occasions including visit of Pope John Paul II (1982)

Access and conditions Open to qualified researchers by appt (tel). Some material available for editorial reproduction and for advertising. No loans; b/w prints and colour transparencies available for a fee. Reproduction rights fees charged. Staff will undertake limited research.

714 • MOCATTA LIBRARY

University College, Gower Street,
London WC1E 6BT
Tel (01) 387 7050 exts 778, 241

Enquiries to Trude Levi, Assistant Librarian

Items About 3000: b/w original and copy photographs, book plates, book illustrations

Dates of subject matter 18th century to *c*. 1955

Dates of photographs *c*. 1850 to *c*. 1955

Subjects Material from the collection of the Jewish Historical Society of England including portraits, caricatures, art objects, Jewish silver

Access and conditions Open to the public by appt, Mon & Wed 10–4. All material available for editorial reproduction and for advertising. No loans; b/w prints available for a fee. Photocopies available. No reproduction rights fees charged. Staff will undertake some research. Copyright clearance is responsibility of user.

Anglo-Jewish Archive

Items About 1000: b/w original photographs

Dates of subject matter 18th century to present

Dates of photographs Late 19th and 20th century

Subjects Anglo-Jewish community including events, conferences, buildings and openings of buildings, youth activities, summer camps, tombstones and inscriptions, personalities including P. S. Waley, Jacob L. Lion, Israel Zangwill, Dr Joseph Herman Hertz, Dr Moses Gaster, David Franklin

Access and conditions Open to the public by appt, Mon & Wed 2–4, Thurs 10–4. Some material available for editorial reproduction, but not for advertising. No loans; material may be copied by outside photographers. Photocopies available. No reproduction rights fees charged.

The Gaster Papers

Items About 3000: b/w original photographs, postcards, greetings cards, posters, illustrated books, ephemera

Dates of subject matter 19th to early 20th century

Dates of photographs 1850 to 1939

Subjects Anglo-Jewish portraits, conferences, meetings; Victoriana, greetings cards, propaganda leaflets, meetings notices, and ephemera of Jewish and general interest from the collection of Dr Moses Gaster (1870–1939)

Access and conditions Open to the public by appt (tel), Mon & Wed 2–4. All material available for editorial reproduction and some for advertising; in some cases permission to publish portraits must be cleared with family. No loans; b/w prints and duplicate transparencies available for a fee. Material may be copied by outside photographers. Photocopies available. No reproduction rights fees charged. Staff will undertake limited research.

715 • PLUSCARDEN ABBEY

Photographic Archives, Pluscarden, Elgin, Grampian IV30 3UA
Tel (034389) 257

Enquiries to Rev Dom Giles Conacher

Items 5000: unprinted film negatives, b/w original photographs, colour transparencies (35mm), postcards, colour photographic prints, glass negatives, lantern slides, architectural drawings

Dates of subject matter BC to present

Dates of photographs Early 20th century to present

Subjects Monastic buildings, abbeys, priories, churches; monastic life and work including prayers, the liturgy, study, pilgrimages, crafts, carving, bookbinding, stained glass, horticulture, restoration work, apiary; Scottish landscapes

Access and conditions Open to qualified researchers by appt (write). All material available for editorial reproduction and for advertising (some restrictions). B/w and colour material loaned free of charge (print fees charged); material may be copied by outside photographers. Reproduction rights and holding fees charged. Some research undertaken. All material copyright. Partial catalogue available.

716 • DR PUSEY MEMORIAL LIBRARY

Pusey House, St Giles, Oxford OX1 3LZ
Tel (0865) 59519

Enquiries to Rev. Dr H. R. Smythe

Items About 2700: b/w original photographs, original cartoons

Dates of subject matter c. 1833 to c. 1940

Dates of photographs c. 1850 to c. 1940

Subjects HALL COLLECTION: Anglican clergymen and Bishops prominent in the Anglo-Catholic Revival (Oxford, or Tractarian, Movement); STONE COLLECTION: Dorchester (Dorset) Missionary College, the town, photographs sent back from the African mission field (1888–1903); prints, engravings, watercolours, portraits, drawings and caricatures relating to the principal figures in the Oxford Movement

Access and conditions Open to qualified researchers by appt (write). All material available for editorial reproduction but not for advertising. B/w prints available for a fee. Colour material loaned or duplicated for a fee. Reproduction rights, service and holding fees charged. Staff of two will undertake limited research. Compulsory credit line.

717 • RELIGIOUS SOCIETY OF FRIENDS

Library, Friends House, Euston Road, London NW1 2BJ
Tel (01) 387 3601

Enquiries to Julius Smit, Picture Librarian

Items About 18,000: b/w original and copy photographs, colour transparencies (35mm), colour photographic prints, glass negatives, lantern slides, postcards, unprinted film negatives, posters, illustrated books

Dates of subject matter 1650 to present

Dates of photographs c. 1850 to present

Subjects History and work of the Society of Friends including portraits of Friends, meeting houses (mostly in UK, some in USA), schools; relief work by Quakers in World Wars I and II including medical care; missionary activity from late 19th century to early 20th century in India, China, Tanzania, Madagascar and Europe; manuscript material including papers, diaries, notebooks representing Quaker thought from 1640 onwards

Access and conditions Open to the public by appt (tel), Mon-Fri 10–5. All material available for editorial reproduction and for advertising. B/w and colour material loaned free of charge for one month; b/w prints and duplicate colour transparencies available for a fee; material may be copied by outside photographers. Photocopies available. Reproduction rights fees charged. Staff will undertake some research. Most material copyright. Duplicated catalogue available.

718 • THE SALVATION ARMY

Archives and Library, International Headquarters, 101 Queen Victoria Street, London EC4P 4EP
Tel (01) 236 5222 ext 229

Enquiries to Archivist and Librarian

Items Over 5000: b/w original and copy photographs, colour transparencies (35mm), glass negatives, lantern slides, postcards, posters, illustrated books

Dates of subject matter 1865 to present

Dates of photographs 1865 to present

Subjects History and work of Salvation Army from its foundation as Christian Mission; portraits of founders and officers; evangelism; social work from 1890s onwards; work overseas from 1880 onwards including contemporary work in 86 countries

Access and conditions Open to the public by appt (tel), Mon-Fri 9–4. All material available for editorial reproduction; advertising use by special arrangement only. B/w and colour material loaned

free of charge by arrangement; material may be copied by outside photographers. Photocopies available. No reproduction rights fees charged but donation appreciated. Staff will undertake some research. Compulsory credit line. Most material copyright. Card catalogue available.

719 • UNITED SOCIETY FOR THE PROPAGATION OF THE GOSPEL

15 Tufton Street, London SW1P 3QQ
Tel (01) 222 4222

Archives Section

Enquiries to Ian Pearson

Items About 50,000: b/w original and copy photographs, colour transparencies (35mm), colour photographic prints, glass negatives, lantern slides, postcards, original cartoons, illustrated maps, unprinted film negatives, posters, greetings cards, architectural drawings, press cuttings, illustrated books, engravings

Dates of subject matter c. 1701 to 1950s

Dates of photographs c. 1855 to 1950s

Subjects History of Christian mission worldwide including Africa, India, Far East, Australia and New Zealand, Central America and Canada with special emphasis on Central and East Africa; landscapes, all aspects of indigenous cultures and lifestyles, agriculture, crafts; church personnel, churches, hospitals, schools

Access and conditions Open to qualified researchers by appt (write), Mon-Thurs 10–5. All material available for editorial reproduction; advertising use by special arrangement only. No loans; b/w prints and duplicate colour transparencies available for a fee; material may be copied by outside photographers. Reproduction rights fees charged. Most material copyright. Partial card catalogue available.

Photo Bureau Section

Enquiries to Mary Harrison

Items About 55,000: colour transparencies (35mm), b/w original photographs, 20th-century fine art prints, illustrated books

Dates of subject matter 1950 to present

Dates of photographs 1950 to present

Subjects Missionary activity worldwide including Africa, India, Pakistan, Burma, Far East, Pacific,

Americas, West Indies, Europe; education, agriculture, crafts, landscape; church personnel and activities; some coverage of painting and sculpture from Zimbabwe, India and China

Access and conditions Open to the public by appt (tel), Mon-Fri 10–5. All material available for editorial reproduction; advertising use by special arrangement only. B/w and colour material loaned free of charge for one month; material may be copied by outside photographers. Reproduction rights fees charged. Staff will undertake limited research. All material copyright.

720 • WESLEY HISTORICAL SOCIETY

Southlands College, 65 Wimbledon Parkside, London SW19 5NN
Tel (01) 946 2234 ext 202

Enquiries to Librarian, Southlands College

Items About 2500: b/w original and copy photographs, colour transparencies (35mm), colour photographic prints, lantern slides, postcards, original cartoons, old fine art prints, art reproductions, unprinted film negatives, posters, greetings cards, architectural drawings, press cuttings, illustrated books

Dates of subject matter 1700 to present

Dates of photographs 1870 to present

Dates of fine art 17th to 19th century

Subjects History and development of Methodism; portraits, buildings worldwide associated with Methodism; circuit plans, manuscripts and newspapers relating to Methodist local history

Access and conditions Open to the public by appt, Mon-Fri 9–5. Most material available for editorial reproduction and for advertising. No loans; b/w prints available for a fee. Photocopies

available. Reproduction rights fees charged. Staff will undertake limited research. All material copyright. Card catalogue available.

721 • YORK MINSTER LIBRARY

Dean's Park, York YO1 2JD
Tel (0904) 25308

Enquiries to Bernard Barr, Sub-Librarian

Items About 15,000: b/w original photographs, colour transparencies (5″ × 4″), glass negatives, lantern slides, old fine art prints, illustrated maps, architectural drawings, press cuttings, illustrated books

Dates of subject matter AD 70 to present

Dates of photographs 1890s to present

Subjects History and development of York Minster including architecture, details of the fabric, stonework, woodwork, metalwork, stained glass, furnishings; excavations and archaeological finds; portraits of Archbishops and Minster staff; history of the choir school, local history of York and Yorkshire including landscapes, architecture, York city churches, social history, personalities; special collections include the GREEN PHOTOGRAPHIC COLLECTION relating to the Minster from 1890s to 1970s, and the HAILSTONE LOCAL HISTORY COLLECTION

Access and conditions Open to the public by appt (write), Mon-Fri 9–5. All material available for editorial reproduction and for advertising by arrangement (some restrictions). No loans; b/w prints and duplicate colour transparencies available for a fee. Photocopies available. Reproduction rights fees charged. Most material copyright. Staff will undertake limited research. Card catalogue available.

Sport

722 • AEROPHOTO

Harrier House, 26 Blandy Avenue, Southmoor, Oxfordshire OX13 5DB
Tel (0865) 820729

Enquiries to Christopher Brooks, Managing Director

Items 12,000: colour transparencies (35mm, 5″ × 4″), b/w original photographs, colour photographic prints

Dates of subject matter 1914 to present

Dates of photographs 1966 to present

Subjects Vintage, civil and military aircraft including air-to-air photographs; vintage and high performance motor cars; motor racing especially Formula One, Two and Group C; English, European and Scandinavian landscapes; skiing and ski resorts; winter scenes; fashion and posed models

Access and conditions Open to qualified researchers by appt (write), Mon-Fri 9–5. All material available for editorial reproduction and for advertising. B/w and colour material loaned free of charge for one month. Reproduction rights, service and holding fees charged; service fees deductible from use fees. Staff of two will undertake some research; fees charged for large projects. All material copyright.

723 • ALL-ACTION PHOTOGRAPHIC

134 Tooley Street, London SE1 2TU
Tel (01) 378 7417/8   Telex 8951182 GECOMS G

Enquiries to Vanessa Colls

Items 65,000: colour transparencies (35mm), b/w original photographs

Dates of photographs 1980 to present

Subjects Sports especially motor sports (motor cycling and motor racing), BMX, football, athletics, golf; American football, cricket, tennis, water sports (surfing, windsurfing, water-skiing, powerboat-racing); minority sports including cycling, polo, croquet, bowls, darts, foreign sports; sports personalities (e.g. Barry Sheene, Daley Thompson, David Gower, Glen Hoddle, Barry McGuigan, Steve Cram) including feature stories, at home, etc.; special events including Triathlons, truck racing, veteran athletes; special effects, unusual and off-beat action shots; special collection of politicians

Access and conditions Open to qualified researchers, Mon-Fri 9–7. All material available for editorial reproduction; advertising use only with permission of agent or personality. B/w and colour material loaned free of charge for four weeks. Reproduction rights, service and holding fees charged; service fee deductible from use fee. Staff of three will undertake research; fee negotiable for large projects. All material copyright.

724 • ALL ENGLAND NETBALL ASSOCIATION LTD

Francis House, Francis Street, London SW1P 1DE
Tel (01) 828 2176

Enquiries to Brian Worrell, National Publicity Officer

Items 3000: b/w original photographs, colour transparencies (35mm)

Dates of subject matter 1977 to present

Dates of photographs 1977 to present

Subjects Netball including most English National events, England players and squads, 6th World Tournament in Singapore; country, regional and schools tournaments

Access and conditions Open to the public by appt (write), Mon-Fri 9–5. All material available for editorial reproduction and for advertising. No loans; b/w prints and duplicate transparencies available for a fee. Reproduction rights fees charged. Staff will carry out some research. All material copyright.

725 • ALL-SPORT PHOTOGRAPHIC LTD

55/57 Martin Way, Morden, Surrey SM4 4AH
Tel (01) 543 0988 Telex 8955022 ASPORT G

Enquiries to Robert McMahon, Library Manager

Items About one million: colour transparencies (35mm), b/w original photographs

Dates of subject matter 1896 to present

Dates of photographs 1896 to present

Subjects Professional and amateur sports including athletics, American football, boxing, cricket, equestrian sports, football, golf, gymnastics, horse racing, hang-gliding, motor racing, Rugby (Union and League), swimming synchro-swimming, diving, tennis, weight-lifting, windsurfing, winter sports including skiing, skating, ice hockey, bobsledding, ski-jumping, speed-skating; famous events including Olympic Games (1896 to 1984), World Cup Football, Commonwealth Games, Cricket Test Matches, Open Golf, Grand National, Derby, Wimbledon Tennis, British Grand Prix; sports grounds including Lords, the Oval, Twickenham, Wembley, Brands Hatch, Los Angeles Coliseum, Caesar's Palace, Crystal Palace, St Andrews; children in sport, games including frisbee, marbles, hot-water-bottle blowing, skateboarding, roller-skating, tug-of-war, fishing; sports personalities including John McEnroe, Daley Thompson, Carl Lewis, Sebastian Coe, Joe Namath, Bryan Robson, Muhammad Ali, Ian Botham, Jack Nicklaus, Lester Piggott, Niki Lauda, Torvill and Dean

Access and conditions Open to qualified researchers by appt (tel), Mon-Fri 9–6. All material available for editorial reproduction; advertising use of photographs of amateur sportsmen and sportswomen must comply with rules governing their status. B/w and colour material loaned free of charge for one month. Prints and duplicate transparencies available for a fee. Reproduction rights, service and holding fees charged. Staff of 12 will carry out research; fees charged for large projects. All material copyright.

726 • ANGLING PRESS SERVICE

53 Cromwell Road, Hounslow, Middlesex TW3 3QG
Tel (01) 570 2811

Enquiries to Bill Howes

Items About 50,000: b/w original photographs, colour transparencies (35mm)

Dates of subject matter 1950 to present

Dates of photographs 1950 to present

Subjects Angling (coarse, game and sea); waterways (canals, rivers, reservoirs); aquatic life (fish, insects, amphibians); angling baits, tackle, locations (home and abroad); coastal and offshore subjects; tourism (USSR, Malta, Gibraltar, Madeira, Italy, Ireland, Scotland, Wales, England); garden flowers, pools, plants

Access and conditions Open to qualified researchers by appt, Mon-Fri 9–5. All material available for editorial reproduction and for advertising. B/w and colour material loaned free of charge for one month. Reproduction rights fees charged. Staff will undertake research within the collection. All material copyright.

727 • ASSOCIATED SPORTS PHOTOGRAPHY

21 Green Walk, Leicester LE3 6SE
Tel (0533) 879666

Enquiries to Christine Silvester

Items Over 50,000: colour transparencies (35mm), b/w original photographs, unprinted film negatives

Dates of photographs 1970 to present

Subjects British, European and world sports and sporting events with emphasis on soccer (World Cup 1982, European Cup Finals 1979–1984, Super-cup, League, League Cup and FAC Internationals), Rugby Union, athletics (Olympics 1964–1984, World Athletics 1983, European Championships 1969, 1971, 1974, 1982, European Cup 1973, 1979, 1983, Commonwealth Games 1966, 1970, 1974), cricket, tennis (including Wimbledon), golf; and also angling, archery, badminton, basketball, boardsailing, boats (Henley Regatta, Boat Race), bowls, boxing, canoeing, cross-country running, cycling, cyclo-cross, diving, fencing, gliding, gymnastics, grid iron, hang-gliding, hockey, ice hockey, ice-skating, horse-racing, jumping, three-day eventing, polo, the Derby, Ascot, Grand National, judo, lacrosse, motor cycles, parachuting, paraplegic games, power boats, rock-climbing, roller-skating, rowing, Rugby League, sailing, speedway, squash, swimming, tug-of-war, volley-ball, water-polo, water-skiing, weight-lifting, wrestling; extensive collection of individual action shots (no portraits) of leading personalities

Access and conditions Open to qualified researchers by appt (tel), Mon-Fri 9–5.30. B/w and colour material loaned free of charge for one month; print fees charged. Photocopies available. Reproduction rights, service and holding fees charged; service fees deductible from use fees. Staff of three will undertake some research.

728 • BEKEN OF COWES LTD

16 Birmingham Road, Cowes, Isle of Wight
PO31 7BH
Tel (0983) 297311

Enquiries to Kenneth J. Beken

Items 145,000: b/w original photographs, colour transparencies (2¼″), glass negatives

Dates of photographs 1880 to present

Subjects Maritime photography: yachting including racing, cruising, dinghies, windsurfing, tall ships, schooners, square riggers, barquentines, boardsailing, ocean races, etc., in UK waters and abroad; ocean liners, powerboats racing and cruising, hovercraft, hydrofoils, steam yachts, Bristol Grand Prix, Cowes, Classic, *Queen Elizabeth II*, *HMS Britannia*, etc.

Access and conditions Open to qualified researchers by appt (tel), Mon-Fri 9–1, 2.15–5.30. All material available for editorial reproduction and for advertising (no calendars). B/w and colour material loaned free of charge for one month. Photocopies available. Reproduction rights, service and holding fees charged. Staff of two will undertake some research.

729 • ALASTAIR BLACK PHOTOGRAPHY

20 Chester Crescent, Lee-on-Solent, Hampshire
PO13 9BH
Tel (0705) 550894

Enquiries to Alastair Black

Items 20,000: colour transparencies (35mm)

Dates of photographs 1974 to present

Subjects Sailing, yachting, windsurfing and wave-jumping (especially in Hawaii); sailing ships including yachts, tall ships, square riggers; ocean liners; marinas and yacht clubs; races including Cowes, Clipper Cup in Hawaii, Admiral's Cup at Cowes, SORC in Florida, etc.

Access and conditions Open to qualified researchers by appt (tel). All material available for editorial reproduction and for advertising. Colour material loaned free of charge for one month. Reproduction rights and holding fees charged; service fees charged when no material is used. Staff will undertake research. All material copyright.

730 • THE BRITISH SPORTING ART TRUST

c/o The Tate Gallery, Millbank, London SW1P 4RG

Organizing Secretary, Picketts Cottage, Medmenham, Marlow, Buckinghamshire SL7 2EZ
Tel (0491) 571294

Enquiries to Mary Dougal, Organizing Secretary

Items About 500: colour transparencies (35mm, 5″ × 4″), b/w original photographs, fine art prints, postcards, greetings cards, illustrated books

Dates of subject matter 1750 to 1950

Dates of photographs 1945 to present

Subjects British sporting art (both paintings and prints) including hunting, shooting, coursing, coaching, farming, fishing, cock-fighting, boxing, archery, riding, baiting, games, horses, dogs, hawking, racing and by the following artists: Emil Adam, Henry Alken, H. B. Chalon, R. B. Davis, George Garrard, John Frederick Herring, Ben Marshall, Robert Pollard, J. M. Sartorius, James Seymour, Thomas Spencer, George Stubbs, John Wootton, and others

Access and conditions Open by appt with the Organizing Secretary; some material on view at the Tate Gallery, the York City Art Gallery and the National Horse Racing Museum. All material available for editorial reproduction and for advertising. B/w and colour material loaned for one month for a fee. Photocopies available. Reproduction rights fees charged. Staff will undertake research; negotiable fee for large projects.

731 • JOHN CLEARE MOUNTAIN CAMERA

67 Vanbrugh Park, London SE3 7JQ
Tel (01) 858 8667

Enquiries to Jo Cleare

Items About 130,000: unprinted film negatives, colour transparencies (35mm), b/w original photographs

Dates of photographs 1960 to present

Subjects Mountain climbing and wilderness sports worldwide including camping, canoeing and river-running, caving, desert travel, fell-running and racing, fell-walking, health and medicine, high-altitude mountaineering, hiking, hill-walking, ice-climbing, jungle-bashing, kayaking and rafting, Operation Drake, orienteering, rescue and safety, rock-climbing, safaris, sailing and Tall Ships, sea canoeing, sea-cliff climbing, skiing (Nordic, cross-country, mountaineering and touring, downhill, speed-skiing), techniques and equipment, trekking; landscapes, geographical, geological and glacial features, flora and fauna, weather; people, villages, agriculture, culture, work and play; the preceding subjects and activities in mountain and wilderness areas worldwide including England, Scotland and Wales and offshore islands, Europe including the Alps (Mont Blanc, the Matterhorn, the Eiger), the Pyrenees, Mt Olympus, areas in Norway, Sweden, Iceland, Greenland, Portugal, Spain, Holland, Czechoslovakia and Germany, North America including most mountain ranges (Sierra Nevada, Yosemite, Tetons, Rockies), deserts of the south-west including Canyonlands, Bryce, Death Valley, Grand Canyon, Monument Valley, Zion, rivers and coastal areas including the Colorado, California coasts and redwood groves, Alaska including an ascent of Mt McKinley, Canadian Rockies and the Bugaboo Range of British Columbia, South America including Peru and the Peruvian Andes (Cordillera Blanca, Huayhuash, Raura, Vilcanota and Vilcabamba), rivers including the sources of the Amazon, Rio Urubamba, the Sacred Valley, Lake Titicaca, Inca ruins, the Inca Trail, Macchu Picchu, deserts and volcanoes in Peru, Ecuador and Mexico, the Falkland Islands; Asia including most regions of the Nepalese Himalayas (Mt Everest, Annapurna), the Trisuli River and Terai jungles, Indian Himalayas and Nanda Devi, Kashmir Himalayas and Nanga Parbat, Ladakh, Karakoram range of Pakistan including K2 and other peaks, Baltoro Glacier and Indus River, China including Xinjiang, Turkestan, Pamirs, Tien Shan, Tibet, Bangladesh, Burma, Bali, Java, New Guinea, Israel and Sinai desert, Africa including Kenya, Mt Kenya, Hell's Gate Gorge, volcanoes, the Rift Valley, lakes, coast, flora and wildlife (especially in Tsavo, Meru and Masai Mara National Parks), Uganda and the Ruwenzori Range (Mountains of the Moon), Murchison and Rwenzori (Queen Elizabeth) National Parks, River Nile, Murchison Falls, Tanzania and Mt. Kilimanjaro, soda lakes, forests and plantations, Ethiopia including landscapes, gorges, villages and markets, Australasia including New Zealand, Fiji, Papua New Guinea, Arctic and Antarctic including Antarctic peninsula, Graham Land, South Georgia, dog-sledging, survey bases, ice-breakers, etc.; sea coasts, sailing, cities (worldwide); industry including aircraft, bridges, construction sites, cooling towers, industrial landscapes, docks, harbours, factories, motorways, oil platforms, oil refineries, power stations, railways, shipbuilding, tunnels and tunnelling; miscellaneous subjects including abstracts, archaeology, avalanches, boats, camels, castles, cathedrals, caves, children, clouds, crowds, curling, elephants, gardens, ghost towns, graffiti, Great Wall of China, Hadrian's Wall, hotsprings, hut circles, icebergs, islands, lighthouses, meteorology, military parades, monuments, moons, native dances, ostriches, ploughing, rainbows, reflections, roads, reservoirs, ruins, scouts, shinty, ships, stately homes, statues, sunrises, sunsets, surf, tents, Uighur tribesmen, waterfalls, windmills, yaks, yurts, zebras

Access and conditions Open to the public by appt (tel), Mon-Fri 9–5.30. All material available for editorial reproduction and for advertising. B/w and colour material loaned free of charge for one month. Reproduction rights and holding fees charged; service fees charged only when no material is used. Staff of two will undertake research. All material copyright.

732 • CLICKSTOP SPORTS PHOTOGRAPHY

Lingholm, Blackheath, Guildford, Surrey GU4 8RD
Tel (0483) 892251

Enquiries to Simon Childs or Mike Johnson

Items Over 3500: colour transparencies (35mm)

Dates of photographs 1981 to present

Subjects Sports and automotive subjects including skiing (European circuit at Garmisch, Wengen, Kitzbuhel), UK powerboating Grand Prix (Royal Victoria Docks, London), gymnastics tournaments (Wembley Coca-Cola International), tennis (Queen's Club, Eastbourne Women's Tournament), motor racing (Formula One, endurance racing in England, Austria, Germany), canoeing in Wales

Access and conditions Open to qualified researchers by appt, Mon-Fri 9–5. All material available for editorial reproduction and for advertising. Colour material loaned free of charge for one month. Reproduction rights and holding fees charged. Staff will undertake research. All material copyright.

733 • MICHAEL COLE CAMERAWORK

The Coach House, 27 The Avenue, Beckenham, Kent BR3 2DP
Tel (01) 658 6120

Enquiries to Michael Cole

Items About 300,000: unprinted film negatives, colour transparencies (35mm, 5" × 4"), glass negatives

Dates of photographs 1900 to present; colour from mid-1950s

Subjects Tennis and history of tennis worldwide including Major Walter Clapton Wingfield and players and games at Wimbledon in the early 1900s, all leading tennis players (Suzanne Lenglen, Rod Laver, John Newcombe, Rosie Casals, Bjorn Borg, John McEnroe, Chris Evert Lloyd, Martina Navratilova, etc.) and major tournaments throughout the world (US Open, French Open, Davis Cup, Monte Carlo, Queen's Club, London, Brighton), both action and portraits. Official photographers to All England Lawn Tennis Club, Wimbledon

Access and conditions Open to qualified researchers by appt (tel), Mon-Fri 9.30–5.30. All material available for editorial reproduction and for advertising (subject to rules governing amateur status). B/w and colour material loaned free of charge for one month. Reproduction rights, service and holding fees charged; service fees deductible from use fees. Photocopies available. Staff will undertake research.

734 • COLORSPORT

44 St Peter's Street, London N1 8JT
Tel (01) 359 2714 Telex 24224 (quote Ref 970)

Enquiries to Colin Elsey, Stewart Fraser, Andrew Cowie

Items 300,000: colour transparencies (35mm), b/w original photographs

Dates of photographs 1881 to present

Subjects Sports and games from around the world including American football, archery, Association football, athletics, Australian rules football, basketball, bobsleighing, bowls, boxing, bull-fighting, canoeing, chess, cresta run, cricket, croquet, curling, cycling, cyclo-cross, darts, diving, fencing, figure-skating, fishing, fox-hunting, Gaelic football, golf, greyhound-racing, gymnastics (inc. M.R.G.), handball, hang-gliding, hockey, horse-racing, hovercraft-racing, hurling, ice-dancing, ice hockey, ice speedway, judo, kung fu, lacrosse, luge, mah-jong, marbles, microlite flying, modern pentathlon, motor cycling, motor racing, motor rallying, orienteering, petanque, polo, pool, powerboat racing, rallycross, rowing, Rugby League, Rugby Union, sailing, sand-yachting, shooting, shove ha'penny, skate-boarding, skiing, ski-jumping, showjumping, snooker, speed-skating, speedway, squash, surfing, swimming, synchronized swimming, table tennis, tennis, three-day event, volleyball, water-skiing, weightlifting, windsurfing, wrestling (Greco-Roman); Association football includes historical material from 1881 to the present and players Sir Stanley Mathews, Dixie Dean, Tom Finney, Billy Meredith, Tommy Taylor, Billy Wright, Stan Mortenson, Duncan Edwards, Jackie Milburn, Pelé, Franz Beckenbauer, Johan Cruyff, George Best, Bobby Moore, Bobby Charlton, Michel Platini, Karl-Heinz Rummenigge, Bryan Robson, Zico, Diego Maradona, etc.; World Cup Finals; FA Cup-winning teams from 1881 to present; European Nations Cup Finals; European Club Competition Finals from 1973; all aspects of British domestic football; cricket includes historical material from 1920 to the present and players Sir Garfield Sobers, Sir Donald Bradman, Sir Leary Constantine, Harold Larwood, Sir Leonard Hutton, Freddie Trueman, Denis Compton, Dennis Lillee, Geoff Boycott, David Gower, Ian Botham, Clive Lloyd, Viv Richards, Greg Chappell, Kapil Dev, Imran Khan and other international and county cricketers of the last 65 years; Rugby Union includes British Lions tours to New Zealand and South Africa since 1974; the Five Nations Championship since 1969; the Varsity match; tours by Australia, Canada, England, Fiji, Japan, New Zealand, South Africa, etc.; club and county championship games and top players since the late 1960s; world-famous events include Olympic Games, World Cup football and cricket, Commonwealth Games, Wimbledon, the Derby, the Grand National, Henley Royal Regatta, Open Golf, Spartakiad, etc.; famous sport venues includes Wembley Stadium, Lord's, The Oval, Twickenham, Wimbledon, Maracana Stadium (Rio), Los Angeles Coliseum, Athens, Madison Square Garden, Caesar's Palace, Cardiff Arms Park, Ellis Park, Giants Stadium, Parc des Princes, Munich, Montreal, Moscow, Sydney Cricket Ground, etc.; famous sports personalities include John McEnroe, Martina Navratilova, Daley Thompson, Seb Coe, Steve Ovett, Steve Cram, Tessa Sanderson, Zola Budd, Carl Lewis, Ed Moses, Muhammad Ali, Larry Holmes, Jack Nicklaus, Severiano Ballesteros, Tom Watson, Tony Jacklin (inc. '69 Open win), Lester Piggott, Willie Carson, Yves Saint-Martin, John Francome, Niki Lauda, Torvill and Dean, Rodnina and Zaitsev, Bill Beaumont, Barry John, Eric Bristow, David Bryant, Steve Davis, Alex Higgins, Lucinda Green, Jahingir Khan, Jean-Claude Killy, Franz Klammer, Mark Spitz, Jackie Stewart, Bjorn Borg, Olga Korbut, Nadia Comaneci, members of the Royal Family attending and participating in several sporting events (Princess Diana at Wimbledon, the Queen at Ascot and Badminton, Princes Charles playing Polo, etc.)

Access and conditions Open to qualified researchers by appt (tel), Mon-Fri 10–6. All material available for editorial reproduction and for advertising (subject to rules governing amateur status and model releases). B/w prints available for a fee; colour material loaned free of charge for four weeks. Reproduction rights, service and holding fees charged; service and holding fees deductible from use fees. Staff of five will undertake research.

735 • GERRY CRANHAM'S COLOUR LIBRARY

80 Fairdene Road, Coulsdon, Surrey CR3 2RE
Tel (07375) 53688

Enquiries to Nan Cranham

Items About 400,000: b/w original photographs, colour transparencies (35mm, 5″ × 4″)

Dates of photographs 1959 to present

Subjects Sports and recreation both amateur and professional, including special emphasis on horse-racing and also athletics, African game parks, archery, American football, American horse-racing, boating, bowls, bobsleighing, billiards, boxing, bicycle polo, cycling, cyclo-cross, canoeing, cricket, cross-country running, curling, croquet, fencing, football, fishing, gymnastics, golf, gliding, greyhound-racing, hockey, hound-trailing, highland games, hill-climbing, ice hockey, karting, Le Mans Motor Race, motor-cycle road racing, motor-cycle scrambling, motor-car racing, mud-larking, National Hunt horse-racing, parachuting, polo, point-to-point racing, power boating, racing stables, rowing, Rugby, sailing, skiing, ski-bobbing, showjumping, shooting, speedway, swimming, tennis, table tennis, tug-of-war, underwater swimming, water polo, wild animals (African), weight lifting, walking, water-skiing, wrestling, yachting; Olympic Games and other major sporting events

Access and conditions Open to qualified researchers by appt, Mon-Fri 9–6. All material available for editorial reproduction and for advertising. B/w and colour material loaned free of charge for one month. Reproduction rights and holding fees charged. Staff of two will undertake some research; negotiable fee for large projects.

736 • PETER DAZELEY PHOTOGRAPHY

5 Heathmans Road, London SW6 4TJ
Tel (01) 736 3171

Enquiries to Peter Dazeley

Items 75,000: unprinted film negatives, colour transparencies (35mm, 2¼″)

Dates of photographs 1970 to present

Subjects Golf, celebrities, trophies

Access and conditions Open to qualified researchers by appt, Mon-Fri 9.30–5.30. All material available for editorial reproduction and for advertising. B/w and colour material loaned free of charge for four weeks. Photocopies available. Reproduction rights and holding fees charged; service fees charged for large orders or bike deliveries. Staff of four will undertake research.

737 • PATRICK EAGAR

5 Ennerdale Road, Kew Gardens, Surrey TW9 3PG
Tel (01) 940 9269

Items About 208,000: b/w original photographs,
colour transparencies (35mm)

Dates of photographs 1965 to present

Subjects Cricket: in England, all Test Matches
from 1972 to present, county cricket from 1965,
one-day competitions/finals, village cricket, cricket
trophies, cricket grounds (all first-class grounds
and Test Match grounds), portraits and action
shots of over 1000 first-class cricketers, landmarks
in cricket (Glenn Turner's 1000th run in May 1973,
Geoff Boycott's 100th century in 1977, Bob Willis'
300th Test wicket, etc.); in Australia, Test Matches
vs England (1974–1975, 1977, 1978–1979, 1979–
1980, 1982–1983) and *vs* West Indies (1975–1976,
1979–1980), Sheffield Shield, cricket grounds (Sydney,
Melbourne, Adelaide, Brisbane, Perth), portraits
and action shots of test cricketers; in West Indies,
Test Matches *vs* Australia (1973, 1978) and *vs*
England (1981), Shell Shield, cricket on beach,
Barbados, informal cricket, Trinidad, cricket
grounds (Port of Spain, Bridgetown, Georgetown);
in India, Test Matches *vs* England (1976–1977, 1980,
1981–1982), Bombay, Calcutta, Madras, portraits
and action shots of players; in Pakistan, Test
Matches *vs* England (1977–1978) and *vs* India (1978),
Karachi, Lahore, portraits and action shots of
players; in New Zealand, Test Matches *vs* England
(1984), Wellington, Christchurch, Auckland,
portraits and action shots of players; Sharjah
(UAE), one-day competitions; wine: France,
vineyards, vines, cellars, winemakers and officials,
ceremonies, Burgundy, Bordeaux, Alsace,
Champagne, Loire, Rhone, Jura, Cognac;
Australia, vineyards, vines, cellars, Barossa
Valley, Coonawarra, Southern Vales (SA), Hunter
Valley (NSW), Ch. Tahbilk (Vic), Swan Valley
(WA); others, England, Greece, Italy, New Zealand

Access and conditions Open to qualified
researchers by appt (tel), Mon-Fri 9–6. B/w and
colour material loaned free of charge for one
month. Reproduction rights, holding and service
fees charged; service fees deductible from use fees.
Staff of three will undertake research. All material
copyright.

738 • FELL AND ROCK CLIMBING CLUB OF THE ENGLISH LAKE DISTRICT

c/o Abbot Hall Art Gallery, Kendal, Cumbria
LA9 5AL
Tel (0539) 22464

Enquiries to June Parker (Club Secretary) for
permission, Mary E. Burkett (Museum Director)
for access

Items 733: glass negatives, b/w original
photographs

Dates of photographs 19th and 20th century

Subjects ABRAHAM COLLECTION: fell- and rock-
climbing, especially by pioneer climbers in the
Lake District, climbers in action, their exploits and
achievements, local scenes and rock faces, portraits
of pioneer climbers

Access and conditions Open to qualified
researchers by appt (write), Mon-Fri 10.30–5.30.
All material available for editorial reproduction but
not for advertising. B/w prints available for a fee.
Photocopies available. Material may be copied by
outside photographers. Reproduction rights and
service fees charged. Staff will undertake limited
research for specific requests; fees charged for large
projects.

739 • DAVID FRITH COLLECTION

6 Beech Lane, Guildford, Surrey GU2 5ES
Tel (0483) 32573

Enquiries to David Frith

Items 100,000: b/w original and copy photographs,
colour transparencies (35mm), colour photographic
prints, glass negatives, postcards, original
cartoons, fine art prints, art reproductions, posters,
greetings cards, press cuttings and tearsheets,
illustrated books, ephemera

Dates of subject matter 1744 to present

Dates of photographs 1862 to present

Subjects Cricket worldwide

Access and conditions Open to qualified
researchers by appt, Mon-Fri 9.30–5.30. All
material available for editorial reproduction and
for advertising. B/w and colour material loaned free
of charge for one month. B/w prints and duplicate
colour transparencies available for a fee.
Reproduction rights, service and holding fees
charged. Staff will undertake some research.

740 • TOMMY HINDLEY

26 Conway Road, London N14 7BA
Tel (01) 882 2555

Enquiries to Tommy Hindley

Items About 50,000: b/w original photographs, colour transparencies (35mm)

Dates of photographs 1960 to present

Subjects Sports including Wimbledon from 1977 to present (personalities, matches, major and minor players), some earlier Wimbledon material (1920s), LTA tournaments, British and British Junior tournaments, Davis Cup, US Open, French Open, Masters, Australian Open; golf, athletics, Rugby, darts, snooker, skiing, handball, water sports, swimming, soccer (FA Cup, Milk Cup, World Cup, main English and Scottish international matches), equestrian sports (Badminton, Hickstead, major trials, Grand National), gymnastics, sailing, hockey, ice hockey, basketball, Rugby League; Olympic Games (Moscow, Los Angeles) including judo, motor racing, squash, speedway, wrestling (professional and amateur), Australian football, badminton, boxing, canoeing, cricket (some Test Matches)

Access and conditions Open to qualified researchers by appt (tel), Mon–Fri 9–5. All material available for editorial reproduction and for advertising. B/w and colour material loaned free of charge for one month. Reproduction rights, service and holding fees charged; service fee deductible from use fee. Staff of four will undertake some research. All material copyright.

741 • THE JOCKEY CLUB

Newmarket, Suffolk CB8 8JL
Tel (0638) 664151

Enquiries to Robert Fellowes

Items Original cartoons, illustrated maps, fine art prints, art reproductions

Dates of subject matter 1660 to present

Subjects English racing and the British thoroughbred from 1660 to the present; paintings of racehorses by George Stubbs, J. N. Sartorius, J. F. Herring Sr, Sir Alfred Munnings, Lynwood Palmer, Emil Adam and others

Access and conditions Open to qualified researchers by appt (write). All material available for editorial reproduction and for advertising.

Agent will arrange for or direct researchers to b/w prints and colour transparencies. Reproduction rights fees charged. Staff will undertake limited research.

742 • BOB LANGRISH EQUESTRIAN PHOTOGRAPHY

1 Whitebeam Close, Longlevens, Gloucester GL2 0UG
Tel (0452) 20371

Enquiries to Bob Langrish

Items 16,000: colour transparencies (35mm, 2¼"), b/w original photographs, colour negatives

Dates of photographs 1968 to present

Subjects International showjumping, eventing, dressage, driving, holidays on horseback; features on riders at home; polo, Pony Club mounted games; breeds, county shows; long-distance riding, Calgary Stampede and American rodeos, working ranches (USA), fox-hunting (UK and USA), ploughing, stable management, racing, mares and foals

Access and conditions Open to qualified researchers by appt (tel), Mon–Fri 9–5. All material available for editorial reproduction and for advertising. B/w and colour material loaned free of charge for one month. Print fee charged for b/w; deductible from use fee. Reproduction rights fees charged. Staff will undertake some research. Card catalogue.

743 • LAT PHOTOGRAPHIC

Standard House, Bonhill Street, London EC2A 4DA
Tel (01) 628 4741 Telex 888602 MONEWS G

Enquiries to Picture Librarian

Items 10,000: b/w original photographs, colour transparencies (35mm)

Dates of subject matter 1947 to present

Dates of photographs B/w 1947 to present; colour 1955 to present

Subjects Motor racing, Grand Prix Formula One, Formulas Two and Three, sports-car racing, national and international rallies (filed by race and date)

Access and conditions Open to qualified
researchers by appt (tel), Mon-Fri 9–5. All material
available for editorial reproduction and for
advertising. B/w prints available for a fee; colour
transparencies loaned for six months for a flat fee.
Reproduction rights fees charged. Staff will
undertake some research.

744 • MARTIAL ARTS COMMISSION

First Floor, Broadway House, 15-16 Deptford
Broadway, London SE8 4PE
Tel (01) 691 8711

Enquiries to David Mitchell

Items About 800: colour photographic prints, b/w
original and copy photographs, colour
transparencies (35mm), illustrated books

Dates of photographs 1977 to present

Subjects Martial arts including aikido, hapkido,
kuk sool, karate, kendo, kung fu, sukido, shominji,
nippon kempo, tai chi

Access and conditions Open to qualified
researchers by appt (write), Mon-Fri 9–5. All
material available for editorial reproduction and
for advertising. B/w and colour material loaned free
of charge by arrangement; material may be copied
by outside photographers. Photocopies available.
No reproduction rights fees charged. All material
copyright.

745 • MARYLEBONE CRICKET CLUB

Lord's Ground, London NW8 8QN
Tel (01) 289 1611

Enquiries to Stephen Green, Curator

Items Unknown: b/w original and copy
photographs, colour transparencies (35mm),
postcards, old fine art prints, 20th-century fine art
prints, glass negatives, lantern slides, original
cartoons, illustrated maps, art reproductions,
posters, greetings cards, architectural drawings,
illustrated books

Dates of subject matter 1550 to present

Dates of photographs c. 1860 to present

Subjects All aspects of history and development
of the game of cricket

Access and conditions Open to the public by
appt (write). Most material available for editorial

reproduction; advertising use by special
arrangement only. No loans; b/w prints and
duplicate colour transparencies available for a fee.
Photocopies available. Reproduction rights fees
charged. Staff will undertake limited research.
Some material copyright. Card catalogue available.

746 • LEO MASON SPORTS PICTURE LIBRARY

100 St Martin's Lane, London WC2N 4AZ
Tel (01) 240 3296

Enquiries to Leo Mason

Items 130,000: colour transparencies (35mm)

Dates of photographs 1975 to present

Subjects Sport worldwide including
comprehensive coverage of domestic and
international events including the Olympics,
Commonwealth Games and World Cup (football);
men and women tennis players (1975 to present) at
Wimbledon and on International Grand Prix
circuit; American sports including grid-iron
football, baseball, basketball, ice hockey; leisure
sports including hang-gliding, windsurfing,
ballooning; minority sports including land-sailing,
wind-skating, parasailing, hotdogging, cresta run;
winter sports including skiing, bobbing, skating,
etc.; 1983 America's Cup

Access and conditions Open to qualified
researchers by appt (tel); letter required for first-
time visitors. All material available for editorial
reproduction and for advertising. Colour material
loaned free of charge for 28 days. Reproduction
rights, service and holding fees charged. Staff will
undertake research. All material copyright.

747 • DON MORLEY INTERNATIONAL SPORTS PHOTO AGENCY

132 Carlton Road, Reigate, Surrey RH2 0JF
Tel (07372) (from London 91) 63765

Enquiries to Don Morley

Items About 500,000: b/w original photographs,
colour transparencies (35mm, 5″ × 4″, larger),
colour photographic prints, glass negatives, press
cuttings and tearsheets, illustrated books

Dates of photographs 1949 to present

Subjects International sport, especially

gymnastics, athletics, tennis, motor and motor-cycle sports (including historical coverage); also darts, football (historic only); collection includes picture library of *Sports World Magazine*

Access and conditions Open to qualified researchers by appt (tel). All material available for editorial reproduction and for advertising. B/w and colour material loaned free of charge for 28 days. Reproduction rights, service and holding fees charged. Staff will undertake research.

748 • NATIONAL HORSERACING MUSEUM

99 High Street, Newmarket, Suffolk CB8 8JL
Tel (0638) 667333

Enquiries to Curator

Items 200: glass negatives, daguerreotypes, old fine art prints

Dates of subject matter 1650 to present

Dates of fine art 1650 to present

Subjects Horse-racing in the British Isles including horses, trainers, owners, jockeys, flat racing, point-to-point, hunt-racing

Access and conditions Open to the public by appt, Tues-Sat 10–5, Sun 2–5. All material available for editorial reproduction and for advertising. No loans; b/w prints and colour transparencies available for a fee; material may be copied by outside photographers. Reproduction rights fees charged. Staff will undertake limited research.

749 • ONLY HORSES PICTURE LIBRARY

27 Greenway Gardens, Greenford, Middlesex UB6 9TU
Tel (01) 578 9047

Enquiries to Mike Roberts

Items 20,000: b/w original photographs, colour transparencies (35mm, 5″ × 4″)

Dates of photographs 1960s to present

Subjects All aspects of horses worldwide including wild and zoo animals, working horses, breeding, foals, yearlings, veterinary care, racing including Ascot, stable management, showing,

coaching, dressage, driving, eventing, gymkhanas, hunting, international events, jumping, the King's Troop, Queen's horses, lunging, military horses, polo, point-to-point, trekking, cross-country

Access and conditions Open to qualified researchers by appt (tel), Mon-Fri 9–6. All material available for editorial reproduction and for advertising. B/w and colour material loaned free of charge for six weeks. Reproduction rights, holding and service fees charged; service fees deductible from use fees. Staff of three will undertake some research. All material copyright.

750 • QUADRANT PICTURE LIBRARY

Business Press International Ltd, Quadrant House, The Quadrant, Sutton, Surrey SM2 5AS
Tel (01) 661 3427/8

Enquiries to Elaine R. Jones, Archivist

Items About 1,250,000: b/w original photographs, colour transparencies (35mm, 5″ × 4″, larger), glass negatives, unprinted film negatives, technical drawings and artwork

Dates of photographs *c.* 1900 to present

Subjects Aviation (civil and military) worldwide from 1906 to present including air shows (Farnborough, Paris, Hanover, etc.); motor cars (all makes) from 1895 to present including sporting pictures and road tests and also races (Brooklands, French and British Grand Prix, etc.); sailing including yachts and races, especially America's Cup from 1930s to present; bicycling including Tour de France and Milk Race; technical drawings and art work; spacecraft (NASA and Ariane shuttles); personalities

Access and conditions Open to the public by appt (tel), Mon-Fri 9–5. All material available for editorial reproduction and for advertising. B/w and colour material loaned free of charge for one month. Reproduction rights, service and holding fees charged; service fees deductible from use fees. Staff will undertake some research. Card catalogue available.

751 • SPORTAPICS LIMITED

43 Main Street, Busby, Glasgow G76 8DT
Tel (041) 638 6143

Enquiries to George Ross Ashton

Items 171,000: b/w original photographs, colour transparencies (35mm)

Dates of photographs 1966 to present

Subjects Sport including boxing, badminton, tennis, golf, Association and Rugby football, athletics

Access and conditions Open to qualified researchers by appt (write). All material available for editorial reproduction and for advertising. B/w and colour material loaned free of charge for 30 days. Reproduction rights, holding and service fees charged; service fees deductible from use fees. Research undertake for a fee. All material copyright. Card catalogue available.

752 • SPORTING PICTURES (UK) LTD

7A Lambs Conduit Passage, London WC1R 4RG
Tel (01) 405 4500 Telex 27924

Enquiries to Steve Brown or Steve Smith, Librarians

Items About two million: b/w original photographs, colour transparencies (35mm)

Dates of subject matter 1970 to present

Dates of photographs 1970 to present

Subjects Coverage of all sporting events in the UK and major events worldwide with particular emphasis on football (Association, Rugby League and Rugby Union), horse racing and motor racing; major sports personalities

Access and conditions Open to qualified researchers by appt (tel), Mon-Fri 10–6. All material available for editorial reproduction and for advertising. B/w and colour material loaned free of charge for one month (print fee charged). Reproduction rights and holding fees charged. Staff of nine will undertake some research. All material copyright.

753 • SPORTSPHOTO AGENCY

12 Castle Road, Scarborough, North Yorkshire YO11 1XA
Tel (0723) 367264, 375454

Enquiries to Stewart Kendall

Items 75,000: b/w original photographs, colour transparencies (35mm), unprinted film negatives

Dates of photographs 1980 to present

Subjects All sports, UK and international, especially golf, football, tennis, athletics, Rugby Union, Rugby League, snooker

Access and conditions Open to qualified researchers by appt (tel). All material available for editorial reproduction and for advertising. B/w and colour material loaned free of charge for four weeks. Photocopies available. Reproduction rights, service and holding fees charged. Staff of three will undertake research.

754 • SUPERSPORT PHOTOGRAPHS

Supersport House, Wayside, White Lodge Lane, Baslow, Via Bakewell, Derbyshire DE14 1RQ
Tel (024 688) 2376

Enquiries to Eileen Langley

Items Over 35,000: b/w original and copy photographs, colour transparencies (35mm, 2¼″)

Dates of photographs Mid-1970s to present

Subjects Sports coverage including badminton, bowls, cycling, dance, hockey, judo, lacrosse, mini-rugby, modern pentathlon, netball, trampolining; football, cricket and swimming in schools; special emphasis on gymnastics (artistic, keepfit, Olympic, rhythmic, sports acrobatics, educational), figure-skating, ice hockey, skiing, athletics, tennis, sport and physical education for young people including schoolchildren, women's sport

Access and conditions Open to qualified researchers by appt (tel), Mon-Fri 9–5. All material available for editorial reproduction and for advertising. Colour material loaned free of charge for six weeks; b/w prints available for a fee. Photocopies available. Reproduction rights and holding fees charged. Staff of two will undertake research for a fee. All material copyright.

755 • BOB THOMAS SPORTS PHOTOGRAPHY

19 Charnwood Avenue, Westone, Northampton NN3 3DX
Tel (0604) 404405

Enquiries to Bob Thomas

Items Over 100,000: colour transparencies (35mm, 5″ × 4″), b/w original photographs, glass negatives

Dates of subject matter 1940 to present

Dates of photographs 1940 to present

Subjects Sports including football (Association, Rugby League, Rugby Union, Australian rules, Gaelic), cricket, athletics, hockey, hurling, baseball, basketball, volleyball, croquet, boxing, golf, squash, badminton, snooker, billiards, weightlifting, cross-country running, rollerskating, hang-gliding, canoeing, rowing and sand-yachting, fishing, surfing, swimming, water-skiing, water polo, windsurfing, powerboat racing, cycling, cyclo-cross, motor-cycle scrambling, speedway, go-karting, motor rallying, field sports (hunting, shooting), showjumping, horse-racing, equestrian trials, ice hockey, skiing, ski-jumping, speed-skating; special collection of international soccer pictures

Access and conditions Open to qualified researchers by appt (tel), Mon-Fri 9–5. All material available for editorial reproduction and for advertising (some restrictions). B/w and colour material loaned free of charge for three months. Photocopies available. Reproduction rights, holding and service fees charged. Staff of seven will undertake research. Photographers available for assignment. All material copyright.

756 • VARLEY PICTURE AGENCY

1 Manor Garth, Ledsham, South Milford, Leeds
LS25 5LZ
Tel (0977) 682134, 683758

Enquiries to Andrew Varley

Items Over 10,000: b/w original photographs, colour transparencies (35mm)

Dates of photographs 1978 to present

Subjects Golf (portraits of contemporary professionals and coverage of 1983 and 1984 British Open); Rugby League football since 1978 including finals, internationals and tour coverage; Association football including World Cup since 1966 and 1984 European Cup Final; Test matches in England sice 1980; news coverage of Leeds and surrounding area; posed models

Access and conditions Open to qualified researchers by appt (write). All material available for editorial reproduction and for advertising. B/w and colour material loaned free of charge for one month (print fees charged). Reproduction rights fees charged; holding fees charged if material returned unused. Staff of three will undertake some research. All material copyright.

757 • FIONA VIGORS LTD

The Old Manor, Upper Lambourn, Newbury,
Berkshire RG16 7RG
Tel (0488) 71657

Enquiries to Fiona Vigors

Items 6000: b/w original photographs, colour transparencies (35mm), colour photographic prints

Dates of subject matter 1967 to present

Dates of photographs 1967 to present

Subjects Thoroughbred racehorses in the UK, Ireland, USA and France including posed pictures of stallions, yearlings and horses in training; studs (general shots), property connected with racing, racing personalities including trainers and jockeys

Access and conditions Open to the public by appt (tel), Mon-Fri 9.30–5.30. All material available for editorial reproduction and for advertising. B/w and colour material loaned free of charge for three months. Reproduction rights fees charged. Staff will undertake some research. Card catalogue.

758 • WILDERNESS PHOTOGRAPHY

2 Kent View, Waterside, Kendal, Cumbria
LA9 4HE
Tel (0539) 28334

Enquiries to John Noble

Items 3000: colour transparencies (35mm)

Dates of photographs 1965 to present

Subjects Mountains and wilderness regions including coverage of USA, Europe, UK, Arctic, Antarctic, Himalayas, Karakoram; exploration, mountaineering, adventure sports including canoeing and skiing; wildlife of polar regions; national parks of USA and UK

Access and conditions Open to qualified researchers by appt (write). All material available for editorial reproduction and for advertising. Colour material loaned free of charge for seven days (print fee charged). Reproduction rights, holding and service fees charged. Research undertaken; negotiable research fee charged. All material copyright.

759 • WORLD OF DARTS LTD

2 Park Lane, Croydon, Surrey CR9 1HA
Tel (01) 681 2837

Enquiries to Anthony Wood

Items About 5000: b/w original photographs, colour transparencies (35mm)

Dates of photographs 1970s to present

Subjects Comprehensive collection relating to the sport of darts both professional and amateur including players, organizers, venues in Britain, northern Europe, Canada, USA and Australia

Access and conditions Open to qualified researchers by appt (tel), Mon-Fri 9–5. All material available for editorial reproduction and for advertising. B/w and colour material loaned free of charge for two months; b/w prints and duplicate colour transparencies available for a fee. Reproduction rights fees charged. Staff will undertake limited research. All material copyright.

760 • JERRY YOUNG

60 Crofton Road, London SE5 8NB
Tel (01) 701 6224

Enquiries to Jerry Young

Items 10,000: colour transparencies (35mm)

Dates of photographs 1974 to present

Subjects Aviation including aerobatics, airlines, airports, airships, airshows, Concorde, commercial aircraft, experimental aircraft, gas balloons, gliders, hang-gliders, helicopters, hot-air balloons, light aircraft, microlight aircraft, military aircraft; sports including bicycle motorcross (BMX), bobsleighing, cresta run, canoeing in the Himalayas and elsewhere, hovercraft-racing, hunting, kite-flying, marathon running, motor sports, motor-cycling, mountaineering, powerboating, parachuting, river-rafting, sailing, skateboarding, skiing, sledging, surfing, water-skiing, windsurfing; travel including Egypt, France, Greek Islands, Iran, Ireland, Kenya, Nepal, Pakistan, Saudi Arabia, Spain, Switzerland, Tunisia, USA (New York, California, Arizona), UK, London (buildings, dockland, fire brigade, National Westminster Tower, parks, St Paul's Cathedral, the Thames, Thames Barrier, Tower of London, Tower Bridge), Humber Bridge, Manchester Ship Canal, Scotland, Wales; general subjects including African animals, beagling, cars, cranes, crafts, farming, ferreting, industry, people, photographers, Pope John-Paul II (UK visit), rare breeds of livestock, ships and boats, steam traction engines, trains, safari parks

Access and conditions Open to qualified researchers by appt (tel), Mon-Fri 9–5. All material available for editorial reproduction and for advertising. Colour material loaned free of charge for one month. Reproduction rights and holding fees charged. Staff will undertake some research.

Medicine

761 • AGE CONCERN ENGLAND

Photo Library, 60 Pitcairn Road, Mitcham, Surrey
CR4 3LL
Tel (01) 640 5431

Enquiries to Graham Williams, Publicity
Assistant

Items 3100: b/w original photographs, colour
transparencies (35mm)

Dates of subject matter Contemporary

Dates of photographs 1940 to present

Subjects Old age including old people working,
recreation, household tasks (shopping, babysitting,
cooking); old people alone, in groups, with spouses
and families, in their own homes, in residential
homes, in hospital, in distress; services for old
people (day centres, lunch clubs, transport
schemes); ethnic minorities, technical aids

Access and conditions Open to qualified
researchers by appt (tel), Mon-Fri 9–5. All material
available for editorial reproduction, but not for
advertising. B/w and colour material loaned free of
charge. Photocopies available. No fees charged;
donations requested. Staff will undertake some
research in answer to specific requests. ACE holds
copyright to 50% of collection; users must negotiate
directly with copyright holders for balance.

762 • CAMERA TALKS LTD

31 North Row, London W1R 2EN
Tel (01) 493 2761

Enquiries to Veronica J. Dorset, Director

Items 30,000: colour transparencies (35mm)

Dates of photographs 1950 to present

Subjects Health sciences including medicine and
dentistry, adoption, anatomy and physiology, care
of the elderly and dying, drug abuse, disabilities,
environmental health, family planning, first aid,
food hygiene, hospitals, health education, health
and safety in industry, industrial accidents, home
safety, mental health, microbiology, midwifery,
nursing, nutrition, obstetrics and gynaecology,
operations, parentcraft, physiotherapy,
occupational therapy, school education, sexual
education, social problems, including hypothermia,
battered wives, child abuse, alcoholism, glue-
sniffing, sexual problems; speech therapy, art and
music therapy

Access and conditions Open to qualified
researchers by appt (tel), Mon-Fri 9–5. All material
available for editorial reproduction and for
advertising subject to approval. Colour material
loaned free of charge for two weeks; duplicate
transparencies available for a fee. Reproduction
rights fees charged. Staff will undertake some
research. Printed catalogue available.

763 • GOWER SCIENTIFIC PHOTOS

Middlesex House, 34-42 Cleveland Street, London
W1P 5FB
Tel (01) 580 9327/8 Telex 21736

Enquiries to Rosemary Allen

Items 20,000: colour transparencies (35mm)

Dates of photographs 1975 to present

Subjects Medicine, anatomy, normal structure
and function, diseases, clinical subjects, X-rays,
histology, pathology, WELLCOME MUSEUM OF
PATHOLOGY COLLECTION: natural history,
photomicrography, photomacrography, plants and
invertebrates, anatomy, life cycles

Access and conditions Open to qualified
researchers by appt (tel), Mon-Fri 9–5. All material
available for editorial reproduction and for
advertising. Colour material loaned free of charge
for one month. Reproduction rights, service and
holding fees charged. Staff will undertake
research.

764 • GRAVES MEDICAL AUDIOVISUAL LIBRARY

Holly House, 220 New London Road, Chelmsford, Essex CM2 9BJ
Tel (0245) 83351

Enquiries to Richard Morton, Director

Items 40,000: colour transparencies (35mm)

Dates of photographs 1957 to present

Subjects Medicine, medical education and health care including abdomen, abortion, accidents, acid-base imbalance, adoption, aged, alcoholism, anaemia, anaesthesia, anatomy, aphasia, arthritis, attitude to death, autism, bacteriology, battered babies, bereavement, blindness, blood, body sounds, bone diseases, breast, breast feeding, breast neoplasms, breast diseases, burns, cardiac disease, cell division, cerebral palsy, cerebrovascular diseases, child abuse, child development, chromosomes, chromosome abnormalities, communicable diseases, contraception, coronary disease, counselling, deafness, dentistry, dermatology, development, diabetes mellitus, diagnosis laboratory, diet, digestive endoscopy, digestive system, disasters, disease, doctor-patient, drug abuse, ear, ear diseases, eczema, education, electrocardiography, electrolyte balance, emergencies, endocrine diseases, endocrine glands, endoscopy, eyes, eye diseases, faecal incontinence, family planning, fever, first aid, foetus, foot, forensic medicine, fractures, gastro-intestinal diseases, general practice, genetics, geriatrics, growth, gynaecology, haematology, haemoglobins, hand, hand injuries, handicapped, health education, hearing aids, heart, heart diseases, heart sounds, hemiplegia, hip joint, histology, history of medicine, history taking, hypothermia, immunology, immunotherapy, infant newborn, infant nutrition, infant welfare, infectious diseases, infestation, injury, internal medicine, intestinal diseases, kidney, kidney diseases, knee joint, labour, laryngeal diseases, law, legislation, libraries (medical), liver diseases, malaria, malocclusion, manipulation (orthopaedic), measurement, medical audit, mental retardation, metabolism, metabolic disorders, microbiology, mother-child relations, mouth, mouth diseases, musculoskeletal diseases, myocardial diseases, neonatology, neoplasms, neurology, nose, nursing, nutrition, obstectrics, occupational health and diseases, occupational therapy, operating-room nursing, opthalmology, orthodontics, orthopaedics, osteoarthritis, otorhinolaryngology, paediatrics, parasitic diseases, parent-child relations, pathology, pharmacology, physical examination, physical therapy, physics, physiology, plastic surgery, play, potassium, pregnancy, psychiatry, psychology, pulmonary, pyrexia, rabies, radiography, radiology, rape, rehabilitation, reimplantation, relaxation techniques, renal, respiratory tract diseases, respiratory tract physiology, resuscitation, rheumatism, sex disorders, sex education, sex offences, sexually transmitted diseases, skin, skin diseases, sleep, sleep disorders, social problems, speech, speech disorders, spina bifida, spine, spinal diseases, spinal injuries, squint, stroke, surgery, suture techniques, terminal care, therapeutics, thyroid gland diseases and neoplasms, tractions, transplantation, trauma, tropical medicine, tuberculosis, urinary incontinence, urology, vascular diseases, venereal diseases, vertigo, vision, voice, water-electrolyte imbalance, wheelchairs, World Health Organization

Access and conditions Open to qualified researchers by appt (tel), Mon-Fri 9–5. Some material available for editorial reproduction and for advertising. Colour material loaned for a rental fee; duplicate transparencies available for a fee. Reproduction rights fees charged. Printed catalogue available. Staff will undertake limited research.

765 • THE INSTITUTE OF PSYCHO-ANALYSIS AND THE BRITISH PSYCHO-ANALYTIC SOCIETY

63 New Cavendish Street, London W1M 7RD
Tel (01) 580 4952

Enquiries to J. Jarrett, General Secretary

Items 500: b/w original and copy photographs, colour photographic prints

Dates of photographs 1900 to present

Subjects Sigmund Freud and his contemporaries; International Psycho-analytical Association Congresses; distinguished British psycho-analysts in portraits, groups, or social events

Access and conditions Open to qualified researchers by appt (write), Mon-Fri 9.30–5.30 (5 on Fri). All material available for editorial reproduction, but not for advertising. Fees and other arrangements at the Secretary's discretion.

766 • INTERNATIONAL PLANNED PARENTHOOD FEDERATION

18-20 Lower Regent Street, London SW1Y 4PW
Tel (01) 839 2911   Telex 919573

Enquiries to Jeremy Hamand, Deputy Publications Editor

Items About 10,000: b/w original and copy photographs, colour transparencies (35mm)

Dates of photographs 1950 to present

Subjects Family planning, its development and environmental problems; technical and historical aspects; portraits of women and children; family planning worldwide with emphasis on Third World; photographs by Mark Edwards

Access and conditions Open to qualified researchers by appt (tel), Mon-Fri 9.30–5.30. All material available for editorial reproduction, but not for advertising. B/w and colour material loaned free of charge for one month. Photocopies available. Reproduction rights and service fees charged.

767 • LONDON AMBULANCE SERVICE

220 Waterloo Road, London SE1 8SD
Tel (01) 928 0333

Enquiries to Kathy Nye, Public Relations Officer

Items 2000: b/w original and copy photographs, colour transparencies (35mm, larger), colour photographic prints, unprinted film negatives, posters

Dates of subject matter 1880 to present

Dates of photographs 1880 to present

Subjects History of London Ambulance vehicles from 1880 to the present, including horse-drawn vehicles, ambulance personnel at work, major accidents, train crashes, road traffic accidents, ambulance stations, ambulance central control rooms (old and new)

Access and conditions Open to qualified researchers by appt (tel), Mon-Fri 9–5. Some material available for editorial reproduction but not for advertising. B/w and colour material loaned free of charge. Material may be copied by outside photographers. Photocopies available. No reproduction rights fees charged. Staff will undertake some research.

768 • MUSEUM OF THE ORDER OF ST JOHN

St John's Gate, St John's Lane, London EC1 4DA
Tel (01) 253 6644 ext 35

Enquiries to Curator

Items About 10,000: b/w original and copy photographs, illustrated books, prints and drawings, colour transparencies (35mm), colour photographic prints, old fine art prints, 20th-century fine art prints, lantern slides, postcards, illustrated maps, posters, ephemera relating to the order of St John

Dates of subject matter 1100 to present

Dates of non-photographic material c. 1490 to present

Dates of photographs c. 1870 to present

Subjects History of the Order of St John and its foundations including the St John Ambulance Brigade and the Ophthalmic Hospital in Jerusalem; the Crusades, Jerusalem, Rhodes and Malta; local history in Britain, portraits of Knights, buildings once in possession of the Order, hospitals, medical equipment and transport

Access and conditions Open to the public by appt (tel), Mon-Fri 9–5. Most material available for editorial reproduction; advertising use by special arrangement only. No loans; b/w prints and duplicate colour transparencies available for a fee; material may be copied by outside photographers. Photocopies available. No reproduction rights fees charged but donation to work of charity required. Staff of three will undertake some research. Some material copyright. Card catalogue available.

769 • PICKER INTERNATIONAL LTD

PO Box 2, East Lane, Wembley, Middlesex HA9 7PR
Tel (01) 904 1288   Telex 922177

Enquiries to Jill Williams

Items 150: b/w original and copy photographs, colour transparencies (35mm), colour photographic prints

Dates of subject matter 1976 to present

Dates of photographs 1976 to present

Subjects Diagnostic imaging equipment including computed tomography, nuclear magnetic resonance, ultrasound and cardiac equipment, X-ray equipment and accessories

Access and conditions Not open; telephone and postal requests only. Most material available for editorial reproduction and for advertising. B/w material loaned free of charge for two weeks; colour material loaned free of charge for 10 days; duplicate colour transparencies available for a fee. Photocopies available. No reproduction rights fees charged. All material copyright.

770 • ROYAL COLLEGE OF PHYSICIANS

11 St Andrews Place, London NW1 4LE
Tel (01) 935 1174

Enquiries to Librarian

Items About 15,000: b/w original and copy photographs, old fine art prints, colour transparencies (35mm), colour photographic prints

Dates of subject matter BC to present

Dates of photographs *c.* 1865 to present

Dates of fine art 17th century to present

Subjects Portraits of physicians with emphasis on members of the Royal College since its foundation in 1518 but also including worldwide coverage of individuals who have made important contributions to medical knowledge

Access and conditions Open to qualified researchers by appt (write), Mon-Fri 10–5. All material available for editorial reproduction but not for advertising. No loans; b/w prints and duplicate colour transparencies available for a fee; material may be copied by outside photographers. Photocopies available. Reproduction rights fees charged. Staff will undertake limited research. Most material copyright. Card catalogue of photographic material available; printed catalogue of engravings available: A. H. Driver, *Catalogue of Engraved Portraits in the Royal College of Physicians of London*, 1952.

771 • ROYAL NATIONAL INSTITUTE FOR THE BLIND

224 Great Portland Street, London W1N 6AA
Tel (01) 388 1266

Enquiries to Gill Pawley, Publications Officer

Items 500: b/w original photographs

Dates of subject matter Early 20th century to present

Dates of photographs Early 20th century to present

Subjects All aspects of the work of the Institute including homes, houses, schools, colleges, hotels, rehabilitation centres, physiotherapy, mobility; professional and executive industrial employment, shorthand typing, computers, switchboards; aids, games, Braille diagrams, maps, Braille production, Kurzweil reading machine, talking books, Moon system, optacons, exhibitions; Louis Braille and Helen Keller, RNIB headquarters and official visits, students' library, National Mobility Centre, sports and special events

Access and conditions Open to the public by appt (write), Mon-Fri 9–5.15. All material available for editorial reproduction but not for advertising. B/w material loaned free of charge for one month; b/w prints available for a fee. Reproduction rights fees charged by arrangement. Staff will undertake some research. All material copyright.

772 • ST BARTHOLOMEW'S HOSPITAL

District Archives, The Clerk's House, West Smithfield, London EC1A 7BE
Tel (01) 600 9000

Enquiries to Janet Foster, District Archivist

Items About 1000: b/w original and copy photographs, illustrated books, fine art prints, illustrated maps, postcards, colour transparencies (35mm)

Dates of subject matter 15th to 20th century

Dates of photographs *c.* 1850 to 1960s

Subjects Scenes and people with medical connections; murals by William Hogarth, *The Good Samaritan* and *The Pool at Bethesda*, paintings by John Everett Millais and Sir Joshua Reynolds, illuminated manuscripts including a 15th-century cartulary, engravings of the hospital buildings from the 18th century, engravings of the church of St Bartholomew the Less, 20th-century watercolours and pen-and-ink drawings of the hospital buildings, 19th- and 20th-century photographs of wards, buildings, staff and a sequence (1940s) of a patient from admission through treatment, operation and discharge

Access and conditions Open to the public by appt (tel), Mon-Fri 10–4.30. Most material available for editorial reproduction and for advertising subject to Archivist's approval. B/w prints available for a fee; colour material loaned free of charge for one month. Material may be copied by outside photographers. Reproduction rights and service fees charged.

773 • C. JAMES WEBB

17 Michleham Down, London N12 7JJ
Tel (01) 445 4506

Items 20,000: b/w original and copy photographs, colour transparencies (35mm), unprinted film negatives

Dates of photographs 1948 to present

Subjects Biology, including human and social subjects; tropical diseases and insects mainly of medical importance, bacteria, fungi, human and animal worms and parasites, anatomy, histology, X-rays

Access and conditions Open to the public by appt (write). All material available for editorial reproduction and for advertising. B/w and colour material loaned free of charge for one month. Reproduction rights and holding fees charged; service fees charged only when no material is used. Staff of three will undertake research.

774 • WELLCOME INSTITUTE FOR THE HISTORY OF MEDICINE

183 Euston Road, London NW1 2BP
Tel (01) 387 4477

Enquiries to Eric Freeman, Librarian (postal)
Enquiry Desk (telephone)

Items Over 100,000: illustrated books, old fine art prints, illustrated manuscripts, paintings, original cartoons, drawings and watercolours, b/w original photographs, archival paintings accompanied by illustrations, postcards, posters, glass negatives, daguerreotypes, lantern slides, 20th-century fine art prints

Dates of subject matter BC to present

Dates of photographs 1860 to present

Subjects History of medicine with special emphasis on pre-20th-century medicine in Europe, Asia and America: experience and treatment of illness, hospitals, physicians' (bedside and consulting), medicine, balneotherapy and hydrotherapy, animal magnetism or mesmeric therapy, electrotherapy, acupuncture, dispensing, lay medical practices, domestic medicine and minor surgery, quackery, afflictions and misfortunes, diagnosis, superstition, poisons, witchcraft; hygiene, gymnastics and sport, disposal of the dead, water supply, public health, innoculation against smallpox, epidemics (including smallpox, cholera and plague), infant nutrition, environmental disruptions, working conditions; medical specialities, psychiatry, paediatrics, gynaecology, obstetrics, surgery and surgical techniques (including bloodletting, amputation, anaesthesia, instruments, acupuncture, wound surgery, lithotomy), radiology, dentistry, orthopaedics, ophthalmology, dermatology, chiropody, military and naval medicine, tropical medicine; bio-medical sciences, anatomy and physiology, phrenology, physiognomy, pharmacy, pharmacology, research into diseases, botany, biology, zoology, chemistry, alchemy, astrology, microscopes; medical personnel; influences on medicine, religious cults, mythology, cosmology, social organization, philanthropy, scientific organization, medical and scientific biography and personalia, education, transport, anthropology, travel and exploration, war, pain, cruelty, attitudes to death and sex; also the Dr Basil Hood album of London hospitals 1900-20; photographs of St Bartholomew's Hospital, London, c. 1914; John Thomson's 19th-century photographs of Hong Kong, China, Vietnam and Cambodia; drug-jars, surgical instruments, diagnostic instruments

Access and conditions Open to qualified researchers by appt (tel), Mon-Fri 9.45–5.15. Some material available for editorial reproduction but not for advertising. No loans; b/w prints and duplicate colour transparencies available for a fee. Photocopies available. Reproduction rights fees charged. Staff will undertake some research. Some material copyright. Partial card catalogue.

Science & Technology

775 • ARCTIC CAMERA

66 Ashburnham Grove, London SE10 8UJ
Tel (01) 692 7651

Enquiries to Derek Fordham

Items About 12,000: colour transparencies
(35mm), some b/w original photographs

Dates of photographs 1968 to present

Subjects Arctic life and environment including
eskimos, dog-sledding, kayaks, igloos, hunting,
settlements, fur clothing, landscapes, icebergs,
pack ice, mountains, glaciers, weather, expeditions,
flora and fauna, modern life, transport, industry

Access and conditions Not open; tel and mail
requests only. All material available for editorial
reproduction and for advertising. B/w and colour
material loaned free of charge for two months.
Reproduction rights, service and holding fees
charged; service fees deductible from use fees. Staff
will undertake research. All material copyright.

776 • ARMAGH OBSERVATORY

College Hill, Armagh BT61 9DG
Tel (0861) 522928 Telex 747937

Enquiries to Dr M. de Groot, Director

Items 6500: b/w original and copy photographs,
glass negatives, colour transparencies (35mm),
unprinted film negatives

Dates of photographs Late 19th century to
present

Subjects Star fields (direct photographs, multiple
exposure and spectral plates); history of
astronomy, optical instruments, observatories and
telescopes; Earth's motions, structure and
atmosphere, celestial mechanics, lunar and
planetary structure, planets, solar system, Sun,
meteors and aurorae, stars, stellar spectra, binary

and variable stars, constellations, galaxies and
universe, space colonization

Access and conditions Open to qualified
researchers by appt (write), Mon-Fri 9–5. All
material available for editorial reproduction and
for advertising. B/w and colour material loaned free
of charge. Print fees charged for lab work.
Photocopies available. Holding fees charged, but no
reproduction rights or service fees. Staff will
undertake limited research. One-third of material
copyrighted by Armagh Observatory; remainder
by individual photographers. Catalogues available.

777 • ASTRO ART

99 Southam Road, Hall Green, Birmingham
B28 0AB
Tel (021) 777 1802

Enquiries to Lawrence Keene

Items Over 1000: colour transparencies (35mm,
2¼″, 5″ × 4″), b/w photographs (to order)

Dates of subject matter Prehistory to present

Dates of photographs 1954 to present

Subjects Original artwork by David Hardy
illustrating astronomy, space travel, science-
fiction, science including energy, air, weather,
geology, technical and cutaway views of rockets,
satellites, etc.; some photographs of Iceland
especially geysers, waterfalls, etc.

Access and conditions Open to qualified
researchers by appt (tel), Mon-Fri, 9.30–5.30. All
material available for editorial reproduction and
for advertising with the artist's approval. B/w and
colour material loaned free of charge for one
month. B/w prints available for a fee. Reproduction
rights fees charged. Staff will undertake some
research.

778 • ASTRONOMICAL SOCIETY OF EDINBURGH

City Observatory, Calton Hill, Edinburgh
EH7 5AA
Tel (031) 556 4365

Enquiries to James Shepherd, Director

Items About 700: lantern slides, colour transparencies (35mm), unprinted film negatives, b/w original photographs, illustrated books, glass negatives, stereographs

Dates of subject matter 1776 to present

Dates of photographs 1896 to present

Subjects Meteors, aurora borealis, noctilucent clouds, forked lightning; early 19th-century telescopes including Fraunhofer & Repsold Transit Telescope (1833), Troughton & Simms Altazimuth Telescope (1831), Cooke 6″ Photovisual refractor telescope (c. 1870); comprehensive collection of photographs of the City Observatory, a fine neo-classical building

Access and conditions Open by appt (write). All material available for editorial reproduction and for advertising. B/w and colour material loaned free of charge for one month. Reproduction rights and service fees charged. Staff will undertake some research.

779 • PAUL BRIERLEY SCIENCE PHOTOGRAPHY

250 Felmongers, Harlow, Essex CM20 3DR
Tel (0279) 25169

Enquiries to Paul Brierley

Items 40,000: b/w original and copy photographs, colour transparencies (2¼″)

Dates of photographs 1950 to present

Subjects Abstracts and concepts, adhesives, automobile engineering, botany, biology, biomedical equipment, chemical engineering, chemistry, ceramics and bricks, clocks and watches, computers, control equipment, cryogenics, crystallography, electrical engineering, electron optics, electronics, engines, environment, fibre optics, fibres and fabrics, gas turbines, geology, glass technology, heat exchangers, holography, industrial components, industrial plant, industrial processes, infra-red technology, instruments, integrated circuits, laboratory equipment, lasers, light, lighting technology, lubrication, machine tools, magnetism, materials science, mechanics, measurement, metalforming, metalworking, microbiology, micro-electronics, micrography, minerals, molecular models, motors, optics, ore and rocks, oscilloscopes and CRTs, petrography, photomicrography, physics, plant structure, plastics, pollution, primary metal production, prime movers, radio-telescopes, relay technology, scientific principles, semiconductor devices, sound, spectra and spectroscopy, superconductivity, television, test equipment, tribology, vacuum techniques, visual display systems, waste, watch movements, welding and cutting

Access and conditions Open to qualified researchers by appt (tel), Mon-Fri 9.30–5.30. All material available for editorial reproduction and for advertising. B/w and colour material loaned free of charge. Reproduction rights fees charged; service and holding fees discretionary. Staff will undertake research. Photographer available for assignment. All material copyright.

780 • BRITISH ANTARCTIC SURVEY

High Cross, Madingley Road, Cambridge CB3 0ET
Tel (0223) 61188   Telex 817725 BASCAM G

Enquiries to Principal Photographer

Items 10,000: colour transparencies (35mm, 5″ × 4″), b/w original photographs, glass negatives

Dates of photographs 1955 to present

Subjects Geographical coverage of British Antarctic Territory, Falkland Islands including South Georgia; Antarctic wildlife including penguins and other seabirds, seals, marine life, insects; plants; research stations, ships and aircraft; research activities including geology, geophysics, glaciology, marine and terrestrial biology, meteorology and atmospheric physics; Trans-Antarctic expedition 1955–58

Access and conditions Open to qualified researchers by appt (tel). All material available for editorial reproduction and for advertising. B/w and colour material loaned free of charge for three months (print fees charged). Reproduction rights fees charged. Staff will undertake limited research. All material copyright.

781 • BRITISH GEOLOGICAL SURVEY

There are three access points for this collection at the following locations:

Geological Museum, Exhibition Road, London SW7 2DE
Tel (01) 589 3444 Telex 8812180 GEOSCI G

Enquiries to Martin Pulsford, Head of Photographic Services

Nicker Hill, Keyworth, Nottingham NG12 5GG
Tel (0607) 76111 ext 3205 Telex 378173 IGSKEY G

Enquiries to Clive Jeffery, Photographic Department

Murchison House, West Mains Road, Edinburgh EH9 3LA
Tel (031) 667 1000 Telex 727343

Enquiries to Colin Will, Librarian and Information Officer

Items Over 180,000: b/w original photographs, colour transparencies (35mm, 5″ × 4″), colour photographic prints, glass negatives, illustrated maps, illustrated books

Dates of subject matter Prehistory to present

Dates of photographs 1900 to present

Subjects Geological field pictures in the UK of topographical features, rock formations, erosion, quarrying, mining, road cutting; minerals, rocks and gemstones worldwide; fossils; models and reconstructions of extinct features such as the Edinburgh volcano; continental drift diagrams; photomicrographs of rock sections; portraits of British geologists; geological maps worldwide

Access and conditions Open to the public by appt (tel), Mon-Fri 10–4. All material available for editorial reproduction and for advertising. Colour material loaned free of charge for one month; b/w prints and duplicate colour transparencies available for a fee; items and specimens from the Geological Museum photographed by staff on request for a fee. Photocopies and dye-line copies of maps available for a fee. Reproduction rights and holding fees charged. Staff will undertake some research. Compulsory credit line. All material copyright. Printed catalogue available: M. O. Morris, *Classified Geological Photographs, selected from the collection of the Geological Survey and Museum,* 3rd edition, 1963, HMSO, London.

782 • BROUGHTY CASTLE MUSEUM

Broughty Ferry, Dundee, Tayside DD5 2BE
Tel (0382) 23141

Enquiries to David Henderson, Assistant Keeper

Items 300: glass negatives

Dates of subject matter 1820 to 1950

Dates of photographs 1890 to 1910

Subjects Arctic whales (photographed between 1890 and 1910); museum artefacts related to whaling including scrimshaw, harpoons, paintings, watercolours, models of ships including Capt. Scott's *Terra Nova*, local men who were among Scott's crew

Access and conditions Open to the public by appt, Mon-Fri 10–1, 2–5.30. All material available for editorial reproduction and for advertising. No loans; b/w prints and duplicate colour transparencies available for a fee. Reproduction rights fees charged. Staff will undertake limited research and order prints or arrange photography.

783 • DARWIN MUSEUM

Down House, Luxted Road, Downe, Orpington, Kent BR6 7JT
Tel (0689) 59119

Enquiries to Philip Titheradge, Custodian

Items About 200: b/w original and copy photographs, colour transparencies (35mm, 5″ × 4″)

Dates of subject matter 600 BC to 1900

Dates of photographs 1860 to present

Subjects Charles Darwin and his family, his microscopes and telescopes, manuscripts, books, published works; Down House

Access and conditions Open to the public by appt (tel), Tues-Thurs 10–12, 1–6. All material available for editorial reproduction and for advertising. B/w prints available for a fee. Colour material loaned free of charge for one month. Reproduction rights and rental fees chared. Staff will undertake some research.

784 • DIRECTORATE OF FISHERIES RESEARCH

Ministry of Agriculture, Fisheries and Food,
Fisheries Laboratory, Lowestoft, Suffolk
NR33 0HT
Tel (0502) 62244 Telex 97490

Enquiries to Information Officer

Items About 500: b/w original photographs, colour transparencies (35mm)

Dates of subject matter 1920 to present

Dates of photographs 1947 to present

Subjects Fisheries research including research boats, apparatus, aquatic pollution, specimens, aquaculture, fish disease

Access and conditions Not open; telephone and postal requests only. All material available for editorial reproduction but not for advertising. B/w and colour material loaned for a fee. Reproduction rights fees charged. All material copyright.

785 • MICHAEL FREEMAN

7 Kendal Steps, St George's Fields, London
W2 2YE
Tel (01) 402 5962

Enquiries to Michael Freeman

Items 30,000: colour transparencies (35mm, 5″ × 4″), b/w original photographs

Dates of subject matter 100 BC to present

Dates of photographs 1970 to present

Subjects Science and technology, with special collections on sub-atomic physics, cosmology, space exploration and relativity (all special effects photography), space and aviation technology (principally at NASA facilities and the National Air and Space Museum, Washington, DC), history of science (exhibits from the National Museum of American History, Washington, DC); anthropology, with special collections on South-east Asian tribes and the Pathan; geography with special collections on South-east Asia and tropical South America; special commodity collections on gold, pearls, jade, oriental food and California wines; special collection on photographic techniques and processes

Access and conditions Open to qualified researchers by appt (tel), Mon-Fri 10–6. All material available for editorial reproduction and for advertising. B/w and colour material loaned free of charge for two months. Reproduction rights and holding fees charged. Staff will undertake some research. All material copyright.

786 • GEOSCIENCE FEATURES PICTURE LIBRARY

6 Orchard Drive, Wye, Nr Ashford, Kent
TN25 5AU
Tel (0233) 812707

Enquiries to Dr Basil Booth

Items About 50,000: colour transparencies (35mm, 5″ × 4″), unprinted film negatives

Dates of subject matter Prehistory to present

Dates of photographs 1946 to present

Subjects World geography and geology including ecology, conservation, pollution, environment, topography, landscapes and moods, mountains (special collection on volcanoes), rocks and minerals, crystallography, palaeontology (fossils), geomorphology, economic and physical geology, meteorology (weather phenomena, seasons, sky, sunsets); natural history including horticulture (flowers, fruits, trees, shrubs, etc.) invertebrates (including insects), amphibians, reptiles, birds, mammals, animals in the wild and in zoos; energy, oil, mining; anthropology and ethnology, ceremonies and customs, religion (non-Christian), rural life, shopping markets; photographic techniques (high-speed flash, micro, macro, ultraviolet); British Isles, Egypt, Ethiopia, Kenya, Sierra Leone, South Africa, Brazil, Bolivia, Chile, Colombia, Ecuador, Peru, Galapagos Islands, Mexico, Martinique, St Vincent, USA, Burma, China, Hong Kong, India, Indonesia, Iran, Nepal, Philippines, Australia, New Zealand, Austria, Azores, Canary Islands, France, Germany, Greece, Greenland, Holland, Iceland, Italy, Madeira, Norway, Sicily, Switzerland, Turkey, Yugoslavia, Afghanistan. Representatives of Solarfilma, Iceland

Access and conditions Open to qualified researchers by appt, Mon-Fri 9–6. All material available for editorial reproduction and for advertising. B/w and colour material loaned free of charge for two months. Reproduction rights, service and holding fees charged. Staff of two will undertake some research; negotiable fee charged for very large projects. Card catalogue.

787 • GREATER MANCHESTER MUSEUM OF SCIENCE AND INDUSTRY

Liverpool Road Station, Liverpool Road, Castlefield, Manchester M3 4JP
Tel (061) 832 2244

Enquiries to Patrick Greene, Director

Items About 28,000: b/w original and copy photographs, colour transparencies (35mm), glass negatives, lantern slides, illustrated books, fine art prints, daguerreotypes

Dates of subject matter *c.* 1700 to present

Dates of photographs 1852 to present

Subjects Science, industry and technology, including locomotives (built by Beyer, Peacock and Co. Ltd, Gorton, Manchester, 1854–1966, and by Sharp, Stewart and Neilson and Co., 1860–1890), the JOHN CLARKE COLLECTION of the last days of steam locomotives in the Northwest (1960s); machine tools (built by Beyer, Peacock, by Craven Brothers and by Shanks); motor cars (bodies built by Joseph Cockshoot and Co., Manchester, 1904–1938); buses (chassis by Crossley Motors Ltd, Gorton, Manchester); gas and diesel engines (built by Crossley Bros, Openshaw, Manchester); portraits of scientists and engineers; stationary steam engines; late 19th-century engineering drawings; textile machinery and illustrations from trade catalogues; railway signalling (northwest, 1950s); paper making; cables and cable laying (by J. T. Glover and Co. Ltd); history of photography including photographs by James Mudd of architecture and locomotives *c.* 1856 and by J. B. Dancer, inventor of micro-photographs, of his family and of British landscapes (mid-19th century)

Access and conditions Open to the public by appt (write) daily. Most material available for editorial reproduction and for advertising by special arrangement. B/w prints available for a fee. Material may be copied by outside photographers. Colour transparencies loaned for a rental fee; duplicate colour transparencies available for a fee. Reproduction rights fees charged. Staff will undertake some research in answer to mail requests. Card catalogue available.

788 • HUNTERIAN MUSEUM

Geology Section

University of Glasgow, Glasgow G12 8QQ
Tel (041) 339 8855 ext 288

Enquiries to Dr W. D. I. Rolfe

Items 4000: b/w original and copy photographs, colour transparencies (35mm), glass negatives, lantern slides, postcards, original cartoons, illustrated maps, fine art prints, posters, greetings cards, press cuttings and tearsheets

Dates of subject matter Pre-Cambrian to present

Dates of photographs 1882 to present

Subjects Victorian and 20th-century photographs especially of amateur field geologists on local excursions; early 20th-century expeditions, e.g., to Spitsbergen; research photographs of fossil plants by Professor John Walton and of fossil productid brachiopods by Dr K. A. G. Shields; miscellaneous fossils, especially East African

Access and conditions Open to the public by appt (write), Mon-Fri 10–5, Sat 9.30–1. Most material available for editorial reproduction and for advertising. B/w and colour material loaned free of charge for two months. B/w prints and duplicate colour transparencies available for a fee. Photocopies available. Reproduction rights, service and holding fees charged. Staff will undertake limited research.

789 • INSTITUTION OF ELECTRICAL ENGINEERS

Savoy Place, London WC2R 0BL
Tel (01) 240 1871 ext 290

Enquiries to Archivist

Items 10,000: glass negatives, b/w original and copy photographs, fine art prints

Dates of subject matter Late 18th to 20th century

Dates of photographs 1890 to present

Subjects Electrical and electronic engineering and related subjects; electric equipment and transport; lighting; the telegraph and early submarine cable laying; IFE building and activities; portraits of eminent scientists and electrical engineers

Access and conditions Open to the public by appt (write), Mon-Fri 9.30–5. Some material available for editorial reproduction. No loans; b/w prints available for a fee. Reproduction rights fees charged. Staff will undertake limited research.

790 • INTERMEDIATE TECHNOLOGY DEVELOPMENT GROUP LTD

Myson House, Railway Terrace, Rugby, Warwickshire CV21 3HT
Tel (0788) 60631

Enquiries to Information Office

Items 5000: b/w original photographs, colour transparencies (35mm)

Dates of photographs 1960 to present

Subjects Appropriate technologies for developing countries, simple low-cost small scale products and processes in agriculture, construction, energy, health, industry, transport, water; some photos of E. F. Schumacher

Access and conditions Open to qualified researchers by appt (write), Mon-Fri 9–5. All material available for editorial reproduction but not for advertising. B/w material loaned free of charge; colour loaned for a rental fee. Photocopies available. Reproduction rights fees charged. Staff will undertake some research.

791 • MARINE LABORATORY LIBRARY

Department of Agriculture and Fisheries for Scotland, PO Box 101, Aberdeen, Grampian AB9 8DB
Tel (0224) 876544 ext 347 Telex 73587

Enquiries to John Burne, Librarian

Items 14,500: colour transparencies (35mm), glass negatives, illustrated books

Dates of photographs 1900 to present

Subjects Seas around the UK, especially the North Sea, equipment especially the Ministry's research ships; fish, mostly species in the laboratory, some underwater; seals, some in habitat, damage to fish by seals (e.g. salmon);

shellfish (commercial varities), lobster, crab, mussels, scampi (live); microphotography of plankton species and phytoplankton; HELEN OGILVIE COLLECTION: early 20th-century drawings of *Diatomaceae* (microscopic algae with silicon in their shells)

Access and conditions Open to the public by appt (tel), Mon-Thurs 9–5, Fri 9–4.30. Some material available for editorial reproduction but not for advertising. B/w prints and duplicate colour transparencies available for a fee. Reproduction rights fees charged. Staff will undertake some research. Crown copyright; compulsory credit line. Card catalogue.

792 • MUSEUM OF THE HISTORY OF SCIENCE

Old Ashmolean Building, Broad Street, Oxford OX1 3AZ
Tel (0865) 243997

Enquiries to A. Simcock, Librarian

Items Unknown number: b/w original and copy photographs, colour transparencies (35mm), glass negatives, daguerreotypes, lantern slides, postcards, original cartoons, stereographs, illustrated books, engravings

Dates of subject matter Prehistory to present

Dates of photographs Mid-19th century to present

Subjects History of science including scientific instruments and apparatus, buildings and laboratories; subject areas include physics, chemistry, electricity, medicine, anatomy, pharmacy, time-telling, clocks and watches, navigation, surveying, astronomy, natural history, optics especially microscopy; history of photography and early photographic materials including images by Herschel and Hill and Adamson

Access and conditions Open to qualified researchers by appt, Mon-Fri 10.30–4.30. Some material available for editorial reproduction but not for advertising. No loans; b/w prints and duplicate colour transparencies available for a fee. Photocopies available. Reproduction rights fees charged. Staff will undertake very limited research. Most material copyright.

793 • NATIONAL CENTRE FOR ALTERNATIVE TECHNOLOGY

Machynlleth, Powys SY20 9AZ
Tel (0654) 2400

Enquiries to Information Officer

Items 70: colour transparencies (35mm), b/w original photographs

Dates of photographs 1970 to present

Subjects Alternative technology including solar, water and wind power, conservation of energy and heat recovery systems, organic gardening

Access and conditions Open to the public, Mon-Fri 9–5. All material available for editorial reproduction; advertising use by special arrangement only. Duplicate colour transparencies available for a fee. Reproduction rights fees charged. Staff will undertake some research. Compulsory credit line. All material copyright. Printed catalogue available.

794 • NATIONAL METEOROLOGICAL LIBRARY

Visual Aids Unit, London Road, Bracknell, Berkshire RG12 2SZ
Tel (0344) 420242 ext 2255 Telex 849801

Enquiries to Ron W. Mason, Visual Aids Officer

Items About 50,000: colour transparencies (35mm), b/w original and copy photographs, colour photographic prints, glass negatives, lantern slides, postcards, unprinted film negatives, posters, b/w transparencies, press cuttings

Dates of subject matter *c*. 1840 to present

Dates of photographs *c*. 1840 to present

Subjects Meteorology, including meteorologists at work, meteorological sites and locations, instruments, data collection, data processing systems, charts, computer output; meteorological phenomena, especially clouds and atmospheric optics, in the UK and north-western Europe (some worldwide coverage) including complete classification of clouds, optical phenomena, lunar and solar coronas, haloes in clouds around the sun, illuminated clouds in sunsets, phenomena formed around head in fog (glories); precipitation including rain, dew, snow, sleet, hail, storms including sleet storms, hurricanes, tornadoes, water spouts, thunder storms, lightning, damage resulting from storms (trees struck by lightning, piers struck by seas, trees deformed by wind, etc.), floods, rainbows, fog bows, ice bows, moon haloes, aurora borealis, drought, dust storms, land erosion

Access and conditions Open to the public by appt (tel), Mon-Thurs 8.30–5, Fri 8.30–4.30. All material available for editorial reproduction and for advertising, subject to copyright clearance. B/w and colour material loaned free of charge for one month. Photocopies available. Reproduction rights fees charged for Crown copyright material; holding and service fees charged. Staff will undertake research; fee charged to commercial users per group of 25 items.

795 • NIGEL PRESS ASSOCIATES LTD

Edenbridge, Kent TN8 6HS
Tel (0732) 865023 Telex 95442 NPALTO G

Enquiries to Bridget Benbow

Items Over 3000: unprinted film negatives, colour transparencies (35mm, 5″ × 4″)

Dates of photographs 1972 to present

Subjects Manned and unmanned satellite coverage of the earth including Landsat, Meteosat, Noaa, Seasat and Spot images

Access and conditions Open to the public by appt (tel), Mon-Fri 9–5. All material available for editorial reproduction and for advertising. B/w and colour material loaned free of charge by arrangement. Photocopies available. Reproduction rights fees charged. Staff will undertake some research. Some material copyright. Printed catalogue available.

796 • R. K. PILSBURY

Nyetimber, Uplands Road, Totland, Isle of Wight PO39 0DU
Tel (0983) 752778

Enquiries to R. K. Pilsbury

Items 6000: colour transparencies (35mm), b/w original photographs, unprinted film negatives

Dates of photographs 1960 to present

Subjects All aspects of meteorology including all types of clouds, optical phenomena (haloes, rainbows, fog bows, mock suns, sunpillars; double white rainbow believed unique); rain, hail, snow, frost, lightning; sunrises, sunsets; alpine and mountain scenery with clouds and snow; rough on-shore seas and wind-damaged trees; British butterflies and moths

Access and conditions Open to qualified researchers by appt (write). All material available for editorial reproduction and for advertising. B/w and colour material loaned free of charge for a month. Reproduction rights fees charged. Research undertaken. All material copyright.

797 • ANN RONAN PICTURE LIBRARY

Wheel Cottage, Bishops Hull, Taunton, Somerset
TA1 5EP
Tel (0823) 52737

Enquiries to Ann Ronan

Items 150,000: b/w original photographs, colour transparencies (35mm, 5″ × 4″), original cartoons, old fine art prints, illustrated periodicals, advertisements, trade cards

Dates of subject matter 1500 to 1900

Dates of photographs Mid-19th century to 1900

Subjects History of science and technology in the UK, Europe and North America covering social sciences, geology, biology, chemistry, physics, engineering, medical science, and including personalities, scientific experiments and discoveries, agricultural practices, manufacturing processes, natural history, working and living conditions, transport, education, child labour, women and work, homeworkers, welfare, family life, communications, religious practices and persecution, natural phenomena

Access and conditions Open to qualified researchers by appt (tel), Mon-Fri 9–5.30. All material available for editorial reproduction and for advertising. B/w and colour material loaned free of charge for one month. Photocopies available for a fee. Reproduction rights, holding and service fees charged. Staff will undertake some research; negotiable fee charged. No material copyright.

798 • ROYAL GEOGRAPHICAL SOCIETY

1 Kensington Gore, London SW7 2AR
Tel (01) 589 5466

Enquiries to Keeper of the Map Room

Items 100,000: b/w original and copy photographs, colour transparencies (35mm), glass negatives, postcards, illustrated maps, stereographs

Dates of subject matter 1930 to present

Dates of photographs Late 19th century to present

Subjects Expeditions (mainly British) including Scott, Shackleton, Livingstone and Fawcett; worldwide contemporary geographical coverage

Access and conditions Open to the public by appt (tel), Mon-Fri 10–5. All material available for editorial reproduction and for advertising. No loans; b/w prints and duplicate colour transparencies available for a fee. Photocopies available. Reproduction rights fees charged. Staff will undertake limited research. Most material copyright. Card catalogue available.

799 • ROYAL GREENWICH OBSERVATORY

Herstmonceux Castle, Hailsham, East Sussex
BN27 1RP
Tel (0323) 833171 Telex 87451

Enquiries to Janet Dudley

Items About 100,000: b/w original photographs, b/w copy photographs, colour transparencies (35mm, 5″ × 4″), colour photographic prints, glass negatives, daguerreotypes, lantern slides, postcards, original cartoons, illustrated maps, posters, architectural drawings, illustrated books, fine art prints, drawings, watercolours

Dates of subject matter c. 16th century to present

Dates of photographs 1860s to present

Dates of fine art 16th century to present

Subjects Astronomical objects and phenomena observed worldwide from the 15th century to present including a collection of solar plates recording solar activity daily from 1870 to 1975; scientific instruments including all types of astronomical and chronometrical instruments from 15th century; portraits of astronomers and physical scientists; illustrations from great voyages of discovery including those of Cook, La Perouse, Parry and Scott; illustrations of Herstmonceux Castle and park and Royal Observatory at Greenwich including watercolours by Turner and Samuel Palmer

Access and conditions Open to the public by appt (write), Mon-Fri 9–6. Most material available for editorial reproduction; advertising use by special arrangement only. B/w prints and duplicate colour transparencies available for a fee. Photocopies and Polaroids available. Reproduction rights fees charged. Staff will undertake limited research. Catalogue in preparation.

800 • ROYAL OBSERVATORY

Blackford Hill, Edinburgh EH9 3HJ
Tel (031) 667 3321 ext 239

Enquiries to Brian Hadley

Items 11,000: b/w original photographs, colour transparencies (35mm), b/w copy photographs, colour photographic prints, postcards, posters

Dates of photographs 1977 to present

Subjects Astronomical research photography including deep space star formations, galaxies, nebulae; telescopes and buildings at Siding Spring Observatory in New South Wales, and Mauna Kea in Hawaii

Access and conditions Open to qualified researchers by appt (write), Mon-Fri 9–12. All material available for editorial reproduction and for advertising. No loans; b/w prints and duplicate colour transparencies available for a fee. Reproduction rights and service fees charged. All material copyright.

801 • SCIENCE MUSEUM

Photographic Order Section

Exhibition Road, London SW7 5NH
Tel (01) 589 3456 Telex 21200

Enquiries to Photographic Order Section, ext 527

Items About 30,000: b/w original and copy photographs, glass negatives, unprinted film negatives

Dates of subject matter Prehistory to present

Dates of photographs Contemporary

Subjects Museum items covering the history and development of science and technology with special emphasis on the physical sciences and their industrial application

Access and conditions Open to the public, Mon-Fri 10–5.30. All material available for editorial reproduction and for advertising. No loans; b/w prints available for a fee; material may be copied by outside photographers. Photocopies available. Reproduction rights fees charged. Staff will undertake limited research. All material copyright. Duplicated catalogue available.

Photography Collection

Tel (01) 589 3456 Telex 21200

Enquiries to John Ward, Curator

Items About 50,000: original photographs, daguerreotypes, photogenic drawings, calotypes, tintypes, ambrotypes, lantern slides, glass negatives, unprinted film negatives, ephemera

Dates of photographs 1835 to present

Subjects History of photographic processes worldwide with emphasis on early development including the work of Fox Talbot, Herschel, Claudet, Ellis, Hill and Adamson, Fenton, Beato and Robertson, Muybridge; ephemera including catalogues and correspondence relating to photographers

Access and conditions Open to the public by appt (tel). Most material available for editorial reproduction; advertising by special arrangement only. No loans; b/w prints and duplicate colour transparencies available for a fee. Photocopies available. Reproduction rights fees charged. Some material copyright.

802 • SCIENCE PHOTO LIBRARY LTD

2 Blenheim Crescent, London W11 1NN
Tel (01) 727 4712, 229 9847

Enquiries to Salim Patel, Sales Director

Items 65,000: colour transparencies (35mm, $5'' \times 4''$), b/w original photographs, colour photographic prints, etchings

Dates of photographs 1960 to present

Subjects Science and technology including: earth sciences – Landsat and other satellite photographs, atmospheric phenomena, lightning, storms, aurora, clouds, north and south poles, ice, glaciers, seas and oceans, oceanography, geophysics, continental drift, volcanoes, earthquakes, minerals, rock strata, fossils, geography, deserts, deltas, agriculture, pollution; botany – plant cell structure, plant sections, plant genetics and reproduction, bacteria, algae, wood sections, pollen and pollination; zoology – protozoa, worms, flukes, rotifers, leeches, crustaceans, insects, bees, wasps, spiders, mites, ticks, sea-snails; genetics and general biology – cell structure, DNA, genes, chromosomes, genetic engineering, biotechnology laboratories, monoclonal antibodies, tissue culture; physics and chemistry – light, optics, magnetism, high-energy physics, bubble-chamber pictures, crystals, vitamins, hormones, drugs; mammalian physiology – skeleton and bones, muscles and tendons, blood, heart, nerve cells, the brain, sense receptors, the eye, the mouth and teeth, intestines, liver, kidneys, lungs, sperm and eggs, fertilization, embryos, cell division, skin and hair, whole-body thermographs and body contour maps; medicine – diseases, clinical medical photographs, cancer and cancer research, injuries, diagnostic techniques, CAT scans, nuclear magnetic resonance, X-rays, hospitals, surgery, dentistry, medical research, obstetrics and gynaecology, general practice; technology – oil, alternative energies, atomic explosions, nuclear power, fusion research, electricity, lasers, holography, robots, optical fibres, communications technology, electronics, integrated circuits, computers, transportation, ocean technology; astronomy – observatories and telescopes, astronomical satellites and spacecraft, meteors, the planets, constellations, nebulae and star formation, star clouds and fields, supernovas and remnants, black holes, the Milky Way, normal and active galaxies, quasars; spaceflight – space organizations and centres including NASA, historical pictures, Mercury, Gemini and Apollo programmes, Skylab, Space Shuttle, space industrialization, communication and other satellites, space colonies; miscellaneous including familiar objects under microscopes, non-destructive testing, portraits of scientists, microscopy, infra-red photography and thermography, schlieren photography, high-speed photography, Kirlian photography, radiography, sonar and radar, ultrasound imagery, computer enhancement

Access and conditions Open to qualified researchers by appt (tel), Mon-Fri 9.30–5.30. All material available for reproduction and for advertising. B/w and colour material loaned free of charge for six weeks. Photocopies available. Reproduction rights fees charged; service and research fees charged only when no material is used. Staff of four will undertake research. Most material copyright. Printed catalogue available free of charge.

803 • SCOTT POLAR RESEARCH INSTITUTE

Lensfield Road, Cambridge CB2 1ER
Tel (0223) 66499 Telex 81240 CAMSPL G

Enquiries to Clive Holland, Archivist

Items 50,000: b/w original and copy photographs, glass negatives, unprinted film negatives, colour transparencies (35mm, 5″ × 4″), b/w copy photographs, watercolours and drawings, lantern slides, old fine art prints, postcards, original cartoons, 20th-century fine art prints, colour photographic prints, press cuttings, illustrated books

Dates of subject matter 1820 to present

Dates of photographs 1858 to present

Subjects History of polar (both Arctic and Antarctic) exploration with emphasis on British expeditions especially in the early 20th century and including Scott and Shackleton; landscapes, ships, ice features, wildlife, native inhabitants

Access and conditions Open to qualified researchers by appt (tel), Mon-Fri 9–5.30. All material available for editorial reproduction and for advertising. B/w prints and duplicate colour transparencies available for a fee; material may be copied by outside photographers. Photocopies available. Reproduction rights and service fees charged. Staff will undertake some research; fees charged for large projects. Most material copyright. Partial card catalogue available.

804 • UNIVERSITY OF CAMBRIDGE

Department of Physics

The Cavendish Laboratory, Madingley Road, Cambridge CB3 0HE
Tel (0223) 66477 Telex 81292 CAV LAB

Enquiries to J. Deakin, Secretary, Department of Physics

Items 250: b/w original and copy photographs, colour transparencies (35mm), glass negatives, lantern slides

Dates of subject matter 1871 to present

Dates of photographs 1920 to present

Subjects The work of the Cavendish Laboratory; scientists and their apparatus, historical and contemporary

Access and conditions Open to qualified researchers by appt (write). Some material available for editorial reproduction but not for advertising. B/w prints and duplicate colour transparencies available for a fee. Photocopies available. Reproduction rights fees charged. Staff will undertake some research. Card catalogue.

805 • ANTHONY WALTHAM

Civil Engineering Department

Trent Polytechnic, Nottingham NG1 4BU
Tel (0602) 418248 ext 2133

Enquiries to Anthony Waltham

Items 11,000: colour transparencies (35mm), b/w original photographs

Dates of subject matter Prehistory to present

Dates of photographs 1970 to present

Subjects Specialist geological and geographical coverage of the UK, north and South America, southern Europe, South-east Asia and China including geomorphology, erosion, rivers, glaciers, landforms, deserts, mountains, limestone landscapes, karst; caves, caverns, potholes; special collection of underground photographs; rocks, fossils, volcanoes, geysers, engineering geology, quarries, mines, ground failure, environmental geography, landscapes, land use, farming communications; geological hazards and disasters including landslides, subsidence, earthquakes, volcanic eruptions

Access and conditions Open to the public by appt (tel), Mon-Fri 9–5. All material available for editorial reproduction and for advertising. B/w and colour material loaned free of charge for one month. Reproduction rights fees charged. Research undertaken. All material copyright.

Industry, Commerce & Agriculture

806 • AE plc

Cawston House, Rugby, Warwickshire CV22 7SB
Tel (0788) 816677   Telex 311259

Enquiries to M. D. J. Hurn, Group Publicity Director

Items 10,000: b/w original photographs, colour transparencies (35mm, 5″ × 4″, 10″ × 8″), colour photographic prints, b/w copy photographs, glass negatives, cuttings and tearsheets

Dates of subject matter 1900 to present

Dates of photographs *c.* 1920 to present

Subjects Manufacturing and application of precision engineering components, especially engine components such as bearings, pistons, piston rings and castings used in the aerospace industry, motor cars and commercial vehicles, marine, construction and general engineering industries

Access and conditions Open to qualified researchers by appt (write), Mon-Fri 9–5. Most material available for editorial reproduction and for advertising. B/w and colour material loaned free of charge. Photocopies available. No reproduction rights fees; service and holding fees occasionally charged. All material copyright. Research undertaken at the discretion of the Publicity Director.

807 • AMEY ROADSTONE CORPORATION LTD

The Ridge, Chipping Sodbury, Avon BS17 6AY
Tel (0454) 316000   Telex 449353

Enquiries to Guy Erwood, Group Communications Officer

Items 20,000: colour transparencies (35mm), b/w original photographs, colour photographic prints

Dates of subject matter Contemporary

Dates of photographs 1950 to present

Subjects Quarrying and processing of stone, sand and gravel; production and laying of asphalt and macadam; production and use of ready-mixed concrete; production and use of pre-cast concrete pipes and blocks; production and processing of sea-dredged aggregates; heavy goods vehicles used in the above; civil engineering, road and bridge construction; production and use of industrial sands for glass and foundry; restoration of quarry and gravel extraction sites; waste disposal by controlled landfill; fish farming

Access and conditions Not open; written requests only. All material available for editorial reproduction and for advertising. B/w and colour material loaned free of charge for one month. B/w prints and duplicate colour transparencies available for a fee. Reproduction rights, service and holding fees not usually charged. Staff will undertake some research, time permitting. All material copyright. Catalogue in preparation.

808 • AVELING-BARFORD LTD

Invicta Works, Grantham, Lincolnshire NG31 6JE
Tel (0476) 65551   Telex 377861

Enquiries to P. Daniele, Photographic Services Manager

Items Over 5000: b/w original photographs, colour photographic prints, colour transparencies (35mm, 5″ × 4″), glass negatives, b/w copy photographs

Dates of subject matter 1850 to present

Dates of photographs *c.* 1850 to present

Subjects Manufacture and use of construction equipment at Grantham, in the UK (site application) and overseas

Access and conditions Open to qualified researchers by appt (tel). All material available for editorial reproduction and for advertising. B/w and colour material loaned free of charge for two weeks; b/w prints and duplicate transparencies available for a fee. Photocopies available. No reproduction rights fees charged. Staff will undertake some research. All material copyright.

809 • AVERY HISTORICAL MUSEUM

Foundry Lane, Smethwick, Warley, West Midlands B66 2LP
Tel (021) 558 1112 Telex 336490

Enquiries to Curator

Items Over 1000: b/w original and copy photographs, lantern slides, illustrated catalogues, illustrated maps, posters

Dates of subject matter 2500 BC to present

Dates of photographs 1927 to present

Subjects Weighing and weighing instruments (scales, balances); Avery products both ancient and modern

Access and conditions Open to the public by appt, Wed & Thurs 9–5. Some material available for editorial reproduction; advertising use by special arrangement only. No loans; b/w prints available for a fee. Material may be copied by outside photographers in some case. Photocopies available. No reproduction rights or service fees charged.

810 • BAKER PERKINS HOLDINGS plc

Westfield Road, Peterborough PE3 6TA
Tel (0733) 261303 Telex 32809

Enquiries to Harry Giltrap, Group Publicity Manager

Items 70,000: b/w original and copy photographs, colour transparencies (35mm, 5″ × 4″, larger), colour photographic prints, glass negatives, lantern slides, cuttings and tearsheets

Dates of subject matter 1860s to present

Dates of photographs 1880s to present

Subjects Bread and biscuit production of all kinds from *c.* 1900 to present, chocolate and

confectionery production, packaging of these products; specialized mixing of chemicals and allied products such as plastics; high-speed web-offset printing presses for colour work; foundry machinery, especially sand mixers; engineering factories, foundries and offices past and present; old and modern machine tools; traditional drawing offices and computer-aided design

Access and conditions Open to qualified researchers by appt (tel), Mon-Fri 8.30–1, 1.45–4.45. Some material available for editorial reproduction and for advertising. Colour material loaned free of charge; duplicate transparencies available for a fee. B/w material not loaned; b/w prints available for a fee. No reproduction rights fees. Staff of four will undertake some research. Card catalogue available.

811 • BANK OF SCOTLAND

The Mound, Edinburgh EH1 1YZ
Tel (031) 229 2555 Telex 72275

Banknote and Coin Collection

Enquiries to Archivist

Dates of subject matter Roman to present

Subjects Scottish banknotes from 1695 to present; coins from Roman period relating to Scotland

Access and conditions Open to qualified researchers by appt (write). Some material available for editorial reproduction at the Bank's discretion. Material may be copied by outside photographers. No reproduction rights fees. Staff will undertake limited research.

Public Affairs Department

Enquiries to Public Affairs Department

Items 500: colour transparencies (35mm), b/w original photographs, colour photographic prints

Dates of photographs Contemporary

Subjects Banking including Head Office, selected branches and officials of the Bank of Scotland

Access and conditions Open to qualified researchers by appt (write). Some material available for editorial reproduction at the Bank's discretion. B/w and colour material loaned. No reproduction rights fees. Staff will undertake limited research.

812 • BASS MUSEUM OF BREWING HISTORY

PO Box 16, Horninglow Street, Burton upon Trent, Staffordshire DE14 1PF
Tel (0283) 45301 ext 2148

Enquiries to J. Brian Curzon, Curator

Items Over 10,000: b/w original and copy photographs, colour transparencies (35mm), colour photographic prints, glass negatives, lantern slides, postcards, original cartoons, posters, architectural drawings, illustrated books

Dates of subject matter 19th and 20th centuries

Dates of photographs *c.* 1860 to present

Subjects Brewing history, especially Bass and breweries absorbed by Bass; postcards, mostly comic, featuring Bass; Burton upon Trent history including local views, paintings, prints, photographs of events from *c.* 1850 to present; products of Orton & Spooner, manufacturer of fairground rides

Access and conditions Open to the public by appt (write), 11–5 daily except Christmas and New Year. Most material available for editorial reproduction; advertising use subject to Bass's approval. B/w and colour material loaned by special arrangement; b/w prints and duplicate colour transparencies available for a fee. Photocopies available.

813 • BATH INDUSTRIAL HISTORY TRUST

Camden Works Museum, Julian Road, Bath, Avon BA1 2RH
Tel (0225) 318348

Enquiries to Frances Repper, Curator

Items 4000: ephemera, trade cards, catalogues, trade journals, graphics, posters, b/w original and copy photographs

Dates of subject matter 1870 to 1930

Dates of photographs 1969

Dates of graphics 1870 to 1930

Subjects BOWLER COLLECTION including full-colour poster calendars advertising Bowler's mineral waters (1881–1914), mineral water trade journals (1870s–1880s), ephemera (bottle labels, advertisements, trade cards) from mineral water trade and from engineering, gas fitting and plumbing trades (1880s–1920s), original factory premises of J. B. Bowler; history of Bath stone including men working in mines, and local architecture and geography

Access and conditions Open to qualified researchers by appt, Mon-Fri 9.30–5.30. Most material available for editorial reproduction and for advertising, subject to copyright clearance. B/w material loaned free of charge for one month; material may be copied by outside photographers. Photocopies available. Reproduction rights and service fees charged.

814 • BERSHAM INDUSTRIAL HERITAGE CENTRE

Bersham, Nr Wrexham, Clwyd LL14 4HT
Tel (0978) 261529

Enquiries to The Curator

Items About 200: colour transparencies (35mm), b/w copy photographs, postcards, unprinted film negatives

Dates of subject matter 18th century to present

Dates of photographs 1900 to 1984

Subjects Bersham Ironworks and Clywedog Industrial trail including past industrial activities and remains in the lead mining area of Minera, the lead spoil heaps, remains of engine houses; at the Bersham Ironworks site, the Ironworks buildings, workers' cottages, weirs, etc.; the Heritage Centre and its collections; DAVIES BROTHERS GATESMITHS COLLECTION: wrought-iron gates made by Davies Brothers, e.g. Chirk Castle gates, Wrexham Parish Church gates; POWELL BROTHERS COLLECTION: old works, original building before demolition, agrricultural machinery, motorcycles, munitions and workers; Cambrian Ironworks, Wrexham; original archive material deposited with County Record Office

Access and conditions Open to the public by appt (tel), Tues-Fri 10–12.30, 1.30–4, Sat 12.30–3.30. Most material available for editorial reproduction and for advertising with the Curator's approval. B/w prints and duplicate colour transparencies available for a fee. Photocopies available. No reproduction rights fees. Staff will undertake some research and mail photocopies.

815 • THE BREWERS' SOCIETY

42 Portman Square, London W1H 0BB
Tel (01) 486 4831   Telex 261946

Enquiries to R. J. Webber, Information Officer

Items About 3000: b/w original and copy photographs, colour transparencies (35mm, 5″ × 4″), lantern slides, colour photographic prints, postcards, cuttings and tearsheets

Dates of subject matter 1900 to 1980

Dates of photographs 1925 to 1980

Subjects Brewing and breweries including brewing process, equipment, transport, training, exhibitions, raw materials, bottles, cans; brewery directors; public house exteriors and inn signs, public house interiors without customers

Access and conditions Open to qualified researchers by appt (tel). Some material available for editorial reproduction but not for advertising. B/w material loaned at the Society's discretion; duplicate colour transparencies available for a fee. Material may be copied by outside photographers. Copyright clearance is responsibility of user. Staff will undertake limited research.

816 • BRISTOL CITY MUSEUM AND ART GALLERY

Technology Section

Queens Road, Bristol, Avon BS8 1RL
Tel (0272) 299771

Enquiries to Curator of Technology

Items 50,000: b/w original and copy photographs, glass negatives, unprinted film negatives, lantern slides, postcards, fine art prints, original cartoons, illustrated maps, posters, architectural drawings

Dates of subject matter c. 1850 to present

Dates of photographs 1850 to present

Subjects Shipping in Bristol and Avonmouth (1880–1950); Great Western Railway (copies of original photographs); photographic records of the Langston Machine Co. (previously known as Brecknell, Munro and Rogers and then as Thrissell Engineering Co.), manufacturers of packaging, handling and paper processing machinery; Bristol commercial vehicles, buses etc., Bristol dock area, including workshops, factories, riggers

Access and conditions Open to the public by appt (write), Mon-Fri 10–5. All material available for editorial reproduction and for advertising subject to committee approval. No loans; b/w prints and duplicate colour transparencies available for a fee. Material may be copied by outside photographers. Photocopies available. Reproduction rights and service fees charged; service fee deductible from use fee. Staff will undertake some research. Card catalogue available.

817 • BRITISH STEEL CORPORATION

East Midlands Regional Record Centre

By-Pass Road, Irthlingborough, Wellingborough, Northamptonshire NN9 5QH
Tel (0933) 650277

Enquiries to Maureen Manson

Items 5000: b/w original photographs, unprinted film negatives, glass negatives, colour photographic prints, art reproductions, illustrated books, press cuttings

Dates of subject matter Prehistory to present

Dates of photographs c. 1880 to present

Subjects Steel making in the UK including the archives of the Corporation and former companies now part of the BSC; steel making processes, workforces, works, plant, major development schemes, job progress

Access and conditions Open to the public by appt. Most material available for editorial reproduction and for advertising. No loans; b/w prints available for a fee; material may be copied by outside photographers. Photocopies available. No reproduction rights fees charged. Staff will undertake some research. Most material copyright; copyright clearance is responsiblity of user. Card catalogue available.

Northern Region Records Centre

Unit F2, Commerce Way, Skippers Lane Industrial Estate, South Bank, Middlesbrough, Cleveland TS7 8QQ
Tel (0642) 467144 ext 544/5

Enquiries to Branch Manager

Items Over 3000: b/w copy and original photographs, colour photographic prints, glass negatives, lantern slides, postcards, architectural drawings

Dates of subject matter 1850 to 1967

Dates of photographs 1850 to 1967

Subjects Iron and steel manufacture and associated processes including ironstone and coal mining and chemical by-products; archive collections of iron and steel companies in Teesside, Sheffield and County Durham nationalized in 1967

Access and conditions Open to the public by appt (write). Most material available for editorial reproduction and for advertising. No loans; b/w prints available for a fee; material may be copied by outside photographers. Photocopies available. No reproduction rights fees charged. Staff will undertake some research. Most material copyright.

818 • BRITOIL plc

Photographic Reference Library, PO Box 120, BRITOIL House, Hill of Rubislaw, Anderson Drive, Aberdeen AB9 8XB
Tel (0224) 574555 ext 3129 Telex 739721

Enquiries to Christine Cook, Information Officer

Items 10,000: colour photographic prints

Dates of photographs 1978 to present

Subjects Offshore oil exploration and drilling, platforms (aerials and on board), on-shore storage terminal, visitors and personnel, social events

Access and conditions Open by appt (write). Material available for editorial reproduction at the discretion of Britoil. Colour transparencies available for a fee. Staff will undertake limited research.

819 • H. P. BULMER LTD

The Cider Mills, Plough Lane, Hereford HR4 0LE
Tel (0432) 276411 Telex 35211

Enquiries to George Thomas, Publicity Manager

Items About 5000: b/w original and copy photographs, colour transparencies (35mm, 5″ × 4″), posters, illustrated books, engravings

Dates of subject matter 17th century to present

Dates of photographs 1850s to present

Subjects Cider and history of cidermaking including orchards in bloom and with apples, apple-picking, cider presses (ancient and modern), barrels, bottles and bottling, cutting and pressing of fruit, cider drinking, advertising; collection of rare 17th-century cider glasses

Access and conditions Not open; telephone and mail requests only. All material available for editorial reproduction but not for advertising. B/w and colour material loaned free of charge. Compulsort credit line. No reproduction rights fees. Staff will undertake some research.

820 • CAMBORNE SCHOOL OF MINES

Geological Museum, Trevenson, Pool, Redruth, Cornwall TR15 3SE
Tel (0209) 714866 Telex 45315

Enquiries to Dr R. L. Atkinson, Curator

Items About 1000: b/w original and copy photographs, colour transparencies (35mm, 5″ × 4″, larger), colour photographic prints, postcards, posters, illustrated books

Dates of subject matter Prehistory to present

Dates of photographs Late 19th century to present

Subjects Mines (tin, etc.) and mining in Cornwall, including surface and underground scenes; engineering projects, mining operations and geology worldwide

Access and conditions Open to the public by appt (tel). Some material available for editorial reproduction and for advertising. B/w and colour material loaned; b/w prints and duplicate colour transparencies available for a fee. Photocopies available. No charge for educational use. Staff will undertake some research.

821 • CARRERAS ROTHMANS LTD

Oxford Road, Aylesbury, Buckinghamshire HP21 8SZ
Tel (0296) 26111 Telex 837553

Enquiries to Graham Wilton, Public Relations Executive

Items 1000: b/w original photographs, colour photographic prints, colour transparencies (35mm)

Dates of subject matter 1870 to present

Dates of photographs 1920 to present

Subjects Tobacco industry including manufacture of cigarettes and cigarette packs, pipe tobacco; cultivation of tobacco in Jamaica, Cyprus and Virginia; sporting events including rally driving, endurance racing (motor cars), aerobatic biplanes, power boating, water-skiing, bobsleighing

Access and conditions Open to qualified researchers by appt. Some material available for editorial reproduction and for advertising; educational use limited to over-sixteens. B/w and colour material loaned free of charge for one month. B/w prints and duplicate colour transparencies available for a fee. Photocopies available. No reproduction rights fees. Staff will undertake limited research.

822 • CEMENT AND CONCRETE ASSOCIATION

Photographs Library, Wexham Springs, Slough, Buckinghamshire SL3 6PL
Tel (02816) 2727   Telex 848352

Enquiries to Jo Searle, Photographs Librarian

Items About 20,000: b/w original and copy photographs, colour transparencies (35mm, 5″ × 4″, larger), colour photographic prints

Dates of photographs 1930 to present

Subjects Cement and concrete industry, manufacture and use including testing equipment and sample testing; pipes, beams, columns, foundations, tunnels; road and rail bridges, roads and road constructions, paving trains; water towers, tanks, reservoirs; agricultural buildings, roads, floors and pavings; pre-cast units, walls, roofs, fencing, chimneys, lighthouses, radio masts; concrete blocks and blocklaying, concrete bricks, paving flags, concrete paved areas; pre-stressing, reinforcing, formwork; domestic and industrial use of concrete block paving (pedestrian precincts, etc.); pedestrian areas, parking areas, shopping precincts; surface finishing, decorative uses; DIY, concrete in home and garden making; concrete in the garden, paving, pools, raised beds, plant containers, walls; concrete structures including bakeries, breweries, sports arenas and facilities, art complexes, churches, schools and colleges, civic buildings, offices, shops, flats, houses

Access and conditions Open to qualified researchers by appt (tel), Mon-Fri 9.30–4.30. All material available for editorial reproduction and for advertising. No loans; b/w prints and duplicate colour transparencies available for a fee. Photocopies available. Reproduction rights fees charged only for advertising and promotional use

and occasionally by copyright holders of non CCA material. Staff of two will undertake some research.

823 • CHATTERLEY WHITFIELD MINING MUSEUM

Tunstall, Stoke-on-Trent, Staffordshire ST6 8UN
Tel (0782) 813337/8

Enquiries to Curatorial Department

Items About 1000: b/w original and copy photographs, colour transparencies (35mm), postcards, architectural drawings, glass negatives

Dates of subject matter c. 1800 to present

Dates of photographs 1850 to present

Subjects Coalmining including accidents and disasters, manpower, coal cutting, collieries, geology, group shots, miners' housing, living conditions, locomotives, mining methods, pitbrow girls, pit ponies, rescues, strikes, tubs and roadways, underground machinery; Chatterley Whitfield Colliery, Norton Colliery, Silverdale Colliery, Talke O'The Hill Colliery and surroundings, Victoria Colliery, Wolstanton Colliery; industrial archaeology, Mill Meece pumping station, public transport, shipping

Access and conditions Open to qualified researchers by appt (tel), Mon-Fri 9–5. All material available for editorial reproduction and for advertising. B/w and colour material loaned free of charge for one month. Photocopies available. Reproduction rights and service fees charged. Staff of two will undertake research.

824 • CLYDE RIVER PURIFICATION BOARD

Rivers House, Murray Road, East Kilbride, Glasgow G75 0LA
Tel (03552) 38181

Enquiries to Dr Gerald A. Best

Items About 3000: colour transparencies (35mm), b/w original photographs, colour photographic prints

Dates of photographs 1960 to present

Subjects Pollution of inland waters by industry (discharges of oil, pollution from steel works, farms, power stations, paper mills, tanneries, dye works, sand and gravel extractors, mines, abandoned mines, water treatment works and sewage treatment works), pollution of tidal waters by oil, sewage and shipyards; agriculture, forestry, industry, local rivers and tidewaters; laboratory instruments, sampling of river and sea water, tables and graphs of survey results; aerial photographs showing views of mines, mills, gravel extractors, water pollution

Access and conditions Open to qualified researchers by appt (write). All material available for editorial use but not for advertising. No loans; b/w prints and duplicate colour transparencies available for a fee. Photocopies available. No reproduction rights fees; service fee charged. Staff will undertake limited research.

825 • CSO VALUATIONS PTY LTD

De Beers Consolidated Mines Ltd, 17 Charterhouse Street, London EC1N 8RA
Tel (01) 404 4444

Enquiries to Rosemary May, Photographer

Items 5000: b/w original and copy photographs, colour transparencies (35mm, 5″ × 4″, larger), colour photographic prints

Dates of photographs 1890 to present

Subjects Diamonds, mining, classification into 300 categories, cutting and polishing, manufacture of jewellery; historical prints of South African diamond mines, sorting, mining and buying activities, etc.

Access and conditions Open to qualified researchers by appt (tel), Mon-Fri 10–12, 2–4. Most material available for editorial reproduction and for advertising. B/w prints and duplicate colour transparencies available for a fee. No reproduction rights fees charged. Staff will undertake limited research.

826 • THE DEVILBISS COMPANY LTD

Ringwood Road, Bournemouth, Dorset BH11 9LH
Tel (0202) 571111 Telex 41213

Enquiries to Ian Bunker, Advertising Manager

Items Over 2000: b/w original and copy photographs, colour photographic prints, colour transparencies (35mm, 5″ × 4″, larger)

Dates of photographs 1965 to present

Subjects Spray guns (many types), sectioned guns; electrostatic liquid and powder coating equipment; complete automatic spray installations, including spray booths; spraying of food, cars, china, leather and wood; air brushes (in use) retouching, modelling; spray-finishing robots; varieties of air compressors

Access and conditions Not open; telephone or postal requests only. All material available for editorial reproduction; for advertising at the Manager's discretion. B/w and colour loaned free of charge for one month. B/w prints and duplicate colour transparencies available; no print fees for small requests. Photocopies available. No reproduction rights fees charged. Staff will undertake some research. Compulsory credit line.

827 • DORMAN PUBLIC RELATIONS

48 Worcester Street, Gloucester GL1 1SL
Tel (0452) 410442

Enquiries to David Dorman, Managing Director

Items 200: colour transparencies (35mm), colour photographic prints, b/w original and copy photographs

Dates of subject matter 19th century to present

Dates of photographs 1980 to present

Subjects Cider manufacturing including apple growing, orchards, processing and bottling; distilling of Scotch whisky (all stages) including bottling

Access and conditions Open to qualified researchers by appt, Mon-Fri 9–5. All material available for editorial reproduction but not for advertising. B/w and colour material loaned free of charge for one month. No reproduction rights fees. Staff will undertake some research.

828 • FARM BUILDINGS INFORMATION CENTRE

National Agriculture Centre, Stoneleigh, Kenilworth, Warwickshire CV8 2LG
Tel (0203) 22345 Telex 31697

Enquiries to Andrea Jacques

Items 500: b/w original and copy photographs, colour transparencies (35mm), colour photographic prints, architectural drawings, cuttings and tearsheets, illustrated books

Dates of subject matter 7th century to present

Dates of photographs 1970 to present

Subjects Farm buildings including details of cow sheds, sheep pens, pigsties; special file on design of buildings and their siting in the landscape

Access and conditions Open to the public by appt (tel), Mon–Fri 9–5. Some material available for editorial reproduction and for advertising. B/w and colour material loaned free of charge for one month. B/w prints and duplicate colour transparencies available for a fee. Photocopies available. No reproduction rights fees. Staff will undertake some research.

829 • *FARMERS' WEEKLY* PICTURE LIBRARY

BUSINESS PRESS INTERNATIONAL

Surrey House, 1 Throwley Way, Sutton, Surrey
SM1 4QQ
Tel (01) 643 8040 ext 4131 Telex 892084 BISPRS
G(ACP)

Enquiries to Sheila Wells

Items About 1,075,000: b/w original photographs, colour transparencies (35mm, 2¼″, 5″ × 4″), unprinted film negatives, fine art prints, original cartoons

Dates of subject matter 1900 to present

Dates of photographs 1934 to present

Subjects Agriculture and rural life, mostly in Great Britain but some material from the USA and Europe; livestock (breeds, feeding, housing, reproduction), arable (crops, cereals, disease, growth, planting, harvesting), machinery (tractors, combine harvesters, drilling rigs, cultivators, contractors and old show machinery), buildings (farmhouses, farm buildings, barns, animal housing), markets and agricultural shows (produce and livestocks marts, showgrounds, show rings, Smithfield Show, Drainage Show), vegetables (growing, planting, processing), weeds, land reclamation, timber, forestry, deforestation, country crafts (basket-making, preserving and pickling, thatching, wheel-making, barrow-making), aerial views, hill and mountain views, snow and floods, *Farmers' Weekly* farms, rural arts, farming worldwide

Access and conditions Open to the public by

appt (tel), Mon–Fri 10–6. All material available for editorial reproduction and for advertising. B/w and colour material loaned free of charge for one month. Photocopies available. Reproduction rights, holding and service fees charged; service fees deductible from use fees. Staff of three will undertake research and mail consignments of photographs. Printed catalogue available.

830 • WALTER FUSSEY & SONS

2 Ferriby Road, Hessle, North Humberside
HU13 0PG
Tel (0482) 648817

Enquiries to Walter Fussey

Items About 1500: b/w original photographs, colour transparencies (35mm), colour photographic prints, glass negatives

Dates of subject matter *c.* 1950 to present

Dates of photographs 1955 to present

Subjects Marine photography, Hull fishing fleet, trawlers, sidewinders, freezers, vessels built in Humberside, tugs, ferries, dredgers, small tankers, small coasters, supply vessels, M.o.D. vessels

Access and conditions Open to the public by appt (tel, 24-hour anwerphone), Mon–Fri 9–5, Sat 8–12. All material available for editorial reproduction and for advertising. B/w negatives and colour transparencies loaned for a fee. B/w prints and duplicate colour transparencies available for a fee. Reproduction rights fees charged. Staff will undertake limited research.

831 • E. GOMME LTD

PO Box 27, Spring Gardens, High Wycombe,
Buckinghamshire HP13 7AD
Tel (0494) 26250 Telex 837110

Enquiries to Alison M. Marvelly

Items 450: colour transparencies (5″ × 4″, larger), b/w original and copy photographs, colour photographic prints

Dates of subject matter 1950 to present

Dates of photographs 1950 to present

Subjects Modern domestic furniture (G-Plan) both upholstered and cabinet, living-room, dining-room, bedroom and occasional pieces, individual pieces and furnished rooms, made of teak, ash, mahogany, elm and other woods

Access and conditions Not open; mail and tel requests only. All material available for editorial reproduction and for advertising. B/w and colour material loaned free of charge for six months. No reproduction rights fees charged. Staff will undertake some research.

832 • WILLIAM GRANT & SONS

The Glenfiddich Distillery, 40 Piccadilly, London W1V 0EL
Tel (01) 734 2316 Telex 21583

Enquiries to Josephine Clark

Items 140: b/w original and copy photographs, colour transparencies (35mm), colour photographic prints, postcards

Dates of subject matter 13th century to present

Dates of photographs Recent

Subjects The Glenfiddich Distillery, distilling process (mashing, malting, fermentation, distillation, spirit safes, filling, cooperage, warehouse, bottling, packaging of bottles and cartons, despatch), pre-1900 photographs of the distillery, distillery tour guides dressed in kilts, the Glenfiddich rose, the Glenfiddich Visitors' Centre (entrance hall, tapestry, Gordon Highlanders display, a/v theatre, Founder's Room, malt barn); Speyside scenery, Scottish castles, Balvenie Castle

Access and conditions Open to qualified researchers by appt, Mon-Fri 9–5. Most material available for editorial reproduction and for advertising. B/w and colour material loaned free of charge; duplicate colour transparencies available for a fee. No reproduction rights fees charged.

833 • HEADWAY PUBLIC RELATIONS

28/29 Southampton Street, London WC2E 7JA
Tel (01) 379 6399

Enquiries to Sharon Masson

Items About 100: b/w original and copy photographs, colour transparencies (35mm)

Dates of photographs Contemporary

Subjects Seiko watches and clocks; Aiwa hi-fi equipment; Martini & Rossi Ltd food and drink,

cocktails, preparation; Slazenger sporting goods and clothing

Access and conditions Open to qualified researchers by appt (tel), Mon-Fri 9–5. All material available for editorial reproduction and for advertising subject to company approval. B/w and colour material loaned free of charge for 10 days; copy prints and duplicates may be made. No reproduction rights fees. Staff will carry out limited research. Compulsory credit lines.

834 • HOLT STUDIOS LTD

Holt Cottage, Newtown Common, Nr Newbury, Berkshire RG15 9BG
Tel (063527) 584

Enquiries to Philip C. Mitchell, Library Manager

Items 25,000: colour transparencies (35mm, $2\frac{1}{4}''$, $5'' \times 4''$), b/w original photographs, colour photographic prints

Dates of photographs 1979 to present

Subjects Worldwide agriculture, crop production and crop protection, examples of excellent and poor crops, weeds, pests, diseases and deficiencies affecting them; agricultural tools, machinery, spraying, cultivation, harvesting and other cultural practices; livestock, horticulture, ornamental plants, ornamental plant pests and diseases, public health pests, biological pest control and beneficial organisms, allied botanical and zoological subjects; worldwide farmland and countryside; speculative and assigned photography in agriculture and related disciplines; livestock breeds, biology and botany, including sequences

Access and conditions Open to qualified researchers by appt (tel), Mon-Fri 9–5. All material available for editorial reproduction and for advertising. B/w and colour material loaned free of charge for one month. Reproduction rights, service and holding fees charged. Staff will undertake research.

835 • HUNDAY NATIONAL TRACTOR AND FARM MUSEUM

Westside, Newton, Stocksfield, Northumberland NE43 7TW
Tel (0661) 842553

Enquiries to Les Blackmore, Curator

Items 3000: b/w original photographs, colour transparencies (35mm), colour photographic prints, b/w transparencies (35mm), ephemera

Dates of subject matter 1850 to 1950

Dates of photographs 1980 to present

Subjects Agricultural machinery, comprehensive picture coverage of tractors in Europe from 1890 to present; agricultural hand tools, horse-drawn machinery, hay-making machinery (1900-1950), binders, hay elevators

Access and conditions Open to the public by appt (tel), Easter-30 Sept daily 10–5, 1 Oct-Easter closed Sat. All material available for editorial reproduction and for advertising. B/w and colour material loaned free of charge for one month. Photocopies available. Reproduction rights and print fees charged. Staff will undertake some research.

836 • IBM UNITED KINGDOM LTD

Photograph Collection

PO Box 41, Baltic House, Kingston Crescent, Portsmouth, Hampshire PO6 3AU
Tel (0705) 694941 ext 5272 Telex 86741 IBMPOR G

Enquiries to Ruth Curtis, Communications Librarian

Items About 16,000: b/w original and copy photographs, colour transparencies (35mm, 5″ × 4″, larger), colour photographic prints

Dates of subject matter 1946 to present

Dates of photographs 1946 to present

Subjects IBM computers, office and other equipment; manufacturing operations; technology (chips, circuitry); IBM plants UK and abroad; early computing equipment and history of computers, chiefly IBM

Access and conditions Not open; telephone and mail requests only. All material available for editorial reproduction and for advertising with IBM's approval. B/w and colour material loaned free of charge. No reproduction rights fees charged. Staff will undertake some research.

837 • INDUSTRIAL DEVELOPMENT AUTHORITY IRELAND

58 Davies Street, London W1Y 1LB
Tel (01) 629 5941 Telex 24751

Enquiries to Brigid Roden, Manager, Press & Public Relations

Items 2000: b/w original photographs, colour transparencies (35mm, 5″ × 4″), colour photographic prints, lantern slides

Dates of photographs 1970 to present

Subjects Industrial development in Ireland including interiors of high-tech companies, exteriors of factories including many multinational companies, universities and colleges of technology, industrial estates, high-tech products made in Ireland including electronics and medical instrumentation

Access and conditions Open to qualified researchers by appt (tel), Mon-Fri 9.15–5.30. All material available for editorial reproduction and for advertising. B/w and colour material loaned free of charge. Photocopies available. No reproduction rights fees charged. Staff will undertake research.

838 • INSTITUTE OF AGRICULTURAL HISTORY AND MUSEUM OF ENGLISH RURAL LIFE

University of Reading, Whiteknights, Reading, Berkshire RG8 0EP
Tel (0734) 875123 ext 477

Enquiries to Dr Sadie Ward, Photograph Librarian

Items About 500,000: b/w original and copy photographs, colour transparencies, glass negatives, unprinted film negatives, lantern slides, fine art prints, postcards

Dates of subject matter Prehistory to present

Dates of photographs *c*. 1850 to present

Subjects History of English agriculture and its related processing and servicing industries; tools and techniques of husbandry and operations of the farming year, rural crafts, buildings, topography, community and domestic life; photographic collections from the following publications: *British Farmer and Stockbreeder*, *Farmers' Weekly*, *Power Farming* (1945–1980), *The Grower* (market gardening and horticulture, 1960s and 1970s); photographs by Sir George Clausen (Victorian painter) of rural labour and field cultivation, by D. Hartley of rural crafts, occupations and pastimes (1920s–1960s), by Noel Long of folk customs and morris dancing, chiefly southern counties (1930s–1940s), by John Read of agriculture, rural life and literature mainly in Somerset (1900–1920s), by

C. F. F. Snow of rural and woodland crafts, southern counties (1940s), by M. Wight of rural crafts, occupations and customs especially in the English and Welsh border counties (1900–1940s); photographs of all items in the museum collection; oil paintings, watercolours, prints, glass pictures and drawings from the 18th century to the present, many of animals

Access and conditions Open to the public by appt (tel), Mon-Fri 9–5, closed August and Sept 1–15. Almost all material available for editorial reproduction and for advertising. No loans; b/w prints and duplicate colour transparencies available for a fee. Photocopies available. Reproduction rights and service fees charged. Staff of three will undertake some research; fees negotiable.

839 • INTERNATIONAL COFFEE ORGANIZATION

22 Berners Street, London W1P 4DD
Tel (01) 580 8591 Telex 267659

Enquiries to Librarian

Items 9000: colour transparencies (35mm)

Dates of photographs 1980 to present

Subjects All aspects of coffee production and consumption in Brazil, Colombia, Indonesia, Kenya, Ivory Coast, USA, Europe, Japan, including seedlings, nurseries, plantations, small coffee farms, hand picking, branches with ripe and unripe cherries, blossoms, mechanical picking, winnowing, labourers, sorting, bagging, loading, transport, shipping, cup-tasting, wet and dry methods of processing coffee cherries, green beans, roasting plants, canning of roast and ground coffee; people drinking coffee including American workers, Viennese cafés, Italian cafés, Japanese women, Norwegian skiers, Greek cafés; preparation and serving of coffee; old coffee houses (prints)

Access and conditions Open to the public by appt (tel), Mon-Fri 9–5. All material available for editorial reproduction and for advertising. No loans; colour transparencies duplicated for a fee. No reproduction rights fees charged. Staff will undertake limited research only.

840 • INTERNATIONAL WHALING COMMISSION

The Red House, Station Road, Histon, Cambridge CB4 4NP
Tel (022023) 3971 Telex 817960

Enquiries to Greg Donovan, Scientific Editor

Items 250: colour transparencies (35mm), b/w original photographs, postcards, posters

Dates of subject matter 1970 to present

Dates of photographs 1978 to present

Subjects Whaling, including catcher boats, land stations, processing; whales and dolphins in the wild

Access and conditions Open to qualified researchers by appt (write), Mon-Fri 8.30–5. All material available for editorial reproduction and for advertising with the Commission's approval. B/w and colour material loaned free of charge for one month. Client may make copy prints and duplicate transparencies. Reproduction rights fees charged. Staff will undertake research and mail photographs.

841 • IRONBRIDGE GORGE MUSEUM TRUST

Photographic Collection

The Library, Ironbridge, Telford, Shropshire TF8 7AW
Tel (095245) 2751, 3522

Enquiries to John Powell, Librarian

Items 12,000: b/w original and copy photographs, colour transparencies (35mm, 5″ × 4″), colour photographic prints, glass negatives, lantern slides, postcards, original cartoons, fine art prints, greetings cards, architectural drawings, illustrated books

Dates of subject matter 1700 to present

Dates of photographs 1870 to present

Subjects Local industry of east Shropshire from the 1850s to the present, products of local companies, particularly castings made by the Coalbrookdale Co., iron and steel goods made by the Lilleshall Co., the Horsehay Co. and others, tiles made by Maw & Co., Craven Dunnill & Co. and others; ELTON COLLECTION: all aspects of the history of industry, and especially early railway history; canals, civil engineering, mining, Great Exhibition of 1851; TELFORD COLLECTION: the life and work of Thomas Telford, civil engineer and builder of outstanding bridges, roads, canals, etc.; *THE SHROPSHIRE STAR*/MORLEY TONKIN COLLECTION: local topographic scenes, especially churches

Access and conditions Open to the public by appt (write), Mon-Fri 10–5 (closed 1–2). All material available for editorial reproduction and for advertising. No loans; b/w prints and duplicate colour transparencies available for a fee. Photocopies available. Reproduction rights fees charged. Staff of three will undertake research. Card catalogue.

842 • KENT INDUSTRIAL MEASUREMENTS LTD

Howard Road, Eaton Socon, St Neots, Huntingdon, Cambridgeshire PE19 3EU
Tel (0480) 75321   Telex 32676

Enquiries to Brian Lazenby, Publicity Manager

Items About 40,000: b/w original and copy photographs, colour transparencies (35mm, 5″ × 4″), colour photographic prints, trade catalogues

Dates of photographs 1975 to present

Subjects Industrial instruments, industrial process control; instrumentation including chart recorders, controllers, indicators, pneumatic display and control equipment, liquids and solids level instruments; application of Kent instrumentation in use in industrial conditions; exhibitions of Kent equipment in static displays and in mobile showroom: factory working and under construction

Access and conditions Not open; postal and telephone requests only. Some material available for editorial reproduction and for advertising with the approval of Kent Industrial Measurements. B/w and colour material loaned free of charge. Photocopies available. No reproduction rights fees charged. Staff will undertake some research.

843 • KEW BRIDGE ENGINES TRUST

Green Dragon Lane, Brentford, Middlesex TW8 0EF
Tel (01) 568 4757

Enquiries to Manager

Items 1500: b/w original photographs, glass negatives, colour transparencies (35mm, 5″ × 4″), colour photographic prints, illustrated books, architectural drawings, postcards

Dates of subject matter 1800 to 1970

Dates of photographs 1900 to 1970

Subjects History of mains water supply in the UK including steam engines, pumping engines, beam engines, public water supply, pumping stations; earliest machine (for this purpose) Boulton and Watt 1820; largest ever working steam engine Sandys Carne Vivian 1847; examples of steam, diesel and electric machines for pumping mains water; associated equipment including an early WANDA computer used to analyse water supply network in the 1960s

Access and conditions Open to the public by appt (tel), Wed-Sun 8am–10pm. All material available for editorial reproduction and for advertising. B/w and colour material loaned free of charge for one month. B/w prints and duplicate colour transparencies also available for a fee. Material may be copied by outside photographers. Reproduction rights and service fees charged. Staff will undertake some research.

844 • KINGSTON UPON HULL CITY MUSEUMS AND ART GALLERIES

Town Docks Museum, Queen Victoria Square, Kingston upon Hull, Humberside HU1 3DX
Tel (0482) 222737

Enquiries to John Bradshaw, Curator

Items Over 5000: b/w original photographs, colour transparencies (35mm, 5″ × 4″), posters, glass negatives, fine art prints, greetings cards

Dates of subject matter 18th century to present

Dates of photographs 19th century to present

Dates of fine art 18th century to present

Subjects Whaling, fishing and trawling, Hull and Humberside shipping; large collection of marine paintings including many by John Ward (local artist, 19th century), posters by Harry Hudson Rodmell of 20th-century ships; scrimshaw collection: carved and engraved objects made by whalers of whale's ivory or whalebone

Access and conditions Open to the public by appt, Mon-Fri 10–5. Most material available for editorial reproduction and for advertising. B/w prints and duplicate colour transparencies available for a fee. Photocopies available. Reproduction rights and service fees charged. Staff will undertake some research. Compulsory credit line.

845 • LEICESTERSHIRE MUSEUM OF TECHNOLOGY

Corporation Road, Leicester LE4 5PW
Tel (0533) 661330

Enquiries to Robert Bracegirdle, Keeper of Technology

Items About 3000: b/w original and copy photographs, glass negatives, lantern slides, postcards, illustrated books

Dates of subject matter 1850 to 1970s

Dates of photographs *c.* 1850 to 1970s

Subjects Industries of Leicestershire including transport, railroads, hosiery and knitting, engineering, mining and quarrying, public utilities including water supply and sewage pumping, stationary steam engines; similar material from adjoining counties; printed ephemera including trade catalogues

Access and conditions Open to the public by appt (tel), Mon-Thurs 10–5.30, closed Fri. All material available for editorial reproduction but not for advertising. B/w prints and duplicate colour transparencies available for a fee. Reproduction rights fees charged. Staff will undertake limited research. Card catalogue.

846 • LEWIS TEXTILE MUSEUM

Museum Street, Blackburn, Lancashire BB1 7AJ
Tel (0254) 667130

Enquiries to Curator

Items About 500: b/w original and copy photographs, colour transparencies (35mm, 5″ × 4″, larger), glass negatives, architectural drawings

Dates of subject matter *c.* 1800 to present

Dates of photographs Late 19th century to present

Subjects Original and reproduction machinery from the Industrial Revolution and later including the original flying shuttle (1820s), replica of the Spinning Jenny, iron and steel frame machines

(the Lancashire Loom), good small collection of spinning wheels; textiles, samples and sample books; local industry, cotton spinning and weaving, mills

Access and conditions Open to the public by appt (write), Mon-Sat 9.30–5. All material available for editorial reproduction and for advertising, with some restrictions. No loans; b/w prints and duplicate colour transparencies available for a fee. Reproduction rights charged. Staff will undertake limited research.

847 • LINNET PHOTOGRAPHIC AND TECHNICAL SERVICES LTD

Denmans, Aller, Langport, Somerset TA10 0QN
Tel (0458) 250387

Enquiries to Pamela Dixon

Items 7000: colour transparencies (35mm)

Dates of subject matter 1960 to present

Dates of photographs 1960 to present

Subjects British agriculture including machinery, buildings, grassland and forage, arable crops, vegetables and fruit, livestock; Mediterranean and tropical agriculture including India, Europe; agricultural machinery at work

Access and conditions Not open; postal and telephone requests only. All material available for editorial reproduction and for advertising. Colour material loaned free of charge for one month. Reproduction rights, service and holding fees charged. Staff will undertake some research. Card catalogue.

848 • MICHELIN TYRE plc

81 Fulham Road, London SW3 6RD
Tel (01) 589 1460   Telex 919071

Enquiries to Chris Rogers, Public Relations Department

Items 1500: b/w original photographs, b/w copy photographs, colour transparencies (35mm)

Dates of photographs 1980 to present

Subjects Michelin tyres including product photographs, tyres fitted to vehicles both stationary and moving; coverage of motor racing events with Michelin-supported teams; company archive material is held at Michelin Headquarters in France but is obtainable through the London office.

Access and conditions Open to qualified researchers by appt (write), Mon-Fri 9–5. All material available for editorial reproduction; advertising use by special arrangement only. B/w and colour material loaned free of charge by arrangement. Reproduction rights fees charged. Staff will undertake limited research. All material copyright.

849 • MIDLAND BANK plc

Midland Bank Group Archives, Mariner House, Pepys Street, London EC3N 4DA
Tel (01) 606 9911 ext 2968

Enquiries to Edwin Green, Archivist

Items 2100: b/w original photographs, colour transparencies (35mm), colour photographic prints, architectural drawings

Dates of subject matter 1830 to present

Dates of photographs *c*. 1890 to present

Subjects Midland Bank buildings exteriors and interiors including buildings designed by Sir Edwin Lutyens; bankers, bank directors and groups

Access and conditions Open to the public by appt (write). All material available for editorial reproduction and for advertising. No loans; b/w prints and duplicate colour transparencies available for a fee. Photocopies available for a fee. No reproduction rights fees charged. Staff will undertake limited research. All material copyright.

850 • THE MUSEUM OF LEATHERCRAFT

60 Bridge Street, Northampton NN1 1PA
Tel (0604) 34881 ext 382

Enquiries to Keeper

Items About 5000: b/w copy photographs, lantern slides, illustrated books, b/w original photographs, colour transparencies (35mm), glass negatives

Dates of subject matter 1500 BC to present

Dates of photographs *c*. 1920 to 1970

Subjects History and development of leather production including modern tannery machinery and processes; leather uses including clothing, footwear, luggage, saddlery and harness, transport (coaches, sedan chairs, coracles), bookbinding, reliquaries and religious items, small boxes and containers, bottles, jars and drinking vessels, military equipment, industrial and scientific uses, sports, games, musical instruments, decorative uses including wall-hangings

Access and conditions Open to the public by appt (tel). Most material available for editorial reproduction and for advertising. No loans; b/w prints and colour transparencies available for a fee. No reproduction rights fees charged. Staff will undertake limited research. All material copyright.

851 • NATIONAL COAL BOARD

Hobart House, Grosvenor Place, London SW1X 7AE
Tel (01) 235 2020   Telex 882161

Enquiries to Press Officer

Items 4000: b/w original photographs, colour photographic prints, colour transparencies (35mm, 2¼″)

Dates of subject matter *c*. 1900 to present

Dates of photographs *c*. 1900 to present

Subjects Coalmining in the UK including colliery surfaces (winding gear and buildings), miners at work on coalface; roadway drivage, coal conveyors, manriding trains, computerized surface control rooms; present and historical methods of coal preparation, coal transport (underground and surface); pit ponies; training; miners' welfare (pithead baths, medical facilities); opencast mining including land restoration and tip removal; research and development including testing of new material and techniques; coal utilization research; use of coal by power stations, industry and domestic consumers; coal exploration including boreholes and seismic surveying; exporting including port arrivals and despatch and coal-handling facilities

Access and conditions Open to qualified researchers by appt (write), Mon-Fri 9–5. All material available for editorial reproduction; advertising use by special arrangement only. B/w and colour material loaned free of charge by arrangement (print fees charged). Photocopies available. Reproduction rights and holding fees charged. Staff will undertake some research. Most material copyright.

852 • NATIONAL DAIRY COUNCIL

5-7 John Princes Street, London W1M 0AP
Tel (01) 499 7822 Telex 298632

Enquiries to Ann Adeline

Items 600: b/w original photographs, b/w copy photographs, colour transparencies (35mm, 7 × 6cm), colour photographic prints, unprinted film negatives, posters, press cuttings

Dates of subject matter Early 20th century to present

Dates of photographs Early 20th century to present

Subjects Milk production and processing, dairy herds, farms, creameries, milk and dairy products; sports events sponsored by the Council (Milk Race and Milk Cup)

Access and conditions Open to qualified researchers by appt (tel). Most material available for editorial reproduction; advertising use by special arrangement only. B/w and colour material loaned free of charge by arrangement. Photocopies available. No reproduction rights fees charged. Staff will undertake limited research. All material copyright.

853 • NATIONAL FARMERS UNION

Agriculture House, Knightsbridge, London SW1X 7NJ
Tel (01) 235 5077 Telex 919669 NFULDN G

Enquiries to Norma Moore

Items 4000: b/w original and copy photographs, colour transparencies (35mm, 5″ × 4″)

Dates of photographs 1900 to present

Subjects Agriculture in the UK (some overseas material) including cultivation of crops, animals, machinery, training, land management, shows, markets and marketing, distribution, buildings, housing, transport, activities of NFU

Access and conditions Open to the public by appt (tel), Mon-Fri 9–5. All material available for editorial reproduction and for advertising. B/w and colour material loaned free of charge for one month; material may be copied by outside photographers. No reproduction rights fees charged. Staff will undertake limited research. Compulsory credit line. All material copyright.

854 • NATIONAL MINING MUSEUM

Lound Hall, Haughton, Retford, Nottinghamshire DN22 8DF
Tel (0623) 860728

Enquiries to Curator

Items About 1000: b/w original and copy photographs, colour transparencies (35mm), colour photographic prints, original cartoons, unprinted film negatives

Dates of subject matter c. 17th century to present

Dates of photographs Early 20th century to present

Subjects History and development of coalmining in the UK including equipment, technology, villages, social history

Access and conditions Open to qualified researchers by appt (write), Mon-Fri 10–5.30. Most material available for editorial reproduction and for advertising. Colour material loaned free of charge by arrangement; material may be copied by outside photographers. Photocopies available. Staff will undertake some research. Some material copyright.

855 • NATIONAL MUSEUM OF LABOUR HISTORY

Limehouse Town Hall, Commercial Road, London E14 7HA
Tel (01) 515 3229

Enquiries to Picture Librarian

Items About 10,000: b/w original and copy photographs, colour transparencies (35mm, 5″ × 4″), postcards, original cartoons, illustrated maps, posters, press cuttings, illustrated books

Dates of subject matter 16th century to present

Dates of photographs 1850 to present

Subjects All aspects of labour history covering industry including sweated industries, poverty, trade unions, Labour Party, women's movement including some early suffragette material, portraits of workers in the London docks 1910 to 1970s from the Port of London Authority Archives; material relating to the French Revolution and the 1926 General Strike

Access and conditions Open to the public, Mon-Fri 9–5. All material available for editorial reproduction and for advertising. Colour material loaned for a fee; b/w prints available for a fee. Polaroids and photocopies available. Reproduction rights, holding and service fees charged. Most material copyright. Card catalogue available.

856 • PETBOW LTD

Sandwich, Kent CT13 9NE
Tel (0304) 613311 Telex 96329

Enquiries to John Ridout, Sales Department

Items About 3000: colour transparencies (35mm, 5″ × 4″), b/w original photographs

Dates of subject matter 1960 to present

Dates of photographs 1960 to present

Subjects Manufacture of diesel generating plant; welding, assembling, flamecutting, packing; generating sets in use in Middle East, Far East, Africa and the UK; industrial product shots

Access and conditions Open to qualified researchers by appt, Mon-Fri 8.30–5. All material available for editorial reproduction and for advertising. No loans; b/w prints and duplicate colour transparencies available for a fee. Reproduction rights and service fees charged. Staff will undertake some research. All material copyright.

857 • PILKINGTON GLASS MUSEUM

Prescot Road, St Helen's, Merseyside WA10 3TT
Tel (0744) 28882

Enquiries to Ian Burgoyne, Curator

Items About 2000: b/w original photographs, colour transparencies (35mm, 5″ × 4″), postcards, old fine art prints, unprinted film negatives, posters, illustrated books

Dates of subject matter 1400 BC to present

Dates of photographs 1963 to present

Subjects All aspects of the history and development of glass-making; manufacturing processes including the core technique, grinding and cutting, casting and pressing glass, blowing and moulding, clear and coloured glass, engraving, etching, sand blasting, decoration; samples of glassware worldwide; applications of glass including stained glass, window glass, mirrors, cameras, optical glass, scientific instruments

Access and conditions Open to the public by appt (tel), Mon-Fri 10–5. Most material available for editorial reproduction; advertising use by special arrangement only. Some b/w and colour material loaned free of charge for two months; b/w prints and duplicate colour transparencies available for a fee; material may be copied by outside photographers. Photocopies available. No reproduction rights fees charged. Staff of two will undertake limited research. Compulsory credit line. All material copyright.

858 • ROYAL DOULTON (UK) LTD

Minton House, London Road, Stoke-on-Trent, Staffordshire ST4 7QD
Tel (0782) 49171 Telex 36502

Enquiries to Public Relations Department

Items About 1500: b/w copy photographs, colour transparencies (35mm, 5″ × 4″), colour photographic prints, illustrated books

Dates of subject matter 1815 to present

Dates of photographs Late 19th century to present

Subjects Ceramic manufacturing processes and products from Royal Doulton, Minton, Royal Crown Derby, Beswick, Royal Albert, Colclough, Paragon and Royal Doulton Crystal; museum pieces including out-of-production figures, exhibition pieces from Crystal Palace Exhibition (1851), Chicago Exhibition (1893) and Philadelphia Exhibition (1904), the Dante vase and the Raby vase

Access and conditions Open to qualified researchers by appt (tel). All material available for editorial reproduction; advertising use by special arrangement only. B/w and colour material loaned free of charge by arrangement. No reproduction rights fees charged. Staff will undertake some research. All material copyright.

859 • RUSTON GAS TURBINES LTD

PO Box 1, Firth Road, Lincoln LN6 7AA
Tel (0522) 36292 Telex 56231

Enquiries to R. E. Hooley, Manager, Technical Reference Section

Items About 25,000: glass negatives, b/w original photographs, b/w copy photographs

Dates of photographs *c*. 1870 to present

Subjects Steam engines, oil engines, gas engines, boilers, excavators, locomotives, pumps, threshing machines, harvesting machinery and their component parts; production, testing and operation of these machines

Access and conditions Open to qualified researchers by appt (tel), Mon-Fri 9.30–5.30. Some material available for editorial reproduction and for advertising. B/w material loaned free of charge. Photocopies available. B/w prints available. Reproduction rights fees charged for commercial use. Staff will undertake limited research. Partial catalogue.

860 • SALFORD MUSEUM OF MINING

Photographic Collection

Buile Hill Park, Eccles Old Road, Salford, Greater Manchester M6 8GL
Tel (061) 736 1832

Enquiries to Geoff Preece, Keeper of Industrial Archaeology

Items 9000: b/w copy photographs, colour transparencies (35mm), b/w original photographs, glass negatives, lantern slides, colour photographic prints, postcards, original cartoons, posters, illustrated maps, machine drawings, illustrated books, 20th-century fine art prints

Dates of subject matter 1600 to present

Dates of photographs 1870 to present

Subjects History and development of mining with emphasis on Lancashire Coalfield but also including some Yorkshire material and including geology, the industrial revolution, canals, railways, mechanization, drainage, ventilation, safety, tools and equipment; health and welfare, trade unions, housing, social life; mining machinery drawings, underground layout plans

Access and conditions Open to the public by appt (tel), Mon-Fri 9.30–4.30. All material available for editorial reproduction; advertising use by special arrangement only. No loans; material may be copied by outside photographers. Photocopies available. Reproduction rights fees charged. Staff will undertake limited research. Some material copyright. Card catalogue in preparation.

861 • THE SALT MUSEUM

162 London Road, Northwich, Cheshire CW9 8AB
Tel (0606) 41331

Enquiries to Margaret Warhurst, Curator

Items About 5000: b/w original and copy photographs, colour transparencies (35mm, 5″ × 4″), glass negatives, postcards, fine art prints, posters, architectural drawings, illustrated books

Dates of subject matter 19th and 20th centuries

Dates of photographs 1860s to present

Subjects Salt production in Cheshire, historical and present day, especially in Northwich, Middlewich and Winsford and including salt mining, open pan salt production, subsidence caused by brine extraction, transport of salt, salt companies; buildings, social history and portraits in Northwich relevant to salt

Access and conditions Open to the public by appt (write), Tues-Sat 2–5, July Aug 10–5. Some material available for editorial reproduction and for advertising. B/w prints available for a fee; colour transparencies rented for a fee. Photocopies available. Reproduction rights fees charged. Staff will undertake limited research. Card catalogue available.

862 • SHEFFIELD CITY MUSEUMS

Industrial Museum, Kelham Island, Sheffield S3 8RY
Tel (0742) 22106

Enquiries to Peter Smithurst, Keeper of Industrial Collections

Items 12,000: b/w original and copy photographs, glass negatives, lantern slides, architectural drawings, illustrated books, oil paintings and watercolours

Dates of subject matter 1200 to present

Dates of photographs Mid-19th century to present

Dates of fine art 1760 to present

Subjects Industrial history and development of Sheffield including plant and equipment, manufacturing processes, products, people at work; manufacturers include Daniel Doncaster Ltd (steel-makers and forge-masters) archive material between 1850 and 1950; Vickers (steel-makers and engineers) material relating to manufacturing processes between 1900 and 1950; Hadfields Ltd incorporating Brown Bayleys (steel-makers), material relating to manufacturing processes, portraits, 1900–1950; Samuel Osborn Ltd (steel-makers, forge-masters, tool-makers), archive material between 1870 and 1950; Firth Brown Co. (steel-makers) archive material, and ciné film of manufacturing processes 1930s to 1960s; trades relating to steel industries including grinding, tool-making, plate manufacture; photomicrographs of steels

Access and conditions Open to qualified researchers by appt (write), Wed-Sat 10–5, Sun 11–5. Some material available for editorial reproduction and for advertising. No loans; b/w prints and duplicate colour transparencies available for a fee; material may be copied by outside photographers. Photocopies available. Reproduction rights fees charged. Staff will undertake limited research. Most material copyright. Partial card catalogue available.

863 • SHELL ADVERTISING ARCHIVE

Shell-Mex House, Strand, London WC2R 0DX
Tel (01) 240 2504 Mon Tues Thurs Fri
(01) 257 1371 Wed   Telex 22585 SHELL G

Enquiries to Ted Sheppard, Marketing Communications Department

Items Over 10,000: b/w original photographs, colour transparencies (35mm), colour photographic prints, oil paintings, watercolours, postcards, original cartoons, unprinted film negatives, posters, greetings cards, architectural drawings, press cuttings, illustrated books

Dates of subject matter Early 20th century to present

Dates of photographs 1930s to present

Subjects Advertising material relating to the former Shell Marketing Ltd and Shell-Mex and BP, and Shell UK from 1974; oil paintings and watercolours including works by Sutherland, Nash, Whistler, Leigh Pemberton, Maurice Wilson, Scott, Shackleton, Edith and Rowland Hilder, Hillier, Badmin; original commercial art collection from the early 1920s including work by McKnight Kauffer and Schleger; the SHELL VALENTINE COLLECTION; SHELL POSTER COLLECTION (1920–52); Shell books from 1934; SHELL POSTCARD COLLECTION (1907–1930s)

Access and conditions Open to qualified researchers by appt (write). All material available

for editorial reproduction and for advertising. B/w and colour material loaned free of charge by arrangement; b/w prints and duplicate colour transparencies available for a fee. Photocopies available. No reproduction rights fees charged. Very limited research undertaken. Compulsory credit line. All material copyright.

864 • SOUTHAMPTON UNIVERSITY INDUSTRIAL ARCHAEOLOGY GROUP

6 Prestwood Road, Hedge End, Southampton SO3 4JL
Tel (04892) 2297

Enquiries to Pamela Moore

Items 25,000: colour transparencies (35mm), b/w original photographs, colour photographic prints, b/w copy photographs, glass negatives, postcards

Dates of subject matter c. 1750 to present

Dates of photographs c. 1850 to present

Subjects Industrial archaeology and history in the UK with special emphasis on Hampshire, and some coverage in Belgium and South Africa, including brewing, brickmaking, milling, iron processing, defence supply, public utilities, textiles, paper manufacture; also transport history including rail, road and canal transport

Access and conditions Not open; tel and postal requests only. Most material available for editorial reproduction; advertising use by special arrangement only. No loans; b/w prints and duplicate colour transparencies available for a fee. No reproduction rights fees charged. Staff will undertake research. Most material copyright.

865 • STANDARD TELEPHONES AND CABLES plc

Company Archives, STC House, 190 Strand, London WC2R 1DU
Tel (01) 836 8055   Telex 22385

Enquiries to Laurie Dennett, Archivist

Items About 14,000: b/w copy photographs, postcards, glass negatives

Dates of subject matter c. 1880 to 1970

Dates of photographs c. 1880 to 1970

Subjects Telecommunications relating to STC and its predecessor Western Electric Company including telephony, land-line cable, submarine cable, switching, broadcasting, microwave and optical fibre technologies; business and office technologies including teleprinters, telex and facsimile processes; site photographs, manufacturing processes, installation and operation

Access and conditions Open to qualified researchers by appt (tel), Mon-Fri 9–5. All material available for editorial reproduction; advertising use by special arrangement only. No loans; b/w prints available; material may be copied by outside photographers. Photocopies available. No reproduction rights fees charged. Staff will undertake limited research. Most material copyright; when copyright not held by STC user must negotiate directly with copyright holder. Catalogue in preparation.

866 • THE TELECOM TECHNOLOGY SHOWCASE

Resource Centre, 135 Queen Victoria Street, London EC4V 4AT
Tel (01) 248 7444 Telex 8956163

Enquiries to Tony Elwood, Assistant Manager, Archives

Items About 6000: b/w copy photographs, colour transparencies (35mm, 5″ × 4″), colour photographic prints, glass negatives, postcards, posters, illustrated books

Dates of subject matter 1830 to present

Dates of photographs Mid-19th century to present

Subjects All aspects of the development of telecommunications since 1830 including telegraphs, telephones, networks, installation, exchanges, buildings, Post Office and British Telecom publicity

Access and conditions Open to the public by appt (tel), Mon-Fri 10–4. Most material available for editorial reproduction and for advertising. B/w material loaned free of charge by arrangement; colour material loaned for a fee. Photocopies available. Reproduction rights and service fees charged. Telecom Technology Showcase owns copyright to 50% of collection; in other cases copyright clearance is responsibility of user.

867 • TELEFOCUS

Telecommunications Photo Library, Floor A3, British Telecom Centre, 81 Newgate Street, London EC1A 7AJ
Tel (01) 356 6591/2/3 Telex 8811510

Enquiries to Jane Marrow, Library Manager

Items About 40,,000: b/w original photographs, colour transparencies (35mm, 2¼″)

Dates of subject matter 1890s to present

Dates of photographs 1890s to present

Subjects Telecommunications, including history of telecommunications (telephones and exchanges from 1890s to present), optical fibres, system X (new electronic system), computers, cable television, Prestel, data systems, men and women at work, business systems, earth stations, satellites, cable ships, product shots, research laboratories, vehicles, remote locations in Scotland and outer islands, BT staff and senior management

Access and conditions Open to qualified researchers by appt (tel), Mon-Fri 9–5. All material available for editorial reproduction and for advertising by arrangement. No loans; b/w prints and duplicate colour transparencies available for a fee. Reproduction rights fees charged. Staff will undertake some research. All material copyright.

868 • THAMES WATER

Nugent House, Vastern Road, Reading RG1 8DB
Tel (0734) 593333

Enquiries to Derek Gregg

Items Over 3000: colour transparencies (35mm, 2¼″), b/w original photographs, colour photographic prints

Dates of subject matter 1974 to present

Dates of photographs 1974 to present

Subjects Water supply and resources in the Thames region including water treatment, sewage treatment and disposal, pollution control, land drainage, flood alleviation (but *not* the Thames Barrier), fisheries; coverage of Thames from Teddington to Lechlade, recreational use of river and reservoirs including fishing

Access and conditions Open to the public by appt (write), Mon-Fri 9–5. All material available for editorial reproduction and for advertising. B/w and colour material loaned by arrangement; b/w and duplicate colour transparencies available for a fee. Reproduction rights fees charged. All material copyright.

869 • TRAIDCRAFT EDUCATIONAL FOUNDATION

Kingsway, Gateshead, Tyne and Wear NE11 0NE
Tel (091) 487 3191

Enquiries to Anne Brown, Slide Librarian

Items About 5500: b/w original photographs, colour transparencies (35mm)

Dates of subject matter 1979 to present

Dates of photographs 1979 to present

Subjects Cottage industries in developing countries including Bangladesh, India, Pakistan, Sri Lanka, Tanzania; some coverage of agriculture, natural history, housing, education, social services, transport, architecture, religion, but special emphasis is on all stages (raw materials, production, premises, workers, equipment) of crafts including basketry, weaving, wood-carving, stonework, block printing, batik printing, shoe-making, carpet-weaving; coffee-growing and processing in Tanzania; tea-growing and processing in Sri Lanka

Access and conditions Open to qualified researchers by appt (tel), Mon-Fri 8.30–4.30. All material available for editorial reproduction; advertising use by special arrangement only. B/w material loaned free of charge for our weeks; b/w prints and duplicate colour transparencies available for a fee. Photocopies available. No reproduction rights fees charged. Staff will undertake limited research. All material copyright.

870 • TROWBRIDGE MUSEUM

Civic Hall, St Stephen's Place, Trowbridge, Wiltshire BA14 8AH
Tel (02214) 65072

Enquiries to John Barton, Assistant Curator

Items About 700: b/w original photographs, b/w copy photographs, postcards, posters

Dates of subject matter 1850 to present

Dates of photographs 1850 to present

Subjects Local history with special emphasis on the local woollen industry including factory interiors, machinery, workers, and print works owned by the Lansdowne family including collection of ephemera and print samples

Access and conditions Open to the public, Tues & Sat 9.30–12. Some material available for editorial reproduction and for advertising; some for private research only. No loans; b/w prints available for a fee. Reproduction rights fees charged. Staff will undertake limited research. Most material copyright. Card catalogue in preparation.

871 • UNITED KINGDOM ATOMIC ENERGY AUTHORITY

Photographic Library, 11 Charles II Street, London SW1Y 4QP
Tel (01) 930 5454 Telex 22565

Enquiries to Evelyn Walker, Photo Librarian

Items About 18,000: b/w original photographs, colour transparencies (35mm)

Dates of photographs 1956 to present

Subjects Nuclear power stations, interiors and exteriors; fuel-manufacture, research and development; fuel-reprocessing, research and development; use of isotopes (medical, industrial); nuclear physics, engineering and chemical research laboratories; monitoring of environment; nuclear reactor systems for producing electricity (magnox reactors, advanced gas-cooled reactors, fast reactors, pressurized water reactors); fission, fusion, isotopes, radioactivity, nuclear waste management

Access and conditions Open to the public by appt, Mon-Fri 9–5. All material available for editorial reproduction and for advertising; UKAEA must approve use and text or caption. B/w colour material loaned free of charge for three months; duplicate transparencies also available for a fee. Photocopies available. Reproduction rights fees and holding fees charged; no charge for educational school textbooks. Staff will undertake some research. All material copyright.

872 • WATSON HAWKSLEY

Terriers House, Amersham Road, High Wycombe, Buckinghamshire HP13 5AJ
Tel (0494) 26240 Telex 83439

Enquiries to Laureen Williamson, Publicity Manager

Items About 3000: architectural drawings, b/w original photographs, colour transparencies (35mm, 5″ × 4″), watercolours

Dates of subject matter 1863 to present

Dates of photographs 1900 to present

Subjects Treatment and supply of potable water in the UK and overseas (Middle and Far East, Africa and Europe) including storage treatment plants, pumping stations, distribution connections and mains, dams, reservoirs, stormwater culverts; irrigation projects; sewerage installations, tunnels, pipes, pumping stations, incinerators, aeration tanks, filter beds, sludge disposal, settlement tanks, computerized control consoles, effluent re-use

Access and conditions Open to qualified researchers by appt (write). Mon-Fri 9–5. Some material available for editorial reproduction and for advertising; some for private research only. B/w material and colour transparencies loaned free of charge for one month; duplicate colour transparencies available for a fee. Photocopies available. No reproduction rights fees charged. Staff will undertake limited research. Compulsory credit line. Most material copyright.

873 • JOSIAH WEDGWOOD AND SONS LTD

Head Office and Museum

Barlaston, Stoke-on-Trent, Staffordshire ST12 9ES
Tel (078139) 4141 Telex 36170

Enquiries to Lynne Miller, Museum Information Officer

Items About 1000: b/w original and copy photographs, colour transparencies (35mm), lantern slides, architectural drawings, illustrated books, pattern books

Dates of subject matter 1759 to present

Dates of photographs 1900 to present

Subjects History of Wedgwood production including manufacturing processes, portraits of workforce, catalogues of products, samples, portraits of Wedgwood family including works by Sir Joshua Reynolds, George Stubbs and George Romney

Access and conditions Open to qualified researchers by appt (write), Mon-Fri 9–5. All material available for editorial reproduction; advertising use by special arrangement only. B/w and colour material loaned free of charge by arrangement (print fees charged). Photocopies available. No reproduction rights fees charged. Staff will undertake research. Compulsory credit line. All material copyright.

Press Office

Wedgwood House, 32-4 Wigmore Street, London W1H 0HU
Tel (01) 486 5181 Telex 25957

Enquiries to Judith Turner, Wedgwood Group Press Officer

Items About 1000: b/w original and copy photographs, colour transparencies (35mm, 5″ × 4″), art reproductions, unprinted film negatives, illustrated books

Dates of photographs 1975 to present

Subjects Production of ceramics by the Wedgwood Group including production processes, samples, workshops, factories; directors' portraits

Access and conditions Open to qualified researchers by appt (write). All material available for editorial reproduction and for advertising. B/w and colour material loaned free of charge for one month; material may be copied by outside photographers. No reproduction rights fees charged. Staff will undertake research. Compulsory credit line. All material copyright.

874 • WELSH WATER AUTHORITY

Slide Library, Cambrian Way, Brecon, Powys LD3 7HP
Tel (0874) 3181

Enquiries to Rod Mackay, Press Officer

Items About 5000: b/w original photographs, colour transparencies (35mm)

Dates of subject matter 1974 to present

Dates of photographs 1978 to present

Subjects All aspects of the work of the Authority including reservoirs, rivers, flow-gauging, water quality, treatment and supply; sewerage, sewage pumping, treatment and disposal; fisheries protection and development work including research, fish breeding and stocking of rivers, protection from poachers and pollution; land drainage and flood protection; health and safety at work, transport, capital works construction; recreational use of rivers and reservoirs

Access and conditions Open to qualified researchers by appt (tel). Some material available for editorial reproduction but not for advertising. B/w and colour material loaned free of charge by arrangement (print fees charged). No reproduction rights fees charged. Staff will undertake limited research. All material copyright.

875 • ERIC WILLIAMS AND PARTNERS (PUBLIC RELATIONS CONSULTANTS) LTD

Ruxley Towers, Claygate, Esher, Surrey
KT10 0HZ
Tel (0372) (from London 78) 67333 Telex 929993

Enquiries to Eric Williams, Chairman

Items 1000: b/w original photographs, colour transparencies (35mm, 5″ × 4″)

Dates of subject matter 1973 to present

Dates of photographs 1973 to present

Subjects Fruit and vegetables at markets throughout the UK, packs, pallet loads; flower, fruit and vegetable growers; samples of produce in field or glasshouse; packaging trade including plastic, steel and fibre drums, stainless steel sinks, metal barrels and closure

Access and conditions Open to qualified researchers by appt (write), Mon-Fri 9–5. All material available for editorial reproduction by special arrangement. B/w and colour material loaned free of charge for one month (print fees charged). Photocopies available. No reproduction rights fees charged. Staff of four will undertake some research for a fee. All material copyright.

Transport

876 • AIR PORTRAITS

131 Welwyndale Road, Sutton Coldfield, West
Midlands B72 1AL
Tel (021) 373 4021

Enquiries to David Davies or Mike Vines

Items 20,000: b/w original photographs, colour
transparencies (35mm, 120mm)

Dates of subject matter 1909 to present

Dates of photographs 1965 to present

Subjects Aircraft worldwide including military
and commercial planes; balloons, gliders, airships,
pilots; comprehensive coverage of the Shuttleworth
collection

Access and conditions Not open; telephone and
postal requests only. All material available for
editorial reproduction and for advertising. B/w and
colour material loaned free of charge for 28 days.
Reproduction rights and holding fees charged;
service fees charged only when no material is used.
Staff will undertake some research. All material
copyright.

877 • AIRSHIP INDUSTRIES (UK) LTD

84/86 Baker Street, London W1M 1DL
Tel (01) 486 9671 Telex 299964

Enquiries to R. A. M. Williams, Public Relations
Manager

Items 2000: b/w original photographs, colour
transparencies (35mm, 5″ × 4″)

Dates of subject matter 1978 to present

Dates of photographs 1978 to present

Subjects Modern non-rigid airships (Skyship
series), interior and exterior views, in flight and on
the ground; production of Skyships 500 and 600
and mission fit

Access and conditions Open to qualified
researchers by appt (write), Mon-Fri 9–5.30. All
material available for editorial reproduction but
not for advertising. B/w and colour material loaned
free of charge for six weeks. Material may be copied
by outside photographers. No reproduction rights,
service or holding fees charged. All material
copyright.

878 • ASHFORD LIBRARY

Railway Collection

Church Road, Ashford, Kent TN23 1QX
Tel (0233) 20649, 35526

Enquiries to D. R. Mole, Group Librarian

Items About 1000: b/w original and copy
photographs, postcards, colour photographic prints,
architectural drawings

Dates of subject matter 1850 to present

Dates of photographs 1880 to present

Subjects Railways of south-east England
including locomotives, stations, lines (permanent
way), Ashford works (staff and machinery),
accidents

Access and conditions Open to the public, Mon-
Tues 9.30–6, Wed 9.30–5, Thurs-Fri 9.30–7, Sat
9–5. All material available for editorial
reproduction and for advertising. No loans; b/w
prints and duplicate colour transparencies
available for a fee. Photocopies available. No
reproduction rights or service fees charged. Staff
will undertake limited research. Some copyright
material requires written permission of copyright
holder.

879 • AUTOMOBILE ASSOCIATION

Picture Library, Publications Division, Fanum
House, Basingstoke, Hampshire RG21 2EA
Tel (0256) 20123

Enquiries to Wyn Voysey

Items About 40,000: colour transparencies
(35mm, 2¼″ × 1⅝″)

Dates of subject matter Prehistory to present

Dates of photographs 1979 to present

Subjects Cities, towns, villages, places of interest, stately homes and castles in the UK and Eire, filed by country; motor cars, driving and maintenance

Access and conditions Open to qualified researchers by appt. All material available for editorial reproduction and for advertising. Colour material loaned free of charge for one month. Reproduction rights, service and holding fees charged; service fees deductible from use fees. Staff will undertake research. All material copyright.

880 • AVIA PRESS ASSOCIATES

75 Elm Tree Road, Locking, Weston-super-Mare, Avon BS24 8EL
Tel (0934) 822524 Telex 44220 COMTEL G Ref 315

Enquiries to Elfan Aprees

Items Over 40,000: unprinted film negatives, b/w original photographs, colour transparencies (35mm), b/w copy photographs, glass negatives, cuttings and tearsheets, illustrated books

Dates of subject matter 1900 to present

Dates of photographs 1900 to present

Subjects Aircraft (worldwide) from c. 1900 to the present; special collection of helicopters and autogyros

Access and conditions Open to qualified researchers by appt. All material available for editorial reproduction and for advertising. B/w and colour material loaned for a fee; colour duplicates available for a fee. Reproduction rights, service and holding fees charged. Staff of two will undertake some research; research fee charged. Partial subject card catalogue.

881 • THE AVIATION PICTURE LIBRARY

3 Berkeley Crescent, Clifton, Bristol BS8 1HA
Tel (0272) 213109

Enquiries to Austin J Brown

Items 140,000: unprinted film negatives, colour transparencies (35mm), colour photographic prints

Dates of subject matter 1900 to present

Dates of photographs 1960 to present

Subjects Aircraft and aircraft industry; aircraft in Europe, USA and Caribbean; civil and military aircraft including ground portraits and air-to-air photos; hang-gliders, microlights, hot-air and gas balloons, airships; spacecraft; rockets and weapons; aircraft at work including search and rescue, firefighting, oil pollution control, submarine tracking; ground facilities, radar, air traffic control, firefighting and emergency systems, ground handling of airliners, radio facilities, ground operations, air crew; historical aircraft and replicas, museum aircraft, airports international and local

Access and conditions Open to qualified researchers by appt (tel). All material available for editorial reproduction and for advertising. B/w and colour material loaned free of charge for one month. Photocopies available. Reproduction rights and holding fees charged. Staff will undertake research. Photographer available for assignments. Compulsory credit line. Subject catalogue available.

882 • THE BOAT MUSEUM

Dockyard Road, Ellesmere Port, South Wirral, Cheshire L65 4EF
Tel (051) 355 5017

Enquiries to Ronald Middleton, Archivist

Items 4000: postcards, b/w original and copy photographs, colour photographic prints, posters, architectural drawings, press cuttings

Dates of subject matter 1750 to present

Dates of photographs 1850 to present

Subjects Inland waterways in the UK including sea and river transport, working and pleasure boats, canal facilities, dockland scenes, harbours, tunnels and bridges; views of Ellesmere Port and its social history; special collections include the MICHAEL WARE COLLECTION of British canal life from the late 19th century

Access and conditions Open to the public by appt (tel), Mon–Fri 9–5. Most material available for editorial reproduction and for advertising. No loans; b/w prints and colour transparencies available for a fee; material may be copied by outside photographers. Photocopies available for a fee. Reproduction rights and service fees charged. Staff will undertake some research. Some material copyright. Card catalogue available.

883 • BRENARD PHOTOGRAPHIC SERVICES

Building 221, Norwood Crescent, Heathrow
Airport North, Hounslow, Middlesex TW6 2SR
Tel (01) 759 1235   Telex 935211

Enquiries to Dawn Khwaja, Librarian

Items 5000: b/w original and copy photographs,
colour transparencies (35mm), lantern slides

Dates of photographs c. 1970 to present, some
1940s

Subjects Heathrow airport, airlines and
personalities, British Airways fleet, terminals,
catering, mechanics, emergency services, take-off
and landing, historical aircraft, Heathrow in the
1940s, personalities (VIPs, pop stars, actors,
politicians)

Access and conditions Open to the public by
appt. All material available for editorial
reproduction and for advertising. B/w prints
available for a fee; colour material loaned free of
charge for one month. Reproduction rights, service
and holding fees charged. Staff will undertake
some research and send material for a fee.

884 • BRITISH HOVERCRAFT CORPORATION LTD

East Cowes, Isle of Wight PO32 6RH
Tel (0983) 294121 ext 42   Telex 86131

Enquiries to Technical Librarian

Items Unknown: b/w original and copy
photographs, colour transparencies (35mm,
larger), colour photographic prints, technical
illustrations, artwork

Dates of subject matter 1920s to present

Dates of photographs 1930s to present

Subjects Products of BHC and its predecessor
Saunders-Roe, including aircraft (c. 1935 to
c. 1955); after 1950, hovercraft, helicopters (Wasps,
Scouts, Skeeters), manufacturing photographs,
displays, in-flight photographs, electronics
including instrumentation measurement and
strain gauge, space rockets including launches at
Woomerang, full range of hovercraft SRN1 (1959),
SRN 2, 3, 4, 5, 6; BH 7, AP1–88

Access and conditions Open to qualified
researchers by appt, Mon-Fri 9–5. Some material
available for editorial reproduction and for
advertising. Fees charged at the Librarian's
discretion. Staff will undertake limited research,
time permitting.

885 • BRITISH RAIL PHOTO LIBRARY

222 Marylebone Road, London NW1 6JJ
From Sept 1986: Euston House, Eversholt Street,
London NW1 1DF
Tel (01) 262 3232 ext 5489   Telex 299431 HQZA

Enquiries to John Barlow, Librarian

Items About 560,000: colour transparencies
(35mm, 2¼″), b/w original and copy photographs,
colour photographic prints

Dates of subject matter 1830s to present

Dates of photographs 1958 to present

Subjects Freight and passenger trains, railway
stations, permanent way, bridges, electrical and
electronic installations such as power signal boxes
and overhead lines, track repairs and construction,
locomotive works, rail coach construction and
interiors, cars on trains, loading and unloading of
container ships, parcel traffic; railway restaurants
and catering, ex-British Rail hotels, rail staff, HQ
and regional offices, TOPS computer; continental
railways; ports, docks, container depots and freight
liners, trains on ships and abroad; research and
testing of high-speed trains and scientists at work
on new projects at Derby research facility;
Channel-tunnel preparations; buses, coaches and
coach-stations; mining, aggregates and industrial
processes, refineries, rail transport of coal, oil, soda
ash, grain, paper, fertilizers and foodstuffs (cider,
whisky, chocolate, fruit, etc.); police work; senior
citizens, families, business men, young people;
scenic shots UK and abroad

Access and conditions Open to the public by
appt (tel), Mon-Fri 9.30–5.30. All material
available for editorial reproduction and for
advertising with very few restrictions. B/w and
colour material loaned free of charge for two weeks;
b/w prints available for a fee. Colour material not
loaned; duplicate colour transparencies available
for a fee. Reproduction rights fees charged. Staff
will undertake some research.

886 • BRITISH WATERWAYS BOARD

Melbury House, Melbury Terrace, London
NW1 6JX
Tel (01) 262 6711 ext 6343 Telex 263605 BWBLDNG

Enquiries to Vanessa Wiggins, Press and
Publicity Assistant

Items 45,000: colour transparencies (35mm, 2¼",
larger) b/w original and copy photographs, colour
photographic prints

Dates of subject matter 1760 to present

Dates of photographs 1900 to present

Subjects Canals and river navigations
administered by the British Waterways Board;
freight including commercial barges, coasters,
tankers, push-tow vessels, docks, depots,
warehouses, loading and unloading; leisure
including views of waterways through BWB's
system, major and minor structures including
bridges, locks, aqueducts, tunnels, details of
paddle-winding gear, lock mechanism, mooring
bollards, canalside buildings including lock
cottages, warehouses, toll offices, boating pictures
and other leisure activities such as sailing (on BWB
reservoirs), canoeing, walking, fishing, using locks;
flora and fauna of waterways; boat interiors with
close-ups of people eating, cooking, etc.;
engineering including before and after
photographs of problem areas (breaches, tunnel
collapses, etc.), progress photographs of major and
minor engineering repairs, lock-gate replacement,
dredging, etc.; major projects upgrading to
Commercial Waterways, restoration projects,
repair yards, engineering craft

Access and conditions Open to qualified
researchers by appt, Mon–Fri 9–5. All material
available for editorial reproduction and for
advertising. B/w and colour material loaned free of
charge for one month. Reproduction rights, service
and holding fees charged. Staff will undertake
some research. Compulsory credit line.

887 • COLOUR-RAIL

5 Treacher's Close, Chesham, Buckinghamshire
HP5 2HD
Tel (0494) 784358

Enquiries to Ron White

Items About 3000: colour transparencies (35mm)

Dates of subject matter 1860s to present

Dates of photographs 1934 to present

Subjects British steam, diesel and electric
locomotives including Great Western Railway,
London Midland and Scottish Railway, London and
North Eastern Railway, British Railways Western
Region, British Railways London Midland Regon,
British Railways Southern Region, British
Railways Eastern Region, British Railways
Scottish Region, Somerset and Dorset Line, London
Transport, preserved steam, narrow gauge, British
Railways diesels and electrics, Irish Railways,
independent railways, tramways

Access and conditions Not open; postal requests
only. Most material available for editorial
reproduction and for advertising. Duplicate colour
transparencies available for a fee. Reproduction
rights fees charged. Staff will undertake some
research. Printed catalogue available; updated
annually.

888 • THE CORRIS RAILWAY SOCIETY

Station Yard, Corris, Machynlleth, Powys
SY20 9RR

Enquiries to Honorary Secretary

Items 150: b/w original and copy photographs,
colour transparencies (35mm), colour photographic
prints, illustrated books

Dates of subject matter 1858 to 1950

Dates of photographs 1890 to 1950

Subjects The Corris Railway (operated 1858 to
1948) including locomotives, stations and staff,
permanent way, passenger trains, goods wagons,
bridges, coal trains, slate wagons, scenic views

Access and conditions Open to the public by
appt (write). Some material available for editorial
reproduction but not for advertising. B/w prints
and duplicate colour transparencies available for a
fee. Photocopies available. No reproduction rights
fees charged.

889 • DERBY INDUSTRIAL MUSEUM

The Silk Mill, Silk Mill Lane, *Off* Full Street, Derby
DE1 3AR
Tel (0332) 31111 ext 740

Enquiries to Brian Waters, Senior Keeper

Items 10,000: b/w original and copy photographs,
postcards, engineering drawings

Dates of subject matter 1840 to present

Dates of photographs 1860 to present

Subjects History of the Midland Railway Works and the London Midland and Scottish Railway Works including locomotives, carriages, wagons, track systems, signals, signal systems, buildings, structures and engineering drawings of all of these items

Access and conditions Not open; postal requests only. Most material available for editorial reproduction but not for advertising. No loans; b/w prints available for a fee. Material may be copied by outside photographers. Reproduction rights fees charged. Staff will undertake limited research.

890 • DEVIZES WHARF CANAL CENTRE

Kennet and Avon Canal Trust, The Wharf, Couch Lane, Devizes, Wiltshire SN10 1EB
Tel: (0380) 71279

Enquiries to Michael Corfield, Honorary Curator

Items 2000: b/w original photographs, posters

Dates of subject matter 18th century to present

Dates of photographs Mid-19th century to present

Subjects Kennet and Avon Canal from Reading to Bristol including landscapes, working boats, pleasure boats, cargoes, fishing, canal restoration

Access and conditions Open to the public by appt, Mon-Fri 9–5. Some material available for editorial reproduction and for advertising; some for private research only. No loans; b/w prints available for a fee. Reproduction rights fees charged. Staff will undertake limited research. Most material copyright. Card catalogue in preparation.

891 • DOLPHIN YARD SAILING BARGE MUSEUM

c/o 117 Plains Avenue, Maidstone, Kent
ME15 7AR
Tel (0622) 62531

Enquiries to Angela Harber, Honorary Secretary

Items 1500: b/w original and copy photographs, glass negatives, postcards, illustrated books

Dates of photographs 1970 to present

Subjects Thames and Medway sailing barges, towns on the Thames and Medway

Access and conditions Open to the public by appt (write). Most material available for editorial reproduction and for advertising. No loans; b/w prints available for a fee. Material may be copied by outside photographers. Photocopies available. Reproduction rights and service fees charged. Staff will undertake limited research.

892 • EXETER MARITIME MUSEUM

The Quay, Exeter, Devon EX2 4AN
Tel (0392) 58075

Enquiries to David Goddard, Director

Items About 200: b/w original and copy photographs, colour transparencies, glass negatives, postcards

Dates of subject matter 1845 to present

Dates of photographs 1970 to present

Subjects Working boats including Danish steam tug, Bedford lifeboat, Exe salmon boat, gig, Irish curraghs, Edwardian river launch, Teifi and Tywi coracles, Severn coracle, Bahraini pearling dhow, huri for pearling dhow, Dubai shahoof, Bahraini fishing dhow, Batinah coast shasha, Lake Titicaca reed boat, Fijian proa, East African dugout, *Cheers*, Tongan canoe, Bahraini jalibot, te bao bao, *Ibis*, Gilbert Islands proa, Sierra Leone dugout, pilot cutter *Cariad*, Bangladeshi sampan, Dutch pram dinghy, Maltese luzzu, Maltese dghajsa, Maltese kajjik, Papuan outrigger, *Cygnet*, Brunei racing canoe, Iraqi guffa, Brunel dredger *Bertha*, Bude tub-boat, Northumberland coble, Westray skiff, Dutch tjotter, Venetian gondola, Colombian dugout, West African dugout, Exe lugger, *Solitaire*, Medway doble, Australian surf boat, Thames racing punt, Nigerian piccin boat, *QE 3* (Grand Banks dory), Aran curragh, Chinese sampan, picarooner, umla, *Miss England*, Arabian Gulf dugout, Philippines dugout, birch-bark canoe, gaff cutter *Sunny South*, Buck's Ledge boat, *Super Silver*, *Britannia II* (rowboat), *Puffin* (rowboat), Tagus lighter, xavega, moliceiro, meia lua, netinha, valboeiro, bateira, rabao, masseira, Taiwan sampan, Cayman Island catboat, Labrador kayak frame, *Britannia* (rowboat), Corfu reed boat, Irrawaddy sampan, Portuguese cod-fishing dory, Lisbon cascais chata, Shetland fourern, kayak, collapsible raiding canoe, pilot cutter *Jolie Brise*,

Lake Baringo (Kenya) ambatch reed boat, steam launch *Hero*, Dordogne boat, international 14-foot racing dinghies *Alarm* and *Lightning*, Morgan Giles international fourteen, Brazilian jangada, Sedgemoor withies punt, Western Samoan outrigger, Tuvalu outrigger, Zaire river dugout, six-oared gig, Western Australian raft, Huanchaco (Peru) beach reed boat, Sedgemoor turf boat, Nigerian sailing dugout, Hong Kong junk, Gizo (Gilbert Islands) dugout, paddling eanoe kiribati, canoa do ribotejo, Sines (Portugal) reed boat, Caribbean expedition canoe, Colchester oyster smack *TSW Shamrock*, Ghana beach boat, flying proa *Britannia*, Malaysian kolek lichang, sometime Alaskan whaling umiak, *Nautica*, Captain Bligh's launch, Azores whaleboat, Portland lerret

Access and conditions Open to qualified researchers by appt, Mon-Fri 10–5. All material available for editorial reproduction and for advertising. No loans; b/w prints and colour transparencies available for a fee. Photocopies available. Reproduction rights fees charged. Staff will undertake some research.

893 • JAMES GILBERT

1 Grafton Square, London SW4 0DE
Tel (01) 622 9253

Enquiries to James Gilbert

Items 10,000: b/w original photographs, colour transparencies (35mm)

Dates of subject matter 1800 to present

Dates of photographs 1900 to present

Subjects Aircraft of all types, worldwide aviation history and modern aviation including ballooning, domestic and military aircraft, airships, biplanes, seaplanes, gliders, airliners, microlight aircraft, aircraft from World Wars I and II; aircraft on the ground, in flight, in formation and stunting; air shows including Paris, Farnborough and Oshkosh, Wisconsin; some wartime action; aircraft from the following countries: UK, USA, France, Germany, Russia

Access and conditions Open to qualified researchers by appt (tel), Mon-Fri 9.30–5.30. All material available for editorial reproduction but not for advertising. B/w and colour material loaned free of charge for three months. B/w prints and duplicate colour transparencies available for a fee. Reproduction rights fees charged. Staff will undertake some research.

894 • HAYNES PUBLISHING GROUP plc

Sparkford, Yeovil, Somerset BA22 7JJ
Tel (0963) 40635 Telex 46212

Enquiries to Judith St Clair-Pedroza

Items About 2500: colour transparencies (35mm, 2½″, 5″ × 4″), unprinted film negatives

Dates of subject matter *c*. 1925 to present

Dates of photographs 1975 to present

Subjects Car and motor cycle maintenance including British and American cars and Japanese, British and European motor cycles; vintage cars and motor cycles including restoration and preservation

Access and conditions Open to qualified researchers by appt (write). Some material available for editorial reproduction and for advertising. B/w prints available for a fee; colour material loaned free of charge for one month and then for a rental fee. Photocopies available. Reproduction rights fees charged. Staff will undertake some research.

895 • MIKE JERRAM AVIATION PHOTOGRAPHY

20 Lindley Avenue, Southsea, Hampshire PO4 9NU
Tel (0705) 832629

Enquiries to Mike Jerram

Items About 10,000: b/w original and copy photographs, colour transparencies (35mm)

Dates of subject matter 1900 to present

Dates of photographs 1900 to present

Subjects Aviation and associated subjects: ground and flying photographs of military and civilian aircraft and helicopters including air-to-air shots, manufacturing processes, aviation personalities, major world air displays, aircraft interiors, private flying

Access and conditions Not open; telephone and mail requests only. All material available for editorial reproduction and for advertising. B/w and colour material loaned free of charge for one month. Photocopies available. Reproduction rights and holding fees charged. Staff will undertake research.

896 • KINGSTON UPON HULL CITY MUSEUMS AND ART GALLERIES

Transport and Archaeology Museum, 36 High Street, Kingston upon Hull, Humberside HU1 1NQ
Tel (0482) 222737

Enquiries to John Bradshaw, Curator

Items 5000: b/w original photographs, colour transparencies (35mm, 5″ × 4″)

Dates of subject matter Prehistory to present

Dates of photographs 1900 to present

Subjects Transport collection: trams, buses, motor cars, public transport, horse-drawn vehicles, motor cycles, bicycles, all in and around Hull; archaeology collection: notable collection of Romano-British mosaics from Humberside; archaeological excavations in East Yorkshire and Humberside including prehistoric, Roman, Anglo-Saxon and medieval sites

Access and conditions Open to the public by appt, Mon-Fri 10–5. Most material available for editorial reproduction and for advertising. B/w prints and duplicate colour transparencies available for a fee. Photocopies available. Reproduction rights and service fees charged. Staff will undertake some research. Compulsory credit line.

897 • THE LOCOMOTIVE CLUB OF GREAT BRITAIN

Ken Nunn Collection

11 Braywood Avenue, Egham, Surrey TW20 9LY

Enquiries to Graham Stacey

Items 12,000: glass negatives, unprinted film negatives

Dates of subject matter c. 1860 to 1962

Dates of photographs 1897 to 1962

Subjects Railway trains and locomotives (no stations and no staff)

Access and conditions Open to qualified researchers by appt (please write). All material available for editorial reproduction and for advertising. B/w prints loaned or available for a fee. Reproduction rights fees charged. Staff will respond to written enquiries by sending relevant duplicated list.

898 • LONDON TRANSPORT LIBRARY

39 Wellington Street, London WC2E 7BB
Tel (01) 379 6344

Enquiries to Librarian

Items Posters, books, maps, ephemera

Dates of items c. 1900 to present

Subjects London Transport posters

Access and conditions Open to the public by appt (tel), Mon-Fri 10–6. Colour transparencies loaned for a fee. Reproduction rights and service fees charged. Staff will undertake limited research.

899 • LONDON TRANSPORT MUSEUM

39 Wellington Street, London WC2E 7BB
Tel (01) 379 6344

Enquiries to Oliver Green, Curator

Items About 23,000: colour transparencies (35mm, 2¼″, 5″ × 4″), posters, b/w original and copy photographs, lantern slides, architectural drawings, postcards, illustrated books

Dates of subject matter c. 1770 to present

Dates of photographs c. 1850 to present

Subjects History of public transport in London including underground railways (1863–present), horse-drawn and motor buses (1829–present), horse-drawn and electric trams (1861–1952), trolley buses (1931–1962), London streetscenes (1830–present), London Transport architecture and design (1860–present), Metroland and suburban development (1870–1939), London Transport at war (1914–1918 & 1939–1945) including women war workers, bomb damage, evacuation, tube shelters, special war work, etc.; lifts and escalators; tickets, staff and staff uniforms; construction of underground railways and stations, repair work

Access and conditions Open to the public by appt (tel), Mon-Fri 10–6. Most material available for editorial reproduction and for advertising. B/w prints available for a fee; colour transparencies rented for a fee. Photocopies available. Reproduction rights and service fees charged.

900 • THE MARITIME TRUST

16 Ebury Street, London SW1W 0LH
Tel (01) 730 0096

Enquiries to Secretary

Items About 600: colour transparencies (35mm), b/w original photographs

Dates of subject matter 19th century to present

Dates of photographs 1970s to present

Subjects Works of the Trust restoring and maintaining historic British ships including *RRS Discovery*, *HMS Warrior*, *HMS Gannet*, *Gipsy Moth IV* and *Lively Lady*

Access and conditions Open to qualified researchers by appt. Most material available for editorial reproduction and for advertising. B/w and colour material loaned free of charge for three months; material may be copied by outside photographers. Photocopies available. No reproduction rights fees charged but donation to work of Trust appreciated. Compulsory credit line. All material copyright.

901 • HUGH McKNIGHT PHOTOGRAPHY

The Clock House, Upper Halliford, Shepperton, Middlesex TW17 8RU
Tel (0932) 783319

Enquiries to Hugh McKnight

Items About 30,000: b/w original photographs, colour transparencies (35mm, 6 × 6cm, 5″ × 4″), b/w copy photographs, postcards, illustrated books, fine art prints, glass negatives

Dates of subject matter Late 18th century to present

Dates of photographs Late 19th century to present

Subjects History of navigable inland waterways (canals and rivers) in 18th-century engravings, late 19th-century and early 20th-century b/w photographs and modern b/w and colour photographs; special collection of early 20th-century views of French waterways; waterways throughout western Europe including British Isles, Ireland, France, Germany, Holland, Belgium, Sweden, Italy; historical material from other parts of the world including USA and Canada; freight and recreational use of waterways

Access and conditions Open to the public by appt (tel). All material available for editorial reproduction and for advertising. B/w and colour material loaned free of charge; period negotiable. Photocopies available. Reproduction rights fees

charged; service and holding fees occasionally charged. Staff will undertake research; negotiable fee for large projects.

902 • MERSEYSIDE TRAMWAY PRESERVATION SOCIETY

9 Cornel Way, Huyton, Liverpool L36 0XN

Enquiries to B. P. Martin

Items About 4000: b/w original photographs, colour transparencies (35mm), colour photographic prints, postcards, illustrated maps, unprinted film negatives, posters, greetings cards, architectural drawings, illustrated books

Dates of subject matter 1897 to 1957

Dates of photographs 1897 to 1957

Subjects Liverpool Corporation tramways, history, development and decline

Access and conditions Open to qualified researchers by appt (write). Some material available for editorial reproduction and for advertising. B/w prints and duplicate colour transparencies available for a fee; colour transparencies loaned for a rental fee. Reproduction rights, service and holding fees charged.

903 • THE MITCHELL LIBRARY

Department of Science & Technology

North Street, Glasgow G3 7DN
Tel (041) 221 7030 Telex 778732

Enquiries to Departmental Librarian

Items About 20,000: b/w original and copy photographs, glass negatives, postcards, illustrated books

Dates of subject matter 1860s to 1960s

Dates of photographs 1860s to 1960s

Subjects North British Locomotive Co. collection covering locomotives manufactured by the Company and its subsidiaries Neilson & Co., Dübs & Co. and Sharp, Stewart & Co. and including construction of locomotives, loading them aboard ship at Glasgow docks for export, and details of finished products; CAMPBELL LAWSON KERR COLLECTION of photographs of steam locomotives in service throughout the British Isles including coverage of almost every class of engine between 1930s and 1964

Access and conditions Open to the public by appt (tel), Mon-Fri 9.30–9, Sat 9.30–5. All material available for editorial reproduction and for advertising (some restrictions). No loans; b/w prints available for a fee; material may be copied by outside photographers. Photocopies available. Reproduction rights fees charged. Staff will undertake limited research. All material copyright. Catalogue in preparation.

904 • N GAUGE SOCIETY

5 Salmond Road, Portway, Andover, Hampshire SP11 8HF
Tel (0264) 61640

Enquiries to M. J. Le Marie

Items About 500: b/w original photographs, colour photographic prints

Dates of photographs 1975 to present

Subjects N gauge locomotives and rolling stock, commercially produced, kit-built and scratch-built; layouts, buildings and scenery

Access and conditions Open to qualified researchers by appt (write). All material available for editorial reproduction and for advertising. B/w and colour material loaned free of charge by arrangement; material may be copied by outside photographers. Reproduction rights fees charged. All material copyright.

905 • NATIONAL BUS COMPANY

Group Photographic Library, 172 Buckingham Palace Road, London SW1W 9TN
Tel (01) 730 3453 Telex 27442

Enquiries to Brian Cooper, Public Affairs Manager

Items 5000: b/w original photographs, colour transparencies (35mm, 2¼"), colour photographic prints, b/w copy photographs

Dates of subject matter 1920 to present

Dates of photographs 1920 to present

Subjects Buses and coaches of all types in service with the company and its 40 subsidiaries in England and Wales; coach excursions, holidays,

travel shots, special services, engineering and maintenance; early vehicles and services

Access and conditions Open to qualified researchers by appt (write). All material available for editorial reproduction; advertising use by special arrangement only. B/w and colour material loaned free of charge for three months (print fees charged). Photocopies available. Reproduction rights fees charged by arrangement. Staff will undertake limited research. Compulsory credit line. Most material copyright.

906 • NATIONAL MARITIME MUSEUM

Romney Road, London SE10 9NF
Tel (01) 858 4422

Historic Photographs Collection

Enquiries to Curator

Items About 500,000: b/w original and copy photographs, 5″ × 4″ glass negatives, lantern slides

Dates of subject matter c. 1845 to present

Dates of photographs c. 1845 to present

Subjects Maritime activity including ship portraits, all aspects of life at sea, shipbuilding

Access and conditions Open to the public by appt (write), Tues Wed Thurs 11–4. Most material available for editorial reproduction and for advertising. No loans; b/w prints and duplicate colour transparencies available for a fee. Reproduction rights fees charged. Some material copyright. Printed catalogue available.

Photo Sales Department

Enquiries to Photographic Sales Section

Items Over 40,000: b/w original photographs, unprinted film negatives, colour transparencies (5″ × 4″, 7″ × 5″, 10″ × 8″)

Dates of photographs 1937 to present

Subjects Objects and paintings in the Museum including portraits, uniforms, medals, events, ships and small vessels, parts of ships and equipment, weapons, navigational and astronomical instruments, maps, charts, globes, ropework, ceramics, documents, ethnography, furniture, glass, jewellery and watches, plate, ship fittings, tools, uniform accessories, textiles

Access and conditions Open to the public by

appt (tel), Apr-Oct Mon-Sat 10–6, Sun 2–5.30, Nov-Mar Mon-Sat 10–5, Sun 2–5. All material available for editorial reproduction and for advertising (some restrictions). No loans; b/w prints and duplicate colour transparencies available for a fee. Reproduction rights fees charged. Staff will undertake limited research. All material copyright.

907 • NATIONAL MOTOR MUSEUM

Motoring Picture Library, John Montagu Building, Beaulieu, Hampshire SO4 7ZN
Tel (0590) 612345

Enquiries to Philip Scott, Photographic Librarian

Items 200,000: b/w original and copy photographs, colour transparencies (35mm, 5″ × 4″), glass negatives, unprinted film negatives, posters

Dates of subject matter 1885 to present

Dates of photographs 1885 to present

Subjects Motoring and motor vehicles from 1885 including motor cars, commercial vehicles, motorcycles, motoring personalities, garages, workshops, factories, showrooms, racing, accidents, advertising, town and country scenes, fashion

Access and conditions Open to the public by appt (tel), Mon-Fri 9–5. All material available for editorial reproduction and for advertising. B/w and colour material loaned free of charge for six weeks. Photocopies available. Reproduction rights, holding and service fees charged; service fees deductible from use fees. Staff of three will undertake limited research. Most material copyright.

908 • NATIONAL RAILWAY MUSEUM

Leeman Road, York YO2 4XJ
Tel (0904) 21261

Enquiries to Library

Items About 200,000: b/w original and copy photographs, colour transparencies (35mm), glass negatives, lantern slides, postcards, original cartoons, posters, illustrated books, engineering drawings

Dates of subject matter c. 1800 to present

Dates of photographs 1866 to present

Subjects History and development of railways in the British Isles including motive power, rolling stock, workshops, stations, bridges, tunnels, trains in motion, railway-owned ships, railway-owned docks, railway-operated road vehicles, railways in wartime, munitions manufacture by railways during World Wars I and II, railway accidents, industrial railways and locomotives; some overseas coverage; special collections include those of E. J. Bedford/G. F. Burtt, J. F. Bruton, E. Craven, R. Cutler, P. C. Dewhurst, M. W. Earley, M. D. England, S. H. P. Higgin, I. C. M. Hill, E. Mason, R. Mills, G. T. Moody, T. B. Sands, S. E. Teasdale, T. E. Williams, G. L. Wilson

Access and conditions Open to the public by appt (tel), Tues-Fri 10.30–5. Most material available for editorial reproduction and for advertising. B/w prints and duplicate colour transparencies available for a fee. Photocopies available. Reproduction rights and service fees charged. Staff will undertake some research. All material copyright. Card catalogue available.

Art Collection

Enquiries to Sue Underwood, Museum Assistant

Items About 7500: posters, prints, engravings, aquatints, lithographs, paintings

Dates of subject matter 1830 to present

Subjects Portraits of railway companies' directors and staff, locomotives; original artwork for posters; Victorian paintings of platform scenes and railway travel; poster collection shows expansion of railway network

Access and conditions Open to the public by appt (tel), Mon-Thurs 10–4.45, Fri 10–4.15. Most material available for editorial reproduction and for advertising. B/w prints and duplicate colour transparencies available for a fee. Reproduction rights and service fees charged. Staff will undertake some research. All material copyright. Card catalogue available.

909 • THE NATIONAL TRAMWAY MUSEUM

Library, Crich, Matlock, Derbyshire DE4 5DP
Tel (077 385) 2565

Enquiries to Librarian

Items 25,000: unprinted film negatives, illustrated books, glass negatives, b/w original and

copy photographs, colour transparencies
(35mm), colour photographic prints, lantern slides,
postcards, old fine art prints, art reproductions,
posters, greetings cards

Dates of subject matter 1860s to present

Dates of photographs 1885 to present

Subjects History and development of tramways
in UK (some coverage of Europe, Australia and
USA) with emphasis on main population centres;
manufacture and operation of horse, steam, cable
and electric street tramway cars and equipment;
trackwork, overhead wire erection, electricity
supply generation; impact of tramways on social
and urban development; trade publications; tickets
and fare collection; special collections include the
ALEC JENSON TICKET COLLECTION and the R. B. PARR
NEGATIVE COLLECTION (excluding Scottish
material)

Access and conditions Open to qualified
researchers by appt (write). Most material
available for editorial reproduction and for
advertising by arrangement. B/w prints available
for a fee; material may be copied by outside
photographers. Polaroids available. Reproduction
rights and service fees charged. Staff of two will
undertake limited research. Most material
copyright. Card catalogue in preparation.

910 • OPC RAILPRINT

BRITISH RAIL & OXFORD PUBLISHING
CO.

302 Holdenhurst Road, Bournemouth, Dorset
BH8 8BX
Tel (0202) 36469

Enquiries to Sue Joslin

Items 250,000: b/w original photographs,
unprinted film negatives, glass negatives,
postcards, architectural drawings

Dates of subject matter 1825 to present

Dates of photographs 1850 to 1870

Subjects British railway history, photographs by
British Rail and constituent company
photographers; locomotives, carriages, wagons,
signalling equipment and installations, permanent
way, railway structures (stations, signal boxes,
viaducts, tunnels), trains, railway stations; railway
track plans, original railway locomotive and rolling
stock drawings

Access and conditions Open to the public by

appt (write). Most material available for editorial
reproduction and for advertising. No loans; b/w
prints available for a fee. Photocopies available.
Reproduction rights and service fees charged. Staff
will undertake research. Printed catalogue
available.

911 • THE PORT OF LONDON AUTHORITY

The Library, Units 39–41, Cannon Workshops,
Cannon Drive, West India Dock, London E14 9SU
Tel (01) 515 1162

Enquiries to Librarian

Items About 28,000: b/w original photographs,
b/w copy photographs, glass negatives, illustrated
maps, posters, architectural drawings, ephemera

Dates of subject matter 1800 to present

Dates of photographs 1860 to present

Subjects History and development of the London
docks including aerial views of the docks, Pool of
London and River Thames; all London bridges;
river views from Teddington to the Nore; transport
including barges, horse-drawn transport, loading
and unloading cargoes, porters handling cargoes by
truck and barrow, cargoes in transit by road and
rail, sheds and warehouses, inspecting and
sampling cargoes including cigars, coffee, drugs,
ivory, meat, rum, sugar, weighing and measuring;
wine vaults; trades associated with the docks and
river including barge skipper, carter, cooper, crane
driver, docker, engine driver, foreman,
immigration officer, lockman, meat porter, pilot,
rat catcher, sampler, seaman, stevedore, timber
porter, waterman; dredging vessels and dry docks
in operation; dock architecture; mechanical
equipment including cranes, elevators, grabs, lock
gates, floating plant, trucks; natural history
including birds, cats, fish, flowers; navigation aids
such as buoys; dock construction and repairs; police
including wartime coverage and women police;
power stations, railways; ships including sailing
ships, tugs; war history including bomb damage,
military personnel in the docks, contraband

Access and conditions Open to the public by
appt (tel). Most material available for editorial
reproduction but not for advertising. B/w material
loaned by arrangement; material may be copied by
outside photographers. Photocopies available.
Reproduction rights and service fees charged;
service fees deductible from use fees. Staff will
undertake limited research. Most material
copyright.

912 • DEREK PRATT PHOTOGRAPHY

WATERWAYS PHOTO LIBRARY

11 Ashchurch Park Villas, London W12 9SP
Tel (01) 743 1824

Enquiries to Derek Pratt

Items About 13,000: b/w original photographs,
colour transparencies (35mm, 2¼″), colour
photographic prints

Dates of photographs 1968 to present

Subjects All aspects of inland waterways in the
UK (some French coverage) including aqueducts,
architecture, bridges, cities, towns, industrial
archaeology, engineering, locks, tunnels,
maintenance, narrow boats, boats, barges, horse-
drawn boats, yachting, hotel boats, holidays,
fishing, swans, waterside wildlife and flowers,
winter scenes

Access and conditions Open to qualified
researchers by appt (tel), Mon-Fri 9–5. All material
available for editorial reproduction and for
advertising. B/w material loaned free of charge by
arrangement; colour material loaned free of charge
for one month. Reproduction rights and holding
fees charged. Staff will undertake some research.
All material copyright.

913 • RAVENGLASS AND ESKDALE RAILWAY CO. LTD

Ravenglass, Cumbria CA18 1SW
Tel (06577) 226

Enquiries to Douglas Ferreira

Items Over 1000: b/w original and copy
photographs, glass negatives, postcards

Dates of subject matter 1874 to present

Dates of photographs 1874 to present

Subjects Landscapes of area adjacent to
Ravenglass and Eskdale narrow-gauge railway
including mining and quarrying activities

Access and conditions Open to qualified
researchers by appt (tel), Mon-Fri 9–5. All material
available for editorial reproduction and for
advertising. B/w material loaned free of charge for
one month; b/w prints available for a fee. No
reproduction rights fees charged. Staff will
undertake limited research. All material copyright.

914 • SWANSEA MARITIME AND INDUSTRIAL MUSEUM

Museum Square, Maritime Quarter, Swansea,
West Glamorgan SA1 1SN
Tel (0792) 50351

Enquiries to David Hoskins, Keeper of
Technology

Items About 4000: b/w original and copy
photographs, colour transparencies (35mm)
unprinted film negatives, glass negatives, lantern
slides, postcards

Dates of subject matter 1856 to present

Dates of photographs 1869 to present

Subjects Shipping and ships which have been
owned by Swansea firms or which have traded with
the port of Swansea including sail, reciprocating-
steam, turbine and internal-combustion powered
vessels; cargo, passenger and warships; Swansea
docks; notable local shipwrecks

Access and conditions Open to qualified
researchers by appt (write), daily 10.30–5.30. Most
material available for editorial reproduction but
not for advertising. No loans; material may be
copied by outside photographers. Photocopies
available. No reproduction rights fees charged.
Staff will undertake very limited research only.
Compulsory credit line.

915 • MICHAEL E. WARE

Schireburn, Beaulieu, Hampshire SO4 7YL
Tel (0590) 612386

Enquiries to Michael Ware

Items 12,000: b/w original and copy photographs,
colour transparencies (35mm, 2¼″)

Dates of subject matter 1854 to present

Dates of photographs 1854 to present

Subjects Comprehensive coverage of canals and
inland waterways of England and Wales with
special emphasis on those canals used by
narrowboats such as Grand Union, Shropshire
Union and River Wey Navigation Canal; some
coverage of Norfolk Broads; narrowboats, barges,
horse-drawn vessels, boat-building yards, people
living and working on canals

Access and conditions Open to qualified
researchers by appt (write), Mon-Fri 9–5. All
material available for editorial reproduction and
for advertising. B/w and colour material loaned free

of charge for six weeks. Photocopies available. Reproduction rights and holding fees charged; service fee sometimes charged, deductible from use fees. Staff will undertake some research. Most material copyright.

916 • WATERWAYS MUSEUM

British Waterways Board, Stoke Bruerne, Nr Towcester, Northamptonshire NN12 7SE
Tel (0604) 862229

Enquiries to Tony Conder, Curator or Roy Jamieson, Museum and Archives Assistant

Items 6000: b/w original and copy photographs, colour transparencies (35mm), glass negatives, postcards, lantern slides, illustrated maps, architectural drawings, old fine art prints

Dates of subject matter 1760 to present

Dates of photographs 1880 to present

Subjects Canals and inland waterways of England, Wales and Scotland, steam and sailing ships, horse-drawn, steam and motor craft, barges, narrowboats, dredgers, lighters, tugs, tunnel tugs, coal boats, timber barges, ice boats, inspection boats, steam paddle boats, passenger launches, boat building and repairs including painting, welding and carpentry; landscapes around canals, docks, wharves, reservoirs, tunnels, cuttings, aqueducts, foot bridges, railway bridges, road bridges, swing bridges, towpaths, lifts, staircases, inclined planes, flood weirs, locks, lock improvement and maintenance including detail of construction, canal maintenance and repair, extreme weather conditions, canal bursts, accidents, pumphouses, warehouses, power stations, public houses, trades and industries associated with waterways, loading and unloading cargoes, maintenance workers (including boys working on the Manchester Ship Canal), boatmen and boatwomen, social events, portraits of people living and working on canals and waterways, some interiors of barges and boats including one of a boat school, boatmen's strike of 1923, advertisements, tolls, notices, timetables; CYRIL ARAPOFF COLLECTION of life on the canals nationwide in the mid-1930s, including Thames lightermen

Access and conditions Open to qualified researchers by appt (tel), Mon-Fri 9–4. Most material available for editorial reproduction and for advertising; 5% for private research only. B/w and colour material loaned free of charge for one month; b/w prints and duplicate colour

transparencies available for a fee; material may be copied by outside photographers. Photocopies available for a fee. Reproduction rights fees charged. Staff of two will undertake some research; fees charged for large projects. All material copyright. Printed catalogue available: *The Waterways Museum Collection*, 1st edition, 1985, from the Waterways Museum.

917 • WORLD SHIP SOCIETY

Photographic Library, 6 Kathkin Avenue, Manchester M8 6QL
Tel (061) 795 5813

Enquiries to Clifford Parsons, Custodian of Negatives

Items 150,000: unprinted film negatives, colour transparencies (35mm, 5″ × 4″), glass negatives, illustrated books

Dates of subject matter 1860 to present

Dates of photographs 1900 to present

Subjects Ships and shipping worldwide including passenger, merchant and naval vessels: warships, Royal Fleet Auxiliaries, tankers, coasters, dredgers, freighters, tugs, pilot vessels, ferries, passenger liners, sailing ships, oil-rig supply vessels, Ro-ro and heavy-lift ships

Access and conditions Open to qualified researchers by appt (write). All material available for editorial reproduction and for advertising. No loans; b/w prints and duplicate colour transparencies available for a fee. Reproduction rights fees charged to non-Society users. Most material copyright.

918 • WORLD'S EDGE PICTURE LIBRARY

9 DeWalden House, Allitsen Road, London NW8 7BA
Tel (01) 586 5243

Enquiries to Dr K. Turnbull

Items About 10,000: b/w transparencies (35mm) and original photographs, colour transparencies (35mm), fine art prints, illustrated maps, illustrated books

Dates of subject matter 15th century to present

Dates of photographs 1950 to present

Subjects Maritime history including shipwreck recoveries (artefacts, treasure, coins and bullion, ship's guns, guns, navigational equipment, etc.); divers, diving boats, excavation and search (undersea) equipment; underwater photos (shipwreck remains, divers, archaeological excavation and survey); historical and general shipwreck illustrations (15th- to 19th-century) including early diving in prints, lithographs, oils, watercolours; naval and maritime history including ships, harbours, views, battles, Spanish galleons, vessels of the East India Company; voyages and exploration from contemporary sources (e.g. *Churchill's Voyages*, *Harleian Voyages*, etc.); naval and maritime topography (prints, lithographs, oils, watercolours), 16th- to 19th-century maps, emphasis on India and Asia

Access and conditions Open to qualified researchers by appt (write), Mon-Fri 9–5. All material available for editorial reproduction and for advertising. B/w and colour material loaned free of charge for one month. Reproduction rights and holding fees charged. Staff will undertake research; fees negotiable.

919 • THE WORLD'S MOTORCYCLES NEWS AGENCY

51 Green Acres, Ludlow, Shropshire SY8 1LY
Tel (0584) 3880

Enquiries to Douglas J. Jackson

Items About 16,500: b/w original and copy photographs, colour transparencies (35mm), colour photographic prints

Dates of subject matter 1900 to present

Dates of photographs 1930 to present

Subjects Motorcycles manufactured outside of the British Isles; some British motorcycles 1960 to present

Access and conditions Open to qualified researchers by appt (write). All material available for editorial reproduction, but not for advertising. B/w material loaned free of charge; colour material loaned for a rental fee. B/w prints and duplicate colour transparencies available for a fee. Photocopies available. Reproduction rights, service and holding fees charged. Staff will undertake some research.

920 • YORK TRAILER COMPANY

St Mark's Road, Corby, Northamptonshire
NN18 8AH
Tel (05363) 3561 Telex 34516

Enquiries to Publicity Department

Items 500,000: b/w original photographs, colour photographic prints, colour transparencies (35mm)

Dates of subject matter 1930 to present

Dates of photographs 1930 to present

Subjects Commercial vehicle bodies manufactured by the company including trailers, articulated trailers, tippers, trucks; ancillary equipment, axles, suspension, landing gear, body repairs, chassis engineering, component manufacture, assembly; vehicle bodies manufactured by Scammell and Anthony Carrimore from 1930 onwards

Access and conditions Open to qualified researchers by appt (write), Mon-Fri 8.30–5. All material available for editorial reproduction and for advertising (some restrictions). B/w and colour material loaned free of charge by arrangement. Service fees but no reproduction rights fees charged. Staff will undertake limited research. Compulsory credit line. All material copyright.

Fine Art & Architecture

921 • ABBOT HALL ART GALLERY

Abbot Hall, Kendal, Cumbria LA9 5AL
Tel (0539) 22464

Enquiries to M. E. Burkett, Director

Items About 35,000: glass negatives, b/w original photographs, colour transparencies (35mm), lantern slides, postcards, fine art prints, greetings cards, original cartoons, b/w copy photographs, unprinted film negatives

Dates of subject matter 3000 BC to present

Subjects British 18th-, 19th- and 20th-century painting and sculpture with emphasis on Lake District and Cumbrian artists and subjects; portraits by George Romney and Daniel Gardner; Lake District views by Julius Caesar Ibbetson, Anthony Devis, Thomas Sunderland, John Constable, Edward Lear and other 18th- and 19th-century watercolourists; watercolours and drawings by John Harden (1772–1847) including interiors (detailing informal costume, hair-styles, entertaining, furniture arrangement, interior decoration, etc.) and landscapes (featuring vernacular architecture, land use, local people, outdoor entertainment, boating, etc.) mainly of Lake District locations; watercolours and sketches of Lake District, Iceland and Norway by W. G. Collingwood; watercolours and drawings by John Ruskin including Turneresque Alpine views, European architecture, natural history specimens and Pre-Raphaelite landscapes; cartoons by Graham Hoggarth; 20th-century artists including Kurt Schwitters, Hilde Goldschmidt, Ben Nicholson, Winifred Nicholson, John Piper, Keith Vaughan, Sheila Fell; Scottish painters including Sir William MacTaggart, Sir William Gillies, S. J. Peploe, Joan Eardley, Anne Redpath and others; decorative arts including 18th-century mahogany and satinwood furniture by Gillows of Lancaster; Chinese ceramics; rare examples of charr plates and dishes – ceramic containers made during the late 18th and early 19th century for the local delicacy potted charr (small fish found in local lakes); 20th-century studio ceramics by Lucie Rie, Hans Coper, Bernard Leach; fine collection of 18th-, 19th- and 20th-century jewellery including jet, paste, cut steel, Scottish pebble, Art Nouveau and Arts and Crafts Movement

Access and conditions Open to qualified researchers by appt (write), Mon-Fri 10.30–5.30. All material available for editorial reproduction and for advertising. B/w prints available for a fee; colour material loaned for a rental fee (duplicate transparencies also available for a fee). Material may be copied by outside photographers. Photocopies available. Reproduction rights, service and holding fees charged. Staff will undertake limited research for specific requests; fees charged for large projects. Abbot Hall owns copyright to part of collection; in other cases copyright clearance is responsibility of user. Printed catalogue available: *Abbot Hall Art Gallery, Kendal: Paintings, Watercolours, Drawings, Sculpture*, ed M. E. Burkett, 1978, available from Abbot Hall Art Gallery, Kendal.

922 • ABERDEEN ART GALLERY AND MUSEUMS

Schoolhill, Aberdeen AB9 1FQ
Tel (0224) 646333

Enquiries to Director

Items 6000: colour transparencies (35mm), fine art prints (old and modern), paintings and drawings, lantern slides, b/w original and copy photographs, glass negatives, illustrated books, posters, stereographs, architectural drawings, postcards, cartoons, art reproductions, daguerreotypes, illustrated maps, colour photographic prints

Dates of subject matter Mesolithic to present

Dates of photographs c. 1860 to present

Subjects British painting and watercolours (17th to 20th century) including works by William Dyce, John Phillip, James McBey, and war artists; MACDONALD COLLECTION of British artists' portraits; European painting, sculpture and prints

(19th and 20th century); photographs by George Washington Wilson; decorative arts including Aberdeen silver, English and 19th-century Venetian glass, Chinese material, costumes, dolls; local industry and technology including natural granite agriculture, paper-making, engineering; archaeology including local digs, medieval sites. The index of Fine Arts collections lists subjects under the following headings: abstracts (mainly 20th-century British works), animals, buildings, caricature, fantasy, figure, genre, history, industry, interiors, landscape, literature, marine, mythology, plants, portraits and self-portraits, religion, seasons, sport, still life, urban landscapes, war

Access and conditions Open to the public; appt (tel) needed for access to reserve collections. All material available for editorial use at the discretion of the Director and with the permission of the copyright holder where applicable. No loans; b/w prints and duplicate colour transparencies available for a fee. Material may be copied by outside photographers. Photocopies available. Reproduction rights fees charged. Staff will undertake some research on computer subject index. Computerized catalogue in preparation.

923 • ARCAID

6 Latchmere Road, Kingston upon Thames, Surrey KT2 5TW
Tel (01) 546 4352

Enquiries to Lynne Bryant

Items 30,000: colour transparencies (35mm, 5″ × 4″, larger), b/w original photographs, architectural drawings, cuttings and tearsheets

Dates of subject matter Roman Britain to present

Dates of photographs 1960 to present

Subjects British, European, American and Asian architecture (industrial, commercial, domestic, public and ecclesiastic), interior design, landscape architecture and famous gardens, special subjects: Britain: English villages, historic houses (some National Trust), Northamptonshire buildings from a 16th-century lodge by Thomas Tresham to a contemporary doctors' surgery by Aldington, Craig and Collinge, Sir John Soane's Museum, Apsley House, Centre Point, National Theatre, Barbican, work by James Stirling including the Leicester Engineering block and the Cambridge Library,

work by Terry Farrell including TV AM, work by Eva Jiricna including high-tech domestic interiors, work by Stirling and Wilfords including the Staatsgalerie in Stuttgart; Europe: architecture and classic architect-designed houses of the 1960s and 1970s, the Pompidou Centre, work by Alvar Aalto including the Concert Hall in Helsinki; USA: weaving mills and related processes, work by Frank Lloyd Wright including Beth Shalom, Fallingwater, Robie House, Oak Park; Sri Lanka: work by Geoffrey Bawa including the new Houses of Parliament and the Triton Hotel, various historic sites; private and public gardens in the UK and abroad including National Trust properties, The Royal Botanic Gardens (Kew), Peradinya Gardens in Sri Lanka; special subjects including the evolution of the lavatory from Roman times to the present day, Victorian railway architecture, street furniture, public houses and graves, use of materials including stone, brick, wood, etc.; photographs by Richard Einzig, Richard Bryant and Lucinda Lambton

Access and conditions Open to qualified researchers by appt (tel), Mon-Fri 9.30–5.30. Most material available for editorial reproduction and for advertising (some restrictions). B/w and colour material loaned free of charge for one month. Reproduction rights fees charged; service fees charged only when no material is used. Staff of two will undertake some research. Photographers available for assignments. All material copyright.

924 • ARCHITECTURAL ASSOCIATION

Slide Library, 36 Bedford Square, London WC1B 3ES
Tel (01) 636 0974

Enquiries to Andrew Higgott, Slide Librarian

Items 90,000: colour transparencies (35mm), lantern slides, glass negatives, b/w original and copy negatives, b/w contact prints (for reference), fine art prints

Dates of subject matter 3000 BC to present

Dates of photographs 1890 to present

Subjects Architecture of all periods and countries but especially of Great Britain, Europe and USA; related subjects including city views, urban environment, gardens, fine and applied art; buildings of historical and artistic importance, vernacular buildings, suburban houses, painted buildings, squatter houses; F. R. YERBURY COLLECTION of historical buildings, work of Le

Corbusier, Mendelsohn, Dudok and others (1920s–1930s), USSR (1932) and USA (1926); E. R. JARRETT COLLECTION of historical buildings, British and European buildings (1930–1950)

Access and conditions Open to qualified researchers by appt (tel), Mon-Fri 10–5.30 (closed mid-Aug to mid-Sept). Most material available for editorial reproduction and for advertising. B/w material not loaned; prints available for a fee. Colour transparencies loaned free of charge for one month. Reproduction rights and holding fees charged; service fees charged only when no material is used. Staff of three will undertake some research. Copyright clearance is responsibility of user.

925 • THE ARCHITECTURAL PRESS LTD

9 Queen Anne's Gate, London SW1H 9BY
Tel (01) 222 4333

Enquiries to Shirley Hind, Photographic Librarian

Items Over 250,000: b/w original photographs, glass negatives, colour transparencies (35mm, 5″ × 4″, larger)

Dates of subject matter 1930 to present

Dates of photographs 1930 to present

Subjects British architecture including towns and town planning, factories, offices, shops and shopping centres, bars and public houses, restaurants, arts centres and art galleries, sports buildings, schools and colleges, museums, exhibition buildings, housing, hotels, country houses; some foreign architecture; Dell and Wainwright photographs (1930s); photographs from *The Architectural Review* and *The Architect's Journal*

Access and conditions Open to qualified researchers by appt (tel), Mon-Fri 2–5.30. Most material available for editorial reproduction and for advertising. B/w material loaned free of charge for one month; duplicate colour transparencies available for a fee. Reproduction rights, service and holding fees charged; service fees deductible from use fees. Staff will undertake some research.

926 • ARMAGH COUNTY MUSEUM

The Mall East, Armagh BT61 9BE
Tel (0861) 523070

Enquiries to D. R. M. Weatherup, Curator

Items 5500: b/w original photographs, b/w copy photographs, colour transparencies (35mm), colour photographic prints, glass negatives, daguerreotypes, lantern slides, postcards, illustrated maps, unprinted film negatives, greetings cards, architectural drawings, cuttings and tearsheets, illustrated books

Dates of subject matter 18th–20th centuries

Dates of photographs *c.* 1850 to present

Subjects Portraits of local interest; works by contemporary Irish artists especially George Russell (AE) of Lurgan and James Sleator of Armagh City; pictures of topographic interest of Ireland and Armagh area

Access and conditions Open to the public by appt (write), Mon-Fri 9–5. Some material available for editorial reproduction, but not for advertising. B/w material loaned by special arrangement; prints available for a fee. Duplicate colour transparencies available for a fee. Reproduction rights and service fees charged. Staff of two will undertake some research.

927 • ARTS COUNCIL OF GREAT BRITAIN

105 Piccadilly, London W1V 0AU
Tel (01) 629 9495

Enquiries to Isobel Johnstone, Curator
Post-War British Art Collection

Items 5000: b/w original photographs, colour transparencies

Dates of subject matter 1944 to present (some from 1900)

Subjects Paintings, prints and sculpture by British artists; some prints by foreign artists

Access and conditions Open to the public by appt (write), Mon-Fri 10–6. All material available for editorial reproduction. B/w prints available for a fee, colour transparencies loaned for a rental fee. Photocopies available. Staff will undertake some research.

British Photographic Collection

Items 1800: b/w original photographs, colour transparencies

Subjects Photographs by 200 leading British photographers including Bill Brandt, Jane Bown, David Montgomery, Fay Godwin, Ian Berry

Access and conditions Open to the public by appt (write), Mon-Fri 10–6. All material available for editorial reproduction and for advertising subject to copyright clearance. B/w prints and duplicate colour transparencies available for a fee. Reproduction rights fee payable to photographers. Photocopies available. Staff will undertake some research.

Arts Council Exhibition Archive

Record copies of photographs used in exhibition catalogues are held. The archive is not open to the public; it is open to qualified researchers in some cases offering a limited access and service for material unobtainable elsewhere.

928 • ATKINSON ART GALLERY

Lord Street, Southport, Merseyside PR8 1DH
Tel (0704) 33133 ext 129

Enquiries to Sheila McGregor, Keeper of Fine Art

Items About 2000: b/w original photographs, unprinted film negatives

Dates of subject matter Classical times to present

Subjects 18th-century portraits; 18th- and 19th-century English watercolours including works by Cotman, Bonington, Crome and Cox; Victorian landscape and genre painting with emphasis on scenes of Victorian rural and domestic life; early 20th-century painting by artists associated with the New English Art Club; contemporary work by local artists; modern prints and sculpture including *Three-Way-Piece-Points* by Henry Moore

Access and conditions Open to the public by appt (write), Mon Wed Fri 10–5, Thur & Sat 10–1. All material available for editorial reproduction and for advertising; in some cases permission of copyright holder is required. B/w material loaned and b/w prints available for a fee. Photocopies available. Reproduction rights fees charged. Staff will undertake limited research. Printed catalogues available, but not comprehensive.

929 • JAMES AUSTIN PHOTOGRAPH LIBRARY

22 Godesdone Road, Cambridge CB5 8HR
Tel (0223) 359763

Enquiries to James Austin

Items 11,000: b/w original photographs, colour transparencies (35mm)

Dates of subject matter 500 BC to present

Dates of photographs 1965 to present

Subjects Greek architecture in Greece, Sicily, Paestum; Roman remains in Pompeii; Romanesque and Gothic architecture and sculpture in France; miscellaneous medieval tapestries, frescoes, stained-glass windows in France and Italy; Romanesque architecture and sculpture in Italy and in Musée Jacquemart-André, Paris; 18th-, 19th- and 20th-century architecture and sculpture in France; miscellaneous architecture and sculpture in Great Britain from medieval to modern times

Access and conditions Open to qualified researchers by appt. All material available for editorial reproduction and for advertising. B/w prints available for a fee; colour transparencies loaned free of charge for one month. Reproduction rights, service and holding fees charged; service fees deductible from use fees. Staff will undertake limited research. All material copyright. Printed catalogue available.

930 • AVONCROFT MUSEUM OF BUILDINGS

Stoke Heath, Bromsgrove, Worcestershire B60 4JR
Tel (0527) 31886

Enquiries to Jennifer Costigan, Assistant Director/Education Officer

Items 7100: b/w original photographs, colour transparencies (35mm), illustrated books, b/w copy photographs, architectural drawings, colour photographic prints, postcards, glass negatives

Dates of subject matter 1300 to present

Dates of photographs Mostly 1960 to present

Subjects Buildings in the Museum collection and their dismantling and re-erection (buildings date from the Middle Ages to the 20th century); related building techniques and crafts; examples of other early buildings not forming part of the Museum collection; processes (blacksmithing, chain-making, flour-milling) that take place within the Museum's exhibits

Access and conditions Open to the public by appt (tel). All material available for editorial reproduction and for advertising. B/w and colour material loaned; b/w prints and duplicate colour transparencies available for a fee. Material may be copied by outside photographers. Photocopies available. Reproduction rights fees charged at the Director's discretion. Card catalogue.

931 • BLACKBURN MUSEUM AND ART GALLERY

Museum Street, Blackburn, Lancashire BB1 7AJ
Tel (0254) 667130

Enquiries to Curator

Items 4500: b/w original and copy photographs, colour transparencies (35mm, 5″ × 4″), colour photographic prints, glass negatives, lantern slides, fine art prints, paintings, watercolours, drawings, illuminated manuscripts

Dates of subject matter *c.* 400 BC to present

Dates of photographs Late 19th century to present

Subjects 19th- and 20th-century English painting and watercolour (mostly landscapes); 13th- to 16th-century medieval manuscript illumination; Persian manuscript illumination; Greek, Roman and British coins; Russian, Greek and Lebanese ikons; Blackburn and district local history and topography, local events and personalities; East Lancashire Regiment (1850s to present) overseas (Canada, India) and at home

Access and conditions Open to the public by appt (write), Mon-Sat 9.30–5. All material available for editorial reproduction and for advertising, with some restrictions. No loans; b/w prints and duplicate colour transparencies available for a fee. Reproduction rights fees charged. Staff will undertake limited research.

932 • THE BRIDGEMAN ART LIBRARY

19 Chepstow Road, London W2 5BP
Tel (01) 727 4065, 229 7420

Enquiries to Harriet Bridgeman or Dominica Blenkinsopp

Items 25,000: colour transparencies (5″ × 4″, larger), b/w original photographs

Dates of subject matter Prehistory to present

Dates of photographs 1960 to present

Subjects Fine art of all kinds, periods and countries accessible under the following headings (and also by artist, etc.): antiquities, arms including armour and militaria, battles, birds, books and book illustrations, botanical illustrations, cards including postcards and ephemera, ceramics, Christmas and seasonal material, clocks including watches and barometers, coins and medals, costume and fashion accessories, enamels, ethnography, furniture, glass, great exhibitions, historical events, icons, inventions, ivories, jade, jewellery, juvenilia, lacquer and japanning, lighting, malachite, manuscripts, historical documents and contracts, maps, medicine, metalwork, miniatures, music, mythology, *objets de vertu*, Oriental and Near-Eastern art, papier-mâché, personalities including writers, explorers, painters, philosophers, social reformers, royalty, statesmen, scientists and sportsmen, photography, posters, prints and drawings, religion, saints, scientific instruments, sculpture, seasons, shellwork, silhouettes, silver, gold and silver gilt, sports and pastimes, stained glass, still lifes, textiles, topography, trade emblems, city crests and coats of arms, transportation, treen, turquoise, wallpaper, insects

Access and conditions Open to the public by appt (tel), Mon-Fri 9.30–5.30. All material available for editorial reproduction and for advertising, subject to permission in a few cases. B/w and colour material loaned free of charge for one month. Reproduction rights, service and holding fees charged. Staff will undertake research; fees charged for large projects. Printed catalogue available in two vols.

933 • BRIGHTON ART GALLERY AND MUSEUMS AND THE ROYAL PAVILION

Brighton BN1 1UE
Tel (0273) 603005

Enquiries to Photographic Enquiries Department

Items 1000: b/w original photographs, colour transparencies (35mm, 5″ × 4″)

Dates of subject matter Prehistory to present

Dates of fine art 17th century to present

Dates of photographs 1950 to present

Subjects ART GALLERY AND MUSEUM: British and European oil paintings, watercolours and drawings including works by Phillippe de Champaigne, Sir Thomas Lawrence, Jan Lievens, Glyn Philpot and Nicolas Poussin; Regency caricatures; designs for the Royal Pavilion; European Art Nouveau and Art Deco furniture and decorative art; WILLETT COLLECTION of commemorative ceramics; ethnography; archaeology and local history of Sussex; toys and games; ROYAL PAVILION: Regency interiors and furnishings and decorative art

Access and conditions Art Gallery and Museum open to the public, Tues-Sat 10–5.45, Sun 2–5; Royal Pavilion open to the public daily, 10–5; July, Aug and Sep 10–6.30; material may be ordered by post only. All material available for editorial reproduction; advertising use by special arrangement only. Items from the collections may be photographed by staff photographer; b/w prints available for a fee; colour transparencies loaned for a fee. Reproduction rights fees charged. All material copyright.

934 • BRISTOL CITY MUSEUM AND ART GALLERY

Museum Collection

Queens Road, Bristol BS8 1RL
Tel (0272) 299771

Enquiries to Francis Greenacre, Curator of Fine Art

Items 5000: unprinted film negatives, glass negatives, lantern slides, illustrated maps, colour transparencies (5" × 4"), original cartoons, architectural drawings

Dates of subject matter Prehistory to present

Dates of photographs 1850 to present

Subjects 17th- to 20th-century British paintings, drawings, watercolours and sculpture, notably of the Bristol School (1810–1840) including view of the Port of Bristol c. 1735, Ernest Board's *Departure of John and Sabastian Cabot*, Nicholas Pocock's drawings of the slave trade, fine Victorian narrative paintings; continental paintings including 13th-century Italian works, fine 19th-century French paintings including works by Gustave Courbet, Auguste Renoir, Alfred Sisley and Jean-Edouard Vuillard

Access and conditions Open to the public by appt (write), Mon-Fri 10–5. All material available for editorial reproduction and for advertising. B/w prints available for a fee; colour transparencies rented for a fee. Reproduction rights and holding fees charged. Staff will undertake some research. Printed catalogue of paintings available.

935 • BRITISH ARCHITECTURAL LIBRARY

Photograph Collection

Royal Institute of British Architects, 66 Portland Place, London W1N 4AD
Tel (01) 580 5533 ext 217

Enquiries to Robert Elwall, Curator

Items 90,000: b/w original and copy photographs, unprinted film negatives, lantern slides, glass negatives, colour photographic prints, illustrated books

Dates of photographs 1850 to present

Subjects British and world architecture, topography, landscape architecture, planning and construction including public, ecclesiastic and vernacular buildings, tube stations, liners, etc.; special collections on British architecture (1850 to present), 19th-century American architecture, foreign architecture from 1858 to the present; Egypt and the Far East; work by the firms of Welch Cachemaille-Day and Lander and by Cornell Ward and Lucas and by the following architects: Sir Reginald Blomfield, William Butterfield, Norman Foster, Henry Stuart Goodhart-Rendel, Eileen Gray, Oliver Hill, Kisho Kurokawa, Sir Edwin Lutyens, Charles Mallows, Sir Edward Maufe, Temple Moore, Brian O'Rorke, Godfrey Samuel, Carlo Scarpa, Marshall Sisson, James Stirling, Sir Walter Tapper, Charles Voysey, George Walton, Cornell Ward, Harry Weedon, Sir Owen Williams, George Wittet; work by Dove Brothers (19th-century builders); photographs by Henry Bedford Lemere, Herbert Felton, Frank Yerbury, Henk Snoek, and others

Access and conditions Open to the public by appt (tel), Mon 10–5, Tues-Thurs 10–8, Fri 10–7, Sat 10–1.30. All material available for editorial reproduction and for advertising with the approval of the Institute. B/w and colour material loaned for a fee; b/w prints and duplicate colour transparencies available for a fee. Reproduction rights fees charged. Staff will undertake research. Copyright clearance is responsibility of user. See also The Royal Institute of British Architects.

936 • BRITISH MUSEUM

Department of Prints and Drawings

Great Russell Street, London WC1B 3DG
Tel (01) 636 1555

Enquiries to Keeper of Prints and Drawings

Items Number unknown: prints, drawings, watercolours, original cartoons, caricatures, portraits, topographical prints, book plates, playing cards, trade cards, albums and sketchbooks, b/w original photographs, colour transparencies

Dates of subject matter Prehistory to present

Dates of photographs Modern

Dates of fine art 15th century to present

Subjects The British Museum collection of graphic arts is one of the largest in the world and contains works by major and minor artists from all over the world. Approach to the collection is by artist or by category and not by subject.

Access and conditions Open to qualified researchers holding a British Museum ticket of admission, Mon-Fri 10–1, 2.15–4, Sat 10–12.30. Most material available for editorial reproduction and for advertising subject to copyright restrictions. B/w prints and colour transparencies available for a fee. Reproduction rights fees charged, but may be waived for scholarly publications. Staff will undertake limited research in answer to specific written requests. Printed and card catalogues.

937 • THE BURRELL COLLECTION

Pollok Country Park, 2060 Pollokshaws Road, Glasgow G43 1AT
Tel (041) 649 7151

Enquiries to Keeper

Items 8000: b/w original photographs, colour transparencies (35mm, 5″ × 4″), postcards, posters

Dates of subject matter 3000 BC to 1910

Dates of photographs 1950 to present

Subjects 19th-century painting of the Hague School mostly by Jacob and Matthew Maris; 19th-century French paintings (Romanticism, Realism, Barbizon School, Impressionism); 18th-century British portraits; 17th-century Dutch painting including works by Franz Hals and Rembrandt; watercolours by Joseph Crawhall (Glasgow

School); Chinese porcelains, bronzes and jades; ancient Egyptian, Greek and Roman art; Mesopotamian stone reliefs; British 16th- and 17th-century oak furniture; Franco-Flemish and German tapestries; 16th- to 18th-century English and Scottish silver; 15th- to 17th-century European sculpture; 12th- and 13th-century Limoges enamels; 14th- and 15th-century European ivories; embroidery and costume (mostly British, 16th to 18th century); 17th-century British glass

Access and conditions Open to the public, Mon-Fri 9–5. All material available for editorial reproduction and for advertising. B/w prints available for a fee; colour transparencies loaned for a rental fee. Reproduction rights, service and holding fees charged. Staff will undertake some research.

938 • BURY ART GALLERY AND MUSEUM

Moss Street, Bury, Lancashire BL9 0DR
Tel (061) 761 4021

Enquiries to William Bennion, Chief Librarian and Arts Officer

Items About 500: b/w original and copy photographs, colour transparencies (35mm, 5″ × 4″), glass negatives, lantern slides, postcards, art reproductions, greetings cards

Dates of subject matter Early 19th century to present

Dates of photographs 1978 to present

Subjects General collection: English and continental seascapes and marine paintings; sheep, cows, dogs, sporting scenes, hunting, etc.; 19th-century portraits (gentry, country people, workers); English, Scottish, Welsh, French and German landscapes; English and continental urban landscapes; 19th-century genre painting (country people, schoolrooms); historical, classical and narrative subjects, mostly 19th-century; WRIGLEY COLLECTION: Victorian paintings including Landseer's *A Random Shot*, J. M. W. Turner's *Calais Sands*, *Ehrenbreitstein* (2), *Liber Studiorum* (etchings) and others; drawings, watercolours and oils by David Cox; works by John Constable, John Linnell, Frederick Goodall, David Roberts, Miles Birket Foster, W. H. Hunt and others

Access and conditions Open to the public by appt (tel), Mon-Fri 10–6, Sat 10–5. All material available for editorial reproduction and for advertising. B/w and colour material loaned; all fees at the discretion of the Librarian. Photocopies available. Staff will undertake limited research. Card catalogue available.

939 • CARLISLE MUSEUM AND ART GALLERY

Castle Street, Carlisle, Cumbria CA3 8TP
Tel (0228) 34781

Enquiries to Laura Hamilton, Arts Assistant

Items 2000: b/w original and copy photographs, fine art prints, colour transparencies (35mm), lantern slides, colour photographic prints, daguerreotypes, postcards, posters, illustrated books

Dates of subject matter Prehistory to present

Dates of photographs 1850 to present

Subjects GORDON BOTTOMLEY BEQUEST (over 600 works) including works by the Pre-Raphaelites, Art Nouveau (Charles Ricketts and Charles Shannon), 20th-century artists (Paul Nash) and also including theatrical designs, landscape, genre, mythological subjects; WILLIAM ROTHENSTEIN COLLECTION of works by 20th-century artists (landscape, genre, portraiture) including William Rothenstein, Paul Nash, Stanley Spencer and Wyndham Lewis; works by Cumberland artists (1700 to 1900) including Sam Bough, W. J. Blacklock, M. E. Nutter, W. H. Nutter, T. Bushby; oriental prints; Presences of Nature: works by 20th-century artists commissioned in 1981 and depicting aspects of the Lake District (sculpture, textiles, ceramics, glass, photographs, prints, paintings)

Access and conditions Open to the public by appt, Mon-Sat 9–5. All material available for editorial reproduction and for advertising, subject to copyright clearance. B/w material loaned; b/w prints and duplicate colour transparencies available for a fee. Photocopies available. Reproduction rights and service fees charged. Staff will undertake some research.

940 • CARMARTHEN MUSEUM
Cultural Services Department

Dyfed County Council, Abergwili, Carmarthen, Dyfed SA31 2JG
Tel (0267) 231691

Enquiries to Christopher Delaney, Curator

Items About 3000: b/w original and copy photographs, colour transparencies (35mm, $5'' \times 4''$), colour photographic prints, glass negatives, daguerreotypes, lantern slides, postcards, original cartoons, illustrated maps, fine art prints, posters, greetings cards, illustrated books, paintings, watercolours, drawings

Dates of subject matter Prehistory to present

Dates of photographs 1850 to present

Subjects Fine and decorative arts: Wales and the old county of Carmarthenshire including 18th- and 19th-century topographical prints and maps (Samuel and Nathaniel Buck, Henry Castineau and others), 19th- and 20th-century drawings, watercolours and paintings by artists working in Carmarthenshire (Alexander Wilson, Edward Morland Lewis, Evan Walters and others), the Gelli Aur Collection of 18th-century portraits of the Vaughan family, 19th-century collection of Llanelly Art Pottery and contemporary work of Carmarthenshire craftsmen; photographic collection: Carmarthenshire trade, industry, folk and social life, landscape, architecture, Llanelly Tinplate Works (19th century), contemporary collection including Welsh landscapes by Fay Godwin

Access and conditions Open to the public by appt (write), Mon-Fri 8.45–5. Most material available for editorial reproduction and for advertising. No loans; b/w prints and duplicate colour transparencies available for a fee. Photocopies available. Reproduction rights and service fees charged. Staff will undertake some research. Card catalogue available.

941 • CHELTENHAM ART GALLERY AND MUSEUMS

40 Clarence Street, Cheltenham, Gloucestershire GL50 3NX
Tel (0242) 37431

Enquiries to George Breeze, Director

Items About 1800: b/w original and copy

photographs, colour transparencies (35mm, larger), lantern slides, postcards, posters, greetings cards

Dates of subject matter 17th century to present

Dates of photographs 1920s to present

Subjects BARON DE FERRIÈRES COLLECTION: 17th- and 19th-century Dutch painting (interiors, religious subjects, streetscenes, landscapes); 17th- to 20th-century British and continental painting; drawings of furniture design by Ernest Gimson and Sidney Barnsley and other designers of the Arts and Crafts movement; works by Edward Bawden, Thomas Hennell, Henry Lamb, John Nash, Paul Nash, John Piper, Sir William Rothenstein, Graham Sutherland, Stephen Bone, Michael Rothenstein (War Artists Advisory Commission Members); GUSTAV HOLST COLLECTION: photographs, pictures, concert programmes and documents associated with the composer's life; HULL GRUNDY JEWELLERY COLLECTION (1780 to the present) including paste and pinchbeck tiaras, shoe buckles and parures, cross pendants, cameos, Vauxhall glass, cut-steel, Berlin ironwork, coral, seed-pearls, ivory, agate, jet, vulcanite and bog oak, silver brooches; Pittville Pump Room (1830) – events associated with the spa; COSTUME COLLECTION: British and European fashion from 1760 to 1960, especially 18th-century silk gowns and men's embroidered waistcoats, Regency, late Victorian and 1920s evening dresses; also gloves, fans, purses, shawls and parasols

Access and conditions Open to the public by appt (write), Mon-Fri 10–5.30. All material available for editorial reproduction and for advertising. B/w prints available for a fee. Colour transparencies available through Bridgeman Art Library (q.v.). Photocopies available. Reproduction rights fees charged. Staff of two will undertake limited research. Printed catalogues; G. Andrews, *Fine Art Checklist*, June 1979; *Catalogue of Designs and Drawings of Artists of Arts and Crafts Movement from the Cheltenham Art Gallery and Museum*, 1984.

942 • CHRIST CHURCH PICTURE GALLERY

Canterbury Quadrangle, Christ Church College, Oxford OX1 1DP
Tel (0865) 242102

Enquiries to Joanna Woodall

Items 2500: b/w original photographs, colour transparencies (35mm, 7″ × 5″, 10″ × 8″, 12″ × 10″), glass negatives, postcards, art reproductions, unprinted film negatives, greetings cards, illustrated books

Dates of subject matter Classical times to present

Subjects 13th- to 18th-century Italian painting; 15th- to 18th-century Italian (Old Master) drawings; Dutch, German, French, English and Spanish paintings and drawings; 18th-century English glass; portraits of people connected with Christ Church College from the 16th to the 20th centuries

Access and conditions Open to qualified researchers by appt (write), Mon-Sat 10.30–1, 2–4.30. All material available for editorial reproduction and for advertising at the Curator's discretion. B/w prints available for a fee; colour transparencies loaned for a rental fee. Reproduction rights fees charged. Printed catalogues available: J. Byam Shaw, *Drawings by the Old Masters at Christ Church, Oxford* and *Paintings by the Old Masters at Christ Church, Oxford* (1967, 1975).

943 • CHRISTIES COLOUR LIBRARY

8 King Street, London SW1Y 6QT
Tel (01) 839 9060 Telex 916429

Enquiries to Araminta Morris, Colour Librarian

Items 50,000: colour transparencies (10″ × 8″), original cartoons, colour separations

Dates of subject matter 5000 BC to present

Dates of photographs 1970 to present

Subjects Paintings (Old Masters, Impressionist, modern), watercolours, drawings, prints, antiquities, arms and armour, books and manuscripts, carpets and rugs, clocks, watches, scientific instruments, coins, medals, orders, European ceramics, glass, Art Nouveau, Art Deco, sculpture and bronzes, furniture, Islamic, Indian and South-east Asian art, jewellery, musical instruments, mechanical music, oriental ceramics and works of art, silver, *objets de vertu*, icons, Russian art, miniatures, stamps, tribal art, toys and dolls, costume, photographica, sporting material, vintage machines

Access and conditions Open to qualified researchers by appt (tel), Mon-Fri 9–5. Most material available for editorial reproduction and for advertising at the librarian's discretion. Colour material loaned free of charge for three months. Reproduction rights fees charged. Staff will undertake some research; fees charged for large projects. Computer-printed catalogue in preparation.

944 • CLIFTON PARK MUSEUM

Clifton Lane, Rotherham, South Yorkshire
S65 2AA
Tel (0709) 2121 ext 3259, 3519

Enquiries to Dr Catherine Ross, Keeper, Fine and Applied Art

Items About 2000: b/w original and copy photographs, colour photographic prints, glass negatives, lantern slides, postcards, original cartoons, fine art prints, art reproductions, posters, greetings cards, architectural drawings, illustrated books

Dates of subject matter 15th to 20th century

Dates of photographs 19th and 20th century

Fine art 18th to 20th century

Subjects Photographs: Rotherham district life and activities including architecture, railways, industry (pottery, iron and steel, brass, glass), canals, shops, streetscenes, inns, church fittings; objects in the museum collection, especially Rockingham porcelain, Yorkshire pottery; fine art: British 18th- and 19th-century oil paintings, watercolours and prints, especially topography of Rotherham District, South Yorkshire and North Derbyshire; portraits of Rotherham notables (Archbishop Thomas Rotherham, Samuel Walker, Ebenezer Elliott), Yorkshire gentry (Rockingham and Fitzwilliam families); South Yorkshire country houses (Wentworth Woodhouse, Wentworth Castle); South Yorkshire picturesque sights (Conisborough Castle, Roche Abbey); Yorkshire artists; 20th-century prints (wood engravings, etchings, lithographs, *c.* 1930–1950); printed ephemera from Rotherham (bill heads, tickets, etc.); special collections of portraits of the Walker family (*c.* 1760–1860); paintings and prints by William Cowen

Access and conditions Open to the public by appt (tel), Mon-Fri 9–5. All material available for editorial reproduction and for advertising. No loans; b/w prints available for a fee. Material may be copied by outside photographers. Reproduction rights fees charged. Staff will undertake some research.

945 • THOMAS CORAM FOUNDATION FOR CHILDREN

40 Brunswick Square, London WC1N 1AZ
Tel (01) 278 2424

Enquiries to Colin Masters, Director and Secretary

Items About 1500: b/w original and copy photographs, glass negatives, unprinted film negatives, fine art prints, postcards, colour transparencies (35mm)

Dates of subject matter 18th to 20th century

Dates of photographs 1860 to present

Subjects British 18th- and 19th-century painting and sculpture including works by William Hogarth, Thomas Gainsborough, Sir Joshua Reynolds, Allan Ramsay, Thomas Hudson, Louis François Roubiliac, John Michael Rysbrack; buildings of the Foundling Hospital and children living there; present-day buildings

Access and conditions Open to qualified researchers by appt (tel), Mon-Fri 10–4. All material available for editorial reproduction and for advertising use at the discretion of the Director. B/w material loaned free of charge for one month. Reproduction rights fees charged. Staff will undertake very limited research only. Catalogue available; see also Benedict Nicolson, *The Treasures of the Foundling Hospital*, Oxford University Press, 1972.

946 • JOSEPH H. CORDINGLEY

83 Sandy Lane, Romiley, Stockport, Greater Manchester SK6 4NH

Enquiries to Joseph H. Cordingley

Items About 20,000: colour transparencies (35mm)

Dates of subject matter 1400 to 1830

Dates of photographs 1964 to present

Subjects History of architecture and decoration of interiors from 1400 to 1830 throughout Europe, especially the Italian Renaissance to the Baroque including French, Portuguese and Spanish architecture and decoration from 1500 to 1800 (also some examples from Greek and Roman periods); extensive collection of German Baroque and Rococo architecture and decoration in Germany, Austria and especially in Czechoslovakia including rare buildings seldom visited and many details of plasterwork and fresco; United Kingdom (but excluding Northern Ireland) and Eire including country houses, town houses and churches from 1550 to 1830, interior decoration including mural and ceiling painting, plasterwork, church fittings, furniture, monuments and heraldry

Access and conditions Open to qualified researchers by appt (write). Most material available for editorial reproduction and for advertising. Colour transparencies duplicated or rented for a fee. Reproduction rights fees charged.

947 • COURTAULD INSTITUTE OF ART

Witt Library, University of London, 20 Portman Square, London W1H 0BE
Tel (01) 935 9292

Enquiries to Witt Library

Items About 1,400,000: b/w original and copy photographs, glass negatives, cuttings and tearsheets

Dates of subject matter *c.* 1200 to present

Dates of photographs *c.* 1890 to present

Subjects Western Art from 1200 to the present day including paintings, drawings and engravings of the British, French, Italian and Netherlands (includes Flemish, Dutch and Belgian) schools. Material filed by name of artist; no subject access except by classification under each artist's name (i.e., religion, mythological, portrait, landscape, genre, etc.)

Access and conditions Open to the public Mon-Fri 10–7 (term time), 10–6 (vacation). Some material available for editorial reproduction and for advertising. No loans; b/w prints available for a fee subject to copyright clearance. Reproduction rights fees charged. Staff of seven will undertake very limited research in answer to written requests only. Catalogue available: *A Check List of Painters c. 1200–1976 Represented in the Witt Library, Courtauld Institute of Art, London*, Mansell, 1978.

948 • CRAFTS COUNCIL

Photograph Library, 12 Waterloo Place, London SW1Y 4AU
Tel (01) 930 4811

Enquiries to Anne French, Index and Information Officer

Items About 22,000: colour transparencies (35mm), b/w original photographs

Dates of subject matter 1973 to present

Dates of photographs 1973 to present

Subjects Selections from the work of 350 craftspeople on the Council's Index including bookbinding, fashion accessories, glass, lettering, metal, musical instruments, ceramics, textiles including batik, weaving, knitting, quilting, embroidery, patchwork, appliqué, rugs, furniture, jewellery, toys, wood

Access and conditions Open to qualified researchers by appt (tel), Tues-Sat 10–5, Sun 2–5. All material available for editorial reproduction and for advertising with permission of the maker or the Crafts Council. B/w material loaned free of charge for four weeks. Reproduction rights and holding fees charged. Staff will undertake some research. Printed catalogue available.

949 • CUMING MUSEUM

155 Walworth Road, London SE17 1RS
Tel (01) 703 5529, 703 3324

Enquiries to Christopher Green, Conservation Officer

Items 3000: lantern slides, glass negatives, colour transparencies (35mm), daguerreotypes, fine art prints, press cuttings and tearsheets

Dates of subject matter AD 43 to present

Dates of photographs 1845 to 1970

Subjects Local archaeological excavations (1960–1970s); sculpture by George Tinworth (local sculptor, mid-19th to early 20th century); 18th- and 19th-century topographical engravings, advertisements, handbills, valentines, early 19th-century trade cards, panorama keys 1800–1850

Access and conditions Open to the public by appt (tel), Mon-Fri 10–5.30, Thurs 10–7. All material available for editorial reproduction and for advertising. No loans; b/w prints available for a fee. Material may be copied by outside photographers. Photocopies available. Reproduction rights fees charged. Staff will undertake limited research.

950 • THE DESIGN COUNCIL PICTURE LIBRARY

28 Haymarket, London SW1Y 4SU
Tel (01) 839 8000 exts 9, 55

Enquiries to Bridget Kinally, Picture Librarian

Items 60,000: colour transparencies (35mm), b/w original and copy photographs, glass negatives, artwork

Dates of subject matter 19th and 20th century

Dates of photographs *c.* 1940 to present

Subjects Historical and contemporary interiors, furniture and product design including textiles, wallcoverings, tableware, domestic appliances, lighting, clocks, toys, furniture (prototypes, domestic, modern classics), graphics and corporate identity (posters, packaging), interior design (shops, offices, domestic interiors), plastics and antique plastics, town planning and environment, transport (air, road, rail, sea); Design Council Awards (consumer and contract goods, engineering products and components, medical equipment, motor vehicles); exhibitions from The Boilerhouse, Camden Arts Centre, Heal's, Hayward Gallery, Victoria & Albert and RCA, including *Penny-in-the-Slot, Classics of Modern Design, The Thirties, Eileen Grey, Bugatti,* etc.; prints from the films *Britain Can Make It* (1946) and *Festival of Britain* (1951); portraits of designers (UK and overseas); artwork from *Design Magazine* and Design Council books

Access and conditions Open to the public, Mon-Fri 10–5. Some material available for editorial reproduction and for advertising. B/w and colour material loaned free of charge for one month. Photocopies available. Reproduction rights, search and holding fees charged; search fees deductible from use fees. Staff of three will undertake research, time permitting.

951 • DUKE OF NORFOLK'S LIBRARY AND ARCHIVES

Arundel Castle, Sussex BN18 9AB

Enquiries to Dr J. M. Robinson, Librarian to the Duke of Norfolk

Items 1000: b/w original and copy photographs, colour transparencies (35mm, 5″ × 4″, larger), illustrated maps, fine art prints, architectural drawings, illustrated books

Dates of subject matter 1067 to present

Dates of photographs 1850 to present

Subjects Paintings in the Duke of Norfolk's collection (mostly Howard family portraits), architecture of Arundel Castle and the Fitzalan Chapel (mid-19th century to present), photographs of the Howard family 19th and 20th centuries; b/w photographs of the paintings available from the Courtauld Institute

Access and conditions Open to qualified researchers by appt (write), Tues-Wed. All material available for editorial reproduction and for advertising. B/w prints available for a fee. Photocopies available. Reproduction rights fees charged. Staff will undertake limited research.

952 • DULWICH PICTURE GALLERY

College Road, London SE21 7AD
Tel (01) 693 5254

Enquiries to John Sheeran, Keeper

Items About 1100: b/w original and copy photographs, colour transparencies (35mm, 5″ × 4″, larger), colour photographic prints, glass negatives, postcards, greetings cards

Dates of subject matter 17th and 18th century

Subjects 17th- and 18th-century European paintings (Italian, French, Spanish, Dutch, Flemish); 17th- and 18th-century British portraiture (Queen Victoria aged 4 by Stephen Poyntz Denning); Dulwich Gallery, interiors and exteriors, designed by Sir John Soane; works by the following artists: Rembrandt, Rubens, Cuyp, Poussin, Claude, Reni, Guercino, Murillo, Gainsborough, Watteau, Tiepolo, G. Dou, Veronese, Kneller, Teniers, Peter Wouwerman, Reynolds, Piero di Cosimo, Lebrun, Hogarth, Van Dyck, Canaletto, Ludolf Bakhuizen; topographical works by C. Bol, *Westminster and the Thames*, and by Canaletto, *Walton Bridge*

Access and conditions Open to the public; appt necessary to inspect stored material (write), Tues-Fri 10–1, 2–5, closed Mon. All material available for editorial reproduction and for advertising. B/w prints available for a fee; colour transparencies rented for a monthly fee. Reproduction rights fees charged. Staff of two will undertake some research. Printed catalogue available.

953 • DUNDEE ART GALLERIES AND MUSEUMS

McManus Galleries, Albert Square, Dundee,
Tayside DD1 1DA
Tel (0382) 23141

Enquiries to Adam B. Ritchie, Curator

Items About 2000: b/w original and copy
photographs, lantern slides, postcards, fine art
prints

Dates of subject matter 3000 BC to present

Dates of photographs 1860 to 1914

Subjects Fine art collection: 18th- to 20th-
century Scottish painting; 17th- to 20th-century
English and European painting; related prints and
drawings; sculpture; Scottish silver and pottery;
antiquities collection: shipping, ethnography,
archaeology, costume and textiles, militaria,
numismatics; world's oldest complete astrolabe
(1555, Portuguese); local history collection:
shipping, jute industry, jam-making industry

Access and conditions Open to the public by
appt, Mon-Fri 9–5. All material available for
editorial reproduction and for advertising. B/w
prints and colour transparencies loaned or
duplicated for a fee. Photocopies available.
Reproduction rights fees charged. Staff will
undertake limited research.

954 • DURHAM UNIVERSITY ORIENTAL MUSEUM

Elvet Hill, Durham DH1 3TH
Tel (0385) 66711

Enquiries to John Ruffle, Keeper

Items About 7600: b/w original photographs,
unprinted film negatives, lantern slides

Dates of subject matter 3000 BC to present

Dates of photographs 1900 to the present

Subjects Chinese ceramics, stone carvings,
metalwork, lacquer, furniture, costume, coins,
scroll paintings and album leaves; Japanese
metalwork, ivory and bone carving, lacquer, some
ceramics (mostly export), prints; South-east Asian
wood carvings, ethnographical material; Indian
religious and court paintings, religious sculpture
and paraphernalia; Tibetan thangkas and religious
paraphernalia; ancient Near Eastern cylinder and
stamp seals, some archaeological material; ancient
Egyptian antiquities, especially small arts and

craft items and amulets; Islamic ceramics, some
metalwork and calligraphy; Tantric art (600 b/w
negatives from the catalogue of the 1971 Arts
Council *Tantra* exhibition at the Hayward
Gallery); MARSHALL COLLECTION: 4000 b/w prints of
Indian monuments photographed by Sir John
Marshall (1902–1935)

Access and conditions Open to the public by
appt (write), Mon-Fri 9.30–1, 2–5. All material
available for editorial reproduction and for
advertising. B/w and colour material loaned free of
charge for two weeks. B/w prints and duplicate
transparencies available for a fee. Photocopies
available. Reproduction rights, service and holding
fees charged; service fees deductible from use fees.
Staff will undertake very limited research only.

955 • EDINBURGH CITY ART CENTRE

2 Market Street, Edinburgh EH1 1DE
Tel (031) 225 2424 ext 6650

Enquiries to Keeper of Fine Art Collections

Items Over 3000: b/w original and copy
photographs, colour transparencies (35mm,
5″ × 4″), architectural drawings, calotypes

Dates of subject matter Prehistory to present

Dates of photographs Mid-19th century

Dates of fine art *c.* 1700 to present

Subjects Scottish painting, sculpture and prints
from the 18th century to the present with a few
earlier portraits; topographical pictures of the city
of Edinburgh and environs, especially views of
Edinburgh buildings by Bruce James Home (1830–
1920) and Jane Stewart Smith (1839–1925);
calotypes by D. O. Hill and Robert Adamson

Access and conditions Open to the public by
appt (tel), Mon-Fri 10–5. All material available for
editorial reproduction and for advertising. B/w
material not loaned; b/w prints available for a fee.
Colour transparencies loaned for a fee. Photocopies
available. Reproduction rights fees charged. Staff
will undertake limited research. Printed catalogue:
E. S. Cuming, *Catalogue of the City of Edinburgh
Art Collection*, 2 vols, 1979.

956 • ET ARCHIVE

Unit 9, Chelsea Wharf, 15 Lots Road, London
SW10 0QH
Tel (01) 352 9671

Enquiries to Anne-Marie Ehrlich or Eileen Tweedy

Items About 15,000: b/w original photographs, colour transparencies (5″ × 4″, larger)

Dates of subject matter 2000 BC to *c.* AD 1930

Dates of photographs 1860 to present

Subjects History and fine art including archaeology, botany, caricatures, ceramics, Empire and emigrations, exploration, fashion, flower arranging, manuscripts, militaria, military and naval paintings and scenes, oriental paintings and miniatures, paintings (classified by artist), portraits (classified by sitter), posters, sporting paintings and engravings, theatre (designs, paintings, posters), topographical views, zoological illustrations, special collections: history of Australia, Garrick Club, Elek archives

Access and conditions Open to qualified researchers by appt (tel), Mon-Fri 9.30–5.30. All material available for editorial reproduction and for advertising. B/w and colour material loaned free of charge for three months. Photocopies available. Reproduction rights, service and holding fees charged. Staff of two will undertake some research. Printed catalogue available.

957 • FERENS ART GALLERY

Queen Victoria Square, Kingston upon Hull, Humberside HU1 3RA
Tel (0482) 222737

Enquiries to John Bradshaw, Curator

Subjects Old Masters (Italian and Dutch Schools, Canaletto, Giovanni, Maffei, Gheeraerts, Ruisdael, Hals), English 18th- to 20th-century portraits and works by Van Dyck, Hogarth, Van de Velde, Reynolds, Romney, Constable, Raeburn, Landseer, B. R. Haydon; Humberside marine paintings; modern collection including Hockney, Augustus John, Paul Nash, Pasmore, Philpot, Sickert, Spencer, Steer, Vasarely, Riley; prints and watercolours by Cotman, Edward Gordon Craig, Thomas Hennell, Edward Lear, John Nash, Samuel Palmer, John Piper, Eric Ravilious, John Singer Sargent, Philip Wilson Steer

Access and conditions Open to the public by appt, Mon-Fri 10–5. Most material available for editorial reproduction and for advertising. B/w prints and duplicate colour transparencies available for a fee. Photocopies available.

Reproduction rights and service fees charged. Staff will undertake some research. Compulsory credit line.

958 • FINE ART PHOTOGRAPHIC LIBRARY LTD

2A Milner Street, London SW3 2PU
Tel (01) 589 3127 Telex 919101 VITIEL

Enquiries to Linda Hammerbeck

Items 10,000: colour transparencies (5″ × 4″, larger)

Dates of subject matter 100 BC to 1940

Dates of photographs 1975 to present

Subjects 16th- to 20th-century paintings and watercolours (mostly English, unpublished and from little-known or private collections) of animals, flowers, fruit, hunting, sport, shooting, fishing, coaching, religion, mythology, historical events, personalities (fictional and historical), landscape and topography, agriculture, social life, domestic scenes, family life, pastimes, tavern scenes, balls, children, games, gardens, seasons, travel, crafts, fashion, ships and the sea, Christmas, snow scenes, Pre-Raphaelites, piano-playing, singing, sewing, gardening; some work by Victorian painters including Atkinson Grimshaw and Myles Birket-Foster; Dutch painting (16th- to 19th-century) by Pieter Bruegel, David Teniers and others; 19th-century French, Spanish and German painting; 18th- to 19th-century Italian painting (Canaletto, Guardi); 19th-century Scandinavian painting

Access and conditions Open to the public by appt (tel), Mon-Fri 9–6. All material available for editorial reproduction and for advertising. Colour material loaned free of charge for one month. Reproduction rights, service and holding fees charged. Staff of three will undertake some research.

959 • FITZ PARK TRUST

Keswick Museum, Keswick, Cumbria CA12 4NF
Tel (0596) 73263

Enquiries to Norman Gandy, Curator

Items 300: b/w original photographs, fine art prints, architectural drawings, watercolours, manuscripts

Dates of subject matter 17th century to present

Dates of photographs c. 1850 to present

Subjects MANUSCRIPT COLLECTION: manuscripts of the work of some of the Romantic poets including Robert Southey, William Wordsworth, Hartley Coleridge and others; manuscripts by Sir Hugh Walpole including the *Rogue Herries* series; PHOTOGRAPH COLLECTION: Lake District scenery, shepherds, Keswick bandsmen's uniforms; PAINTING COLLECTION: portraits of Sir Hugh Walpole, Robert Southey, groups of local personalities, groups skating, local landscapes, figures, portraits of the Ratcliffe family (Earls of Derwentwater)

Access and conditions Open to the public, Apr 1-Oct 30 Mon-Fri 10–12.30, 2–5.30, Nov-Mar open by appt. All material available for editorial reproduction and for advertising with the Curator's permission. B/w prints and duplicate colour transparencies available for a fee. Photocopies available. Reproduction rights fees charged. Staff will undertake research. Compulsory credit line. Card catalogue.

960 • FITZWILLIAM MUSEUM

Trumpington Street, Cambridge CB2 1RB
Tel (0223) 69501

Enquiries to Melissa Dalziel, Photographic Sales Officer

Items About 25,000: unprinted film negatives, colour transparencies (35mm, 5″ × 4″, larger), glass negatives, original cartoons, illustrated maps, fine art prints, architectural drawings, illustrated books

Dates of subject matter c. 12,000 BC to present

Dates of photographs c. 1950 to present

Subjects Museum collection contains material from prehistoric, Egyptian and classical (Greek and Roman) antiquity, coins and medals, arms and armour, ceramics, glass, metalwork, sculpture, furniture, ivory, musical instruments, clocks and watches, jewellery, oriental decorative arts, bronze, silver and gold, illuminated manuscripts, music, literary and autograph manuscripts; paintings, drawings and prints from Europe, Asia, America, the Orient and Britain, and from all periods

Access and conditions Open to the public, Tues-Sat 10–5, Sun 2.15–5. Most material available for editorial reproduction and for advertising. B/w prints available for a fee; colour transparencies

duplicated or loaned for a rental fee. Reproduction rights fees charged. Staff will undertake limited research in answer to specific requests only and commission new photography if needed.

961 • FOX TALBOT MUSEUM

Lacock, Wiltshire SN15 2LG
Tel (024 973) 459

Enquiries to Robert Lassam, Curator

Items About 500: calotypes, daguerreotypes, lantern slides, art reproductions, unprinted film negatives, stereographs, illustrated books

Dates of subject matter 1835 to present

Dates of photographs 1835 to present

Subjects History of photography including calotypes by Fox Talbot between 1835 and 1856 including portraits, still life, landscapes, architecture and photogenic drawings; photographs representing the development of photographic processes to the present day

Access and conditions Open to qualified researchers by appt (write). All material available for editorial reproduction and for advertising by special arrangement only. No loans; b/w prints available for a fee. Reproduction rights and service fees charged.

962 • THE FRANCIS FRITH COLLECTION

Charlton Road, Andover, Hampshire SP10 3LE
Tel (0264) 53113/4

Enquiries to John Buck

Items 310,000: b/w original photographs, glass negatives, postcards

Dates of photographs 1860 to 1970

Subjects Topographic views of about 4000 towns and villages throughout the British Isles 1860 to 1970 including social history and architecture; general collection including armed forces, blacksmiths and smithies, boating, boats and ships, brewing and breweries, buses, butchers, camping, canals, carriages and carts, cars, castles, characters, children at play, colleges and universities, commercial buildings, crafts, cricket, croquet and bowls, cycles, docks and harbours, domestic chores, fairgrounds and amusement parks, farming, fashion, fishing, golf, groups, harvesting, hospitals, horticulture, horse-riding and hunting, lifeboats and lifeboat men, lighthouses, locomotives and trains, markets, perambulators, homes of famous people, piers, polo, public buildings, racehorse meetings, railways and stations, royalty, schools, sculpture, seaside scenes, seascapes, snowscenes, stage shows and Pierrots, steamships, street furniture, streetscenes, swimming, teatime, tennis, trams, watermills, windmills

Access and conditions Open to qualified researchers by appt, Mon–Sat 9–5. All material available for editorial reproduction and for advertising. B/w prints available for a fee. Photocopies available. Reproduction rights and service fees charged; service fees deductible from use fees. Staff of seven will undertake research. Several printed catalogues available.

963 • GAINSBOROUGH'S HOUSE

Sudbury, Suffolk CO10 6EU
Tel (0787) 72958

Enquiries to Hugh Belsey, Curator

Items Over 2000: colour transparencies (35mm, 5″ × 4″), b/w original photographs, lantern slides, glass negatives

Dates of subject matter 18th century

Dates of photographs 1960 to present

Subjects The paintings of Thomas Gainsborough and his contemporaries including works by Henry William Dunbury, George Frost, Gainsborough Dupont and other artists with Suffolk or East Anglian connections; representative collection of drawings by 18th-century artists including John Hamilton Mortimer, Allan Ramsay and John Flaxman

Access and conditions Open to qualified researchers by appt, 24-hour answerphone. Most material available for editorial reproduction and for advertising. B/w prints and colour transparencies loaned free of charge for one month. Photocopies available. Reproduction rights fees charged at the Curator's discretion; holding fees charged. Staff will undertake some research.

964 • GLASGOW MUSEUMS AND ART GALLERIES

Kelvingrove, Glasgow G3 8AG
Tel (041) 357 3929

Enquiries to Anne Donald, Keeper of Art

Items 8000: b/w original and copy photographs, colour transparencies (35mm, 5″ × 4″, larger), colour photographic prints, postcards, fine art prints, art reproductions, posters, greetings cards

Dates of subject matter 14th century to present

Dates of photographs 20th century

Subjects Old Master paintings by Rembrandt, Giorgione, Rubens, Giovanni Bellini, Tintoretto, Paris Bordone, Palma Giovane, Guardi, Francesco Zuccarelli and others; Flemish and early Netherlandish painting by Bernard Van Orley, Jan van Scorel, Jacob Jordaens, David Teniers the Younger; Dutch painting by Albert Cuyp, Jacob Ruisdael, Philip Wouwerman, Jacob and Willem Maris; German painting by Rottenhammer, Christoph Amberger; French painting by Chardin, Delacroix, Gericault, Millet, Decamps, Meissonier, Michel, Legros, Corot, Barbizon School including Troyon, Daubigny, Diaz, Jacque, Impressionist and Post-Impressionist Schools including Degas, Monet, Boudin, Pisarro, Renoir, Fantin-Latour, Sisley, Cézanne, Van Gogh, Braque, Derain, Dufy, Picasso, Utrillo, Vuillard; British School including 18th-century portraiture by Allan Ramsay and Sir Henry Raeburn and also paintings by Reynolds, Romney, Gainsborough, Hogarth, Constable, Turner, William McTaggart, Horatio McCulloch, Samuel Bough, James McNeill Whistler, Ford Madox Brown, David Roberts, Alma-Tadema, George Henry, Sir David Cameron, Joseph Crawhall, Sir James Guthrie, Augustus John, Wyndham Lewis, Walter Sickert, Graham Sutherland, Ben Nicholson, Stanley Spencer, Duncan Grant, L. S. Lowry, Paul Nash; sculpture by Rodin, Degas, Renoir, Carpeaux, Houdon, Rysbrack, Flaxman, Chantrey, Epstein, Zadkine

Access and conditions Open to the public by appt (write), Mon–Sat 10–5, Sun 2–5. Most material available for editorial reproduction and for advertising. B/w prints available for a fee; colour material loaned for a rental fee. Photocopies available. Reproduction rights and service fees charged. Staff will undertake some research. Printed catalogues available.

965 • GRAVES ART GALLERY

1 Surrey Street, Sheffield S1 1XZ
Tel (0742) 734781

Enquiries to David Alston, Deputy Director

Items About 6500: b/w copy photographs, colour transparencies (35mm)

Dates of subject matter BC to present

Dates of photographs *c*. 1930 to present

Subjects British and European paintings of the 19th and 20th centuries including works by Murillo, Ribera, Cézanne, Corot, Matisse and John Singer Sargent; English watercolours including works by Turner, Girtin and Cotman; 17th to 20th centuries portrait collection; Persian and Indian miniatures, Graeco-Roman sculpture, Islamic pottery; ceramics and tribal masks of Central America and Africa; Aboriginal bark paintings; work of contemporary photographers including Brandt and Brassai. The MAPPIN ART GALLERY is the sister gallery of the Graves and holds mainly British art of 18th to 20th centuries including works by Turner, Constable, Morland, Millais, Landseer, Moore, Caro, Hoyland, Greaves and Jones; photographic sales for this gallery are available *only* through the Graves.

Access and conditions Open to the public by appt (tel). All material available for editorial reproduction and for advertising. Colour material loaned for a fee; b/w prints available for a fee. Photocopies available. Reproduction rights and holding fees charged. Staff will undertake some research. All material copyright. Card catalogue available.

966 • GRAY ART GALLERY AND MUSEUM

Clarence Road, Hartlepool, Cleveland TS24 8BT
Tel (0429) 66522 ext 259

Enquiries to John O. Mennear, Curator

Items 400: b/w original photographs, glass negatives, postcards, fine art prints, art reproductions, posters, architectural drawings

Dates of subject matter 14th century to present

Dates of photographs 1880 to present

Subjects 19th- and early 20th-century British oil painting, 19th-century British watercolours by Hartlepool and other north-eastern artists; decorative arts including ceramics and locally-made pottery; oriental collection including 19th-century netsuke (Japanese), Indian religious objects, Buddhas, Chinese porcelain; ethnography collection including African weapons, medieval tile, pottery, glass and bronze brooches; local history collection, Hartlepool streetscenes, buildings, World War II bomb damage (along with Scarborough, first place to be bombarded)

Access and conditions Open to the public by appt (tel), Mon–Sat 10–5.30. All material available for editorial reproduction and for advertising with the Curator's approval. B/w material loaned free of charge; b/w prints available for a fee. Colour material photographed for a fee. Photocopies available. Reproduction rights and service fees charged. Staff will undertake limited research. Card catalogue available.

967 • HARRIS MUSEUM AND ART GALLERY

Market Place, Preston, Lancashire PR1 2PP
Tel (0772) 58248

Enquiries to Michael Cross, Museum and Arts Officer

Items Over 11,000: b/w original and copy photographs, glass negatives, postcards, greetings cards, fine art prints, lantern slides, stereographs, daguerreotypes, watercolours

Subjects Fine Art Collection: 19th- and 20th-century British oil paintings, watercolours and drawings by J. M. W. Turner, Samuel Palmer, William Holman Hunt, John Frederick Lewis, David Roberts, Spencer Gore, Walter Sickert, Daniel Maclise, John Linnell, Sir Alfred Munnings, Augustus John, Harold Knight, Laura Knight, William Roberts, Sir Stanley Spencer, Lucian Freud; works by Arthur Devis (1712–1787) including miniature portraits, conversation pieces, prints, woodcuts, engravings, caricatures, topography, natural history prints, and Preston and environs in oil paintings, watercolours and prints; works by Anthony Devis (1780–1810) including picturesque watercolours and topography; Photography Collection: local history and survey photographs, Preston docks, town and environs (1860 to 1960)

Access and conditions Open to the public by appt, Mon–Fri 10–5. Most material available for editorial reproduction. B/w prints and duplicate colour transparencies available for a fee. Colour material loaned free of charge for three months. Reproduction rights fees charged. Staff will undertake limited research.

968 • HARROGATE MUSEUMS AND ART GALLERY

Department of Technical Services

Knapping Mount, West Grove Road, Harrogate, North Yorkshire HG2 2AE
Tel (0423) 503340

Enquiries to Patricia Clegg, Curator

Items Over 2000: b/w original photographs, colour transparencies (35mm, 5″ × 4″), glass negatives, daguerreotypes, lantern slides, postcards, original cartoons, illustrated maps, fine art prints, art reproductions, greetings cards, architectural drawings, cartes-de-visite

Dates of subject matter Prehistory to present

Dates of photographs *c.* 1850 to present

Subjects 18th- to 20th-century British painting and prints including many landscapes; large collection of cartes-de-visite, valentines, Christmas cards and postcards; the spa at Harrogate, potteries at Leeds, Castleford, Rockingham and from Yorkshire; HULL GRUNDY COLLECTION: jewellery and European costume jewellery; local archaeology and flint tools; Mediterranean antiquities including Greek pottery, Cretan pottery, Egyptian artefacts, Coptic textiles; ethnographic material including costumes from Romania, India and Jordan

Access and conditions Open to qualified researchers by appt (write), Mon-Sat 10.30–5. Most material available for editorial reproduction and for advertising. B/w material loaned free of charge for one month; colour material loaned for three months for a rental fee. Reproduction rights and holding fees charged. Staff will undertake some research.

969 • HASTINGS MUSEUM AND ART GALLERY

Johns Place, Cambridge Road, Hastings, East Sussex TN34 1ET
Tel (0424) 435952

Enquiries to Victoria Williams, Curator

Items 5000: b/w original and copy photographs, colour transparencies (35mm), glass negatives, lantern slides, original cartoons, illustrated maps, fine art prints, stereographs, posters, architectural drawings, press cuttings and tearsheets

Dates of subject matter Prehistory to present

Dates of photographs 1850 to present

Subjects 18th- and 19th-century British watercolours; 20th-century watercolours by local artists; Japanese prints; cartoons by Harry Furniss; architectural drawings by James and Decimus Burton; photographs by George Woods of local fishing, tourism and agriculture (late 19th century); paintings of Sussex windmills; English and European ceramics including Sussex pottery; Sussex ironwork including firebacks; ethnographic collection with emphasis on the Pacific and Australasia, American Indians; oriental art including Chinese, Japanese, Indian and South-east Asian ceramics, textiles, jewellery

Access and conditions Open to the public by appt, Mon-Fri 10–1, 2–5. Most material available for editorial reproduction and for advertising. B/w prints and duplicate colour transparencies available for a fee. Reproduction rights fees charged. Staff will undertake some research. Card catalogue available.

970 • HERBERT ART GALLERY AND MUSEUM

Jordan Well, Coventry, West Midlands CV1 5RW
Tel (0203) 25555

Social History Section

Enquiries to Jenny Mattingly, Keeper, Social History

Items About 6250: lantern slides, postcards, woven silk pictures (Stevengraphs)

Dates of subject matter *c.* 1850 to 1900

Subjects STEVENGRAPH COLLECTION: local topography, royal weddings, Prime Ministers, sport, hunting scenes, Lady Godiva procession, Royal Jubilee Exhibition (Manchester, 1887), silk postcards, bookmarks and favours; 19th-century b/w and colour lantern slides of Japan; domestic machinery and equipment, civic life, law and order; costume (1800 to present); silk-ribbon weaving, Coventry ribbons and sample books; watch-making (equipment and products), reconstruction of watch-making shops

Access and conditions Open to the public by appt (tel), Mon-Fri 8.30–5 (Fri 4.30). Some material available for editorial reproduction and for advertising. B/w prints and duplicate colour transparencies available for a fee. All material can be photographed. Reproduction rights and service fees charged. Staff will undertake some research.

Visual Arts Section

Enquiries to Patrick Day, Keeper, Visual Arts

Dates of subject matter 1586 to present

Subjects Topography of Coventry and Warwickshire (prints, drawings, watercolours) *c.* 1700 to 1980; British landscapes, mainly watercolours, *c.* 1780 to 1980 by J. M. W. Turner, John Varley, David Cox, Thomas Baker; British figure drawings (very good collection) *c.* 1870 to 1980; Graham Sutherland's sketches and studies for the Coventry Cathedral tapestry; modern British painting (1900–1980) including works by Robert Bevan, Paul Nash, Ben Nicholson, Matthew Smith (pre-1950); contemporary art (*c.* 1950–1980) including works by L. S. Lowry, Carel Weight, Derek Southall; civic portraits; sculpture and ceramics

Access and conditions Open to the public by appt (write), Mon-Sat 10.30–5.30. All material available for editorial reproduction but not for advertising. B/w and colour material loaned free of charge for four weeks. B/w prints and duplicate colour transparencies available for a fee. Reproduction rights and service fees charged. Staff will undertake research.

Natural History Section

Enquiries to Adam Wright, Keeper, Natural History

Dates of subject matter Early 20th century

Subjects 250 paintings of British wildflowers and fungi by Angela Brazil

Access and conditions Open to the public by appt (write), Mon-Sat 10.30–5.30. All material available for editorial reproduction and for advertising.

971 • THE CECIL HIGGINS ART GALLERY

Castle Close, Bedford MK40 3NY
Tel (0234) 211222

Enquiries to Halina Grubert, Curator

Items About 6000: b/w original and copy photographs, colour transparencies (35mm, 5″ × 4″, larger), colour photographic prints, greetings cards, architectural drawings, daguerreotypes, postcards, press cuttings and tearsheets

Dates of subject matter *c.* 800 BC to present

Dates of photographs *c.* 1850 to present

Subjects 17th- to 20th-century British and European paintings, drawings and prints; English watercolours (*c.* 1760 to 1840); 18th- to 20th-century British and European ceramics, especially 18th-century Chelsea and Meissen figures; 17th- and 18th-century British and European glass, especially Queen Anne glass, and a few Roman and Ancient Egyptian pieces; 17th- to 20th-century British furniture (a few European and American pieces) especially late 19th-century including pieces by William Burges; 17th- to 19th-century English miniatures; 17th- to 20th-century English costume and accessories, especially 19th-century; 18th- to 20th-century English and European sculpture; 18th- and 19th-century English silver, silver-gilt and Sheffield plate; 18th- and 19th-century English pewter; 19th-century English metalwork by William Burges, W.A.S. Benson, John Paul Cooper and others; 18th-century European silver; 19th-century Bedfordshire Maltese pillow lace; 17th- to 20th-century English curtains, samplers and needlework; 19th-century English valentines; 19th-century English jewellery; toys, *objets d'art*, carpets and rugs, European and other lace; Gallery activities from 1976 to the present

Access and conditions Open to the public by appt (tel), Tues-Fri 12.30–5, Sat 11–5, Sun 2–5. All material available for editorial reproduction but not for advertising. B/w material not loaned; b/w prints available for a fee. Colour material loaned for a rental fee; duplicate colour transparencies available for a fee. Reproduction rights and holding fees charged. Staff of four will undertake some research. Card catalogue available.

972 • HISTORIC CHURCHES PRESERVATION TRUST

Fulham Palace, London SW6 6EA
Tel (01) 736 3054

Enquiries to P. Fraser

Items About 10,000: b/w original photographs, colour photographic prints, lantern slides

Dates of subject matter Saxon times to 1884

Dates of photographs 1953 to present

Subjects Churches (no cathedrals) in England (not Scotland and Wales), mostly country parish churches; some 19th-century town churches

Access and conditions Open to qualified researchers by appt (write), Mon-Fri 9–5.30. All material available for editorial reproduction but not for advertising. B/w material loaned free of charge for one month; colour material rented for a fee. Reproduction rights charged at the discretion of the copyright holder; holding fees charged. Staff will undertake limited research.

973 • MICHAEL HOLFORD PHOTOGRAPHS

119 Queens Road, Loughton, Essex IG10 1RR
Tel (01) 508 4358

Enquiries to Michael Holford

Items 30,000: colour transparencies (5″ × 4″), b/w original photographs

Dates of subject matter Prehistory to present

Dates of photographs 1960 to present

Subjects Art history including architecture, textiles, ceramics, sculpture, coins, maps, prints, paintings, history of science, manuscripts, ethnography, Greek vase painting, Bayeux tapestry, navigational instruments, jewellery and prehistoric tools and including material from the following cultures: Sumerian, Babylonian, Assyrian, Egyptian, Greek, Roman, Chinese, Indian, Japanese, Russian, pre-Colombian (Central and South America), Polynesian, Melanesian, Viking, Anglo-Saxon and also material from medieval and 15th- to 19th-century Europe

Access and conditions Open to qualified researchers by appt (tel), Mon-Fri 9–5.30. All material available for editorial reproduction but most not for advertising. B/w and colour material loaned free of charge. Reproduction rights fees charged. Staff will undertake research.

974 • ANGELO HORNAK LIBRARY

17 Alwyne Villas, London N1 2HG
Tel (01) 354 1790

Enquiries to Angelo Hornak

Items About 5000: colour transparencies (5″ × 4″)

Dates of subject matter 6000 BC to present

Dates of photographs 1973 to present

Subjects History of architecture in the United Kingdom, France, Italy, Germany, Austria, Eire, USA, Lebanon, Syria, Egypt, India; antiques and museum subjects (furniture, ceramics, metalwork, glass, textiles, etc.) from museums and private collections; botanical engravings and illustrations; material from the National Museum, New Delhi, India

Access and conditions Open to the public by appt (tel), Mon-Fri 9–6. All material available for editorial reproduction and for advertising. Colour material loaned free of charge for one month. Reproduction rights and holding fees charged. Staff will undertake research.

975 • HOVE MUSEUM AND ART GALLERY

19 New Church Road, Hove, Sussex BN3 4AB
Tel (0273) 779410

Enquiries to John Boyden

Items 500: b/w original photographs, colour transparencies (5″ × 4″), colour photographic prints, daguerreotypes

Dates of subject matter 18th century to present

Dates of photographs 1978 to present

Subjects 20th-century British landscapes, portraits and figure studies in oil, watercolour and pencil by Duncan Grant, Gwen John, Stanley Spencer, Patrick Procktor; 18th- and early 19th-century British and European portraits and landscapes including a landscape by Gainsborough and some Sussex landscapes; Brighton and Hove (18th to 20th centuries) watercolours and Regency prints

Access and conditions Open to the public, Tues-Fri 10–5, Sat 10–4.30. Some material available for editorial reproduction and for advertising. B/w and colour material loaned free of charge for two months. Material may be copied by outside photographers. Reproduction rights fees charged.

976 • THE HOWARTH-LOOMES COLLECTION

London
Tel (01) 445 3297

Enquiries to B. E. C. Howarth-Loomes

Items About 25,000: b/w copy photographs, colour transparencies (35mm), daguerreotypes, postcards, original cartoons, stereographs, posters, illustrated books, ambrotypes, tintypes, cartes-de-visite, photographs on ceramics, early colour photographs

Dates of photographs 1840 to 1918

Subjects History of photography with emphasis on general and commercial photography of the 19th century including portraits, landscapes, streetscenes, architecture, travel scenes, social documentation; 19th-century photographic display materials including cases, decorative albums, stereoscopes and other viewing devices, photographic jewellery and photographic novelties; photographic ephemera including bills, receipts, catalogues, advertisements and instructions; work by Julia Margaret Cameron, Antoine Claudet, Roger Fenton, Peter Henry Emerson, and others

Access and conditions Not open; tel requests only, Mon-Fri 9.30–7. All material available for editorial reproduction and for advertising. No loans; b/w prints and duplicate colour transparencies available for a fee. Reproduction rights fees charged. Staff will undertake limited research.

977 • HPR PUBLICITY

9 Fitzroy Square, London W1P 6AE
Tel (01) 380 0517 Telex 28221

Enquiries to Gwyn Headley

Items About 3000: b/w original and copy photographs, colour transparencies (35mm, $5'' \times 4''$), colour photographic prints, postcards, fine art prints, unprinted film negatives, posters, architectural drawings, press cuttings and tearsheets, illustrated books

Dates of subject matter 1550 to present

Dates of photographs 1952 to present

Subjects Architectural follies (about 1100) organized by county and including Ralph Allen's Sham Castle, the Monkey Island Follies, Hop Castle, Ringo's Folly, the Newby Demesne Gazebos, Lady Anne Clifford's Follies, the Fingringhoe Hall Bear Pit, the Rokeby Cave and Urn, Jackdaw's Castle, The Chapel in the Woods, the Siamese Garage, St Antholin's Spire, the Kirk House Gothic Pigsty, the Parbold Bottle, the Royal Follies at Osborne, the Scarborough Pagoda, the Haugh Head Dovecote, the Biddulph Grange Chinese Garden, the Tattingstone Wonder, etc.

Access and conditions Open to qualified researchers by appt daily. All material available for editorial reproduction and for advertising. B/w and colour material loaned free of charge for three months. Photocopies available. Reproduction rights and holding fees charged. Staff will undertake research; negotiable research fee for long projects.

978 • IPSWICH MUSEUM AND GALLERIES

Department of Recreation and Amenities

Civic Centre, Civic Drive, Ipswich, Suffolk
IP1 3QH
Tel (0473) 213761

Enquiries to Chris Kitchener, Registrar

Items About 10,500: b/w original photographs, fine art prints, lantern slides, architectural drawings, postcards, glass negatives, illustrated maps, original cartoons, stereographs, posters, greetings cards, watercolours, ephemera

Dates of subject matter Pre-Cambrian to present

Dates of photographs c. 1870 to present

Subjects Suffolk County topography, architecture, measured drawings, church restorations, tomb monuments, portraits, landscapes, events; paintings of the East Anglian school by Gainsborough, Constable, Thomas Churchyard, John Moore, Edward Robert and Thomas Smythe, George Frost, Robert Burrows, Samuel Read, Henry Bright; Dutch paintings; modern works by local artists; modern prints by Picasso, Matisse, Chagall, Moore; portraits of local people; cartoons of early and mid-19th-century local politics; posters of Ipswich entertainments and politics in the 19th century; Christmas and valentine cards; photographs of Africa and Tibet by Fenwick Owen, and of Salao in Malaya

Access and conditions Open to the public by appt (tel), Mon-Sat 10–5. All material available for editorial reproduction and for advertising. No loans; b/w prints and duplicate colour transparencies available for a fee. Photocopies available. Reproduction rights fees charged. Staff will undertake limited research. Card and printed catalogues.

979 • KEELE UNIVERSITY

Keele, Staffordshire ST5 5BG
Tel (0782) 621111 ext 489

Enquiries to Registrar

Items About 500: b/w original photographs, colour photographic prints, illustrated maps, fine art prints, art reproductions, posters, illustrated books

Dates of subject matter 17th century to present

Dates of photographs Contemporary

Subjects SNEYD COLLECTION: drawings and watercolours by the Sneyd family (18th and 19th centuries); AIR PHOTOGRAPH COLLECTION: covers most of UK; DUKE OF NEWCASTLE'S BEQUEST; BARNETT-STROSS COLLECTION: landscapes by Gaspar Dughet, Alstan Emery, Leslie Gilbert, F. J. Errill, F. England, L. S. Lowry, Rowley Smart; prints by E. Ardizzone, M. Ayrton, J. Trevelyan; figures by Jiri Borsky, Augustus John; sculpture by Barbara Hepworth, Henry Moore; ceramics

Access and conditions Open to the public by appt (tel). Most material available for editorial reproduction but not for advertising. B/w prints and duplicate colour transparencies available for a fee. Reproduction rights fees charged.

980 • KIRKLEES LIBRARY AND ART GALLERY

Alexandra Walk, Huddersfield, West Yorkshire HD1 2SU
Tel (0484) 513808

Enquiries to Robert Hall, Curator

Items About 10,000: b/w original photographs, colour transparencies (5″ × 4″), fine art prints, original cartoons

Dates of subject matter 18th century to present

Subjects British 20th-century painting including works by Francis Bacon, L. S. Lowry; Harold Gilman and others of the Camden Town Group; 19th-century Japanese prints; British 18th- and 19th-century watercolours; some British sculpture, drawing and prints

Access and conditions Open to the public by appt (tel), Mon-Fri 10–6, Sat 10–4. All material available for editorial reproduction and for advertising. B/w prints and duplicate colour transparencies available for a fee. Photocopies available. Reproduction rights fees charged. Staff will undertake some research.

981 • LEEDS CITY ART GALLERIES

City Art Gallery, Temple Newsam House, Lotherton Hall

Municipal Buildings, The Headrow, Leeds, West Yorkshire LS1 3AA
Tel (0532) 462495

Enquiries to Alex Robertson, Senior Assistant Keeper

Items About 3500: colour transparencies (35mm, 5″ × 4″, 10″ × 8″), b/w original photographs

Dates of subject matter 1600 to present

Dates of photographs 1975 to present

Subjects Old Master paintings, especially 17th-century Dutch and Italian baroque; 18th-century English painting; Victorian painting; strong collection of 20th-century British painting and sculpture, especially work by Henry Moore; English prints and watercolours from the 16th to 20th centuries; Temple Newsam House and Lotherton Hall collections include furniture, silver (Doncaster Race Cups), ceramics especially Leeds ware; costume collection including modern fashions; important collection of Chinese ceramics

Access and conditions Open to the public by appt, Mon-Fri, 10–5. Some material available for editorial reproduction and for advertising use at the Keeper's discretion. B/w prints and duplicate colour transparencies available for a fee. Photocopies available. Reproduction rights fees charged. Staff will undertake some research. Printed catalogue.

982 • LEEDS CIVIC TRUST

Claremont, 23 Clarendon Road, Leeds, West Yorkshire LS2 9NZ
Tel (0532) 439594

Enquiries to Parry Thornton, Secretary

Items About 1400: b/w original and copy photographs, glass negatives, press cuttings and tearsheets

Dates of subject matter 18th century to present

Dates of photographs c. 1890 to 1980

Subjects Leeds, especially architecture of the central city and of buildings now demolished or damaged, some suburban areas and people; FRANKS COLLECTION: late 19th- and early 20th-century Leeds; suburban area of Bramley just before demolition in the 1960s

Access and conditions Open to qualified researchers by appt (tel), Mon-Fri 9–30–1. All material available for editorial reproduction but not for advertising. B/w prints available for a fee. Photocopies available. Reproduction rights fees charged. Staff will undertake some research; fee charged for long projects.

983 • LEIGHTON HOUSE MUSEUM

12 Holland Park Road, London W14 8LZ
Tel (01) 602 3316

Enquiries to Stephen Jones, Curator

Items 1083: b/w original and copy photographs, colour photographic prints, colour transparencies (35mm, 5″ × 4″), glass negatives, postcards

Dates of subject matter 1845 to 1940

Dates of photographs 19th century to present

Subjects Oil paintings, drawings and sculpture by Frederic Leighton, Baron Leighton; works by other 19th-century artists including Eleanor Fortescu Brickdale, Edward Burne-Jones, John Wiston Byam Shaw, Louis Grimshaw, Solomon J. Solomon, George Frederick Watts; sculpture by Hamo Thornycroft; photographic record of Leighton's works not in the museum collection; photographs by Julia Margaret Cameron

Access and conditions Open to the public by appt (tel), Mon-Sat 11–5. All material available for editorial reproduction but not for advertising. B/w prints available for a fee; colour transparencies loaned for a rental fee. Photocopies available. Reproduction rights and service fees charged. Staff will undertake some research.

984 • LILLIE ART GALLERY

Station Road, Milngavie, Glasgow Strathclyde
G62 8AQ
Tel (041) 956 2351 ext 46

Enquiries to Elizabeth M. Dent, Curator

Items 200: colour transparencies (35mm, 5″ × 4″), b/w original photographs, fine art prints, posters

Dates of subject matter 1880 to present

Subjects 20th-century Scottish painting including work by members of the Glasgow School and the Scottish Colourists

Access and conditions Open to the public by appt, Tues-Fri 11–5, Sat & Sun 2–5, closed Mon. Some material available for editorial reproduction and for advertising. B/w material loaned free of charge for three months. Reproduction rights fees charged. Staff will undertake research. Card catalogue.

985 • LIVERPOOL CITY LIBRARIES

William Brown Street, Liverpool L3 8EW
Tel (051) 207 2147

Reference Library

Enquiries to Reference Librarian

Items About 200: b/w original photographs

Subjects History of photography including photographs by Julia Margaret Cameron, Roger Fenton and Walter Frith

Access and conditions Open to the public by appt (tel), Mon-Fri 9–9. Most material available for editorial reproduction and for advertising. B/w prints available for a fee. Photocopies available. Reproduction rights fees charged. Staff will undertake some research.

Hornby Library

Enquiries to Librarian

Items Over 8000: fine art prints, illustrated books

Dates of subject matter Prehistory to present

Dates of fine art 15th century to present

Subjects Engravings, etchings, mezzotints, etc.; engraved portraits (pre-1850); castles and stately homes (pre-1850)

Access and conditions Open to the public by appt (tel), Mon-Fri 9–9. Some material available for editorial reproduction and for advertising. B/w prints available for a fee. Reproduction rights fees charged. Staff will undertake limited research.

986 • LONGLEAT HOUSE

Warminster, Wiltshire BA12 7NN
Tel (09853) 551

Enquiries to Jane Fowles, Librarian and Archivist

Items About 450: b/w original photographs, colour

transparencies (35mm, 5″ × 4″), colour photographic prints, lantern slides, postcards, original cartoons, illustrated maps, fine art prints, greetings cards, architectural drawings, illustrated books

Dates of subject matter c. 1500 to 1960

Dates of photographs 1950 to present

Subjects English portraits (16th to 20th centuries); Dutch landscapes (16th and 17th centuries); series of hunting scenes by John Wootton (18th century); religious scenes by Bassano, Credi, Lotto, Johann Rottenhammer, Titian and others; views of Longleat and its surroundings by Siberechts, Robert Thacker and others (17th to 19th centuries); cartoons of nursery rhymes by Richard Doyle (19th century); drawings by Ernest Shepard, Kate Greenaway and others; landscapes

Access and conditions Open to the public by appt (write), Easter-Oct daily 10–6, Oct-Easter daily 10–4. All material available for editorial reproduction and for advertising. B/w prints available for a fee; colour transparencies loaned for a rental fee. Reproduction rights fees payable in advance. Marquess of Bath retains copyright. Staff will undertake research; nominal fee for long projects.

987 • LORDS GALLERY

26 Wellington Road, London NW8 9SP
Tel (01) 722 4444

Enquiries to Philip Granville

Items About 3500: posters, colour transparencies (35mm), colour photographic prints, b/w original photographs, fine art prints

Dates of subject matter 1866 to present

Dates of photographs 1960 to present

Subjects Posters (1866 to present) from Europe, USA, USSR, China and the Far East, French Colonies, British Empire, and including Art Nouveau, Art Deco, World Wars I and II and political and social events of the last 100 years: entertainment and entertainers, dance, circuses, music hall, theatre, opera, sports; literature and writers, magazines, newspapers, books, history; products, cosmetics, drinks, food, clothes, shoes, lighting, etc.; social questions, abortion, drug addiction, education, health, hygiene, religion, the occult, politics (anti-Semitism, Fascism, communism, Labour Party, Conservative Party,

Women's Lib, road safety); travel, aviation, boats, cars, cycles, railways and space and by the following artists: Henri de Toulouse-Lautrec, Jules Cheret, Adolphe Mouron Cassandre, Alphonse Mucha, Paul Colin, Charles Kiffer, Ludwig Hohlwein, Kolo Moser, Wassily Kandinsky, Ashley (Havinden), Will H. Bradley, McKnight Kauffer, Vladimir Mayakovsky, Kurruniks, and others; paintings and prints by Friedrich Meckseper, prints by Martin Cornelius Escher, paintings and watercolours by Henry Simpson, sculpture by Medardo Rosso

Access and conditions Open to the public by appt (tel), Mon-Fri 10–6. All material available for editorial reproduction and for advertising. B/w prints and duplicate colour transparencies available for a fee. Reproduction rights fees charged. Staff will undertake research; fee charged for long projects.

988 • LUTON MUSEUM AND ART GALLERY

Wardown Park, Luton, Bedfordshire LU2 7HA
Tel (0582) 36941/2

Enquiries to Frank Hackett, Curator

Items About 10,000: b/w original and copy photographs, colour transparencies (35mm), glass negatives, daguerreotypes, lantern slides, postcards, illustrated maps, fine art prints, art reproductions, stereographs, posters, greetings cards, architectural drawings, illustrated books

Dates of subject matter 1700 to present

Dates of photographs 1860 to present

Subjects Photographs and prints: local topography and social history, trades, crafts, industry; photographs by Julia Margaret Cameron and by local photographer Frederick Thurston; paintings: watercolours and oil paintings of local topography including works by Henry Sylvester Stannard, Thomas Fisher, Theodore Kern, Amy Katherine Browning, Thomas Cantrell Dugdale, Edward Callam, T. Hennell, Samuel Lucas, Sutton Palmer, Carlton A. Smith, George Shephard; museum collection: straw marquetry, 19th-century children's books, scrap albums, fashion plates (especially hats), Pyne's *Microcosm*; illuminated manuscripts: register of the Luton Guild of the Holy Trinity (1474–1547) and register of the fraternity of St John the Baptist (1442–1547)

Access and conditions Open to qualified

researchers by appt (tel), Mon Wed-Fri 10–5. Most material available for editorial reproduction and for advertising. No loans; b/w prints and duplicate colour transparencies available for a fee. Photocopies available. Reproduction rights and service fees charged.

989 • MANCHESTER CITY ART GALLERIES

Mosley Street, Manchester M2 3JL
Tel (061) 236 9422

Enquiries to Julian Spaulding, Director

Items About 12,000: b/w original and copy photographs, colour transparencies (35mm, 5″ × 4″, larger), colour photographic prints, glass negatives, daguerreotypes, lantern slides, postcards, original cartoons, illustrated maps, fine art prints, art reproductions, posters, greetings cards, architectural drawings, press cuttings and tearsheets, illustrated books

Dates of subject matter 3000 BC to present

Dates of photographs 1845 to 1980

Subjects Fine art: British painting, especially of the 18th and 19th centuries, including works by George Stubbs, Thomas Gainsborough, Sir Joshua Reynolds, James Barry, William Etty and others; famous PRE-RAPHAELITE COLLECTION, including works by Ford Madox Brown, Edward Burne-Jones, William Holman Hunt, John Everett Millais; High Victorian art including works by George Frederick Watts, James Leader, Frederic Leighton, Baron Leighton, Briton Rivière, Sir Lawrence Alma Tadema, William Powell Frith, Herkomer, Daniel Maclise; CHARLES RUTHERSTON COLLECTION of late 19th- and early 20th-century British art including works by Charles Augustus John, Henry Lamb, Walter Sickert, Philip Wilson Steer; foreign painting and sculpture including works by Francesco Guardi, Pompeo Batoni, Bernardo Bellotto, Antonio Canaletto, Algardi; ASSHETON-BENNETT COLLECTION of 17th-century Dutch paintings; decorative arts: 18th-century English silver, Greg Collection of English earthenware, Royal Lancastrian pottery, important collection of English costume 17th century to the present especially 18th-century brocaded and embroidered garments; photograph collection includes Victorian and Edwardian local scenes and views, cartes-de-visite and cabinet portraits of people in the costume collection

Access and conditions Open to the public by appt (tel), Mon-Sat 10–6. Most material available for editorial reproduction but not for advertising. B/w prints available for a fee; colour transparencies loaned for a rental fee. Reproduction rights and service fees charged. Staff will undertake limited research. Catalogues of paintings and watercolours available.

990 • McLEAN MUSEUM AND ART GALLERY

9 Union Street, Greenock, Strathclyde PA16 8JH
Tel (0475) 23741

Enquiries to Valerie Boa, Curator

Items About 10,000: b/w original photographs, posters, lantern slides, postcards, unprinted film negatives, old fine art prints, illustrated books, b/w copy photographs, colour transparencies (35mm), glass negatives, daguerreotypes, illustrated maps, architectural drawings, press cuttings, oil paintings, drawings and watercolours

Dates of subject matter Prehistory to present

Dates of photographs 1850 to 1930s

Subjects Photographs of Western Scotland, landscapes and steamships especially paddlesteamers; poster collection of World War I propaganda, mainly UK but also including material from USA, Australia and Greece; CAIRD COLLECTION of paintings, prints and drawings by mainly Scottish artists; museum collection includes ethnography (particularly Oceanic), Egyptology, ship models, natural history, geology, technology, decorative arts

Access and conditions Open to the public by appt (tel), Mon-Sat 10–5. All material available for editorial reproduction; advertising use by special arrangement only. No loans; b/w prints and duplicate colour transparencies available for a fee; material may be copied by outside photographers. Photocopies and Polaroids available. No reproduction rights fees charged. Staff will undertake limited research. Compulsory credit line. Some material copyright. Card catalogue available; printed catalogue for Caird collection: Ian Phillips and William Armour, *The Caird Collection Catalogue*, 1972.

991 • MICHELHAM PRIORY

SUSSEX ARCHAEOLOGICAL SOCIETY

Upper Dicker, Hailsham, East Sussex BN27 3QS
Tel (0323) 844224

Enquiries to G. W. R. Harrison, Honorary
Curator

Items 450: unprinted film negatives, old fine art
prints, drawings, watercolours, engravings

Dates of subject matter 1100 to present

Dates of photographs 1740 to present

Subjects SHARPE COLLECTION of watercolour
drawings of Sussex churches between 1797 and
1809 by Henry Petrie including some interiors and
architectural details; watercolours, drawings,
prints of Sussex landscapes and buildings from
1740

Access and conditions Open to the public by
appt (write). All material available for editorial
reproduction and for advertising by special
arrangement only. No loans; b/w prints and
duplicate colour transparencies available for a fee.
Photocopies available. Reproduction rights and
service fees charged; service fees deductible from
use fees. Some material copyright. Printed
catalogue to Sharpe collection available.

992 • LEE MILLER ARCHIVES

Burgh Hill House, Chiddingly, Nr Lewes, East
Sussex BN8 6JF
Tel (0825) 872691

Enquiries to Suzanna Penrose

Items About 45,000: unprinted film negatives, b/w
original and copy photographs, colour
transparencies (35mm, 5″ × 4″), fine art prints,
press cuttings, illustrated books

Dates of photographs 1907 to present

Subjects Photographs by Lee Miller including her
work in Egypt, Syria and the Lebanon (1936–
1939), fashion photographs in Paris and New York
early 1930s, London 1940–1949, Paris 1944; World
War II London blitz (1940–1941), France (siege of
St Malo, liberation of Paris), Russian-American
link-up at Torgau, Brussels, Loire River bridges,
fighting in Alsace and Luxembourg, Cologne,
Leipzig, Ludwigshaven; Munich, Dachau and
Buchenwald concentration camps, Berchtesgaden
in flames; post-armistice in Vienna, Salzburg,
Denmark, Hungary (including many folk
costumes), Romania; 20th-century artists
including Pablo Picasso, Joan Miro, Max Ernst,
Paul Eluard, Paul Delvaux, René Magritte, Jean
Cocteau, Christian Berard, Man Ray, Henry
Moore, Antonio Tapies, Eileen Agar, Leonora
Carrington, Dorothea Tanning, Roland Penrose;
portraits and photographs of Lee Miller by Edward
Steichen, Arnold Genthe, Nickolas Muray (New
York, 1925)

Access and conditions Open to qualified
researchers by appt (write), Mon-Fri 9.30–4. All
material available for editorial reproduction but
not for advertising or political purposes. B/w and
colour material loaned free of charge for four
weeks. Photocopies available. Reproduction rights,
service and holding fees charged. Staff will
undertake some research. Card catalogue;
computer index in preparation.

993 • WILLIAM MORRIS GALLERY

Water House, Lloyd Park, Forest Road, London
E17 4PP
Tel (01) 527 5544 ext 4390

Enquiries to Peter Cormack, Deputy Keeper

Items About 4000: b/w copy photographs, old fine
art prints, glass negatives, b/w original
photographs, illustrated books, architectural
drawings, designs, cartoons

Dates of subject matter 1850 to present

Dates of photographs 1860 to present

Subjects Designs for printed and woven textiles,
ceramics, stained glass, carpets and rugs, mural
decoration by William Morris, Sir Edward Burne-
Jones, Dante Gabriel Rossetti, Ford Madox Brown,
Philip Webb, May Morris, J. H. Dearle; designs for
architecture and the applied arts by Arthur
Mackmurdo and the Century Guild, Herbert Horne
and Selwyn Image; designs for stained glass by
Christopher Whall; printed books by Williams
Morris including the Kelmscott Press, Walter
Crane and the Century Guild's *Hobby Horse*
magazine; photographs of William Morris and
family and friends including Arthur Mackmurdo,
Selwyn Image and Sir Frank Brangwyn

Access and conditions Open to the public by
appt (write), Tues-Sat 10–5. All material available
for editorial reproduction; advertising use by
special arrangement only. No loans; b/w prints and
duplicate colour transparencies available for a fee;
material may be copied by outside photographers.

Photocopies available. Reproduction rights and access fees for special photography charged. Staff will undertake some research. Compulsory credit line. All material copyright.

994 • NATIONAL GALLERIES OF SCOTLAND

COMPRISING NATIONAL GALLERY OF SCOTLAND, SCOTTISH NATIONAL PORTRAIT GALLERY, SCOTTISH NATIONAL GALLERY OF MODERN ART

All enquiries relating to reproduction-quality material must be made to the Publications Department, National Galleries of Scotland, The Mound, Edinburgh EH2 2EL Tel (031) 556 8921 Research enquiries should be addressed to individual Keepers in charge of collections.

National Gallery of Scotland

The Mound, Edinburgh EH2 2EL Tel (031) 556 8921

Enquiries to Keeper

Items About 10,000: fine art

Dates of subject matter *c.* 1400 to 1900

Subjects European painting from 15th century including works by Titian, Canaletto, Poussin, Watteau, Delacroix, Monet, Renoir, Degas, Cézanne, Van Gogh, Gauguin; important collection of Dutch paintings including works by Rembrandt, Vermeer, Hobbema, Jan Steen, Avercamp, Van Dyck and Rubens; English artists include Bonington, Constable, Cotman, Hogarth, Gainsborough, Reynolds, Romney, Turner; Scottish artists include Sir Henry Raeburn, Andrew Geddes, William Dyce, William McTaggart

Department of Prints and Drawings

Items About 19,000: prints and drawings

Dates of subject matter *c.* 1500 to 1900

Subjects Old Master drawings and prints including work by Italian, German, French, Spanish, English and Scottish artists

Access and conditions Gallery open to the public Mon-Sat 10–5, Sun 2–5. For other conditions see below.

Scottish National Portrait Gallery

Queen Street, Edinburgh EH2 1JD Tel (031) 556 8921

Enquiries to Keeper

Items About 20,000: fine art and engravings

Dates of subject matter *c.* 1500 to present

Subjects Portraits of influential people from Scotland's history including royalty, statesmen, political figures, artists, writers, scientists

Photographic Collections

Enquiries to Sara Stevenson, Keeper

Items 10,000: b/w original photographs

Dates of subject matter 1843 to present

Dates of photographs 1843 to present

Subjects Photography as an art form including work by Hill and Adamson, Thomas Rodger, Thomas Keith, James Craig Annan, William Carrick

Reference Section

Enquiries to Dr Rosalind Marshall

Items 20,000: b/w copy photographs

Dates of subject matter *c.* 1500 to present

Dates of photographs Contemporary

Subjects Photographs of portraits of individuals in both private and public collections in Scotland (some English coverage) – important reference source for tracing Scottish portraits; reference material including photographs and biographical details relating to Scottish artists

Access and conditions Open to the public by appt (tel), Mon-Fri 10–5. Gallery open to the public, Mon-Sat 9–5, Sun 2–5. For other conditions see below.

Scottish National Gallery of Modern Art

Belford Road, Edinburgh EH4 3DR Tel (031) 556 8921

Enquiries to Keeper

Items About 3000: fine art, graphic art, sculpture

Dates of subject matter Early 20th century to present

Subjects 20th-century painting, sculpture and graphic art including work by major British,

European and American artists; artists represented include Matisse, Picasso, Utrillo, Magritte, Max Ernst, Klee, de Stael, Wilson Steer, Sickert, Paul Nash, Ben Nicholson, S. J. Peploe, Leslie Hunter, John Maxwell, Joan Eardley

Access and conditions Open to the public, Mon-Sat 10–6, Sun 2–6.

Access and conditions for all collections All material available for editorial reproduction and for advertising. Colour transparencies loaned for a fee; b/w prints available for a fee; material may be copied by outside photographers by arrangement. Reproduction rights fees charged.

995 • NATIONAL PORTRAIT GALLERY

15 Carlton House Terrace, London SW1Y 5AH
Tel (01) 930 1552

Enquiries to Research Assistant

Library and Archive

Items Over two million: b/w copy photographs, original cartoons, old fine art prints, 20th-century fine art prints, art reproductions, press cuttings, illustrated books, woodcuts, engravings, magazines, catalogues

Dates of subject matter 16th century to present

Dates of photographs 1840s to present

Subjects Portraits of eminent Britons including military, royal, political, religious and artistic figures from earliest British history to present; portfolios and engravings of fine art, costume, heraldry, country houses, family history and biography

Access and conditions Open to the public by appt (tel), Mon-Fri 9.30–5.30. Most material available for editorial reproduction and for advertising. No loans; b/w prints available for a fee.

Photographic Collection

Items About one million: b/w original and copy photographs, glass negatives, unprinted film negatives, autochromes, daguerreotypes, lantern slides, postcards, stereographs, ambrotypes, tintypes, colour photographic prints

Dates of subject matter 1840 to present

Dates of photographs 1840 to present

Subjects Photographic portraits of eminent figures in British history; most photographic processes are represented; special collections include two albums of Hill and Adamson; portraits by Julia Margaret Cameron; Day Books of Camille Silvy; parliamentary photographs of Sir Benjamin Stone; autochromes by Olive Edis Galsworthy; National Photographic Record coverage of formal portraits of politicians, military personnel and diplomats between 1917 and 1972; Dorothy Wilding's studio portrait collection; negatives from the studios of Lenare, Bassano and Vandyke, Elliot and Fry; formal portraits of Bishops of the Anglican communion from *c.* 1860

Access and conditions Open to the public by appt (tel), Mon-Fri 9.30–5.30. Most material available for editorial reproduction and for advertising (some restrictions). No loans; b/w prints available for a fee. Photocopies and Polaroids available. Reproduction rights fees charged. Staff will undertake limited research. Most material copyright. Card catalogue available.

Publications Department

2 St Martin's Place, London WC2H 0HE
Tel (01) 930 1552

Enquiries to Judith Prendergast

Items About 6000: b/w original photographs, colour transparencies (35mm, 10″ × 8″), glass negatives

Dates of subject matter 1500 to present

Dates of photographs Contemporary

Subjects Portraits of renowned British subjects including royal, political, military, literary, artistic and scientific figures

Access and conditions Open to the public, Mon-Fri 10–5. Most material available for editorial reproduction; advertising use by special arrangement only. Colour material loaned for a fee; b/w prints available for a fee. Reproduction rights and holding fees charged. All material copyright. Printed catalogue available: K. K. Yung, *National Portrait Gallery Complete Illustrated Catalogue*, 1981.

996 • NENE COLLEGE

Osborne Robinson Poster Collection

The Library, Avenue Campus, St George's Avenue, Northampton NN2 6JB
Tel (0604) 714101 ext 223, (0604) 715000 ext 209

Enquiries to Reader Services Librarian

Items About 2000: posters, colour transparencies (35mm)

Dates of subject matter 1890 to 1970

Subjects Poster design worldwide from the 1890s onwards covering material from France including work by Cheret, Rasel, Cassandre, Mucha, Dali, Matthieu and Villemot; Germany including work by Gutschow, Spiro and Strom; UK including work by Bawden, Beggarstaff, Cooper, Greiffenhagen, Kauffer, Mason, Nash, Nicholson, Paine, Purvis, Taylor, Whistler and Zero; Italy; Poland including work by Flejsar, Cieslewicz, Kipinski and Swierzy; Australia, Belgium, Canada, Czechoslovakia, Denmark, Greece, Holland, Japan, India, Middle East, Portugal, South America, Spain, USA, USSR and Yugoslavia

Access and conditions Open to qualified researchers by appt. Most material available for editorial reproduction but not for advertising. No loans; duplicate colour transparencies available for a fee. No reproduction rights fees charged. Staff will undertake limited research. Most material copyright. Partial card catalogue available.

997 • NEW LANARK CONSERVATION TRUST

Counting House, New Lanark, Lanark ML11 9DG
Tel (0555) 61345

Enquiries to Manager

Items 1000: colour transparencies (35mm), b/w original photographs, architectural drawings

Dates of subject matter 1785 to present

Dates of photographs 1880 to present

Subjects Restoration work in New Lanark; architectural and landscape coverage from 19th century

Access and conditions Open to qualified researchers by appt (write), Mon-Fri 9–5. Most material available for editorial reproduction and for advertising. B/w material loaned by arrangement; material may be copied by outside photographers. No reproduction rights fees charged. Compulsory credit line. Most material copyright.

998 • NEWBY HALL ESTATE

The Estate Office, Newby Hall, Ripon, North Yorkshire HG4 5AE
Tel (09012) 2583

Enquiries to Rory Wardroper

Items About 600: colour transparencies (35mm), colour photographic prints, b/w copy photographs, original cartoons, illustrated maps, old fine art prints, architectural drawings, illustrated books

Dates of subject matter 1740 to present

Subjects Portraits of the Grantham family; equestrian 18th- and 19th- century pictures; architectural drawings relating to Newby Hall including designs by Robert Adam, William Chambers and John Carr of York

Access and conditions Open to the public by appt (write). Some material available for editorial reproduction and for advertising by special arrangement only. B/w prints and colour transparencies available for a fee. Reproduction rights fees charged. All material copyright.

999 • NORTH WEST CIVIC TRUST

The Environmental Institute, Greaves School, Bolton Road, Swinton, Manchester M27 2UX
Tel (061) 794 9314

Enquiries to Norman Bilsborough

Items 4000: colour transparencies (35mm), b/w original photographs, unprinted film negatives

Dates of subject matter Medieval to present

Dates of photographs 1965 to present

Subjects Conservation and improvement of the environment and buildings in north-west England

Access and conditions Open to the public by appt (write), Mon-Fri 9–5. All material available for editorial reproduction and for advertising. B/w material loaned free of charge for two months; colour material loaned for a fee. No reproduction rights fees charged. All material copyright. Printed catalogue available.

1000 • NORWICH CASTLE MUSEUM

Castle Museum, Norwich NR1 3JU
Tel (0603) 611277 ext 291

Enquiries to Art Department

Items About 1000: b/w original photographs, colour transparencies (35mm, 5″ × 4″), old fine art prints, 20th-century fine art prints

Dates of subject matter 16th century to present

Dates of photographs 1960 to present

Subjects Landscapes by artists of Norwich School including John Sell Cotman and John Crome; 18th- and 19th-century English oil paintings and watercolours; 17th- and 18th-century Dutch paintings; Norwich civic portraits from 16th to 19th centuries; prints and drawings of Norfolk

Access and conditions Open to the public by appt (write). All material available for editorial reproduction and for advertising. B/w prints available for a fee; colour material loaned free of charge by arrangement. Reproduction rights and holding fees charged. All material copyright. Printed catalogues available.

1001 • NOTTINGHAM CASTLE MUSEUM AND ART GALLERY

Nottingham NG1 6EL
Tel (0602) 411881

Enquiries to Ann Gunn, Keeper of Fine Art

Items About 4000: b/w original photographs, colour transparencies (35mm, 5″ × 4″), glass negatives, postcards, unprinted film negatives, posters, greetings cards

Dates of subject matter 1400 to present

Dates of photographs 1878 to present

Subjects British painting (oils, watercolours, etc.) from the 17th to the 20th century including works by Paul Sandby, Richard Parkes Bonington, Ben Nicholson, Dame Laura Knight, Sir Jacob Epstein, L. S. Lowry); 17th-century Dutch painting; 16th-century Italian painting and drawing; prints; ceramics, especially Nottingham stoneware and Wedgwood; English glass; important English silver collection (18th and 19th century); Nottingham medieval alabaster sculpture of religious figures; archaeology including some Greek, Roman and Hellenistic objects; ethnography comprising a miscellaneous collection from Africa, Japan, India, and of American Indian objects collected by Victorian travellers

Access and conditions Open to the public by appt Mon-Sat 10–4.45 (Oct-Easter), 10–5.45 (Easter-Sept). Most material available for editorial

reproduction and for advertising. No loans; b/w prints and duplicate colour transparencies available for a fee; Reproduction rights and holding fees charged. Staff will undertake very limited research. Printed catalogue available.

1002 • PETERBOROUGH CITY MUSEUM AND ART GALLERY

Priestgate, Peterborough, Cambridgeshire PE1 1LF
Tel (0733) 43329

Enquiries to Martin Howe, Curator

Items 5000: Unprinted film negatives, glass negatives, daguerreotypes, lantern slides, postcards, original cartoons, fine art prints, stereographs, greetings cards, architectural drawings, colour transparencies (35mm), illustrated books

Dates of subject matter Prehistory to present

Dates of photographs Mid-19th century to present

Subjects Fine art: British portraits (16th to 18th century), British and European landscapes and genre paintings (17th to 20th century), local topography, contemporary art including works by Sally Hargreaves, Peter Moss, Ricardo Cinelli, Doug Cocker, David Weisman, Therese Alton, Keith Brown, Christine Walsh; museum collection: archaeology and industrial archaeology, folklife, ceramics and glass, watch-making, geology and natural history, material associated with the life and work of John Clare; photograph collection: local history and topography of the Peterborough area

Access and conditions Open to the public by appt, Oct-Mar Tues-Sat 12–5, Apr-Sept Tues-Sat 10–5. All material available for editorial reproduction and for advertising. No loans; b/w prints and colour transparencies available for a fee. Reproduction rights fees charged. Staff will undertake research.

1003 • POLLOK HOUSE

2060 Pollokshaws Road, Glasgow G43 1AT
Tel (041) 632 0274

Enquiries to Sheenah Smith, Deputy Keeper of Fine Art

Items About 200: b/w original photographs, colour transparencies (35mm, 5″ × 4″)

Dates of subject matter 16th to 19th century

Subjects STIRLING MAXWELL COLLECTION: paintings of the British School including a portrait of Elizabeth I and works by Hogarth, Romney, Kneller, Blake and William Etty; of the Spanish School including works by Murillo, Goya, Velázquez and El Greco; of the Italian School including works by Signorelli, Guardi, the school of Canaletto; of the Dutch School including works by Jordaens and Berchem

Access and conditions Open to the public by appt (write), Mon-Fri 9–5. Most material available for editorial reproduction and for advertising. B/w prints available for a fee; colour material loaned for a rental fee. Photocopies available. Reproduction rights and service fees charged. Staff will undertake some research. Printed catalogue available.

1004 • PORTSMOUTH CITY MUSEUM AND ART GALLERY

Art Department

Museum Road, Old Portsmouth, Hampshire PO1 1LJ
Tel (0705) 827261

Enquiries to Keeper of Art

Items About 2000: paintings, old fine art prints, 20th-century fine art prints, b/w original and copy photographs, colour transparencies (35mm), lantern slides, postcards

Dates of subject matter 1500 to present

Dates of photographs 1880 to present

Subjects British paintings, prints, drawings and sculpture from 18th to 20th centuries; special collections of 20th-century paintings and prints including works by Wodsworth, Burra, Wyndham Lewis, Duncan Grant and Derek Boshier; decorative art including painted furniture with some important pieces by Duncan Grant and Vanessa Bell; ceramics and glassware; tapestries

Access and conditions Open to the public by appt (write), Mon-Fri 10.30–5. Most material available for editorial reproduction and for advertising. B/w and colour material loaned by arrangement (print fees charged); material may be copied by outside photographers. Some photocopies available. Reproduction rights fees charged. Staff

will undertake limited research. Most material copyright. Card catalogue available.

1005 • PRESTON MANOR

Preston Park, Brighton BN1 6SD
Tel (0273) 603005 ext 59

Enquiries to Keeper

Items About 2000: b/w original and copy photographs, lantern slides, unprinted film negatives, greetings cards, architectural drawings, press cuttings, illustrated maps

Dates of subject matter c. 16th century to present

Dates of photographs 1900 to present

Subjects Family portraits of the Stanford family including works by Etty, J. J. Shannon and William Orpen; landscapes by Nasmyth, Pether, Leader, T. S. Cooper and J. Clayton Adams; series of weather drawings made for the *Daily Graphic* c. 1890s illustrating the daily weather forecast

Access and conditions Open to the public by appt (tel). All material available for editorial reproduction and for advertising. No loans; b/w prints and duplicate colour transparencies available for a fee. Photocopies available. Reproduction rights fees charged. Staff will undertake some research. Compulsory credit line. All material copyright. Card catalogue and computer list available.

1006 • RENFREW DISTRICT COUNCIL MUSEUMS AND ART GALLERIES SERVICE

Art Department

High Street, Paisley, Strathclyde PA1 2BA
Tel (041) 889 3151

Enquiries to David Shearer, Chief Curator

Items About 10,000: colour transparencies (35mm), unprinted film negatives, b/w copy photographs, old fine art prints, 20th-century fine art prints, art reproductions, architectural drawings

Dates of subject matter 300 BC to present

Dates of photographs 1975 to present

Subjects British 19th- and 20th- century painting and sculpture with emphasis on Scottish artists; Barbizon School of French painting; ceramics especially studio ceramics of 19th and 20th centuries; decorative arts including glass and silver

Access and conditions Open to qualified researchers by appt (write). All material available for editorial reproduction but not for advertising. B/w and colour material loaned free of charge by arrangement; material may be copied by outside photographers. Photocopies available. No reproduction rights fees charged. Staff will undertake some research. All material copyright. Card catalogue available, printed catalogue available: *The Studio Ceramics Collection at the Paisley Museum and Art Galleries*, 1984, published by Scottish Development Agency.

1007 • ROCHDALE ART GALLERY

Esplanade, Rochdale, Lancashire OL16 1AQ
Tel (0706) 47474 ext 269, 764

Enquiries to Bev Bytheway, Assistant Arts and Exhibition Officer

Items 1500: b/w original photographs, colour transparencies (35mm), postcards, art reproductions, posters, catalogues

Dates of subject matter Late 14th century to present

Dates of photographs 1980 to present

Subjects British 18th- and 19th-century watercolours; Victorian narrative and landscape paintings including works by women artists; contemporary British paintings; photographic collection includes coverage of contemporary social issues in Rochdale

Access and conditions Open to the public by appt (tel), Mon Tues Thurs & Fri 10–5, Wed 10–1, Sat 10–4. All material available for editorial reproduction and for advertising. Colour material loaned for a fee; b/w prints available for a fee; material may be copied by outside photographers. Photocopies available. Reproduction rights and service fees charged; service fees deductible from use fees. Staff will undertake limited research. All material copyright. Card catalogue available.

1008 • ROYAL INCORPORATION OF ARCHITECTS IN SCOTLAND

Photographic Collection

15 Rutland Square, Edinburgh EH1 2BE
Tel (031) 229 7205

Enquiries to Charles McKean

Items About 3000: b/w original and copy photographs, colour transparencies (35mm), lantern slides, architectural drawings, glass negatives

Dates of subject matter AD 500 to present

Dates of photographs 1970s to present

Subjects Historic and contemporary architecture in Scotland with emphasis on Edinburgh, Dundee and Stirling and work of Sir Robert Lorimer; some coverage of architecture in East Anglia and London

Access and conditions Open to the public by appt (write). All material available for editorial reproduction and for advertising by special arrangement only. B/w and colour material loaned free of charge by arrangement (print fees charged). Photocopies available. Reproduction rights fees charged. Staff will undertake limited research. Most material copyright. Catalogue in preparation.

1009 • THE ROYAL INSTITUTE OF BRITISH ARCHITECTS

British Architectural Library Drawings Collection

21 Portman Square, London W1H 9HF
Tel (01) 580 5533

Enquiries to John Harris, Curator

Items About 300,000: architectural drawings

Dates of subject matter 15th century to present

Subjects Architecture with special emphasis on Great Britain but also including overseas material; most significant collections of drawings are those by Inigo Jones, Palladio and Webb, the Smythsons, Waterhouse, Scott and Comper; other important collections include drawings by Sir Edwin Lutyens, Webb and Herbert Baker, Voysey, Philip Webb and Norman Shaw; also material by the Wyatt family and the Pugins; complete archives of the firms of Dove Brothers, Norman and Burt, and Bowman and Son of Stamford, also the archive of the architect Erno Goldfinger

Access and conditions Open to the public by appt (tel), Mon-Fri 10–1 (closed Aug). All material available for editorial reproduction and for advertising. No loans; b/w prints and duplicate colour transparencies available for a fee. Reproduction rights and service fees charged. Staff of four will undertake some research. All material copyright. Card and printed catalogues available.

See also **British Architectural Library.**

1010 • THE ROYAL PHOTOGRAPHIC SOCIETY

The Octagon, Milsom Street, Bath, Avon BA1 1DN
Tel (0225) 62841

Enquiries to Pamela Roberts, Collection Librarian

Items About 60,000: b/w original and copy photographs, glass negatives, lantern slides, stereo cards, daguerreotypes, colour transparencies (35mm, 5″ × 4″), unprinted paper negatives, illustrated books, periodicals, ambrotypes, tintypes, ferrotypes, collodion opal prints, autochromes

Dates of subject matter 1839 to present

Dates of photographs 1839 to present

Subjects History and development of photography including portrait photography of the 19th and 20th centuries; landscapes of Britain, Italy, Middle East, India; architecture including material from Britain, India, Burma and China; coverage of the Crimean and Boer Wars; some coverage of conflicts in Abyssinia and Vietnam; natural history; social history and political life of Britain in early 20th century; British Royal Family with emphasis on Victorian and Edwardian material; special collections include the NATURE CONSERVANCY COUNCIL COLLECTION, the JAMES JARCHÉ COLLECTION of sports, theatre, film and television personalities, and the HOUSTON ROGERS COLLECTION of ballet, theatre and opera

Access and conditions Open to the public by appt, Mon-Fri 9.30–5.30. All material available for editorial reproduction and for advertising by arrangement. B/w and colour material loaned for a fee (print fees charged); material may be copied by outside photographers. Photocopies and Polaroids available for a fee. Reproduction rights, holding and service fees charged. Staff will undertake some research. Most material copyright. Card catalogue available.

1011 • ROYAL SOCIETY OF PAINTERS IN WATERCOLOURS

Bankside Gallery, 48 Hopton Street, London SE1 9JH
Tel (01) 928 7521

Enquiries to Michael Spender, Curator

Items 380: colour transparencies (35mm)

Dates of subject matter 1800 to present

Dates of photographs 1984 to present

Subjects Watercolours by British artists including works by Helen Allingham, William Callow, David Cox, Sir William Russell Flint, Myles Birkett Foster, John Jessop Hardwick, Sir Edward Burne-Jones, Dame Laura Knight, Samuel Palmer, Alfred Parsons, Arthur Rackham, William Collingwood Smith, Sir Lawrence Alma Tadema and Sir Ernest A. Waterlow

Access and conditions Open to the public by appt (tel), Tues-Sat 10–5, Sun 2–6. Some material available for editorial reproduction and for advertising. Colour material loaned free of charge by arrangement (print fees charged); material may be copied by outside photographers. Reproduction rights fees charged. Staff will undertake limited research. Compulsory credit line. Some material copyright. Duplicated subject list available.

1012 • SAINSBURY CENTRE FOR VISUAL ARTS

University of East Anglia, Norwich, Norfolk NR4 7TJ
Tel (0603) 56161

Enquiries to Veronica Sekules, Acting Keeper

Items About 500: b/w original and copy photographs, colour transparencies (35mm, 5″ × 4″), lantern slides, postcards, 20th-century fine art prints, posters, greetings cards

Dates of subject matter Prehistory to present

Dates of photographs 1930 to present

Subjects ROBERT AND LISA SAINSBURY COLLECTION: paintings, drawings and prints by 20th-century figurative artists including works by Francis Bacon, Alberto Giacometti, Amedeo Modigliani, Henry Moore, Pablo Picasso, Antonio Saura, John Davies, Balthus, Jules Pascin, Charles Despiau and Chaim Soutine; works by 19th-century artists such as Edgar Degas, Auguste Rodin and Berthe Morisot; Egyptian faience and bronze figures, Greek Cycladic sculpture, Etruscan and Roman bronzes, Indian miniatures, Japanese scroll paintings; African tribal sculpture, traditional sculpture from Pacific Islands, North American Indian and Eskimo artefacts, Pre-Columbian art of Middle and South America; UNIVERSITY COLLECTION OF ABSTRACT ART AND DESIGN: paintings, drawings, and prints by artists including David Bomberg, Van der Leck, Moholy-Nagy, Amédée Ozenfant, Ben Nicholson, Kenneth Martin, Auguste Herbin, Adrian Heath, Tess Jaray and Frank Stella; ANDERSON COLLECTION OF ART NOUVEAU: sculpture, glassware, art pottery, furniture, silverware, metalware, textiles, graphic art and jewellery including work by Gallé, Loetz, Tiffany, Majorelle and Alfonse Mucha

Access and conditions Open to the public, Tues-Sun 12–5. All material available for editorial reproduction but not for advertising. B/w prints and duplicate colour transparencies available for a fee. Photocopies available. Reproduction rights fees charged. Staff will undertake very limited research. Printed catalogues available.

1013 • ST HELEN'S MUSEUM AND ART GALLERY

College Street, St Helen's WA10 1TW
Tel (0744) 24061 ext 2572

Enquiries to Janice Murray, Curator

Items 3000: b/w copy photographs, colour transparencies (35mm), b/w original photographs

Dates of subject matter BC to present

Dates of photographs 1972 to present

Subjects British 19th-century oil paintings; Pilkington collection of British 19th-century landscape watercolours; archaeological material from the Sir Flinders Petrie dig at Megada in Egypt; local natural history and local social history; decorative arts including ceramics and glass and a collection of Chinese ceramics; military memorabilia connected with the Lancashire Hussars

Access and conditions Open to qualified researchers by appt (tel before 10), Mon-Fri 10–5, Sat 10–1. All material available for editorial reproduction and for advertising. No loans; b/w prints and duplicate colour transparencies available for a fee. Reproduction rights and service fees charged. Most material copyright. Card catalogue available.

1014 • SALFORD ART GALLERY

Peel Park, Salford, Greater Manchester M5 4WU
Tel (061) 736 2649

Enquiries to Judith Sandling, Keeper of Art

Items About 3500: colour transparencies (35mm, 5″ × 4″), glass negatives, old fine art prints, 20th-century fine art prints, art reproductions

Dates of subject matter BC to present

Dates of fine art 14th century to present

Subjects British 19th- and 20th-century oil paintings, watercolours and drawings, including major collection of works by L. S. Lowry but also works by Harold Riley, Geoffrey Key, William Roberts, Vanessa Bell, Duncan Grant, Graham Sutherland; contemporary sculpture including works by Elizabeth Frink and Jacob Epstein; local history painting collection of Salford and Manchester streetscenes; Greek and Roman pottery; pottery and glassware including Wedgwood, Georgian and Victorian work

Access and conditions Open to the public by appt (tel), Mon-Fri 10–5, Sun 2–5. Some material available for editorial reproduction and for advertising. B/w and colour material loaned free of charge by arrangement; b/w prints and duplicate colour transparencies available for a fee; material may be copied by outside photographers. Reproduction rights fees charged. Staff will undertake limited research. Some material copyright. Card catalogue available; printed catalogues available: *L. S. Lowry – The Salford Collection*, 1975, *L. S. Lowry – his life and work*, 1984, both from Salford Art Gallery.

1015 • SALISBURY AND SOUTH WILTSHIRE MUSEUM

The Job Edwards Collection of Prints

65 The Close, Salisbury, Wiltshire SP1 2EN
Tel (0722) 332151

Enquiries to Simon Olding, Assistant Curator

Items About 3000: b/w copy photographs, colour transparencies (35mm, 5″ × 4″), b/w original photographs, postcards, illustrated maps, unprinted film negatives, posters, greetings cards

Dates of subject matter 1700 to present

Dates of photographs 1870s to present

Subjects Prints, paintings and drawings from the

18th century onwards relating to people, events and places in Salisbury and South Wiltshire including a collection of watercolours and engravings by artists including Turner, Sandby, Rowlandson and Constable, a collection of drawings, watercolours and lithographs including works by local artists such as Robert Kemm, R. G. Heape, Walter Tiffin; small collection of oil paintings including works by George Beare and Augustus John

Access and conditions Open to the public by appt (write), Oct–Mar Mon–Sat 10–4, Apr–Sep Mon–Sat 10–5. All material available for editorial reproduction; advertising use by special arrangement only. B/w and colour material loaned free of charge by arrangement; b/w prints and duplicate colour transparencies available for a fee; material may be copied by outside photographers. Photocopies available. Reproduction rights and service fees charged. Staff of three will undertake some research. All material copyright. Card catalogue available.

1016 • SCOTTISH DEVELOPMENT AGENCY

Small Business Division, Rosebery House, Haymarket Terrace, Edinburgh EH12 5EZ
Tel (031) 337 9595

Enquiries to Crafts Manager or Nick Allen for Conservation Bureau enquiries

Items About 2000: colour transparencies (35mm, 5″ × 4″), b/w original photographs

Dates of subject matter Late 16th century to present

Dates of photographs 1980 to present

Subjects Craftwork of artists living or working in Scotland and including ceramics, batik, jewellery, leatherwork, glassblowing, weaving, tapestry-making, textiles, knitwear, furniture, calligraphy; conservation work either *in situ* in historic houses in Scotland or in workshops and including restoration of architectural paintwork, painted ceilings, stained glass and glass vessels, plasterwork, furniture, clocks, books and documents

Access and conditions Open to the public by appt (tel). All material available for editorial reproduction and for advertising. B/w and colour material loaned free of charge by arrangement; material may be copied by outside photographers.

Photocopies available. Reproduction rights fees charged by arrangement. Staff of two will undertake limited research. All material copyright.

1017 • CHARLES SKILTON & FRY LTD

Balmoral Publishing Works, Cheddar, Somerset BS27 3JD
Tel (0934) 743737

Enquiries to Charles Skilton

Items About 2000: colour transparencies (2¼″, 5″ × 4″), b/w original photographs

Dates of subject matter Prehistory to 1980

Dates of photographs 1960 to 1980

Subjects Scottish architecture including historic buildings (civic, ecclesiastic and vernacular), castles, ruins, general views and landscapes

Access and conditions Open to the public by appt (write), Mon–Fri 9–5.30. All material available for editorial reproduction and for advertising. B/w and colour material loaned free of charge for one month. Reproduction rights and holding fees charged. Staff will undertake some research. All material copyright.

1018 • J. C. D. SMITH

Old Arch, Four Forks, Spaxton, Bridgwater, Somerset TA5 1AA
Tel (027867) 404

Enquiries to Colin Smith

Items 3000: b/w original photographs, unprinted film negatives, colour transparencies (35mm)

Dates of subject matter 1200 to 1700

Dates of photographs 1970s to present

Subjects Church woodcarvings in England, Wales and Holland with emphasis on medieval period including misericords and bench-ends, pulpits, font covers, screens; types of carvings include Biblical scenes, saints, devils, medieval trades and occupations, musicians, entertainers, games and pastimes, domestic scenes, animals, birds, fishes, grotesques, mythology, heraldry, humour, satire

Access and conditions Open to the public by appt (tel). All material available for editorial reproduction and for advertising. B/w and colour material loaned free of charge for one month; b/w prints and duplicate colour transparencies available for a fee. Photocopies available. Reproduction rights and holding fees charged. Research undertaken. All material copyright.

1019 • THE SUTCLIFFE GALLERY

1 Flowergate, Whitby, North Yorkshire YO21 3BA
Tel (0947) 602239

Enquiries to Bill Shaw, Director

Items About 2000: glass negatives, b/w copy photographs, postcards, illustrated books, hand-finished photographic prints

Dates of subject matter 1871 to 1900

Dates of photographs 1971 to 1900

Subjects FRANK MEADOW SUTCLIFFE COLLECTION of photographs of Whitby and surrounding area including genre scenes of fishing and farming community, coastal trading vessels, inshore fishing vessels, railway construction, landscapes, streetscenes

Access and conditions Open to the public, Mon-Sat 9–5. (Telephone before visiting as opening hours are shorter in winter.) All material available for editorial reproduction and for advertising. No loans; b/w prints available for a fee (for some items there may be a waiting period of up to six weeks). Reproduction rights and service fees charged; service fees deductible from use fees. Staff of four will undertake research; search fees charged in some cases. All material copyright. Printed catalogue available: *The Sutcliffe Gallery Catalogue*, 1983.

1020 • WIM SWAAN ARCHIVE

c/o Moira L. Johnston, 5 Priory Avenue, London W4 1TX
Tel (01) 994 2497

Enquiries to Moira L. Johnston

Items About 4000: b/w original photographs, colour transparencies (35mm, 5″ × 4″)

Dates of subject matter 10th to 19th centuries

Dates of photographs Contemporary

Subjects Architecture (interiors and exteriors), sculpture, art objects and paintings in Britain, France, Italy, Germany, Spain, Portugal, Belgium, Holland, Greece (Hellenistic), Turkey (Istanbul), Egypt (objects in Cairo Museum), Morocco (including streetscenes), Iran (Isfahan, Persepolis), India (Mughal period), Sri Lanka, Burma, Kampuchea, Tibetan thangkas; in Europe, emphasis on Romanesque, Gothic and baroque styles

Access and conditions Open to qualified researchers by appt (tel), Mon-Fri 9.30–5.30. All material available for editorial reproduction and for advertising. B/w and colour material loaned free of charge for one month. Photocopies available. Reproduction rights and holding fees charged. Staff will undertake research.

1021 • TATE GALLERY

Millbank, London SW1P 4RG
Tel (01) 821 1313

Archive

Items Unknown number: b/w original and copy photographs, colour transparencies (35mm, 5″ × 4″, 10″ × 8″), colour photographic prints, glass negatives, posters, press cuttings

Dates of photographs 1930s to present

Subjects Photographs within the Archive relate to the life and work of 20th-century British artists and their associates worldwide including portraits of artists and their studios; special collection of photographs by Paul Nash; posters designed by contemporary artists

Access and conditions Open to qualified researchers by appt (write), Thurs & Fri 10–5.30. Most material available for editorial reproduction; advertising use by special arrangement only. No loans; b/w prints and duplicate colour transparencies available for a fee. Reproduction rights and service fees charged. Staff will undertake limited research. All material copyright.

Publications Department

Enquiries to Graham Langton

Items Unknown number: b/w original photographs, colour transparencies (10″ × 8″)

Dates of subject matter 1545 to present

Dates of photographs 1960s to present

Subjects British paintings from 16th century to 1860 including works by Blake, Constable, Turner and Gainsborough; paintings and prints by modern artists worldwide including Picasso, Matisse,

Renoir, Cézanne, Van Gogh, Patrick Caulfield and Francis Bacon

Access and conditions Open to the public by appt (tel). All material available for editorial reproduction; advertising use by special arrangement only. Colour material loaned for a fee; b/w prints available for a fee. Reproduction rights fees charged. All material copyright. Printed catalogue available.

1022 • THAMESDOWN MUSEUMS AND ART GALLERY

Bath Road, Swindon, Wiltshire SN1 4BA
Tel (0793) 26161 ext 3129

Enquiries to Robert Dickinson, Assistant Curator

Items About 6000: lantern slides, postcards, paintings

Dates of subject matter Late 19th century to present

Dates of photographs Early 20th century to present

Subjects FRED STEVENS COLLECTION of postcards in the late 19th and early 20th century covering landscapes, streetscenes, local events in Swindon and north-east Wiltshire; ERIC ARMAN COLLECTION of lantern slides covering life in Swindon and surrounding area; contemporary paintings and ceramics by British artists and potters including Hamilton, Hilton, Lowry, Moore, Nicholson, Smith, Steer, Sutherland, Batterham, Coper, Finch, Leach, Martin, Rie and Rogers

Access and conditions Open to the public by appt (tel), Mon-Fri 10–5.30. All material available for editorial reproduction and for advertising. No loans; b/w prints and duplicate colour transparencies available for a fee; material may be copied by outside photographers. Reproduction rights fees charged. Staff of three will undertake limited research. All material copyright. Card catalogue.

1023 • TOWNELEY HALL ART GALLERY AND MUSEUMS

Burnley, Lancashire BB11 3RQ
Tel (0282) 24213

Enquiries to Hubert R. Rigg, Curator

Items About 3000: b/w original photographs, original book illustrations, oil paintings and watercolours, architectural drawings

Dates of subject matter Prehistory to present

Dates of photographs Mid-19th century to present

Subjects Photographs: Burnley and environs including local natural history, landscapes and towns, architecture, people; fine art: 18th- and 19th-century English watercolours and oil paintings of rural scenes, seascapes, historical and genre scenes, including Zoffany's *Charles Towneley in the Park Street Gallery, Westminster* and Marten Van Valkenborch's *Tower of Babel*; 19th- and 20th-century original children's and adults' book illustrations on a wide variety of topics, good collection of 17th-century English oak furniture

Access and conditions Open to the public by appt (tel), Mon-Fri 9–5. All material available for editorial reproduction and for advertising at the discretion of the Curator. B/w prints available for a fee; duplicate colour transparencies available for a fee. Reproduction rights and service fees charged. Staff will undertake limited research. Catalogue of fine art available: Susan Bourne, *Catalogue of Oil Paintings and Watercolours,* (Burnley Borough Council).

1024 • TOWNER ART GALLERY AND LOCAL HISTORY MUSEUM

Manor Gardens, High Street, Old Town, Eastbourne, East Sussex BN20 8BB
Tel (0323) 21635, 25112

Enquiries to Patricia Andrew, Curator

Items Over 3000: b/w original and copy photographs, glass negatives, postcards, original cartoons, old fine art prints, 20th-century fine art prints, posters

Dates of subject matter Prehistory to present

Dates of photographs 1870 to present

Subjects Comprehensive collection of British oil paintings, watercolours and prints by mainly 19th- and 20th-century artists including works by Eric Ravilious, Christopher Wood, Duncan Grant, Vanessa Bell, Ceri Richards and Alfred Wallace; small collection of sculpture; cartoons by Cruickshank and contemporaries; local history collection includes Neolithic flints, Roman remains,

Anglo-Saxon burial complete with skeleton, reconstructed medieval well, and a Victorian kitchen; photographic collection covers the local history of Eastbourne and surrounding area including landscapes, architecture, transport, social history, portraits, local events, activities associated with the seafront; CECIL BELL COLLECTION of British butterflies and moths; the Towner Art Gallery manages the collection of the SOUTH EAST ARTS ASSOCIATION which covers a wide range of work (paintings, drawings, prints, sculpture and crafts) by contemporary artists living or working in the area

Access and conditions Open to the public by appt (tel), Mon-Sat 10–5, Sun 2–5, in winter closed Mon. All material available for editorial reproduction; advertising use by special arrangement only. B/w prints and duplicate colour transparencies available for a fee by arrangement. Reproduction rights fees charged depending on use. Staff of two will undertake limited research. Most material copyright. Card catalogue available; printed catalogue in preparation.

1025 • ULSTER MUSEUM

Department of Art

Botanic Gardens, Belfast BT9 5AB
Tel (0232) 668251

Enquiries to Ted Hickey, Keeper of Art

Items 4500: b/w original photographs, colour transparencies (35mm)

Dates of subject matter 17th century to present

Dates of photographs Late 19th century to present

Subjects Irish paintings from the 17th century to present including works by Thomas Bate, Joseph Wilson, William Conor and William Scott; British paintings from the 17th century to present including works by Gainsborough, Reynolds, and the LLOYD PATTERSON COLLECTION OF BRITISH ART (1900-1937) containing works by Vanessa Bell, Roger Fry, Duncan Grant, J. D. Innes, Augustus John, Ambrose McEvoy, John and Paul Nash, Stanley Spencer and P. W. Steer; small collection of old masters including works by Jacob Jordaens, Jan van Bylert, Lorenzo Lippi, Jacob van Oost the Elder and Jan Pynas; modern paintings including works by Sam Francis, Morris Louis, Kenneth Noland and Joan Mitchell; British and Irish watercolours; drawings by Paul Sandby, John

Henry Fuseli, Myles Birket Foster; prints, etchings and wood engravings; British and Irish sculpture from 18th century mainly of portrait busts; 20th-century sculpture includes works by Anthony Caro, John Davies, Gaudier-Brzeska, Barbara Hepworth, Henry Moore, Philip King and F. E. McWilliam; decorative arts including glass, ceramics, silver and metalwork, furniture and woodwork of Irish manufacture or significance; textiles including costume from 17th century with particular emphasis on 20th-century dress; jewellery from 16th century

Access and conditions Open to the public by appt, Mon-Fri 10–5. All material available for editorial reproduction and for advertising. Colour material loaned for a fee; b/w prints available for a fee. Photocopies available. Reproduction rights and holding fees charged. Staff of three will undertake some research. Compulsory credit line. All material copyright. Catalogue in preparation.

1026 • UNIVERSITY OF LIVERPOOL

Art Gallery, University of Liverpool, Liverpool L69 3BX
Tel (051) 709 6022 ext 3170

Enquiries to Janice Carpenter, Curator

Items Over 2000: colour transparencies (35mm, 5″ × 4″), b/w original photographs, lantern slides, original cartoons, illustrated maps, old fine art prints, 20th-century fine art prints, unprinted film negatives, posters, greetings cards, architectural drawings, oils, watercolours, drawings

Dates of subject matter Late 17th century to present

Dates of photographs Contemporary

Subjects Paintings (mainly British) from the 17th century including works by Joseph Wright, Isaak van Ostade, J. M. W. Turner, William Taverner, Joseph Heard, Samuel Walters, John Joseph Audubon, Victor Pasmore; SIR SYDNEY JONES COLLECTION of watercolours including works by Paul Sandby, Nicholas Pocock, John Robert Cozens, Thomas Girtin, David Cox, John Linnell, William Callow; drawings including set of cartoons by Edward Burne-Jones; antique furniture, clocks, tapestry, ceramics, silver and glassware; sculpture including works by Barbara Hepworth, Phillip King, Jacob Epstein and Elizabeth Frink

Access and conditions Open to the public by appt (tel). All material available for editorial reproduction and for advertising. Colour material loaned free of charge by arrangement; b/w prints and duplicate colour transparencies available for a fee; material may be copied by outside photographers. Reproduction rights fees charged. Staff will undertake some research. Most material copyright. Card catalogue available.

1027 • USHER GALLERY

Lindum Road, Lincoln LN2 1NN
Tel (0522) 27980

Enquiries to Richard Wood, Keeper of Art

Items About 5000: b/w copy photographs, colour transparencies (35mm, 5″ × 4″)

Dates of subject matter BC to present

Dates of photographs *c.* 1960 to present

Subjects Paintings of the 15th-, 16th- and 17th-century Italian Schools; paintings of the 16th-, 17th- and 18th-century Dutch and Flemish Schools including works by Nicholas Van Schoors, Cornelius Verdonck and Henri Voordecker; major collection of drawings and paintings by Peter De Wint; Lincolnshire topographical paintings including works by J. M. W. Turner, Thomas Girtin, Augustus Pugin, Samuel Prout, William Callow and J. W. Carmichael; works by Lincolnshire artists including James Bourne, Charles Haslewood Shannon, William Logsdail and William Warrener; 19th- and 20th-century British paintings including works by Ferneley, J. E. Herring, John Collier, W. R. Sickert, Vanessa Bell, John Piper and L. S. Lowry; sculpture including works by John Gibson, Joseph Nollekens, William Theed and Jacob Epstein; English and Continental portrait miniatures from the late 16th to the 19th century; English and French clocks and watches of the 17th and 18th centuries; English silver from the 16th century to the late 19th century; Chinese porcelain of the K'ang Hsi period 1662 to 1722; 18th- and 19th-century porcelain from the Sèvres and Meissen factories; 18th- and 19th- century English porcelain from the Chelsea, Derby, Worcester and Nantgarw factories; 18th-century Battersea and Staffordshire enamels; studio pottery including works by Michael Cardew, Shoji Hamada, Bernard Leach and Charles Vyse; portraits and personal effects of Alfred Lord Tennyson; coins and medals with special emphasis on items connected with Lincolnshire

Access and conditions Open to the public by appt (tel), Mon-Sat 10–5.30, Sun 2.30–5. Most

material available for editorial reproduction and for advertising. B/w and colour material loaned by arrangement; material may be copied by outside photographers. Photocopies available. Reproduction rights fees charged. Staff of three will undertake limited research. All material copyright. Partial printed catalogue available.

1028 • VICTORIA AND ALBERT MUSEUM

Cromwell Road, London SW7 2RL
Tel (01) 589 6371

Department of Prints, Drawings and Photographs

Enquiries to Print Room

Items 300,000: b/w original photographs, colour photographic prints, glass negatives, daguerreotypes, lantern slides, postcards, stereographs, original cartoons, old fine art prints, 20th-century fine art prints, art reproductions, posters, greetings cards, architectural drawings, ephemera

Dates of subject matter BC to present

Dates of photographs *c.* 1840 to present

Subjects British and European drawings and graphic art from 15th century to present; pattern books for textiles, industrial design, cartoons, record sleeves, valentine and Christmas cards, cigarette cards, calendars, book covers; drawings for furniture, glass, ceramics, sculpture, textiles; photographic collection contains material by Hill and Adamson, Fenton, Fox Talbot, Julia Margaret Cameron and Eadweard Muybridge

Access and conditions Open to the public, Mon-Thurs 10–4.30. Some material available for editorial reproduction and for advertising. Requests for reproduction-quality material should be made initially to the Photographic Sales Department – see below. Reproduction rights fees charged. Staff will undertake limited research. Card catalogue available.

Photographic Sales Department

Enquiries to Photographic Sales

Items About one million: colour transparencies (5″ × 4″, 10″ × 8″), glass negatives, unprinted film negatives

Dates of subject matter BC to present

Dates of photographs 1850 to present

Subjects Objects in the Museum (material relating to fine and applied art of many different countries, periods and styles) including sculpture: the work of European sculptors from AD 300; ceramics: particularly strong collection of English porcelain and Italian maiolica; Far Eastern: Oriental art, ceramics, metalwork and textiles; furniture and woodwork: European furniture from medieval times, also musical instruments, treen leatherwork and woodwork; prints, drawings & photographs (see above); textiles: including carpets, batik, costumes, ecclesiastical embroidery, tapestries; paintings and watercolours: British paintings 1700–1900 including works by Gainsborough, Reynolds and Morland, Mulready, Landseer, Frith and Turner; watercolours by British artists such as Sandby, Cozens, Girton, Cox, Turner and de Wint; Theatre Museum (entry 1082)

Access and conditions Open to the public, Mon-Thurs 10–5. All material available for editorial reproduction and for advertising. Colour material loaned for a fee; b/w prints available for a fee; material may be copied by outside photographers. Reproduction rights and holding fees charged. Most material copyright. Research enquiries should be addressed to individual departments.

1029 • VICTORIA ART GALLERY

Bridge Street, Bath, Avon BA2 4AT
Tel (0225) 61111 ext 416

Enquiries to Jill Knight, Keeper of Art

Items About 5000: b/w original and copy photographs, colour transparencies (35mm, 5″ × 4″), old fine art prints, 20th-century fine art prints, postcards, original cartoons

Dates of subject matter 17th century to present

Dates of photographs 1970s to present

Subjects British and European oil paintings and watercolours from the 17th century onwards; early Dutch and Flemish paintings; topographical watercolours and prints including works by Thomas Malton, Thomas Rowlandson and John Claude Nattes; 20th-century artists include Walter Sickert, Thérèse Lessore, Lord Methuen, John Nash, Gilbert Spencer, William Roberts and Matthew Smith; ceramics, glass, sculpture and domestic items

Access and conditions Open to qualified

researchers by appt (tel), Mon-Fri 10–5. Most material available for editorial reproduction and for advertising. B/w prints and duplicate colour transparencies available for a fee. Reproduction rights fees charged. Staff will undertake some research. Compulsory credit line. All material copyright.

1030 • VISUAL ARTS LIBRARY

82 Sinclair Road, London W14 0NJ
Tel (01) 603 7945

Enquiries to Celestine Dars

Items 500,000: microfiche prints

Dates of subject matter Prehistory to present

Dates of photographs 1860 to present

Subjects Decorative and fine art in the following collections: Victoria and Albert Museum; Wallace Collection; Imperial War Museum; Royal Library, Windsor; Burrell Collection, Glasgow; British Museum; Christies archives; Design Council; British *Vogue*; French National Art Collections; Caisse Nationale des Monuments Historiques; Alinari collection of early Italian photographs

Access and conditions Open to the public by appt (tel), Mon-Fri 10–6. This is a reference collection only; users must negotiate directly with collections for use of material, copyright clearance and fees. Consultation fee charged.

1031 • GLYNN VIVIAN ART GALLERY AND MUSEUM

Alexandra Road, Swansea SA1 5DZ
Tel (0792) 55006

Enquiries to Hilary J. Woolley, Director of Museums Services

Items 5000: b/w original photographs, colour transparencies (35mm, 5″ × 4″), glass negatives, original cartoons, fine art prints, architectural drawings, illustrated books

Dates of subject matter 17th century to present

Subjects Oil paintings, drawings and prints by Ceri Richards; oil paintings by Evan Walters, death mask; cartoons for British Empire Panels and the panels themselves by Frank Brangwyn; Old Master drawings; marine oil paintings and watercolours; miniatures; work by John Dickson

Innes, Augustus John and Gwen John; work by Welsh artists, Welsh subjects

Access and conditions Open to the public by appt (write). Most material available for editorial reproduction but not for advertising. B/w prints available for a fee; colour transparencies loaned for a rental fee or duplicated for a fee. Reproduction rights fees charged. Staff will undertake limited research only.

1032 • WAKEFIELD ART GALLERY AND MUSEUMS

Wentworth Terrace, Wakefield, West Yorkshire WF1 3QW
Tel (0924) 370211 ext 8031

Enquiries to Gillian Spencer, Museums and Art Galleries Officer

Items About 13,000: glass negatives, b/w original and copy photographs, colour transparencies (35mm, 5″ × 4″), daguerreotypes, lantern slides, postcards, fine art prints, stereographs, posters, architectural drawings

Dates of subject matter 1680 to present

Dates of photographs 1870 to present

Subjects British 20th-century painting and sculpture including works by Barbara Hepworth, Henry Moore, Norman Adams, Euan Uglow, Keith Grant, Nicholas Pope; Old Master paintings, mostly Flemish; painting and prints of the Wakefield district, especially 18th- and 19th-century views by Reinagle, Louis Grimshaw; 20th-century Pontefract portrait photographs

Access and conditions Open to the public by appt (write), Mon-Sat 10.30–12.30, 1–5. Most material available for editorial reproduction and for advertising, subject to the Curator's approval. No loans; b/w prints and duplicate colour transparencies available for a fee. Photocopies available. Reproduction rights fees charged. Staff will undertake some research. Partial catalogue available.

1033 • WALKER ART GALLERY, SUDLEY ART GALLERY, LADY LEVER ART GALLERY

William Brown Street, Liverpool L3 8EL
Tel (051) 227 5234 Telex 629018 MERCTY G

Enquiries to Christine Parry, Publications Officer

Items About 15,400: b/w original and copy photographs, fine art prints, postcards, colour transparencies (35mm, 5″ × 4″, larger), architectural drawings, original cartoons, posters, watercolours, drawings, art reproductions, unprinted film negatives, greetings cards, illustrated books, colour photographic prints

Dates of subject matter c. 1300 to present

Dates of photographs c. 1922 to present

Subjects WALKER ART GALLERY: European oil paintings, watercolours, drawings, prints and sculptures; early Italian and Flemish works by Simone Martini, Ercole de Roberti and Jan Mostaert; later work of the Dutch, English and German Schools by Rubens, Rembrandt, Hogarth, Signorelli, Johann Zoffany, George Stubbs, Richard Wilson, works of the Liverpool School and the Pre-Raphaelites, late Victorian academic paintings and some 20th-century work; SUDLEY ART GALLERY: 18th- and 19th-century English painting by Turner, Gainsborough, Romney, Sir David Wilkie, William Mulready, Holman Hunt; LADY LEVER ART GALLERY: Wedgwood pottery, Chinese porcelain, 18th-century furniture, tapestry, needlework, miniatures; Napoleoniana

Access and conditions Open to the public by appt (tel), Mon-Sat 10–5, Sun 2–5. Most material available for editorial reproduction and for advertising with some restrictions. B/w prints available for a fee; colour transparencies loaned for a rental fee. Reproduction rights fees charged. Staff will undertake some research. Printed catalogue available.

1034 • THE WALLACE COLLECTION

Hertford House, Manchester Square, London W1M 6BN
Tel (01) 935 0687

Enquiries to John Larkworthy, Publications Manager

Items About 10,000: unprinted film negatives, b/w original photographs, colour transparencies (35mm, 8″ × 6″, 10″ × 8″), glass negatives, postcards, 20th-century fine art prints, greetings cards, illustrated books

Dates of subject matter 1100 to present

Dates of photographs 1900 to present

Dates of fine art 1700 to present

Subjects Old Master paintings of the Italian, Dutch, Flemish, French and Spanish Schools including works by Titian, Canaletto, Guardi, Rembrandt, Hals, Rubens, Poussin, Velázquez; 18th-century French and English paintings including works by Watteau, Boucher, Fragonard, Reynolds, Gainsborough and Lawrence; European arms and armour from medieval times to the late 18th century, Oriental (Persia eastwards) arms and armour of the 18th and 19th centuries, Sèvres porcelain, gilt-bronzes, clocks, gold snuff-boxes, French 18th-century furniture, English and continental miniatures, paintings by Richard Parkes Bonington, Italian 16th-century bronzes and maiolica, medieval and Renaissance works of art including Venetian glass, Limoges enamels, silver-gilt, cuttings from illuminated manuscripts, carved ivory, rock crystal and boxwood

Access and conditions Open to the public Mon-Sat, Sun 2–5. All material available for editorial reproduction and for advertising. Colour transparencies loaned for a fee; b/w prints and duplicate colour transparencies available for a fee. Reproduction rights and hire fees charged. Staff will undertake limited research. Compulsory credit line. All material copyright. Printed catalogues available: *Sculpture*, 1931 (with supplement 1982); *Furniture*, 1956; *European Arms and Armour* (2 vols), 1962, reprinting; *Oriental Arms and Armour*, 1913 (with supplement 1978); *Ceramics* (vol 1: Pottery, Maiolica, Faience and Stoneware), 1976; *Summary Illustrated Catalogue of Pictures*, 1979; *Miniatures*, 1980; *Illuminated Manuscript Cuttings*, 1980; all from the Wallace Collection.

1035 • WALSALL LIBRARY AND MUSEUM SERVICES

Garman-Ryan Collection and Permanent Collection of Fine Art

Central Library, Lichfield Street, Walsall, West Midlands WS1 1TR
Tel (0922) 21244 ext 3124

Enquiries to Linda Brooks, Keeper of Fine Art

Items Over 650: b/w copy photographs, colour transparencies (35mm), 20th-century fine art prints

Dates of subject matter Medieval period to present

Dates of photographs 1975 to present

Dates of fine art 1497 to present

Subjects British and French 19th- and 20th-century oil paintings, watercolours, drawings, prints including works by Blake, Constable, Delacroix, Monet, Renoir, Turner, Van Gogh; sculpture, watercolours and drawings by Jacob Epstein; woodcuts by Dürer; etchings by Goya and Rembrandt; Victorian genre paintings including works by William Powell Frith and Walter Langley; contemporary prints

Access and conditions Open to the public, Mon-Fri 10–6, Sat 9–4.45. All material available for editorial reproduction and for advertising. Colour material loaned free of charge for one month; b/w prints and duplicate colour transparencies available for a fee. Photocopies available. Reproduction rights and service fees charged. Staff will undertake limited research. All material copyright. Printed catalogue available: Peter Vigurs, *The Garman-Ryan Collection*, Metropolitan Borough Council, 1976.

1036 • WELSH ARTS COLLECTION

The Slide Library, Museum Place, Cardiff CF1 3NX
Tel (0222) 394711

Enquiries to Nicholas Pearson, Visual Art Marketing Officer

Items 4800: colour transparencies (35mm)

Dates of subject matter 1980 to present

Subjects Work of contemporary artists including painters, sculptors, graphic designers and craftspeople living or working in Wales

Access and conditions Open to the public by appt (tel), Mon-Fri 9–5. All material available for editorial reproduction and for advertising by special arrangement with individual artist. Reference prints available through the Welsh Arts Collection who will provide contact address for artist; method of copying items and reproduction fees charged by arrangement with individual artist. Computer list in preparation.

1037 • WELSH ARTS COUNCIL

The Welsh Collection

Museum Place, Cardiff CF1 3NX
Tel (0222) 394711

Enquiries to Valmai Ward, Administrative Assistant

Items 600: colour transparencies (35mm), b/w original photographs

Dates of photographs 1950s to present

Subjects Original works of art including paintings, prints and sculpture produced mainly in Wales between 1950 and 1979

Access and conditions Open to qualified researchers by appt (write), Mon-Fri 9–5. All material available for editorial reproduction and for advertising by special arrangement with individual artists. No loans; b/w and colour material loaned free of charge for one month; material may be copied by outside photographers. Reproduction rights fees charged depending on use of material. Staff will undertake some research. All material copyright of individual artists. Printed catalogue available free of charge.

1038 • ELIZABETH WHITING AND ASSOCIATES

21 Albert Street, London NW1 7LU
Tel (01) 388 2828

Enquiries to Liz Whiting, Director

Items Over 100,000: colour transparencies (35mm, 5″ × 4″)

Dates of subject matter 1950 to present

Dates of photographs 1950 to present

Subjects Interior decoration and home interest from one-room living to architect-designed homes; family houses, conversions, extension, flats, country houses; individual rooms classified by usage; decorating styles, soft furnishings, paint techniques, lighting, shelving, entertaining, table settings; balconies, patios, gardens, swimming pools; some coverage from Italy, Germany and the USA

Access and conditions Open to qualified researchers by appt (tel), Mon-Fri 10–6. All material available for editorial reproduction and for advertising (some restrictions). Colour transparencies loaned free of charge for one month. Reproduction rights and service fees charged. Staff of three will undertake some research; fees charged for large projects. Photographers available for assignment. All material copyright.

1039 • WHITWORTH ART GALLERY

University of Manchester, Whitworth Park, Oxford Road, Manchester M15 6ER
Tel (061) 273 4865

Enquiries to Francis Hawcroft, Principal Keeper

Items About 25,000: fine art prints, art reproductions, b/w original and copy photographs, colour transparencies (35mm, 5″ × 4″), postcards, posters, greetings cards, illustrated books and catalogues

Dates of fine art *c.* 1300 to present

Dates of photographs Contemporary

Subjects Old Master paintings by Willem van de Velde II, David Teniers II, John Wootton and Sir Thomas Lawrence's *Portrait of Richard Payne Knight*; British drawings and watercolours from the 18th century to the present, especially works by Thomas Gainsborough, J. R. Cozens, William Blake (including the *Ancient of Days*), Thomas Girtin, J. M. W. Turner, the Pre-Raphaelites and World War II artists; Old Master and contemporary prints including works by A. Pollaiuolo, A. Mantegna, A. Dürer, Rembrandt, Piranesi and Picasso; modern European watercolours by Cézanne, Van Gogh, Klee and Picasso; Japanese colour woodcuts; contemporary British paintings including Francis Bacon's *Portrait of Lucian Freud*, Lucian Freud's *Self Portrait 1963*, Peter Blake's *Got a Girl,* Howard Hodgkin's *Interior at Oakwood Court*

Access and conditions Open to the public by appt (write), Mon-Fri 9–5. Most material available for editorial reproduction and for advertising. Colour transparencies loaned for a fee; b/w prints available for a fee. Photocopies available. Staff of seven will undertake research. Reproduction rights fees charged. All material copyright. Card catalogue.

1040 • WILLIAMSON ART GALLERY AND MUSEUM

Slatey Road, Birkenhead, Wirral, Merseyside L43 4UE
Tel (051) 652 4177

Enquiries to Clifford Thornton, Curator

Items About 13,000: watercolours, oil painting, artefacts

Dates of subject matter BC to present

Dates of fine art 16th century to present

Subjects English watercolours from the 18th to 20th centuries including works by Constable, Turner and Cozens; 19th-century oil paintings by Liverpool artists; ship models; pattern books, designs, samples of embroidery and block printing from the Arthur H. Lee Tapestry Works at Birkenhead; ethnographic material from West Africa including artefacts and wooden carvings

Access and conditions Open to the public, Mon-Fri 10–4. All material available for editorial reproduction and for advertising. B/w prints and duplicate colour transparencies available for a fee. Photocopies and Polaroids available for a fee. Reproduction rights fees charged. Staff will undertake some research. Compulsory credit line. Most material copyright. Printed catalogues to Museum and Art Gallery collections.

1041 • WISBECH AND FENLAND MUSEUM

Museum Square, Wisbech, Cambridgeshire
PE13 1ES
Tel (0945) 583817

Enquiries to Curator and Librarian

Items About 10,000: unprinted film negatives, illustrated books, b/w copy photographs, postcards, watercolours and drawings, b/w original photographs, old fine art prints, glass negatives, illustrated maps, oil paintings, architectural drawings, lantern slides, press cuttings

Dates of subject matter 15th century to present

Dates of photographs 1850 to present

Dates of fine art 17th century to present

Subjects British oil paintings from 18th century with emphasis on 19th century and including works by Richard Wilson, T. Van Sil, David Bates, T. S. Cooper, W. H. Williamson, G. Chambers, J. Doyle-Penrose and Geoffrey Lefeaver; 19th-century watercolours of Europe and the Middle East by the Rev. C. H. Townsend and the Peckover family, sketchbooks of the Rev. Townsend, Coats family postcard collection of 20th-century East Anglian landscapes, villages and towns; Samuel Smith collection of calotypes c. 1850–60 covering Wisbech especially churches and including Ely and Peterborough Cathedrals; PECKOVER COLLECTION of early atlases including 1486 edition of Ptolemy atlas and maps by Speed and Saxton, also two volumes of Piranesi etchings of *Views of Rome*;

Peckover family photograph albums covering both European travel and domestic life at home in Wisbech; local history collection of Wisbech and surrounding area covering landscapes, social history, architecture, transport, local industry, trade including 19th-century Wisbech woad industry, and soft fruit and bulb growing in the 20th century

Access and conditions Open to qualified researchers by appt (write), summer Tues-Sat 10–5, winter Tues-Sat 10–4. All material available for editorial reproduction and for advertising by special arrangement only. No loans; b/w prints and duplicate colour transparencies available for a fee; material may be copied by outside photographers. Photocopies available for a fee. Reproduction rights fees charged. Staff will undertake some research; fees charged for large projects. Wisbech and Fenland Museum owns copyright to 20% of collections; in other cases copyright clearance is the responsibility of user. Card catalogue.

1042 • MICHAEL WOODWARD ASSOCIATES

Barkston Towers, Barkston Ash, Tadcaster, North Yorkshire LS24 9PS
Tel (093781) 598 Telex 55293 CHACOM G

Enquiries to Michael Woodward

Items 30,000: colour transparencies (5″ × 4″)

Dates of photographs 1980 to present

Subjects Artwork including animals, birds, flowers, transport, landscape, cartoons, children, graphics, Victorian lithographs, Oriental design and pattern, specialist photography

Access and conditions Open to qualified researchers by appt (tel), Mon-Fri 9–5.30. Most material available for editorial reproduction and for advertising. Colour material loaned free of charge for one month. Reproduction rights, holding and service fees charged. Staff will undertake some research. Most material copyright.

1043 • WORCESTER CITY MUSEUM SERVICE

City Museum and Art Gallery, Foregate Street, Worcester WR1 1DT
Tel (0905) 25371

Enquiries to Curator

Items 250,000: natural history specimens, artefacts, fine art

Dates of subject matter Prehistory to present

Dates of fine art 1650 to present

Subjects Natural history of Worcestershire (now part of Hereford and Worcester) including mineral, rock and fossil samples, mounted plant specimens, mounted birds and mammals, UK freshwater and marine mollusc shells, worldwide tropical mollusc shells, entomological collection of mainly British insects; archaeological material found in Worcester and Malvern area from the Iron Age, Romano-British, Anglo-Saxon and Norman periods; domestic items, tools and agricultural implements from medieval times onwards, including those relating to hop cultivation in north and west Worcestershire; handtools, machinery and samples of glove-making, sample tins and a tin body maker from the Metal Box Company canning factory in the 1920s; official regimental collection of the Worcestershire Regiment and Yeomanry Cavalry including uniforms, medals, weapons and campaign relics; regalia and medals of General Sir Richard Gale, GCB, KBE, DSO, MC; oil paintings and watercolours including works by David Bates, William Callow, John Collier, David Cox, Julius Caesar Ibbotson, Dame Laura Knight, Benjamin Leader, Peter de Wint and Thomas Woodward; prints and drawings from the 1960s onwards

Access and conditions Open to the public Mon-Fri 9.30–6, closed Thurs, Sat 9.30–5. Most material available for editorial reproduction and for advertising. B/w prints and duplicate colour transparencies available for a fee; material may be copied by outside photographers. Reproduction rights fees charged. Staff will undertake limited research. Most material out of copyright.

1044 • THE WORSHIPFUL COMPANY OF GOLDSMITHS

Goldsmiths' Hall, Foster Lane, London EC2V 6BN
Tel (01) 606 8971

Enquiries to David Beasley, Assistant to the Librarian

Items About 20,000: colour transparencies (35mm), unprinted film negatives

Dates of subject matter Antiquity to present

Subjects Gold and silver wares including antique and modern silver and jewellery, portraits of past members of the Company, events including prize-giving and dinners, views of past and present Halls; items in permanent collection including dish and ewer by Paul de Lamerie, ewer by James Garrard, candelabra by Paul Storr; hallmarking process, details of hallmarks on objects, history of hall-marking over 500 years

Access and conditions Open to qualified researchers by appt, Mon-Fri 10–5.30. Some material available for editorial reproduction and for advertising. B/w and duplicate colour transparencies available for a fee. Reproduction rights fees charged. Staff will undertake limited research.

1045 • YERBURY OF EDINBURGH

46 Arden Street, Edinburgh EH9 1BW
Tel (031) 447 1063

Enquiries to Trevor E. R. Yerbury

Items Over 500: glass negatives, lantern slides, b/w original photographs, colour transparencies (10″ × 8″), daguerreotypes

Dates of photographs 1845 to 1967

Subjects History of photography, including daguerreotypes, paper negatives, albumen and platinum prints, glass negatives and lantern slides; material from the photographic firm E. R. Yerbury (Edinburgh, founded 1864) and other studio collections; works by the following photographers: E. R. Yerbury, William Crooke, Moffat, Balmain & Tunney, G. W. Wilson; subjects include Edinburgh city centre and environs in the 19th century, golf in the 1880s, Scottish and other personalities including Gladstone, Andrew Carnegie, George IV, Edinburgh steamers on the Firth of Forth, London in the 1890s

Access and conditions Open to qualified researchers by appt (write). All material available for editorial reproduction and for advertising. B/w and colour material loaned free of charge for two weeks. Reproduction rights, service and holding fees charged. Staff of three will undertake research. Printed catalogue available.

Performing Arts

1046 • AQUARIUS PICTURE LIBRARY

PO Box 78, London SE19 2QS
Tel (01) 653 8457

Enquiries to Gilbert Gibson, Managing Director

Items 130,000: b/w original and copy photographs, colour transparencies (35mm, 5″ × 4″, larger), unprinted film negatives, glass negatives

Dates of photographs 1915 to present

Subjects Entertainment including films (by title and actor), vintage Hollywood candids, South African films, silent film stills, on-the-set photos, premières; popular music and musicians including vintage and current pop stars; television; contemporary American and British showbusiness personalities; material from Cosmos Agency (Tokyo) and Bertil Unger (Hollywood)

Access and conditions Not open: telephone and mail requests only. All material available for editorial reproduction; some restrictions on advertising use. B/w and colour material loaned free of charge for two months. Photocopies available. Reproduction rights, service and holding fees charged. Staff will undertake research. Printed catalogue available.

1047 • ERICH AUERBACH COLLECTION

Flat 161, 29 Abercorn Place, London NW8 9DU
Tel (01) 624 5208

Enquiries to Lizzy Auerbach

Items 7000: b/w original photographs, unprinted film negatives, colour transparencies (35mm, 5″ × 4″, larger), colour photographic prints

Dates of photographs 1945 to 1977; some earlier

Subjects English and international musicians, orchestras, quartets, trios, choirs; performances of chamber music, concerts, operas, ballet; actors, artists, personalities including Claudio Abbado, Amadeus Quartet, Marian Anderson, Victoria de los Angeles, Ernest Ansermet, Louis Armstrong,

Dame Janet Baker, Wilhelm Backhaus, Sir John Barbirolli, Daniel Barenboim, Sidney Bechet, Sir Thomas Beecham, Richard Rodney Bennett, Jussi Bjöerling, Nadia Boulanger, Grace Bumbry, Montserrat Caballé, Maria Callas, Pablo Casals, Shura Cherkassky, Aaron Copland, Alfred Cortot, Clifford Curzon, Colin Davis, Alfred Deller, Antonin Dvořák, Duke Ellington, Sir Geraint Evans, Dietrich Fischer-Dieskau, Nicolai Gedda, Beniamino Gigli, Emil Gilels, Carlo Maria Guilini, Tito Gobbi, Benny Goodman, Glenn Gould, Bernard Haitink, Hans Werner Henze, Hans Hotter, Leoš Janáček, Gwyneth Jones, Herbert von Karajan, Julius Katchen, Rudolf Kempe, Otto Klemperer, Cleo Laine, Lotte Lehmann, Lotte Lenya, Christa Ludwig, Lorin Maazel, Zubin Mehta, Gian Carlo Menotti, Yehudi Menuhin, Olivier Messiaen, Arturo Benedetti Michelangeli, Gerald Moore, Birgit Nilsson, Seiji Ozawa, Peter Pears, Gervase de Peyer, Jacqueline du Pré, Hermann Prey, Sviatoslav Richter, Paul Robeson, Mstislav Rostropovich, Sir Malcolm Sargent, Elisabeth Schwarzkopf, Andres Segovia, Tullio Serafin, Ravi Shankar, Anja Silja, Solomon, Georg Solti, Gerard Souzay, Karl-Heinz Stockhausen, Joan Sutherland, Georg Szell, Dame Maggie Teyte, Paul Tortelier, Rosalyn Tureck, Heitor Villa-Lobos, Bruno Walter, Sir William Walton, Ralph Vaughan Williams, Pinchas Zuckermann, and many others

Access and conditions Open to qualified researchers by appt. All material available for editorial reproduction and for advertising. B/w and colour material loaned free of charge for two weeks. Photocopies available. Reproduction rights fees, service and holding fees charged; service fee deductible from use fee. Staff will undertake research. Card catalogue.

1048 • BALLET RAMBERT

94 Chiswick High Road, London W4 1SH
Tel (01) 995 4246

Enquiries to Jane Pritchard, Archivist

Items 3500: b/w original photographs, colour transparencies (35mm), b/w copy photographs, postcards, posters, ephemera

Dates of photographs 1900 to present

Subjects Ballet and contemporary dance including works in the repertoire of the Ballet Rambert and artists who have performed with the company (Dame Marie Rambert, Frederick Ashton, Anthony Tudor, Glenn Tetley, Robert North, Christopher Bruce, Richard Alston, etc.)

Access and conditions Open to qualified researchers by appt (write). Some material available for editorial reproduction and for advertising. B/w material loaned; colour transparencies loaned for a rental fee. Reproduction rights fees charged. Staff will undertake limited research.

1049 • CLIVE BARDA

50 Agate Road, London W6 0AH
Tel (01) 741 0805 Telex 291829 BARDA

Enquiries to Clive Barda

Items 250,000: b/w original photographs, colour transparencies (35mm, 2¼")

Dates of photographs 1969 to present

Subjects Classical music and opera including music personalities working and relaxing, formal and informal; orchestras, concerts, sections of the orchestra, individual instruments, singers, conductors, instrumentalists, musical events (e.g. Last Night of the Proms, a night at the opera), operas on stage, in costume, including close-ups of important roles, full stage shots, Covent Garden, Glyndebourne, English National Opera, Welsh National Opera, some foreign venues

Access and conditions Open to qualified researchers by appt (tel), Mon-Fri 9.30–6. All material available for editorial reproduction; some not available for advertising. B/w and colour material loaned free of charge for one month. Reproduction rights fees charged. Staff of two will undertake research. All material copyright.

1050 • BARNES MUSEUM OF CINEMATOGRAPHY

44 Fore Street, St Ives, Cornwall TR26 1HE

Enquiries to John Barnes, Curator

Items About 1000: b/w original and copy photographs, daguerreotypes, lantern slides, postcards, fine art prints, stereographs, posters, cuttings and tearsheets, illustrated books

Dates of subject matter 17th to 20th century

Dates of photographs 1842 to 1930

Subjects History of moving pictures and the photographic image including shadowgraphy, panoramas, dioramas, peepshows, magic lanterns and optical projection, optical illuminants, toys, stereoscopy, photography, cinematography

Access and conditions Open to written requests year round; museum closed in June and from Oct to Easter. All material available for editorial reproduction and for advertising. No loans; b/w prints available for a fee. Material may be copied by outside photographers. Photocopies available. Reproduction rights fees charged. Staff will undertake some research.

1051 • BIRMINGHAM PUBLIC LIBRARIES

The Shakespeare Library

Language and Literature Department

Central Library, Chamberlain Square, Birmingham B3 3HQ
Tel (021) 235 4227 Telex 337655 BIRLIB G

Enquiries to Nicola Rathbone, Shakespeare Librarian

Dates of subject matter 17th to 20th century

Dates of photographs 20th century

Dates of fine art 17th to 19th century

Subjects Shakespeare including portraits, life, contemporaries, Stratford, London, theatres, Shakespearean actors and actresses, artist's representations of the plays, stage productions (prints, engravings, photos), film and TV production photos; the H. R. FORREST COLLECTION comprising an extra-illustrated, indexed Shakespeare in 76 folio volumes containing portraits, illustrations, playbills and theatre programmes; the JAMES TURNER COLLECTION of 37 volumes (one for each play) with portraits and illustrations; the HOWARD S. PEARSON COLLECTION of 39 folio volumes (indexed) of portraits and illustrations mainly of stage productions during the late 19th and early 20th century; the WILLIAM BENNETT COLLECTION of four volumes (1630 to

1922) of playbills, portraits, newspaper cuttings and other material relating to Covent Garden, Drury Lane and other London theatres; contemporary professional and amateur productions in the UK and also foreign productions

Access and conditions Open to the public, Mon-Fri 9–8, Sat 9–5. All material available for editorial reproduction and for advertising; copyrighted material must be cleared with copyright owner. No loans; b/w prints and colour transparencies available for a fee. Photocopies available at the discretion of the Dept Head. Material may be copied by outside photographers. Reproduction rights fees charged. Staff will undertake limited research. Card and printed catalogue available: *A Shakespeare Bibliography: the Catalogue of the Birmingham Shakespeare Library,* Mansell, 1971.

1052 • TED BOTTLE COLLECTION

114 Meadow Lane, Agar Nook, Coalville, Leicestershire LE6 3DZ
Tel (0533) 714941, (0530) 34133 evenings

Enquiries to Ted Bottle

Items About 4000: colour transparencies (35mm)

Dates of subject matter 1811 to present

Dates of photographs 1977 to present

Subjects Nearly 100 English theatres and music halls, interiors, details, backstage including mechanical remains, dressing rooms, fly galleries. Some of these buildings are no longer extant. Collection includes Hippodrome, Bishop Auckland; Winter Gardens Theatre, Blackpool; Royal, Macclesfield; Queens, Whitehaven; Empire, Maryport; Balmbras Music Hall, Newcastle; etc.

Access and conditions Open to qualified researchers by appt (write). All material available for editorial reproduction and for advertising. Colour material loaned free of charge for one month. Reproduction rights fees charged; service fees charged only when no material is used. All material copyright.

1053 • BRITISH FILM INSTITUTE

Stills, Posters and Design Collection

National Film Archive, 81 Dean Street, London W1V 6AA
Tel (01) 437 4355 exts 45, 23 Telex 27624

Enquiries to Michelle Snapes, Head of Dept.

Items About three million: b/w original photographs, colour transparencies (35mm, 5″ × 4″, larger), glass negatives, posters, lantern slides, postcards, colour photographic prints, original cartoons, set & costume designs, pressbooks and brochures, maquettes of studio sets, fine art prints

Dates of subject matter *c.* 1895 to present

Dates of photographs *c.* 1895 to present

Subjects History of world cinematography (over 100 countries represented), films (by titles, actors, directors, producers and technical crew), film studios, cinema apparatus (projectors, cameras, sound equipment, editing machines, etc.), cinema buildings, newsreels; history of television, television (by programmes, actors, directors, producers, writers), television studios, television apparatus, television news; special emphasis throughout on British cinema and television

Access and conditions Open to the public by appt (tel), Tues-Fri 11–5.30. All material available for editorial reproduction subject to permission of copyright owners. No loans; b/w prints and duplicate colour transparencies or prints available for a fee. No reproduction rights fees; service fees charged. Staff will undertake limited research; fees charged for large projects. Copyright clearance responsibility of user. Printed catalogue available: Markku Salmi (ed), *National Film Archive Catalogue of Stills, Posters & Designs,* British Film Institute, 1982.

1054 • THE CINEMA BOOKSHOP

13/14 Great Russell Street, London WC1B 3NH
Tel (01) 637-0206

Enquiries to Pauline Sheffield

Items 750,000: b/w original and copy photographs, colour transparencies (35mm, 5″ × 4″, larger), colour photographic prints, posters, illustrated books, press books, campaign sheets

Dates of photographs 1920 to present

Subjects Cinema mostly British and American, some foreign material including Italian neo-realist films; cartoons; extensive collection of posters and lobby cards; stills filed by title and personality

Access and conditions Open to qualified researchers by appt (tel), Mon-Sat 10.30–5.30. All material available for editorial reproduction and for advertising subject to copyright clearance by user. B/w and colour material loaned free of charge for 14 days. B/w printed available for a fee. Reproduction rights and holding fees charged. Staff will undertake some research.

1055 • JOE COCKS STUDIO

19 Sheep Street, Stratford-upon-Avon, Warwickshire CV37 6EF
Tel (0789) 293630

Enquiries to Hildegard Cocks

Items About 3000: b/w negatives, colour transparencies (35mm), colour photographic prints

Dates of photographs 1969 to present

Subjects Productions of plays at the Royal Shakespeare Company's theatre at Stratford-upon-Avon, portraits of actors and actresses

Access and conditions Open to the public, Mon-Sat 10–5.30. All material available for editorial reproduction and for advertising. B/w prints and duplicate colour transparencies available for a fee. Reproduction rights fees charged. Staff will undertake research.

1056 • DONALD COOPER PHOTOGRAPHY

21 Wellington Street, London WC2E 7DN
Tel (01) 240 1910

Enquiries to Donald Cooper

Items About 200,000: b/w original photographs, colour transparencies (35mm), illustrated books

Dates of photographs 1969 to present

Subjects Theatre production, principally in London and Stratford-upon-Avon, and including musicals, straight plays, comedies, premières, revivals; Royal Shakespeare Company and National Theatre (comprehensive coverage); West End (extensive coverage) and major fringe theatres (Royal Court, Hampstead, Bush, ICA, Half Moon, etc.); pre-production (i.e. non-costume) and rehearsal photographs, stage lighting, backstage activity, off-stage portraits, candids, theatre buildings; opera productions, principally at Covent Garden, London Coliseum and Camden Festival

Access and conditions Open to qualified researchers by appt (tel), Mon-Fri 9.30–5.30. All

material available for editorial reproduction; some for advertising. B/w and colour material loaned free of charge; period negotiable. Photocopies available. Reproduction rights, service and holding fees charged. Staff will undertake some research.

1057 • MALCOLM CROWTHERS

40 Buckingham Palace Road, London SW1W 0RE
Tel (01) 828 4894

Enquiries to Malcolm Crowthers

Items 75,000: b/w original photographs, colour transparencies (35mm, larger)

Dates of subject matter Prehistory to present

Dates of photographs Contemporary

Subjects Classical music including personalities (portraits and action shots, rehearsals and concerts), conductors (Carlo-Maria Giulini, Pierre Boulez, etc.), composers (Olivier Messiaen, Karlheinz Stockhausen, Sir Michael Tippett, etc.), instrumentalists (Yehudi Menuhin, Christoph Eschenbach, Ivo Pogorelich, etc.), singers (Jessye Norman, Sir Peter Pears, Ghena Dimitrova, etc.), orchestras (BBC Symphony Orchestra, Royal Philharmonic Orchestra, etc.), choirs (BBC Singers, London Sinfonietta Voices, etc.), ensembles (Consort of Musicke, etc.), opera with emphasis on contemporary opera (György Ligeti's *Le Grand Macabre* (ENO), Sir Michael Tippett's *Knot Garden* (Opera Factory), Alban Berg's *Lulu* (Royal Opera House), etc.), London concert halls, musical instruments (organ at Beauvais, 18th-century flute, harpsichords, etc.), dance; geography including Europe and especially Italy and the UK, Middle East (Petra, marsh Arabs), North Africa, USSR, Hong Kong, Singapore, New Zealand (North Island, Maori sculpture), coastal and mountain scenery in Western Scotland, cityscapes, architecture, churches, Torcello Cathedral, St. Mark's Venice (detail of horses), ziggurat at Ur, mosaics, Romanesque architecture, sculpture by Elizabeth Frink; natural history including plants, particularly orchids, kaori trees, gum trees, and birds, especially puffins and gannets

Access and conditions Open to qualified researchers by appt (tel). All material available for editorial reproduction; most for advertising. B/w and colour material loaned free of charge for one month. Reproduction rights and holding fees charged. Staff will undertake research.

1058 • THE DANCE LIBRARY

13 Lexham Mews, London W8 6JW
Tel (01) 937 8634

Enquiries to Darryl Williams or Jan Dalley

Items About 20,000: colour transparencies
(35mm, 5″ × 4″), b/w original and copy
photographs, postcards, original cartoons, fine art
prints, uprinted film negatives

Dates of subject matter Prehistory to present

Dates of photographs 20th century

Subjects Contemporary and historical
international dance including ballet, street
dancing, ballroom dancing, disco, tap dancing, jazz
dancing, folk dancing, ethnic dancing, carnival,
tribal rites, rituals and ceremonies, ice-dancing,
musical comedy, variety, initiation rites, death
rites, national customs, events and personalities;
dance in prehistory and antiquity; photostories;
anthropology, sociology, health and beauty, keep-
fit, theatres, archaeology, art, behaviour,
shamanism, carnivals and pageants, religion,
cinema, fashion, costume, festivals and folk lore,
education, youth, energy, erotica, glamour, posed
models, legends, historical scenes, music, primitive
cultures, showbusiness, teenagers, tourism,
photographic techniques

Access and conditions Open to qualified
researchers by appt (tel), Mon-Fri 9.30–5.30. All
material available for editorial reproduction and
for advertising. B/w and colour material loaned free
of charge for one month. Reproduction rights,
service and holding fees charged; service fees
deductible from use fees. Staff of three will
undertake research; negotiable fee for large
projects.

1059 • DAT'S JAZZ PICTURE LIBRARY

38 Kings Way, Harrow, Middlesex HA1 1XU
Tel (01) 427 7384

Enquiries to Derick A. Thomas

Items About 5000: colour transparencies (35mm),
b/w original photographs, colour photographic
prints

Dates of photographs 1979 to present

Subjects Jazz, rock and classical musicians in
performance; personalities; geography of France,
Spain, Oman, Singapore, Hong Kong, Thailand

Access and conditions Open to the public by

appt (tel), Mon-Fri 10am–11pm. All material
available for editorial reproduction and for
advertising. B/w and colour material loaned free of
charge for one month. Reproduction rights, service
and holding fees charged. Staff will undertake
research. Catalogue available.

1060 • DOMINIC PHOTOGRAPHY

Zoë Dominic and Catherine Ashmore

9A Netherton Grove, London SW10 9TQ
Tel (01) 352 6118

Enquiries to Catherine Ashmore

Items About 400,000: b/w original photographs,
colour transparencies (35mm, 2¼″, 5″ × 4″)

Dates of photographs 1956 to present

Subjects Performing arts including theatre
(actors, actresses, directors, designers, exteriors,
auditoriums, backstage, playwrights, production
pictures), opera (productions, singers, backstage),
ballet (productions, dancers, designers,
choreographers), music, conductors and soloists;
pantomime, musicals, films including some
production shots

Access and conditions Open to qualified
researchers by appt (tel). All material available for
editorial reproduction and for advertising. B/w and
colour material loaned free of charge for one
month. Polaroids available. Reproduction rights,
holding and service fees charged; service fees
deductible from use fees. Staff will undertake
research.

1061 • EDINBURGH UNIVERSITY

Historic Musical Instrument Archive, Reid
Concert Hall, Bristo Square, Edinburgh EH8 9AG
Tel (031) 667 1011 ext 2573

Enquiries to Arnold Myers, Curator and
Archivist

Items About 500: b/w original and copy
photographs

Dates of subject matter 1580 to present

Dates of photographs *c.* 1930 to present

Subjects Musical instruments (excluding
keyboard instruments) worldwide, with emphasis
on Western culture, string, woodwind, brass and
percussion instruments including a special

collection of European guitars from 1580 to present, Scottish bagpipes (1780 to present), British brass-band instruments (1830 to present), 20th-century percussion instruments, mainstream orchestral instruments (flutes, clarinets, horns, oboes, harps, bassoons, etc.) from 1700 to present

Access and conditions Open to the public by appt, Wed 3–5, Sat 10–1 and by appt. All material available for editorial reproduction and for advertising. No loans; b/w prints and duplicate colour transparencies available for a fee. Reproduction rights fees charged. Staff will undertake some research. Catalogue in preparation.

1062 • ENGLISH FOLK DANCE AND SONG SOCIETY

Vaughan Williams Memorial Library, Cecil Sharp House, 2 Regent's Park Road, London NW1 7AY
Tel (01) 485 2206

Enquiries to Malcolm H. Taylor

Items 3500: b/w original and copy photographs, colour transparencies (35mm), lantern slides

Dates of photographs 1870 to present

Subjects World folk and calendar customs including maypole and May-Day celebrations, may-pole dancing, morris dancing, sword dancing, traditional English and also foreign equivalents such as sword dancing in the Basque countries; ritual animal disguises including Padstow hobby horse play on May 1, Minehead hobby horse, etc.; performers, collectors, informants, folk singers including Cecil Sharpe, Percy Grainger, Vaughan Williams, Harry Cox; festivals countrywide (music and dance), traditional drama, including Stratford-upon-Avon Dance Festival from 1920s to present, Keele University Music Festival 1960s to present; performances of Mummers' Plays

Access and conditions Open to the public by appt (tel), Tues-Fri 9.30–5.30, closed Mondays. All material available for editorial reproduction and for advertising. No loans; b/w prints and colour transparencies available for a fee. Photocopies available. Reproduction rights and service fees charged. Staff will undertake some research. Card catalogue.

1063 • THE EURO COLLECTION

82 Gladstone Road, London SW19 1QT
Tel (01) 437 9694

Enquiries to Peter Cargin

Items 45,000: b/w original and copy photographs, colour transparencies (35mm), colour photographic prints, posters

Dates of photographs 1950 to present

Subjects European cinema (1954 to present) including European actors, actresses, directors, on-set material; British, German, Italian, French, Scandinavian and Eastern European cinema; *nouvelle vague*, comedy, horror; accessories, ballet, novel in film, Bible in film, art in film, glamour, baths and sex in film; Australian cinema, directors at work

Access and conditions Open to qualified researchers by appt (write), Mon-Fri 9.30–5.30. All material available for editorial reproduction. B/w and colour material loaned free of charge; period negotiable. Reproduction rights, service and holding fees charged.

1064 • JOEL FINLER COLLECTION

7A Belsize Square, London NW3 4HT
Tel (01) 794 7175

Enquiries to Joel Finler

Items 45,000: b/w original photographs, colour transparencies (35mm, 5″ × 4″), b/w copy photographs, colour photographic prints, posters

Dates of photographs Early 20th century to present

Subjects World cinema including stills from films, actors, actresses, directors at work

Access and conditions Open to the public by appt (tel), Mon-Fri 9–5. All material available for editorial reproduction and for advertising. B/w and colour material loaned free of charge by arrangement. Reproduction rights fees charged. Research undertaken; negotiable research fee charged.

1065 • THE FRIENDS OF ST CECILIA'S HALL AND THE RUSSELL COLLECTION

St Cecilia's Hall, Niddry Street, Edinburgh
EH1 1LJ
Tel (031) 667 1011 ext 4415

Enquiries to Charles Napier, Publications Officer

Items About 300: b/w copy photographs, colour transparencies (35mm, 5″ × 4″), b/w original photographs, colour photographic prints, postcards, technical plans

Dates of subject matter 1600 to 1900

Dates of photographs 1950 to present

Subjects Early keyboard instruments including virginals, harpsichords, clavichords, spinets, pianos and organs; complete views and details of component parts

Access and conditions Open to the public by appt (write). Most material available for editorial reproduction and for advertising. B/w and colour material loaned for a fee. Reproduction rights fees charged. Staff will undertake some research; negotiable research fee charged. Most material copyright. Printed subject list available.

1066 • GO ENTERTAINMENTS

Chapel House, Chapel Street, Congleton, Cheshire
CW12 4AB
Tel (0260) 276627

Enquiries to John Machin

Items Unknown number: b/w original and copy photographs, colour transparencies (35mm, 5″ × 4″, larger), colour photographic prints, lantern slides, postcards, original cartoons, fine art prints, art reproductions, unprinted film negatives, posters, greetings cards, press cuttings and tearsheets, ephemera

Dates of subject matter *c.* 1770 to present

Dates of photographs Mid-19th century to present

Subjects Circuses and circus history including acts, tents, equipment, history of specific circus companies, animals and trainers, portraits, buildings, circus families and their history (up to four generations), clowns, jugglers, acrobats, etc.; posters and ephemera related to circuses

Access and conditions Open to qualified researchers by appt (write). Some material available for editorial reproduction and for advertising. Go Entertainments are agents for travelling circus people and have access to private and family collections of performers. Terms and conditions for use of material have to be negotiated on an individual basis.

1067 • RONALD GRANT ARCHIVE

1-3 Effra Road, London SW2 1BU
Tel (01) 737 3208

Enquiries to Ronald Grant

Items Over 250,000: b/w original and copy photographs, colour photographic prints, colour transparencies (35mm, 5″ × 4″, larger), posters and lobby cards, ephemera, postcards, lantern slides

Dates of subject matter 1896 to present

Dates of photographs 1896 to present

Subjects History of motion pictures including film stills, production shots, portraits of actors and actresses, directors at work, studio personnel, film-making, cinema façades and interiors, posters, lobby cards, cinema programmes, advertising material, silent and sound film projection apparatus, staff uniforms, foyer-stills frames, light fittings, door pulls, carpets and other items of period cinema decor; films from UK, USA, China, Russia and Europe including France, Italy, Poland and Czechoslovakia; GRAHAM HEAD COLLECTION: silent and sound films from 1896 to the present classified as actuality films (i.e. actual events, newsreels, story films, early trick films, nature films, some with stop motion technique), some stills available

Access and conditions Open to qualified researchers by appt (tel) Mon-Fri 11–5. All material available for editorial reproduction; out-of-copyright material also available for advertising. B/w material loaned free of charge for one month. Photocopies available. Reproduction rights, service and holding fees charged. Staff will undertake some research; negotiable fee for long projects.

1068 • DAVID JAMIESON CIRCUS PHOTOGRAPHY

53 Park Court, Harlow, Essex CM20 2PZ
Tel (0279) 419574

Enquiries to David Jamieson

Items 12,000: b/w original photographs, colour transparencies (35mm), colour photographic prints, postcards, posters

Dates of photographs 1970 to present

Subjects Circuses worldwide (UK, USA, Europe, Australia, Africa), interiors, exteriors, circus acts, action shots, personalities, especially flying trapeze and wild animal acts

Access and conditions Open to qualified researchers by appt (write). All material available for editorial reproduction and for advertising. B/w and colour material loaned free of charge for four weeks. Reproduction rights, service and holding fees charged. Staff will undertake research.

1069 • ALAN JOHNSON PHOTOGRAPHY

6 St Peter's Road, Harborne, Birmingham, West Midlands B17 0AS
Tel (021) 426 1654

Enquiries to Alan Johnson

Items 3000: b/w original photographs, colour transparencies (35mm, 5″ × 4″)

Dates of subject matter 1968 to 1982

Dates of photographs 1968 to 1982

Subjects Jazz, blues, rock, pop and progressive music, singers and musicians mostly in concert in Britain; personalities of the entertainment world including British comedians

Access and conditions Open to qualified researchers by appt (write), Mon-Fri 9–5. All material available for editorial reproduction and for advertising. B/w and colour material loaned free of charge for one month. Photocopies available. Reproduction rights and holding fees charged. Staff will undertake research.

1070 • THE KOBAL COLLECTION

1st Floor, 28-32 Shelton Street, London WC2H 9HP
Tel (01) 240 9565

Enquiries to Alex Lascelles

Items 300,000: b/w original photographs, colour transparencies (35mm, 5″ × 4″, 10″ × 8″), postcards, 20th-century fine art prints

Dates of subject matter 1896 to present

Dates of photographs 1896 to present

Subjects All aspects of the cinema and film industry including portraits of film actors and actresses, special effects, animation, premières, studios, directors, cameramen, television

Access and conditions Open to qualified researchers by appt (tel). All material available for editorial reproduction; advertising use by special arrangement only. B/w and colour material loaned free of charge for one month. Reproduction rights and holding fees charged. Staff will undertake some research; fees charged for large projects.

1071 • LONDON FEATURES INTERNATIONAL LTD

8 Dorset Square, London NW1 6PU
Tel (01) 723 4204/5 Telex 25884 LONPIX G

Enquiries to John Halsall

Items Three-and-a-half million: b/w original and copy photographs, colour transparencies (35mm, 6 × 6cm, 7 × 6cm)

Dates of photographs 1950 to present

Subjects Show business, film, television, sport, royal and political personalities (1972 to present); pop and rock music personalities 1950 to present

Access and conditions Open to qualified researchers by appt (tel), Mon-Fri 9–6. All material available for editorial reproduction. B/w and colour material loaned free of charge for 28 days. Photocopies available. Reproduction rights, service and holding fees charged. Staff of seven will undertake research.

1072 • LONDON FESTIVAL BALLET

Festival Ballet House, 39 Jay Mews, London SW7 2ES
Tel (01) 581 1245

Enquiries to John Travis or Jane Pritchard, Archivists

Items 5000: b/w original and copy photographs, colour transparencies (35mm, 5″ × 4″), colour photographic prints, posters, postcards, illustrated books, ephemera

Dates of subject matter 20th century

Dates of photographs 20th century

Subjects Primary collection: complete record of

LFB ballet productions, sets, repertoire, posters, publicity photos, portraits of dancers, designers, original designs; smaller collection on other ballet companies worldwide, mainly ephemera

Access and conditions Open to qualified researchers by appt (write). Some material available for editorial reproduction and for advertising. B/w prints available for a fee; colour transparencies loaned for a rental fee. Photocopies available. Reproduction rights fees charged, but occasionally waived. Staff will undertake some research.

1073 • OPERA NORTH

Grand Theatre, 46 New Briggate, Leeds LS1 6NU
Tel (0532) 439999

Enquiries to Kate Quick, Press Officer

Items About 2500: b/w original photographs

Dates of subject matter 1978 to present

Dates of photographs 1978 to present

Subjects Production photographs taken at dress rehearsals since formation of company in 1978

Access and conditions Open to qualified researchers by appt (tel), Mon-Sat 10–6. All material available for editorial reproduction and for advertising. B/w material loaned free of charge by arrangement. No reproduction rights fees charged. Staff will undertake limited research. All material copyright.

1074 • THE QUESTORS THEATRE

Mattock Lane, London W5 5BQ
Tel (01) 567 0011

Enquiries to Wilfrid Sharp, Archivist

Items Over 3000: b/w original photographs, colour transparencies (5″ × 4″), colour photographic prints, unprinted film negatives, posters, architectural drawings, press cuttings, lantern slides, postcards

Dates of subject matter 1929 to present

Dates of photographs 1929 to present

Subjects Amateur productions at the theatre, tours by the company both in the UK and overseas, personalities visiting the theatre, visits by overseas companies including those from France, Italy, Poland and the USA

Access and conditions Open to qualified researchers by appt (write). All material available for editorial reproduction; advertising use by special arrangement only. No loans; b/w prints available for a fee; material may be copied by outside photographers. Reproduction rights fees charged. Staff will undertake limited research. Most material copyright. Subject lists available.

1075 • DAVID REDFERN PHOTOGRAPHY

83/4 Long Acre, London WC2E 9NG
Tel (01) 240 1883   Telex 28221 REDFOTG

Enquiries to Caroline Thistlethwaite

Items 85,000: colour transparencies (35mm, 5″ × 4″), b/w original and copy photographs

Dates of photographs 1939 to present

Subjects All aspects and types of popular music covering jazz, folk, rock, blues, soul, heavy metal, country and western, and including musicians, festivals, concerts, discotheques, recording studios and record production, instruments; special collection of American jazz music, 1939–1945

Access and conditions Open to the public by appt (write), Mon-Fri 9.30–5.30. All material available for editorial reproduction; portraits of musicians not available for advertising use. B/w and colour material loaned free of charge for one month. Photocopies available. Reproduction rights and holding fees charged; service fees charged only when no material is used. Staff of three will undertake some research. All material copyright. Printed subject list available.

1076 • ROYAL COLLEGE OF MUSIC

Department of Portraits

Prince Consort Road, London SW7 2BS
Tel (01) 589 3643 ext 23

Enquiries to Nathalie McCanse, Assistant Keeper of Portraits

Items About 10,000: illustrated books, old fine art prints, postcards, b/w original photographs, colour transparencies (35mm), posters, original cartoons, illustrated sheet music title pages

Dates of subject matter 16th century to present

Dates of photographs 1850 to present

Subjects Portraits of classical composers, musicans and singers worldwide with emphasis on historical material; collection of Victorian and other sheet music, concert programmes

Access and conditions Open to the public by appt (tel), Mon-Fri 10–5. All material available for editorial reproduction and for advertising. Colour material loaned for a fee; b/w prints and duplicate colour transparencies available for a fee. Photocopies available. Reproduction rights fees charged. Staff of five will undertake some research. Most material copyright. Card catalogue in preparation.

1077 • ROYAL OPERA HOUSE

Covent Garden, London WC2 9DD
Tel (01) 240 1200

Enquiries to Francesca Franchi, Archivist

Items About 100,000: b/w original and copy photographs, colour transparencies (35mm, 5″ × 4″), colour photographic prints, glass negatives, postcards, illustrated maps, old fine art prints, architectural drawings, press cuttings, illustrated books, original cartoons, art reproductions, programmes, costume and set designs, periodicals, libretti, music scores, song sheets

Dates of subject matter 1732 to present

Dates of photographs Late 19th century to present

Subjects History of three Covent Garden theatres since first opening in 1732 and related historical material including portraits of actors, actresses, playwrights, scenes from productions, dancers, singers; ballet, pantomimes, circuses, social dances; theatre in use as Mecca Dance Hall during World War II; record of performances of resident ballet and opera companies since 1946 including performances on tour and covering composers, conductors, librettists, choreographers, designers, producers, premières of operas and ballets at other theatres; collection of architectural drawings, illustrations of exteriors and interiors

Access and conditions Open to qualified researchers by appt (write). Most material available for editorial reproduction and for advertising. B/w material loaned free of charge for one month; colour material loaned for a fee. Photocopies available. Reproduction rights and

holding fees charged. Staff will undertake some research; fees charged for large projects. Most material copyright. Card catalogue available.

1078 • THE SHAKESPEARE BIRTHPLACE TRUST

The Shakespeare Centre, Henley Street, Stratford-upon-Avon, Warwickshire CV37 6QW
Tel (0789) 204016

Enquiries to Levi Fox, Director

Items 35,000: b/w original and copy photographs, colour transparencies (35mm, 5″ × 4″), press cuttings, posters, unprinted film negatives, colour photographic prints, glass negatives, lantern slides, postcards, illustrated maps, old fine art prints, illustrated books

Dates of subject matter c. 1550 to present

Dates of photographs c. 1850 to present

Subjects SHAKESPEARE CENTRE LIBRARY COLLECTION and SHAKESPEARE BIRTHPLACE TRUST RECORDS OFFICE COLLECTION including portraits of William Shakespeare, illustrated editions of his works, stage history of the plays, actors in Shakespearian roles, portraits of actors, designs for Shakespeare productions from 19th century onwards; engravings and reproductions of all aspects of English 16th- and 17th-century life; local history of Stratford-upon-Avon and south Warwickshire including landscapes, agriculture, architecture, urban development from 18th century onwards; paintings of Shakespeare properties including Anne Hathaway's cottage; special collections include the Royal Shakespeare Company Library and Archive covering production photographs, set photographs, designs (including some originals) from 1880 to present, non-Shakespeare productions at all theatres used by the Company: photographers include Ernest Daniels, Angus McBean, Gordon Goode, Tom Holte; BRAM STOKER COLLECTION on Henry Irving

Access and conditions Open to the public by appt (tel), Mon-Fri 10–5, Sat 9.30–12.30. Most material available for editorial reproduction and for advertising. No loans; b/w prints and duplicate colour transparencies available for a fee. Photocopies available for a fee. Reproduction rights and service fees charged. Staff of five will undertake limited research. Most material copyright.

1079 • TYNEWEAR THEATRE COMPANY

Newcastle Playhouse, Barras Bridge,
Newcastle upon Tyne NE1 7RH
Tel (0632) 323335

Enquiries to Bernard Martin, Publicity Director

Items About 2000: b/w original photographs,
colour transparencies (35mm), postcards, posters,
greetings cards, press cuttings

Dates of subject matter 1978 to present

Dates of photographs 1978 to present

Subjects Productions by the company since its
formation in 1978 including national and regional
tours, pantomimes at Newcastle Theatre Royal,
workshops and educational activities organized in
Newcastle and the North-East, portraits of actors
and directors

Access and conditions Open to qualified
researchers by appt (write). Most material
available for editorial reproduction; advertising use
by special arrangement only. B/w material loaned
free of charge by arrangement; duplicate colour
transparencies available for a fee. Photocopies
available. Reproduction rights and service fees
sometimes charged. Staff will undertake some
research. All material copyright.

1080 • UNIVERSITY OF BRISTOL THEATRE COLLECTION

Department of Drama

29 Park Row, Bristol BS1 5LT
Tel (0272) 24161

Enquiries to Ann Brooke Barnett, Keeper of the
Theatre Collection

Items Over 150,000: b/w original photographs,
engravings, press cuttings, fine art prints,
ephemera, colour transparencies

Dates of photographs 1880 to present

Subjects RICHARD SOUTHERN COLLECTION:
100,000 prints and photographs of all aspects of
theatre architecture, costume and scene design;
engravings, playbills, paintings and illustrated
books; theatre models including Georgian Theatre,
Richmond, Yorks. and the Wren Drury Lane
theatre; unpublished manuscript notebooks of
theatre historian William John Lawrence (1880s);
BEERBOHM TREE COLLECTION: original ground plans
and elevations for Her Majesty's Theatre built by
Tree in 1897; prompt books, especially for his

productions of Shakespeare; Tree's diaries,
personal papers and correspondence; 50 books of
press cuttings; ERIC JONES EVANS COLLECTION:
theatrical memorabilia including scripts, playbills,
prompt books, letters, music scores, photographs
and artefacts, props, costumes and personal effects,
many related to Sir Henry Irving; record of the life
of a touring provincial actor between the wars;
ALAN TAGG COLLECTION: designs, models and
photographs of productions spanning his career
from 1956 to the present; ROBINSON COLLECTION:
18th- and 19th- century playbills from West
Country theatres; LANDSTONE BEQUEST:
programmes for all London productions 1944-1969;
FRENCH THEATRE COLLECTION: pictorial material
illustrating theatre designs, production and
costume from the Middle Ages to the present;
German Theatre: material on Max Reinhardt's life
and work; facsimiles of Appia's designs for
Wagner's operas; *Monumenta Scenica* by Joseph
Gregor, representing the Court Theatres of the
classical and baroque periods; THE OLD VIC
ARCHIVE; paintings of David Garrick, Charles
Kean, Sarah Siddons, Edmund Kean, John
Kemble, Sir John Vanbrugh

Access and conditions Open to the public by
appt, Mon-Fri 10–5. All material available for
editorial reproduction and for advertising with the
Keeper's permission. B/w prints and duplicate
colour transparencies available for a fee.
Photocopies available. Reproduction rights fees
charged. Staff will undertake limited research.
Catalogue available.

1081 • JOHN VICKERS THEATRE COLLECTION

27 Shorrolds Road, London SW6 7TR
Tel (01) 385 5774

Enquiries to Laurence Bernes, Director

Items 35,000: b/w original photographs, glass
negatives, colour photographic prints

Dates of photographs 1938 to 1974

Subjects English theatre, personalities,
musicians, composers, including Old Vic
productions (1942-1955), Laurence Olivier, Ralph
Richardson, Alec Guinness, Peggy Ashcroft, Sybil
Thorndike, Michael Redgrave, etc.

Access and conditions Open to qualified
researchers by appt (tel). All material available for
editorial reproduction and for advertising. B/w and
colour material loaned free of charge for four to six
weeks. Reproduction rights, service and holding

fees charged. Staff of three will undertake research. Catalogue available.

1082 • VICTORIA AND ALBERT MUSEUM

Theatre Museum, Cromwell Road, London SW7 2RL
Tel (01) 589 6371

Enquiries to Theatre Museum

Items About 150,000: b/w original and copy photographs, colour transparencies (35mm, 5″ × 4″), colour photographic prints, glass negatives, lantern slides, postcards, original cartoons, old fine art prints, 20th-century fine art prints, art reproductions, unprinted film negatives, posters, press cuttings

Dates of subject matter *c.* 17th century to present

Dates of photographs *c.* 1860 to present

Subjects British and European theatre including original designs for sets and costumes since 1700; portraits of performers since *c.* 1600; stage personalities and productions with special emphasis on British 19th-century and post-World War II theatre; dance productions and dancers worldwide with special emphasis on the development of British ballet; theatre buildings throughout the UK; British and some European opera productions (mainly Covent Garden post-1945); circuses, puppetry

Access and conditions Open to qualified researchers by appt (write), Tues-Thurs 10–4.30. All material available for editorial reproduction and for advertising subject to copyright clearance. Requests for reproduction-quality material should be made to the Photographic Sales Department – see entry no. 1028. Reproduction rights and holding fees charged. Staff will undertake research for a fee. Most material copyright; where copyright is not held by the Theatre Museum, clearance is the responsibility of the user. Partial card catalogue available.

1083 • GEOFFREY WHEELER (PHOTOGRAPHS) LONDON

195 Gloucester Place, London NW1 6BU
Tel (01) 262 2558 day, 402 6494 eve

Enquiries to Geoffrey Wheeler

Items About 1500: b/w original photographs, colour transparencies (35mm), b/w copy photographs, colour photographic prints

Dates of subject matter 1450 to present

Dates of photographs 1960 to present

Subjects Richard III and the Wars of the Roses including panel portraits, engravings, illuminated manuscripts, manuscript letters, castles, churches, stained glass, monumental effigies, tombs and monumental brasses, memorials, battlefields; stills of productions of Shakespeare's history plays on stage, film and television; stills from filmed adaptations of Shakespeare with emphasis on parts played by Sir Lawrence Olivier

Access and conditions Open to the public by appt. All material available for editorial reproduction. B/w material loaned free of charge for three months; colour material loaned free of charge for three weeks. Reproduction rights fees charged. Staff will undertake some research. Most material copyright.

1084 • REG WILSON PHOTOGRAPHY

55 Beechwood Avenue, London N3 3BB
Tel (01) 346 7776

Enquiries to Reg Wilson

Items Over one million; b/w original photographs, colour transparencies (35mm, 2¼″), postcards, unprinted film negatives, illustrations, engravings

Dates of subject matter 19th century to present

Dates of photographs 1960 to present

Subjects Comprehensive collection relating to the performing arts with special emphasis on productions in the UK but also including coverage of overseas companies and productions especially on tour in this country; opera, ballet, theatre, musicians, composers, authors, playwrights; historical material covers old illustrations and European concert and opera programmes, ephemera with special emphasis on operatic performances and concerts

Access and conditions Open to qualified researchers by appt (write), Mon-Fri 9–5. All material available for editorial reproduction but not for advertising or exhibition use. B/w and colour material loaned free of charge by arrangement. Reproduction rights fees charged. Staff of three will undertake some research. Photographer available for assignment. All material copyright. Card catalogue available.

Specialized Collections

Charity & Youth

1085 • DR BARNARDO'S

Barnardo Photographic Archive

Tanners Lane, Barkingside, Ilford, Essex IG6 1QG
Tel (01) 550 8822

Enquiries to Roy Ainsworth, Chief Photographer

Items 250,000: b/w and sepia original photographs

Dates of photographs 1870 to present

Subjects Children who have been helped by Dr Barnardo's including destitute children of the late 1800s upon admission to the Homes, workshop pictures of young apprentices learning their trade, life in Dr Barnardo's Homes of that period and up to 1910; from 1926 to present, photographs of child-care work with the Barnardo organization

Access and conditions Open to qualified researchers by appt (write). Some material available for editorial reproduction (photographs must be over 20 years old) at the discretion of Dr Barnardo's. No loans; b/w prints available for a fee. Photocopies of popular subjects from the archives are available by post for a fee. Reproduction rights fees charged.

1086 • THE CHILDREN'S SOCIETY

Old Town Hall, Kennington Road, London
SE11 4QD
Tel (01) 735 2441

Enquiries to Miranda Melbourn, Archivist

Items About 3000: b/w original and copy photographs, lantern slides, colour photographic prints, postcards, colour transparencies (35mm), fine art prints, architectural drawings, illustrated books

Dates of photographs 1880 to present

Subjects Children in care c. 1890 in small cottage homes, industrial schools and farms; life on an industrial farm showing ploughing, tailoring, printing, house parlour-maids, ceremonies of laying foundation stones, early committees, daily life, emigration to Canada; World Wars I and II, including evacuation of children, gas masks, young recruits, war nurseries, Canadian Red Cross parcels; Depression years, streetscenes; Royal patronage (Queen Mary, Queen Elizabeth II); early photographs of crippled and multi-handicapped children, diabetic children, childcare procedures; adoption and fostering, large children's homes; modern projects (including a gypsy encampment), patronage of present-day personalities, e.g. the Beatles

Access and conditions Open to the public by appt (write). All material available for editorial reproduction and for advertising subject to the Society's approval. B/w material loaned; b/w prints available; photocopies available. Donation requested in lieu of reproduction rights fees; postage payable. Staff will undertake some research.

1087 • COMMUNITY SERVICE VOLUNTEERS

237 Pentonville Road, London N1 9NJ
Tel (01) 278 6601

Enquiries to Anne Webster, Information and Press Officer

Items About 100: b/w original photographs, colour transparencies (35mm), colour photographic prints

Dates of photographs 1970 to present

Subjects Young volunteers (aged 16-35) working in community service projects throughout the UK including with young children, with the mentally handicapped, with the elderly, in hospitals, with young people in trouble, with the physically disabled, with the single homeless, in probation hostels, borstals and prison; young unemployed people working on CSV's youth employment and training schemes; pupils working on community involvement projects in schools

Access and conditions Open to qualified researchers by appt (tel). All material available for editorial reproduction subject to CSV approval. B/w and colour material loaned free of charge for one month. No reproduction rights fees. Staff will undertake some research.

1088 • THE DUKE OF EDINBURGH'S AWARD

5 Prince of Wales Terrace, London W8 5PG
Tel (01) 937 5205

Enquiries to Deborah Dowdall, Public Relations Executive

Items About 1000: b/w original and copy photographs, colour transparencies (35mm, 5″ × 4″), colour photographic prints, glass negatives, posters

Dates of photographs 1956 to present

Subjects Youth activities worldwide in 43 countries (mostly Commonwealth, and many in India and Africa) including community service, expeditions (climbing, wild-country walking, camping); non-physical skills (video filming, photography, painting, handicrafts, cooking, gardening, engineering, dance, drama, music), sports and physical recreation; tours and visits by HRH the Duke of Edinburgh; award presentation ceremonies

Access and conditions Open to the public by appt, Mon-Fri 10–4. Some material available for editorial reproduction but not for advertising. B/w and colour material loaned free of charge for two months. B/w prints and duplicate colour transparencies available for a fee. Photocopies available. No reproduction rights fees. Staff will undertake limited research. Compulsory credit line.

1089 • SAVE THE CHILDREN FUND

Mary Datchelor House, 17 Grove Lane, London SE5 8RD
Tel (01) 703 5400

Enquiries to Alison Fowles, Library Assistant, Audio-Visual Materials

Items About 20,000: b/w copy photographs, colour transparencies (35mm)

Dates of subject matter 1919 to present

Dates of photographs 1919 to present

Subjects Work of the Fund in developing countries including mother and child health clinics, nutrition and feeding, education, training, immunization, emergency relief, sponsorship, refugees; coverage of work in the UK including family centres, playgroups, residential schools, hospital playschemes, gypsies, Vietnamese refugees

Access and conditions Open to the public by appt (tel), Mon-Thurs 9.30–5.30, Fri 9.30–5. All material available for editorial reproduction but not for advertising. B/w and colour material loaned by arrangement; b/w prints and duplicate colour transparencies available for a fee. No reproduction rights fees charged. All material copyright. Catalogue in preparation.

1090 • THE SCOUT ASSOCIATION

Baden-Powell House, Queen's Gate, London SW7 5JS
Tel (01) 584 7030

Enquiries to Jack Olden, Public Relations Officer

Items About 7000: b/w original and copy photographs, colour transparencies (35mm), colour photographic prints, glass negatives, original cartoons

Dates of subject matter 1907 to present

Dates of photographs 1907 to present

Subjects History of and activities relating to Scouting in the UK including portraits of founder, Robert Baden-Powell, and all subsequent Chief Scouts; camping, hiking, canoeing, sailing; community service projects, public duties

Access and conditions Open to the public by appt (write), Mon-Fri 9–5. All material available for editorial reproduction and for advertising. B/w and colour material loaned free of charge for three months; material may be copied by outside photographers. Reproduction rights and service fees charged. No research undertaken.

Costume & Fashion

1091 • BIRMINGHAM PUBLIC LIBRARIES

Social Sciences Department

Central Library, Chamberlain Square,
Birmingham B3 3HQ
Tel (021) 235 4545 Telex 337655 BIRLIB G

Enquiries to Marion Large, Head of Department

Items About 11,000: postcards, b/w original photographs, 18th- and 19th-century colour and b/w engravings and lithographs, architectural drawings

Dates of subject matter 1772 to present

Dates of photographs 1890 to c. 1970

Subjects R. CROMPTON RHODES COLLECTION of fashion plates (1772-1893) of male and female fashions from British and French periodicals (b/w and colour); women's fashions including general fashions (1930 to 1961), teenage fashions (1950s and 1960s), women's hats (1950s), women's hairstyles (1930 to 1960) in b/w only; history of railways including architectural drawings of stations and bridges of pre-nationalized railway companies especially the Great Western Railway Company (1840s to 1930s), stations built by the Great Western Railway and railways it absorbed (1950s and 1960s), foreign railway stations (1890 to 1914)

Access and conditions Open to the public, Mon-Fri 9–8, Sat 9–5. All material available for editorial reproduction and for advertising; copyrighted material must be cleared with owner of copyright. No loans; b/w prints and colour transparencies available for a fee. Photocopies available. Reproduction rights fees charged. Staff will undertake limited research.

1092 • GALLERY OF ENGLISH COSTUME

Platt Hall, Platt Fields, Rusholme, Manchester
M14 5LL
Tel (061) 224 5217

Enquiries to Keeper

Items About 11,000: b/w original and copy photographs, colour transparencies (35mm), fine art prints, stereographs, daguerreotypes, ambrotypes, greetings cards, architectural drawings, illustrated books, ephemera

Dates of subject matter 1400 to present

Dates of photographs c. 1840 to present

Subjects Costume made or worn in England, or worn by English people abroad; history of fashionable and unfashionable dress; occupational dress, clothing trades, crafts and manufacture; social history of dress, etiquette; sports clothes, trade catalogues, dress patterns, fashion plates; caricatures and lampoons; studio portraits, cabinet and cartes-de-visite photographs; 19th-century working people (including Welsh steel-workers, both men and women), rational and aesthetic dress

Access and conditions Open to qualified researchers by appt, Mon-Fri 9–5. All material available for editorial reproduction and for advertising. No loans; b/w prints available for a fee. Material may be copied by outside photographers. Reproduction rights fees charged. Staff will undertake very limited research in response to out-of-town requests.

1093 • MUSEUM OF COSTUME AND FASHION RESEARCH CENTRE

4 Circus, Bath, Avon BA1 2EW
Tel (0225) 61111 ext 425

Enquiries to P. C. Byrde, Keeper of Costume

Items About 10,000: b/w original photographs, colour transparencies (35mm), press cuttings, hand-coloured engravings, illustrated trade catalogues, fashion periodicals, daguerreotypes

Dates of subject matter Medieval to present

Dates of photographs c. 1850s to present

Subjects History and development of male and female textiles and needlework costume including British and European paintings and sculpture illustrating clothes of earlier periods; millinery, underwear, jewellery, royal and ceremonial clothes; 19th-century cartes-de-visite, family photographs and albums illustrating fashionable British dress in the 19th and 20th centuries; special collections include the *SUNDAY TIMES* fashion ARCHIVE 1957–72, and the WORTH and PAQUIN ARCHIVES; children's toys and games

Access and conditions Open to the public by appt (write). Some material available for editorial reproduction; advertising use by special arrangement only. No loans; b/w prints and duplicate colour transparencies available for a fee. Photocopies available. Reproduction rights and service fees charged; service fees deductible from use fees. Most material copyright. Card catalogue available.

1094 • UNITED TRADE PRESS LTD

33 Bowling Green Lane, London EC1R 0DA
Tel (01) 837 1212 Telex 229049

Enquiries to Judith Bains, Promotions Secretary

Items Thousands: illustrated magazines

Dates of subject matter 1860s to 1960s

Subjects Bound copies of magazines relating to the tailoring and dressmaking trades from the mid-19th century onwards including *Tailor and Cutter*, *Women's Wear*, *Gentleman's Tailor*, *Clerical Tailor* and *American Gentlemen's Tailor*; magazines contain illustrations of finished garments and scaled-down patterns for making-up

Access and conditions Open to the public by appt (tel), Mon-Fri 9–5. All material available for editorial reproduction; advertising use by special arrangement only. No loans; b/w prints available for a fee. Photocopies available. Reproduction rights and service fees charged. All material copyright.

Ephemera

1095 • CHRISTMAS ARCHIVES INTERNATIONAL

Wassail House, 64 Severn Road, Canton, Cardiff CF1 9EA
Tel (0222) 41120

Enquiries to Count Andrzej von Staufer

Items 30,000: colour transparencies (35mm, 5″ × 4″), b/w original photographs, lantern slides, postcards, original cartoons, illustrated maps, fine art prints, art reproductions, posters, greetings cards, press cuttings and tearsheets, ephemera

Dates of subject matter AD 100 to present

Dates of fine art *c*. 1600 to 1930s

Dates of photographs Current

Subjects Christmas and related subjects including Christmas cards (1850 to present); posters, menus, books, magazines and illustrated papers (1600 to present); traditional seasonal characters including Babouska, Tomten, Misrule, and others worldwide; giftbringers of the world, worldwide nativity scenes, early celebrations of Christmas, images of Santa Claus, Christmas crafts, Christmas in architectural details, frescoes; customs, decorations; pantomime, foods, Christmas trees, Christmas in other countries, contemporary Christmas scenes, children, winter and snow scenes; religious, commercial, educational, historical Christmas subjects; stores and streetscenes; historical commercial design; non-seasonal greetings cards and related material including toys, fairies, flora, Art Nouveau, Art Deco, children; folklore, Easter designs; gastronomy including food, bills of fare, accounts, advertisements, old kitchens, equipment, wartime food and related topics

Access and conditions Open to qualified researchers by appt, written and telephone requests preferred, Mon-Fri 10–6. Most material available for editorial reproduction and for advertising, subject to copyright clearance. B/w material loaned free of charge for 21 days, colour for 28 days. B/w prints and duplicate colour transparencies available for a fee.

1096 • ROBERT OPIE COLLECTION

120 Gordon Road, London W13 8PJ
Tel (01) 997 6419, (0452) 32309

Enquiries to Robert Opie

Items 200,000: commercial packaging, postcards, promotional material, ephemera, posters, greetings cards, colour transparencies (35mm), illustrated books, lantern slides

Dates of subject matter 1800 to present

Subjects Commercial artefacts with special emphasis on consumer products, retail packaging, promotional material, posters, leaflets, brochures, trade and cigarette cards; ephemera including luggage labels, tickets, travel brochures, theatre posters, calendars, telegrams, postal items, greetings cards, postcards, toys, games, store catalogues, magazines, comics and wartime ephemera; all aspects of daily life covered including fashion, sports, pastimes, events (festivities, coronations), buildings, transport, consumer products and commodities especially food, drink, cosmetics, toiletries, medicines, household goods, tobacco products, matches

Access and conditions Open to the public by appt (tel). Most material available for editorial reproduction and for advertising. B/w and colour material loaned free of charge for two months (print fees charged). Material may be copied by outside photographers. Photocopies available. Reproduction rights fees charged. Staff will undertake some research; negotiable research fee charged. Some material copyright.

1097 • RETROGRAPH DESIGN AND PACKAGING LIBRARY

164 Kensington Park Road, London W11 2ER
Tel (01) 727 9378

Enquiries to Martin and Jilliana Ranicar-Breese

Items Over 10,000: ephemera, lantern slides, postcards, posters, greetings cards, artwork, sample books

Dates of subject matter 1880 to 1960

Subjects European Packaging 1880–1960 including labels, boxes, chocolate wrappers, perfume and soap labels, cotton-bale labels, cheese labels, food labels, beer, wine and liquor labels, jam and general canning subject labels; cigar labels; fashion: wide range of deco fashion advertisements and invitations (mainly French); food and drink: menus, wine catalogues, labels and packaging; publicity: French perfume publicity, tinned coffee and beverages, shop display signs, 3D examples of animals in publicity (cats, pigs, frogs, etc.); advertising fans: good examples from France; hotel and transport: hotel labels (1930 to 1960), printer's stock, airline labels and tags (1940–1960); airline time schedules: shipping, ballooning and early aviation ephemera; bookmarks: publicity bookmarks; performing arts: important pre-cinema collection of magic lanterns, slides, optical toys and related ephemera; magic and illusion: large collection of magical prints, antique magic apparatus and ephemera; optical illusion: ephemera and objects, transformation examples, hold-to-light cards; photography: images of the photographer and the tripod; greetings cards: examples covering period 1900 to 1925; social and religious: black memorabilia and ephemera, Judaica 1880 to 1944, large collection of documentation; militaria: specialist collection relating to Boer War from French point of view; sports: images of the pennyfarthing; motoring: ephemera, publicity and advertising; printing art: examples of lettering, letterheads, printer's sample books covering packaging, design, specialist metallic and embossed printing; trade: manufacturer's catalogues, printer's samples of calendars 1900–1930; European songsheets 1920–1930

Access and conditions Open to qualified researchers by appt (tel), Mon-Fri 9.30–5.30. Most material available for editorial reproduction and for advertising. B/w material loaned free of charge for one week; colour negotiable. Photocopies and Polaroids available. Reproduction rights, holding and service fees charged; service fees deductible from use fees. Staff will undertake research; negotiable fee for large projects.

Concerning one Person

1098 • CHURCHILL COLLEGE ARCHIVES CENTRE

The Archives Centre, Churchill College,
Cambridge CB3 0DS
Tel (0223) 61200

Enquiries to M. M. Stewart

Items Unknown number: b/w original and copy photographs, colour photographic prints, glass negatives, postcards, original cartoons, illustrated maps, unprinted film negatives, posters, greetings cards, architectural drawings, illustrated books

Subjects Scientific, military and political papers of Sir Winston Churchill in 15,000 boxes with photographs *passim;* important collection of Churchill's photograph albums

Access and conditions Open to qualified researchers with a letter of introduction, Mon-Fri 9–12.30, 1.30–5. Some material available for editorial reproduction. No loans; colour and b/w material may be copied by local photographer for a fee. Photocopies available. Copyright clearance responsibility of user. Reproduction rights and service fees charged in some cases. Staff will undertake limited research in response to specific requests.

1099 • THE DICKENS' HOUSE MUSEUM

48 Doughty Street, London WC1N 2LF
Tel (01) 405 2127

Enquiries to Dr David Parker, Curator

Items About 8000: b/w original and copy photographs, colour transparencies (35mm, 5″ × 4″, larger), colour photographic prints, glass negatives, lantern slides, press cuttings and tearsheets, illustrated books, postcards, fine art prints, greetings cards, art reproductions, illustrated maps, original cartoons, daguerreotypes, posters

Dates of subject matter 1750 to present

Dates of photographs 1840s to present

Subjects Portraits of Charles Dickens (about 500), his family and pets and his circle including Hablôt Knight Browne (Phiz), George Cruikshank, John Forster, Daniel Maclise, Alfred Tennyson;

illustrations to the novels from almost any edition; Dickens memorabilia including cigarette cards and postcards; contemporary cartoons and caricatures; facsimiles of letters, manuscripts, legal documents, printed matter related to Dickens; Dickens' works in other media including film stills, scenes from plays, playbills and advertisements; Dickens scholars, the Dickens Fellowship and their activities; the T.W. TYRRELL COLLECTION including extensive topographical material covering every imaginable area associated with the life and works of Dickens, many areas of London since radically altered, prints showing contemporary conditions; SUZANNET COLLECTION: original illustrations to Dickens' novels, books, presentation copies, letters, manuscripts

Access and conditions Open to the public by appt, Mon-Fri 10–5. All material available for editorial reproduction and for advertising. B/w prints available for a fee; colour transparencies loaned free of charge for one month or duplicated for a fee. Photocopies available. Reproduction rights fees charged. Staff will undertake half a day of research free of charge; search fee charged for longer projects.

1100 • THE ERNST DRYDEN COLLECTION

25 Onslow Road, Burwood Park, Walton-on-Thames, Surrey KT12 5BB
Tel (0932) 227333

Enquiries to Anthony Lipmann

Items About 4000: colour transparencies (5″ × 4″), b/w negatives, colour negatives

Dates of subject matter 1911 to 1938

Dates of photographs 1921 to 1938; some earlier

Subjects Graphic work of the Austrian artist Ernst Deutsch Dryden (1883–1938) including posters, advertisements, magazine covers, fashion illustrations, fashion design and film costume design; photographs of the artist, working tracings for fashion design with fabric samples attached, letters, a film storyboard (*The Garden of Allah,* 1936), costume stills; subjects advertised include automobiles, cigarettes, sun-tan oil, sportswear, couture, preserves, fruit, beer, spirits, tea, library, washing products, loudspeakers, coloured crayons, biscuits, Christmas shopping, shipping line, pen & pencil manufacturers, tailor, clocks, ties, newspaper, shampoo, *eau de vie*, suspenders, anti-nicotine, swimwear, (advertisers: Berliet, Bibliothèque Nationale des Beaux Arts (Paris), Blaupunkt, Bugatti, Chanel, Canadian Club Whisky, Cinzano, Hapag, Knize, Lux, Persil, Jane Regny, *Paris Matinal*, Voisin, Wolsey); fashion design including day wear 1923 to 1938, dresses, suits, bridal gowns, casual, beachwear, cocktail dresses, evening wear male and female, accessories (belts, hats, coats, shoes) and designed for Saks Fifth Avenue, Macy's, Marshall Field, Chanel, Germaine Monteil, Knize, Hello (Vienna); designs and illustrations including covers for *Die Dame* (1926–1933), *Neue Freie Presse*, *Adam* – including dresses, social occasions, interior design, automobiles, sport and leisure, art and theatre; Hollywood costume design (1933–1938) for many films including *The Adventures of Tom Sawyer*, *Alibi for Murder*, *Devil's Playground*, *The Garden of Allah*, *The King Steps Out*, *Lost Horizon*, *Remember Last Night*, *The Prisoner of Zenda*, *Dr Rhythm* and for Marlene Dietrich, Tilly Losch, Grace Moore, Jane Wyatt, Constance Cummings, Madeleine Carroll, Dolores del Rio, Beatrice Lillie, Mae West and many others

Access and conditions Open to qualified researchers by appt (write). Some material available for editorial reproduction and for advertising at the discretion of the owners. B/w and colour material loaned free of charge for one month. B/w prints and duplicate colour transparencies available for a fee. Reproduction rights, service and holding fees charged. Staff will undertake some research. Catalogue available.

1101 • KEATS HOUSE

Wentworth Place, Keats Grove, London NW3 2RR
Tel (01) 435 2062

Enquiries to Curator

Items About 2000: b/w original and copy photographs, colour transparencies (35mm), glass negatives, lantern slides, postcards, unprinted film negatives, greetings cards, illustrated books

Dates of subject matter 1790 to present

Dates of photographs Late 19th century to present

Subjects Illustrative material relating to the life of John Keats and his circle including Percy Bysshe Shelley, Joseph Severn, Benjamin Robert Haydon, Samuel Taylor Coleridge, Charles Lamb and others; portraits of Keats, some paintings by Haydon; places where Keats lived in UK and Rome; KATE GREENAWAY COLLECTION: material related to her book and card production including early proofs, birthday books, cards, original artwork, printed material

Access and conditions Open to the public by appt (write), Mon-Sat 10–1, 2–6, Sun 2–5. All material available for editorial reproduction but not for advertising. B/w prints and duplicate colour transparencies available for a fee. Photocopies available. Reproduction rights fees charged. Staff will undertake some research. Compulsory credit line. Card catalogue.

1102 • MARX MEMORIAL LIBRARY

37A Clerkenwell Green, London EC1R 0DU
Tel (01) 253 1485

Enquiries to Andrew Davies or Max Egelnick

Items About 1000: b/w original and copy photographs, posters, glass negatives, unprinted film negatives, greetings cards, illustrated books

Dates of subject matter 1870 to present

Dates of photographs 1900 to present

Subjects Karl Marx, Friedrich Engels, V. I. Lenin, Marx Memorial Library, London dock strike (1889), General Strike (1926), scenes from the Russian Revolution, the *DAILY WORKER* COLLECTION

Access and conditions Open to library members (you may join), Mon & Fri 2–6, Tues-Thurs 2–9. All material available for editorial reproduction and for advertising. No loans; material may be copied by outside photographers. Photocopies available. Reproduction rights and service fees charged. Staff will undertake limited research. Compulsory credit line.

1103 • MARYLEBONE LIBRARY

Sherlock Holmes Collection

Marylebone Road, London NW1 5PS
Tel (01) 828 8070 ext 4028 Telex 263305

Enquiries to Catherine Cooke, Librarian

Items About 500: b/w original and copy photographs, postcards, colour photographic prints, illustrated books, press cuttings, unprinted film negatives, colour transparencies (35mm), glass negatives, lantern slides, original cartoons, illustrated maps, posters, greetings cards, magazines, advertising matter, pamphlets

Dates of subject matter 1890 to present

Dates of photographs 1890 to present

Subjects Sir Arthur Conan Doyle and the character of Sherlock Holmes with special emphasis on material from the US; Conan Doyle's life, family, beliefs, work; background, sources and locations for Holmes stories; lives, families and work of Holmes and Dr Watson; artwork for publications including *Strand Magazine*, societies, media photographs of actors and sets, use of characters in advertising and exhibitions including 1951 Festival of Britain; complete run of *Strand Magazine* from 1891 to 1930; illustrations by artists including Sidney Paget and Frank Wiles, stills from films and television productions

Access and conditions Open to the public by appt (tel), Mon-Fri 9.30–7, Sat 9.30–5. Some material available for editorial reproduction and for advertising. Colour transparencies loaned free of charge for three weeks; b/w prints and duplicate colour transparencies available for a fee; material may be copied by outside photographers. Photocopies available. Reproduction rights fees charged. Staff will undertake limited research. Some material copyright; copyright clearance is responsibility of user. Card catalogue.

1104 • SCOTTISH NATIONAL MEMORIAL TO DAVID LIVINGSTONE TRUST

David Livingstone Centre, Blantyre, Glasgow G72 9BT
Tel (0698) 823140

Enquiries to William Cunningham

Items About 300: b/w copy photographs, colour transparencies (35mm), lantern slides

Dates of subject matter 1785 to 1875

Dates of photographs c. 1850 to 1875

Subjects Life and work of David Livingstone including miniature painted before African travels, personal belongings, diaries, equipment, African relics

Access and conditions Open to the public, Mon-Sat 10–6, Sun 2–6. All material available for editorial reproduction and for advertising. B/w prints and duplicate colour transparencies available for a fee. No reproduction rights fees charged. Compulsory credit line. All material copyright.

Newspapers & Magazines

1105 • BACKNUMBERS

81 Theberton Street, London N1 0QY
Tel (01) 602 4472 (day), 262 4711 (eve)

Enquiries to Patrick Robertson

Items 18,000: ephemera (old newspapers), colour transparencies (35mm)

Dates of Items c. 1698 to 1975

Subjects Magazines and newspapers, especially English and American, but also British Commonwealth and foreign material, daily and Sunday newspapers (200), magazines (4000 titles) in the following categories: fashion, film and theatre, motoring, aviation, sport, business, sex, juvenile and comics; special collection of underground newspapers from the 1960s

Access and conditions Open to qualified researchers by appt (tel). All material available for editorial reproduction and for advertising. B/w and colour material loaned free of charge to picture researchers only for one month. Material may be copied by outside photographers. Reproduction rights and holding fees charged. Staff will undertake limited research; in-depth projects must be undertaken in person.

1106 • BRITISH LIBRARY

Newspaper Library

Colindale Avenue, London NW9 5HE
Tel (01) 200 5515

Enquiries to John Westmancoat, Information Officer

Items Newspapers

Dates of subject matter *c.* 1700 to present

Subjects Daily and weekly newspapers and periodicals including London newspapers from 1801 to present; English provincial, Scottish, Irish and Welsh newspapers from 1700 to present; Commonwealth and English-language foreign newspapers

Access and conditions Open to the public, Mon-Sat 10–4.45. Some material available for editorial reproduction and for advertising. No loans; b/w prints available for a fee (4–6 weeks). Material may be copied by outside photographers. Reproduction rights fees charged at the Librarian's discretion. Staff cannot undertake research, but will supply copies by post if accurate publication dates are supplied. Copyright clearance is responsibility of user. Printed catalogue available from British Library Publications, Great Russell Street, London WC1B 3DG.

1107 • JOHN FROST HISTORICAL NEWSPAPER SERVICE

8 Monks Avenue, New Barnet, Hertfordshire EN5 1DB
Tel (01) 440 3159

Enquiries to John Frost

Items Over 25,000: original newspapers and reproductions, periodicals

Dates of subject matter 1640 to present

Subjects Newspapers recording coronation and death of every British monarch since 1761, election of every American president since 1832, every major event in the life of Winston Churchill from Omdurman in 1898 until his death; British and American editions covering the American Civil War, Boer War, Crimean War, World Wars I and II, Korean War, Vietnam, famous trials, disasters, obituaries of famous people, space travel, royal events, records on land, sea and air

Access and conditions Open to qualified researchers by appt (tel), Mon-Fri 9–5. All material

available for editorial reproduction and for advertising. B/w and colour original material loaned free of charge for two weeks. Photocopies available. Material may be copied by outside photographers. Reproduction rights, service and holding fees charged. Staff will undertake some research.

1108 • NATIONAL MAGAZINE COMPANY LTD

Library and Syndication Department

72 Broadwick Street, London W1V 2BP
Tel (01) 439 7144 Telex 263879

Enquiries to Library and Syndication Manager

Items About 10,000: b/w original and copy photographs, colour transparencies (35mm, $5'' \times 4''$)

Dates of subject matter 1862 to present

Dates of photographs 1970s to present

Subjects Illustrative material and photographs from *Harpers & Queen, Company, Good Housekeeping, Antique Collector* covering fashion, cooking, design, homes, gardens, personalities, antiques and including material from former *Queen* magazine (1862–1970) and *Harper's Bazaar* (1929–1970)

Access and conditions Open to the public by appt (tel), Mon-Fri 10–5. Most material available for editorial reproduction; advertising use by special arrangement only. B/w and colour material loaned for three months (print fees charged). Photocopies available. Reproduction rights and holding fees charged. Staff will undertake limited research. All material copyright.

1109 • VINTAGE MAGAZINE CO LTD

39-41 Brewer Street, London W1R 3HP
Tel (01) 439 8525

Enquiries to Danny Posner, Director

Items Over one million: illustrated magazines, b/w original and copy photographs, colour photographic prints

Dates of magazines 1840 to 1980

Subjects British, American, French, German and Italian magazines on the following subjects:

cinema, theatre, sport, fashion, 19th- and 20th-century news, glamour, humour, advertising, war and militaria, politics, topography, shops, society, motoring, shipping, aircraft, travel, food, hobbies, fads, architecture, exploration, design, personalities

Access and conditions Open to the public. All

material available for editorial reproduction and for advertising. B/w prints loaned free of charge for three months; colour transparencies loaned for a rental fee or duplicated for a fee. Photocopies available. Reproduction rights, service and holding fees charged. Staff of 11 will undertake research; fee for large projects.

Politics & Government

1110 • COMMUNIST PARTY PICTURE LIBRARY AND ARCHIVE

16 St John Street, London EC1M 4AL
Tel (01) 251 4406

Enquiries to Betty Reid or George Matthews

Items About 5000: b/w original and copy photographs, original cartoons, prints, stereographs, posters, illustrated books, ephemera

Dates of subject matter Mostly 19th and 20th century

Dates of photographs 1920s to present

Subjects JAMES KLUGMANN PICTURE COLLECTION including portraits of leading personalities in British and working-class history, 19th- and 20th-century social conditions, Radicalism, Chartism, history of the trade union movement, women, peace and disarmament, unemployment, Ireland, anti-Fascism, anti-colonialism, the Paris Commune, the General Strike (UK), history of the Communist Party, history of the Labour movement; general collection including radical movement, elections, industries, textile factories, crafts, trade union emblems, agricultural workers, dockers, engineers, miners, hunger marches, poverty, French Revolution, suffragettes, Social Democractic Federation, William Morris, Tom Paine, Independent Labour Party, World Wars, May Day celebrations, Karl Marx, Friederich Engels, Nikolai Lenin, the Russian Revolution, China, the First International, Spain, Germany (pre-1939)

Access and conditions Open to qualified researchers by appt (tel), Mon-Fri 10–4.30. All

material available for editorial reproduction and for advertising. B/w prints and duplicate colour transparencies available for a fee. Photocopies available. Reproduction rights fees charged. Staff will undertake some research.

1111 • HOUSE OF COMMONS LIBRARY

Public Information Office, House of Commons, Norman Shaw Building (North), Victoria Embankment, London SW1A 2JF
Tel (01) 219 4272

Enquiries to Gillian Howarth

Items 15: b/w original photographs

Dates of photographs Recent

Subjects Commons Chamber, Deputy Serjeant-at-Arms in formal dress, doorkeeper with badge, Clerks' desk in Division Lobby, Houses of Parliament (exterior view), Mace, Serjeant-at-Arms in formal dress and also with Mace, Speaker's Chair, Select Committee Room, Standing Committee Room, Speaker in State Robes, Speaker's Procession before a State Opening (no photographs of individual MPs)

Access and conditions Not open: tel and written requests only, 9.30 to rising of the House on sitting days, 10–5 during recesses. All material available for editorial reproduction and for advertising. B/w material supplied free of charge. A/v material available for hire from CFL Vision, Chalfont Grove, Gerrards Cross, Bucks SL9 8TN (tel 02407 4111).

1112 • HOUSE OF LORDS RECORD OFFICE

House of Lords, London SW1A 0PW
Tel (01) 219 3074

Enquiries to Clerk of the Records

Items About 1000: b/w original and copy photographs, colour transparencies (35mm), colour photographic prints, glass negatives, architectural drawings

Dates of subject matter 13th century to present

Dates of photographs 1890 to present

Subjects Historic Parliamentary documents (1497 to present); architectural drawings of the Houses of Parliament; members and officers of both Houses of Parliament; interior and exterior views of the Palace of Westminster, including early meeting places (chambers) of the Commons and the Lords and works of art in the Lords; ceremonies, especially the State Opening of Parliament; E. J. FARMER COLLECTION of photographs including negatives and prints of photographs of the Palace of Westminster and its contents c. 1905; STONE COLLECTION of photographs of the Palace of Westminster, the Opening of Parliament and other events in the Palace c. 1892-1911) and of historical documents and other objects connected with the Palace by Sir John Benjamin Stone

Access and conditions Open to the public by appt, Mon-Fri 9–5 (closed last two weeks in Nov and day after Bank Holiday). Some material available for editorial reproduction and for advertising with the approval of the Clerk of the Records. Reference-quality prints available; for reproduction, material may be copied by outside photographers. Photocopies available. Reproduction rights fees charged. Staff will undertake limited research.

1113 • THE LABOUR PARTY LIBRARY

150 Walworth Road, London SE17 1JT
Tel (01) 703 0833

Enquiries to Ruby Ranaweera or Ursula Alexis

Items About 40,000: b/w original and copy photographs, colour transparencies (35mm), original cartoons, posters

Dates of subject matter 1900 to present

Dates of photographs c. 1906 to present

Subjects History of the Labour movement from 1900 to the present, social conditions, housing, hospitals; portraits of politicians, political events

Access and conditions Open to qualified researchers by appt (tel), Mon-Fri 10–4.45. Some material available for editorial reproduction and for advertising. B/w material loaned free of charge for three weeks. Out-of-copyright material may be copied by outside photographers. Reproduction rights and service fees charged; service fees deductible from use fees. Staff will undertake limited research for a fee. Card catalogue.

1114 • LIBERAL PARTY ORGANIZATION

Liberal News Photo Files, 1 Whitehall Place, London SW1A 2HE
Tel (01) 839 4092 ext 43

Enquiries to Paul Sample, Press Office

Items 2000: b/w original photographs, postcards, posters, illustrated books

Dates of subject matter c. 1920 to present

Dates of photographs c. 1920 to present

Subjects Liberal party leaders, officials and candidates

Access and conditions Open to qualified researchers by appt (write), Mon-Fri 10–4.30. Some material available for editorial reproduction but not for advertising. B/w prints loaned free of charge. No reproduction rights fees charged. Staff will undertake very limited research only.

Royalty & Portraits

1115 • BASSANO STUDIOS

35 Moreton Street, London SW1V 2NY
Tel (01) 828 3931

Enquiries to Keith Herschell

Items 250,000: b/w original photographs, glass negatives

Dates of subject matter 1860 to present

Dates of photographs 1860 to present

Subjects Portraits of famous people by the Bassano, Vandyke and Elliot & Fry studios, including the Royal Family (Queen Victoria to Queen Elizabeth II); Prime Ministers (Disraeli and Gladstone to present); writers including Mark Twain, Oscar Wilde, H. G. Wells, Rudyard Kipling, George Bernard Shaw, D. H. Lawrence; army officers including Lord Montgomery of Alamein, Kitchener of Khartoum; musicians including Gustav Holst, Edward Elgar, Edvard Grieg, Maurice Ravel; inventors and scientists including Logie Baird, Albert Einstein, Louis Pasteur; leaders including General Smuts, Franklin Delano Roosevelt, Mohandas K. (Mahatma) Gandhi, Cecil Rhodes, Golda Meir

Access and conditions Open to qualified researchers by appt (tel), Mon-Fri 9–5.30. All material available for editorial reproduction and for advertising. No loans; b/w prints available for a fee. Photocopies available. Reproduction rights fees charged. Additional material from this collection is held by Camera Press and by the National Portrait Gallery (q.v.).

1116 • LIONEL CHERRUAULT

21 Ulysses Road, London NW6 1ED
Tel (01) 794 9770

Enquiries to Lionel Cherruault or Christine Black

Items 7000: colour transparencies (35mm)

Dates of photographs 1980 to present

Subjects Formal and informal photographs of the British Royal Family, including the Queen and the Duke of Edinburgh, the Prince and Princess of Wales, Prince William, Prince Harry, Princess Anne and Capt. Mark Phillips, Zara Phillips, Peter Phillips, Princess Margaret, Lady Sarah Armstrong-Jones, Lord Linley, Prince Edward, Prince Andrew, the Duke and Duchess of Kent, Lady Helen Windsor, Lord Nicholas Windsor, the Duke and Duchess of Gloucester, Prince and Princess Michael of Kent, Lord Frederick, Lady Gabriella, Princess Alexandra, Angus Ogilvy, Marina Ogilvy, Princess Alice, the Queen Mother, other minor royals; most royal tours

Access and conditions Open to qualified researchers by appt (tel), Mon-Fri 9–5. All material available for editorial reproduction; for advertising by special arrangement only. Colour material loaned free of charge for 30 days. Reproduction rights and holding fees charged. Staff will undertake research. All material copyright.

1117 • REGINALD DAVIS

29 Heriot Road, London NW4 2EG
Tel (01) 202 7941

Enquiries to A. Fields

Items 35,000: colour transparencies (35mm, 2¼″, larger)

Dates of photographs 1955 to present

Subjects Royalty worldwide (1955 to present), heralds, guards, etc.; personalities including Sophia Loren, Joan Collins, Isabella Rossellini, Ira von Furstenbourg, Caroll Baker, Elizabeth Taylor, Lilli Palmer, Hildegard Knef, Princess Soraya, Golda Meir and family, Indira Gandhi and family, Duke and Duchess of Windsor, Valéry Giscard d'Estaing, Haile Selassie

Access and conditions Open to qualified researchers by appt (write). All material available for editorial reproduction; some for advertising. Colour material loaned free of charge for two to four weeks. Reproduction rights, service and holding fees charged. Staff will undertake some research.

1118 • MARK GERSON PHOTOGRAPHY

24 Cavendish Avenue, London NW8 9JE
Tel (01)286 5894

Enquiries to Mark Gerson

Items 20,000: b/w original photographs, colour transparencies (35mm, 2¼")

Dates of photographs 1950 to present

Subjects Portraits of literary personalities, mostly British and Commmonwealth, including authors, playwrights, poets

Access and conditions Open to qualified researchers by appt Mon-Fri 9–6, Sat 12–4. All material available for editorial reproduction and for advertising. B/w and colour material loaned free of charge for five days. Reproduction rights, service and holdings fees charged. Staff will undertake limited research.

1119 • TIM GRAHAM PICTURE LIBRARY LTD

31 Ferncroft Avenue, London NW3 7PG
Tel (01) 435 7693

Enquiries to Tim Graham

Items Over 100,000: colour transparencies (35mm), b/w original photographs

Dates of photographs 1970 to present

Subjects All members of the British Royal Family including formal and informal photographs, in the UK and on royal tours abroad, portraits, fashions, public engagements, banquets, state visits, state occasions, annual ceremonies, at home, sporting interests, family groups, homes, cars, planes, boats; foreign royals and heads of state, foreign countries, English scenes

Access and conditions Open to qualified researchers by appt (tel), Mon-Fri 10–6. All material available for editorial reproduction; royal pictures not for advertising use. B/w and colour material loaned free of charge for one month. Reproduction rights, service and holding fees charged; service fees deductible from use fees. Staff of six will undertake research. Printed catalogue available.

1120 • ANWAR HUSSEIN PICTURE LIBRARY

29 Wyndham Street, London W1H 1DD
Tel (01) 723 2158

Enquiries to Anwar Hussein

Items 300,000: colour transparencies (35mm, 5" × 4"), colour photographic prints

Dates of photographs 1960 to present

Subjects The British Royal Family including portraits, events formal and informal, overseas tours, sports, fashion, children; royalty in general, including Belgian, Dutch, Spanish, Luxembourg and Middle Eastern Royal Families; travel photography, landscapes, people; personalities in show business, politicians, world leaders including the Pope

Access and conditions Open to the public by appt (tel), Mon-Fri 9–5. All material available for editorial reproduction and for advertising. B/w and colour material loaned free of charge for two weeks. Reproduction rights, service and holding fees charged; service fee deductible from use fee. Staff of two will undertake some research.

1121 • JS LIBRARY INTERNATIONAL

101A Brondesbury Park, London NW2 5JL
Tel (01) 451 2668, 459 0223 Telex 912881

Enquiries to John Shelley, Manager

Items 40,000: colour transparencies (35mm), b/w original photographs, illustrated books

Dates of subject matter 1978 to present

Dates of photographs 1978 to present

Subjects Coverage of the British Royal Family at the Badminton Horse Trials, Royal Windsor Show, Windsor Horse Trials, Trooping of the Colour, Royal Ascot, Braemar Games, Christmas Day morning service at St George's Chapel, Windsor, Maundy Thursday service, Remembrance Day service, sporting events, official visits to industry, institutions, film and play premières, overseas tours; foreign royalty of Europe, the Middle East and Africa; visit of Pope John Paul II to the UK in 1982; television, stage and screen personalities

Access and conditions Open to qualified researchers by appt (tel), Mon-Fri 10–6. All material available for editorial reproduction; advertising use by special arrangement only. B/w and colour material loaned free of charge for one month; b/w prints and duplicate colour transparencies available for a fee. Reproduction rights and holding fees charged. Staff of three will undertake research. All material copyright. Duplicated catalogue available.

Miscellaneous

1122 • CLIFFORD C. ASHTON

20 Kingsway, Rochdale OL16 4UU
Tel (0706) 44914

Enquiries to Clifford C. Ashton

Items 15,000: unprinted film negatives, glass negatives

Dates of subject matter 1932 to present

Dates of photographs 1932 to present

Subjects Fires, both burning and resultant damage, including behaviour of material during fires; press photography Rochdale area; Gracie Fields in Rochdale

Access and conditions Open to qualified researchers by appt. All material available for editorial reproduction and for advertising. No loans; b/w prints available for a fee. Reproduction rights and service fees charged. Staff will undertake some research; research fee negotiable.

1123 • CENTRE FOR THE STUDY OF CARTOONS AND CARICATURE

The Library, University of Kent, Canterbury CT2 7NU
Tel (0227) 66822 ext 573

Enquiries to Curator

Items About 70,000: original cartoons

Dates of subject matter 1900 to present

Subjects Original cartoons from British newspapers and journals from 1900 onwards including political, humorous, wartime and social-comment cartoons; artists represented include Low, Strube, Vicky, Cummings, Zee, Lee, Haselden, Smythe, Jensen, Garland, Dyson, Trog, Horner, Hewison, Mac and Illingworth

Access and conditions Open to qualified researchers by appt (tel). All material available for editorial reproduction but not for advertising. No loans; b/w prints available for a fee; material may be copied by outside photographers. Photocopies available. Reproduction rights fees sometimes charged; service fees charged. Staff of two will undertake research for a fee. Card catalogue available.

1124 • CHARTERHOUSE

Godalming, Surrey GU7 2DX
Tel (04868) 7105 after 2 pm

Enquiries to Brian Souter

Items About 5000: b/w original photographs, colour photographic prints, original cartoons, illustrated maps, old fine art prints, 20th-century fine art prints, art reproductions, architectural drawings

Dates of photographs 1860 to present

Subjects History of Charterhouse School including photographs of old boys, and history of Association football; material relating to and sketches and painting by Baden-Powell

Access and conditions Open to qualified researchers by appt (write). All material available for editorial reproduction and for advertising by permission of the Headmaster. No loans; b/w prints and duplicate colour transparencies available for a fee. Photocopies available. Reproduction rights and service fees charged. All material copyright.

1125 • CHELSEA COLLEGE LIBRARY

Manresa Road, London SW3 6LX
Tel (01) 351 2488

Enquiries to Site Librarian

Items 200: b/w original and copy photographs, architectural drawings

Dates of subject matter 1900 to present

Dates of photographs 1900 to present

Subjects College activities including student functions, ceremonies; classes in art, chiropody and science; laboratories, college buildings, sports teams, teaching staff

Access and conditions Open to qualified researchers by appt (write), Mon-Fri 9–5. Some material available for editorial reproduction and for advertising. No loans; b/w prints available for a fee. Material may be copied by outside photographers. Reproduction rights fees charged.

1126 • JOHN H. CUTTEN ASSOCIATES

22 Belsize Park, London NW3 4DU
Tel (01) 794 3972, 431 0848

Enquiries to John H. Cutten, Director

Items 2000: b/w original and copy photographs,
colour transparencies (35mm), colour photographic
prints, glass negatives, lantern slides, unprinted
film negatives

Dates of subject matter c. 1200 BC to present

Subjects Parapsychology and psychical research,
including portraits of well-known investigators,
instruments and equipment used in research,
Kirlian photography, ghost pictures and fantasies;
early aircraft and World War I aircraft; fashion
(19th and 20th century); British and foreign
royalty including the Tsar Nicholas II and his
family

Access and conditions Open to qualified
researchers by appt, Mon-Fri 9–5. All material
available for editorial reproduction and for
advertising. B/w and colour material loaned free of
charge for one month. Photocopies available.
Reproduction rights, service and holding fees
charged. Staff will undertake limited research.

1127 • DUNDEE UNIVERSITY LIBRARY

University Photographic Archive

Photographic Department
Dundee, Tayside DD1 4HN
Tel (0382) 23181 ext 204 Telex 76293

Enquiries to Library Photographic Department

Items 4000: b/w original photographs, colour
transparencies (35mm), colour photographic prints

Dates of subject matter 1840 to present

Dates of photographs 1880 to present

Subjects University of Dundee (formerly known
as University College, then as Queen's College,
then as St Andrew's University), laboratories,
classes, buildings, staff and students, ceremonies
including Rectoral Drag Monday and former
Rectors including Peter Ustinov and Clement
Freud

Access and conditions Open to the public by
appt, Mon-Fri 9–5. All material available for
editorial reproduction and for advertising. No
loans; b/w prints and duplicate colour

transparencies available for a fee. Photocopies
available. Reproduction rights fees charged. Staff
will undertake some research.

1128 • FIRE DEFENCE COLLECTION

Wiltshire Fire Brigade, Manor House, Worton
Road, Potterne, Wiltshire SN10 5PP
Tel (0380) 3601

Enquiries to Rod Priddle, Station Officer

Items About 1000: b/w original and copy
photographs, colour photographic prints

Dates of subject matter Late 19th century to
present

Dates of photographs Late 19th century to
present

Subjects Fire-engines (including horse-drawn
vehicles), fire crews, fire-stations, some action
material, wartime coverage, appliances and
equipment, presentation of medals, funerals of
firemen

Access and conditions Open to qualified
researchers by appt (write). Some material
available for editorial reproduction and for
advertising; some for private research only. No
loans; b/w prints available for a fee. Reproduction
rights fees charged. Staff will undertake limited
research. Most material copyright. Card catalogue
in preparation.

1129 • FORTEAN PICTURE LIBRARY

Melangell House, Princes Street, Montgomery,
Powys SY15 6PY
Tel (068681) 405

Enquiries to Janet Bord

Items 10,000: b/w original and copy photographs,
colour transparencies (35mm)

Dates of subject matter c. 1600 to present

Dates of photographs 1880 to present

Subjects Accidents, alchemy, alternative senses
(sight via skin, etc.), ancient technology, animals
(strange, rare), angels, antigravity, antiquities,
anthropoids (Yeti, Bigfoot), apparitions, apport
phenomena, archaeological enigmas, artificial
creation of life, astral projection, astronomical
mysteries, atmospheric lights (beams, glows,
parhelia, rainbows, aurorae), attacks by animals,

aura, beached whales, behaviour (strange, of animals, people, crowds), birds (strange, giant), biological curiosities, bioluminescence, black dogs, calculating prodigies, clouds (strange), coincidences, cults, deaths (strange, animal, people), devils, discoveries, divination, dowsing, dreams, dwarves, elves, earthquakes, ecstasy, electric people, embeddings (toads in stones, coins in wood, etc.), energies (new, unknown), evolution, exorcism, falls (of fish, frogs, ice, objects, metal, matter), fairies, feral humans, fire-walking, fires, fish (strange, rare), floods, drought, flows (bleeding statues, weeping icons, etc.), folklore, footprints, tracks (mystery, fossil), fossils, freaks (animal, human), geological curiosities, ghosts, ghouls (grave-robbing), giants, gravity anomalies, hail, snow, hallucinations, hollow earth, illnesses (mystery), images, immunity, insects (strange), lake monsters, levitation, lights (mystery, in sky, sea, land), lightning (ball lightning, tricks of, deaths from), lost cities, continents and tribes, machines, magic (ritual, black, white, weather), migrations, miracles, mirages, multiple personalities, murders, mutations, mutilations, omens, portents, signs, perpetual motion, plants (strange), poltergeists, haunted houses, possession, precognition, psychic surgery, faith healing, psychic phenomena, psychic photography, psychics, pyramids, rain-making, reincarnation, religious phenomena, relics, sea monsters, shamanism, scientific mysteries, Surrey puma (mystery large cats, etc.), stigmata, swarmings, telekinesis, trance phenomena, twins (coincidences between), UFOs (in sky, landings, encounters, etc.), vampires, vanishing (ships, people, objects), visions, winds, whirlwinds, storms, werewolves, witchcraft, yogic feats

Access and conditions Open to qualified researchers by appt, Mon-Fri 9–5. All material available for editorial reproduction and for advertising. B/w and colour material loaned free of charge. Reproduction rights fees charged. Staff will undertake research. Card catalogue.

1130 • THE GEFFRYE MUSEUM

Kingsland Road, London E2 8EA
Tel (01) 739 8368

Enquiries to Jeffrey Daniels, Director

Items 500,000: b/w original photographs, colour transparencies (35mm, 5″ × 4″), lantern slides, posters, greetings cards, trade catalogues

Dates of subject matter *c.* 1600 to 1945

Dates of photographs 1950 to present

Subjects Development of domestic design in series of room settings 1600 to 1939 showing furniture, ceramics, textiles, metalwork, paintings, prints and drawings in context; 18th-century kitchen and domestic utensils; 18th-century woodworker's shop and woodworking tools; costume gallery with display of utility clothing; 19th- and 20th-century fashions

Access and conditions Open to the public by appt, Tues-Sat 10–5, Sun 2–5. All material available for editorial reproduction and for advertising. B/w prints available for a fee; colour transparencies loaned for a rental fee. Photocopies available. Reproduction rights fees charged. Staff will undertake some research. Card catalogue.

1131 • HER MAJESTY'S STATIONERY OFFICE

St Crispins, Duke Street, Norwich, Norfolk NR3 1PD
Tel (0603) 622211 Telex 97301

Enquiries to Jill Ward, Copyright Section

Items 70: colour transparencies (5″ × 4″, larger), b/w original photographs, illustrated books

Dates of photographs 1975 to present

Subjects English royal regalia kept in the Tower of London Jewel House (Crown Jewels)

Access and conditions Open to qualified researchers by appt (tel), Mon-Fri 8.30–5. All material available for editorial reproduction but not for advertising. B/w prints available for a fee. Colour transparencies loaned for a rental fee. Reproduction rights fees charged. Staff will undertake limited research. Printed guidebook available.

1132 • INTERNATIONAL DEFENCE AND AID FUND FOR SOUTHERN AFRICA

Canon Collins House, 64 Essex Road, London N1 8LR
Tel (01) 359 9181

Enquiries to Barry Feinberg, Director of Research, Information and Publications

Items 35,000: b/w original and copy photographs, colour transparencies (35mm)

Dates of subject matter 1700 to present

Dates of photographs *c.* 1860 to present

Subjects South Africa and Namibia, living conditions, squatter camps and resettlement, health, education, work conditions, unions and labour, apparatus of repression including military, police, security; political prisoners, deaths in detention, refugees, demonstrations, liberation movements, personalities; special collection on South Africa in the 19th and early 20th centuries; ELI WEINBERG COLLECTION including South Africa and conditions of life under apartheid and history of the struggles against apartheid (1940s to 1970s)

Access and conditions Open to qualified researchers by appt (tel), Mon-Fri 9.30–5.30. All material available for editorial reproduction and for advertising. No loans; b/w prints and duplicate colour transparencies available for a fee. Photocopies available. Reproduction rights fees charged. Staff will undertake some research but encourage personal visits.

1133 • PETER JENNINGS

26 Rowan Close, St Albans, Hertfordshire AL4 0ST
Tel (0727) (from London 56) 61835

Enquiries to Peter Jennings

Items 3500: b/w original and copy photographs, colour transparencies (35mm, 9 × 6cm), postcards, unprinted film negatives, press cuttings and tearsheets, illustrated books

Dates of subject matter 1600 to present

Dates of photographs 1900 to present

Subjects Windmills in Britain, exteriors and interiors, close-ups of machinery; some historical material, some Mediterranean windmills

Access and conditions Open to qualified researchers by appt (tel), Mon-Fri 9–5. All material available for editorial reproduction and for advertising. B/w material loaned free of charge for two months; colour for one. Reproduction rights fees charged. Staff will undertake some research.

1134 • PIERS INFORMATION BUREAU

38 Holte Road, Atherstone, Warwickshire
CV9 1HN
Tel (08277) 2640

Enquiries to Timothy J. Mickleburgh

Items About 500 postcards

Dates of subject matter *c.* 1800 to present

Dates of photographs 1900 to present

Subjects Piers in the UK including those now not in existence; some overseas coverage including Holland, Belgium and the USA

Access and conditions Open to qualified researchers by appt (write). Most material available for editorial reproduction and for advertising. No loans; material may be copied by outside photographers. Photocopies available. Reproduction rights fees charged. Some research undertaken. Most material copyright; copyright clearance is responsibility of user.

1135 • JOHN RYLANDS UNIVERSITY LIBRARY OF MANCHESTER

Oxford Road, Manchester M13 9PP
Tel (061) 834 5343

Enquiries to David Riley, Keeper of Printed Books

Items 2000: b/w original photographs, unprinted film negatives, glass negatives

Dates of subject matter 19th to early 20th century

Dates of photographs 1920 to 1930

Subjects E. MITFORD ABRAHAMS COLLECTION: windmills and watermills in Cambridgeshire, Cheshire, Cumberland, Hertfordshire, Huntingdonshire, Lancashire, Leicestershire, Lincolnshire, Norfolk, Northamptonshire, Nottinghamshire, Rutland, Suffolk, Westmoreland, Yorkshire; interiors and exteriors

Access and conditions Open to qualified researchers by appt (write), Mon-Fri 10–5.30, Sat 10–1. All material available for editorial reproduction but not for advertising. B/w prints available for a fee. Photocopies available. Reproduction rights fees charged. Staff will undertake limited research.

1136 • SHREWSBURY SCHOOL LIBRARY

Shrewsbury School, The Schools, Shrewsbury, Shropshire SY3 7BA
Tel (0743) 62926

Enquiries to Librarian

Items About 10,000: b/w original photographs, colour transparencies (35mm), old fine art prints, architectural drawings, lantern slides, original cartoons, illustrated maps, illustrated books, watercolours

Dates of subject matter BC to present

Dates of photographs 1860 to present

Dates of fine art 1100 to present

Subjects School life from 1860 including portraits, groups, buildings, sports (football, cricket, rowing, athletics and cross-country); Shropshire local history; architectural drawings of Shrewsbury School and local churches from 1830; maps of Shrewsbury and Shropshire from 1830-1900; illustrated books from 1470 to 1800 including 16th- and 17th-century volumes on science, physics, chemistry, medicine, surgery, natural history, botany and mathematics; special collections of material relating to Charles Darwin, Sir Philip Sidney and Samuel Butler; books from the Kelmscott Press; English 19th-century watercolours

Access and conditions Open to qualified researchers by appt (write). All material available for editorial reproduction and for advertising by special arrangement only. B/w prints and duplicate colour transparencies available for a fee. Photocopies available. Reproduction rights fees charged by arrangement. Staff will undertake some research. All material copyright.

1137 • HOMER SYKES

19 Kenilworth Avenue, London SW19 7LN
Tel (01) 947 7975

Enquiries to Homer Sykes

Items 500: b/w original photographs, colour transparencies (35mm)

Dates of photographs 1970 to present

Subjects Traditional English and Scottish country customs taking place on one day each year and unique to the specific village or town

Access and conditions Open to qualified researchers by appt (tel). All material available for editorial reproduction and for advertising. B/w and colour material loaned free of charge for one month. Reproduction rights, service and holding fees charged. Staff will undertake research.

1138 • UNIVERSITY OF BRISTOL LIBRARY ARCHIVES

Tyndall Avenue, Bristol BS8 1TJ
Tel (0272) 303030 Telex 449174

Enquiries to Norman Higham, University Librarian

Items About 5000: b/w original and copy photographs, colour transparencies (35mm), glass negatives, lantern slides, postcards, illustrated maps, unprinted film negatives, posters, architectural drawings, fine art prints, illustrated books

Dates of photographs c. 1870 to present

Subjects Bristol University history, architecture (exteriors and interiors), staff, students, ceremonies, royal visits (King George V and Queen Mary, Queen Elizabeth II), visits by Chancellor Winston Churchill (1929)

Access and conditions Open to qualified researchers by appt (tel), Mon-Fri 9.15–4.45. Most material available for editorial reproduction. No loans; b/w prints and duplicate colour transparencies available for a fee. Photocopies available. Reproduction rights fees charged. Staff will undertake limited research.

1139 • UNIVERSITY COLLEGE LONDON LIBRARY

Gower Street, London WC1E 6BT
Tel (01) 387 7050

Enquiries to Janet Percival, Assistant Librarian

Items 1000: b/w original and copy photographs, colour photographic prints, glass negatives, lantern slides, illustrated maps, posters, architectural drawings, press cuttings, illustrated books

Dates of subject matter 1860 to present

Dates of photographs 1860 to present

Subjects Life, family and work of George Orwell; photographs relating to University College including portraits of benefactors, staff and students, special events, buildings

Access and conditions Open to the public by appt (write). All material available for editorial reproduction and for advertising. No loans; b/w prints available for a fee; material may be copied by outside photographers. Photocopies available. Reproduction rights and service fees charged. Staff will undertake limited research. All material copyright.

1140 • WARWICK DOLL MUSEUM

Oken's House, Castle Street, Warwick CV34 4JH
Tel (0926) 495546, 491600

Enquiries to Perry Nesbitt, 29 St Nicholas Church Street, Warwick

Items About 3000: antique dolls, automata, puzzles, books, pictures

Dates of subject matter 1700 to 1930

Subjects Children's dolls and toys from the UK, France, Germany, Italy and USA since 1700 including doll's houses, prams, automata, puzzles, miniatures

Access and conditions Open to the public by appt (write), Mon-Fri 10.30–5. All material available for editorial reproduction; advertising use by special arrangement only. Material may be

copied by outside photographers. Compulsory credit line. All material copyright.

1141 • WILBERFORCE HOUSE

25 High Street, Kingston upon Hull, Humberside HU1 1NE
Tel (0482) 222737

Enquiries to John Bradshaw, Curator

Items 10,000: b/w original and copy photographs, colour transparencies (35mm, 5″ × 4″), glass negatives, daguerreotypes, lantern slides, postcards, original cartoons, fine art prints, posters, greetings cards

Dates of subject matter c. 1750 to 1945

Dates of photographs 1854 to 1945

Subjects The Atlantic slave trade in the 18th and 19th centuries; William Wilberforce and the Wilberforce family; antislavery and abolition campaigns especially 1787 to 1833; views of Hull and of the East Riding of Yorkshire, architecture, portraits of Hull people; transport, local railway

Access and conditions Open to the public by appt, Mon-Fri 10–5. Most material available for editorial reproduction and for advertising. B/w prints and duplicate colour transparencies available for a fee. Photocopies available. Reproduction rights and service fees charged. Staff will undertake some research. Compulsory credit line.

Index of collections and sub-collections

Major collections are indicated as follows: Bodleian Library 24; sub-collections are indicated as follows: John Johnson Collection of Printed Ephemera (Bodleian Library) 24

Abbot Hall Art Gallery 921
Aberdeen Art Gallery and Museums 922
Aberdeen Central Library 266
Aberdeen Journals Ltd 267
Aberdeen University Library 1
Abergavenny Museum 268
Aberystwyth Public Library 269
Abingdon Museum 270
Abington Museum 271
Abraham Collection (Fell and Rock Climbing Club of the English Lake District) 738
E. Mitford Abrahams Collection (Rylands University Library of Manchester) 1135
Ace Photo Agency 2
Acton Historical Library (Cambridge University Library) 32
Adams Picture Library 3
Adespoton Film Services (Jo Bond Words and Pictures) 26
AE plc 806
Aerial Archaeology Air Photographs Collection 258
Aerofilms Ltd 259
Aerophoto 722
Age Concern England 761
Air Photograph Collection (Keele University) 979
Air Portraits 876
Airship Industries (UK) Ltd 877
Aldus Archive 4
Bryan and Cherry Alexander Photography 5
Bernard Alfieri Picture Library 6
Alfreton Library 272
All-Action Photographic 723
All England Netball Association Ltd 724
All-Sport Photographic Ltd 725
J. Catling Allen Photographic

Library 7
Amey Roadstone Corporation Ltd 807
Ancient Art and Architecture Collection 623
Anderson Collection of Art Nouveau (Sainsbury Centre for Visual Arts) 1012
Andes Press Agency 8
Ken Andrew 9
Heather Angel (Biofotos) 632
Angling Press Service 726
Anglo-Chinese Educational Institute 580
Anglo-Jewish Archives (Mocatta Library) 714
Angus District Council 273
Animal Photography Ltd 624
Animals Unlimited 625
Gordon Anthony Collection (BBC Hulton Picture Library) 16
Aquarius Picture Library 1046
Aquila Photographics 626
Cyril Arapoff Collection (Waterways Museum) 916
Arbroath Library (Angus District Council) 273
Arbroath Museum (Angus District Council) 273
Arcaid 923
Architectural Association 924
The Architectural Press Ltd 925
Archive of St Kilda (National Trust for Scotland) 145
Arctic Camera 775
Ardea London Ltd 627
Argyll and Bute District Library 274
Armagh County Museum 926
Armagh Observatory 776
Eric Arman Collection (Thamesdown Museums and Art Gallery) 1022
Army Museums Ogilby Trust 601
Arnold Library 275
Robert Arnold 628
Art Directors Photo Library 10
Art, Medallion and Poster Collections (Imperial War Museum) 607
Arts Council Exhibition Archive (Arts Council of Great Britain) 927
Arts Council of Great Britain 927

Ashbridge Collection (Marylebone Library) 453
Ashford Library – Local Studies Collection 276
Ashford Library – Railway Collection 878
Clifford C. Ashton 1122
Aspect Picture Library 11
Assheton-Bennett Collection (Manchester City Art Galleries) 989
Associated Press Limited 12
Associated Sports Photography 727
Astral Aerial Surveys Ltd 260
Astro Art 777
Astronomical Society of Edinburgh 778
Athelstan Museum 277
Atkinson Art Gallery 928
The Auckland Collection 602
Erich Auerbach Collection 1047
James Austin Photograph Library 929
Automobile Association 879
Auty-Hastings Collection (Newcastle Upon Tyne Central Library) 474
Aveling-Barford Ltd 808
Avery Collection (Greater London Council Photograph Library) 391
Avery Historical Museum 809
Avia Press Associates 880
The Aviation Picture Library 881
Aviemore Photographic 13
Avoncroft Museum of Buildings 930
A–Z Botanical Collection 629

B & B Photographs 630
Backnumbers 1105
Baker Perkins Holdings plc 810
Ballet Rambert 1048
Bandphotos 14
Bank of Scotland 811
Banknote and Coin Collection (Bank of Scotland) 811
Clive Barda 1049
Barnaby's Picture Library 15
Dr Barnardo's 1085
Barnes Museum of Cinematography 1050

Museum of London 467
Museum of the Middlesex Regiment Collection (Bruce Castle Museum) 304
Museum of the Order of St John 768
Mustograph Collection (Barnaby's Picture Library) 15

N Gauge Society 904
NAAS Limited 142
Edmund Nägele 143
National Anti-Vivisection Society Limited 663
National Army Museum 612
National Art Survey Drawings (Royal Commission on Ancient and Historical Monuments of Scotland) 680
National Bus Company 905
National Centre for Alternative Technology 793
National Coal Board 851
National Dairy Council 852
National Farmers' Union 853
National Galleries of Scotland 994
National Horseracing Museum 748
National Library of Scotland 468
National Library of Wales 469
National Magazine Company Ltd 1108
National Maritime Museum 906
National Meteorological Library 794
National Mining Museum 854
National Motor Museum 907
National Museum of Antiquities of Scotland 470
National Museum of Labour History 855
National Portrait Gallery 995
National Railway Museum 908
The National Tramway Museum 909
The National Trust 144
The National Trust for Scotland 145
Natural History and Archaeology Photographs 664
Natural History Photographic Agency 665
Natural Science Photographs 666
Nature Conservancy Council (Royal Photographic Society) 1010
Nature Photographers Ltd 667
Nautical Photo Library (Popperfoto) 177
Nene College 996
Network Photographers 146
Neverovsky Collection (Royal Anthropological Institute) 679
New Lanark Conservation Trust 997
Newark Advertiser Collection (Newark District Council Museum) 471

Newark District Council Museum 471
Newarke Houses Museum 472
Peter Newark's Western Americana 147
Newbury Hall Estate 998
Newcastle Under Lyme Public Library 473
Newcastle Upon Tyne Central Library 474
Newslink Africa Ltd 148
Newspaper Library (British Library) 1106
Newton Collection (Leicestershire Record Office) 437
Nigel Press Associates Ltd 795
Maurice Nimmo 668
Norfolk Archaeological Unit 669
Norfolk Rural Life Museum 475
Philip Norman Collection (Guildhall Library Print Room) 396
Norris Library and Museum 476
North British Locomotive Co. Collection (The Mitchell Library) 903
North East Fife District Library 477
North of England Newspapers 149
North West Civic Trust 999
North West Counties Press Ltd 150
North Yorkshire County Library 478
Northamptonshire Record Office 479
Northern Ireland Information Service 151
Northern Ireland Tourist Board 152
Northern Picture Library 153
Norwich Castle Museum 1000
Norwich Central Library 480
Nottingham Castle Museum and Art Gallery 1001
Nottingham Central Library 481
Nottinghamshire County Council 261
Novosti Press Agency 593
Ken Nunn Collection (Locomotive Club of Great Britain) 897

Helen Ogilvie Collection (Marine Laboratory Library) 791
Old Mill House Museum 482
Old Theatre Bills and Programmes Collection (Guildhall Library Print Room) 396
The Old Vic Archive (University of Bristol Theatre Collection) 1080
Oldfield Collection (Hertfordshire Record Office) 417
Only Horses Picture Library 749
Onslow Collection (Guildford Muniment Room) 79
OPC Railprint 910
Open Eye Gallery 483
Openeye Photo Agency 154
Opera North 1073

Robert Opie Collection 1096
Orpix 155
Christine Osborne 156
Ron Oulds Colour Library 157
Oxford Scientific Films Ltd 670
Oxfordshire County Libraries 484
Oxon and Bucks News-Photo Agency 485

Pagden Collection (Entomology Library, British Museum) 638
Palmers of Merton Collection (Surrey Record Office) 537
Paquin Archive (Museum of Costume and Fashion Research Centre) 1093
Dr Parker Collection (Wells Museum) 560
N. Parker Collection (Palaeontology Collection, British Museum) 638
Tom Parker Colour Library 158
R. B. Parr Negative Collection (National Tramway Museum) 909
Parry Collection (South Tyneside Central Library) 524
Parsons Peebles Ltd (Scottish Record Office) 512
Lloyd Patterson Collection (Ulster Museum) 1025
Pavlova Collection (Museum of London) 467
Howard S. Pearson Collection (Birmingham Public Libraries) 1051
Ann and Bury Peerless 159
The Pembrokeshire Record Office 486
People's Dispensary for Sick Animals 671
Perth Museum and Art Gallery 487
Petbow Ltd 856
Peterborough Central Library 488
Peterborough City Museum and Art Gallery 1002
Peterhead Arbuthnot Museum 489
Michael Peto Collection (Dundee University Library) 57
Philips Collection (Manchester Central Library) 451
Phillips Collection (BBC Hulton Picture Library) 16
Phillips Collection (Wells Museum) 560
Peter Phipp Photo Library 160
Phipson Collection (Manchester Central Library) 451
Photo Co-Op 161
Photo Library International 162
The Photo Source 163
Photofile International Ltd 164
The Photographers' Library 165
Photon Photo Library 166
Photopress 613
Photopress Press Agency Collection

Subject Index